Henry Cowles

Ezekiel and Daniel

With notes, critical, explanatory, and practical, designed for both pastors and people

Henry Cowles

Ezekiel and Daniel
With notes, critical, explanatory, and practical, designed for both pastors and people

ISBN/EAN: 9783337285296

Printed in Europe, USA, Canada, Australia, Japan

Cover: Foto ©Lupo / pixelio.de

More available books at **www.hansebooks.com**

EZEKIEL AND DANIEL;

WITH

NOTES,

CRITICAL, EXPLANATORY, AND PRACTICAL,

DESIGNED FOR BOTH PASTORS AND PEOPLE.

BY

REV. HENRY COWLES, D. D.

"Understandest thou what thou readest? And he said, How can I, except some man should guide me?"—ACTS 8 : 30, 31.

NEW YORK:
D. APPLETON AND COMPANY,
443 & 445 BROADWAY.
1867.

Entered, according to Act of Congress, in the year 1867, by

REV. HENRY COWLES,

In the Clerk's Office of the District Court of the United States, for the Northern District of Ohio.

PREFACE.

This volume is a continuation of the series on all the prophets which was commenced in the autumn of the last year by the publication of "The Minor Prophets." The preface and general introduction to the prophetic books, prefixed to that volume, need not be repeated here, inasmuch as the greater part, at least, of the readers of this volume may be supposed to have access to that. This pursues the same general plan, aiming to be concise and yet lucid, and to bring out the true and precise sense of the original, with extended discussion only upon points of special interest and difficulty.

The reader will notice that Italics are used in the text, as in our English Bibles, to signify that there are no precisely corresponding words in the original Hebrew; but in the notes they are used for emphasis.

It is hoped that the remaining volumes on the prophets, viz., on Isaiah and on Jeremiah, will follow at no distant day.

OBERLIN, OHIO, July, 1867.

EZEKIEL.

INTRODUCTION.

THE just interpretation of Ezekiel will turn very much upon his circumstances as a prophet. Hence the usual introductory questions respecting the author, his date, his residence, and his people, will, in his case, conduce greatly to disclose the main purposes of his prophetic life, and consequently the true sense of his prophecies. Let us then, in the outset, give these points our careful attention.——Of the early history of Ezekiel we know only that he was the son of Buzi, was a *priest*, and was taken as a captive to Chaldea in the second great deportation, which occurred in the first year of Jehoiachin, B. C. 600. In what part of Judea he had previously lived, under what circumstances he received his early training, and at what age he was made a captive, are points not on record. They can be reached only by doubtful conjecture. The fact that he was by birth and training a *priest* accounts for the remarkable type of the last nine chapters of his book. Such minute detail as we find in that vision of the temple, its rituals and surroundings, could by no means be expected in any prophet who was not perfectly familiar with those matters. The divine Spirit adapts himself to the prophets through whom he speaks, evermore using terms, figures, and modes of illustration, with which each one severally may be conversant.

The *date* of his several prophecies is mostly given with care and thus placed beyond reasonable doubt. The captivity of Jehoiachin (B. C. 600) is his epoch. Prophesying and writing with and for the Jews in captivity, this epoch was for them altogether appropriate, and was doubtless their own in current use.——His book opens with another epoch in the words, "In the thirtieth year," etc. This has given rise to much speculation. I reject the three theories following, viz.: that this refers to his own age; that it dates from the discovery of the book of the law in the reign of Josiah; and that it dates from the last Jubilee. Either of these theories is too capricious to be adopted. I accede to the opinion that these words allude to the new Chaldean epoch of Nabopolassar, the father of Nebuchadnezzar, which dates from the fall of Nineveh, B. C., 625, and was the great epoch of the profane historians of those and of subsequent times. As Ezekiel wrote among the Chaldeans, it was pertinent that he should make so much allusion to their great national epoch. Yet since his prophecies were intended chiefly for the use of the Jews, it was fitting that after this brief allusion to the Chaldean epoch, he should drop it, and in all other cases use only the epoch of his own people. Such is the fact.——Following this Jewish epoch, his prophecies commence with the fifth year (chap. 1: 2), and close (chap. 29: 17) with the twenty-seventh. The last nine chapters date in the twenty-fifth year. Between these extremes are a large number of definite dates, to be noticed in their place.

. Ezekiel's *residence* in Chaldea is said to have been "by the river of *Chebar*." Some commentators have identified this river with the Chaboras of Upper Mesopotamia, which falls into the Euphrates at Circesium, while others have sought traces of its name in the province of "Habor by the river of Gozan" (2 Kings 17: 6), where the king of

Assyria located some of his captives when he subverted the kingdom of the ten tribes. I accept the more recent view, which finds this "river of Chebar" in the *royal canal* built by Nebuchadnezzar, the greatest of all those artificial water-courses which were among the stupendous works of his reign. The word Chebar implies something great and *long*. The Hebrew orthography is not the same with that of the word rendered Habor (2 Kings 17 : 6).——The testimony of all history, sacred and profane, locates these Hebrew captives near Babylon, and not in the remote districts of Upper Mesopotamia. It scarcely admits of question that the Jewish captives were employed in excavating these immense canals, and hence would naturally have their homes along their line. This view may explain that inimitable ode (Ps. 137): "By the rivers of Babylon there we sat down; yea, we wept when we remembered Zion." Along side of those artificial water-courses, the scenes of their daily toil and weary tasks, how often had they sat down, exhausted and heart-sick, to weep as they thought of their dear but desolate Zion!——It was among those exiles, and in the midst of such surroundings, that Ezekiel spent his prophetic life. His great mission from God was to bring moral appliances to coöperate with physical for the regeneration of those exiles. The Lord had thrown them into his crucible of sore affliction; he therefore sent Ezekiel with truths divine—warnings, exhortations, counsels, and promises, to perfect the work of moral renovation for which those afflictions were designed.——Let it not be forgotten that the great national sin of the Jews had long been *idolatry*. The history of the rent kingdoms from Jeroboam to Hoshea, and from Rehoboam to Zedekiah, coupled with the testimony of the Lord's prophets during those ages, shows this most conclusively. For this sin the people of Judah were doomed to captivity in Babylon. To cure them of this sin, the Lord first selected the better portion to go into captivity, and let the baser portion fall by the sword, famine or pestilence, or remain in the land to go down madly into Egypt to perish miserably there.

Jer. 24 is a special prophecy indicating that this sifting process lay distinctly in the plan of God. But to make this plan successful, other agencies were requisite besides captivity in a foreign land.

Among these other agencies, the mission of Ezekiel was prominent. The Lord sent him forth among those captives to rebuke idolatry; to keep vividly before them the enormity of this national sin; to show them how horribly corrupt their brethren, yet remaining in Judah and Jerusalem, had become; and then (as in chaps. 8–11) to receive from the Lord a great panoramic vision of those sins, and of God's ministering and avenging angels, marking, and scourging, and slaying those hoary sinners; and then, by reporting, reproduce it to the eyes of his fellow captives. This was one striking method of making the judgments for idolatry inflicted in Jerusalem available for moral warning and impression upon the captives in Babylon. With a kindred moral aim, the Lord sent by Ezekiel many a tender, precious promise of mercy to the penitent, and of restoration to the faithful in the fullness of his own time.

——Striking analogies appear between Ezekiel and Jeremiah, and for the obvious reason that both had the same idolatrous people to deal with; both were sent of God to convict the people of the guilt of the same great national sin; both were God's instruments to supplement with moral warnings and promises the influence which his providences were exerting, yet needed those moral appliances for their more sure interpretation and best efficiency. Thus the major points in the life of these two prophets were analogous, yet there were minor points of unlike character. Jeremiah spent his prophetic life in Judea and in Egypt; Ezekiel, his in Chaldea. Jeremiah's public labors spanned the last eighteen years of Josiah's reign, the three months' reign of Jehoahaz, the eleven years' reign of Jehoiakim, and five years into the captivity of Jehoiachin, before Ezekiel began his prophetic ministry; while the twenty-two years of Ezekiel's prophetic life (named as its *minimum* length) probably extended somewhat beyond the close of Jeremiah's.—— Again, Jeremiah had to do with the mass of Jewish corruption—with the very worst class of her princes and people; while Ezekiel had only the better part—base, indeed, but yet not the basest—the captivity having been made, under God, itself a sifting process, to destroy and otherwise eliminate the vilest portion, and to save the more hopeful and less contaminated. Jeremiah came constantly in contact with kings on their thrones, the wicked and weak sons of the good Josiah, and found his trials intensified exceedingly by these relations of prophetic messenger from Him who fills the infinite throne of heaven to those base but proud men who disgraced their little seats of power over God's covenant people.——Ezekiel's mission lay among the people and their elders and head men, but no proud and morally rotten thrones lay in his way. The Lord had broken down that barrier to a spiritual reform of his people.——Jeremiah and Ezekiel both prophesy not of Jerusalem and the Jews only, but of other and contiguous nations also, and each of them for the same general reason. The Lord involved those other nations, to a greater or less extent, in the same fearful calamities which subverted the Jewish kingdom. They had been guilty of the same great national sins, and, therefore, must needs share the same fearful doom. They had even given the Jews their own idols, and must now bear the responsibility of this sin before the Most High God and before mankind. Some of them had maliciously exulted over the fall of Jerusalem, and had thus drawn down upon themselves the vengeance of Israel's God; and in general it was a time of retribution on the guilty, idolatrous nations of the age. Hence, vengeance having begun at the house of God, it might fitly be asked, "Where shall the ungodly and the sinner appear?" (1 Pet. 4: 17, 18.) They could not go altogether unpunished. (See Jer. 25: 29, and 49: 12.) Hence, the prophets Jeremiah and Ezekiel both speak of these fearful judgments on Ammon, Tyre, Edom, and Egypt, to which list Jeremiah adds Babylon and many others. The main objects of these prophecies seem to have been to assure the Jews that their own God shaped the destinies of all these heathen kingdoms, and that he had his own plans in mind beforehand, and, therefore, could predict them through his servants; but especially to impress them with a more deep and vivid sense of God's sure retribution on guilty nations for their national sins. This sense of certain retribution would be of the utmost moment in its bearings on their own case.

No complaint lies against Ezekiel for any lack of *order* and *date* in his several prophecies. His book may be comprehensively divided into two equal parts. Of his forty-eight chapters, the first twenty-four bear to the same point and treat of the same general theme, being addressed directly to the exiles, recounting their own sins and those of their brethren in Judea, especially in the line of idolatry and heart-apostasy from God.——The second portion is more miscellaneous, embracing prophecies against other nations; and then, in the line of God's jealousy for his own insulted name, there shines forth his glorious purpose to avenge himself upon his enemies, and to purify and save his own people. The book closes with far-reaching, magnificent prophecies of ultimate victory on Zion's side over all his foes, and of unsurpassed efficiency in the institutions, the truth, and the Spirit of the living God, now become gloriously present among his people.——The subdivisions of these parts will appear as we proceed.

Remarkably we find in Ezekiel all the varieties of style that appear within the entire range of the Hebrew prophets. He has pure visions, clearly indicated to be such by the language which introduces or closes the record; *c. g.*, chaps. 1, 8–11, 37 and 40–48. He has symbolic actions, also indicated in the record itself; *e. g.*, chap. 4, 5 and 12. He has similitudes, as of the vine-tree, chap. 15; of the watchman, chap. 33; and of the shepherd and his flock, chap. 35. He has also parables, as in chap. 17; an elegiac song in highly poetic costume in chap. 19; extended allegories in chaps. 23 and 24; and, finally, plain, unembellished prophecy coupled with solemn admonition, or with tender, hope-inspiring promise.——His style does not often lack elegance; never, force. He has remarkable power in grouping a mass of somewhat minute details in a way to heighten the effect exceedingly. Witness his portrayal of the horrible impurities of idolatry in Jerusalem and Samaria, chap. 23; or his description of the commerce, the splendor, and the fall of ancient Tyre, chaps. 27 and 28.——His spirit and style have elicited the admiration of able and learned critics. Havernick speaks of him as "coming forward with all abruptness and iron consistency in an age when prophecy was most rare. Has he to contend with a people of brazen front and unbending neck? He possesses, on his own part, an unbending nature, opposing the evil with an unflinching spirit of boldness and with words of consuming fire." "The glow of divine indignation, the mighty rushing of the Spirit of the Lord, and the holy majesty of Jehovah as the seer beheld it, are remarkably reflected in his writings. The lofty action, the torrent of his eloquence, rest on the same combination of power and consistency—the one as unwearied as the other is imposing."——Hengstenberg also gives his glowing testimony to the same points: "The Lord began to fulfill his good word, given to the exiles through Jeremiah, by causing Ezekiel to appear in the midst of them, who raised his voice like a trumpet and showed to Israel his misdeeds; whose word, like a threshing machine, passed over all those sweet hopes and purposes and ground them to the dust; whose whole manifestations furnished the strongest proof that the Lord was still among his people; who was himself a temple of the Lord, before whom the apparent temple, which still stood at Jerusalem for a short time sunk back into its own nothingness; a spiritual Samson, who, with a strong arm, seized the pillars of the temple and dashed it to the ground; an energetic, gigantic nature, who was thereby suited effectually to counteract the Babylonish spirit of the time, which loved to manifest itself in violent, gigantic, and grotesque forms; one who stood alone, but was yet equal to a hundred of the scholars of the prophets. The extent of his influence appears from the fact that the oldest of the people were accustomed to assemble in his house in order to hear the words of the Lord through him—a sign of the public and formal acknowledgment of his spiritual dignity in the colony."—Christology, vol. 3, pp. 459, 460.——The general style of his symbols, especially in his first and tenth chapters, is largely Chaldean, and, so far forth, is due to his Chaldean surroundings. The Jews for whom he wrote, residing in Chaldea, had become familiar there with these modes of representation. The Chaldeans who might read his writings would readily appreciate the beauty and force of these symbols. His own mind had felt their power as presented in Chaldean works of art. Hence the divine Spirit revealed himself to the prophet's mind in these symbols because they were, in that age and to that people, a readily intelligible and even forcible mode of representation. They were almost the language of the common people. If obscure to us, their obscurity is mainly due to their being a foreign tongue—a sort of symbolic speech which had its home in the valley of the Euphrates, and in the age of proud Nineveh and Babylon, but which has long since ceased to be a living tongue. The recent disinterment of so many sculptures and various works of art from the ruins of those cities affords us a pertinent key to the significance of these symbols and an ample explanation of their appearance in the prophecies of Ezekiel.*

---

* Those who have read Layard's Nineveh, or who have made them-

The style of representation in this first vision is, in part, Jewish, and, in so far forth, will be illustrated in the notes.

selves familiar otherwise with the modern discoveries in the ruins of ancient Nineveh and Babylon, will readily recall those figures, either sculptured or painted, of a composite character, made up of selected portions of various animals; *c. g.* " winged, human-headed bulls (Layard, p. 85); "gigantic winged bulls;" "small winged lions" (p. 32); a figure "with the head of the lion, the body of a man, and the feet of a bird" (p. 229). Or, again, "a human body clothed in robes, with the head of an eagle or a vulture; a curved beak, half open, disclosing a narrow-pointed tongue; over the shoulders, the usual curled, bushy hair of the Assyrian images; a comb of feathers rising on the top of the head; two wings springing from the back; and in either hand was the usual square vessel and the fir cone—the former supposed to be significant of gifts bestowed by the gods; the latter, being specially inflammable, may have symbolized fire—an element associated, in oriental minds, with the qualities or the home of the gods." Layard suggests that " this effigy probably typified by its mystic forms the union of certain divine attributes" (pp. 45-47).——Again, on pp. 51, 52, is an extended description of a second pair of winged, human-headed lions, the human shape continued to the waist, with human arms and with the legs of a lion; twelve feet in height, and as many in length; expanded wings sprang from the shoulder and spread over the back. A knotted girdle, ending in tassels, encircled the loins. All was found in a state of perfect preservation.——Of these figures, Mr. Layard expresses his views and reflections thus: "I used to contemplate for hours these mysterious emblems, and muse over their intent and history. What more noble forms could have ushered the people into the temple of their gods? What more sublime images could have been borrowed from nature by men who sought, unaided by the light of revelation, to embody their conception of the wisdom, power, and ubiquity of a Supreme Being? They could find no better type of intellect and knowledge than the head of the man; of strength, than the body of a lion; of ubiquity, than the wings of a bird. These winged, human-headed lions were not idle creations, the offspring of mere fancy; their meaning was written upon them. They had awed and instructed races which flourished three thousand years ago " (p. 52).

CHAPTER I.

The remarkable vision recorded in this chapter served to introduce Ezekiel to his prophetic work. It was a species of theophany analogous to that made to Isaiah, as recorded in his sixth chapter, and to John, Rev. 1: 10–20. How admirably it was adapted to prepare him for his mission will be better seen when we have carefully studied its import and in some good measure comprehended its symbols. We shall find them richly significant.

1. Now it came to pass in the thirtieth year, in the fourth month, in the fifth day of the month, as I was among the captives by the river of Chebar, that the heavens were opened, and I saw visions of God.

2. In the fifth day of the month, which was the fifth year of king Jehoiachin's captivity,

3. The word of the Lord came expressly unto Ezekiel the priest, the son of Buzi, in the land of the Chaldeans by the river Chebar; and the hand of the Lord was there upon him.

As said above in the general introduction, I find this "thirtieth year" in the new Chaldean epoch of Nabopolassar, father of Nebuchadnezzar, which reckoned its years from the fall of Nineveh, B. C. 625. Every other theory is capricious and without adequate foundation. This is natural, and meets all the conditions of the case; for the very brevity of the allusion shows that the epoch must have been well known, and goes far to prove that it was the common epoch of the place, the people, and the age—in other words, that it was *Chaldean.* A prophecy written in Chaldea should naturally, first of all, connect itself with the current Chaldean epoch. So much deference to their national history would seem due to that people. Yet, since the prophecy was chiefly for the Jews, no more than this brief connecting link could be demanded. This would enable the Chaldeans to compare Jewish dates with their own, and thus locate each several message. For his common epoch Ezekiel would manifestly prefer the Jewish.

These captives are, of course, the Jewish exiles, located, as shown in the introduction, along the royal canal of Nebuchadnezzar, the great and *long river,* as the word Chebar without much doubt indicates. These "visions of God" are not merely visions given by God through his revealing Spirit, but visions *of God,* visions, the special purpose of which was to reveal God himself in certain great aspects of his providential agency. The "fifth year of king Jehoiachin's captivity" follows the Jewish epoch, dating from the captivity of Jehoiachin, son of Jehoiakim, and last king of Judah save one, his uncle Zedekiah. This captivity occurred, B. C. 600. Hence both this epoch and the Chaldean locate this first vision of Ezekiel B. C. 595. See 2 Chron. 36: 9, 10, and 2 Kings 24: 1–16. The words "came expressly" translate the usual emphatic Hebrew phrase which repeats the infinite absolute before the finite verb; "coming, it came, i. e., it certainly came; came with the clearest demonstrations of its actuality. "The hand of the Lord was there upon him," is the usual phrase to indicate the special agency of the divine Spirit in revealing himself to his servants the prophets. See other cases of its use in chap. 3: 14–22, and 37: 1, and in the same sense, though with various phrase, Jer. 1: 7, 10, and 20: 7.

4. And I looked, and, behold, a whirlwind came out of the north, a great cloud, and a fire infolding itself, and a brightness was about it, and out of the midst thereof as the color of amber, out of the midst of the fire.

Before I enter upon the particular description of this wonderful vision, it may aid the reader if I state in few words what I take to be its general import.

I do not regard it as an unmeaning display of things magnificent, grotesque, and marvelous, nor, strictly speaking, as an attempt to represent by symbols the essential nature of the Infinite God; but I suppose it to be *a symbolic representation of the moveable base of the throne of God incarnate*—this incarnate God being considered as manifesting himself in his providential government of our world. As here represented, his throne rests on a lofty, magnificent platform or solid floor, which floor itself reposes on the bodies and wings of "the living creatures" that are so graphically portrayed in this vision. The whole representation contemplates the varied agencies of God's providence as combining the utmost energy, wisdom, celerity, efficiency, and grandeur, and is designed to show how He moves among the nations of men, lifting up and casting down at his will, scourging for sin, and purifying by discipline, evermore just and righteous, and making his movements conspire to the exalted and worthy ends of his own glory and of human salvation.——Let us now look carefully into the several features of this delineation. The vision opens with surpassing grandeur. A whirlwind rolls up from the north with a great cloud and a fire which perpetually *takes hold of itself* (so the Heb.), making one vast continuous sheet of flame. A brightness invests the whole, of the color of "amber," or, as many modern critics prefer, of "burnished brass." All the ideas of that age seem to have located the home of the gods in the north—a sentiment due perhaps to the Aurora Borealis, which they seem to have thought of as the occasional illumination of the palace halls of the gods. Thus Isaiah (14: 13) makes his proud Lucifer (the great monarch of Babylon) say, "I will exalt my throne above the stars of God; I will sit also upon the mount of the congregation, *in the sides of the north.*" Perhaps it was with some reference to those ideas that this magnificent vision of Jehovah's moving throne comes forth from the north.

5. Also out of the midst thereof came the likeness of four living creatures. And this was their appearance; they had the likeness of a man.

6. And every one had four faces, and every one had four wings.

7. And their feet were straight feet; the sole of their feet was like the sole of a calf's foot; and they sparkled like the color of burnished brass.

8. And they had the hands of a man under their wings on their four sides; and they four had their faces and their wings.

9. Their wings were joined one to another; they turned not when they went; they went every one straight forward.

Now there came forth from the blaze of this effulgence what seemed like four living creatures in whom the human form predominates. Yet each one had four faces and also four wings. Their feet, moreover, were not those of a man, but of a calf or ox, yet sparkling with radiance like that of burnished brass. They had also the hand of a man under their wings. Two of these wings, making one pair, were joined together. Remarkably they made no turn in their movements, but went in straight lines, evermore straight forward. Probably this fact takes its significance from that law of mind which associates moral perversity with turning from a right line. The path of right and duty is thought of as being straight, but never crooked. God's providential agencies are evermore true and righteous altogether. It may indicate that in both discipline and retribution God moves straight on to his purposed end. The symbol of the calf or ox may have a place here to indicate the solid, massive strength requisite to support so vast a structure as the throne of the Almighty. The reader will note that many of these symbols appeared to the Jews in actual life in the vast "molten sea" connected with Solomon's temple. This sea stood on twelve oxen, and, moreover, had in its ornamental work sculptured lions, oxen, and cherubim, coupled also with wheels as in this vision of Ezekiel. See 1 Kings 7: 23–33. In some respects, therefore, this grouping of symbols was Hebraic, while in others it was Chaldean. The grouping of diverse animal figures in one nondescript symbol is very common, as above shown, in the Chaldean monuments of that age.

10. As for the likeness of their faces, they four had the face of a man, and the face of a lion, on the right side: and they four had the face of an ox on the left side; they four also had the face of an eagle.

11. Thus were their faces: and their wings were stretched upward; two wings of every one were joined one to another, and two covered their bodies.

12. And they went every one straight forward: whither the spirit was to go, they went; and they turned not when they went.

This account of the location of the several faces is not quite explicit, but there can scarcely be a doubt that these four diverse faces looked each in its several direction, the human face in front, the lion face to the right, the face like the ox to the left, and that of the eagle backward to the rear. Of their four wings, two were joined and stretched upward, while the other two fell and covered their bodies. Somewhat like this were the wings of the cherubim as seen by Isaiah (chap. 6: 2). They had each six wings: one pair covering the face, one the feet, and the other used for flight. Here again we may note that all movement is straight forward, with no turning. They go as the spirit in them impels; this whole representation being designed to show that the magnificent agencies of God's universal providence are every-where and for evermore permeated and controlled by his own ever-present will—the one Infinite Mind guiding and ruling all.

13. As for the likeness of the living creatures, their appearance was like burning coals of fire, and like the appearance of lamps: it went up and down among the living creatures; and the fire was bright, and out of the fire went forth lightning.

14. And the living creatures ran and returned as the appearance of a flash of lightning.

To heighten the grandeur of this magnificent portrayal, these living creatures now seem to have the appearance of coals of fire that burn like lamps. One clause seems to say that this fire shoots and darts among these living creatures—a fire invested with a glorious radiance out of which lightnings flashed; while another clause has it that the living creatures themselves ran and returned like flashes of lightning. Probably he meant to say both these things; probably both were seen in the vision. How grand and sublime must that scene have been!

15. Now as I beheld the living creatures, behold one wheel upon the earth by the living creatures, with his four faces.

16. The appearance of the wheels and their work was like unto the color of a beryl: and they four had one likeness: and their appearance and their work was as it were a wheel in the middle of a wheel.

17. When they went, they went upon their four sides; and they turned not when they went.

Wheels are an expressive symbol of power and rapid motion.

As to the number of wheels in this combination of symbols, v. 15, seems to indicate but one; but vs. 16 and 18 both speak of four, and so also does the coördinate description in chap. 10: 9, 10. These wheels were sparkling and brilliant, shining like polished gems. But the most remarkable feature was their combination, said to be "as it were a wheel in the middle of a wheel." According to this description, they might be concentric and in the same plane, or they might be concentric and yet in different planes, say at right angles. From the account of their motion in any direction without turning, the latter seems to have been their form. This is the view of the ablest modern commentators. We need not trouble ourselves with the fact that no axletree could be made to work in two such concentric double wheels, so that they could run in planes at right angles to each other. For this moveable base for the throne of God was *seen in prophetic vision*, and not in the actual world; was constituted *to be seen*—not to run in the business of real life; and had for its object a certain impression on the mind of the prophet, and not any particular result in the mechanical world.

18. As for their rings, they were so high that they were dreadful; and their rings were full of eyes round about them four.

"Rings," as used here, mean the *rims*, the periphery, or felloes of the wheels. Their height, so great that they seemed "dreadful," represents the wheels as of immense size, towering aloft in the air with magnificence fearfully sublime. Then the periphery of these wheels was full of eyes all round about, indicating perfect intelligence, and giving the impression of piercing thought and most vivid expressiveness.

19. And when the living creatures went, the wheels went by them: and when the living creatures were lifted up from the earth, the wheels were lifted up.

20. Whithersoever the spirit was to go, they went, thither was their spirit to go; and the wheels were lifted up over against them: for the spirit of the living creature was in the wheels.

21. When those went, these went; and when those stood, these stood; and when those were lifted up from the earth, the wheels were lifted up over against them: for the spirit of the living creature was in the wheels.

Next we have the same elements of life and self-acting inspiration in these wheels as in the living creatures themselves. The wheels constantly attend the living creatures as if moved by one common impulse and will. This was one of the most striking features in this wonderful combination of symbols. It could not signify less or other than that God's providences always have a meaning; always aim at some wise purpose; are evermore guided by one and the same supreme and all-pervading divine will.

22. And the likeness of the firmament upon the heads of the living creature was, as the color of the terrible crystal, stretched forth over their heads above.

23. And under the firmament were their wings straight, the one toward the other: every one had two, which covered on this side, and every one had two, which covered on that side, their bodies.

Here we begin to reach the purpose and work of this remarkable combination of symbols. These living creatures bear upon their heads and upon their straight wings, a firmament, *i. e.*, a solid expanse, platform, or elevated floor. Its appearance was in color "like the terrible crystal"—so brilliant and dazzling as to be even fearful to behold. Upon this base, as we shall soon see, reposed the throne of the incarnate God.——The prophet again refers to the position of the two sets of wings, one set straight and joined together, assisting to support the firmament, somewhat like the wings of the cherubim in the most holy place. When the living creatures stood, the other set fell gracefully down and protected their bodies.

24. And when they went, I heard the noise of their wings, like the noise of great waters, as the voice of the Almighty, the voice of speech, as the noise of an host: when they stood, they let down their wings.

25. And there was a voice from the firmament that was over their heads, when they stood, and had let down their wings.

As if to combine every element of grandeur and sublimity, and appeal to every sense, the sound of their wings, when in motion, was as the roar of great waters, like the voice of the Almighty God himself. In the clause, "The voice of speech as the noise of an host," the Hebrew does not imply the utterance of articulate words, but should rather be rendered, "The sound of their noise was as the sound of an host," *i, e.*, of an army rushing to battle. There may have been the voice of articulate words from above the firmament, *i. e.*, from the glorious personage who sat on the throne; v. 25 seems to imply this.——The reader will readily recall the manifestations made by the "Alpha and Omega," by Him who is both the first and the last, to John, the Revelator, as in Rev. 1: 10–16, "His voice was as the sound of many waters, and his face as the sun when he shineth in his strength."

26. And above the firmament that was over their heads was the likeness of a throne, as the appearance of a sapphire

stone: and upon the likeness of the throne was the likeness as the appearance of a man above it.

27. And I saw as the color of amber, as the appearance of fire round about within it, from the appearance of his loins even upward, and from the appearance of his loins even downward, I saw as it were the appearance of fire, and it had brightness round about.

The vital points in this description are plain, and they are also richly significant and sublime. Here is the throne, for the sake of supporting which, and of moving it also, we have seen a wonderful combination of living creatures, wings and wheels, with various accompanying symbols of intelligence, energy, splendor, and majesty. Here also—more really sublime than all the rest-- is the appearance of a *man* upon this throne. From his loins upward, and from his loins downward, he seemed as one begirt with fire—the brightness of fire, and the effulgence of the most magnificent pearls and gems, combining to invest him with ineffable glory. This personage can be no other than the incarnate Son of God, the great Lord of universal providence, appearing in this majestic form to his servant Ezekiel, much as the same personage appeared to Isaiah (chap. 6), of which case, John in his Gospel (chap. 12: 41) tells us that Isaiah then and there "saw the glory of Jesus and spake of him." Numerous proofs might be adduced to show that repeatedly, during the course of the Old Testament age, Jesus Christ anticipated his incarnation by appearing in human form to his people. He appeared thus to Manoah and his wife (Judges 13: 2–23), giving them his name, "Wonderful" (not "secret"), using the identical word which Isaiah gives as one of his names (Isa. 9: 6), "*Wonderful*, Counsellor, the Mighty God," etc.——"This is also He who was with his church in the wilderness," as Stephen affirms (Acts 7: 38), and as the narrative (Ex. 23: 20–23) most plainly indicates. It was therefore only a subsequent appearance of the same glorious personage which was vouchsafed to John in Patmos with a luster and effulgence of glories closely analogous to what we have here.

28. As the appearance of the bow that is in the cloud in the day of rain, so was the appearance of the brightness round about. This was the appearance of the likeness of the glory of the Lord. And when I saw it, I fell upon my face, and I heard the voice of one that spake.

The final touch to this inimitable representation compares it to the radiance of the "bow in the cloud in the day of rain." Such was the brightness and glory that invested the incarnate Deity. Thus the Shechinah revealed himself to Ezekiel to impress his soul with the magnificence, the energy, and the glory of Him whose work he was now to undertake, whose mission as a prophet he was to fulfill, whose words he was to hear and then to bear to his people. What an installation this into his prophetic work! No wonder he fell on his face as one overwhelmed with reverence and awe!——Let it be noted yet further that this portrayal was specially pertinent in view of the fact that God's providential agencies were then intensely active among the nations, and especially toward the Jews in both discipline and judgment—the discipline that chastened to reclaim, and the judgments that scourged in stern and awful retribution. Into the midst of these agencies Ezekiel was thrown. He was commissioned as a prophet of God to coöperate by the use of moral agencies with those providential agencies of the Almighty. He was to interpret the significance of those judgments. He was to warn the people to repent, as they would escape such inflictions. He was to press them to repentance by the promise of pardoning mercy. In every appropriate way he was to supplement those agencies of providence with the concurrent influences of God's revealed truth. Hence nothing could be more vital than to impress upon his mind the qualities of that fearfully glorious and energetic divine providence which in its intensified forms was now being manifested toward the chosen people.——Moreover, nothing could have been better adapted to impart to him a baptism of reverence, docility, energy, and self-sacrificing devotion. Under the influence of such views of the glorious Being whose behests he is commissioned to bear to the people, how could he falter before hardship or danger? How could he fail to carry with him through life a sense of the glory of his Divine Master, saying evermore: "*I serve the ineffably glorious incarnate God; and I must be true and faithful!*"

Some minds will naturally ask, What proof do you give your readers that your interpretation of this chapter is the true one? To such I answer briefly: *The fact that it meets all the conditions of the case.* It fits every circumstance. It is pertinent to an inauguration of Ezekiel to his prophetic office, as it should be; it fits his relations as a prophet to the captives at Babylon; fits their relations to the Omnipresent and then specially active agencies of God's providence over nations; fits the style of illustrating the attributes of God which prevailed in Chaldea, and also that which was developed to some extent in the Jewish temple; in short, this construction fits in all possible points, and therefore must be the true one. Out of a dozen trial keys, that one which enters the lock, moves without obstruction and with the least possible friction through its wards, and throws its bolt readily, must be the right one. No rational man ever doubts such proof.

CHAPTER II.

The glorious personage brought to view in the previous chapter here gives the prophet his commission and instructions.

1. And he said unto me, Son of man, stand upon thy feet, and I will speak unto thee.
2. And the spirit entered into me when he spake unto me, and set me upon my feet, that I heard him that spake unto me.

The overwhelming impressions of solemnity and awe under which the prophet sank to the ground, and also the kind words and imparted spirit which set him upon his feet again and restored calmness to his soul, are noted here with entire simplicity. This case is closely analogous to that of Isaiah as in his sixth chapter, and that of Daniel, (chap. 10: 15–19,) or of the revelator John (chap. 1: 17). It can not surprise us that John should say, "When I saw him, I fell at his feet as dead;" or that Daniel should testify, "O my Lord, by the vision my sorrows are turned upon me, and I have retained no strength, neither is any breath left in me." In each of these cases, as in this case of Ezekiel, the Lord kindly renewed their strength and prepared them to hear his words.

3. And he said unto me, Son of man, I send thee to the children of Israel, to a rebellious nation that hath rebelled against me; they and their fathers have transgressed against me, even unto this very day.
4. For *they are* impudent children and stiff-hearted. I do send thee unto them; and thou shalt say unto them, Thus saith the Lord God.
5. And they, whether they will hear, or whether they will forbear, (for they *are* a rebellious house,) yet shall know that there hath been a prophet among them.

"Impudent," in v. 4, is in the original *hard-faced*. The prophet is to assure them that he brings them a message, not from himself, but from the Lord God. "Will forbear," means will refuse to hear. The Lord intimates that they will have occasion to know that he has certainly sent his prophet among them. His judgments would verify the prophet's commission and leave the people no room to doubt this appalling truth. This introduction shows that the exiles in Chaldea, though less hardened and hopeless than their brethren in Judea, were yet exceedingly stubborn and perverse. It was a great and very difficult work for Ezekiel to accomplish, to impress upon them the fear of the Lord and to recall them to repentance and a new life.

6. And thou, son of man, be not afraid of them, neither be afraid of their words, though briers and thorns *be* with thee, and thou dost dwell among scorpions: be not afraid of their words, nor be dismayed at their looks, though they *be* a rebellious house.

7. And thou shalt speak my words unto them, whether they will hear, or whether they will forbear; for they *are* most rebellious.

The clause, "Though briers and thorns be with thee," Gesenius prefers to render, "though they be rebels and thorns toward thee." Maurer, favoring greater congruity between the two words, makes the sense "nettles and thorns." The general sense is clear. Though they are hostile, malign, severe, and even savage toward thee, yet be thou firm and fearless before them, and do thy duty. The Lord would have him anticipate stern opposition and a painfully trying life, and gird his soul to meet it. So evermore, he who will live godly in Christ Jesus and *for* Christ Jesus must suffer more or less persecution. Let him expect it and seek grace to meet it with Christian fortitude.

8. But thou, son of man, hear what I say unto thee; Be not thou rebellious like that rebellious house: open thy mouth, and eat that I give thee.

9. And when I looked, behold, a hand *was* sent unto me; and, lo, a roll of a book *was* therein;

10. And he spread it before me: and it *was* written within and without: and *there was* written therein lamentations, and mourning, and woe.

This eating was in vision, and not done in the actual world. As a thing of vision, it was admirably significant, implying that he must take the messages of God to his heart and shrink not from any service for God which they might involve. This roll, like the ancient book, was a long strip of parchment, fitted to roll up, which was written upon both sides ("within and without"). Its contents, the matters therein written, were wholly of "lamentation, and mourning, and woe"—all mournful exposures of guilt and crime; messages of swift judgment and of awful doom! How sad to Ezekiel must have been this preintimation of his painfully trying work! Must his messages to his own people testify only to their guilt and shame; speak but rarely of promise and hope, and mainly of judgment without mercy and of woe "too wide to see beyond!" If so, may he have grace to be true to his God and true to the souls of the guilty people; for it were a fearful thing for mortal man to falter in duty where the destiny of souls is at stake!

CHAPTER III.

This chapter continues and completes what pertains properly to Ezekiel's introduction to his prophetic work. The Lord explains and defines his commission; warns him of the opposition he has to encounter, and girds him with the requisite firmness and energy to meet it; discloses the great responsibilities of his work as bearing on the life or death of souls; and finally signifies to him that he is not to speak on his own motion, but only as the Lord shall give him a message from himself for the people.

1. Moreover he said unto me, Son of man, eat that thou findest; eat this roll, and go speak unto the house of Israel.

2. So I opened my mouth, and he caused me to eat that roll.

3. And he said unto me, Son of man, cause thy belly to eat, and fill thy bowels with this roll that I give thee. Then did I eat *it;* and it was in my mouth as honey for sweetness.

As already indicated in the notes on chap. 2: 8, the eating of this roll, done only in vision, signified that he should take the messages of God home to his very heart, give them his most solemn attention, make himself thoroughly master of their contents, and hold himself at God's command to deliver them faithfully as directed.——That they were in his mouth as honey for sweetness, implied his joy in accepting his prophetic mission, showing that at least his *first* impressions in receiving this honor were those of willing and cheerful obedience, and the consequent joy of yielding to the will of God. He does not say here in explicit terms as John does (Rev. 10: 9, 10), "As soon as I had eaten it, my belly was bitter;" yet v. 14 seems to imply this: "I went in bitterness, in the heat of my spirit." There would be sore trials to the flesh, trials to his human sensibilities, in the painful service of bearing such messages to a people so dear to him and yet so guilty and refractory toward God.——So evermore the faithful Christian life on earth will blend the joy of pleasing God with the pain of coming in contact with sin in the case of those who stand in relations near and dear to our hearts.

4. And he said unto me, Son of man, go, get thee unto the house of Israel, and speak with my words unto them.

5. For thou *art* not sent to a people of a strange speech and of an hard language, *but* to the house of Israel;

6. Not to many people of a strange speech and of an hard language, whose words thou canst not understand. Surely, had I sent thee to them, they would have hearkened unto thee.

7. But the house of Israel will not hearken unto thee; for they will not hearken unto me: for all the house of Israel *are* impudent and hard-hearted.

"Strange," as usual, means *foreign*. The Lord says to his prophet, "I send thee only to the house of Israel; not to a foreign nation of an unknown language; not to many tribes or people of unknown tongue. If I had sent thee to such a people, they would have hearkened to thee, for such perverseness and obduracy of heart could be found nowhere among the heathen.——Underneath this statement lies a great law of human sinning. It is only by the long abuse of great light and of rich mercies that men reach such a degree of moral hardihood and such depths of intense depravity. It is appalling to think of the influence of resisted light, of mercies abused, of obligations seen yet repelled and finally scorned! With what fearful rapidity, especially in the later stages, do such sinners become seven-fold more the children of hell than before!——Our Savior met and fully recognized this law of human sinning in his intercourse with the Jews of his time. See Mat. 11: 20-24, John 9: 39, 41, and 15: 22, 24.

8. Behold, I have made thy face strong against their faces, and thy forehead strong against their foreheads.

9. As an adamant harder than flint have I made thy forehead: fear them not, neither be dismayed at their looks, though they *be* a rebellious house.

These are bold figures, but are readily understood. The Lord was preparing his servant to confront the most brazen-faced sinners with firm unflinching heart. This is said with a double purpose—to forewarn and to forearm; to signify to him what he must expect, and to gird his soul to meet it.

10. Moreover he said unto me, Son of man, all my words that I shall speak unto thee receive in thine heart, and hear with thine ears.

11. And go, get thee to them of the captivity, unto the children of thy people, and speak unto them, and tell them, Thus saith the Lord God; whether they will hear, or whether they will forbear.

V. 10 seems to express without a figure what the act of eating the roll implies.——The expressive clause, "whether they will hear or not hear" ("will forbear"), seems to be not merely a part of the Lord's instructions to his prophet, but a part also of his message to the people. The prophet must give them to understand that God lays on them the fearful responsibility of deciding whether they would hear or would not. They must determine this question for themselves and bear its consequences.

12. Then the spirit took me up, and I heard behind me a voice of a great rushing, *saying*, Blessed *be* the glory of the Lord from his place.

This being "taken up by the Spirit" was done in vision only. It seems to be bearing him away from the scenes described in the first chapter. Hence he receives his last impressions from these sounds behind him as he is leaving. The great rush corresponds to the account in chap. 1: 24, the sound of the wings of flying cherubim and of their voices, here praising God and celebrating his glories as revealed from the place of these manifestations.

13. *I heard* also the noise of the wings of the living creatures that touched one another, and the noise of the wheels over against them, and a noise of a great rushing.

In the phrase, "the wings that touched one another," the Hebrew has the beautiful figure, "wings that kissed each that of her sister."

14. So the spirit lifted me up, and took me away, and I went in bitterness, in the heat of my spirit; but the hand of the Lord was strong upon me.

This scene must have been immensely exciting to the youthful prophet. Probably he begins to appreciate the responsibilities and trials of the work now devolved upon him, and hence feels pangs of bitterness in his soul, and a sense as of intense heat in his spirit. But the hand of the Lord is strong upon him, and he can not withstand the summons to painful duty, and would not if he could. The experiences of Jeremiah were much the same. See notes on Jer. 20: 7–9.

15. Then I came to them of the captivity at Tel abib, that dwelt by the river of Chebar, and I sat where they sat, and remained there astonished among them seven days.

Here we pass from scenes of prophetic vision to scenes not visional but purely in the actual world. He comes to the exiles, and soon begins to speak to them from the Lord his God. As they were in the real world only, and not at all in prophetic vision, so must his words and acts, relating to them, be understood as in the actual and not the ideal world.——Tel-abib (corn-hill) was the residence of a large body of these exiles, and probably of the prophet himself.——The first Hebrew verb of the phrase, "I *sat* where they sat," is variously read and translated by the best critics. Our English translation follows the vowel points of the Hebrew text and not the consonants, and is not generally approved as the most reliable reading. Gesenius prefers a reading of the original, which means, "I saw them sitting there, and I sat down with them astonished seven days." Maurer, preferring another root, renders, "I turned aside where they were sitting, and sat down with them."——As the verb rendered "*remained*," is precisely the usual Hebrew verb to *sit*, our received translation repeats itself; "I sat where they sat, and *sat* astonished;" which is scarcely admissible. ——But no important sentiment is involved in these diversities of reading.——"Seven days," a round indefinite number, meaning a considerable time. See the same usage under somewhat similar circumstances in the case of Job's three friends (Job 2: 13).

16. And it came to pass at the end of seven days, that the word of the Lord came unto me, saying,

17. Son of man, I have made thee a watchman unto the house of Israel: therefore hear the word at my mouth, and give them warning from me.

18. When I say unto the wicked, Thou shalt surely die; and thou givest him not warning, nor speakest to warn the wicked from his wicked way, to save his life; the same wicked *man* shall die in his iniquity, but his blood will I require at thy hand.

19. Yet if thou warn the wicked, and he turn not from his wickedness, nor from his wicked way, he shall die in his iniquity; but thou hast delivered thy soul.

20. Again, When a righteous *man* doth turn from his righteousness, and commit iniquity, and I lay a stumbling-block before him, he shall die: because thou hast not given him warning, he shall die in his sin, and his righteousness which he hath done shall not be remembered; but his blood will I require at thy hand.

21. Nevertheless if thou warn the righteous *man*, that the righteous sin not, and he doth not sin, he shall surely live, because he is warned; also thou hast delivered thy soul.

These words were specially addressed by the Lord to his prophet. They may or may not have been announced by the prophet to the people. Essentially the same ideas are drawn out somewhat more fully in chap. 33. There, they are rehearsed to the people. Their intensely solemn import is plain. The watchman or sentinel stands guard in war to give notice of impending danger. If he does his duty faithfully, and the people disregard his warnings, his hands are clear of their blood: they perish in their own folly. If he neglects his duty and the people perish unwarned, they perish indeed, but their blood is required at his hand.——So of the prophet. So of all Christian ministers, and indeed of all Christians in every sphere in their relations to the people among whom the Lord in his providence may place them. They must admonish those who are in their sins of their danger, as they would free themselves from blood-guiltiness in the death of unwarned souls. The case of a righteous man apostatizing from a pious life falls under the same law. Every good and true servant of God is bound to admonish him of his peril, else his blood may be required of those who have neglected to give him such warning.——The "stumbling-block" spoken of here (v. 20) is not a temptation to sin, but a means of destruction, an agency employed of God to destroy the sinner.

22. And the hand of the Lord was there upon me; and he said unto me, Arise, go forth into the plain, and I will there talk with thee.

23. Then I arose, and went forth into the plain: and, behold, the glory of the Lord stood there, as the glory which I saw by the river of Chebar: and I fell on my face.

This "plain" or valley stands contrasted with the hill (Tell Abib) where the people resided. The spirit of the call is, Go down to a retired place; I have another personal charge to give thee in private.——The prophet obeyed; and there he saw again the same manifestation of the glory of the Lord which he had seen by the river Chebar. Here also, as there, he falls prostrate on his face.——This going to the valley seems to have been done in the external world. What followed there was said and shown to him in prophetic vision.

24. Then the spirit entered into me, and set me upon my feet, and spake with me, and said unto me, Go, shut thyself within thy house.

25. But thou, O son of man, behold, they shall put bands upon thee, and shall bind thee with them, and thou shalt not go out among them:

26. And I will make thy tongue cleave to the roof of thy mouth, that thou shalt be dumb, and shalt not be to them a reprover: for they *are* a rebellious house.

27. But when I speak with thee, I will open thy mouth, and thou shalt say unto them, Thus saith the Lord God; He that heareth, let him hear: and he that forbeareth, let him forbear: for they *are* a rebellious house.

I take the general import of these instructions to be this: Thy mission, Ezekiel, is simply and only to speak the words of God; not thine own words. Shut up thyself, therefore, in thine own house, and remain there till the Spirit of God shall lead thee forth. The people will withstand thee; but let not their opposition instigate thee to any rash words of thine own. Wait in silence till the Lord shall give thee his own message to deliver to them. However much the greatness or the guilt of their sins may fire thy soul with indignation, take care to say only what the Lord shall give thee to say. Restrict thyself absolutely to the messages that are given thee of the Lord thy God. When I open thy mouth, then speak and fear nothing. Till then be silent.

CHAPTER IV.

THE object of the symbolic transactions recorded in this chapter was to impress the exiles with the facts that Jerusalem was soon to be besieged; that this siege would be exceedingly severe, involving great famine and distress; and that it was to come upon the city and the people for their great sins.——The date of the prophecies in chaps. 4-7, can not be much later than the fifth year of Jehoiachin's captivity, since no new date appears between chaps. 1: 2, and 8: 1. The latter was the sixth year and sixth month. Zedekiah's reign began very soon after the captivity of Jehoiachin. The siege of Jerusalem commenced in the tenth month of his ninth year. (Jer. 52: 4.) Hence this prophecy preceded the beginning of the siege by some four or four and a half years only.——The two significant symbolic transactions recorded in this chapter are closely related to each other—are indeed parts of the same whole; viz. (1.) The delineation of the city of Jerusalem on a tile, and formally laying siege to it: and, (2.) The prophet's lying on his left side three hundred and ninety days, and on his right, forty, and taking his bread and water by measure during those periods—to indicate both the straitness of the siege and its moral causes in the nation's great sins.

1. Thou also, son of man, take thee a tile, and lay it before thee, and portray upon it the city, *even* Jerusalem:

2. And lay siege against it, and build a fort against it, and cast a mount against it; set the camp also against it, and set *battering* rams against it round about.

3. Moreover take thou unto thee an iron pan, and set it *for* a wall of iron between thee and the city: and set thy face against it, and it shall be besieged, and thou shalt lay siege against it. This *shall be* a sign to the house of Israel.

The ruins of Nineveh and of Babylon have furnished the world during the present century large quantities of "*tile*," sun-baked or kiln-burnt brick, *covered with inscriptions*. Hence this symbol was perfectly familiar to Ezekiel and to his fellow-exiles. To portray a city on a tile and let it represent Jerusalem was altogether in harmony with the usages of the Chaldean people.——This symbolic transaction was throughout in keeping with the modes of ancient warfare. Towers were built, mounds raised, often to the full height of the walls of the besieged city; a camp was fitted up; battering rams provided. Then, to protect the besiegers, strong ramparts were raised between them and the city, indicated in this transaction by the "iron pan." All this was for a "*sign*" to the house of Israel, a thoroughly symbolic process, to signify the siege of their beloved city.——There can be no reasonable doubt that this was really *done* as here stated, and not merely *seen in vision* without being done in fact. For the record has none of the usual intimations of a vision, *e. g.*, "I looked;" "I saw;" "the Lord showed me;" "I was in the spirit and saw," etc., etc. On the contrary, the prophet is simply commanded to do precisely this thing, and the Lord said it should be a "*sign*," a visible, significant symbol, to the people.

4. Lie thou also upon thy left side, and lay the iniquity of the house of Israel upon it: *according* to the number of the days that thou shalt lie upon it thou shalt bear their iniquity.

5. For I have laid upon thee the years of their iniquity, according to the number of the days, three hundred and ninety days: so shalt thou bear the iniquity of the house of Israel.

6. And when thou hast accomplished them, lie again on thy right side, and thou shalt bear the iniquity of the house of Judah forty days: I have appointed thee each day for a year.

This also we must interpret as an actual transaction, symbolic of course in its purpose, but not an unreal vision. It proceeds in the same strain as the previous symbol, a simple command to *do*. Manifestly this lying on either side, as well as the preparation and eating of his food, were to be done "*in the sight of the people*" (see v. 12). Now, since the people are in the external world only, and not in prophetic vision, this must have been an actual proceeding, and not a thing of mere vision.——It can not be supposed that this lying on one side was absolutely continuous and unbroken by any rising up during the entire thirteen months in the former case and one and one-third months in the latter. For, according to the record, the prophet prepared his own food and ate it from time to time. The necessities of his physical being were therefore to be provided for as an exception to the general law of his fixed position.

It will meet all the conditions of the case if we suppose that his lying on his side was so public as to be well known, and so continuous as to fill out the greater part of the time and as to involve great hardship and suffering. So much we must admit, else it would not forcibly symbolize his bearing of the iniquities of Israel and Judah, and the sore straitness of the besieged city and its people. The restraint which the Lord put upon him (v. 8) prevented his turning from side to side to relieve himself, but did not prevent his preparing and eating his necessary food.——These periods of time (three hundred and ninety days, and forty) were not capricious. They were sufficiently long to involve much discomfort and even suffering. There was probably some special significance in both periods. Critics have generally agreed that the long period looks to the interval from the revolt under Jeroboam to the destruction of the city, which the common chronology makes three hundred and eighty-eight years—in round numbers three hundred and ninety. During this period the two nations had been relapsing into idolatry—a fact which would itself give ample significance to the symbol of lying three hundred and ninety days on his left side to bear the iniquities of Israel.——The special significance of the number *forty* for the years of Judah is less obvious. Rosenmueller and Maurer agree in commencing it with the twelfth year of Josiah when his great reform was inaugurated, and in closing it with the destruction of the city—this period beginning hopefully but closing wofully with horrible apostasy—the bitter disappointment of fondly cherished hopes of national reform, and the aggravated guilt of broken covenants and of light rejected. There was manifestly good reason why the special attention of the Jews should be called to the more aggravated course of their nation within these last forty years.——This explanation is on the whole to be preferred to any other that has been before me. The forty years' wandering in the wilderness is too remote in time, and not sufficiently pertinent to the present case.——I doubt if any other special significance pertains to the distinction between Israel and Judah except what is readily seen in the historic circumstances as above indicated. The three hundred and ninety years of Israel began with the revolt of Jeroboam. In that revolt, Israel as distinct from Judah was prominent. There, in her revolt, and in the idolatrous decree of the golden calves, the terrible relapse of the whole nation into idolatry began. ——On the other hand the forty years' period, as above explained, related specially to Judah, marking the period of her last guilty relapse from God, and suggesting the great light she had sinned against. That God's special appointment should make each day's lying by the prophet on his side, symbolic of one year, need occasion no surprise or difficulty. Once indicated, the significance was clear and unmistakable. But, that interpreters of prophecy should find here authority for the theory that in all prophetic notations of time, "day" means "year," and "year" means three hundred and sixty years, is in the last degree capricious and unfounded. How can those who embrace this theory fail to see that throughout this passage the words "day" and "year" are used evermore in their ordinary and common sense, and not at all with the special extension or rather multiplication which they claim for them? Did the prophet lie on his left side three hundred and ninety *years*, and on his right side forty *years*? That would be simply monstrous, yet not more so than the theory that the word "day" in prophecy means "year."——In the present case the only reason why each day's confined posture on the side represents a year lies in the symbol (not in the word day), and is there by special divine arrangement. It is not at all in the sense of the words "day" and "year." The Lord told the prophet and also the people that his lying a certain number of *days* on either side should remind the people of so many *years* of their national sin. This is all.——That Israel was indicated by the prophet's left side may look to the fact that geographically, that kingdom lay on their left, since in locating the points of compass, the Orientals stood with their faces to the east. Note also chap. 16: 46, "Thine elder sister is Samaria, she and her daughters that dwell at thy left hand."

7. Therefore thou shalt set thy face toward the siege of Jerusalem, and thine arm *shall be* uncovered, and thou shalt prophesy against it.

8. And behold, I will lay bands upon thee, and thou shalt not turn thee from one side to another, till thou hast ended the days of thy siege.

This is a remarkable combination of symbols—a man lying prostrate on one side to signify that he bears the iniquity of the house of Israel; yet setting his face toward his tile, which represents Jerusalem, to indicate that he is (in symbol) besieging the city, and having his arm bare and his loins girded to show that the assailing party is alert and unimpeded in his assault. Making bare the arm by girding the loins is one of the most common, well defined, and expressive symbols of oriental life. See Isa. 52: 10.——"Thou shalt prophesy against," may include in its meaning these significant symbols which would themselves speak with no doubtful voice. But very probably he added explanatory words.——The "bands that God laid upon him," seem to have restrained him from turning from side to side, to relieve himself, but manifestly did not prevent his rising to prepare and take his food.

9. Take thou also unto thee wheat, and barley, and beans, and lentiles, and millet, and fitches, and put them in one vessel, and make thee bread thereof, *according* to the number of the days that thou shalt lie upon thy side; three hundred and ninety days shalt thou eat thereof.

10. And thy meat which thou shalt eat *shall be* by weight, twenty shekels a day: from time to time shalt thou eat it.

11. Thou shalt drink also water by measure, the sixth part of a hin: from time to time shalt thou drink.

Directions as to his food, and the quantity of bread and water allowed him.——The reader will notice that our translators (unlike ourselves) make no broad distinction between "bread" and "meat." What is "bread" in v. 9 is "meat" in v. 10. The Hebrew word in v. 10 comprehends every thing eaten. Our translators seem to have used the word "meat" in this comprehensive sense.——A shekel is equal to half an ounce. Consequently twenty shekels are ten ounces—a light ration of mere vegetables, and designed to represent the extreme scarcity in the besieged city.——A hin, according to Gesenius, is five English quarts. One-sixth part of it consequently is five-sixths of a quart.

12. And thou shalt eat it *as* barley cakes, and thou shalt bake it with dung that cometh out of man, in their sight.

13. And the Lord said, Even thus shall the children of Israel eat their defiled bread among the Gentiles, whither I will drive them.

14. Then said I, Ah Lord God! behold, my soul hath not been polluted: for from my youth up even till now have I not eaten of that which dieth of itself, or is torn in pieces; neither came there abominable flesh into my mouth.

15. Then he said unto me, Lo, I have given thee cow's dung for man's dung, and thou shalt prepare thy bread therewith.

Under the general scarcity of other fuel in the unwooded regions of the East, the offal of domestic animals is much used for fuel, even in cooking. Ezekiel manifestly regarded the use of human offal for this purpose as not only offensive but ceremonially polluting. He therefore pleads for some relief from this injunction. It was kindly granted him.——The Lord wished to show by this symbol that the Jews were doomed to eat defiled bread in their captivity among the heathen.

16. Moreover he said unto me, Son of man, behold, I will break the staff of bread in Jerusalem: and they shall eat bread by weight, and with care; and they shall drink water by measure, and with astonishment:

17. That they may want bread and water, and be astonished one with another, and consume away for their iniquity.

The phrase, "to eat bread with care," should take the stronger sense of extreme anxiety, dreadful apprehension. Famine and terror should consume them—a fearful doom!——Before we pass from this chapter let us note the fact that the scenes it describes filled out (at 365 days per year) one year, two months and a fraction of five days over, while the interval between the dates in chap. 1: 1, 2, and in chap. 8: 1, is one year and two months. As the numbers in chap. 4 are obviously *round* numbers, it can scarcely be doubted that the two periods are identically the same.

That is, the symbolic transaction, representing the siege of Jerusalem and the bearing of the iniquities of Israel and Judah, filled up the first stage of his prophetic life—the entire interval between his call with the vision accompanying it, and the second great vision recorded, chaps. 8–11. This symbolical scene, therefore, was properly his introduction before the people in his new character as a prophet. As such, it was adapted to make strong impressions on their minds. They could not but observe the strangeness of the scene and say, "Verily, here is a prophet of the Lord among us, and it behooves us to mark his words and his no less significant deeds."——Let us also note that these symbolic transactions recorded in this chap. 4 are the text for the sermon which fills chapters 5, 6, and 7. These latter chapters for the most part drop all symbol and announce in plain but terrible words, the judgments of siege, conquest and destruction, then within four or five years of being realized upon the long guilty and doomed city of the Jews. These lessons were full of terrible significance to their captive brethren now in Chaldea, as we shall see.

CHAPTER V.

This chapter presents a new symbol, but continues the same course of thought. Manifestly, the destiny of the doomed city and people of Jerusalem is the theme illustrated here by the prophet's cutting off the hairs of his head and of his beard, dividing the mass into three equal parts, and then by a triple process destroying them. The body of the chapter explains this symbolic trans action and unfolds in various forms this revealed destiny of ruin to the people and the city.

1. And thou, son of man, take thee a sharp knife, take thee a barber's razor, and cause *it* to pass upon thy head and upon thy beard: then take thee balances to weigh, and divide the *hair*.
2. Thou shalt burn with fire a third part in the midst of the city, when the days of the siege are fulfilled; and thou shalt take a third part, *and* smite about it with a knife: and a third part thou shalt scatter in the wind; and I will draw out a sword after them.

Cutting off the hair of the head, and especially of the beard, indicated sometimes the highest indignity, but usually extreme calamity. The feeling of the Orientals toward their beard and hair involved strong affection, sometimes rising to real veneration. Hence it became a most expressive token of bitter grief to tear out the hair, and a symbol of mourning over great calamity to cut it off. Comp. 2 Sam. 10: 4, 5, and Jer. 41: 5, and 48: 37.——This cutting of the prophet's hair was a real transaction, having a symbolic import to the people. The balances were to divide the hair into three equal parts, each of which was to have its own peculiar mode of destruction.——"The days of the siege" form a connecting link between this chapter and the preceding one.——V. 12 is God's own interpretation of this symbol. One third part of the people are to die with pestilence and famine in the city; another third by the sword in the siege and capture; and the remaining third were to be scattered to every wind of heaven, and the sword of the Lord would pursue even these to their destruction.

3. Thou shalt also take thereof a few in number, and bind them in thy skirts.

4. Then take of them again, and cast them into the midst of the fire, and burn them in the fire: *for* thereof shall a fire come forth into all the house of Israel.

A small remnant were to be gathered carefully and bound up in his skirts, yet even of them some would be cast into the fire, and a fire go forth from them into all the house of Israel. If this has special reference to any particular portion of the Jewish people, it would naturally be to that small remnant who remained in the land, but were either cut off with Gedaliah, or went down into Egypt to perish there. The general sense is, manifestly, that only the smallest part of a small remnant should survive these sweeping calamities.——A better remnant were saved out of the exiles in Chaldea—this revelation of exterminating judgments on those who remained in Judah being one of the divinely ordained means for their moral culture and restoration to piety and to their own land.

5. Thus saith the Lord God; This *is* Jerusalem: I have set it in the midst of the nations and countries *that are* round about her.

Here the interpretation of the symbols begins. This represents the doom of Jerusalem—the long-loved and honored city of the exiles in Chaldea, to whom Ezekiel is prophesying. He is setting before them the judgments about to fall on her—long and richly due for her great sins.——That she is "in the midst of the nations and countries about her," looks to her central position among the nations of Western Asia and Northeastern Africa, and to her prominence before all those nations as a people governed and judged by the only living God.

6. And she hath changed my judgments into wickedness more than the nations, and my statutes more than the countries that *are* round about her: for they have refused

my judgments and my statutes, they have not walked in them.

The Heb. verb rendered "changed," which our translators derived from *moor*, modern critics with good reason take from *marah*, and so render it, "And she hath impiously resisted my judgments"— *i. e.*, with perverse and bitter spirit hath discarded them, more than the heathen nations. This comparison of the Jews with the heathen about them refers to the common moralities of the laws of nature. The Jews had outraged these laws more than the heathen had done.

7. Therefore thus saith the Lord God; Because ye multiplied more than the nations that *are* round about you, *and* have not walked in my statutes, neither have kept my judgments, neither have done according to the judgments of the nations that *are* round about you;

The phrase, "multiplied more than the nations" is not explicit, since it does not necessarily involve moral wrong. The original gives it a better turn, and makes it clear. "Because ye have been *tumultuous*, outbreaking in sin, more than those contiguous nations." Compare the same word in Ps. 2: 1, "Why do the heathen *rage*," etc. She had been violent, reckless, desperate.

8. Therefore thus saith the Lord God; Behold, I, even I, *am* against thee, and will execute judgments in the midst of thee in the sight of the nations.

9. And I will do in thee that which I have not done, and whereunto I will not do any more the like, because of all thine abominations.

10. Therefore the fathers shall eat the sons in the midst of thee, and the sons shall eat their fathers; and I will execute judgments in thee, and the whole remnant of thee will I scatter into all the winds.

The Lord would show most clearly that he was against that guilty city. The language puts this idea in the most emphatic form. Stress is laid also on the thought that judgment on Jerusalem would be inflicted *in the sight of all the nations*. It had a lesson for them. Moreover this prediction was adapted to humble the national pride of the Jews, and might thus be salutary.—— That the fathers should eat the sons, and the sons the fathers, probably refers here, not to the eating of human flesh in the straitness of the siege, but to civil war—terrible feuds which should array fathers against sons and sons against fathers.

11. Wherefore, *as* I live, saith the Lord God; Surely, because thou hast defiled my sanctuary with all thy detest-

able things, and with all thine abominations, therefore will I also diminish *thee;* neither shall mine eye spare, neither will I have any pity.

In this verse the word "diminish" gives a sense too feeble for the demands of the case. The original verb means to withhold or withdraw; to which we must subjoin as the object either the word *eye*, or the word *myself*. In the former case the word "eye" is put forward from the clause that immediately follows, giving the sense, I will not look upon or heed thy bitterest woes. In the latter case with substantially the same sense, I will withhold myself from compassion. I will suppress all the impulses of pity and let judgment take its course without mercy. In either case it is a threat of awful import, yet had its just occasion in the outrageous sin of defiling his sanctuary with idol gods and with pollutions too horrid to name.

12. A third part of thee shall die with the pestilence, and with famine shall they be consumed in the midst of thee: and a third part shall fall by the sword round about thee; and I will scatter a third part into all the winds, and I will draw out a sword after them.

As already said, this verse is the Lord's interpretation of the symbol with which the chapter opens.

13. Thus shall mine anger be accomplished, and I will cause my fury to rest upon them, and I will be comforted: and they shall know that I the Lord have spoken *it* in my zeal, when I have accomplished my fury in them.

14. Moreover I will make thee waste, and a reproach among the nations that *are* round about thee, in the sight of all that pass by.

15. So it shall be a reproach and a taunt, an instruction and an astonishment unto the nations that *are* round about thee, when I shall execute judgments in thee in anger and in fury and in furious rebukes. I the Lord have spoken *it*.

16. When I shall send upon them the evil arrows of famine, which shall be for *their* destruction, *and* which I will send to destroy you: and I will increase the famine upon you, and will break your staff of bread:

17. So will I send upon you famine and evil beasts, and they shall bereave thee; and pestilence and blood shall pass through thee; and I will bring the sword upon thee. I the Lord have spoken *it*.

These verses expand and reiterate the thought that these judgments are the stern demand of divine justice and the outburst of irrepressible indignation, designed not only as a fearful retribution upon the guilty Jews, but as a lesson of solemn instruction and admonition to all surrounding nations.——This assumes that the principles on which God dealt with the Jewish nation were not unique and special, but *general*, and applicable, therefore, to all nations of every age and clime, and hence to our *own nation and people*. This fact deserves to be seriously pondered. In the case of the Jews, God has taught *us* how he will judge and punish every other guilty nation, including, of course, our own. In v. 15, the phrase, "*furious rebukes*," involves the two ideas of *infliction* and of *wrath;* as Rosenmuller fitly suggests, "not castigation as of sons, but vengeance as against enemies." Yet let no one doubt that these appalling judgments on the guilty Jews and their polluted city were really demanded by the largest benevolence and the truest wisdom. For the Infinite Sovereign *must* maintain the honor of his throne; *must* frown fearfully upon such horrible insults and outrages upon his house and worship; *must* impress the nations with a salutary fear of sinning;—else would the universe go down before the powers of sin and hell, and its well-being be forever blasted.——If it be asked, Why such threatenings against Jerusalem and the Jews of Judea, *in the prophecies of Ezekiel*, borne only to the exiles in Chaldea? The answer is at hand. Those Jews in their native land were their own brethren and fathers; that city was their own loved home. These judgments, therefore, appealed to their tenderest sympathies, and were brought thus vividly before their mind for their moral good. The Divine hope and purpose were to impress them with God's abhorrence of idolatry, to open their eyes to its guilt, and turn their heart effectually from this great national sin.

CHAPTER VI.

This chapter is in the same strain with chapters 4, 5, and 7—predicting fearful judgments on the land and people of Judah—this strain being broken only by a brief reference to a remnant that should survive and repent (vs. 8, 9).

1. And the word of the Lord came unto me, saying,
2. Son of man, set thy face toward the mountains of Israel, and prophesy against them,
3. And say, Ye mountains of Israel, hear the word of the Lord God: Thus saith the Lord God to the mountains, and to the hills, to the rivers, and to the valleys; Behold, I, *even* I, will bring a sword upon you, and I will destroy your high places.
4. And your altars shall be desolate, and your images

shall be broken: and I will cast down your slain *men* before your idols.

5. And I will lay the dead carcasses of the children of Israel before their idols; and I will scatter your bones round about your altars.

6. In all your dwelling-places the cities shall be laid waste, and the high places shall be desolate; that your altars may be laid waste and made desolate, and your idols may be broken and cease, and your images may be cut down, and your works may be abolished.

7. And the slain shall fall in the midst of you, and ye shall know that I *am* the Lord.

With a bold personification, the mountains, hills, ravines and valleys, desecrated by the horrid rites of idolatry, are here addressed as if intelligent and conscious of guilt and danger. The Lord threatens to bring the sword upon those desecrated places, and to cut down the guilty idolaters so that their dead bodies shall lie unburied around their altars and before their idols. Carrying out this bold personification to the letter, the Lord closes—"Ye" (the mountains, hills and valleys) "shall yourselves know that I am the Lord;" *i. e.*, when ye shall see the slain idolaters fallen on every side of the altars of the idol gods they had wickedly worshiped there.——In v. 4, the Hebrew rendered "your images," implies that they were images in honor of the sun; probably used in the worship of Baal.——In v. 6, the last word, rendered "abolished," has the strong sense of *wiped out, obliterated;* implying that God would wash the land clean of these abominations.

8. Yet will I leave a remnant, that ye may have *some* that shall escape the sword among the nations, when ye shall be scattered through the countries.

9. And they that escape of you shall remember me among the nations whither they shall be carried captives, because I am broken with their whorish heart, which hath departed from me, and with their eyes which go a whoring after their idols: and they shall loathe themselves for the evils which they have committed in all their abominations.

10. And they shall know that I *am* the Lord, *and that* I have not said in vain that I would do this evil unto them.

The destruction of the covenant people will not be universal and utter. A small remnant of the captives will be spared and ultimately brought to repentance. This precious truth is interposed here for the comfort of those who still retained some fear of God, and for the encouragement of those who could be moved to serious thought toward repentance.——In the middle clause of v. 9, the course of thought is more natural and easy if we read, not "Because I am broken," etc., but, "*When I shall have broken* their whorish heart . . . . . and [subdued to tears] those eyes that went a whoring after their idols," etc. The form of the Hebrew verb fully admits this construction. The precise sense would be, When I shall have broken *for myself*, for my own glory—the Niphal conjugation having here the sense of the Greek middle voice. Thus the sentiment corresponds with that in Ezek. 36: 31, 32; "Then shall ye remember your own evil ways, and your doings that were not good, and shall loathe yourselves in your own sight for your iniquities and for all your abominations. Not for your sakes do I this, saith the Lord God, be it known unto you: be ashamed and confounded for your own ways, O house of Israel!"——"Shall remember me"—shall recall to mind their obligations to me, their sins against me, and the love I have shown them. This is the main antecedent step to repentance. "I thought on my ways, and turned my feet to thy testimonies." So Ezek. 36: 31 (above cited), and Zech. 10: 9, "They shall remember me in far countries, and they shall *live* with their children, and turn again."

11. Thus saith the Lord God; Smite with thy hand, and stamp with thy foot, and say, Alas, for all the evil abominations of the house of Israel! for they shall fall by the sword, by the famine, and by the pestilence.

12. He that is far off shall die of the pestilence; and he that is near shall fall by the sword; and he that remaineth and is besieged shall die by the famine: thus will I accomplish my fury upon them.

13. Then shall ye know that I *am* the Lord, when their slain *men* shall be among their idols round about their altars, upon every high hill, in all the tops of the mountains, and under every green tree, and under every thick oak, the place where they did offer sweet savor to all their idols.

Ezekiel is usually very emphatic and demonstrative—here, by special divine direction. These strong gestures would bespeak the earnestness of his soul, or rather, of God's own heart in the utterance of these solemn warnings.——The people would have convincing proof that God had spoken these words of doom when they should see the idol-worshipers lying dead among their idols and around their altars in every place where they had made offerings to idol gods.——In v. 12, the word rendered "besieged" demands the good sense—who has been *preserved, kept*, i. e., from the sword. He, though saved from the sword, shall die of famine.

14. So will I stretch out my hand upon them, and make the land desolate, yea, more desolate than the wilderness toward Diblath, in all their habitations: and they shall know that I *am* the Lord.

The strength of critical testimony is decidedly in favor of *Riblah*, rather than "Diblath"—the whole clause to be rendered, "desolate from the wilderness unto Riblah," *i, e.*, throughout its whole extent, since "the wilderness" is probably that which lay on the south of Judah, and Riblah was just outside their northern border. This city became prominent in Jewish history as the head-quarters of the king of Babylon when Jerusalem fell before his arms.

CHAPTER VII.

This chapter continues and closes this particular message, and announces the fearful doom of the guilty Jews and of their city. The points made specially prominent are—that this day of judgment is *very near*, and that the ruin it shall bring upon the city, the land and the people, shall be extreme and utter.

1. Moreover the word of the Lord came unto me, saying,
2. Also, thou son of man, thus saith the Lord God unto the land of Israel; An end, the end is come upon the four corners of the land.
3. Now *is* the end *come* upon thee, and I will send mine anger upon thee, and will judge thee according to thy ways, and will recompense upon thee all thine abominations.
4. And mine eye shall not spare thee, neither will I have pity: but I will recompense thy ways upon thee, and thine abominations shall be in the midst of thee: and ye shall know that I *am* the Lord.

A terrible emphasis is laid upon the oft repeated words, "*the end is come.*" The land is to be made utterly desolate. Its beauty and glory will go down in the darkness of night. God will pour out his wrath upon them and requite them for all their abominable idolatries. "Thine abominations shall be in the midst of thee," implies that they will be there, not as sins being committed and enjoyed, but as sins calling loudly for retribution and bringing it down terribly upon the long sinning people.

5. Thus saith the Lord God; An evil, an only evil, behold, is come.
6. An end is come, the end is come: it watcheth for thee; behold, it is come.

In v. 5, "an only evil"—literally, *a one evil*, I understand to mean, not strictly a pure, unmixed evil, but rather, one all-comprehensive calamity, which at one fell blow should smite down all their happiness and well-being.——In v. 6, "the end" is the predestined, long predicted and deserved end. In the next clause I prefer to read, not "it *watcheth* for thee;" but it *awaketh and riseth up against thee*—as if it had been a slumbering giant, but now starts from its slumbers and puts itself on the alert to do its work.

7. The morning is come upon thee, O thou that dwellest in the land: the time is come, the day of trouble *is* near; and not the sounding again of the mountains.

The sense of the first word is not *morning*, as of the opening of the predicted day; but *cycle; the cycle has come round to thee;* the fixed divine order which brings judgment after and upon great sin. The Hebrew word here is not the usual one for morning.—— The last clause, "and not the sounding again of the mountains," contains an allusion not patent to the casual reader, and not easily traced without the aid of the original. The word here rendered "sounding again" is a shorter form of the word which is used either for the shouting of those who tread grapes, or for the shouts of victory in battle. Isaiah plays upon this twofold use of the word when he says of Moab (chap. 16: 9, 10), "I will water thee with my tears, because upon thy summer fruits and thy harvests, the war-shout" (not the grape-treaders' shout) "has fallen." By an analogous play upon the two current senses of this word, this prophet, alluding to the outcries common in the orgies of idol-worship on the hills, says, There shall be no more such shouts of idol-worshipers on your high places, but instead of it, the battle-cry of thy conquerors. The latter is rather implied than expressed; but is manifestly involved by the force of prophetic usage in this special play on the word. Jeremiah (51: 14) has the same usage. ——The reference to "the mountains" looks to the passages (Ezek. 6: 2, 3, 13) which locate their idol-worship on the high places.

8. Now will I shortly pour out my fury upon thee, and accomplish mine anger upon thee: and I will judge thee according to thy ways, and will recompense thee for all thine abominations.

9. And mine eye shall not spare, neither will I have pity: I will recompense thee according to thy ways, and thine abominations *that* are in the midst of thee; and ye shall know that I *am* the Lord that smiteth.

10. Behold the day, behold, it is come; the morning is gone forth; the rod hath blossomed, pride hath budded.

11. Violence is risen up into a rod of wickedness: none of them *shall remain*, nor of their multitude, nor of any of theirs: neither *shall there be* wailing for them.

In v. 10 the word "morning" is the same as in v. 7, and in the same sense. The *cycle* of the divine order brings thee thy day of doom.——"The rod hath blossomed"—the rod for thy scourging hath developed itself and is in readiness for service; the pride of thy conquerors flowers out, *i. e.*, into action and life, impelling them on to war and destruction against thee. The figure in regard to pride follows the previous figure of the rod. Violence becomes a rod to scourge and punish thy wickedness.——Critics disagree somewhat in the interpretation of the middle clause of v. 11, where our translators have supplied the words, "shall remain." Yet it can not well be doubted that the general sense is, This violence shall bring upon the Jews a sweeping unsparing destruction, one which nothing shall survive. The precise rendering of the original may be, "There shall be nothing *of them*, nor of their *multitude*, nor of their *wealth*." The Hebrew presents a striking *paranomasia* in these three leading words here italicized. ——The last clause Gesenius renders, "Nor shall aught splendid remain among them." This is in better harmony with the scope of the verse than the sense given in the English translation, which follows the ancient Jewish interpreters.

12. The time is come, the day draweth near: let not the buyer rejoice, nor the seller mourn: for wrath *is* upon all the multitude thereof.

13. For the seller shall not return to that which is sold, although they were yet alive: for the vision *is* touching the whole multitude thereof, *which* shall not return; neither shall any strengthen himself in the iniquity of his life.

The customary business transactions of life will cease, and with them the consequent feelings of joy or sorrow which they occasion. Let not the buyer rejoice in his purchase and new acquisition; it shall avail him nothing. Let not the seller mourn as one compelled to part with things of fond endearment; it is all the same to him, for none can retain the choice things they prize most. The wrath of God is upon all the people, to poison all the enjoyments of life.——To see the force of this passage, one needs to bear in mind the wide distinction between the business dealings of oriental and Hebrew life, and those of our own age and country. Selling, especially of real estate, was then not a business, but a necessity. Men sold only when poverty or necessity compelled them. Hence the presumption that the seller would mourn and the buyer rejoice.——The seller's returning to what he has sold contemplates that provision of the Hebrew law by which real estate, having been sold, returned to its former owner at the Jubilee. (Lev. 25: 23.) The prophet says that although the seller should live to the next Jubilee, yet the country would then be desolate; there would be no returning to the possession of land sold. This prophetic vision relates to the whole people, and not one shall escape this visitation of judgment and doom. It could avail nothing for any man to make himself strong in his iniquity.

He could by no means withstand the terrible foes whom God was about to bring down upon the land.

14. They have blown the trumpet, even to make all ready; but none goeth to the battle: for my wrath *is* upon all the multitude thereof.

15. The sword *is* without, and the pestilence and the famine within: he that *is* in the field shall die with the sword; and he that *is* in the city, famine and pestilence shall devour him.

The thought continues from the previous verses. The power of the Jews to withstand their enemies avails nothing. They blow the trumpet to call forth the people to war; but none go forth. They are powerless against those enemies because God's wrath is upon the whole nation; and what can men do in self-protection when the mighty God arises in wrath for their destruction?

16. But they that escape of them shall escape, and shall be on the mountains like doves of the valleys, all of them mourning, every one for his iniquity.

Here, as often elsewhere, amid the most terrific threatenings of universal doom, there breaks forth a glimmering ray of hope for a very small remnant—a few who shall (as said here) be mourning over their great sins, even as doves of the valley are noted for mourning the loss of their mates. Blessed hope! that some will repent in bitterness for their sin and return to God sorrowing, to become the nucleus of the future Zion.

17. All hands shall be feeble, and all knees shall be weak *as* water.

18. They shall also gird *themselves* with sackcloth, and horror shall cover them: and shame *shall be* upon all faces, and baldness upon all their heads.

The discourse returns to its former theme—the fearful retributions coming on Judah and her people for their great sins. "All knees shall be weak as water;" the original puts in the bolder form, "All knees shall *flow* with water;" become liquid and weak as if they were only water.——V. 18 groups together the customary tokens of intense grief and mourning. Horror *invests* them, becoming like an outside garment, apparent on every face and in every act and motion.

19. They shall cast their silver in the streets, and their gold shall be removed: their silver and their gold shall not be able to deliver them in the day of the wrath of the Lord: they shall not satisfy their souls, neither fill their bowels: because it is the stumbling-block of their iniquity.

20. As for the beauty of his ornament, he set it in majesty: but they made the images of their abominations *and* of their detestable things therein: therefore have I set it far from them.

In a day of such calamity, their silver and gold would be of no account. They would cast their silver down in the public streets, and throw away their gold as a thing loathed and abominated, for such is the sense of the Hebrew word rendered "*removed*"—this word, as used by our translators, covering an allusion to a special form of uncleanness, which the original fully sustains. Compare Ezek. 36: 17.——Gold and silver will not avail them to withstand the wrath of God or to satisfy their personal wants, because it has been their temptation—in this sense "the stumbling-block of their iniquity"—an occasion of their falling into sin.——I understand v. 20 to say, The people made use of their beautiful ornaments for purposes of pride and display. They also made their images of idols and abominations out of this gold and silver (as in Ex. 32), and therefore God made this wealth a thing loathed, abhorred and cast away.——Thus God is wont to send judgments so plainly in the line of men's sins as to remind them perpetually of the sins which they were sent to scourge.

21. And I will give it into the hands of the strangers for a prey, and to the wicked of the earth for a spoil; and they shall pollute it.

22. My face will I turn also from them, and they shall pollute my secret *place:* for the robbers shall enter into it, and defile it.

God will turn his face away from his nominal people, hearing their prayer and granting them aid no more. Consequently their enemies shall pollute the Lord's secret place, his inner sanctuary, the "holy of holies," where his glory had long dwelt.——"Robbers" are men of notorious violence; here, the Chaldean armies.

23. Make a chain: for the land is full of bloody crimes, and the city is full of violence.

24. Wherefore I will bring the worst of the heathen, and they shall possess their houses: I will also make the pomp of the strong to cease, and their holy places shall be defiled.

"Make a chain," a new symbol, as if the very land was to be bound and delivered over a culprit into the hands of the officers of justice. Their bloody crimes, crimes worthy of death, deserved such retribution. The passage indicates that atrocious immoralities filled the land—the natural fruit of such extreme apostasy from God and of such debasing and polluting idolatry.——The word rendered, "their holy places," may mean *their priests*, the class who by profession consecrated the people to God. Even this sacred order of men will be dishonored, treated with extreme indignity and violence. So the pomp of the strong and the sanctity of the holy ones should alike fail to screen and save them; should rather conduct down upon their heads the vengeance of God for their great sins.

25. Destruction cometh; and they shall seek peace, and *there shall be* none.

Instead of "destruction," I prefer "*horror*," as more close to the sense of the Hebrew and in better keeping with the context. When a horror of great fear shall fall on them, they shall seek peace, but in vain.

26. Mischief shall come upon mischief, and rumor shall be upon rumor; then shall they seek a vision of the prophet; but the law shall perish from the priest, and counsel from the ancients.

27. The king shall mourn, and the prince shall be clothed with desolation, and the hands of the people of the land shall be troubled: I will do unto them after their way, and according to their deserts will I judge them, and they shall know that I *am* the Lord.

Like king Saul when the Lord had forsaken him, they shall seek some vision from the Lord, but he shall make them no reply. He shuts his ear and gives them no counsel in the day of their imploring cry. So he said (Prov. 1: 28), "Then shall they call upon me, but I will not answer; they shall seek me early [earnestly], but they shall not find me."——Even the king is not too high in station or too much above the reach of calamity, to come down in the dust as a bitter mourner. These terrible judgments would reach the throne and carry terror and woe to all hearts.——Then the nations abroad, and the Jewish people no less, will know that the Lord Jehovah is indeed the Lord—the King of nations and the righteous Judge and Avenger of the guilty.

Thus closes this section of Ezekiel's prophecies, including chapters 4–7, freighted with threatenings of terrific judgments upon Jerusalem and Judah for their grievous idolatries and utter apostasy from their own God. Let us bear in mind that these announcements are made to the Jewish exiles in Chaldea, now only some five years out from their dear native land, and up to this moment, doubtless, full of hope for the future of their country, and very probably, with high anticipations of themselves returning at no distant day to enjoy peace and good there. Over these fond hopes, such predictions must have passed rough-shod like the terrible threshing sledge of oriental times, crushing them down into shapeless ruin. Yet this bitter wreck of their cherished hopes was kindly purposed on God's part to give them a new sense of the awful sin of idolatry and to open their eyes to the wrath of God against their nation for this great national sin. It was the Lord's thought of mercy to reclaim and save a remnant out of these captives, and it was vital to its realization that precisely this portrayal of their nation's guilt and doom should be set vividly before their eyes, that so the moral power of what was being done in Judah might come with force undiminished by distance upon the hearts of the exiles in Chaldea.——We, too, may fitly pause over these chapters and say, Thus the Lord shows his high and holy displeasure against sin in his apostate people. It *is true* of him that he abhors sin, and that, after long forbearance, the hour of judgment without mercy will surely come. When it does come, alas! there will be a fearfulness in the doom of the guilty before which the stoutest hearts are appalled with terror! Verily, it can not be well for sinners to provoke the Almighty to vengeance! When God says, "Mine eye shall not spare, neither will I have pity," woe be to the guilty and helpless sinner! Why did he not take the kind forewarning and avert that wrath which no heart can endure?

CHAPTER VIII.

This chapter opens a very extraordinary vision, the details of which fill four chapters (8–11). It has its well-defined date—precisely two years and two months later than his first vision (chap. 1), which brought to him the Lord's call into his prophetic office. As already shown in the notes near the close of chapter 4, the symbolic transaction of besieging Jerusalem and bearing the iniquities of Israel and Judah, filled up the interval between that vision and this, and was now just closed.——That the transactions recorded in these four chapters were all *seen* in vision and not *done* in the external world, is made abundantly clear by the language which records them. "The hand of the Lord fell upon me;" "I saw a likeness;" "He put forth the form of a hand and took me by a lock of mine head," and "the Spirit lifted me up between the earth and the heaven, and brought me *in the visions of God* to Jerusalem." There he saw the Shekinah—the visible manifestation of the glory of the Lord. The scene closes with the statement (chap. 11: 24, 25), "After that, the Spirit took me up and *brought me back in a vision by the Spirit of God* into Chaldea to them of the captivity. So the vision that I had seen went up from me. Then I spake unto them of the captivity all the things that the Lord had showed me." All this is perfectly explicit to the point that the scene here is purely prophetic vision. None of his fellow-captives saw it. It was shown to the prophet only. When it closed, he reported it to them entire. Every feature in this description conspires to make a clear and unquestionable case of a pure prophetic vision.——The great moral purposes of this vision are obvious. The Lord aimed to reveal to his prophet and through him to the exiles, (1.) The horrible abominations of idol worship in various forms as they existed in Jerusalem and within the very temple of Jehovah: and (2.) The discriminating judgments by which the Lord would assuredly sift out and cut down in his unsparing vengeance all the guilty idolaters among his people. These points it was of the utmost consequence to the captives in Chaldea to understand. As bearing on their own moral state, it was vital that they should know how deeply guilty the masses of the people in their native land had become; how much the elders and the priests were involved in this guilt as indeed the prime leaders in it by their position and example; and how terribly the Lord would destroy them for such horrible apostasy and depravity. These things would show the exiles that they had no occasion to sympathize with their suffering brethren as if punished too severely in the terrible calamities of siege and ruin then closely impending. They would also be a forcible and most pertinent warning to themselves to turn away from those same sins as they would escape a like terrible vengeance.

1. And it came to pass in the sixth year, in the sixth *month*, in the fifth *day* of the month, *as* I sat in my house, and the elders of Judah sat before me, that the hand of the Lord God fell there upon me.

2. Then I beheld, and lo a likeness as the appearance of fire: from the appearance of his loins even downward, fire; and from his loins even upward, as the appearance of brightness, as the color of amber.

3. And he put forth the form of a hand, and took me by a lock of my head; and the spirit lifted me up between the earth and the heaven, and brought me in the visions of God to Jerusalem, to the door of the inner gate that looketh toward the north; where was the seat of the image of jealousy, which provoketh to jealousy.

As already shown, the days of his lying on his side (chap. 4) have just closed. He is now at home, sitting quietly in his own house. The elders of Judah are sitting there before him, deeply impressed (we may suppose) by the strangeness of that scene, by its fearful significance, and by the threatenings of judgment on the guilty city which we have been reading in chapters 5–7. The Lord proceeds now to another method of presenting, first to the prophet and then through him to the people, essentially the same ideas—the sin and the doom of the Jews yet remaining in Jerusalem. The method of presenting these truths is obviously varied in the hope of more effectually securing thereby the desired moral impression.—— Let us note that this method of presenting to the prophet and to his fellow-exiles the sin and doom of Jerusalem, reveals not any human view of those points, but emphatically and precisely *God's view* of them. The facts are shown from God's own stand-point. The observer sees them only and wholly as seen and shown by God himself. Hence this vision teaches us how God looks upon such sins as those, among his own covenant people, within his very sanctuary, and also how he discriminates between the innocent and the guilty; by what marks he knows and points out the innocent, and with what unsparing vengeance he punishes and even exterminates all save those who bear his mark.——The glorious personage, present to the mind's eye of the prophet in this vision, is the same who was seen on the movable throne in chap. 1, bearing essentially the same description as in chap. 1: 26–28, all begirt with fire, and with a resplendent radiance as of polished brass; the word rendered "the color of amber," being the same as in chap. 1: 4.——The impression of being transported through the air is not unknown in the phenomena of dreams. How closely analogous this case of prophetic vision may be to the experience of dreams, it is impossible for any to say save the prophets themselves. Let it suffice us to rest in the fact that He who made the mind of man must have ample means for making any impression upon it which he may wish to make.——"The door of the inner gate that looketh toward the north" IS THE TEMPLE.——This "image of jealousy" is an idol image which provoked the jealousy of Almighty God. The thought looks toward the second command, "Thou shalt not make unto thee any graven image," etc.—"thou shalt not bow down thyself to them nor serve them, *for I the Lord thy God am a jealous God.*"——In the last clause of verse 3, the Heb. for the last word is supposed by Gesenius to mean, "which *sells* the nation into bondage." Our translators supposed the word to be only another form of the verb for being jealous. Neither sense is bad. Some of the ablest modern critics still adhere to the view of our translators.

4. And behold, the glory of the God of Israel *was* there, according to the vision that I saw in the plain.

5. Then said he unto me, Son of man, lift up thine eyes now the way toward the north. So I lifted up mine eyes the way toward the north, and behold northward at the gate of the altar this image of jealousy in the entry.

6. He said furthermore unto me, Son of man, seest thou what they do? *even* the great abominations that the house of Israel committeth here, that I should go far off from my sanctuary? But turn thee yet again, *and* thou shalt see greater abominations.

The "vision seen in the plain" refers to chap. 3: 22, 23. Here he meets again the same glorious personage as there, in the form of the ancient Shekinah. This personage speaks to him and leads him on through the scenes of this vision.——Standing in the temple at Jerusalem and looking toward the north, he sees at the temple gate, near the great altar of burnt-offering, this idol-image which provoked the God of Israel to jealousy. His divine Guide calls his special attention to this first abomination.——The clause, "That I should go far off from my sanctuary," speaks of those abominations as *compelling* him to abandon his temple and give it up to destruction. This was a vital point—the more so because the Jews presumptuously assumed that God could not let the city be destroyed so long as his temple stood there, but must protect the city for his temple's sake. See Notes on Jer. 7: 4. It seems never to have occurred to them that such abominations would compel the Lord to abandon his temple and give up both city and temple to destruction.

7. And he brought me to the door of the court; and when I looked, behold a hole in the wall.

8. Then said he unto me, Son of man, dig now in the wall: and when I had digged in the wall, behold a door.

9. And he said unto me, Go in, and behold the wicked abominations that they do here.

10. So I went in and saw; and behold every form of creeping things, and abominable beasts, and all the idols of the house of Israel, portrayed upon the wall round about.

11. And there stood before them seventy men of the ancients of the house of Israel, and in the midst of them stood Jaazaniah the son of Shaphan, with every man his censer in his hand; and a thick cloud of incense went up.

12. Then said he unto me, Son of man, hast thou seen what the ancients of the house of Israel do in the dark, every man in the chambers of his imagery? for they say, The Lord seeth us not; the Lord hath forsaken the earth.

There is now opened to the prophet's view a secret "chamber of imagery," the walls of which are covered with delineations of all unclean beasts and insects, portrayed here as objects of idolatrous worship. This species of idols and the manner of delineating them were obviously *Egyptian*, borrowed from that land where almost every known animal was included among their objects of reverence and worship. It would seem that this base form of idolatry was kept somewhat back from public view, in the secret chambers of the temple.——These seventy men of the ancients of the house of Israel were obviously the Jewish *Sanhedrim*, the well-known supreme council of the nation, always chosen from the elders of the people. It was their sacred duty to suppress all idolatry; yet here they are in their retired chambers with every man his censer in his hand to burn incense to toads and snakes—to every base and abominable creature! To aggravate the case yet more, there stood in the midst of them, probably as president of the council, Jaazaniah, the son of Shaphan. This Shaphan appears in the history of Josiah's great reformation as a true and noble man; also in the life of Jeremiah as the father of Ahikam, that prophet's powerful friend. See 2 Kings 22, and Jer. 26: 24. If Jaazaniah was now at the head of the Sanhedrim, and if he was also the son (and not the grandson) of Shaphan, he must on both grounds have been at this time far advanced in years, and for this reason his sin in this idol worship was the greater and the more appalling. Shaphan was somewhat advanced in years when he appears prominently in Josiah's reformation; *i. e.*, in this king's eighteenth year; full thirty years before this vision. It was, therefore, for many reasons a strong case that Jaazaniah, the son of the good Shaphan and now the president of the Sanhedrim, hoary with years and perhaps trembling on the brink of the grave, should be leading on his younger brethren of this great council in these most base and debasing idolatries. Alas! how were the noble fallen! And how manifestly hopeless of reform must the nation have become!——The Lord saw their deeds of darkness and revealed them in vision to his prophet. "Son of man, hast thou seen?" Take note of it, for it testifies to the deep and hopeless corruption of the whole people!——Observe what they say. "The Lord seeth us not; the Lord hath forsaken the earth." This was at least the language of their heart—that inner thought with which they cast off all fear of God and all just sense of his presence. Perhaps the Lord does not mean to say that they openly taught this doctrine to others, or even publicly avowed it; yet even this would not be incredible, and if true, would only evince their confirmed moral hardihood and infatuation.——Rosenmuller cites from Ammianus Marcellinus, a Latin historian, to the effect that the Egyptians practiced precisely this form of idol worship in subterranean recesses, sculpturing on house-walls many kinds of fowls and of wild beasts which they designated with hieroglyphic characters.

13. He said also unto me, turn thee yet again, *and* thou shalt see greater abominations that they do.

14. Then he brought me to the door of the gate of the Lord's house, which *was* toward the north; and behold, there sat women weeping for Tammuz.

15. Then said he unto me, Hast thou seen *this*, O son of man? Turn thee yet again, *and* thou shalt see greater abominations than these.

This form of idolatry was Syrian, Tammuz being probably the celebrated youthful Adonis, over whose untimely (supposed) death, the Syrian damsels held an annual mourning. As the legend runs, Adonis was subsequently found alive, or restored from the dead, whereupon their mourning turns to exuberant joy. Foul and licentious practices followed. "The finding again was the commencement of *a wake*, accompanied by all the usages which in the East attend such a ceremony—prostitution, cutting off the hair, cutting the breast with knives, and playing on pipes." (Smith's Bible Dictionary.)

16. And he brought me into the inner court of the Lord's house, and behold, at the door of the temple of the Lord, between the porch and the altar, *were* about five and twenty

men, with their backs toward the temple of the Lord, and their faces toward the east; and they worshiped the sun toward the east.

17. Then he said unto me, Hast thou seen *this*, O son of man? Is it a light thing to the house of Judah that they commit the abominations which they commit here? for they have filled the land with violence, and have returned to provoke me to anger: and lo, they put the branch to their nose.

18. Therefore will I also deal in fury; mine eye shall not spare, neither will I have pity: and though they cry in mine ears with a loud voice, *yet* will I not hear them.

Here are twenty-five men, their backs to the temple of the Lord, and their faces eastward, worshiping the sun. As the other special forms of idolatry were Egyptian and Syrian in their origin, this is nationally Persian, yet was in most ancient times widespread, and very probably was the earliest form of idolatry. Job refers to it, chap. 31: 26–28, "If I beheld the sun when it shined, or the moon, walking in brightness, and my heart hath been secretly enticed, or my mouth hath kissed my hand; this also were an iniquity to be punished by the judge; for I should have denied the God above."——The revealing personage now appeals to the prophet to say if such base idolatries can be accounted a small thing. Especially considered as practiced by the house of Judah, the ancient covenant people of the living God, *ought* He not to be jealous for his holy name, and take vengeance on such sinners?——Nor was their sin limited to idol worship. Under the influence of idolatry, the people had become grossly immoral. They had "filled the land with violence"—the usual phrase to indicate assaults and murders. Idolatry is the legitimate mother of extreme immorality. It discards the fear of God, and breaks down all the restraints that come upon the minds of men from just views of the great, the pure and the ever-glorious Jehovah. Thus it opens the floodgates of human depravity.——"Putting the branch to the nose" is thought to refer to a Persian ceremony, practiced in their worship of the sun and of its symbol, fire.——For all these grievous sins, the Lord will surely scourge and punish his apostate people; he will not spare; and however imploring their cry, he will not hear! There is a time for prayer; but, that time once past, there comes another hour which is *not* the time for prayer. Woe to the sinner who waits till then ere he lifts up his beseeching cry for mercy!——As bearing on the fearful doom of the incorrigibly wicked in the future world, this testimony from God himself is fearfully in point to show that there *is* a time when cries for mercy will be unavailing. If there come such hours in the lighter judgments of time, what must we not expect amid the far sorer judgments of eternity!

CHAPTER IX.

This chapter continues the subject of the chapter preceding. The prophet is shown in vision how the Lord discriminates between his friends and his enemies, to spare the one and to slay the other without mercy.

1. He cried also in mine ears with a loud voice, saying, Cause them that have charge over the city to draw near, even every man *with* his destroying weapon in his hand.

2. And behold, six men came from the way of the higher gate, which lieth toward the north, and every man a slaughter-weapon in his hand; and one man among them *was* clothed with linen, with a writer's inkhorn by his side: and they went in and stood beside the brazen altar.

These men represent the executive agents or ministers of the Lord's providential government over the city. The object of this vision is to set before the eye of the prophet the fact of God's retributive judgments upon the city, and the manner in which his agents perform their mission.——The "man clothed with linen" is not attired for slaughter. Linen, so commonly worn by the priests, would have been out of place on the men who bore the "slaughter-weapons."——It was the custom of official scribes to attach their inkhorn to their girdles.——The executioners take their stand first beside the brazen altar, to begin their work at the point which best indicated the great sin of the people—the desecration of God's holy altar.

3. And the glory of the God of Israel was gone up from the cherub, whereupon he was, to the threshold of the house. And he called to the man clothed with linen, which *had* the writer's inkhorn by his side.

4. And the Lord said unto him, Go through the midst of the city, through the midst of Jerusalem, and set a mark upon the foreheads of the men that sigh and that cry for all the abominations that be done in the midst thereof.

This "glory of the God of Israel" I take to be the Shekinah of the Mosaic economy (see Ex. 29: 43, and 40: 34, 35, and 1 Kings 8: 11). Its resting-place was over and upon the cherubim whose outspread wings covered the mercy-seat or lid of the ark of testimony. This removal to the threshold seems to have the twofold object; (1) of indicating that he was soon to withdraw from this desecrated and doomed temple; and (2) of placing himself in nearer proximity to the executioners of his vengeance as if to supervise and direct their movements. Chap. 10 · 18 notes the return of this Shekinah to his usual position.——The godly men of the city must first be discriminated and marked before the wicked are slain. So in the end of the world: "He shall separate them one from another as a shepherd divideth his sheep from the goats, and he shall set the sheep on his right hand and the goats on his left" (Mat. 25: 32, 33). Judgment can never proceed till this separation is first provided for.——The bearer of the writer's inkhorn knows his men by their tears and sighs. It is assumed to be impossible that any one can be truly the friend of God and not be agonized in view of the abominations done in the holy city.

This then is the sole criterion for the discrimination. The man with the inkhorn asks for no one's professions, or claims, or hopes. He asks only for these most reliable tests of the *heart*—the tears and outcries of bitter grief by which those whose hearts were really with God must indicate the anguish they feel in view of such awful abominations. Man may look on the outward appearance; God looks on the heart.

5. And to the others he said in mine hearing, Go ye after him through the city, and smite: let not your eye spare, neither have ye pity:

6. Slay utterly old *and* young, both maids, and little children, and women: but come not near any man upon whom *is* the mark; and begin at my sanctuary. Then they began at the ancient men which *were* before the house.

7. And he said unto them, Defile the house, and fill the courts with the slain: go ye forth. And they went forth, and slew in the city.

The destroyers followed—did not precede—the man with the inkhorn. But they followed close behind him. They spared every man who bore the mark, but none other. Whoever was not *for God*, decidedly, strongly, with his real heart—was adjudged to be *against* him, and was cut down accordingly. There was no recognition of any neutral class. The commissions given respectively to the man who marked and to the men who slew, utterly precluded the possibility of any neutrality in the case. The men who did not care for the honor of God, and who had no tears to shed over these abominations, were at once cut down as God's enemies. No matter how civil and quiet they may have been; no matter how much they may have consulted their ease or their personal standing and influence, or any other form of personal consideration; if they did not sigh and cry over the utter desecration of Jehovah's name and temple, law and worship, they were accounted his enemies and met their doom with the wicked.——"Begin at my sanctuary"—there where the nation's sin had culminated and assumed its most outrageous and horrid forms,—there let judgment begin. Those "ancient men" were obviously the Jewish Council. See 8: 11.—— Some might think that God would spare his temple the defilement of this scene of slaughter. No, indeed. The guilty Jews have desecrated it with their abominations: let it be cleansed with their blood. The Lord accounts it no defilement, but rather a cleansing by means of righteous retribution, to fill the courts of the temple with mangled corpses and fresh gore.

8. And it came to pass while they were slaying them, and I was left, that I fell upon my face, and cried, and said, Ah, Lord God! wilt thou destroy all the residue of Israel in thy pouring out of thy fury upon Jerusalem?

9. Then said he unto me, The iniquity of the house of Israel and Judah *is* exceeding great, and the land is full of blood, and the city full of perverseness: for they say, The Lord hath forsaken the earth; and the Lord seeth not.

10. And as for me also, mine eye shall not spare, neither will I have pity, *but* I will recompense their way upon their head.

The impulses of the prophet's humanity and love for his country and people stand out here with beautiful simplicity. Seeming to himself to stand almost alone, one living man among the heaps of dead, his natural thought and utterance are, "Ah, my God! Wilt thou destroy the whole nation? In this scene of retribution on the guilty Jews, are there none at all to be spared?"——The Lord answers that their iniquity is *exceeding great;* that the land is full of the blood of personal violence, outrages and murders; and the city full of perverseness—the wresting of judgment, the violation of every personal and sacred right—these sinners practically saying, "There is no God here; he does not see us; he has gone up from the earth." See 8: 12. Because of these outrages and horrible abominations and immoralities, the Lord must give scope to judgment without mercy. He can not pardon; he must not spare.

11. And behold, the man clothed with linen, which *had* the inkhorn by his side, reported the matter, saying, I have done as thou hast commanded me.

The man with the inkhorn reports the fulfillment of his commission. It is not intimated that the men with slaughter-weapons made any report. The difference in the two cases indicates the special interest felt by the Lord in the men who are to be saved and in the faithful execution of his commission in their behalf. Judgment, here as ever, is his strange work; mercy, his delight. The spirit of vengeance does not for one moment eclipse his love for his people, or abate from his wakeful and never-waning interest in their welfare.——The moral force of this entire scene is of the very highest order, and is scarcely surpassed by any thing found in the sacred scriptures. The Jerusalem of that age represents the corrupt church of God—the case of his chosen people when fearfully apostate from God, so utterly corrupt indeed that the Lord can spare no longer, but turns to terrible judgment. One of the points of most vital significance (as already shown) is the principle on which the discrimination is made between God's friends and his enemies.

This can not be studied too carefully or with too much close and thorough self-application. How many on this principle would be spared in our church or community? Should I be among them? Judged by the test of my heart's real and expressed sympathy, should I have my place with God's friends or his foes?

CHAPTER X.

This chapter is a continuation of the same vision. The scene presented here is substantially a reappearance of that recorded in chap. 1. The glorious Shekinah, the cherubim, their wings, bodies, the wheels attending them, the common inspiration that moved them all, and the same law of their motion directly forward without turning; these are the leading features here and also there. This description differs from that in a few minor points. The word "cherub" here answers for the most part to the word "living creature" there. Here the entire number of cherubim seem to constitute one "living creature" (vs. 15, 20). The "throne" is named here, only in v. 1. In other cases the "living creature" appears directly under the God of Israel (vs. 4, 19, 20).——While these symbols have the same objects as those of chap. 1, viz., to impress the prophet's mind with the unutterable majesty and glory of the God of Israel, especially as developed in his providential agencies for the government of nations and for judgment on the guilty, they have each their specific differences. The scenes of chap. 1 were specially adapted to the inauguration of the prophet into his work. Those of chap. 10 were adapted to the purposes of this vision (chaps. 8–11), particularly to show that the consuming fire, cast upon the guilty city came forth from underneath the throne of God, wielded by the omnipotent agencies which underlie that moving throne; and further, to show also that the manifested presence of the glory of God was preparing to leave his long occupied place in the sacred temple.——These general remarks comprise most of the explanations which this chapter requires.

1. Then I looked, and behold, in the firmament that *was* above the head of the cherubims there appeared over them as it were a sapphire stone, and the appearance of the likeness of a throne.

I understand this passage to say that what seemed to be a throne was brilliant like a sapphire stone and rested on the firmament which itself reposed on the heads of the cherubim.

2. And he spake unto the man clothed with linen, and said, Go in between the wheels, *even* under the cherub, and fill thy hand with coals of fire from between the cherubims,

and scatter *them* over the city. And he went in in my sight.

The throne before spoken of implied the presence of the king who sat upon it, who now accosts the man clothed in linen.——As already intimated, this fire taken from between the wheels underneath the cherubim, to be cast upon the guilty city, indicated that terrific judgments from the agencies of God's providence were about to consume it. It is a significant fact that the executive agent here should be the man in linen who in chap. 9 has no other function save to mark in their foreheads the men who bewailed the abominations of the guilty people. But God has no class of servants too holy or sacred to act as his agents, if need be, in the execution of his righteous judgments. It certainly corresponds with his arrangements *in this world* to use them in representing, symbolizing and setting before the minds of the people, these most fearful judgments. The gospel minister who wears holy linen in God's temple must not shrink from proclaiming to the wicked both their guilt and their fiery doom.

3. Now the cherubims stood on the right side of the house, when the man went in; and the cloud filled the inner court.

4. Then the glory of the Lord went up from the cherub, *and stood* over the threshold of the house; and the house was filled with the cloud, and the court was full of the brightness of the Lord's glory.

5. And the sound of the cherubims' wings was heard *even* to the outer court, as the voice of the Almighty God when he speaketh.

That the Shekinah removed from his usual place over the mercy-seat and stood over the threshold indicates (as said in notes on chap. 9: 3) that he was preparing to depart from that polluted temple. It may also have been a more appropriate position from which to direct and observe the movements then at hand.——The sublime and impressive sound of the wings of the cherubims when they moved was prominent in the vision of chap. 1. See chap. 1: 24, 25.

6. And it came to pass, *that* when he had commanded the man clothed with linen, saying, Take fire from between the wheels, from between the cherubims; then he went in and stood beside the wheels.

7. And *one* cherub stretched forth his hand from between the cherubims unto the fire that *was* between the cherubims, and took *thereof*, and put *it* into the hands of *him that was* clothed with linen: who took *it*, and went out.

8. And there appeared in the cherubims the form of a man's hand under their wings.

That a man clothed with linen should take both hands full of fire, unharmed, would be a most impressive symbol. Nothing is incongruous in dreams. The symbol, however, has none the less force because the thing would be impossible in real life.

9. And when I looked, behold the four wheels by the cherubims, one wheel by one cherub, and another wheel by another cherub: and the appearance of the wheels *was* as the color of beryl stone.

10. And *as for* their appearances, they four had one likeness, as if a wheel had been in the midst of a wheel.

11. When they went, they went upon their four sides; they turned not as they went, but to the place whither the head looked they followed it; they turned not as they went.

12. And their whole body, and their backs, and their hands, and their wings, and the wheels, *were* full of eyes round about, *even* the wheels that they four had.

13. As for the wheels, it was cried unto them in my hearing, O wheel!

14. And every one had four faces: the first face *was* the face of a cherub, and the second face *was* the face of a man, and the third the face of a lion, and the fourth the face of an eagle.

15. And the cherubims were lifted up. This *is* the living creature that I saw by the river of Chebar.

The points made here were mostly presented in chap. 1. The cry, "O wheel!" seems intended to recognize them as inspired with intelligence and consciousness—the Spirit of God dwelling within them and energizing all their activities. This view is given also in chapter 1. The clause (vs. 1, 5), "This is the living creature that I saw by the river Chebar," refers to the scenes of the first chapter.

16. And when the cherubims went, the wheels went by them: and when the cherubims lifted up their wings to mount up from the earth, the same wheels also turned not from beside them.

17. When they stood, *these* stood; and when they were lifted up, *these* lifted up themselves *also:* for the spirit of the living creature was in them.

18. Then the glory of the Lord departed from off the threshold of the house and stood over the cherubims.

19. And the cherubims lifted up their wings, and mounted up from the earth in my sight: when they went out, the wheels also *were* beside them, and *every one* stood at the door of the east gate of the Lord's house; and the glory of the God of Israel *was* over them above.

20. This *is* the living creature that I saw under the God of Israel by the river of Chebar; and I knew that they *were* the cherubims.

21. Every one had four faces apiece, and every one four wings; and the likeness of the hands of a man *was* under their wings.

22. And the likeness of their faces *was* the same faces which I saw by the river of Chebar, their appearances and themselves: they went every one straight forward.

These points have been before us. It only remains to suggest that these symbols are repeated in this vision of judgments on Jerusalem to show that the agencies for its destruction were precisely those which were symbolized by the wonderful phenomena of the moving throne of God. In his government over the nations of men, God wields the agencies of judgment and retribution at his pleasure, with resources ineffably vast and glorious. O, if we might only see them with unveiled eye, it might befall us as it befell the servant of Elisha when his master prayed, "Lord, open his eyes that he may see." "And the Lord opened the eyes of the young man and he saw, and behold, the mountain was full of horses and chariots of fire round about Elisha" (2 Kings 6: 17).

CHAPTER XI.

This chapter continues the same vision and brings it to its close. ——While the prophet is in vision at Jerusalem, he sees some of the princes of leading influence in wickedness and is directed to prophesy to them. While doing so, one of them, Pelatiah, falls dead. From this point, the strain of the vision changes. In answer to the prophet's expostulation, the Lord shows him that although the Jews in Jerusalem are proud, exclusive, and hopelessly hardened, yet it is his purpose to save a precious remnant from among the exiles and give them wholly a new spirit and a tender heart. With this, the vision closes.

1. Moreover, the spirit lifted me up, and brought me unto the east gate of the Lord's house, which looketh eastward: and behold at the door of the gate five and twenty men; among whom I saw Jaazaniah the son of Azur, and Pelatiah the son of Benaiah, princes of the people.

2. Then said he unto me, Son of man, these *are* the men that devise mischief, and give wicked counsel in this city:

3. Which say, *It is* not near; let us build houses: this *city is* the caldron, and we *be* the flesh.

A new scene opens. The divine Spirit puts the prophet into a new position at the east gate of the temple where he sees twenty-five men of leading influence, among whom he recognizes and names two who were princes among the people. These are the men who had seduced the people into deeper sin, perpetually counteracting the labors of the Lord's faithful prophets. V. 3 quotes some of their language. The English version of the first clause, "It is not near; let us build houses," means, The judgments threatened against us are yet far remote; let us go on as usual in the pursuits of peaceful life. The original, however, presents some rather serious difficulties in this construction, particularly in the form of the verb rendered, "Let us build," which is the infinitive construct. A different view is, therefore, proposed, thus: "The time for building houses is not near; we have war upon us, or near impending; this is a time of calamity. Let us meet it with whatever sacrifices of the common comforts of life may be necessary. We need not fear being ousted from the city. This city is to us the caldron—the pot in which flesh is boiled. We are the flesh. As the flesh remains in the pot as its place and home, so shall we remain in this city."——The latter of these two constructions, I, on the whole, prefer.——The figure of the pot or caldron appears again somewhat amplified in chap. 24. So far as its significance is developed here, it obviously meant one thing as used by the princes, and another as used by the prophet. As indicated above, they used it only in a good sense—the pot making a home for the flesh put therein, as the city was in their view to be the home for its population, in contradistinction to being driven out into exile.——The prophet, by a quick turn, plays on the figure and gives it a new significance. The city is indeed (he would say) your caldron, and ye are flesh in it, but not flesh in the sense of living men sheltered in a peaceful home, but in a sense more in keeping with the figure—dead flesh put into the pot to be boiled thoroughly and then brought forth for another form of destruction!

4. Therefore prophesy against them, prophesy, O son of man.

5. And the spirit of the Lord fell upon me, and said unto me, Speak; Thus saith the Lord; Thus have ye said, O house of Israel: for I know the things that come into your mind, *every one of* them.

In the clause, "The things that come up into your mind," the prominent Hebrew word seems rather to mean, the aspirations; the high and raised hopes of your souls. God knew how full they were of vain self-confidence.

6. Ye have multiplied your slain in this city, and ye have filled the streets thereof with the slain.

7. Therefore thus saith the Lord God; Your slain whom ye have laid in the midst of it, they *are* the flesh, and this

city is the caldron: but I will bring you forth out of the midst of it.

8. Ye have feared the sword; and I will bring a sword upon you, saith the Lord God.

9. And I will bring you out of the midst thereof, and deliver you into the hands of strangers, and will execute judgments among you.

10. Ye shall fall by the sword; I will judge you in the border of Israel; and ye shall know that I *am* the Lord.

11. This *city* shall not be your caldron, neither shall ye be the flesh in the midst thereof; *but* I will judge you in the border of Israel:

12. And ye shall know that I *am* the Lord: for ye have not walked in my statutes, neither executed my judgments, but have done after the manners of the heathen that *are* round about you.

It is supposable that this slaughter was then yet future but near and thought of as certain, and as the legitimate fruit of their pernicious influence. Hence they might well be charged with the responsible guilt of it.——The prophet turns their figure to a terrible significance. The heaps of slaughtered men, soon to fill this city, are to be the flesh, held by this city as a caldron holds animal flesh. The living God will bring them forth out of this city into a bitter exile. "The hands of strangers" will bear them far away. ——When the Lord said (v. 11), "This city shall *not* be your caldron," etc., he meant, it shall not be so *in your sense* of that figure. For they would surely be driven out of their city and land.——" I will judge you in the border of Israel," implies that they shall be removed from the city, and shall meet some of their judgments on the borders of their land. This may allude to the fact that Zedekiah and many of his princes were brought to trial at Riblah, just on the northern border of Israel, and there received their sentence and doom (Jer. 52: 8–11, 26, 27). The reason for this terrible doom is fitly stated: "For ye have not walked in my statutes, neither executed my judgments, but have done after the manner of the heathen."

13. And it came to pass, when I prophesied, that Pelatiah the son of Benaiah died. Then fell I down upon my face, and cried with a loud voice, and said, Ah Lord God! wilt thou make a full end of the remnant of Israel?

In order to confirm this prophecy to the people, and not least, to give the prophet himself an impressive sense of the terrible significance of the things now shown to him and announced by him, all suddenly while he is speaking, Pelatiah falls dead! The prophet falls on his face and cries out, "Ah, Lord God, wilt thou make a full end of the remnant of Israel?" Shall none be left? Are the people of God to be exterminated and no seed be left to replant the land, and rebuild the Zion of the Lord?——The shock of such an appalling death impresses him with this painful fear, to which the Lord kindly responds in the verses following.

14. Again the word of the Lord came unto me, saying,
15. Son of man, thy brethren, *even* thy brethren, the men of thy kindred, and all the house of Israel wholly *are* they unto whom the inhabitants of Jerusalem have said, Get you from the Lord: unto us is this land given in possession.
16. Therefore say, Thus saith the Lord God; Although I have cast them far off among the heathen, and although I have scattered them among the countries, yet will I be to them as a little sanctuary in the countries where they shall come.

The import of v. 15 I take to be this: The people now remaining in Jerusalem, in their proud exclusiveness and vain self-confidence, are saying to yourself, to your relatives, and to all the house of Israel who are with you in your present exile in Chaldea, "*Be gone!* The Lord has cast you out of his city and far away from his presence. You shall have no part any more in this city or in the God of your fathers. The city and land are given to us for our permanent possession."——To which the Lord replies; "Although I have cast out the people who are with you into exile, yet I will surely befriend them; will bless to them this very exile; and will be their sanctuary in the sense of refuge in the countries where they shall be."——I prefer to construe the word "*little*," not as meaning *small* applied to *sanctuary*, but as meaning *short* in reference to *time*, indicating that for a little time he will reveal himself as their refuge and help in this foreign land. The exile should be short. Through its brief duration God would be their sanctuary. Although they were cast forth from the outward sanctuary at Jerusalem, yet God would be their real sanctuary in their exile. His presence was infinitely more and better than the temple walls reared by Solomon.——Shortly afterward, the prophet sees the Lord leaving the earthly temple (v. 23).

17. Therefore say, Thus saith the Lord God; I will even gather you from the people, and assemble you out of the countries where ye have been scattered, and I will give you the land of Israel.
18. And they shall come thither, and they shall take away all the detestable things thereof and all the abominations thereof from thence.
19. And I will give them one heart, and I will put a new spirit within you; and I will take the stony heart out of their flesh, and will give them an heart of flesh:

20. That they may walk in my statutes, and keep mine ordinances, and do them: and they shall be my people, and I will be their God.

The Lord will bring this remnant home to their native land. They shall exterminate every vestige of idolatry and put away all those abominations which had been the ruin of their nation; and to crown all, God will give them "*one heart*"—not a heart divided between God and Satan—the holy temple and abominable idols; but *one heart*, true and pure; and "a new spirit," all unlike what they had before. These precious promises, clothed in strong but plain words, reappear somewhat amplified in chap. 36. Their rich and precious significance lies in the point that the Lord will put his own hand to the work of their thorough reformation; that he will reach their very hearts; that he will radically cure their horrible propensity to idolatry, and will turn their heart wholly to himself. So turned and so renewed in heart and spirit, they will walk in his statutes and keep his ordinances with a willing, loving heart. They will be truly the Lord's people, and the Lord himself will be their God.——Let us bless the God of love for such promises, and pray that their fullness of meaning may be granted in glorious measure to his Zion of these latter days.——As these words stand here, their first installment of realization must be assigned to the restoration under Zerubbabel;—their first, but not their last. For, beyond a question, these promises in their ample range are Messianic, and pertain to the gospel age, and preëminently to those latter times of this age when "all shall know the Lord from the least to the greatest."

21. But *as for them* whose heart walketh after the heart of their detestable things and their abominations, I will recompense their way upon their own heads, saith the Lord God.

Some will repel the divine mercy, and will still walk after their detestable idols. All such must receive the terribly fearful but just retribution of God upon their guilty heads.——It was of the utmost importance for its moral bearings that this statement should be made, fastening on every man his own responsibility for his own moral conduct. Even this great baptism of regenerating mercy and power does not shut off the personal agency of the people. Those who thrust God away and will "always resist the Holy Ghost," giving their heart still to their abominations, must perish in their sins.

22. Then did the cherubims lift up their wings, and the wheels beside them; and the glory of the God of Israel *was* over them above.

23. And the glory of the Lord went up from the midst

of the city, and stood upon the mountain which *is* on the east side of the city.

The visible divine glory now leaves the city and rests on the mountain toward the east, Mount Olivet; indicating that he is soon to depart and leave the city to its doom.

24. Afterward the spirit took me up, and brought me in a vision by the Spirit of God into Chaldea, to them of the captivity. So the vision that I had seen went up from me.

25. Then I spake unto them of the captivity all the things that the Lord had shewed me.

The scenes of the vision have closed; the prophet is consciously brought back to Chaldea; and now rehearses to the people in exile there, all that the Lord had shown him. It was the main purpose in placing these matters in vision before the prophet that he might present them to the people then in exile. The points made in the various scenes of this one vision were all of them intensely vital to their moral position—adapted to dissipate their vain hopes in regard to the permanence of the city, to impress them with a sense of its horrid guilt, and to show them that God had designs of mercy toward themselves, if only they would turn from their idols and give him their heart undivided.

CHAPTER XII.

In this chapter the prophet by divine direction makes himself a suggestive sign of the people going into captivity, vs. 1–10; eats his bread with trembling to denote the terror of the inhabitants of Jerusalem and Israel, vs. 17–20; and rebukes their presumption in assuming that the predictions of judgments borne to them by the prophets referred only to some far-distant time, vs. 21–28.

1. The word of the Lord also came unto me, saying,

2. Son of man, thou dwellest in the midst of a rebellious house, which have eyes to see, and see not; they have ears to hear, and hear not: for they *are* a rebellious house.

It is implied here that the spirit of rebellion blinded the people, becoming a perpetual temptation to them to shut their eyes and refuse to see God and their duty—to hear his warnings and their doom. They *might* see, but *would* not. This is the precise sense of having eyes to see, but yet seeing not. Compare Isa. 6: 9, and 42: 20; Mat. 13: 13–15, and Acts 28: 25–27.——This propensity to self-blindness is adduced here as a reason for one more effort to put the near impending captivity of Judah and Jerusalem palpably before the eyes of the exiles in Chaldea, in the hope that so they will be made to see and apprehend it as true.——It is well here to note definitely how the subject matter of this chapter stands related on the one hand to the exiles among whom Ezekiel was living, and on the other, to the people yet remaining in Judah and Jerusalem to whom those prophecies referred more or less directly. We must assume the closest sympathy between the exiles and their brethren yet in their native land. The exiles clung to the belief that the city and the nation were safe, and that they themselves were soon to return. Now there was practically no hope of their being brought to repentance till these illusions were dispelled. Hence these varied and persistent efforts of the Lord through Ezekiel to impress the exiles with a sense of the incorrigible wickedness, the damning guilt, and the certain and near impending doom of the holy city and of the people of Judah.——Here "the rebellious house" (v. 2) is primarily the body of the exiles among whom the prophet then lived. This significant symbol of removing into captivity was placed before them in order to make a strong impression on their mind. The captivity referred to was that of Zedekiah, then king of Judah. ——In like manner, the prophet (vs. 17–20) eats his bread with trembling to give the exiles a more impressive sense of the condition of the people of Jerusalem in the approaching siege.——The proverb referred to (v. 22) was in vogue "*in the land of Israel;*" but its rebuke and refutation were immensely needed for the exiles in Chaldea. These points are important toward a clear apprehension of the scope of this chapter.

3. Therefore, thou son of man, prepare thee stuff for removing, and remove by day in their sight; and thou shalt remove from thy place to another place in their sight; it may be they will consider, though they *be* a rebellious house.

4. Then shalt thou bring forth thy stuff by day in their sight, as stuff for removing: and thou shalt go forth at even in their sight, as they that go forth into captivity.

5. Dig thou through the wall in their sight, and carry out thereby.

6. In their sight shalt thou bear *it* upon *thy* shoulders, *and* carry *it* forth in the twilight: thou shalt cover thy face, that thou see not the ground: for I have set thee *for* a sign unto the house of Israel.

7. And I did so as I was commanded: I brought forth my stuff by day, as stuff for captivity, and in the even I digged through the wall with my hand; I brought *it* forth in the twilight, *and* I bare *it* upon *my* shoulder in their sight.

This is not a thing seen in vision, but a thing done in fact. For the prophet is commanded to *do it*, and to do it "*in the sight*" of the people; and he testifies that he *did do* it. Its symbolic import was to represent the going forth of the prince and people of Jerusalem from their city into captivity. The special points of the representation were, (1.) Providing for himself the requisite apparatus for carrying a few indispensable things—his knapsack or traveling bag—for this is the meaning of the Hebrew word rendered "*stuff*," which is not his baggage, but his *bag*—that in which he carried his baggage.——(2.) He was to go out of his house, not through the door, but through a hole which he dug in the wall. This represented the mode of Zedekiah's escape from the city, as given by Jeremiah (chap. 39: 4); "And when Zedekiah the king of Judah saw them (the Chaldean officers) and all the men of war (*i. e.*, saw them to be really within the city) then they fled and went forth out of the city by night by the way of the king's garden, between the two walls (a private exit), and he went out the way of the plain." This corresponded to digging through the wall of one's house instead of going out at the door. Compare also Jer. 52: 7, and 2 Kings 25: 4–6.——(3.) He was to go out by night, bearing his valuables on his shoulder. This corresponds also with the time of Zedekiah's flight.——(4.) He covered his face so as not to see the ground, to indicate the bitter grief of the king and of his people when at last their hopes were crushed and they were compelled to leave—he his throne and they their city and homes—for the doubtful chances of escape, and the probable doom of death or captivity. So David, fleeing from Absalom, "went weeping and with his head covered" (2 Sam. 15: 30). This may also have referred to the fact that Zedekiah had his eyes put out at Riblah and was taken blind as well as bound to Babylon (Jer. 39: 7).

8. And in the morning came the word of the Lord unto me, saying,

9. Son of man, hath not the house of Israel, the rebellious house, said unto thee, What doest thou?

10. Say thou unto them, Thus saith the Lord God, This burden *concerneth* the prince in Jerusalem, and all the house of Israel that *are* among them.

11. Say I *am* your sign: like as I have done, so shall it be done unto them: they shall remove *and* go into captivity.

Has this symbolic and strange transaction failed to excite the attention of this stupid, self-blinded people? This seems to be the implication in this question v. 9. But if so, let us still persist in the effort to get this truth into their mind. Go therefore and say unto them, "This *burden*" (always a prediction of calamity) "refers to the king in Jerusalem" (Zedekiah) "and to all the house of Israel that are among them"—the house of Israel being the people of the city, and the word "*them*" among whom they were, referring perhaps to the army largely drawn from other parts of the country. It therefore related especially to the king and his army, not excluding the people of the city yet surviving. Ezekiel is accustomed to call the king by this name, "the prince." (See chap. 7: 27, and 21: 25.——Say also, "I am your sign." The Lord directed me to do this thing to represent to you the doom of Jerusalem, and of its king and people. They are destined to go into captivity.

12. And the prince that *is* among them shall bear upon *his* shoulder in the twilight, and shall go forth: they shall dig through the wall to carry out thereby: he shall cover his face, that he see not the ground with *his* eyes.

13. My net also will I spread upon him, and he shall be taken in my snare: and I will bring him to Babylon *to* the land of the Chaldeans, yet shall he not see it, though he shall die there.

14. And I will scatter toward every wind all that *are* about him to help him and all his bands; and I will draw out the sword after them.

15. And they shall know that I *am* the Lord, when I shall scatter them among the nations, and disperse them in the countries.

The symbol was to have its precise fulfillment in Zedekiah who should in like manner bear away his little parcel of valuables; dig through the wall for a private exit, and go away in the sadness of his grief as one whose face is covered and who sees not the ground.——Remarkably Ezekiel makes no mention of Zedekiah's loss of his eyes, and gives no clue to explain the apparent enigma of his being brought to Babylon and dying there, yet never seeing it. Jeremiah solves this enigma by recording that the king of Babylon put out his eyes at Riblah, and afterward bound him with chains to carry him to Babylon (Jer. 39: 7). Ezekiel had no solicitude to make out the truth of his own predictions by showing their fulfillment.——To this fact of his not seeing Babylon, the prophet's going forth with his face so covered that he saw not the ground, seems to have had a somewhat special reference.——God did scatter his army widely, first over the country of Judah and ultimately into Egypt and elsewhere. (See Jer. 39: 4, 5, and 40: 7-10, and 41: 11-18, and chap. 42: 44.

16. But I will leave a few men of them from the sword, from the famine, and from the pestilence; that they may declare all their abominations among the heathen whither they come; and they shall know that I *am* the Lord.

One purpose in sparing a small remnant was that they might testify among the heathen nations that the destruction of Jerusalem and Judah was a judgment from God for their great sins of idol-worship. They might bear this testimony either orally and purposely; or indirectly and without purpose, by what was apparent in their life and in their doom.

17. Moreover the word of the Lord came to me, saying,
18. Son of man, eat thy bread with quaking, and drink thy water with trembling and with carefulness;
19. And say unto the people of the land, Thus saith the Lord God of the inhabitants of Jerusalem, *and* of the land of Israel; They shall eat their bread with carefulness, and drink their water with astonishment, that her land may be desolate from all that is therein, because of the violence of all them that dwell therein.
20. And the cities that are inhabited shall be laid waste, and the land shall be desolate; and ye shall know that I *am* the Lord.

This too was a symbolic act. The prophet was to eat his bread and drink his water with manifest perturbation, as one trembling in dread of some dire calamity. This the Lord himself applies to the people of Jerusalem and of the land of Israel. It indicated the terror they were doomed to feel. The comprehensive thing here named as the moral cause of this terror is, "the *violence* of all" the people in the land. So God sent the flood because "the earth was full of violence." Assaults, assassinations, murders, were rife—testifying how utterly men had lost the fear of God and cast off the restraints of even common morality.——But here, as ever, men shall know that the Lord is truly God, the fearful Judge and Destroyer of the wicked.

21. And the word of the Lord came unto me, saying,
22. Son of man, what *is* that proverb *that* ye have in the land of Israel, saying, The days are prolonged, and every vision faileth?
23. Tell them therefore, Thus saith the Lord God: I will make this proverb to cease, and they shall no more use it as a proverb in Israel; but say unto them, The days are at hand, and the effect of every vision.
24. For there shall be no more any vain vision nor flattering divination within the house of Israel.
25. For I *am* the Lord: I will speak, and the word that I shall speak shall come to pass; it shall be no more prolonged: for in your days, O rebellious house, will I say the word, and will perform it, saith the Lord God.

"Because sentence against an evil work is not executed speedily, therefore the heart of the sons of men is fully set in them to do evil" (Ec. 8: 11). In those days also, "there were scoffers who said, Where is the promise of his coming?" This presumption manifested itself in the Israel of that age. It had even passed into a proverb—so commonly was it said and so persistently was this delusion cherished—that the days of predicted evil had been postponed far into the future, and every vision was failing as to any practical application to the generation then living.——The prophet is commanded to confront this delusion and assure the people that the days were near at hand, and that the *real thing predicted* in every vision would soon be fulfilled. The word "effect" does not so precisely express the Hebrew as *event*—*i. e.*, the fact predicted to take place.——The Lord would soon put an end to the flattering and false predictions of the prophets by astounding the people with the judgments he had long since foretold. He says, I will speak and the thing shall be speedily done and no more "prolonged," *i. e.*, postponed or delayed.——So it often happens that wicked men cut short the period of God's forbearance, and hasten up the day of swift, inexorable retribution by their scoffing and their abuse of his long forbearance and delay. Ah, how terribly must those judgments fall which the wicked thus madly pluck down on their own guilty heads! As if they were weary of waiting through the long period in which God waits in long-suffering mercy for them to repent! Their bold and scoffing impiety contemns the Almighty and compels him to close the period of his sparing mercy suddenly, and bid Justice do its work!

26. Again the word of the Lord came to me, saying,

27. Son of man, behold, *they of* the house of Israel say, The vision that he seeth *is* for many days *to come*, and he prophesieth of the times *that are* far off.

28. Therefore say unto them, Thus saith the Lord God; There shall none of my words be prolonged any more, but the word which I have spoken shall be done, saith the Lord God.

Essentially the same thought is here repeated. They say, The prophet's visions are ofttimes far remote; but God responds; None of my words are to be long deferred; what I have said shall be done speedily.——Let no man trifle with the threatened judgments of the Almighty! That doom which overhangs all the wicked in the world to come may break all suddenly, and O, how fearfully, on the head of any one of the proud sinners who to-day are presuming it will come only in the far distant future, and perhaps never! Such presumption often cuts short the day of grace which God would fain prolong.

CHAPTER XIII.

In this chapter the Lord rebukes the false prophets, vs. 1–16, and the false prophetesses vs. 17–23, denouncing wars and judgments upon them, and pledging himself to deliver his people from their pernicious influence.

1. And the word of the Lord came unto me, saying,
2. Son of man, prophesy against the prophets of Israel that prophesy, and say thou unto them that prophesy out of their own hearts, Hear ye the word of the Lord;
3. Thus saith the Lord God; Wo unto the foolish prophets, that follow their own spirit, and have seen nothing!

False prophets were a fearful curse to the people in this corrupt age. Jeremiah had occasion to expose and rebuke their devices repeatedly. See Jer. 14: 13–16, and 23: 9–40, and 27 and 28. It appears, even in Jeremiah, that there were false prophets not in Judea only, but among the exiles in Chaldea. See Jer. 29: 15–32 and notes there. Consequently, they withstood Ezekiel's influence in Chaldea as they had Jeremiah's in Judea. The Lord, therefore, most pertinently sends them, by his prophet, this caustic and scathing message.——They are here described forcibly and truly as those who prophesied out of their own heart and not from God; following their own spirit, and not the Spirit of the Lord; foolish in the sense of lying and impious; men who pretended to have seen visions from God, but who had seen nothing.

4. O Israel, thy prophets are like the foxes in the deserts.
5. Ye have not gone up into the gaps, neither made up the hedge for the house of Israel to stand in the battle in the day of the Lord.

False prophets are pertinently compared to foxes, since Israel was the Lord's vine, and "the little foxes spoiled the vines" (Cant. 2: 5); and because they came in through the breaches in the garden wall, and the rents in the inclosing hedge, and thus did the more mischief because of these weak points in the gardener's means of protection. They never set themselves to repair these breaches, as God's true shepherds would have done; but they either perpetrate the more mischief, or slink away into the desert, reckless of all responsibility for repairing the vineyard walls and hedges. See Ezek. 22: 30. "And I sought for a man among them, that should make up the hedge, and stand in the gap before me for the land, that I should not destroy it: but I found none."——In v. 5 there seems to be a double figure; a breach in the inclosure of the vineyard as above explained; and a breach in the city walls through which the enemy are forcing their way in battle in the day of the Lord's vengeance upon the city. In the latter emergency, all true patriots rush to the breach, to repair it if possible, or at least to confront the foe at this point of chief peril. These false prophets had no such patriotism.——A change of person as from "they," addressed to "Israel," in v. 4, to "ye," the false prophets in v. 5, is by no means uncommon in the Hebrew writers.

6. They have seen vanity and lying divination, saying, The Lord saith: and the Lord hath not sent them: and they have made *others* to hope that they would confirm the word.

7. Have ye not seen a vain vision, and have ye not spoken a lying divination, whereas ye say, The Lord saith *it;* albeit I have not spoken?

"Vanity," here, (as usual) in the sense of falsehood. They claimed to be sent of God, and made use of the established formula of prophecy, "the Lord saith;" when in fact the Lord had said nothing to them at all. Yet they made some of the people believe them, or at least *hope* that their words would prove true.——In v. 7 the interrogative repeats the thought in a stronger form, appealing to themselves to say if this charge of lying were not true.

8. Therefore thus saith the Lord God; Because ye have spoken vanity, and seen lies, therefore, behold, I *am* against you, saith the Lord God.

9. And my hand shall be upon the prophets that see vanity, and that divine lies: they shall not be in the assembly of my people, neither shall they be written in the writing of the house of Israel, neither shall they enter into the land of Israel; and ye shall know that I *am* the Lord God.

Because of this great sin, the Lord declares himself committed against them for their destruction. They shall not be counted in the assemblies of God's people, but shall be excommunicated, cut off utterly, never more to have any portion in the land of the Lord.——"Written in the writing of the house of Israel," means, having their names stand in the register of his people, with allusion to the early Hebrew practice of keeping a genealogical list of all the tribes, families, and souls, that belonged to the nation. Extracts from this register appear repeatedly, *e. g.*, 1 Chron. chapters 1–9.—— When God should fulfill this threatening, they would know that he is truly God, faithful to his word and mighty in resources to fulfill all he ever threatens.

10. Because, even because they have seduced my people, saying, Peace; and *there was* no peace: and one built up a wall, and lo, others daubed it with untempered *mortar:*

11. Say unto them which daub *it* with untempered *mortar*, that it shall fall: there shall be an overflowing shower; and ye, O great hailstones, shall fall; and a stormy wind shall rend *it*.

12. Lo, when the wall is fallen, shall it not be said unto you, Where *is* the daubing wherewith ye have daubed *it?*

13. Therefore thus saith the Lord God; I will even rend *it* with a stormy wind in my fury; and there shall be an overflowing shower in mine anger, and great hailstones in *my* fury to consume *it.*

14. So will I break down the wall that ye have daubed with untempered *mortar*, and bring it down to the ground, so that the foundation thereof shall be discovered, and it shall fall, and ye shall be consumed in the midst thereof: and ye shall know that I *am* the Lord.

15. Thus will I accomplish my wrath upon the wall, and upon them that have daubed it with untempered *mortar*, and will say unto you, The wall *is* no *more*, neither they that daubed it;

16. *To wit*, the prophets of Israel which prophesy concerning Jerusalem, and which see visions of peace for her, and *there is* no peace, saith the Lord God.

The false prophets seduced the people by promising them peace from God when God had not promised peace, but had predicted ruin.——The figure of a wall, built up and plastered with worthless mortar, looks somewhat to the similar allusion in v. 5. The false prophets did not rush into the deadly breach and breast the foe there, nor did they labor to close up the rent hedge; but they did build up a miserable wall of protection for the people and plaster it with mortar that had no cohesive power; in other words, their lies allayed those fears of the people which God sought to arouse, and also inspired hopes of peace which God sought to dispel, that he might press them to look to himself alone for refuge.——A "wall" should naturally be a symbol of strength and protection—here, against the judgments with which God had threatened the nation. The figure of the worthless wall and its treacherous mortar is carried out fully. It shall surely fall. The Lord will overwhelm it with terrific showers, great hailstones, and a furious wind; its very foundations shall be laid bare, and its builders (even all these false prophets) *shall be utterly consumed under its ruins*—for v. 16 is entirely explicit in applying this figure.

17. Likewise, thou son of man, set thy face against the daughters of thy people, which prophesy out of their own heart; and prophesy thou against them,

18. And say, Thus saith the Lord God; Woe to the *women* that sew pillows to all arm-holes, and make kerchiefs upon the head of every stature to hunt souls! Will ye hunt the souls of my people, and will ye save the souls alive *that come* unto you?

EZEKIEL.—CHAP. XIII. 73

19. And will ye pollute me among my people for handfuls of barley and for pieces of bread, to slay the souls that should not die, and to save the souls alive that should not live, by your lying to my people that hear *your* lies?

Some women also as well as men were guilty of this horrible sin of lying prophecy to deceive souls to their ruin. To such the remainder of the chapter relates.——The figures which represent their seductive influence belong to their sex, being drawn from things which women manufacture. The male prophets are builders of walls; the female sew pillows, cushions, quilts; providing every luxury in that line to allure people away from God and into deeper sin.——The word rendered "arm-holes" clearly means the finger-joints. Pillows for the head are not deemed extravagant; but cushions for the elbows savor of luxury, and much more pillows for every finger-joint. The prophet intended to make a strong case of effeminacy. ——"The head of every stature" means the heads of people of every height, boys and men of all ages. By "kerchiefs" our translators probably meant head-coverings. The original word favors the sense of quilt, mattress, or *spread.* In the clause rendered "upon the head," perhaps the thought may be that they are large and long enough to cover the entire person, however tall, even to the head. The general sense is, who provide luxuries for the tastes of the people and use their feminine skill to ensnare souls.——By yet another special figure, they are thought of as hunters of game, meaning however, hunters of human souls, to kill those whom they should let live, and to promise life to those whom God would destroy.—— In the last clause of v. 18, the words "that come" have no corresponding words in the original. The sense of the clause seems to be, Will ye save souls alive *for yourselves*—for the sake merely of your own personal interests?——V. 19 shows that they dishonored God and recklessly *profaned* his name and word (this is the sense of the Hebrew word for "pollute") for the sake of gifts and bribes of barley and bread. For a consideration so small and so purely selfish, they would predict ruin to the righteous, but life to the wicked. For they are said to slay or to spare those whom their influence tended or their purpose sought to slay or to spare. See the same use of language Jer. 1: 10.

20. Wherefore thus saith the Lord God; Behold, I *am* against your pillows, wherewith ye there hunt the souls to make *them* fly, and I will tear them from your arms, and will let the souls go, *even* the souls that ye hunt to make *them* fly.

21. Your kerchiefs also will I tear, and deliver my people out of your hand, and they shall be no more in your hand to be hunted; and ye shall know that I *am* the Lord.

22. Because with lies ye have made the heart of the righteous sad, whom I have not made sad; and strength-

4

ened the hands of the wicked, that he should not return from his wicked way, by promising him life:

23. Therefore ye shall see no more vanity, nor divine divinations: for I will deliver my people out of your hand: and ye shall know that I *am* the Lord.

God is utterly against these female deceivers also, and dooms them to ruin and their efforts to failure, in terms adapted to their sex and to their influence.——In the clause v. 20, "hunt souls to make them fly," Gesenius gives the sense, "hunt souls after the manner of hunting birds—*as* men hunt the flying ones. This relieves the incongruity of the idea of hunting animals to make them fly.——V. 22 interprets the figures above used into literal language. These prophetesses had made the heart of the righteous sad, as God did not, and as they should not; and on the other hand, they had strengthened the heart of the wicked in his sins by promising him life however wicked—as God would not, never does, and can not bear to have lying prophetesses do.——A word of warning to men who fail to discriminate between those who serve God and those who serve him not—to men who promise peace to the wicked for whom God has no peace here or hereafter. It is indeed a fearful crime against both God and man to mar the threatenings of his holy word and fritter away their solemn significance! When God in infinite love would fain warn the wicked of his danger and press him to escape for his life from the doom that awaits him, it is awful that men or women either should interpose their lies to foster hopes that God would fain destroy, and to comfort souls in sin whom God would arouse by fear of damnation to flee from the wrath to come! ——It was a fearfully solemn responsibility assumed by those lying men and women in Ezekiel's day, when they sought thus to thwart the benevolent efforts of the great and holy God. No less solemn to-day is the responsibility assumed by men who abate from the doom threatened against all persistent sinners and encourage men to make the most of sinful pleasures while they can, till the day of mercy ends all suddenly in the night of eternal death!

CHAPTER XIV.

AGAIN certain of the elders of Israel come and sit before the prophet, and the Lord gives him another message in continuation of the subject of the previous chapter. The Lord will not let men come to him asking favors, with their idols enthroned in their hearts. If they do, he will answer them according to their idols and abominations. If they seduce a prophet to inquire of the Lord for them, God will let that prophet be deceived and then deceive those who try in this way to make use of his prophetic functions. The only right thing a guilty people can do is to repent of their sins and put away all their abominations.——Another turn is given to this leading thought in vs. 12–21. If, for the great wickedness of the land, God shall send upon them his sore judgments, he will not be entreated in their behalf. Though even those great and good men, distinguished as intercessors high in favor with God, Noah, Daniel, and Job, were in it, they should save their own souls only. Their prayers or their presence could not save so wicked a people. ——Such is the scope of the chapter.

1. Then came certain of the elders of Israel unto me, and sat before me.
2. And the word of the Lord came unto me, saying,
3. Son of man, these men have set up their idols in their heart, and put the stumbling-block of their iniquity before their face: should I be inquired of at all by them?

"Then came," etc. This seems to have been shortly after the prophecy narrated in the previous chapter. This chapter and that are closely connected in thought. That denunciation of the false prophets may have made some impression upon certain of the elders, and they may have been consequently in an attitude to listen to something further on the same and kindred points. The language, "these men," etc., somewhat strongly implies a reference to the elders then before him.——"To set up their idols in their hearts," is precisely to enthrone them there—to give them a standing, a fixed position in their very heart as in a temple prepared for the purpose.——"Stumbling-block" is used here in the sense of temptation to sin, put directly before their own face, so that it shall have its greatest power to ensnare and thus destroy their own souls.—— While they are in this moral state, God asks, "Shall I be inquired of at all by them?" Of course he will not be.

4. Therefore speak unto them, and say unto them, Thus saith the Lord God; Every man of the house of Israel that setteth up his idols in his heart, and putteth the stumbling-block of his iniquity before his face, and cometh to the prophet; I the Lord will answer him that cometh according to the multitude of his idols.
5. That I may take the house of Israel in their own heart, because they are all estranged from me through their idols.

If such a man shall go to a prophet to engage him to intercede for himself with God, God will answer him through that prophet *according to his sins;* that is, will give him no such answer as he desires; but will let him be deceived to his ruin.——In v. 5, "That I may take," etc., means, that I may *take hold violently and effectually* of their heart; *i. e.*, by spurning them away and visiting them with sore judgments, grasping their heart so that they shall feel it—taking hold, not to restore or to comfort, but to chasten or punish.

This construction, both the general sense of the verb and the demands of the context combine to require and sustain.

6. Therefore say unto the house of Israel, Thus saith the Lord God; Repent, and turn *yourselves* from your idols; and turn away your faces from all your abominations.

"Therefore say" this—that there is no evading this manifest and imperative duty of repentance. Seeking God with your abominations still in power in your hearts can be of no avail save to curse you the more fearfully. The effort to reach God through his prophets by seducing them to your aid will only involve those wicked prophets as well as yourself in deception and calamity. "Therefore say to the house of Israel, Repent and turn from all your idols;" "turn away your faces from all your abominations." This last phrase refers to vs. 3, 4, where they are said to have set their idols in their heart and before their face—of course with their face toward those idols.——This is one application of the universal truth that sinners can never find any relief or real good save through repentance.

7. For every one of the house of Israel, or of the stranger that sojourneth in Israel, which separateth himself from me, and setteth up his idols in his heart, and putteth the stumbling-block of his iniquity before his face, and cometh to a prophet to inquire of him concerning me; I the Lord will answer him by myself:

8. And I will set my face against that man, and will make him a sign and a proverb, and I will cut him off from the midst of my people; and ye shall know that I *am* the Lord.

The meaning of these verses is plain and has been already brought out. Whether the inquirer be an Israelite or a foreigner, if he sever himself from God and give his heart to idols, and then shall go to a prophet to learn something respecting God, or to gain some favor from God (*e. g.*, like king Saul in his distress), God will answer him in his own way and for his own righteous ends.——In v. 8, the Hebrew verb rendered "*will make*" "him a sign and a proverb," involves a critical question respecting the true reading. Our translators adopted the more easy reading, which certainly harmonizes well with the context and with the usual phraseology of the prophet. Others, in deference to the rule, "Follow the more difficult reading," make it from another root, in the sense, "I will *destroy* him for a sign and a proverb." The ultimate meaning is essentially the same—as happens in a great majority of cases where the original text is doubtful.

9. And if the prophet be deceived when he hath spoken a thing, I the Lord have deceived that prophet, and I will

stretch out my hand upon him, and will destroy him from the midst of my people Israel.

10. And they shall bear the punishment of their iniquity: the punishment of the prophet shall be even as the punishment of him that seeketh *unto him;*

11. That the house of Israel may go no more astray from me, neither be polluted any more with all their transgressions; but that they·may be my people, and I may be their God, saith the Lord God.

What is said here affords no good reason for impugning the justice or even the goodness of God. All candid minds will see this if they carefully consider and duly appreciate these three points: (1.) That the case supposed is that of a wicked man, seducing and bribing a prophet to give him a favorable answer from God, while he yet cleaves to his sins. God declares that he will not be tampered with by a wicked man for so vile a purpose. He will let both the prophet and the sinner who tries to bribe him be deceived and ruined.——(2.) No other form of divine agency need be implied here than what is properly *permissive.* God will *let* that prophet be deceived. He will leave him to make mistakes—leave him in the darkness of his own perverse heart. God will not reveal truth to his mind; will not help him carry out the wicked purpose and desire of the sinner who has bribed him to try to extort something from God for his own selfish advantage. The usage of all Scripture, and indeed of all human language, sustains this construction. God is said to *do* what he only *suffers* or *permits* to be done. And in this case, who can say that God does not most righteously and justly leave the sinner to be frustrated in his impious purpose?——(3.) The divine intent in this proceeding is infinitely wise and good. As declared by himself in this very connection, it is "that the house of Israel may go no more astray from me, neither be polluted any more with all their transgressions; but that they may be my people, and I may be their God." The Lord frustrates the counsels of the wicked and baffles their vile schemes to overreach himself, for the very purpose of reducing to the lowest possible amount the good they may find in sin, that so he may press them with the strongest possible motives to repent and seek their good in the Lord their God. And who shall say that this is not altogether right; nay more, infinitely good and glorious? How else *should* the Lord deal with the wicked in a world of moral probation like this? How better than so could he restrain them in their wickedness and press them to turn to obedience?

12. The word of the Lord came again to me, saying,

13. Son of man, when the land sinneth against me by trespassing grievously, then will I stretch out my hand upon it, and will break the staff of the bread thereof, and will send famine upon it, and will cut off man and beast from it.

14. Though these three men, Noah, Daniel, and Job, were in it, they should deliver *but* their own souls by their righteousness, saith the Lord God.

15. If I cause noisome beasts to pass through the land, and they spoil it, so that it be desolate, that no man may pass through because of the beasts:

16. *Though* these three men *were* in it, *as* I live, saith the Lord God, they shall deliver neither sons nor daughters; they only shall be delivered, but the land shall be desolate.

17. Or *if* I bring a sword upon that land, and say, Sword, go through the land; so that I cut off man and beast from it:

18. Though these three men *were* in it, *as* I live, saith the Lord God, they shall deliver neither sons nor daughters, but they only shall be delivered themselves.

19. Or *if* I send a pestilence into that land, and pour out my fury upon it in blood, to cut off from it man and beast:

20. Though Noah, Daniel, and Job, *were* in it, *as* I live, saith the Lord God, they shall deliver neither son nor daughter; they shall *but* deliver their own souls by their righteousness.

21. For thus saith the Lord God; How much more when I send my four sore judgments upon Jerusalem, the sword, and the famine, and the noisome beast, and the pestilence, to cut off from it man and beast?

The fearful truth involved here is that when the sins of a people imperatively demand the visitations of divine judgment, God will not hear the intercessory prayer of even good men in their behalf and so reverse his purpose of judgment.——The points of this case are made entirely plain. It is presented for the most part as a *case supposed* in a hypothetical way. *If* any land should become grievously wicked, beyond the divine endurance, then would I scourge them with my four great and sore judgments: famine; destructive beasts; the sword of war; and pestilence;—and then, though these three men, preëminent for their availing intercession, viz., Noah, Daniel, and Job, were in that land, they should save themselves only; they could not save that land from my judgments. They could not save from any one of these forms of judgment coming singly:—how much less from all combined?——Of the godly men named here, the reader will recall in the case of Noah the fact that God forewarned him of the flood one hundred and twenty years before it came, during which time we may suppose that his prayers were unceasing that the Lord would defer this judgment and spare the guilty race. So far, "the long-suffering of God did wait in the days of Noah" (1 Pet. 3: 20), and, no doubt, in answer to his prayer. Good men in such circumstances always pray.——Job prayed for his three friends, and the Lord accepted his prayer and blessed both them and him therefor. Job 42: 8, 10.——Daniel's remarkable prayer for the restoration of his people as recorded chap. 9 had not yet transpired; but Daniel was already a praying man; already bore his people continually on his heart; was known to God as a prominent intercessor, and probably was known in that respect among the exiles in Chaldea. His influence among them became great at a very early period of his life and of their exile.——If we date this prophecy in the sixth year of Jehoiachin's captivity, Daniel had then been in Chaldea fully fourteen years, and in power at the court of the king, thirteen. This reference to him was not necessarily prophetic—in anticipation of his future developments.

Let us turn to the broad fact that the sins of the Jewish people had become such that God could not pardon, but must punish. So he had said of the sins of Manasseh (2 Kings 24: 4). Repeatedly through Jeremiah the Lord had signified that he could not hear prayer in their behalf to turn from his purposed judgments. See Jer. 7: 16, and 11: 14, and 14: 11, 12, and not least, 15: 1. "Though Moses and Samuel stood before me" (*i. e.*, as intercessors), "yet my mind could not be toward this people; cast them out of my sight and let them go forth."——Fearful is the doom that awaits either a nation or an individual when the point is reached where prayer avails nothing! Let the guilty who are thoughtlessly hardening their heart in sin consider and take warning! There is a limit beyond which men abuse the mercy of God to their certain destruction. It can not be well to reach and pass that limit. The only safe course is to desist from sin and turn to God at once while yet mercy is possible.

22. Yet behold, therein shall be left a remnant that shall be brought forth, *both* sons and daughters: behold, they shall come forth unto you, and ye shall see their way and their doings: and ye shall be comforted concerning the evil that I have brought upon Jerusalem, *even* concerning all that I have brought upon it.

23. And they shall comfort you, when ye see their ways and their doings: and ye shall know that I have not done without cause all that I have done in it, saith the Lord God.

The thought here is that God would yet save a remnant out of this last final wreck of the nation at the fall of Jerusalem, and that this remnant should be brought, captives, to Babylon, and there join the captives previously brought out, among whom Ezekiel was then living and prophesying. He says to these elders now before him; When ye see this last company of captives, and learn from personal observation the horrible corruption of their hearts and lives, ye will be comforted concerning the evil which God has brought on Jerusalem, for ye will see that it must have been richly deserved, and that God did not scourge that city to its utter destruction without good cause. If they had felt any misgiving in view of a judgment so terrible, they would surely see in the character of the captives that God had amply justifying cause for the severity of those judgments.——It is a comfort to the people of God to see that his most terrible judgments are not excessive or in any wise unduly severe. The Lord is careful to show his confiding people that whatever else he may do, he never can punish *too severely*. He may punish *less* than man's iniquities deserve; but never, more.

CHAPTER XV.

1. And the word of the Lord came unto me, saying,

2. Son of man, What is the vine-tree more than any tree, or *than* a branch which is among the trees of the forest?

3. Shall wood be taken thereof to do any work? or will *men* take a pin of it to hang any vessel thereon?

4. Behold, it is cast into the fire for fuel; the fire devoureth both the ends of it, and the midst of it is burned. Is it meet for *any* work?

5. Behold, when it was whole, it was meet for no work: how much less shall it be meet yet for *any* work, when the fire hath devoured it, and it is burned?

6. Therefore thus saith the Lord God; As the vine-tree among the trees of the forest, which I have given to the fire for fuel, so will I give the inhabitants of Jerusalem.

7. And I will set my face against them; they shall go out from *one* fire, and *another* fire shall devour them; and ye shall know that I *am* the Lord, when I set my face against them.

8. And I will make the land desolate, because they have committed a trespass, saith the Lord God.

This short chapter makes but one point and makes that plainly. Jerusalem and Israel had often been thought and spoken of as a *vine* under the culture of their own God. See Isa. 5: 1–7, and 27: 2, and Jer. 2: 21, and Ps. 80: 8–16. But now she has altogether ceased to bring forth grapes. She bears no fruits of holiness; renders to God no acceptable service.——The phrase (v. 8), "committed a trespass," is not said of some trivial sin, but of desperate wickedness; most grievous sin. The phrase means, they have been shamefully treacherous.——What then is she good for? What is a vine-tree good for when it has ceased to bring forth grapes? Can the wood of it be wrought into any work of utility or of art? Is it even fit to make a pin, i. e., a peg to hang vessels upon?——The oriental tent made great use of these projecting pegs for hanging up household utensils. See Isa. 22: 23–25 where the same Hebrew word used here is rendered "nail." The wood of the vine was too slender for tent nails or pins. It might, however, answer to burn for fuel. It was used for this purpose, and was fit for nothing else. So of the people of Jerusalem. They might serve as an example to illustrate God's justice in punishing the incorrigibly guilty. They might answer some useful purpose to *burn up*. To this purpose the Lord would consign them and would lay their land utterly desolate.——A fearful truth is this, as applied to all sinners who will bear no fruit of obedience and love to God; from whom he can extract no other service in his universe save to make them an example of his righteous justice in their damnation! Actively, of their free will and honest intent, they will do nothing for God, or for his creatures and the general good: hence, passively, by suffering, and against their will, the Lord will turn them to the only good account possible in their case, and make them fuel for his justice to burn—a living, eternal testimony before the universe to his holy and intense abhorrence of rebellion. They shall know, and all intelligent beings in God's kingdom shall learn in their case that he is the Lord God Omnipotent, holy and righteous for evermore!

CHAPTER XVI.

This chapter embraces one general theme—the idolatry of Jerusalem, set forth in vivid, glaring, appalling colors under the figure common to the prophets, by which idolatry is thought of as adultery. The key-note is struck in v. 2: "Cause Jerusalem to know her abominations." Set them before her eyes in forms and figures so expressive that she can not but see them, and so sickening that, seeing, she can not fail to loathe and abhor herself for all she has done.——Let us also bear in mind that this exposé of Jerusalem is made before the exiles in Chaldea to show them how righteously that city is about to suffer utter destruction; to impress them with the enormity of their great national sin, in which themselves were deeply guilty; and to urge them to deep self-condemnation and bitter repentance.

1. Again the word of the Lord came unto me, saying,
2. Son of man, cause Jerusalem to know her abominations,

3. And say, Thus saith the Lord God unto Jerusalem; Thy birth and thy nativity *is* of the land of Canaan; thy father *was* an Amorite, and thy mother a Hittite.

No one will take this allusion to her "birth and nativity" in the literal sense. Men and nations are spoken of as the children of those whose ways they follow, as our Lord accosted the Pharisees; "Ye generation of vipers" (Matt. 23: 33), and "Ye are of your father the devil" (John 8: 44). Isaiah (chap. 1: 10) addresses the Jews as "rulers of Sodom and people of Gomorrah."——This was the more caustic and cutting because of the haughty scorn with which the Jews looked on those Canaanites, and especially the Amorite and the Hittite. They are not unfrequently named as chief in guilt and baseness. See Gen. 15: 16, and 24: 3, and 26: 34, 35, and 27: 46; Amos 2: 9; 1 Kings 21: 26, and 2 Kings 21: 11. The general contempt felt by the Jews for the Canaanites, may be seen in such passages as Hos. 12: 7 and Zech. 14: 21. In the New Testament age, Jew scorned Galilean with the same national feeling. Hence the pungency of the rebuke, "Thy father was an Amorite and thy mother a Hittite. Thy spirit shows thy parentage to be utterly base.

4. And *as for* thy nativity, in the day thou wast born thy navel was not cut, neither wast thou washed in water to supple *thee;* thou wast not salted at all, nor swaddled at all.

5. None eye pitied thee, to do any of these unto thee, to have compassion upon thee; but thou wast cast out in the open field, to the loathing of thy person, in the day that thou wast born.

This is the early history of the Hebrews as they were passing from a small family to a populous nation, specially in their Egyptian life. Outcast, friendless, as an infant cast forth uncared for upon the cold, waste world—so was Israel in that age.——The word rendered "supple," the older critics read, "to cleanse;" the modern (Gesenius) "to make fit to be seen;" to prepare for presentation to parents and friends; from a verb which means, *to see*.——"To the loathing of thy person," Gesenius reads, "To the loathing of thyself;" "to thine own self-loathing"—virtually dropping the figure of the infant. Others, better; to be an object of loathing to all; as our received translation implies.

6. And when I passed by thee, and saw thee polluted in thine own blood, I said unto thee *when thou wast* in thy blood, Live; yea, I said unto thee *when thou wast* in thy blood, Live.

7. I have caused thee to multiply as the bud of the field, and thou hast increased and waxen great, and thou art come

to excellent ornaments: *thy* breasts are fashioned, and thy hair is grown, whereas thou *wast* naked and bare.

8. Now when I passed by thee, and looked upon thee, behold, thy time *was* the time of love; and I spread my skirt over thee, and covered thy nakedness: yea, I sware unto thee, and entered into a covenant with thee, saith the Lord God, and thou becamest mine.

9. Then washed I thee with water: yea, I thoroughly washed away thy blood from thee, and I anointed thee with oil.

10. I clothed thee also with broidered work, and shod thee with badgers' skin, and I girded thee about with fine linen, and I covered thee with silk.

11. I decked thee also with ornaments, and I put bracelets upon thy hands, and a chain on thy neck.

12. And I put a jewel on thy forehead, and ear-rings in thine ears, and a beautiful crown upon thine head.

13. Thus wast thou decked with gold and silver; and thy raiment *was of* fine linen, and silk, and broidered work; thou didst eat fine flour and honey, and oil: and thou wast exceeding beautiful, and thou didst prosper into a kingdom.

14. And thy renown went forth among the heathen for thy beauty: for it *was* perfect through my comeliness, which I had put upon thee, saith the Lord God.

These figures are plain and refer manifestly to the early development of the religious life and of the national strength and wealth of the Hebrew people in the wilderness and in Canaan. God's first interposition broke the yoke of Pharaoh and brought them forth from their national bondage. Then he entered into the solemn marriage covenant with them, and they became truly and avowedly his own people. The entire book of Exodus is a special comment on these verses.——In v. 6 the original word is not precisely "polluted," but rather *trodden under foot*—indicating their state in Egypt.——The announcement, "Live," is solemnly repeated for emphasis. It was this majestic and paternal voice which restored their national life, when else they had died nationally under Egyptian servitude.——The reader will not fail to note that this setting forth of God's loving kindness to the nation in its birth and youth is intended to show (and does) how deeply indebted the Hebrew nation were to their own covenant God, and hence, how intensely flagrant, mean and wicked was their apostasy from their own God to idols; their spiritual adultery.

15. But thou didst trust in thine own beauty, and playedst the harlot because of thy renown, and pouredst out thy fornications on every one that passed by; his it was.

The clause, "playedst the harlot because of thy renown," was supposed by our translators to mean that under the influence of national pride, the Hebrews departed from God and fell into idolatry. But the original may (perhaps better) be read, Thou didst commit whoredom *against* or *despite of thy name; i. e.*, the name of thy husband, the living God. Despite of thy solemn marriage covenant with Jehovah in which thou didst assume the name, *the people of God*, thou didst give up thy heart and thyself to idols.

16. And of thy garments thou didst take, and deckedst thy high places with divers colors, and playedst the harlot thereupon: *the like things* shall not come, neither shall it be *so*.

17. Thou hast also taken thy fair jewels of my gold and of my silver, which I had given thee, and madest to thyself images of men, and didst commit whoredom with them.

18. And tookest thy broidered garments, and coveredst them: and thou hast set mine oil and mine incense before them.

19. My meat also which I gave thee, fine flour, and oil, and honey, *wherewith* I fed thee, thou hast even set it before them for a sweet savor: and *thus* it was, saith the Lord God.

The wealth and abundance, but especially the gold and silver which God had given them, they had used in the manufacture of idols; to deck them also with ornaments and provide costly offerings at their shrines. See the same thought in Hos. 2: 8, 13.——This is the very thing that wicked men do in all ages—take the good gifts of God's providence and make them into idol gods for their own hearts to love and to trust; let the earthly good which God gives them be a power, not to lead their hearts *to* God in grateful love, trust, and obedience, but to lead their hearts utterly away *from* God into lower sensual gratifications, utter forgetfulness of God, and more reckless sinning.

20. Moreover, thou hast taken thy sons and thy daughters, whom thou hast borne unto me, and these hast thou sacrificed unto them to be devoured. *Is this* of thy whoredoms a small matter,

21. That thou hast slain my children, and delivered them to cause them to pass through *the fire* for them?

Was this crime of thy whoredom in making and serving other gods too small a thing to satisfy thy wicked heart, that thou shouldst needs go on to more horrid guilt, and burn thine own sons and daughters in the fire to these cruel idols? With equal force and beauty, the Lord says, "Thou hast slain *my* children"—as if his parental heart yearned over the innocent little ones hurled by their unnatural fathers and mothers into the deadly fire to Moloch and Saturn!

22. And in all thine abominations and thy whoredoms thou hast not remembered the days of thy youth, when thou wast naked and bare, *and* wast polluted in thy blood.

It had aggravated her guilt all along that she would not suitably remember the goodness of her God manifested toward her in the early days of her national life. In this chapter (vs. 4–14) the Lord has been pressing this urgently upon her attention. This was the burden of many an earnest exhortation from the Lord through Moses and the prophets. See Deut. 8: 2, and 5: 15, and 15: 15, and 16: 12, and 24: 18, 22. She did not love to remember how abject and forlorn she was in the day when the mercy of the Lord met her in Egypt.——So sinners are slow and reluctant to remember the special favors shown them by that Great Benefactor whose name they revile, whose law they discard, and whose love to them they will not think of requiting with responsive love in return.

23. And it came to pass, after all thy wickedness, (woe, woe unto thee! saith the Lord God,)

24. *That* thou hast also built unto thee an eminent place, and hast made thee a high place in every street.

25. Thou hast built thy high place at every head of the way, and hast made thy beauty to be abhorred, and hast opened thy feet to every one that passed by, and multiplied thy whoredoms.

The reader will the better appreciate the force of this description of the painfully loathsome abominations of Jerusalem, if it be suggested that the word used by Ezekiel for 'eminent place" (vs. 24, 31) means a brothel.——"High places" look to the general fact that high grounds were selected for the rites of idolatry.——Without discussing the propriety of such minute allusions and "great plainness of speech" in regard to lewdness as we find in this chapter and elsewhere in the Scriptures, let it suffice to say; (1.) That the taste of oriental writers and readers must not be judged by our standard: and (2.) That in deference to the sensibilities of our own times, in which both the writer and his readers are presumed to participate, he will feel himself excused from minute comment, and will explain only so far as may be requisite to give the ultimate moral bearing of the chapter.

26. Thou hast also committed fornications with the Egyptians thy neighbors, great of flesh; and hast increased thy whoredoms, to provoke me to anger.

27. Behold, therefore I have stretched out my hand over thee, and have diminished thine ordinary *food*, and delivered

thee unto the will of them that hate thee, the daughters of the Philistines, which are ashamed of thy lewd way.

28. Thou hast played the whore also with the Assyrians, because thou wast unsatiable; yea, thou hast played the harlot with them, and yet couldst not be satisfied.

29. Thou hast moreover multiplied thy fornication in the land of Canaan unto Chaldea; and yet thou wast not satisfied herewith.

In fact the Jews had sought, borrowed, and worshiped the idol gods of Egypt, of Assyria, and even of Chaldea. Her spirit of idolatry seemed indeed insatiable.

30. How weak is thy heart, saith the Lord God, seeing thou doest all these *things*, the work of an imperious whorish woman;

31. In that thou buildest thine eminent place in the head of every way, and makest thy high place in every street; and hast not been as a harlot, in that thou scornest hire;

32. But as a wife that committeth adultery *which* taketh strangers instead of her husband!

33. They give gifts to all whores: but thou givest thy gifts to all thy lovers, and hirest them, that they may come unto thee on every side for thy whoredom.

34. And the contrary is in thee from *other* women in thy whoredoms, whereas none followeth thee to commit whoredoms: and in that thou givest a reward, and no reward is given unto thee; therefore thou art contrary.

"How weak is thine heart" as to any stamina of womanly character—any thing noble, dignified, worthy of an intelligent being! ——The depth of her debasement is measured by the fact that instead of *receiving* the wages of prostitution, she *gives* them to her paramours! She had gone abroad to *seek after idol gods*, taking up greedily the meanest and vilest objects ever worshiped by the heathen.——The prophet assumes it to be the custom of harlots to "scorn hire," yet not in the sense of being above its meanness, but in the sense of decrying the offered wages as a bid for higher! Even this disgusting, ineffable meanness was entirely above the harlot-life of Jerusalem! She had sunk indefinitely lower!

35. Wherefore, O harlot, hear the word of the Lord:

36. Thus saith the Lord God; Because thy filthiness was poured out, and thy nakedness discovered through thy whoredoms with thy lovers, and with all the idols of thy abominations, and by the blood of thy children, which thou didst give unto them;

37. Behold therefore, I will gather all thy lovers, with

whom thou hast taken pleasure, and all *them* that thou hast loved, with all *them* that thou hast hated; I will even gather them round about against thee, and will discover thy nakedness unto them, that they may see all thy nakedness.

38. And I will judge thee, as women that break wedlock and shed blood are judged; and I will give thee blood in fury and jealousy.

39. And I will also give thee into their hand, and they shall throw down thine eminent place, and shall break down thy high places; they shall strip thee also of thy clothes, and shall take thy fair jewels, and leave thee naked and bare.

40. They shall also bring up a company against thee, and they shall stone thee with stones, and thrust thee through with their swords.

41. And they shall burn thy houses with fire, and execute judgments upon thee in the sight of many women: and I will cause thee to cease from playing the harlot, and thou also shalt give no hire any more.

The Hebrew law had stringent penalties for the crime of adultery. See Deut. 22: 22-24—the stoning of both the guilty parties, in the public "gate of the city."——With rare exceptions, all nations, civilized or savage, punish this crime severely. Indeed, human society can not exist without some respect, free or forced, for the seventh commandment. Where there is no such respect, society is already rotten, and decomposing; nations are dying; men are too corrupt to live.——In this passage, v. 38 alludes with terrible power to the jealousy and fury with which men often avenge the crime of adultery when their own hearts are torn and their own homes ruined by it. So God will shed the blood of Jerusalem in his fury and jealousy! What could be more fearfully expressive! He will make an example of her before many cities and nations, as the adulteress suffered her deserved doom "in the sight of many women."

42. So will I make my fury toward thee to rest, and my jealousy shall depart from thee, and I will be quiet, and will be no more angry.

43. Because thou hast not remembered the days of thy youth, but has fretted me in all these *things;* behold therefore, I also will recompense thy way upon *thy* head, saith the Lord God: and thou shalt not commit this lewdness above all thine abominations.

"Will make my fury toward thee to rest," assumes that this appalling execution of judgment would satisfy God's sense of justice and ease his heart from the painful burden of its demands.——

In v. 43 is a renewed mention of the sin of "not remembering the days of her youth" to be moved thereby to a better life. See v. 22 and notes there.——In the phrase, "hast fretted me," the original scarcely bears the transitive sense in this form of the verb. Better thus: "Thou hast raged against me"—hast been violent and outbreaking in thy wickedness. The same verb appears in Gen. 45: 24, there rendered, "See that ye *fall not out* by the way." Also Prov. 29: 9; and much in point, 2 Kings 19: 27, 28; God saying to the proud Assyrian monarch; "I know thy *rage* against me."——The last clause means, Thy lewdness, not "above," but *in addition to* all thine other abominations; implying that Jerusalem was guilty of gross immoralities besides her lewdness, *i. e.*, idolatry. There are references to violence—sins against personal safety and life—which show that common morality had sunk fearfully low—as it might be said, below the living point.

44. Behold, every one that useth proverbs shall use *this* proverb against thee, saying, As *is* the mother, *so is* her daughter.

45. Thou *art* thy mother's daughter, that loatheth her husband and her children; and thou *art* the sister of thy sisters, which loathed their husbands and their children; your mother *was* an Hittite, and your father an Amorite.

See v. 3, and notes there. Jerusalem has imitated and even surpassed the immoralities and crimes of the debased nations of Canaan.

46. And thine elder sister *is* Samaria, she and her daughters that dwell at thy left hand: and thy younger sister, that dwelleth at thy right hand, *is* Sodom and her daughters.

47. Yet hast thou not walked after their ways, nor done after their abominations: but as *if that were* a very little *thing*, thou wast corrupted more than they in all thy ways.

To humble the national pride of Jerusalem and set forth her monstrous guilt, she is compared to Samaria as her sister on the left hand, and to Sodom, her sister on the right. Jerusalem sits geographically between these two cities with her face to the east.——"She did not walk after their ways," for she had done indefinitely worse than they. So utterly had her crimes surpassed theirs, as to throw them quite into the shade.——In v. 47, the original word rendered, "a very little thing," means a *thing of disgust*, as if it disgusted her as *too small sinning*. Jerusalem piques herself upon sinning on a grander scale, with more daring, horrible impiety!

48. *As* I live, saith the Lord God, Sodom thy sister hath not done, she nor her daughters, as thou hast done, thou and thy daughters.

49. Behold, this was the iniquity of thy sister Sodom,

pride, fullness of bread, and abundance of idleness was in her and in her daughters, neither did she strengthen the hand of the poor and needy.

50. And they were haughty and committed abomination before me: therefore I took them away as I saw *good*.

This comparison with Sodom is full of intense significance and power. There stood the history of Sodom and her fearful doom before the very eyes of the Jewish people. The record of it lifts up its columns of smoke and flame before the generations of history, standing on their own sacred page, and it would seem that they must have learned from their childhood to abhor such crimes and dread such a doom! Yet here the burning tongue of their prophet puts it to them that their own guilt is indefinitely greater!——The clause rendered, "abundance of idleness," seems more strictly to mean, the most perfect quiet; exemption from all fear of national disaster. Like Moab, she was "settled on her lees, and had not been emptied from vessel to vessel." See Jer. 48: 11. It seems to be assumed here that national calamity checked the growth of national depravity and crime.——In the last clause of v. 50, the word *good* is without authority. The original seems to mean, "When I saw it," alluding to Gen. 18: 20, 21, "I will go down now and *see* if they have done altogether according to the cry that is come unto me."

51. Neither hath Samaria committed half of thy sins; but thou hast multiplied thine abominations more than they, and hast justified thy sisters in all thine abominations which thou hast done.

52. Thou also, which hast judged thy sisters, bear thine own shame for thy sins that thou hast committed more abominable than they: they are more righteous than thou: yea, be thou confounded also, and bear thy shame, in that thou hast justified thy sisters.

Jerusalem in her abominations had justified Samaria only in the sense that her greater crimes made the sins of Samaria appear to be almost virtues.——V. 52 might be translated, "Bear thou (Jerusalem) that disgrace which thou hast adjudged to thy sisters, for thy sins in which thou hast been more abominable than they," etc. Jerusalem had condemned her sisters, Sodom and Samaria, adjudging to them deep disgrace. Let her bear all this herself and more, for her greater abominations.

53. When I shall bring again their captivity, the captivity of Sodom and her daughters, and the captivity of Samaria and her daughters, then *will I bring again* the captivity of thy captives in the midst of them:

54. That thou mayest bear thine own shame, and mayest

be confounded in all that thou hast done, in that thou art a comfort unto them.

55. When thy sisters, Sodom and her daughters, shall return to their former estate, and Samaria and her daughters shall return to their former estate, then thou and thy daughters shall return to your former estate.

This also must have been acutely mortifying to the pride of Jerusalem. Sodom and Samaria shall stand before thee, or at least fully up with thee, in the matter of being restored in mercy from their captivity. Only when they shall return from their captivity canst thou hope to return from thine!——[The restoration of Sodom literally from her captivity being quite impossible, this passage can not be taken as a prophecy of such restoration. With almost equal certainty may the same be said of the ten tribes (Samaria), those tribes being obviously lost to history so that no possible restoration could ever be identified. The phrase therefore, "Bring again their captivity," must be taken as figurative, equivalent to "returning to their former estate," as virtually explained in v. 55. The statements are put in this shape because the Lord had occasion to speak of restoring Judah again from her captivity, and meant to say that her guilt so much surpassed that of Sodom and Samaria that these latter would be as soon restored to their former estate as Judah to hers.]

56. For thy sister Sodom was not mentioned by thy mouth in the day of thy pride,

57. Before thy wickedness was discovered, as at the time of *thy* reproach of the daughters of Syria, and all *that are* round about her, the daughters of the Philistines, which despise thee round about.

58. Thou hast borne thy lewdness and thine abominations, saith the Lord.

59. For thus saith the Lord God; I will even deal with thee as thou hast done, which hast despised the oath in breaking the covenant.

Jerusalem was too proud and felt herself too much above Sodom to take that name into her lips.——V. 57 applies this remark to her pride *before* the guilt and consequent weakness of Jerusalem were disclosed by the victories gained over her by the Syrians. This refers probably to victories gained over Ahaz in consequence of his fearful strides into idolatry. See 2 Kings 15: 37.——In v. 58 the sense seems to be, Thou hast borne and shalt yet bear the punishment for thy lewdness, etc. The tense of the verb looks to the nearer future as well as to the past.——Her guilt in despising her oath and breaking her covenant with her God was that especially which so greatly surpassed the guilt of Sodom and Samaria, and which made her doom so dreadful. She had sinned against great light and infinite obligations. "If I had not come and spoken to them, they had not had sin; but now they have no cloak for their sin."

60. Nevertheless I will remember my covenant with thee in the days of thy youth, and I will establish unto thee an everlasting covenant.

61. Then thou shalt remember thy ways, and be ashamed, when thou shalt receive thy sisters, thine elder and thy younger: and I will give them unto thee for daughters, but not by thy covenant.

62. And I will establish my covenant with thee; and thou shalt know that I am the Lord:

63. That thou mayest remember, and be confounded, and never open thy mouth any more because of thy shame, when I am pacified toward thee for all that thou hast done, saith the Lord God.

What unutterable compassion and forgiving love are in these words! Thou, Jerusalem, wilt not remember the days of thy youth and of my mercy to thee then;—but I will remember my covenant with thee, made in those days of thy youth, and I will establish it with thee for an everlasting covenant! Is not such love as this *sovereign*—a love that owes nothing to antecedent love on the part of his people, but lifts itself high above the mountains of sin and spans the deep abysses of guilt and the sinks of human abominations to find subjects on which loving-kindness and divine compassion may rest! O indeed this is the loving-kindness of the ever-blessed God! Well may it be said, "The Lord is pitiful and of tender mercy. He hath not dealt with us after our sins nor rewarded us according to our iniquities." Fitly does the Lord himself testify, "For my thoughts are not your thoughts, neither are your ways my ways, saith the Lord. For as the heavens are higher than the earth, so are my ways higher than your ways and my thoughts than your thoughts." (Isa. 55: 8, 9).——In that day such manifestations of mercy and compassion will melt the hardest heart. Jerusalem shall remember her ways and be ashamed and confounded and never open her mouth any more (in the way of her old pride) because of her shame for her abominations.——It will heighten both her shame for her own sins and her sense of divine mercy that God will give her for sisters, both Sodom and Samaria, yet not on the strength of her fidelity to her covenant.—— So the conversion of Gentile nations should rather deepen the humility than flatter the pride of God's people, since it comes not of her self-moved fidelity but of God's self-moved mercy.——In the close of v. 63 "pacified" stands for the usual Hebrew word to denote *pardon*—the covering of sins from the sight of the Lord through an atonement. So all salvation comes through atoning blood. The deep apostasies of God's professed sons and daughters find mercy there and there only.

CHAPTER XVII.

The riddle or parable which constitutes the subject throughout this chapter is explained in the chapter itself vs. 11–21. This explanation makes the significance entirely clear and certain.——The first eagle (v. 3–6) is Nebuchadnezzar of Babylon: the second (v. 7) is Pharaoh of Egypt. The highest branch of the cedar cropped by the first eagle and carried to a land of traffic, etc., (vs. 3, 4) was Jehoiachin, taken from the throne of Judah into captivity to Babylon. Then "the seed of the land, planted in a fruitful field, by great waters, and becoming a spreading vine of low stature (vs. 5, 6) was Zedekiah, made king by Nebuchadnezzar over the remnant left in the land. He was, of course, bound by solemn covenant to a faithful allegiance to his conqueror and sovereign. Turning toward Egypt to solicit help thence that he might maintain himself in breaking faith with the king of Babylon, was base treachery and rebellion, which God abhorred, and here declares that he will punish. This is the general scope of the chapter.——The historical facts which are the basis of this parable may be seen in 2 Kings 24: 8–20, and 2 Chron. 36: 9–13, and Jer. 52: 1–7.

1. And the word of the Lord came unto me, saying,
2. Son of man, put forth a riddle, and speak a parable unto the house of Israel;
3. And say, Thus saith the Lord God; A great eagle with great wings, long-winged, full of feathers, which had divers colors, came unto Lebanon, and took the highest branch of the cedar:
4. He cropped off the top of his young twigs, and carried it into a land of traffic; he set it in a city of merchants.

This representation partakes of the nature of both the riddle and the parable. In its points of analogy it is a parable: in its enigma—in the fact that its significance is somewhat recondite and obscure; it is a riddle.——The eagle, king of birds, not unfitly represents the kings of Chaldea and Egypt. So, also a tree, whether the cedar or the vine-tree, with its magnificent foliage and abundant fruit, making homes and furnishing food for whole families of birds, not unaptly represents a great king, the father of his people. This figure was not altogether foreign to Chaldea, for we find it applied beautifully to Nebuchadnezzar in Dan. 4.

5. He took also of the seed of the land, and planted it in a fruitful field; he placed *it* by great waters, *and* set it *as* a willow tree.
6. And it grew, and became a spreading vine of low stature, whose branches turned toward him, and the roots

thereof were under him: so it became a vine, and brought forth branches, and shot forth sprigs.

This eagle, (Nebuchadnezzar) now takes of the seed of the land, a scion of the royal family of Judah, and plants it under favorable auspices in a fruitful field and by abundant waters, where it might become,—not indeed a great cedar, but a humble yet useful vine. If Zedekiah had remained true to his sovereign, and especially, if true also to God, he and his people might have enjoyed a career of honor and prosperity. His comparatively humble condition— a vine of low stature—looks to the fact that all the chief princes and the more active, intelligent and useful citizens, had been taken to Babylon as captives. See 2 Kings 24: 14–16, and Jer. 24.

7. There was also another great eagle with great wings and many feathers: and behold, this vine did bend her roots toward him, and shot forth her branches toward him, that he might water it by the furrows of her plantation.

8. It was planted in a good soil by great waters, that it might bring forth branches, and that it might bear fruit, that it might be a goodly vine.

The historical facts represented here are simply that Zedekiah rebelled against Nebuchadnezzar and sent ambassadors to Egypt for aid. This policy the Lord by his prophet sharply condemned. It was the burden of repeated remonstrances through Jeremiah.

9. Say thou, Thus saith the Lord God; Shall it prosper? shall he not pull up the roots thereof, and cut off the fruit thereof, that it wither? it shall wither in all the leaves of her spring, even without great power, or many people to pluck it up by the roots thereof.

10. Yea, behold, *being* planted, shall it prosper? shall it not utterly wither, when the east wind toucheth it? it shall wither in the furrows where it grew.

The Lord now begins to make the moral application of this parable. Shall such treachery prosper? Can such ingratitude and baseness result well in the end? Will not the first great eagle (Nebuchadnezzar) take revenge upon this vine (Zedekiah); tear it up by its roots and leave it to wither and die?——The passage intimates that this will be done easily. Judah was now greatly reduced in military strength by the loss of her citizens already taken captive; by her immoralities; and not least, by God's wrath against her. The king of Babylon could easily punish her "without great power or many people to pluck her up by her roots."

11. Moreover the word of the Lord came unto me, saying,

12. Say now to the rebellious house, Know ye not what

these *things* mean? Tell *them*, Behold, the king of Babylon is come to Jerusalem, and hath taken the king thereof, and the princes thereof, and led them with him to Babylon;

13. And hath taken of the king's seed, and made a covenant with him, and hath taken an oath of him: he hath also taken the mighty of the land:

14. That the kingdom might be base, that it might not lift itself up, *but* that by keeping of his covenant it might stand.

15. But he rebelled against him in sending his ambassadors into Egypt, that they might give him horses and much people. Shall he prosper? shall he escape that doeth such *things?* or shall he break the covenant, and be delivered?

16. *As* I live, saith the Lord God, surely in the place *where* the king *dwelleth* that made him king, whose oath he despised, and whose covenant he brake, *even* with him in the midst of Babylon he shall die.

This explanation is itself plain and most amply unfolds the meaning of this riddle or parable. The great facts of Zedekiah's treachery were just about transpiring now in the sixth year of his reign. It was essential that the exiles in Chaldea should know these facts, and should see the justice of God's wrath against Zedekiah and his people for this rebellion against the king of Babylon. Hence this representation held a vitally important place in Ezekiel's prophecies to his captive brethren.——V. 16 disclosed to them the pertinent prophecy that King Zedekiah should be brought to the place where his real sovereign lived, under the power of the king against whom he had perjured himself and whose covenant he had broken, and should die there in Babylon. This announcement must have sufficed to crush out any fond hopes they might have had as to the reign of Zedekiah.

17. Neither shall Pharaoh, with *his* mighty army and great company, make for him in the war, by casting up mounts, and building forts, to cut off many persons:

18. Seeing he despised the oath by breaking the covenant, when lo, he had given his hand, and hath done all these *things*, he shall not escape.

19. Therefore thus saith the Lord God; *As* I live, surely mine oath that he hath despised, and my covenant that he hath broken, even it will I recompense upon his own head.

20. And I will spread my net upon him, and he shall be taken in my snare, and I will bring him to Babylon, and will plead with him there for his trespass that he hath trespassed against me.

21. And all his fugitives with all his bands shall fall by the sword, and they that remain shall be scattered toward all winds: and ye shall know that I the Lord have spoken it.

The help of Egypt, though promised him, should avail nothing. Deservedly this passage lays stress upon the base treachery and rebellion of Zedekiah as the ground of the Lord's last judgments on himself, his family and his throne.——So true and right it is that God holds even kings to the morality of good faith in their solemn compacts. Why should he not? Why should kings be privileged to perjure themselves with impunity? Could the influence of such an example on whole masses of people be endured under the government of God?——Need it be said that this principle applies to all rulers under every form of human government? Or that the curse of God against national bad faith is not a whit lessened but is greatly aggravated by the weakness of the party to whom the nation's faith is pledged? What must God think and what ought the wide world to say of the violation of American treaties with the feeble Indian tribes? And what if the good faith of the nation should be broken with the Anglo-African race after they have saved the nation by their fidelity and bravery in arms under the national guarantee of freedom and protection?

22. Thus saith the Lord God, I will also take of the highest branch of the high cedar, and will set *it;* I will crop off from the top of his young twigs a tender one, and will plant *it* upon a high mountain and eminent:

23. In the mountain of the height of Israel will I plant it: and it shall bring forth boughs, and bear fruit, and be a goodly cedar: and under it shall dwell all fowl of every wing; in the shadow of the branches thereof shall they dwell.

24. And all the trees of the field shall know that I the Lord have brought down the high tree, have exalted the low tree, have dried up the green tree, and have made the dry tree to flourish: I the Lord have spoken and have done *it.*

The tone of this chapter thus far might naturally be depressing to the exiles, adapted to extinguish their hopes for all the future of God's kingdom and cause on earth. Hence the special fitness of this beautiful closing prophecy. It not only counteracted their discouragement, but it laid the foundation for sweet and glorious hope.——Is the eagle able to pluck the highest branch of the proud cedar, and set it where he will? So God—a loftier monarch than he of Babylon—will pluck a tender scion from his high cedar and will set it in his high and holy mountain—the ever honored temple mountain in Jerusalem, for this must be "the mountain in the height of Israel." Compare such passages as Isa. 2: 2–4, Micah

4: 1–3, and in Ezekiel himself, chap. 20: 40: "For in mine holy mountain, in the mountain of the height of Israel, there shall all the house of Israel serve me; there will I accept them and there will I require your offerings," etc. See also chap. 34: 14.——To the glory of *this* goodly cedar, there shall be no eclipse. No decay shall ever reach it, neither shall violence pluck it up; there shall be no limit to the blessings it shall diffuse. "Under it shall dwell all fowl of every wing; in the shadow of the branch thereof shall they dwell." It shall forever illustrate the sovereign power of God who takes down the loftiest monarchs of earth at his pleasure, and lifts up the lowest; who "withers the green tree and makes the dry tree flourish," and who, according to this promise of his love, will cast down all opposing thrones and will establish the one universal throne of his own glorious Son that "the kingdoms of this world may become the kingdom of our Lord and of his Christ, and he shall reign for ever and ever."——There can be no good reason to doubt the application of these verses to the then future Messiah. All the kings of David's line were in the succession of promise between him and his greater Son. Hence the sad fall of the two last prior to the captivity afforded a pertinent occasion for thus alluding to the greater glories—never to be despaired of—that were sure to the future Zion in her blessed King. The hopes of God's people need not go down in the eclipse that came over the royal house of David through the crimes, the captivity, and the death, of these two kings. Their doom forcibly suggested the contrasted destiny of "the Righteous Branch" that should reign and prosper" and fill the earth with his blessings. The Lord could not forego such an opportunity for promises so timely, so refreshing, so inspiring to his true people in all ages.

CHAPTER XVIII.

This chapter refutes the implication of injustice in God, involved in the use of the proverb, "The fathers have eaten sour grapes and the children's teeth are set on edge."——The whole subject demands careful attention and candid, intelligent discriminations. For it should be remembered that in the standard moral law embraced in the ten commandments the Lord appends to the penalties of the second commandment, forbidding idolatry, these words: "Visiting the iniquities of the fathers upon the children unto the third and fourth generation of those that hate me;" and further, that the prophets had declared that God would and did send the Jews into captivity for the sins of Manasseh;—*e. g.*, 2 Kings 24: 3, 4, and 23: 26, 27, and 21: 11–16. But these judgments fell, not on Manasseh himself, but on his sons of the third and fourth generation—Josiah being in the second; his sons Jehoiakim and Zedekiah in the third, and Jehoiachin in the fourth. It need not surprise us therefore that this proverb should come to the lips of men who sought to justify themselves in their sins, and who were gratified to have even the least apology for arraigning the justice of God and for persisting in their sins, refusing to repent.——The chapter will show us how the Lord meets this implication and how he enforces upon the people their personal duty.

1. The word of the Lord came unto me again, saying,
2. What mean ye, that ye use this proverb concerning the land of Israel, saying, The fathers have eaten sour grapes, and the children's teeth are set on edge?
3. *As* I live, saith the Lord God, ye shall not have *occasion* any more to use this proverb in Israel.

The original rendered—"What mean ye?" demands rather the reason than the meaning. The sense is, *Why* should ye thus implicate the justice of God? and not merely this; What precisely do you *mean* by this proverb? The Hebrew would read literally; "What is it to you who are using this proverb?" etc.; equal to, *Why* do ye use this proverb? Nearly the same phrase has occurred chap. 12: 22; "What to you is that proverb concerning the land of Israel?" *i. e.*, What business have you to use it? For what reason?——In v. 3 the word "occasion," supplied by our translators with no corresponding word in the original, should not by any means be construed so as to imply that the Jews previously had good reason for using this proverb, but should have it no longer. The original simply affirms, "There shall not be to you any more the using of this proverb;" which naturally means, *Ye shall no more use it.* The Lord would set the case in a light so clear that they must see the injustice of the implication which it involved. It does not by any means appear that the Lord proposes to change his policy, *i. e.*, either his principles or his practice in his government, so that henceforth there should be no more occasion for using this proverb, while previously there may have been occasion.
——The phrase, "Set on edge," is in common use for that peculiar sensation and effect produced sometimes by using acid fruit. It is singular that while this phrase seems most naturally to mean *sharpened*, the original Hebrew means *to make dull.* The sensation best explains itself. Its meaning as a proverb is simply, The fathers sin and the children suffer its penalty.

4. Behold, all souls are mine; as the soul of the father, so also the soul of the son is mine: the soul that sinneth, it shall die.

This is the first point of the Lord's reply. The affirmation, "*are mine,*" implies not only ownership but parental care and responsibility, and especially the governmental responsibility of dealing with them according to justice and never in violation of justice. The Infinite Father who has given existence to all human souls affirms of himself that he holds the solemn trust of administering his moral government over them all—over fathers and sons alike—on such principles as can never involve any injustice. The sinning soul and he only shall die. He dies for his own sins and not for another's. The same Lord is equally just to all. Bound to be just toward the son as truly as toward the father—loving the son as he loves the father—how can he visit upon the son the proper penalty of the sin of which the father only is guilty? He never can.——The Hebrew phrase rendered "are mine," occurs elsewhere, chap. 29: 3, where Pharaoh says of the Nile, "My river is *mine own;* I have made it for myself." Also Exod. 13: 2, where the Lord says of every first-born in Israel, "*It is mine;*" and Ps. 50: 10, where the same is affirmed of "every beast of the forest and of the cattle on a thousand hills." The ownership which God claims in human souls involves higher responsibilities than his ownership of the beasts of the field because they have nobler powers and sustain higher relations.——The words "die" and "death" are used in the Scriptures in at least three diverse senses: (1.) For the well-known dissolution of soul and body—natural death. (2.) For a state of heart in which sin has absolute dominion and the soul is committed to sinning past all hope of recovery by its own exertions—a state often called spiritual death. (3.) For the penalty of the divine law for sin—an amount of suffering and evil thought of as indefinitely great, and called death because this word stands for the greatest earthly evil—the ultimate infliction possible for man to inflict on his fellow-man.——The two former are not to be thought of in this connection. Only the third meets the conditions of the case. See the term used in the same sense by Jeremiah (chap. 31: 30) in the same connection as here, rebuking the people for using this same proverb. Also by Ezekiel (chap. 3: 18-20), and by Hosea (chap 13: 1); "When Ephraim offended in the matter of Baal, *he died;* and now they sin more and more," etc.—implying that the terrible penalty of death was in their case still suspended. It should be noted that these principles—"all souls are mine;" and "the sinning soul shall die"—are immutable and eternal. They had not been adopted *since* the Jews had begun to use this proverb and in consequence of this use. They had not come into existence as a modification of the Lord's recent course toward the Jewish nation. The possible implication which our received translation ("shall not have *occasion* any more") might be thought to favor, finds no support in this first grand point made in the reply of the Lord.

5. But if a man be just, and do that which is lawful and right,

6. *And* hath not eaten upon the mountains, neither hath lifted up his eyes to the idols of the house of Israel, neither hath defiled his neighbor's wife, neither hath come near to a menstruous woman,

7. And hath not oppressed any, *but* hath restored to the debtor his pledge, hath spoiled none by violence, hath given his bread to the hungry, and hath covered the naked with a garment;

8. He *that* hath not given forth upon usury, neither hath taken any increase, *that* hath withdrawn his hand from iniquity, hath executed true judgment between man and man,

9. Hath walked in my statutes, and hath kept my judgments, to deal truly; he *is* just, he shall surely live, saith the Lord God.

This is a description of a good man, drawn for those times, in view of the morals and immoralities of that age, and also of the precepts and prohibitions of the Mosaic law.——" Eaten upon the mountains," means, eaten at idol feasts, of flesh offered to idols and in their honor.——"High places" were chosen as sites for idol temples and worship.——"Restored to the debtor his pledge." The Hebrew law, protecting the poor debtor, prescribed very specific rules in regard to receiving and restoring pledges.given for the payment of debts. See Ex. 22: 25-27 and Deut. 24: 6, 10-13. The main points were that raiment taken in pledge must be restored before sunset so that the debtor might use it for his bedcovering; that neither the upper nor nether mill-stone might be taken at all—this being a necessity for every family, however poor; and that the creditor must not go into the debtor's house to get his pledge, but must "stand abroad" and wait for the poor man to bring it out. With such jealous care did the gracious Lord protect the rights and interests of the poor against the not infrequent inhumanities of the rich.——The law against loaning upon usury and taking increase, rested on the same principle—the protection of the poor and unfortunate—who in those ages were the borrowers contemplated in these laws. Using other people's money to make more money was quite unknown in legitimate Hebrew life. In circumstances where such business is legitimate and useful, it can not be inferred from the Hebrew law that it would be wrong to take interest for the use of money.——Of this just man, thus described in detail, the Lord declares, "*he shall surely live;*" *i. e.,* he shall not die in the sense of *death* as used in this chapter. He shall have the favor and blessing of God, and not his frown and curse. The point of the affirmation is that God deals with individual men on principles that never violate simple justice.——Here let us carefully note that while the Lord conducts his defense and states the policy of his moral government by means of *hypothetical cases*—"*If* a man"—any man—do so and so, such and such shall be the result; yet his supposed cases would naturally suggest the names of various kings well known in their recent history. Thus, *e. g.*, under this hypothetical case (vs. 5-9) they might naturally write the names of Hezekiah and Josiah. They were good men. They shall live and not die. The hypothetical form would apply the principle to every good man: the character living in their thought and prominent in the recent history of their kings, would give it vitality and force.

10. If he beget a son *that is* a robber, a shedder of blood, and *that* doeth the like to *any* one of these *things*,

11. And that doeth not any of those *duties*, but even hath eaten upon the mountains, and defiled his neighbor's wife,

12. Hath oppressed the poor and needy, hath spoiled by violence, hath not restored the pledge, and hath lifted up his eyes to the idols, hath committed abomination,

13. Hath given forth upon usury, and hath taken increase: shall he then live? he shall not live: he hath done all these abominations; he shall surely die; his blood shall be upon him.

The case here supposed is that of an apostate and recreant son of this just and good father. He is wicked—all the more so for the light of a godly and just example which he perpetually sins against.——In v. 10, last clause, the Hebrew makes prominent the word "brother," which our translators construed rather harshly, thus;—"Who doeth deeds that are *brother* to robbery and bloodshedding." Usage scarcely sustains this construction, and v. 18—a renewed mention of the same case—forbids it. Better thus; Who doeth such deeds as robbery and murder *to his brother; i. e.*, probably to his brother-man—to those whom he is bound to account as his brethren—a thought which puts his sin in a most aggravated light.——Shall this man *live?* Nay, verily; by no means. He shall not live because his father was so good a man. For this very reason is his guilt the greater, and therefore for this reason all the more shall he die. His blood shall be on his own head. This is justice, and thus God evinces himself just.——Of this case also there were royal examples painfully recent and fresh in every mind. The good Josiah had three wicked sons and one wicked grandson who filled the throne after him till their crimes sank that throne and kingdom in ruin. Did they live in the favor of God for their good father's sake? Utterly far from it. For his goodness, all the greater was their sin and all the more terrible their doom!
——Manasseh for a long time ran the same career, and but for his late repentance, would have been another illustration of this case.

14. Now lo, *if* he beget a son, that seeth all his father's sins which he hath done, and considereth, and doeth not such like,

15. *That* hath not eaten upon the mountains, neither hath lifted up his eyes to the idols of the house of Israel, hath not defiled his neighbor's wife,

16. Neither hath oppressed any, hath not withholden the pledge, neither hath spoiled by violence, *but* hath given his

bread to the hungry, and hath covered the naked with a garment,

17. *That* hath taken off his hand from the poor, *that* hath not received usury nor increase, hath executed my judgments, hath walked in my statutes; he shall not die for the iniquity of his father, he shall surely live.

Here this wicked son becomes a father, and has a son who sees, abhors, and forsakes his father's sins. This case came directly to the main point of the proverb. The father has eaten sour grapes: shall the son's teeth be blunted thereby? Shall the upright son die. for the sins of his wicked father? Nay, verily. His virtue is really the greater because of the unpropitious circumstances under which and despite of which it has been developed.——"That hath taken off his hand from the poor," means, hath taken off a *hard hand*—one that is overbearing, oppressive.——Here let us specially note that the Lord confronts the implication of the proverb by explicitly affirming that he always, sooner or later, deals with individual men according to their own personal guilt or innocence. From this just principle he never deviates. This is what justice demands—is what the just God invariably does.——The royal family furnished examples to fill this case. Hezekiah succeeded the wicked Ahaz; Josiah, the wicked Amon; but neither followed his father's crimes. Each turned away from the wicked course of his father and did what was lawful and right; and each lived thereby.

18. *As for* his father, because he cruelly oppressed, spoiled his brother by violence, and did *that* which *is* not good among his people, lo, even he shall die in his iniquity.

To make the application of this case to the proverb the more palpable, the prophet recurs again to the ungodly father, described fully vs. 10–13. He, being a wicked man, must die in his iniquity. His own sins demand this terrible doom! His doom is in no sense mitigated by his having a godly son. Ahaz and Amon were none the more favored of God for having such sons as Hezekiah and Josiah.

19. Yet say ye, Why? doth not the son bear the iniquity of the father? When the son hath done that which is lawful and right, *and* hath kept all my statutes, and hath done them, he shall surely live.

20. The soul that sinneth, it shall die. The son shall not bear the iniquity of the father, neither shall the father bear the iniquity of the son: the righteousness of the righteous shall be upon him, and the wickedness of the wicked shall be upon him.

The prophet here supposes the people to reaffirm their position, though somewhat modestly, and in the form only of a question. But after all you have said, *is it not true that sons bear the iniquity of their fathers?*———The Lord answers; When the son, even of a wicked father, does right, he shall live. The soul that sinneth (and he *only*) shall die. The son shall not bear the iniquity of the father, nor the father, the iniquity of the son. The righteousness of the righteous shall determine his destiny: the wickedness of the wicked shall decide his doom.

21. But if the wicked will turn from all his sins that he hath committed, and keep all my statutes, and do that which is lawful and right, he shall surely live, he shall not die.

22. All his transgressions that he hath committed, they shall not be mentioned unto him: in his righteousness that he hath done he shall live.

The people doubtless made use of this proverb and of its unjust implication of wrong on God's part, to *relieve their conscience from the pressure of obligation to repent*. Hence the tone of these and the following verses bears directly to the point of counteracting this influence and of persuading them to repent. Though you have sinned, yet if you will turn from all your sin and do only right, you shall live and not die. All your transgressions shall be forgiven and not be mentioned any more against you. Because of the new moral course unto which ye turn, ye shall live. It was vital to the best moral results that the people should see that repentance brings salvation, even to the chief of sinners.———Here came in the strong case of Manasseh, who, after many years of awfully wicked life, repented, humbled himself greatly, was brought back from his captivity in Babylon, and found mercy of God. See the record 2 Chron. 33: 11–13, 18, 19. · It was this repentance that averted the divine judgments from himself and gave a new lease of life to the nation. Because of this repentance, the national ruin was delayed for yet another great effort toward their salvation.

23. Have I any pleasure at all that the wicked should die? saith the Lord God: *and* not that he should return from his ways, and live?

Is it any pleasure to me that the wicked man should die? Is it not rather my supreme pleasure that he should turn from his wicked ways and so should live? The people may have thought otherwise. It may have seemed to them that God took delight in visiting the penalties of an awful death on the wicked. If they had thought so, they did not know the heart of God; they had entirely misapprehended his nature; they had never seen and appreciated his deep eternal love! For, the most glorious, most blessed truth ever revealed of God to this sinning world is here—that God has compassion toward even very guilty sinners; is pained and not pleased when he must punish; is delighted, even to infinite joy, when the sinner turns from his wicked ways and lives. Out of this loving compassion came the scheme of atonement through the incarnation and death of his own beloved Son, making pardon safe to his kingdom—possible without peril to the vital interests of his government. For all this, let the heavens rejoice and let the earth be glad!

24. But when the righteous turneth away from his righteousness, and committeth iniquity, *and* doeth according to all the abominations that the wicked *man* doeth, shall he live? All his righteousness that he hath done shall not be mentioned: in his trespass that he hath trespassed, and in his sin that he hath sinned, in them shall he die.

Still another phase of the general question requires notice. Suppose a man has lived righteously a long time and has accumulated what might be accounted a stock of righteousness. If then he turns from his righteousness and commits iniquity, shall he live? By no means. All his stock of accumulated righteousness goes for nothing—"shall not be mentioned;" in his sins he must die. So men must abandon all hope of God's favor on the ground of having once done right—if they turn from that righteousness and commit iniquity.

25. Yet ye say, The way of the Lord is not equal. Hear now, O house of Israel; Is not my way equal? are not your ways unequal?

26. When a righteous *man* turneth away from his righteousness, and committeth iniquity, and dieth in them; for his iniquity that he hath done shall he die.

27. Again, when the wicked *man* turneth away from his wickedness that he hath committed, and doeth that which is lawful and right, he shall save his soul alive.

28. Because he considereth, and turneth away from all his transgressions that he hath committed, he shall surely live, he shall not die.

Here the implication, tacitly involved in the proverb, is brought out palpably—a charge of injustice in God. They say the course of God's moral administration is not equitable. It violates justice. This is the charge of the people against God.——To this the Lord replies, squarely asserting the perfect justice of his own ways, and the injustice of theirs. It is *your* ways that are unequal: mine are always equal.——The points of argument made here are these two: (1.) That a righteous man, turning from his righteousness and doing wrong, shall die for his iniquity: (2.) That a wicked man, considering his ways and turning from his wickedness, shall surely live and not die. These great features of God's moral administration over a sinning world are so obviously equitable; they so plainly cover the whole ground of justice and of mercy, and so commend themselves to every man's conscience and moral sense as intrinsically right and good, that they are naturally the end of all argument. More is superfluous.

29. Yet saith the house of Israel, The way of the Lord is not equal. O house of Israel, are not my ways equal? are not your ways unequal?

30. Therefore I will judge you, O house of Israel, every one according to his ways, saith the Lord God. Repent, and turn *yourselves* from all your transgressions; so iniquity shall not be your ruin.

31. Cast away from you all your transgressions, whereby ye have transgressed; and make you a new heart and a new spirit: for why will ye die, O house of Israel?

32. For I have no pleasure in the death of him that dieth, saith the Lord God: wherefore turn *yourselves*, and live ye.

Yet the people are supposed to reiterate their charge of injustice against God. The Lord reaffirms his perfect justice in the same terms as before, v. 25; declares that he will judge them every one according to his ways; and exhorts them therefore to repent and turn from all their transgressions: else iniquity must be their ruin. So doing, it shall not be.——"Casting away all transgression," is here essentially equivalent to "making to themselves a new heart and a new spirit." The putting away of sin supposes sin to be abhorred, supposes that the heart turns to God to obey and to love him supremely. This and nothing less than this, God implies in this exhortation; this and nothing less God demands of every sinner, and demands it with infinite reason. This reasonable duty God presses here as the only alternative to the doom of death. Do this—for why will ye die, O house of Israel? Do this —*else you must die*, past all mercy, past all possibility of salvation. And *why should you choose death?* Why doom yourselves to so dire an end when life is before you, and when God so earnestly longs to see you turning from your sins to accept and insure it for evermore!——And this is truly the attitude and this the language of the All-glorious Father to every sinner! No one need say; "Such mercy can never apply to me; such words are too good to be said of me!" "*Whosoever will*, let him take the water of life freely!"

Before we pass on from this great discussion, vindicating the justice of God, let us turn our attention yet more distinctly to the circumstances which probably gave rise to the proverb and note also the method in which the Lord rebuts its implication of injustice.——In those ages, idolatry was the great national sin of the Jews—the special cause of the judgments of God on their city and land. In the second command of the decalogue, the recital of penalty has these words; "Visiting the iniquity of the fathers upon the children unto the third and fourth generation of them that hate me." Ex. 20: 5. As shown above, this special statement was precisely fulfilled in the fact that the sins of Manasseh are repeatedly represented to be those which the Lord "could not pardon" and must punish; while yet the punishment in the form of dethronement, captivity, and a violent death, fell upon his children of the third and fourth generation.——Now it was probably in view of these facts that the people brought into current use this proverb—cited also by Jeremiah (chap. 31: 29, 30) and rebutted there in the same way as here. *How* does the Lord reply and rebut this allegation?——Not by any attempt, even the least, to explain the philosophy of the penalty attached to the second commandment; not by showing *why* he governs nations with much long-suffering and waits through many generations of individual men, far down in the nation's life, still pressing his agencies for reform and laboring to save the whole people from the ruin toward which they are tending. Not thus does he condescend to debate this matter, although he *might* have done so;—but he makes his response directly and squarely *practical*, to the heart and conscience of the people. He says to them virtually, There is no need just now that ye concern yourselves with the policy of God in his government of nations *as such*. Suffice it for you that ye personally stand or fall before God on your individual life. With every individual man, whether king or subject, I deal in perfect equity, never punishing any one sinner for the guilt of another sinner; never the son for the sins of his father. Do right and you live: but persist in sinning, turn from righteousness to sin, and you surely die. I have no pleasure in your death; I long to see you repenting and living righteously with a new heart and a new spirit. So shall my heart be cheered and gladdened in your eternal peace and life.——This was the vital thing that needed to be said. This was all that the case really demanded. This rebutted the allegation of injustice on God's part, and brought the greatest possible pressure upon the heart and conscience toward repentance and salvation. It was doubtless wise in God to omit all philosophical discussion upon the further question of his policy *toward nations as such*, and to hold their attention simply and closely to the one far greater theme—their own personal responsibilities, perils, and possibilities of life.——But as already hinted, the Lord might have replied by expounding the philosophy of that remarkable penalty attached to the second commandment. He might have said—Nations are not precisely the same as individuals. A nation's life runs through a period which includes the lifetime of many individual generations. Why may I not exercise long-suffering toward a nation as well as toward an individual? And hence, what can forbid my bearing with a nation through several generations of fathers and sons, plying every moral agency to turn them from their sins to righteousness? Especially, he might have said; What principle of justice is violated, *provided* that always and every-where, sooner or later, I deal with every individual sinner in that nation, king or subject, according to his personal deserts?——The retribution of nations as such is not closed up and exhausted each successive day nor each year, nor in each generation. It waits far into the nation's life for its fullness of time, much as God waits upon some one individual sinner past many sins, through many months or years it may be of his sinning, yet never loses sight of his case; never fails to administer perfect justice in the end.——Thus are the ways of the Lord true and righteous altogether. Thus the laws of his moral administration over nations are in some respects peculiar and unique, resting on their own good reasons, and having evermore due regard to what is peculiar in the life of nations as such in this world.——Still further, let us recur again to the fact that the sins of Manasseh were made prominent as involving the nation in guilt which the Lord could not pardon; also, that in the event the national ruin fell on his children of the third and fourth generation; and that this fact may have had some influence to bring into vogue the proverb which leads the discussion in this chapter. Here then note that this discussion brings out the very principle on which the Lord spared Manasseh. *He repented; broke off his sins by righteousness; and found mercy.* The case was one of exceedingly great and rich moral power as an encouragement to the vilest of sinners to return to the Lord their God. Was it not, at least mainly, for the sake of affording scope for the influence of this example that the Lord delayed the infliction of his judgments upon the nation, and yet prolonged their space for repentance!——In this point the Lord has the same policy with nations as with individuals, suddenly arresting his judgments at the very moment when they are ready to smite the guilty, if any new circumstances inspire fresh hope or develop some yet untried influence which may possibly lead to repentance. Manasseh's long-continued wickedness had depraved and almost sunk the nation; his late repentance cast a gleam of hope athwart the darkness; and God therefore not only spared him, but postponed his annihilating judgments for the sake of one other earnest effort to reclaim and save a guilty people.

CHAPTER XIX.

This chapter sets before the exiles the fall of the royal house of Judah and ultimately of the nation. With high poetic beauty this is done by conceiving of the whole people as "thy mother;" of this mother as first a lioness who puts her young lions one after another on the throne: and next, as a vine whose strong shoots become scepters for her kings, but which is finally itself plucked up in fury, dried by the east wind, and burned in the fire. So perish the kings of Judah, the people also, and the whole frame of organized society and government—a cluster of painful facts taken up here for a lamentation among the exiles of Chaldea.——Some of these events had already transpired: the rest of them were near at hand. There was no hope of saving these exiles morally and spiritually without bringing to bear upon them the entire moral power of those judgments with which God was scourging and wasting their mother people and country. Hence these topics appear in Ezekiel "line upon line," reiterated with wonderful variety of representation, and we might say, in forms which exhaust the entire wealth of symbols and figures known to Hebrew or Chaldean literature.

1. Moreover take thou up a lamentation for the princes of Israel,

2. And say, What *is* thy mother? A lioness: she lay down among lions, she nourished her whelps among young lions.

"Take up," in the sense of prepare and present to the exiles; announce and record it, for their moral instruction. Since the theme is one of bitter sorrow, let it be an *elegy*, to be used in public lamentation over the fall of their mother country.——"For the princes of Israel," refers to the *kings* on the throne of David. Ezekiel currently uses the word "prince" for those kings.——The term "Israel" looks not to the kingdom of the ten tribes, now extinct, but rather, back to David, to indicate the fall of the last kings in his line.——Naturally, "mother" represents the people, as "daughter" often does the chief cities, especially Jerusalem.—— The lion, king of beasts, fitly represents a king in the nation. The figure was at home in Chaldea, as is shown by their abundant use of it, evinced at this day in the ruins of their cities and temples.

3. And she brought up one of her whelps: it became a young lion, and it learned to catch the prey; it devoured men.

4. The nations also heard of him; he was taken in their pit, and they brought him with chains unto the land of Egypt.

This first young lion-king was Jehoahaz, recognized by three marks:—(1.) He was the first among the sons of Josiah to succeed him on his throne, and is the first in order here: (2.) He was put on the throne *by the people*, as the history specially affirms, 2 Kings 23: 30, and 2 Chron. 36: 1: (3.) He and he only, having been deposed by Pharoah Necho, was carried (as here stated) to Egypt and died there.——The figure is carried out to the life. This young lion caught the ways of lion-kings; he "learned to catch the prey and devoured men." Even the original word for "chain" keeps up the figure, denoting the hook or ring fixed in the nose of wild animals to control them.

5. Now, when she saw that she had waited, *and* her hope

was lost, she took another of her whelps, *and* made him a young lion.

6. And he went up and down among the lions, he became a young lion, and learned to catch the prey, *and* devoured men.

7. And he knew their desolate palaces, and he laid waste their cities; and the land was desolate, and the fullness thereof, by the noise of his roaring.

8. Then the nations set against him on every side from the provinces, and spread their net over him: he was taken in their pit.

9. And they put him in ward in chains, and brought him to the king of Babylon: they brought him into holds, that his voice should no more be heard upon the mountains of Israel.

This second young lion is not Jehoiakim, the immediate successor of Jehoahaz, but is Jehoiachin, his son. For the former (the father) was put on the throne, not by the people, but by the king of Babylon; and he seems not to have been carried to Babylon, but to have died in disgrace at Jerusalem. See Jer. 22: 18, 19 and 36: 30. On the other hand, Jehoiachin was in favor with the people, and for aught that appears was put on the throne by them; was taken captive to Babylon and remained there in captivity at least thirty-seven years; and finally his fall was specially afflictive to the exiles. They had many fond hopes of his restoration. See Lam. 4: 20. The people hoped that Jehoahaz might be restored to them, till this hope perished (v. 5).——In v. 7 the word rendered "desolate palaces," stands in our Hebrew text, *widows*. If this reading be accepted, the word "knew" must mean *violated*, giving us a dark view of his moral purity.

10. Thy mother *is* like a vine in thy blood, planted by the waters: she was fruitful and full of branches by reason of many waters.

11. And she had strong rods for the scepters of them that bare rule, and her stature was exalted among the thick branches, and she appeared in her height with the multitude of her branches.

12. But she was plucked up in fury, she was cast down to the ground, and the east wind dried up her fruit: her strong rods were broken and withered; the fire consumed them.

13. And now she *is* planted in the wilderness, in a dry and thirsty ground.

14. And fire is gone out of a rod of her branches, *which* hath devoured her fruit, so that she hath no strong

rod *to be* a scepter to rule. This *is* a lamentation, and shall be for a lamentation.

By a sudden change of figure the Jewish people become a *vine*—a figure of somewhat frequent occurrence in the Scriptures and recently used by Ezekiel himself. See chap. 15: 6 and 17: 6. See also Isa. 5: 1-7 and 27: 2-7; Ps. 80: 8-16 and Jer. 2: 21.—— Her strong shoots are scepters for kings, and virtually in the figure, represent kings themselves. She rose to prominence among the nations, but she was suddenly plucked up by the fury of the Almighty. The east wind—terribly withering in that climate—dried up her roots: her strong rods (scepters) were broken, and the fires of divine judgments consumed both kings and people.—— A few of her people had been taken into captivity—a fact represented here by her being transplanted to a wilderness and set in a dry and thirsty ground. Her last king, Zedekiah, by his treachery to the king of Babylon, had brought down the final stroke of vengeance—corresponding to a fire going out from one of the rods (scepters) of her foliage, which devoured her fruit, so that she had no successor for her throne. The royal house is utterly broken down. The throne of Judah is in ruins. To the Hebrew exiles, this was and should still be "for a lamentation."——In v. 10 the word translated "in thy blood," involves great critical difficulties. Probably the reading is not correct. What it should be, it is perhaps impossible to determine with certainty. Fortunately no sentiment of special importance is involved in the question. Gesenius says, most probably thus;—"like a vine of thy vineyard." Others variously.

CHAPTER XX.

This chapter, with a new date, has its special *occasion*—the coming of certain elders of Israel to inquire of the Lord through the prophet. It has also its special strain of reply—essentially a resumé or historical review of the great trials which the Lord experienced with the Hebrew people on the point of their propensity to idolatry, showing that, over and over again, he had forbidden them to worship idols, had solemnly sworn that he would exterminate them with his judgments for this sin, but had spared them for his great mercy's sake.——As a historical sketch, the chapter corresponds somewhat closely with Neh. 9; Ps. 78; and the speech of Stephen in Ac. 7. Here preëminently the historical facts cited bear on the great points now present and prominent—viz., that the people were strangely infatuated toward idolatry; that they had been on the verge of national ruin repeatedly for this sin; and that they had been spared only through the great mercy of God and to save the honor of his throne before the heathen; and not at all for their own sake or merit.

EZEKIEL.—CHAP. XX.

1. And it came to pass in the seventh year, in the fifth *month*, the tenth *day* of the month, *that* certain of the elders of Israel came to inquire of the Lord, and sat before me.

This new date is about eleven months later than the last named —(8: 1).——It is obvious both from the strain of the chapter and from the relation of these exiles to their fatherland that they came to inquire of the Lord, not specially for themselves, but for their nation and their beloved but now doomed city. The Lord's reply is not this: "I can not hear you in the thing you ask for yourselves;" but, "I can not spare that guilty nation!"——They came and sat before the prophet to confer with him in the matter, and probably to enlist his sympathies with their own if they could.

2. Then came the word of the Lord unto me, saying,

3. Son of man, speak unto the elders of Israel, and say unto them, Thus saith the Lord God; Are ye come to inquire of me? *As* I live, saith the Lord God, I will not be inquired of by you.

The Lord understood their thought before their words had disclosed it and promptly replied with a most solemn refusal. The doom of the guilty people and city was fixed and no prayer could reverse it. God "would not pardon." See 2 Kings 24: 4, Ezek. 14, and Jer. 15, and 7: 16, and 11: 14, and 14: 11.——On the clause, "I will not be inquired of by you," Jerome has this fine comment: "To the holy and to those who ask for right things, the promise is given; 'While they are yet speaking, I will say—Here I am.' But to sinners, such as these elders of Israel were, and as those whose sins the prophet proceeds to describe, no answer is given, but only a fierce rebuke for their sins, to which He adds his oath; 'As I live,' to strengthen his solemn refusal."

4. Wilt thou judge them, son of man, wilt thou judge *them?* cause them to know the abominations of their fathers:

This question, "Wilt thou judge them?" can not be taken as implying that he *ought not* to do it, thus; Wilt thou do a thing so wrong as to judge them? On the contrary, it manifestly implies an affirmative and enjoins the duty of judging them. The Hebrew interrogative particle used here sometimes implies a negative particle with it; *e. g.*, Jer. 31: 20—"Is (*i. e.*, is *not*) Ephraim my dear son?" Is he (not) a pleasant child?" Also Job 20: 4: "Knowest thou (not) this of old that the triumphing of the wicked is short?"—— "Judge," is here used in the forensic sense—bring them to trial; prefer charges against them; recite the catalogue of their crimes; and, as the parallel clause has it, show them the abominable sins of their fathers.——This v. 4 indicates the course of thought throughout vs. 5–32. Instead of allowing himself to be inquired of in prayer to avert his threatened judgments against the Jews, the Lord directs the prophet to set before these elders the long record of their national sins and provocations.

5. And say unto them, Thus saith the Lord God; In the day when I chose Israel, and lifted up my hand unto the seed of the house of Jacob, and made myself known unto them in the land of Egypt, when I lifted up my hand unto them, saying, I *am* the Lord your God;

6. In the day *that* I lifted up my hand unto them, to bring them forth of the land of Egypt into a land that I had espied for them, flowing with milk and honey, which *is* the glory of all lands:

7. Then said I unto them, Cast ye away every man the abominations of his eyes, and defile not yourselves with the idols of Egypt: I *am* the Lord your God.

"Chose Israel." See Deut. 7: 6–8 and 14: 2. "For thou art an holy people unto the Lord thy God. The Lord *hath chosen thee* to be a special people unto himself above all people that are upon the face of the earth," etc.——"Lifted up mine hands," *i. e.*, in the solemn oath, as in Deut. 32: 40, "For I lift up my hand to heaven and say, 'I live forever:'" or Dan. 12: 7 and Rev. 10: 5.——"Had espied," *i. e.*, explored and selected.——In these verses and in their context, it is implied that while yet the people were in Egypt, the Lord solemnly admonished them against idolatry, but they would not hear. The Scripture narrative omits this, except in so far as it may be implied in the proposal to go out from Egypt into the desert to offer sacrifice unto the Lord their God. Yet there can be no doubt of the fact that even there in Egypt the Lord admonished his people against being seduced into the worship of their idols.

8. But they rebelled against me, and would not hearken unto me: they did not every man cast away the abominations of their eyes, neither did they forsake the idols of Egypt: then I said, I will pour out my fury upon them, to accomplish mine anger against them in the midst of the land of Egypt.

9. But I wrought for my name's sake, that it should not be polluted before the heathen, among whom they *were*, in whose sight I made myself known unto them, in bringing them forth out of the land of Egypt.

They would not hearken to the Lord: hence while they were in Egypt, the Lord solemnly threatened to pour out his fury and to exhaust ("accomplish") his anger upon them. But he spared and saved his people then for his name's sake, that the heathen might not reproach him as unable to save his own people.

10. Wherefore I caused them to go forth out of the land of Egypt, and brought them into the wilderness.

11. And I gave them my statutes, and shewed them my judgments, which *if* a man do, he shall even live in them.

"Do and live," looks to that stubborn and stringent alternative put by the Lord through Moses, Deut. 30: 15-20, "See, I have set before thee this day life and good—death and evil." "I call heaven and earth to record this day against you that I have set before you life and death, blessing and cursing," etc.——The ancient Chaldee paraphrast expands the last clause of v. 11; "He shall live in them *with eternal life.*" This represents the current theology held by the Jews on this point before and near the Christian era, and hence has an important bearing on the interpretation of our Savior's language on this subject. It shows in what sense his language must have been understood, and hence in what sense he must have used it.

12. Moreover also I gave them my sabbaths, to be a sign between me and them, that they might know that I *am* the Lord that sanctify them.

This verse is specially important because of its supposed and real bearings on the nature and perpetuity of the Sabbath.——Why is the term here in the plural form, "*Sabbaths?*" Does it include other festal days than those enjoined in the fourth commandment?—— Under some circumstances it might; for God did enjoin upon the Jews other seasons of rest from labor, *e. g.*, during the three great feasts; on the great day of atonement, etc. But the reference in this passage to Exo. 31: 13-17 is so manifest that we must allow that passage to interpret this. There we read, "Verily my sabbaths" (plural) "shall ye keep;" yet the plural refers to many successive sabbaths—each seventh day—fifty-two in each year; and not to various days of required rest, other than this seventh day. Hence our passage in Ezekiel probably speaks only of the day enjoined in the fourth command.——In what sense did the Lord give the Jews the seventh-day sabbath "*as a sign?*"——The passage in Exodus reads; "Verily my sabbaths ye shall keep; for it is a sign between me and you throughout your generations, that ye may know that I am the Lord that doth sanctify you." "Wherefore the children of Israel shall keep the Sabbath to observe the Sabbath throughout their generations for a perpetual covenant. It is a sign between me and the children of Israel forever; for in six days the Lord made heaven and earth, and on the seventh day he rested and was refreshed."——In this passage the word "*sign*" manifestly means a standing memorial and witness of his relations to his people. It witnessed that he would have them imitate himself in his seventh-day rest after the six days' work of creation, and that he was devoting himself to their sanctification as his people;—"that ye may know that I am the Lord that doth sanctify you." God gave them the Sabbath to indicate these relations: they should observe it as a means of recognizing these relations on their part and of responding to them in observing the duties they involved.

We may now come to the question of more special interest in our age. Does this passage thus expounded, or indeed on any just exposition, teach that the Sabbath is exclusively a Jewish institution? Was it Mosaic or even Hebraic in such a sense that its obligations ceased with the expiration of that system and have no binding force in the Christian age?——I reply; the fact that God enjoined it upon the Hebrew people is no reason why he should not enjoin it also upon all mankind. On the contrary, if his revealed purposes and objects in enjoining it upon them are of a general nature, applicable in the main to all mankind, then his enjoining it upon them proves it to be binding universally on the race. Now it admits of ample proof that the reasons given of God for enjoining the observance of the Sabbath—given specially in the fourth command itself, and in the passage Exodus 31: 13–17, which is specially under Ezekiel's eye in our text—*are of universal application.* The Great Father of the race wrought six days in the creation and rested the seventh. He puts his own example, not before Israel only, but before the race, and invites—nay more, *commands* them to follow it. He signifies to them that he *would be remembered* as their Creator and Father, and would have them set apart time for an object so vital. Then Ex. 31: 13–17 (cited above) develops yet more fully the thought that in the Sabbath God aims to sanctify his people and to make it a visible sign of a special relationship between himself and them. Yet here let it be carefully noted, it is his relation to them not as Hebrews, but as his children, his people. All these points are general, not special; good for the race, not restricted and of value to the Hebrews only. Indeed they show the Sabbath to be a glorious *boon* which no tribe or nation or age can afford to forego.——Thus far the discussion of this great question respecting the universal obligation of the Sabbath as a divine institution comes fairly within the province of the expositor of Ezekiel because it is legitimately involved in the sense of his words. Other points bearing on the question, *e. g.*, its institution in Eden; the traces of it in the seven-day periods during the deluge; its existence among the Hebrews prior to its announcement from Sinai (see Exod. 16: 22–30), and the proofs of its reindorsement in the beginning of the Christian age, must be omitted as not germain to the scope of this commentary.

13. But the house of Israel rebelled against me in the wilderness: they walked not in my statutes, and they despised my judgments, which *if* a man do, he shall even live in them; and my sabbaths they greatly polluted: then I said, I would pour out my fury upon them in the wilderness, to consume them.

14. But I wrought for my name's sake, that it should not

be polluted before the heathen, in whose sight I brought them out.

15. Yet also I lifted up my hand unto them in the wilderness, that I would not bring them into the land which I had given *them*, flowing with milk and honey, which *is* the glory of all lands;

16. Because they despised my judgments, and walked not in my statutes, but polluted my sabbaths: for their heart went after their idols.

17. Nevertheless mine eye spared them from destroying them, neither did I make an end of them in the wilderness.

This brief reference to the wilderness-life of the children of Israel is most abundantly confirmed in the Pentateuch, especially in the history of the golden calf, Ex. 32 and 33, and in the unbelief and murmuring consequent on the report of the spies, Num. 13 and 14. See also Ps. 78 and 95. That stage of Hebrew life was a mournful illustration of human depravity, and especially of the corrupting influence exerted upon the fathers during their long residence in Egypt and long familiarity with idol-worship there.

18. But I said unto their children in the wilderness, Walk ye not in the statutes of your fathers, neither observe their judgments, nor defile yourselves with their idols:

19. I *am* the Lord your God; walk in my statutes, and keep my judgments, and do them;

20. And hallow my sabbaths; and they shall be a sign between me and you, that ye may know that I *am* the Lord your God.

21. Notwithstanding the children rebelled against me: they walked not in my statutes, neither kept my judgments to do them, which *if* a man do, he shall even live in them: they polluted my sabbaths: then I said, I would pour out my fury upon them, to accomplish mine anger against them in the wilderness.

22. Nevertheless I withdrew my hand, and wrought for my name's sake, that it should not be polluted in the sight of the heathen, in whose sight I brought them forth.

It was indeed most true that the Lord reiterated his admonitions, warnings and threatenings, continually during the forty years' life of the nation in the wilderness. It was one constant scene of moral labor to train and reform the people. It availed in great measure to save the children and youth—those who were under twenty years of age when they came out of Egypt; but seems to have mostly failed to reclaim those more advanced in years and more confirmed in their habits of thought and of life.——The strain of this chapter is that the Lord's patience was repeatedly tried to the utmost, so that he was often on the point of exterminating the guilty people by his swift judgments; but restrained himself through his great mercy, and to save his holy name from reproach before the heathen in whose sight he had brought them forth from Egypt and adopted them as his own peculiar people.—— This view of their national history was eminently pertinent and forcible for Ezekiel's time and for the circumstances of both the exiles and their brethren then just on the brink of exterminating ruin in their native land.

23. I lifted up my hand unto them also in the wilderness, that I would scatter them among the heathen, and disperse them through the countries;

24. Because they had not executed my judgments, but had despised my statutes, and had polluted my sabbaths, and their eyes were after their fathers' idols.

25. Wherefore I gave them also statutes *that were* not good, and judgments whereby they should not live;

26. And I polluted them in their own gifts, in that they caused to pass through *the fire* all that openeth the womb, that I might make them desolate, to the end that they might know that I *am* the Lord.

The points specially requiring attention here stand in vs. 25, 26. *What statutes and judgments* are here referred to? In what sense did God "give them?" And for what purpose? The laws of language compel us to take the words, "Statutes and judgments" in a sense similar and analogous to that in which they are used elsewhere throughout this chapter; *e. g.*, in vs. 11, 13, 16, 18, 19, 21, 24,—yet not as referring to precisely and identically the same statutes and judgments, for it was because they did not execute those judgments but despised them (v. 24), that God says (v. 25), "Therefore I gave them also statutes not good," etc. Hence the latter were somewhat yet not altogether different from the former.——These conditions are met in "the Statutes of Omri," (See Mic. 6: 16, where the same word is used as here by Ezekiel), and in the decree of Jeroboam (1 Kings 12: 28-33). These were royal statutes and judgments establishing idol-worship by public authority.——In what sense did God give the people these statutes?——Only in the sense of suffering their wicked kings to enjoin them. Not unfrequently God is said in the Scriptures to do what he only permits to be done. He was said to harden Pharaoh's heart, when, in fact, according to the record, he only suffered him to harden his own heart, and when the most direct agency which he exerted toward that result was *in removing the plagues* under which that proud king quailed and relented. So far as the Scriptures explain *how* his heart was hardened, they attribute it in small part to the influence of his own magicians, but in large part, to the divine mercy in lifting the plagues from him and from his land. See the former in Ex. 7: 10–13, 22, and the latter, in Ex. 8: 15, 32, and 9: 34, 35, and 10: 19, 20.——According to the doctrine of the Scriptures, God's agencies in some form reach all events. Some events he brings to pass without the intermediate agency of his creatures; some, with such intermediate agency. In the latter class, his own work is often only *permissive*—suffering these intermediate agents to do what they choose to do. In this case the Lord is said sometimes to do them.——It remains to inquire—*For what purpose* in this case did the Lord give the people "statutes not good and judgments whereby they should not live?"——The passage itself supplies the answer. Because they did not execute his judgments but despised his statutes, polluted his Sabbaths and set their eyes on their fathers' idols, therefore God suffered them to be ensnared into deeper idolatry by the royal influence of Jeroboam, Ahab, Omri, and Manasseh. It was a divine judgment upon them for their persistent love of idols. The Lord gave them their way to let them see and to let all the world in coming ages see what idolatry is; what it leads to; how fearfully it curses a people of itself, and how terribly God will punish it. On the same principle God gave up the heathen nations to idolatry and to deep moral corruption. So Paul affirms Rom. 1: 21, 24, 26, 28, in the language; "Because that when they knew God, they glorified him not as God, neither were thankful, but became vain in their imaginations, and their foolish heart was darkened:" "*Wherefore, i. e.*, for this reason, God gave them up to uncleanness," etc. "*For this cause* God gave them up to vile affections." "And even as they did not like to retain God in their knowledge, God gave them over to a reprobate mind." Paul also develops the same law of God's moral administration in 2 Thess. 2: 11; "And for this cause God shall send them strong delusion that they should believe a lie." So far as we can know, this may be a necessary measure of policy in a moral government, to give some persistent sinners a larger range for possible sin and less restraint, that they may exemplify for the warning of others the fearful power of sin on the soul and its terrible and certain curse in the line both of natural consequences and of divine judgments therefor. Hence no reasonable objection can lie against the All-wise and All-good Ruler of the moral universe for this policy.——The scope of this passage, v. 25, appears also in v. 39.——V. 26 bears the same interpretation and sustains it. 1 suffered them to become more and more polluted in their gifts at the shrine of their idols even to the extent of burning to death all their first-born sons and daughters, consecrating them to Moloch and Saturn and not to God. I did this in order that I might bring utter desolation on their land, under which desolation both they themselves and all men should learn that I am the Lord. An evil so horrible as this virus of idolatry must be suffered to ripen and develop itself into its legitimate fruits before its punishment could have the highest and best moral effects.

27. Therefore, son of man, speak unto the house of Israel, and say unto them, Thus saith the Lord God; Yet in this your fathers have blasphemed me, in that they have committed a trespass against me.

28. *For* when I had brought them into the land, *for* the which I lifted up my hand to give it to them, then they saw every high hill, and all the thick trees, and they offered there their sacrifices, and there they presented the provocation of their offering: there also they made their sweet savor, and poured out there their drink-offerings.

29. Then I said unto them, What *is* the high place whereunto ye go? And the name thereof is called Bamah unto this day.

"Yet in this" same idol-worship, your fathers have *blasphemed* me—provoked and insulted me exceedingly; for when I brought them into the goodly land of Canaan, they sought out every beautiful location, every high hill and thick grove, and located their idol-worship there. Then I said to them, Why go ye to those high places rather than to the temple, the "one place" which God had ordained? What special attraction draws you thither? But they answer only by persisting in their custom, and by giving those high places a distinguished name unto this day.——The significance of this v. 29, seems to be that God protested against those localities for worship; but the people insisted and still kept up the usage under that name well known among themselves and deeply offensive and odious to their God. In harmony with this the Psalmist says (78: 58), "For they provoked him to anger with their *high places.*"

30. Wherefore say unto the house of Israel, Thus saith the Lord God; Are ye polluted after the manner of your fathers? and commit ye whoredom after their abominations?

31. For when ye offer your gifts, when ye make your sons to pass through the fire, ye pollute yourselves with all your idols, even unto this day: and shall I be inquired of by you, O house of Israel? *As* I live, saith the Lord God, I will not be inquired of by you.

Are not ye of this generation as deeply polluted as your fathers ever were? And now, shall I be inquired of by you? By no means.

32. And that which cometh into your mind shall not be at all, that ye say, We will be as the heathen, as the families of the countries, to serve wood and stone.

33. *As* I live, saith the Lord God, surely with a mighty

hand, and with a stretched-out arm, and with fury poured out, will I rule over you:

34. And I will bring you out from the people, and will gather you out of the countries wherein ye are scattered, with a mighty hand, and with a stretched-out arm, and with fury poured out.

35. And I will bring you into the wilderness of the people, and there will I plead with you face to face.

36. Like as I pleaded with your fathers in the wilderness of the land of Egypt, so will I plead with you, saith the Lord God.

37. And I will cause you to pass under the rod, and I will bring you into the bond of the covenant.

38. And I will purge out from among you the rebels, and them that transgress against me: I will bring them forth out of the country where they sojourn, and they shall not enter into the land of Israel: and ye shall know that I *am* the Lord.

Here the tone changes to exhortation and promise. The Lord will yet put forth his mighty hand to redeem a remnant and restore them to piety and to consequent prosperity. The temptation to be like the heathen must be withstood and its very thought repelled. Verses 35, 36 are a beautiful analogy between this process of discipline and that by which the Lord sifted, proved, and tried his people in the wilderness of Sinai. So also in Hos. 2: 14–23. The cases are not only analogous in the principle involved but in the means used and even partially in the minute point of a wilderness life, for these exiles were led forth through a long wilderness route from Canaan to Chaldea.——"I will cause you to pass under the rod," looks to the usage of shepherds in numbering their flocks, perhaps nightly as they entered the fold, or after a purchase, to verify the number. So God will bring his dear people carefully into his fold, taking pains to see that all are there, and consecrating them to himself. The sifting processes of his providence will expel the rebels of unsubdued heart. They will never return to his land.

39. As for you, O house of Israel, thus saith the Lord God; Go ye, serve ye every one his idols, and hereafter *also*, if ye will not hearken unto me: but pollute ye my holy name no more with your gifts, and with your idols.

40. For in my holy mountain, in the mountain of the height of Israel, saith the Lord God, there shall all the house of Israel, all of them in the land, serve me: there will I accept them, and there will I require your offerings, and the first fruits of your oblations, with all your holy things.

41. I will accept you with your sweet savor, when I bring you out from the people, and gather you out of the countries wherein ye have been scattered; and I will be sanctified in you before the heathen.

42. And ye shall know that I *am* the Lord, when I shall bring you into the land of Israel, into the country *for* the which I lifted up my hand to give it to your fathers.

43. And there shall ye remember your ways, and all your doings wherein ye have been defiled; and ye shall loathe yourselves in your own sight for all your evils that ye have committed.

44. And ye shall know that I *am* the Lord, when I have wrought with you for my name's sake, not according to your wicked ways, nor according to your corrupt doings, O ye house of Israel, saith the Lord God.

The scope of v. 39, I take to be—Play the hypocrite with me no longer. If ye will persist in serving idols, go on; but cease to mix up the worship of idols with the worship of the living God! No more pollute me, my name and my temple, with your gifts and idols. For lo, in my holy mountain there shall be none but pure hearts and true lives. Hypocrites can have no place there. There I will accept the honest and faithful worshipers; they shall penitently loathe and forsake their abominations, and shall know in their own blessed experience that I am the Lord their Savior and Redeemer.——This strain of promise is eminently precious after so long and so terrible a recital of God's holy displeasure against his apostate people, his grievous heart-trials with them, and his fearful judgments upon them.——At this point, our Hebrew Bibles close this chapter. It is manifestly the close of this special theme and strain. The remaining verses (45–49) belong properly to the next chapter.

45. Moreover the word of the Lord came unto me, saying,

46. Son of man, set thy face toward the south, and drop *thy word* toward the south, and prophesy against the forest of the south field;

47. And say to the forest of the south, Hear the word of the Lord; Thus saith the Lord God; Behold, I will kindle a fire in thee, and it shall devour every green tree in thee, and every dry tree: the flaming flame shall not be quenched, and all faces from the south to the north shall be burned therein.

48. And all flesh shall see that I the Lord have kindled it: it shall not be quenched.

Remarkably the prophets set the face toward the country or the people to whom their prophecies were addressed. See chap. 6: 2, and 13 : 17, etc.——"The south," and "the forest of the south field," as here used, are manifestly Jerusalem and Judah, thought of as "the south" for the same reason that Babylon—Ezekiel's residence then—was "the north." See Jer. 1 : 14–15. Ezek. 21 : 2, 3 confirms this reference to Judah.——"Drop thy word"—let thy speech *distil*—fall in drops (such is the figure). It occurs elsewhere: Job 29 : 22 and Amos 7 : 16.——Judah and Jerusalem are thought of as a forest which is combustible—fit material for the fires of Jehovah's judgments. A terrible figure of a ruin before which nothing can stand!

49. Then said I, Ah, Lord God! they say of me, Doth he not speak parables?

A feeling of sad discouragement comes over the prophet as he thinks of delivering this message (vs. 46–48), for he remembers how the people received his threatenings from the Lord before, when they were clothed in strongly figurative language. Hence he cries out, "Alas! alas! O Lord God; they are saying of me (this is the precise tense of his language); they have been saying and doubtless they will say again of me—"Does he not use strong figures? Must we not make large allowance for his vivid imagination? Have his words much meaning after all? So I understand their question, "Doth he not speak parables?" For to suppose they simply ask; What rhetorical terms, according to the best authorities, should be applied to such forms of expression? is to misapprehend entirely both their feelings and his.——Rosenmueller, however, gives it this turn; Does he not talk very blindly, confusedly, with dark figures that we can not understand? But if this had been their meaning the prophet would have understood it, and then, instead of groaning deeply over their perverseness, he would have said—Brethren, this matter can readily be made clear, and it *shall be!*——The case exemplifies both the spirit and the manner in which perverse sinners who are annoyed by what the Bible says of an eternal hell seek to fritter away its meaning and evade its force. Is it not altogether figurative, say they? How then can we know much about its real meaning? Does not the whole description bear the aspect of great exaggeration?——To questions like these, it may be replied briefly but most truthfully; Figures of speech are used in every human language, in all ages of time. They come nearer to the idea of a *universal language*, clearly intelligible to all, than any other form or mode of speech. To the popular mind, nothing can better or more accurately describe suffering than the language used in the Bible of hell. Who does not know the effect of fire on human flesh? Who does not understand fire as an agency of ruin among the works of men? How utterly infatuated then must the man be who decries all wholesome fear of hell and of the wrath of God because the appeal to such fear comes to us from our divine Father, clothed in figurative language? Alas for the madness of men when they *will sin on* to their own damnation, and *will choose such delusions* to smooth their pathway thither!

CHAPTER XXI.

In this description of judgments from God upon Jerusalem vs. 1-25, and upon Ammon vs. 28-32, the *sword* is made signally prominent—drawn out from the Lord's scabbard, sharpened, polished, gleaming, flashing, and coming down fearfully for its work of slaughter! It is the *chapter of the sword*.——If we may suppose a tacit connection with the closing words of the chapter previous, we shall see a special pertinence in this figure. The people are saying; These figures and symbols, parables and things of that sort;—who can tell how much they mean?——To which the Lord replies; "Ye must certainly know what the *sword* means: ye have seen and heard of the *sword;* let the sword therefore be the figure—yet scarcely a figure so much as a terrible reality—in the prophet's foretelling of your doom!"

1. And the word of the Lord came unto me, saying,

2. Son of man, set thy face toward Jerusalem, and drop *thy word* toward the holy places, and prophesy against the land of Israel,

3. And say to the land of Israel, Thus saith the Lord; Behold I *am* against thee, and will draw forth my sword out of his sheath, and will cut off from thee the righteous and the wicked.

4. Seeing then that I will cut off from thee the righteous and the wicked, therefore shall my sword go forth out of his sheath against all flesh from the south to the north.

5. That all flesh may know that I the Lord have drawn forth my sword out of his sheath: it shall not return any more.

Set thy face toward the city to which the predicted judgments pertain, as in v. 46, and elsewhere.——The destruction must be general, embracing both the righteous and the wicked. Since no discrimination is made on the ground of moral character, there can be no discrimination whatever (vs. 4, 5), but the sword shall cut down all the living from south to north in the land. The Lord's sword is drawn, and will not return to its scabbard till this work is done.

6. Sigh therefore, thou son of man, with the breaking of *thy* loins; and with bitterness sigh before their eyes.

7. And it shall be, when they say say unto thee, Wherefore sighest thou? that thou shall answer, for the tidings; because it cometh; and every heart shall melt, and all hands shall be feeble, and every spirit shall faint, and all knees

shall be weak *as* water: behold, it cometh, and shall be brought to pass, saith the Lord God.

To make the deeper impression on the heart of the people, the prophet is commanded to sigh and groan bitterly in their presence with his hands upon his loins as one under intense and crushing grief. When the attention of the people should be arrested and they should inquire the cause, he must answer; "Because of what I hear, for it cometh"—not the *tidings* merely come, but the thing itself, the *calamity* is near at hand.——The Hebrew is, "All knees shall flow with water," *i, e.*, become water, having no more firmness than water.

8. Again the word of the Lord came unto me, saying,

9. Son of man, prophesy and say, Thus saith the Lord; Say, A sword, a sword is sharpened, and also furbished:

10. It is sharpened to make a sore slaughter: it is furbished that it may glitter: should we then make mirth? it contemneth the rod of my son, *as* every tree.

In this extended description of the sword (vs. 9–23), we shall find several clauses in which modern criticism has furnished the means of improving somewhat the received translation. Thus, in the last clause of v. 10, this translation brings out no intelligible sense in harmony with the context. But, guided by the Septuagint, a very slight change is made in two Hebrew letters, one in each of two words, whereby we read *cl* for *ov*, and nasce for nasces, and then we translate the entire verse thus; "It is sharpened to make a great slaughter; it is polished that it may have the flash as of lightning *against the prince of the tribes of my son* (my people) *who scorn all wooden rods;*" *i. e.*, who are thoroughly hardened against the lighter scourging with saplings, and must needs be scourged, slain, with my glittering sword.——The prince represents the people, so that the sword upon him falls upon the whole people.

11. And he hath given it to be furbished, that it may be handled: this sword is sharpened, and it is furbished, to give it into the hand of the slayer.

Is made sharp and bright that it may pass into the hand of God's destroying angel, "the slayer."

12. Cry and howl, son of man: for it shall be upon my people, it *shall be* upon all the princes of Israel: terrors by reason of the sword shall be upon my people: smite therefore upon *thy* thigh.

In the middle clause, better—"Upon all the princes of Israel who are consigned over to the sword along with my people;"—*i. e.*

all the princes as well as all the people are delivered over to the sword. Therefore smite upon thy thigh in bitter grief.

13. Because *it is* a trial, and what if *the sword* contemn even the rod? it shall be no *more*, saith the Lord God.

The literal rendering here is impressive, "For it" (the sword) "has been proved," (*i. e.*, on other people), "and what if even this scornful tribe" (Israel) "shall be no more" (shall be utterly annihilated), "saith the Lord God."

14. Thou therefore, son of man, prophesy, and smite *thy* hands together, and let the sword be doubled the third time, the sword of the slain: it *is* the sword of the great men *that are* slain, which entereth into their privy chambers.

"Let the sword be doubled," in the sense of doubling its blow; "let it smite the third time," etc.——" The sword of the great men that are slain," is the sword that has slain the great men. I would not read, "Which entereth into their privy chambers;" but, "which besieges, begirts them round about as the walls of a chamber inclose its occupants:—*i. e.*, the sword is on every side of them, so that none can possibly escape.

15. I have set the point of the sword against all their gates, that *their* heart may faint, and *their* ruins be multiplied: ah! *it is* made bright, *it is* wrapped up for the slaughter.

The word rendered, "point" of the sword, occurs in Hebrew only here. Hence naturally the precise meaning is doubtful. Yet the general sense is clear. Gesenius says, "The *turning* of the sword," meaning that the sword's point is turned toward all her gates; "or more probably by a change in one letter, the *slaughter* of the sword."——"Wrapped up for slaughter," should doubtless be, *made smooth, polished* for use in slaughter. This translation assumes a different root from that supposed in the received version.

16. Go thee one way or other, *either* on the right hand, *or* on the left, whithersoever thy face *is* set.

This verse is an address to the sword.——Critics suggest that the form of this address is that of military command: "Close up ranks, right: to your post, left." The first verb means *stand as one*. By a bold personification, the sword becomes an armed host, now being marshaled for battle and ordered to be in readiness for a charge.

17. I will also smite my hands together, and I will cause my fury to rest: I the Lord have said *it*.

This seems to be the language of God, spoken of himself.—— "Cause my fury to rest," as above chap. 5: 13, and 16: 42, and below chap. 24: 13. The sense seems to be, to *abide*, remain long, and not be evanescent.

18. The word of the Lord came unto me again, saying,
19. Also, thou son of man, appoint thee two ways, that the sword of the king of Babylon may come: both twain shall come forth out of one land: and choose thou a place, choose *it* at the head of the way to the city.
20. Appoint a way, that the sword may come to Rabbath of the Ammonites, and to Judah in Jerusalem the defensed.

The object here seems to be to indicate the process by which the king of Babylon would decide by a sort of lot which course to take first, whether toward Ammon or toward Jerusalem. The statements imply that the prophet was to go through the usual ceremonies symbolically, to make a stronger impression of the facts upon the people. Taking his position at the head of the way leading to the city, he marked out one way leading to Jerusalem; another, to the country of Ammon. Both led out from the one land of Babylon. ——In the last part of the verse the sense is better given by reading *or* instead of "*and;*" "To Rabbath of the Ammonites, *or* to Judah in Jerusalem."

21. For the king of Babylon stood at the parting of the way, at the head of the two ways, to use divination; he made *his* arrows bright, he consulted with images, he looked in the liver.
22. At his right hand was the divination for Jerusalem, to appoint captains, to open the mouth in the slaughter, to lift up the voice with shouting, to appoint *battering* rams against the gates, to cast a mount, *and* to build a fort.

This refers to ancient customs of learning the will of the gods (as supposed) by various forms of divination. Three forms are here.——(1.) Not, "making the arrows bright," but shaking the arrows (previously labeled) in a bag, and then drawing out one, the label of which would give the desired answer.——Nos. 2 and 3 are noticed frequently in the old classic authors; consulting images of the gods, and examining the liver of an animal slain for the purpose.——If the indications led toward the right hand, then the king of Babylon would (not "appoint captains" but) "put up battering rams"—the same word which the last clause renders in this way. He would also give command for slaughter, or, perhaps, open the mouth in outcry. (So Gesenius.)

23. And it shall be unto them as a false divination in their sight, to them that have sworn oaths: but he will call to remembrance the iniquity, that they may be taken.

24. Therefore thus saith the Lord God; Because ye have made your iniquity to be remembered, in that your transgressions are discovered, so that in all your doings your sins do appear; because, *I say*, that ye are come to remembrance, ye shall be taken with the hand.

I understand these verses to mean that this divination, taken by the king of Babylon and directing him to besiege Jerusalem, would be held by the Jews as false and of no account because they had been in sworn allegiance to that king and assumed that they could have peace with him on easy terms again. But that king remembers their iniquity in violating those oaths, and this exasperates him to sterner vengeance. It should be borne in mind that this very king placed Zedekiah on his throne (2 Chron. 36: 10, 13, and Jer. 52: 3, and Ezek. 17: 15, 18) under a solemn oath of fidelity to himself as his liege lord.

25. And thou, profane wicked prince of Israel, whose day is come, when iniquity *shall have* an end,

26. Thus saith the Lord God; Remove the diadem, and take off the crown: this *shall* not *be* the same: exalt *him that is* low, and abase *him that is* high.

27. I will overturn, overturn, overturn it: and it shall be no *more*, until he come whose right it is; and I will give it *him*.

From a view of the intense depravity and horrible idolatry of the king and his people, now culminating in perjury against the king of Babylon, the course of thought passes suddenly to direct address to the guilty king now to be slain and of course deposed and stripped of his crown. The passage might be translated, almost literally, thus: "And thou, most wicked prince of Israel; pierced through with the sword, whose day has come in the time of fatal sin: Thus saith the Lord God; The sacred headband is removed; the regal crown is taken off; this shall be no longer this (what it has been); the lowly is exalted; the lofty is brought down: I will utterly overturn, and even then it shall not be permanent until he comes to whom it belongs; then I will give it to him."——In Zedekiah's utter fall, the crown of Judah is vilely cast away: the ancient throne of David seems to be fearfully subverted:—but the Lord's hand is in these revolutions: he will push them on for his own purposes until the greater Prince of David's line shall come to whom the eternal promise of David's throne stands sure. Then God will give him that crown and kingdom.——The word rendered "profane" should be rendered, "pierced through," both because this is the usual sense of the word, and because the scope of the chapter, so full of the *sword*, contemplates him as smitten fatally thereby, and thus dethroned and his kingdom destroyed. Dr. Hengstenberg insists that *pierced through, slain,* is the only admissible, well-established, sense of this Hebrew word. He supposes it used here with some lattitude of meaning, indicating not certainly that he died from a sword-thrust, but that he fell by violence; his nation and himself overpowered by the arms of the king of Babylon.——"When iniquity shall have an end," is literally, "in the time of the sin of the end"—meaning, in the time of the last, the fatal, the damning sin for which there can be no pardon, and the vengeance for which can be delayed no longer.——The word rendered "diadem," is used in this precise form only for the sacred fillet of the High Priest, *e. g.*, Ex. 28: 4, 37, 39 and 29: 6 and 39: 28, 31 and Lev. 8: 9 and 16: 4. It was specially appropriate that this prophecy should indicate the suspension of the functions of the high priest as well as those of the king.——Remarkably both were restored by special promise according to the prophecies of Zechariah (chap. 4: 14 and 6: 13) after the return from captivity. Both were united under one head and given to the great Messiah when he ultimately came. Both went down together in this fearful judgment upon the nation for its sin. Both returned together when, through the repentance of the people and the divine mercy, they returned again to become the Lord's.—— "This shall not be the same"—(literally, "this shall not be this") obviously means that all is changed; nothing of the old remains. As said in the next clause, "the low is made high;" "the high is made low." These verbs are in the infinitive, not the imperative, to indicate simply the action in general without defining it specifically.——The repetition, "I will make it a thing overturned, overturned, overturned," is a common Hebrew mode of strong emphasis, meaning—I will overturn *utterly*.——He to whom "the judgment," or the *right* is, can be none other than the great Messiah. The idea of his "*coming*" may tacitly refer to Gen. 49: 10, "*Until Shiloh shall come.*" The term "*come*" is in Hebrew use to designate the Messiah as "*he that should come;*" *e. g.* "Art thou he that should come, or look we for another? Matt. 11: 3. Onkelos, the best of the Chaldee paraphrasts, gives us his paraphrase of Gen. 49: 10, with his eye on our passage; "Until Messiah come whose is the kingdom."——Thus the prediction of fearful ruin on Jerusalem and her king and high priest, suggests the consummation of the kingdom of God on earth under that great Personage, both King and Priest, who fills the throne of David forever—a glorious priest on his throne for the joyful salvation of his redeemed people. From the ashes of ruin a Phenix arises, surpassing all the strangeness of things fabled, glorious like the loving purposes of its Infinite Author.——This passage is rich in its suggestive resources;—*c. g.*, that none need fear the results of the revolutions of earthly thrones, determined in the providence of God: that the helm of universal dominion is in hands equal to every emergency, guided by a far-seeing wisdom and evermore evolving events toward the sublime and blessed consummation of God's great purposes of human redemption.——These lessons bear toward a peaceful, joyful trust in our divine Father and Lord, and bid us wait on him in faith and prayer, and with such labor as we may, till he bring forth his righteousness as the light, and his faithfulness in promise as the noonday!

28. And thou, son of man, prophesy and say, Thus saith the Lord God concerning the Ammonites, and concerning their reproach; even say thou, The sword, the sword *is* drawn: for the slaughter *it is* furbished, to consume because of the glittering;

29. While they see vanity unto thee, while they divine a lie unto thee, to bring thee upon the necks of *them that are* slain, of the wicked, whose day is come, when their iniquity *shall have* an end.

30. Shall I cause *it* to return into his sheath? I will judge thee in the place where thou wast created, in the land of thy nativity.

31. And I will pour out mine indignation upon thee; I will blow against thee in the fire of my wrath, and deliver thee into the hand of brutish men, *and* skillful to destroy.

32. Thou shalt be for fuel to the fire; thy blood shall be in the midst of the land; thou shalt be no *more* remembered: for I the Lord have spoken *it*.

It was indicated (vs. 19-22) that the king of Babylon sought divination to determine which city to attack first in order, Jerusalem, or Ammon. Both were in his plan and in God's plan. The one being finished, the other follows as here. Perhaps it stands in this connection with the fall of Jerusalem to show that the Lord tenderly remembers his true people; that he resents the reproaches cast on them by the heathen under their great calamities; and that it is only *as apostates* that God scourges his own city and nation; while his sympathies are none the less *against* the wicked heathen nations round about them and *with* his own chosen people.——Another prophecy against Ammon, similar in its general tone, appears chap. 25: 1-7.——In form, this passage is legitimately a continuation of the sword-chapter, the figure of the devouring sword being prominent throughout.——In v. 28, "their reproach" is that which they cast on the suffering Jews. See the same idea more fully drawn out, chap. 25: 3-7.——Verse 29 implies that in Ammon also, as well as in Jerusalem, false prophets and diviners were gainsaying the word of the Lord and misleading the people to their destruction—the results of which would be to bring down the prophet, armed with the Lord's glittering, devouring sword, upon the necks of their slain in the day of their fatal damning sin. The phraseology here looks back to the case of Jerusalem, vs. 14, 23, 25.——In v. 30, the form of the Hebrew verb "return" is imperative. I prefer to translate it thus and apply it to the sword of the Ammonites, admonishing them to abstain from all resistance of the Chaldean arms. Thus: "Put it (the sword) back into its scabbard. In the place where thou wast created, in thy birth-place will I judge thee;" and hence it can be of no avail to withstand the Almighty. The first clause gives no intimation of being a question, nor of being in the first person.——The scope of the passage denounces fearful and even exterminating judgments on Ammon.

CHAPTER XXII.

The word of the Lord in this chapter sets forth the varied and enormous wickedness of Jerusalem and of Judah. It shows that they were guilty of other sins besides idolatry—indeed, of *every* other sin named in the decalogue or known in this depraved world.——Here let us bear in mind that this rehearsal and exposé of the sins of the Jews still resident in Jerusalem and Judah and now on the eve of their destruction are made before the exiles in Chaldea for the sake specially of the resulting moral influence toward the reformation of those exiles. God would have them understand *why* those terrible judgments were sent on their brethren and fathers and on the city and land of their early homes and early love. He would have them feel the full moral impression of those judgments as his own terribly earnest admonition against sin and persuasive to obedience. His heart was set on reclaiming those exiles to a new life. Hence the mission of Ezekiel, and hence these pertinent appliances of truth, bearing mightily upon their sympathies, their conscience and their hearts.

1. Moreover the word of the Lord came unto me, saying,
2. Now, thou son of man, wilt thou judge the bloody city? yea, thou shalt shew her all her abominations.

"Judge," must be taken here in the same sense as in chap. 20: 4. See notes there.——"The bloody city," so called because stained with crimes of personal violence, innocent blood, rudely and wickedly shed.

3. Then say thou, Thus saith the Lord God; The city sheddeth blood in the midst of it, that her time may come, and maketh idols against herself to defile herself.
4. Thou art become guilty in thy blood that thou hast shed; and hast defiled thyself in thine idols which thou hast made; and thou hast caused thy days to draw near, and art come *even* unto thy years; therefore have I made thee a reproach unto the heathen, and a mocking to all countries.
5. *Those that be* near, and *those that be* far from thee, shall mock thee, *which art* infamous *and* much vexed.

The city sheddeth blood *to hasten her time* of destruction—this being the *result* of such bloody violence. In the same sense is v. 4; "Thou hast caused thy days" (*i. e.*, of vengeance from God) "to draw near."——The last words of v. 5 would read literally; "defiled in name and great in tumult;" *i. e.*, in social disorders, commotions. Society was practically broken up by the explosive force of outbreaking wickedness.

6. Behold, the princes of Israel, every one were in thee to their power to shed blood.

This seems to mean that even the princes who ought to have set a virtuous example were really using their great influence toward brutal violence and murder, doing all they could to excite the people to outrages and bloody crimes.

7. In thee have they set light by father and mother: in the midst of thee have they dealt by oppression with the stranger: in thee have they vexed the fatherless and the widow.

8. Thou hast despised my holy things, and hast profaned my sabbaths.

9. In thee are men that carry tales to shed blood: and in thee they eat upon the mountains: in the midst of thee they commit lewdness.

10. In thee have they discovered their fathers' nakedness: in thee have they humbled her that was set apart for pollution.

11. And one hath committed abomination with his neighbor's wife; and another hath lewdly defiled his daughter-in-law; and another in thee hath humbled his sister, his father's daughter.

12. In thee have they taken gifts to shed blood; thou hast taken usury and increase, and thou hast greedily gained of thy neighbors by extortion, and hast forgotten me, saith the Lord God.

This is a sad, appalling catalogue of the foulest immoralities.—— "To carry tales to shed blood" is to get up false accusations and retail slanders against the life of their fellow-citizens.——Lewdness, here, is to be taken in its literal, not its figurative sense.

13. Behold, therefore I have smitten my hand at thy dishonest gain which thou hast made, and at thy blood which hath been in the midst of thee.

14. Can thy heart endure, or can thy hands be strong, in the days that I shall deal with thee? I the Lord have spoken *it*, and will do *it*.

15. And I will scatter thee among the heathen, and disperse thee in the countries, and will consume thy filthiness out of thee.

"Smitten my hand at thy dishonest gain," is a significant gesture, indicating his purpose to scatter those gains to the winds of heaven and to make solemn requisition for that blood. It was God's own intimation that he would call her to account for those horrible sins. When the hour of her judgment should come, "Could her heart endure or her hands be strong" *against the Infinite God?* Alas, she would find that God never lacks agencies and resources for terrific punishment! How vain for frail, weak creatures to stand up against the Almighty! How surely will sinners learn this to their unutterable consternation when the wrath of God shall fall on them to the uttermost!

16. And thou shalt take thine inheritance in thyself in the sight of the heathen, and thou shalt know that I *am* the Lord.

"Thou shalt take thine inheritance in thyself in the sight of the heathen," fails to give any pertinent sense in harmony with the context. The verb should be taken not from the root *nahal*, but from the root *halal*, in the sense, to violate, to profane. *Thou shalt be dishonored, abused, treated as profane before the heathen.* This word occurs in the same sense in chap. 7: 24.

17. And the word of the Lord came unto me, saying,

18. Son of man, the house of Israel is to me become dross: all they *are* brass, and tin, and iron, and lead, in the midst of the furnace, they are *even* the dross of silver.

19. Therefore thus saith the Lord God; Because ye are all become dross, behold, therefore I will gather you into the midst of Jerusalem.

20. *As* they gather silver, and brass, and iron, and lead, and tin, into the midst of the furnace, to blow the fire upon it, to melt *it;* so will I gather *you* in mine anger and in my fury, and I will leave *you there,* and melt you.

21. Yea, I will gather you, and blow upon you in the fire of my wrath, and ye shall be melted in the midst thereof.

22. As silver is melted in the midst of the furnace, so shall ye be melted in the midst thereof; and ye shall know that I the Lord have poured out my fury upon you.

By a new and expressive figure, the people are all said to be mere dross; not gold and silver, but only the refuse matter which is mixed with those precious metals and requires to be expelled by intense heat in the furnace. So the Lord would gather this wicked people, put them into his great furnace, blow upon them in the fierceness of his wrath, and expel all the impure, worthless matter.——In the last clause of v. 20 the verb rendered, "leave you there," is better translated, "*cast you in*"—*i. e.*, to the furnace to melt you there. Literally, to cause you to rest there; put you in to stay permanently.——This figure is intensely expressive.

23. And the word of the Lord came unto me, saying,
24. Son of man, say unto her, Thou *art* the land that is not cleansed, nor rained upon in the day of indignation.

By yet another figure, the land of Judah is like a field not cleansed of its briars, thorns and weeds, which are fatal to the production of useful plants,—nor had it been rained upon. Of course it can be only barren.

25. *There is* a conspiracy of her prophets in the midst thereof, like a roaring lion ravening the prey; they have devoured souls; they have taken the treasure and precious things; they have made her many widows in the midst thereof.
26. Her priests have violated my law, and have profaned my holy things; they have put no difference between the holy and profane, neither have they shewed *difference* between the unclean and the clean, and have hid their eyes from my sabbaths, and I am profaned among them.
27. Her princes in the midst thereof *are* like wolves ravening the prey, to shed blood, *and* to destroy souls, to get dishonest gain.

Her prophets, priests and princes—the three classes of leading influence—are successively arraigned as each horribly guilty of corruption in their respective offices and of most flagrant immoralities. They mislead and ruin souls, wielding their great influence, not to save men from sin and death, but to destroy.

28. And her prophets have daubed them with untempered *mortar*, seeing vanity, and divining lies unto them, saying, Thus saith the Lord God, when the Lord hath not spoken.
29. The people of the land have used oppression, and exercised robbery, and have vexed the poor and needy: yea, they have oppressed the stranger wrongfully.

The worst class of all in their influence call for renewed remark. False prophets were the most terrible curse; no other influence could be so bad as theirs. They throw it solid *against* the true prophets to break down the confidence of the people in the real word of the Lord and to win their confidence to their own lies.—— See this figure—"untempered mortar"—explained chap. 13: 10–16. ——"Robbery and oppression of the poor," invariably appear foremost among the sins of a people so deeply corrupt in general morals. It is one of the terrible manifestations of human depravity and uncurbed selfishness.

30. And I sought for a man among them, that should make up the hedge, and stand in the gap before me for the land, that I should not destroy it: but I found none.

31. Therefore have I poured out mine indignation upon them; I have consumed them with the fire of my wrath: their own way have I recompensed upon their heads, saith the Lord God.

See the figure of the "hedge and the gap" in chap 13: 5. The hedge here seems to be a wall built up to withstand the judgments of God. No man is found in the land to rush into the breach, rebuild the broken wall, or stand against the foe at the point of deadly peril. The moral power of the people to recover themselves from their horrible corruptions is prostrate; there is no recuperative force left. Not a man appeared to stem the torrent of this corruption. If the Lord could have found one such strong man to work with himself for the salvation of the people, he would at least have deferred this final outpouring of his wrath in exterminating judgments. But he found none, and hence their ruin was inevitable, and no reason existed for its being longer delayed.

CHAPTER XXIII.

In this chapter, the figure by which the Lord represents the idolatry of his people as adultery assumes a bolder form than usual, and is carried out with very great minuteness both in respect to the sin and its punishment. The whole representation is intensely keen and caustic, setting forth in a most revolting light the great crimes of the Jewish people in the line of idolatry, and adapted to fill them with a sense of shame and self-loathing. In a few passages our translation fails to give the full strength of the original, but the nature of the subject ought perhaps to excuse the omission of any more amplifying details.——The ultimate sense of the whole is plain. Samaria and Jerusalem are called "Aholah" and "Aholibah." As harlots, they began their harlot life with Egypt; continued it with Assyria, the Chaldeans and the people of the desert; pushed their idolatry even to the extent of burning alive their children, God's own sons and daughters, and of desecrating his very sanctuary with their idols: and then, being put on trial under Hebrew law before righteous men, they suffer the doom of adulteresses, on whose hands is the blood of murder also:—they are stoned with stones and their houses burned with fire.——Thus the land is cleansed of the abominations of its spiritual whoredom; it bears the sins of its idols, and Desolation sits upon the ruins of those cities—a living memorial of God's righteous jealousy against his apostate people!

1. The word of the Lord came again unto me, saying,
2. Son of man, there were two women, the daughters of one mother:
3. And they committed whoredoms in Egypt; they committed whoredoms in their youth: there were their breasts pressed, and there they bruised the teats of their virginity.
4. And the names of them *were* Aholah the elder, and Aholibah her sister: and they were mine, and they bare sons and daughters. Thus *were* their names; Samaria *is* Aholah, and Jerusalem Aholibah.
5. And Aholah played the harlot when she was mine; and she doted on her lovers, on the Assyrians, *her* neighbors,
6. *Which were* clothed with blue, captains and rulers, and all of them desirable young men, horsemen riding upon horses.
7. Thus she committed her whoredoms with them, with all them *that were* the chosen men of Assyria, and with all on whom she doted; with all their idols she defiled herself.

Her young Assyrian neighbors are presented in these forms of beauty and splendor to indicate the strong attractions of taste, art, and sensual pleasure, thrown around idol-worship in that age. It has always been the policy of Satan to invest idolatry with every attraction possible—beautiful sites, charming groves, gorgeous temples, luxurious feasts, and enchanting music—to say nothing of the charms of dress and of female beauty, or of the baser passions of lasciviousness and lust.——Syria is probably included under the comprehensive term, "Assyria." There is abundant historical evidence that, in Syria, during the period of the revolt, idolatry was invested with strong artistic and sensual attractions. See 2 Kings 16: 10, and 2 Chron. 28: 2-4, 23-25.

8. Neither left she her whoredoms *brought* from Egypt: for in her youth they lay with her, and they bruised the breasts of her virginity, and poured their whoredom upon her.
9. Wherefore, I have delivered her into the hand of her lovers, into the hand of the Assyrians, upon whom she doted.

10. These discovered her nakedness: they took her sons and her daughters and slew her with the sword: and she became famous among women; for they had executed judgment upon her.

Samaria, the elder sister, is put foremost as having led off in this great sin. The reference is to Jeroboam and his successors.

11. And when her sister Aholibah saw *this*, she was more corrupt in her inordinate love than she, and in her whoredoms more than her sister in *her* whoredoms.

12. She doted upon the Assyrians *her* neighbors, captains and rulers clothed most gorgeously, horsemen riding upon horses, all of them desirable young men.

Jerusalem was worse than Samaria as having sinned against greater light, more sacred vows and obligations, and especially, in the presence of the very temple of the holy God!

13. Then I saw that she was defiled, *that* they *took* both one way:

14. And *that* she increased her whoredoms: for when she saw men portrayed upon the wall, the images of the Chaldeans portrayed with vermilion,

15. Girded with girdles upon their loins, exceeding in dyed attire upon their heads, all of them princes to look to, after the manner of the Babylonians of Chaldea, the land of their nativity:

16. And as soon as she saw them with her eyes, she doted upon them, and sent messengers unto them into Chaldea.

17. And the Babylonians came to her into the bed of love, and they defiled her with their whoredom, and she was polluted with them, and her mind was alienated from them.

18. So she discovered her whoredoms, and discovered her nakedness: then my mind was alienated from her, like as my mind was alienated from her sister.

19. Yet she multiplied her whoredoms, in calling to remembrance the days of her youth, wherein she had played the harlot in the land of Egypt.

20. For she doted upon their paramours, whose flesh *is as* the flesh of asses, and whose issue *is like* the issue of horses.

21. Thus thou calledst to memory the lewdness of thy youth, in bruising thy teats by the Egyptians for the paps of thy youth.

The reader will notice the reference to the attractions which art had thrown around the idol-worship of Chaldea. On this subject the historical portions of Daniel give additional light. The portrayal of idol images on the walls of her temples corresponds entirely with the testimony recently brought to light from the ruins of Nineveh and Babylon.——This representation was specially pertinent from the lips of Ezekiel to the Jewish exiles then in Chaldea, being well adapted to make them abhor these seductive temptations which addressed themselves not unfrequently (we must suppose) to their eyes.

22. Therefore, O Aholibah, thus saith the Lord God; Behold, I will raise up thy lovers against thee, from whom thy mind is alienated, and I will bring them against thee on every side;

23. The Babylonians, and all the Chaldeans, Pekod, and Shoa, and Koa, *and* all the Assyrians with them: all of them desirable young men, captains and rulers, great lords and renowned, all of them riding upon horses.

24. And they shall come against thee with chariots, wagons, and wheels, and with an assembly of people, *which* shall set against thee buckler and shield and helmet round about: and I will set judgment before them, and they shall judge thee according to their judgments.

In v. 23, "Pekod" "Shoa," and "Koa" were taken by our translators as proper nouns—names of either cities or countries. Modern critics take them to be common nouns, descriptive of office or class;—"pekod," the overseer; "shoa," the rich; "koa," literally, the male camel, but here the princes. This corresponds with what immediately follows—"all of them desirable young men, captains and rulers," etc.——In the last clause of v. 24, the sense of "setting judgment before them" is, I will commit the judgment upon your case into their hands.

25. And I will set my jealousy against thee, and they shall deal furiously with thee : they shall take away thy nose and thine ears; and thy remnant shall fall by the sword: they shall take thy sons and thy daughters; and thy residue shall be devoured by the fire.

26. They shall also strip thee out of thy clothes, and take away thy fair jewels.

27. Thus I will make thy lewdness to cease from thee, and thy whoredom *brought* from the land of Egypt: so that thou shalt not lift up thine eyes unto them, nor remember Egypt any more.

28. For thus saith the Lord God; Behold, I will deliver thee into the hand *of them* whom thou hatest, into the hand *of them* from whom thy mind is alienated:

29. And they shall deal with thee hatefully, and shall take away all thy labor, and shall leave thee naked and bare: and the nakedness of thy whoredoms shall be discovered, both thy lewdness and thy whoredoms.

30. I will do these *things* unto thee, because thou hast gone a whoring after the heathen, *and* because thou art polluted with their idols.

Jealousy is the very feeling which is wont to manifest itself most fearfully in the punishment of adultery. So here. Cutting off the nose and ears was the punishment of adultery in Egypt.——In v. 29, "hatefully" means with intense hatred—with a sense of the loathsomeness of the crimes and with personal hatred of the offender.

31. Thou hast walked in the way of thy sister; therefore will I give her cup into thy hand.

32. Thus saith the Lord God; Thou shalt drink of thy sister's cup deep and large: thou shalt be laughed to scorn and had in derision; it containeth much.

33. Thou shalt be filled with drunkenness and sorrow, with the cup of astonishment and desolation, with the cup of thy sister Samaria.

34. Thou shalt even drink it and suck *it* out, and thou shalt break the sherds thereof, and pluck off thine own breasts: for I have spoken *it*, saith the Lord God.

Jerusalem drinks from the same cup as Samaria—drinks it to the dregs and even sucks every drop that adheres to the broken sherds of that cup. In her drunkenness and misery she tears her own breasts—one of the extreme indications of wretchedness.

35. Therefore thus saith the Lord God; Because thou hast forgotten me, and cast me behind thy back, therefore bear thou also thy lewdness and thy whoredoms.

36. The Lord said moreover unto me; Son of man, wilt thou judge Aholah and Aholibah? yea, declare unto them their abominations;

37. That they have committed adultery, and blood *is* in their hands, and with their idols have they committed adultery, and have also caused their sons, whom they bare unto me, to pass for them through *the fire*, to devour *them*.

38. Moreover this they have done unto me: they have defiled my sanctuary in the same day, and have profaned my sabbaths.

39. For when they had slain their children to their idols, then they came the same day into my sanctuary to pro-

fane it; and lo, thus have they done in the midst of my house.

The figure is here in part dropped and literal statements appear, perhaps because no possible turn of the figure could adequately represent the enormity of burning their own children in the fire, or of desecrating the very temple of the living God with their idols.——The view given of the dreadful guilt of the Jews is heightened by the repeated statement that after burning their own children to idol gods, they went *on the same day* into God's holy temple with their bloody hands and there profaned his sanctuary, as if they had no sense of God's abhorrence of their unnatural and bloody crimes!

40. And furthermore, that ye have sent for men to come from far, unto whom a messenger *was* sent; and lo, they came: for whom thou didst wash thyself, paintedst thy eyes, and deckedst thyself with ornaments,

41. And satest upon a stately bed, and a table prepared before it, whereupon thou hast set mine incense and mine oil.

42. And a voice of a multitude being at ease *was* with her: and with the men of the common sort *were* brought Sabeans from the wilderness, which put bracelets upon their hands, and beautiful crowns upon their heads.

43. Then said I unto *her that was* old in adulteries, Will they now commit whoredoms with her, and she *with them?*

44. Yet they went in unto her, as they go in unto a woman that playeth the harlot: so went they in unto Aholah and unto Aholibah, the lewd women.

In v. 42, the word "Sabeans" is probably a common and not a proper noun—meaning *drunkards*, and not the Sabean people. The prophet represents them as the basest of men, the very lowest of the human race, to show that nothing was too low or mean for this debased and guilty people to do in the line of idolatry.

45. And the righteous men, they shall judge them after the manner of adulteresses, and after the manner of women that shed blood; because they *are* adulteresses, and blood *is* in their hands.

46. For thus saith the Lord God; I will bring up a company upon them, and will give them to be removed and spoiled.

47. And the company shall stone them with stones, and dispatch them with their swords; they shall slay their sons and daughters, and burn up their houses with fire.

48. Thus will I cause lewdness to cease out of the land,

that all women may be taught not to do after your lewdness.

49. And they shall recompense your lewdness upon you, and ye shall bear the sins of your idols: and ye shall know that I *am* the Lord God.

The judgment, administered by righteous men in its awful severity upon adulteresses, polluted with life-long crime and standing before the court with their bloody hands—closes this appalling scene. Abating the intensely revolting nature of this description and the repugnance of its details to our sense of delicacy, the whole description is pungent and thrilling, and must have been full of moral power upon the heart and conscience of the men to whom it was originally spoken. One may well suppose it would make their ears tingle and their cheeks crimson with a sense of shame for their people and their beloved city. We naturally incline to pass by such a chapter unread; yet let us not forget that to the Jewish exiles of Ezekiel's day its features that are revolting to us would be scarcely if at all objectionable, and then that its caustic and terribly truthful severity must have made its testimony against the guilt of Jerusalem burn itself into the very heart and soul of the people.——Let us hope that this chapter was greatly blessed of God to open their dull eyes to the enormity of their national sin and to a sense of the justice of that dreadful doom which was ready even then to fall with crushing, annihilating force on the doomed city. The siege was within a few months of its commencement. These were the last words of the prophet prior to his announcement that the siege had begun.

CHAPTER XXIV.

This chapter bears a new date, viz., the very day in which Nebuchadnezzar commenced the siege of Jerusalem, and two years and five months later than the last preceding date (20: 1.) It is in two parts—the first part (vs. 3–14) presenting the confirmed wickedness of Jerusalem and God's efforts to cleanse it out, under the figure of a pot foul with rust, yet not cleansed by use, and incapable of being cleansed till it is set empty upon a hot fire and the very brass itself thoroughly heated and burned.——In the second part (vs. 15–27) the prophet's wife suddenly dies; he is forbidden to manifest his grief in the usual modes, showing the people thus that the calamities of their nation will be too great to admit of the common public manifestations of mourning.

1. Again in the ninth year, in the tenth month, in the tenth *day* of the month, the word of the Lord came unto me, saying,

2. Son of man, write thee the name of the day, *even* of this same day: the king of Babylon set himself against Jerusalem this same day.

The precise day on which the siege of Jerusalem commenced is on record 2 Kings 25:1, and Jer. 52:4; precisely as here. Omitting only the day of the month, the same date appears in Jer. 39:1. Of course this was one of the ever-memorable days of Jewish history, long observed as a day of fasting. See Zech. 8:19.——It was an impressive fact to the exiles. They must have seen in it new proof of the failure of their long-cherished hopes.

3. And utter a parable unto the rebellious house, and say unto them, Thus saith the Lord God; Set on a pot, set *it* on, and also pour water into it:

4. Gather the pieces thereof into it, *even* every good piece, the thigh, and the shoulder; fill *it* with the choice bones.

5. Take the choice of the flock, and burn also the bones under it, *and* make it boil well, and let them seethe the bones of it therein.

Inasmuch as this is distinctly declared to be a *parable*, we can not suppose it to have been a real symbolic transaction performed before the eyes of the people, nor yet a vision shown to the prophet by the divine Spirit. It is rather a *supposed transaction*, designed to represent certain analogous points in the case of the city of Jerusalem, its people and its pollutions. The pot of brass represents the city; its contents of flesh and bones are the inhabitants; and the rust ("scum") and foulness of the pot stand for the abominations of the city, the deep pollutions of society which had hardened and become incrusted upon the inner surface of the pot, and could be removed by no ordinary process. The first step in the operation is described in these verses. Fill it with water, flesh, and bones; set it over a hot fire, and boil it thoroughly. See what *discipline* will do toward reform.

6. Wherefore thus saith the Lord God; Wo to the bloody city, to the pot whose scum *is* therein, and whose scum is not gone out of it! bring it out piece by piece; let no lot fall upon it.

7. For her blood is in the midst of her; she set it upon the top of a rock; she poured it not upon the ground, to cover it with dust;

8. That it might cause fury to come up to take vengeance; I have set her blood upon the top of a rock, that it should not be covered.

9. Therefore thus saith the Lord God; Wo to the bloody city! I will even make the pile for fire great.

10. Heap on wood, kindle the fire, consume the flesh, and spice it well, and let the bones be burned.

New points in the process are blended here with explanations of its moral significance. The pot is shown to mean the city. Its filth and rust represent the blood of the city which has not been poured out upon the earth to be absorbed, but thrown upon the sunny surface of a rock, where it would only dry down and remain—a standing witness of crime—a defilement removable only with the utmost labor.——The Lord would push this boiling process with the utmost energy to see what can be done toward cleansing the pot from its filth and rust. Vs. 6 and 11 intimate that after the failure of this effort, the pot is entirely emptied of its flesh and bones—*i. e.*, the city is emptied of its people, and then the city itself (the pot) is subjected to intense heat, to burn off its pollutions.

11. Then set it empty upon the coals thereof, that the brass of it may be hot, and may burn, and *that* the filthiness of it may be molten in it, *that* the scum of it may be consumed.

12. She hath wearied *herself* with lies, and her great scum went not forth out of her: her scum *shall be* in the fire.

13. In thy filthiness *is* lewdness: because I have purged thee, and thou wast not purged, thou shalt not be purged from thy filthiness any more, till I have caused my fury to rest upon thee.

14. I the Lord have spoken *it*: it shall come to pass, and I will do *it*; I will not go back, neither will I spare, neither will I repent; according to thy ways, and according to thy doings, shall they judge thee, saith the Lord God.

Now the last effort is made to cleanse the pot by means of the fierce ordeal of fire upon it when empty. The aim is to reduce its filth to a molten state, and thus consume its rust ("scum.")——V. 12 should rather be read, "It," the pot, "has wearied itself, not with "lies," but with its great "*labor*"—*i. e.*, to cleanse itself of its rust and filth;—"but its great filth will not go forth from it, not even by the fire.——This verse aims to say that this long protracted and varied effort of God in his providence to reform the people and cleanse the city had been in vain. So v. 13 teaches. "In thy filthiness is *purposed* wickedness (so the Hebrew implies)—the deep, persistent, malign purpose to push madly on in rebellion. Because I have sought to purge thee, yet with no success, I shall make no further effort till I pour out my wrath on thee to abide upon thee, through a long captivity. God has spoken and will do it!——This is the outcome of the "parable." The Lord despairs of cleansing the city from its fixed incrustations of corruption—the residuum of crime hardened on at the bottom of society, and consequently leavening the whole mass with its pollution; and withal adhering so tenaciously that no ordinary heat and no other possible appliances will remove it and cleanse the vessel. So the city must be emptied of all its inhabitants and then be thoroughly burned to the ground.

15. Also the word of the Lord came unto me, saying,

16. Son of man, behold, I take away from thee the desire of thine eyes with a stroke: yet neither shalt thou mourn nor weep, neither shall thy tears run down.

17. Forbear to cry, make no mourning for the dead, bind the tire of thy head upon thee, and put on thy shoes upon thy feet, and cover not *thy* lips, and eat not the bread of men.

18. So I spake unto the people in the morning: and at even my wife died; and I did in the morning as I was commanded.

This beautiful descriptive epithet, "the desire of thine eyes," is shown (v. 18) to mean his wife—an object ever grateful to the eye and dear to the heart. The Lord says, I am about to take her away at one stroke, and you must refrain from all the usual manifestations of grief. The shock of a sore calamity is sometimes too great for tears, too overwhelming to allow one thought upon the forms and manifestations of sorrow. When men die by tens of thousands on the field of battle, who finds time or thought for sighs or for the drapery of woe!——So, in the destruction of the temple and the fall of the great city of their fathers' sepulchers, in the slaughter by thousands of their own fathers, brothers, sisters—they might well spare the habiliments of grief and omit all its usual symbols.——Such seems to have been the lesson intended in this startling, appalling scene.——V. 17 defines and forbids the usual indications of public mourning. "Forbear to cry; smother thy sighs; literally, "*sob; be silent;*" push back the tears. "Bind the tiara upon thine head," for in grief, this was removed and the hair suffered to stream out dishevelled. "Put thy shoes on thy feet;" for the mourner removed his shoes and walked barefoot. "Cover not thy mustache," which the mourner was wont to do; and "eat not the bread furnished by other men;" according to the custom of friends to furnish bread for the mourners. See Jer. 16: 5–8 and notes there.——" So I spake to the people in the morning," rehearsing to them this fearful word from the Lord; "at even my wife died," and I did in the morning [of the next day] as I was commanded." Since it was to be done before the people for a *sign* to them, the morning of the ensuing day would be the earliest time possible and the proper time for obeying this divine command.

19. And the people said unto me, Wilt thou not tell us what these *things are* to us, that thou doest so?

20. Then I answered them, The word of the Lord came unto me, saying,

21. Speak unto the house of Israel, Thus saith the Lord God; Behold, I will profane my sanctuary, the excellency of your strength, the desire of your eyes, and that which your soul pitieth; and your sons and your daughters whom ye have left shall fall by the sword.

22. And ye shall do as I have done: ye shall not cover *your* lips, nor eat the bread of men.

23. And your tires *shall* be upon your heads, and your shoes upon your feet: ye shall not mourn nor weep; but ye shall pine away for your iniquities, and mourn one toward another.

The attention of the people is arrested, and they inquire what all this signifies *to themselves*. The answer is definite. Remarkably it makes special account of the destruction of the temple and of the slaughter of their own sons and daughters left behind in their fatherland. They had fondly cherished the temple in their hearts, accounting it both the glory and the strength of their nation, so regarding it especially because they deemed it a guaranty of the presence and favor of Almighty God. This was to them what Ezekiel's wife was to him; "The desire of their eyes;" the object of their heart's tenderest, deepest sympathy; "what thy soul pities." No doubt it was literally true that the fall of the city involved the slaughter of many of their own sons and daughters. Under this terrible stroke, which fell on them suddenly like the blow which smote down the prophet's wife, they were forbidden to mourn in public, but would pine away in their iniquity, *i. e.*, under this terrible infliction for their sin, and might silently groan ("mourn") "one to another,"

24. Thus Ezekiel is unto you a sign: according to all that he hath done shall ye do: and when this cometh, ye shall know that I *am* the Lord God.

"A *sign* unto you;" a visible, significant symbol of what is to befall you and of what you must do and also of what you may *not* do, under an infliction of calamity analogous to his.——This word rendered "sign"* implies something specially striking, astounding, often rendered, "a wonder."

25. Also, thou son of man, *shall it* not *be* in the day when I take from them their strength, the joy of their glory, the desire of their eyes, and that whereupon they set their minds, their sons and their daughters,

26. *That* he that escapeth in that day shall come unto thee, to cause *thee* to hear *it* with *thine* ears?

---

* Not אות, which is the more common word in such connections, but מופת

27. In that day shall thy mouth be opened to him which is escaped, and thou shalt speak, and be no more dumb: and thou shalt be a sign unto them; and they shall know that I *am* the Lord.

When the city shall fall and the glorious temple go down under the general ruin, and this great calamity shall overwhelm the exiles with grief, then shall there not come to thee a messenger escaping from the city to announce these heavy tidings in thine ears? Then thy mouth shall be opened to him; thou shalt speak thenceforth freely and be no more dumb; and the significance of this sign shall become obvious to all the people, so that they also shall at last know that I am the Lord.——In view of this case of the death of the prophet's wife, let us not omit to note that the Lord spared no pains and shrunk from no sacrifices to make deep and solemn impressions on the minds of the exiles. A death so sudden as this; predicted in the morning; occurring by one swift blow in the evening; falling on the beloved wife of the venerable man who had stood before them as the messenger of God; the suppression of his tears and sighs; the withholding of every usual token of grief; and then the interpretation of these scenes as referring to the fall of their own beloved temple and the slaughter of their own sons and daughters in that land of their tenderest love—constitute a combination of circumstances at once startling and solemnly impressive. Truly might the Lord say, "What could I have done more to my vineyard," (my people) "that I have not done" to bring home to their heart the full sense of my wrath against them for their sins?——What shall we think of this divinely commissioned prophet? How did he feel? What did he say in the whisperings of his unuttered thought? Did he shudder and recoil, inwardly saying, This costs me too much! Must I be a sign to the people at such awful expense, at the cost of such harrowing grief? And then, as if to lose my dear wife at one blow were not enough, that God should not let me shed one tear! nor breathe out one audible sigh!—— With joy let us note that this record gives not the slightest hint of one thought of this sort. So far as appears, he bowed himself in the dust and said—"It is the Lord; let him do what seemeth him good." We may presume that he had human sensibilities; but we may also presume that grace given him of God brought him such moral strength that his spirit was sweetly submissive and unmurmuring, and his soul placid under this sorest of trials ever known to the human heart. What can not the grace of God do for his trusting, obedient people!

At this point, the first part of Ezekiel's prophecies ends and the second begins. He closes a long series of messages, varied in their forms and modes of revealing truth, but scarcely varying at all in their grand theme and purpose, viz., to set before the exiles the enormity of their national sin, the great wickedness and the deep corruption of Judah and Jerusalem; the certainty that the Lord would abandon his temple, city and people there to destruction, and the terribleness of that doom.——The manifest purpose of God in these revelations to the exiles was to convince them of his justice in those judgments; to give them a full sense of those sins, and to lead them to personal and sincere repentance and radical reformation, until they should themselves be ashamed and confounded, and never open their mouth any more for shame for their own sins and those of their people and land.——So a remnant are to be reclaimed and made the nucleus in future years for replanting the land of promise, and for restoring both their political and religious institutions.

CHAPTER XXV.

Exterminating judgments are announced against Ammon, vs. 1–7; against Moab, vs. 8–11; against Edom, vs. 12–14; and against Philistia, vs. 15–17—uniformly for the same national sin, viz., proud exultation over the fall of Judah and Jerusalem, and reproach cast on the name of Israel's God by reason of their fall.——Obadiah, nearly at the same time, wrote in the same strain against Edom. Ezek. 35 expands this prophecy against Edom.——Jeremiah prophesied against the same four neighboring powers, yet with a somewhat broader view of their national sins and especially of their pride; viz., against Ammon, chap. 49: 1–6; Moab, chap. 48; Edom, chap. 49: 7–22; and Philistia, chap. 47. So also Isaiah and some of the Minor Prophets.——The scope of these prophecies is designedly consolatory to the true people of God, assuring them that he still remembered Zion with tender affection, regarded her true interests as his own; and therefore would avenge her upon her proud and scornful foes. In this point of light, these prophecies hold an important place among the messages sent of God by Ezekiel to the exiled Jews in Chaldea. Their city in ruins, their nationality prostrate, and themselves in exile and under circumstances of the deepest national discouragement, they needed precisely such assurances of the Lord's tender mercy and of his identity of interest and sympathy with their people as still bearing his name and yet to bear it before all the nations of the earth. All the more did they need such words from Ezekiel, because thus far his messages had spoken of little else than national sin, judgments, and ruin. From this point their subject and tone change. Henceforward, with scarce an exception, his messages are encouraging and consolatory to all whose hearts were still true to their God.

1. The word of the Lord came again unto me, saying,

2. Son of man, set thy face against the Ammonites, and prophesy against them;

3. And say unto the Ammonites, Hear the word of the Lord God; Thus saith the Lord God; Because thou saidst,

Aha, against my sanctuary, when it was profaned; and against the land of Israel, when it was desolate; and against the house of Judah, when they went into captivity;

4. Behold, therefore, I will deliver thee to the men of the east for a posssesion, and they shall set their palaces in thee, and make their dwellings in thee: they shall eat thy fruit, and they shall drink thy milk.

5. And I will make Rabbah a stable for camels, and the Ammonites a couching-place for flocks: and ye shall know that I *am* the Lord.

The sin for which Ammon is doomed is here made very definite—exulting triumph over God's polluted temple, desolate land, and captive people. Why should not the Lord frown fearfully on such manifestations of proud hostility against himself and his people, and make such enemies an example of his righteous justice before all the nations of men in all time? There the record stands, equally in prophecy and in their history, witnessing that the Lord Almighty will let no people, however powerful or however proud, contemn his name with impunity.——"The men of the East"—God's executioners of vengeance upon Ammon—were the Chaldeans, raised up in his providence for judgment, not on Judah and Jerusalem alone, but on those contiguous nations which had long been deeply sunk in the same forms of debasing idolatry, and had now filled up the cup of their national sin by malign hostility against Israel and scornful exultation over her fall. They would seize the whole country of Ammon and make her proud capital a stable for camels—significant of an utter overthrow of her nationality.

6. For thus saith the Lord God; Because thou hast clapped *thy* hands, and stamped with the feet, and rejoiced in heart with all thy despite against the land of Israel;

7. Behold, therefore I will stretch out my hand upon thee; and will deliver thee for a spoil to the heathen; and I will cut thee off from the people, and I will cause thee to perish out of the countries: I will destroy thee; and thou shalt know that I *am* the Lord.

Her exultation manifests itself in these violent gestures. "With all thy despite," means with all thy pride, in the form of the utmost proud and haughty scorn. For these sins the Lord would cut them off from being a nation and blot out their very name;—a prophecy which had its first fulfillment in the sweep of ruin brought over their land by the Chaldean power shortly after the fall of Jerusalem. It was consummated in subsequent ages.

8. Thus saith the Lord God; Because that Moab and Seir do say, Behold, the house of Judah *is* like unto all the heathen;

9. Therefore, behold, I will open the side of Moab from the cities, from his cities *which are* on his frontiers, the glory of the country, Beth-jeshimoth, Baalmeon, and Kiriathaim.

10. Unto the men of the east with the Ammonites, and will give them in possession, that the Ammonites may not be remembered among the nations.

11. And I will execute judgments upon Moab; and they shall know that I *am* the Lord.

The spirit of Moab and Seir is essentially the same with that of Ammon. They exult over Judah as being like all the nations in having a patron God no mightier than their own gods, and hence as being, at least equally with themselves, subject to defeat, captivity, and national ruin. This was dishonor and even contempt toward the Infinite God. Therefore the Lord will open the side of Moab to the assaults of foreign enemies in the very point where she had imagined her chief strength lay, viz., in those great cities on her frontiers which had been her reliance and her glory.—— The men of the east who subdued Ammon subdued *her*.——" With the Ammonites," does not mean that the men of the east had them as allies in this invasion, but that they subdued Moab *in addition to* the Ammonites.

12. Thus saith the Lord God; Because that Edom hath dealt against the house of Judah by taking vengeance, and hath greatly offended, and revenged himself upon them;

13. Therefore thus saith the Lord God; I will also stretch out my hand upon Edom, and will cut off man and beast from it; and I will make it desolate from Teman; and they of Dedan shall fall by the sword.

14. And I will lay my vengeance upon Edom by the hand of my people Israel; and they shall do in Edom according to mine anger and according to my fury; and they shall know my vengeance, saith the Lord God.

Special stress is laid on the spirit of retaliation and revenge manifest against Israel in Edom. Of all the nations adjacent to Israel, none seem to have cherished a deeper animosity or a meaner revenge than the descendants of Esau. It was a national spirit, and was specially offensive to God because of their early relationship. Moreover as a Great Father of nations, bound to promote fraternal relations between them, he could not but frown on this unnatural, supremely selfish and hateful spirit. Let it stand and be understood as God's rebuke against this spirit, whether in nations, families, or individuals.——" Cutting off man and beast from it," leaves it an utter desolation, as it is this day and has been for many ages.——The last clause should probably read, "And even to Dedan they shall fall by the sword;" *i. e.*, from Teman on the south to

Dedan on the north, the whole country shall be laid in ruins.——
V. 14 states that this vengeance on Edom is to be executed in part at least "by the hand of God's people Israel." So history shows. The final destruction of their nationality was effected by the Jews under John Hyrcanus, B. C. 128. Josephus (Ant. 13: 9: 1) gives a brief account of this subjugation, adding that Hyrcanus compelled them to accept circumcision, and thus destroyed their nationality and merged them into the Jewish community.

15. Thus saith the Lord God; Because the Philistines have dealt by revenge, and have taken vengeance with a despiteful heart, to destroy *it* for the old hatred;

16. Therefore thus saith the Lord God; Behold, I will stretch out my hand upon the Philistines, and I will cut off the Cherethims, and destroy the remnant of the sea-coast.

17. And I will execute great vengeance upon them with furious rebukes; and they shall know that I *am* the Lord, when I shall lay my vengeance upon them.

The fatal sin of the Philistines also was their spirit of revenge, animosity, and proud disdain toward Israel.——"Cherethim" is nearly synonymous with "Philistines"—the two words being at least sometimes used for the same people. See 1 Sam. 30: 14, 16, and Zeph. 2: 5. They occupied the country of the sea-coast, *i. e.*, along the eastern shore of the Mediterranean.——In the fulfillment of this prophecy, the Lord's vengeance was visited upon them first by the hands of the Chaldeans. From this devastation they never rose again to power.

CHAPTER XXVI.

From Ezekiel's stand-point of view at Babylon, the great nations of the West and South-west were Tyre and Egypt;—Tyre, the mistress of the seas, the great emporium of commerce for the civilized world of that age; and Egypt, then as through all ancient time, the powerful sovereignty of North-eastern Africa, sitting upon her fertile Nile, and enjoying a civilization even at that time hoary with the lapse of centuries. Ammon, Moab, Edom, and the Philistines were subordinate powers, closely contiguous to Palestine indeed, but far less formidable to the great central power at Babylon. Hence a very few words only sufficed to note their fortunes and their fall; while the prophecies against Tyre and Egypt are expanded with very considerable detail—three chapters being devoted to Tyre and four to Egypt.——Territorially, Tyre had little more than a foothold upon the soil of Western Asia. The city was the empire; but that city, built partly on the main land yet mostly on a small island which it completely covered, was exceedingly strong by its maritime position; strong by its absolute control over the waters which embosomed it; strong in its vast wealth and consequent ability to hire soldiers and maintain a large army without drawing upon its own population. It must have been strong also through its commercial and intimate relations, *e. g.*, with Carthage, a colony of its own citizens, and with Tartessus in Spain, another of its great trading outposts. Convincing proof of the great strength of Tyre lies in the fact that she withstood the assaults of Nebuchadnezzar during a siege of thirteen years.

1. And it came to pass in the eleventh year, in the first *day* of the month, *that* the word of the Lord came unto me, saying,

Comparing this date with that of the fall of Jerusalem, as in Jer. 42: 6, and 39: 2, it will be seen that this was within the same year. Here, the month is not given; yet partly for this reason it is supposed to have been the first, since if it had been any other, the month would have been named. Jerusalem was "broken up" and burned in the fourth month and ninth day in the same year. At the date here given, the city had not yet fallen, but its speedy fall was morally certain.

2. Son of man, because that Tyrus hath said against Jerusalem, Aha, she is broken *that was* the gates of the people: she is turned unto me: I shall be replenished, *now* she is laid waste:

Tyre regarded Jerusalem as her rival in commerce, in magnificence, and in population. She was the "gate of the people" in the sense of a place of concourse for masses of people. Hence when she was broken down, Tyre exulted in her proud selfishness, confident that the fall of her rival would conduce to her own advantage, saying, *Her* wealth, trade, and population will come round to augment mine; "I shall be replenished" by her being laid waste.

3. Therefore thus saith the Lord God; Behold, I *am* against thee, O Tyrus, and will cause many nations to come up against thee, as the sea causeth his waves to come up.

4. And they shall destroy the walls of Tyrus, and break down her towers: I will also scrape her dust from her, and make her like the top of a rock.

5. It shall be *a place for* the spreading of nets in the midst of the sea: for I have spoken *it*, saith the Lord God: and it shall become a spoil to the nations.

6. And her daughters which *are* in the fields shall be slain by the sword; and they shall know that I *am* the Lord.

EZEKIEL.—CHAP. XXVI. 149

The great King of nations must hold them, even the proudest of them, to a just standard of national morality. Hence he could not let proud Tyre go on fostering such intense and mean selfishness with impunity. "For this sin, saith the Lord, I am against thee, O Tyrus." God would bring up many nations against her, even as the great sea heaves up its mighty waves against the bulwarks that feeble men rear. This maritime figure is entirely in place in a prophecy against Tyre. The island city was built on the top of a huge rock. When the city became utterly desolate, and all its vast walls, forts and structures were demolished, the surface of this rock was laid bare and became precisely a place for fishermen to spread and dry their nets. This prophecy has long since been literally fulfilled. Her great wealth, accumulated during ages of lucrative commerce, became a spoil to the nations.

7. For thus saith the Lord God; Behold, I will bring upon Tyrus Nebuchadnezzar king of Babylon, a king of kings from the north, with horses, and with chariots, and with horsemen, and companies, and much people.

8. He shall slay with the sword thy daughters in the field: and he shall make a fort against thee, and cast a mount against thee, and lift up the buckler against thee.

9. And he shall set engines of war against thy walls, and with his axes he shall break down thy towers.

10. By reason of the abundance of his horses their dust shall cover thee: thy walls shall shake at the noise of the horsemen, and of the wheels, and of the chariots, when he shall enter into thy gates, as men enter into a city wherein is made a breach.

11. With the hoofs of his horses shall he tread down all thy streets: he shall slay thy people by the sword, and thy strong garrisons shall go down to the ground.

12. And they shall make a spoil of thy riches, and make a prey of thy merchandise: and they shall break down thy walls, and destroy thy pleasant houses: and they shall lay thy stones and thy timber and thy dust in the midst of the water.

This passage predicts the celebrated siege of Tyre by Nebuchadnezzar which occurred not long after. Josephus refers to it in two distinct passages (Ant. 10: 11: 1, and against Apion 1: 21); in the former, citing Philostratus as saying that "this king besieged Tyre thirteen years while Ethbaal reigned at Tyre;" and in the latter, quoting in general from the records of the Phenicians to the same effect.——Precisely how this siege of Tyre terminated, whether with its absolute subjugation, or by capitulation, or by the withdrawal of the besiegers, is still in dispute among antiquarians.

The testimony of Jerome, in his commentary on Ezek. 29: 8, is quite explicit to the point that Nebuchadnezzar did capture the city, but found nothing of any account within it because the Tyrians had previously removed every thing valuable in their ships. There can be no reasonable doubt that a thirteen years' siege laid and left the city mainly in ruins. It was a stern and terrible siege, as Ezekiel's own statements (29: 18) abundantly attest. "Nebuchadnezzar caused his army to serve a great service against Tyrus; every head was made bald and every shoulder was peeled."——In v. 9, the *effect* of a battering ram is described in place of giving its distinctive name. "He shall bring against thy walls the stroke of what is over against." Was this mode adopted because Ezekiel and his readers were not familiar with an appropriate name for this engine?——In the last clause of v. 11, instead of reading, "strong garrison," read—"The statues of the gods," in which lay their supposed strength. Down went those statues, significant of the utter prostration of their political and military power.——That "her stones, timber and dust went into the midst of the waters" resulted from her location upon an island, built out to the very water's edge.

13. And I will cause the noise of thy songs to cease; and the sound of thy harps shall be no more heard.

14. And I will make thee like the top of a rock: thou shalt be *a place* to spread nets upon: thou shalt be built no more: for I the Lord have spoken *it*, saith the Lord God.

Her "songs" and "harps" indicate that music was in a somewhat advanced stage of cultivation.——"Thou shalt be built no more," *i. e.*, with like magnificence and strength. The city rose again—to be besieged more than two centuries later by Alexander—after which it never regained its independence, nor its former magnificence.

15. Thus saith the Lord God to Tyrus; Shall not the isles shake at the sound of thy fall, when the wounded cry, when the slaughter is made in the midst of thee?

16. Then all the princes of the sea shall come down from their thrones, and lay away their robes, and put off their broidered garments: they shall clothe themselves with trembling: they shall sit upon the ground, and shall tremble at *every* moment, and be astonished at thee.

17. And they shall take up a lamentation for thee, and say to thee, How art thou destroyed, *that wast* inhabited of seafaring men, the renowned city, which was strong in the sea, she and her inhabitants, which cause their terror *to be* on all that haunt it!

18. Now shall the isles tremble in the day of thy fall;

yea, the isles that *are* in the sea shall be troubled at thy departure.

The term "*isles*" as usual stands for all maritime countries reached by sea, and here has special reference to Carthage, Tartessus, and all those regions of Northern Africa and Southern Europe which had sustained close commercial relations with Tyre. At the sound of her fall those isles would shake; their princes would come down from their thrones, lay off their robes, and put on trembling, and sit on the ground as men brought down, despite of all their honor, to their mother dust! Their mourning comes to us in the life-like form of the very words of their bitter wail over her fall: "How art thou destroyed whose inhabitants were from the seas—a city renowned, which was strong, she and her people, in the sea; impressing her terror on all its dwellers!"——The isles of the sea may have been troubled at her departure through fear that the same enemy might come down upon themselves next!

19. For thus saith the Lord God; When I shall make thee a desolate city, like the cities that are not inhabited; when I shall bring up the deep upon thee, and great waters shall cover thee;

20. When I shall bring thee down with them that descend into the pit, with the people of old time, and shall set thee in the low parts of the earth, in places desolate of old, with them that go down to the pit, that thou be not inhabited; and I shall set glory in the land of the living;

21. I wilt make thee a terror, and thou *shalt be* no *more:* though thou be sought for, yet shalt thou never be found again, saith the Lord God.

I prefer to read v. 20 as the apodosis, *i. e.*, the corresponding second part of the sentence, thus; "When I shall make thee desolate," etc., (v. 19); "*Then* (v. 20) I will bring thee down with those that descend into the pit *to* the ancient people, and will make thee dwell in the under-world—in the everlasting desolations—to the end that thou shalt be inhabited no more, (*i. e.*, upon this earth); "but I will set glory in the land of the living"—the land of my own people Israel over whose fall thou hast exulted. The idea is that Tyre goes down to the under-world, to live no more among the nations of this fair earth, while the Lord will raise up Judah and make her again the glory of all lands.——The word "glory" here is the same as in chap. 20: 6, 15, and elsewhere, Dan. 8: 9, and 11: 16, 41.——This conception of the grave or pit as an under-world where the ancient dead have their long abode, is applied here beautifully to cities and kingdoms which go down to ruin to rise no more.——Over against this doom of Tyre, thus perished and gone, never to rise in her glory again, the Lord promises to make the land of his own people Israel once more the glory of the earth.——So perish the nations and the people that set themselves proudly and defiantly against the mighty God, while to his people, there ariseth new joy out of their grief; new light from their darkness; and from every eclipse, a new radiance of glory!——Who shall say it is not well to take one's lot with the oft-despised people of God! Why should men fear the trials and the darkness that may be for a moment when their eternal future is so sure and so ineffably glorious!

CHAPTER XXVII.

This remarkable chapter is a sort of inventory of the wealth, greatness, and glory of ancient Tyre, showing the sources whence she drew her materials and men for the commerce and the carrying trade of the world. No ancient historian has ever approximated toward a statement so full and complete as this of the business relations which existed in that age among the nations of the world. Here is Tyre, the commercial center of the world, reaching forth her arms in every direction to make every land contribute its best products in men, in wisdom, martial prowess, nautical skill, and in every sort of material to stock her markets, or to minister to her facilities for transportation. It is a wonderful description; yet it stands here, not to give us the barren facts of so much commerce and so much splendor in the arts, but to show how much human greatness and glory went down in one fearful fall when the Almighty arose in his wrath to smite her bulwarks and sink all her glory in the depths of ruin. By how much the more sublime the height of her glory, by so much the more astounding was the crash of her fall!——The revelator John had his eye on this chapter in his magnificent description of the fall of Babylon the Great (Rev. 18).

1. The word of the Lord came again unto me, saying,
2. Now, thou son of man, take up a lamentation for Tyrus;
3. And say unto Tyrus, O thou that art situate at the entry of the sea, *which art* a merchant of the people for many isles, Thus saith the Lord God; O Tyrus, thou hast said, I *am* of perfect beauty.

Tyre was proud of her wealth and splendor. This was her national sin, and wrought her ruin. She gloried in her perfect beauty, and so became reckless of the claims of God and regardless of the obligations of common humanity and morality. The mean selfishness in which she gloated over the fall of Jerusalem is made prominent in the previous chapter (26: 2). The prophet Amos (1: 9) gives yet another telling fact; viz., that she sold all her captives taken in war into slavery in Edom—as if any thing were right in trade and for gain! V. 13 refers to her slave-trade.——"At the entry of the sea." Tyre was the commercial port for the whole eastern shore of the Mediterranean. This vast body of water was practically in those times what its name indicates, the *midland sea* of the nations, begirt on every side with the civilization, the industry, and the wealth of the known world.——The word rendered "merchant" implies that she had the carrying trade of the world, transporting the commodities of the great East to the West, and of the great West to the East.

4. Thy borders *are* in the midst of the seas, thy builders. have perfected thy beauty.

5. They have made all thy *ship*-boards of fir-trees of Senir: they have taken cedars from Lebanon to make masts for thee.

6. *Of* the oaks of Bashan have they made thine oars; the company of the Ashurites have made thy benches *of* ivory, *brought* out of the isles of Chittim.

7. Fine linen with broidered work from Egypt was that which thou spreadest forth to be thy sail; blue and purple from the isles of Elishah was that which covered thee.

In v. 5, "Senir" is used for a part or the whole of Mt. Hermon in the country of Ammon. These "ship-boards" were *ship-decks*, made double, as the dual number of the noun indicates.——In v. 6 Gesenius translates, not—"the company of the Ashurites"—but, "thy benches"(for the rowers to sit upon) "were of ivory inlaid in the Sherbin cedar:" literally, "were of ivory, the daughter of the Sherbin cedar." The statement illustrates the magnificence and finish of her appointments for her carrying trade. This cedar, noted for being straight and tall, came from the Island of Cyprus.
——"Fine linen of Egypt was spread for her *flag*, her banners—not her "sail"—for the sails would require strength rather than beauty.——"Elishah" is probably Elis, a district of Peloponnesus, in Greece.

8. The inhabitants of Zidon and Arvad were thy mariners: thy wise *men*, O Tyrus, *that* were in thee, were thy pilots.

9. The ancients of Gebal and the wise *men* thereof were in thee thy calkers: all the ships of the sea with their mariners were in thee to occupy thy merchandise.

10. They of Persia and of Lud and of Phut were in thine army, thy men of war: they hanged the shield and helmet in thee; they set forth thy comeliness.

11. The men of Arvad with thine army *were* upon thy walls round about, and the Gammadims were in thy towers:

they hanged their shields upon thy walls round about; they made thy beauty perfect.

In v. 8 the word for "mariners" means *rowers*, indicating the great fact of that age, viz., that human muscle was the chief reliance for propelling power. The application of steam power was then unknown and skill in the use of sails was in its infancy.—— The word for "pilots" bears the wider sense of *seamen*.—— "Calkers;" literally, men to make the joints strong, water-tight. ——The last clause of v. 9 means, not precisely to "occupy thy merchandise, but rather, to exchange thy commodities; to do the business of traffic, barter, commerce.——She hired her soldiers from Persia, in the far east; and from Lud and Phut, countries of northern Africa, lying west of Egypt, descendants of Ham.—— Shields and helmets were hung up when not in immediate use. These men were perhaps her standing army on garrison duty for home defense. They heightened her splendor (" comeliness)."—— In v. 11, "Gammadim" is a common (not a proper) noun, meaning (by etymology) *the brave warriors* who cut down the enemy as the woodman fells trees.

12. Tarshish *was* thy merchant by reason of the multitude of all *kind of* riches; with silver, iron, tin, and lead, they traded in thy fairs.

13. Javan, Tubal, and Meshech, they *were* thy merchants: they traded the persons of men and vessels of brass in thy market.

14. They of the house of Togarmah traded in thy fairs with horses and horsemen and mules.

15. The men of Dedan *were* thy merchants; many isles *were* the merchandise of thy hand: they brought thee *for* a present, horns of ivory and ebony.

16. Syria *was* thy merchant by reason of the multitude of the wares of thy making: they occupied in thy fairs with emeralds, purple, and broidered work, and fine linen, and coral, and agate.

"Tarshish," Tartessus in Spain, supplied largely the minerals most used in the arts. So ancient history testifies.——The last clause means; They replenished thy markets with these commodities. "Javan," strictly ancient Ionia; "Tubal and Meshech," also countries of Asia Minor, sold slaves in her market. "Togarmah" was a region yet farther north, supposed to be Armenia, peopled with descendants of Gomer through Torgom. They abounded in horses.——Dedan on the Persian Gulf, far in the south, is supposed to have been an ancient Phenician colony. The maritime places adjacent are referred to here as the "many isles" which supplied merchandise to the hand of Tyre. Ivory, and ebony (literally *stone-wood* for its hardness), were their products.——Syria was pre-eminently the manufacturing country.

17. Judah, and the land of Israel, they *were* thy merchants; they traded in thy market wheat of Minnith and Pannag, and honey, and oil, and balm.

18. Damascus *was* thy merchant in the multitude of the wares of thy making, for the multitude of all riches; in the wine of Helbon, and white wool.

19. Dan also and Javan going to and fro occupied in thy fairs: bright iron, cassia, and calamus, were in thy market.

20. Dedan *was* thy merchant in precious clothes for chariots.

Judah and Israel supplied the staple articles of food.——"Minnith" was a place in the land of Ammon whence choice wheat came. "Pannag" is probably a common noun, meaning *sweet cake*.——The same view as to the nature of the trade between Tyre and Israel appears in the negotiations between Hiram and Solomon (1 Kings 5: 9-11). Hiram said, "Thou shalt accomplish my desire in giving food for my household." "Solomon gave Hiram twenty thousand measures of wheat for food for his household and twenty measures of pure oil year by year."——Damascus was even then celebrated for her manufactures. Her skill in fine cloths and especially in silks has given the term " *Damasks* " an enduring place in human language.——In v. 19 Gesenius reads, not "Dan also," but Vedan—making the first letter a component part of the proper name. This was a city of Arabia, said to have produced anciently these very commodities. "Javan," in this verse, he supposes to have been also an Arabian city, as well as Dedan. The word rendered, "going to and fro," is thought to refer to *spinning;* so that the clause means, "they set out spun-work in thy fairs."

21. Arabia, and all the princes of Kedar, they occupied with thee in lambs, and rams, and goats: in these *were they* thy merchants.

22. The merchants of Sheba and Raamah, they *were* thy merchants: they occupied in thy fairs with chief of all spices, and with all precious stones, and gold.

23. Haran, and Canneh, and Eden, the merchants of Sheba, Asshur, *and* Chilmad, *were* thy merchants.

24. These were thy merchants in all sorts *of things*, in blue clothes, and broidered work, and in chests of rich apparel, bound with cords, and made of cedar, among thy merchandise.

That herds and flocks were the commodities of Arabia and Kedar is in harmony with all antiquity. Isaiah sang of "the flocks of Kedar" (chap. 60: 7), and in the same connection, of "the gold and incense of Sheba" (chap. 60: 6).——This Raamah lay in south-east Arabia, associated naturally with Sheba. So in Gen. 10: 7, and 1 Chron. 1: 9.——V. 23 groups several points in ancient Assyria; Haran, known in the early history of Abraham; Canneh, probably the "Calno" of Isaiah's time, (chap. 10: 9) and the Ctesiphon of the Greeks; Eden and Chilmad are not well known.—— The general showing is to the effect that the whole civilized world brought their commodities to one grand emporium in ancient Tyre.

25. The ships of Tarshish did sing of thee in thy market; and thou wast replenished, and made very glorious in the midst of the seas.

The original seems to mean; not, "did sing of thee," etc., but were carriers of thy merchandise. So Gesenius and Maurer. This completes the category.

26. Thy rowers have brought thee into great waters: the east wind hath broken thee in the midst of the seas.

27. Thy riches, and thy fairs, thy merchandise, thy mariners, and thy pilots, thy calkers, and the occupiers of thy merchandise, and all thy men of war, that *are* in thee, and in all thy company which *is* in the midst of thee, shall fall into the midst of the seas in the day of thy ruin.

Here the discourse turns from her glory and greatness to her fall. It was as if her rowers had brought her into great waters, to be sunk there with all her wealth by the mighty east winds of that inland sea. Then by how much the greater her freight of wealth, merchandise, mariners, mercenary soldiers, men of all business and population of every sort; by so much the more terrible the fearful fall that would engulf her in the mighty deep to rise no more!

28. The suburbs shall shake at the sound of the cry of thy pilots.

29. And all that handle the oar, the mariners, *and* all the pilots of the sea, shall come down from their ships, they shall stand upon the land;

30. And shall cause their voice to be heard against thee, and shall cry bitterly, and shall cast up dust upon their heads; they shall wallow themselves in the ashes:

31. And they shall make themselves utterly bald for thee, and gird them with sackcloth, and they shall weep for for thee with bitterness of heart *and* bitter wailing.

32. And in their wailing they shall take up a lamentation for thee, and lament over thee, *saying*, What *city is* like Tyrus, like the destroyed in the midst of the sea?

This is the mourning and the wailing over her fall. The prophet groups together all the usual oriental symbols and modes of expressing the most intense grief. The last clause of v. 32 is specially expressive, where instead of, "like the destroyed," etc., I would read, "*as one hushed to dead silence* in the midst of the sea," in contrast with the hum and noise of her busy commerce and the myriad sounds of a great city of trade.

33. When thy wares went forth out of the seas, thou filledst many people; thou didst enrich the kings of the earth with the multitude of thy riches and of thy merchandise.

34. In the time *when* thou shalt be broken by the seas in the depths of the waters, thy merchandise and all thy company in the midst of thee shall fall.

35. All the inhabitants of the isles shall be astonished at thee, and their kings shall be sore afraid, they shall be troubled in *their* countenance.

36. The merchants among the people shall hiss at thee; thou shalt be a terror, and never *shalt be* any more.

Once so great, enriching kings from thy stores of wealth; now broken, impoverished; the isles astonished at thy fall; the kings of the earth appalled before such retribution and the merchants of the earth, once joyous in thy traffic, now hissing contemptuously over thy ruin:—what a scene is this! How fraught with impressive lessons on the frailty of human wealth and grandeur, and the folly of human pride!——Let those who give their hearts to the attractions of wealth and splendor, or to the charms of business and gain, pause over this lesson and ask, What wisdom is here for us? Let the nations that are treading in the steps of ancient Tyre think of her sins and of her consequent doom! No securities are too substantial to be utterly broken down. No guaranty for the permanence of wealth and glory will stand when God arises to call men to their moral account!

CHAPTER XXVIII.

In this chapter judgments on Tyre continue through vs. 1-19; then on Zidon through vs. 20-26. The judgments against Tyre are specially directed to "the prince of Tyrus," (v. 2,) and to "the king" (v. 12), for his great pride. The king is probably a representative man; first, the embodiment of the nation's pride; then, the symbol of her doom.

1. The word of the Lord came again unto me, saying,

2. Son of man, say unto the prince of Tyrus, Thus saith the Lord God; Because thy heart *is* lifted up, and thou hast said, I *am* a god, I sit *in* the seat of God, in the midst of the seas; yet thou *art* a man, and not God, though thou set thy heart as the heart of God:

3. Behold, thou *art* wiser than Daniel; there is no secret that they can hide from thee:

4. With thy wisdom and with thine understanding thou hast gotten thee riches, and hast gotten gold and silver into thy treasures:

5. By thy great wisdom *and* by thy traffic hast thou increased thy riches, and thy heart is lifted up because of thy riches.

The latter part of v. 2 I would translate thus: "Because thou hast said, I am God; I sit in the seat of God in the midst of the seas;—but thou art man and not God, and yet thou dost set thy heart as the heart of God." "Man" here is *frail* man, of dust. The special point of the affirmation is that, being only frail and mortal—nothing but man in his weak estate—he should yet most unreasonably, proudly and wickedly, assume to be God and think of himself and bear himself as the Almighty Lord of all.——The words, "Thou art wiser than Daniel," give not the view of God but the view of this prince of Tyre. So he thinks of himself.—— Tyre had manifested worldly wisdom in her business and trade, and becoming rich thereby had also become excessively proud—no uncommon result of that business capacity which insures wealth. ——The Lord intends to make her case an admonition to every man of like wisdom and of similar success, against a similar pride and a like fearful doom.

6. Therefore thus saith the Lord God; Because thou hast set thy heart as the heart of God;

7. Behold, therefore I will bring strangers upon thee, the terrible of the nations: and they shall draw their swords against the beauty of thy wisdom, and they shall defile thy brightness.

8. They shall bring thee down to the pit, and thou shalt die the deaths of *them that are* slain in the midst of the seas.

9. Wilt thou yet say before him that slayeth thee, I *am* God? but thou *shalt be* a man, and no God, in the hand of him that slayeth thee.

10. Thou shalt die the deaths of the uncircumcised by the hand of strangers: for I have spoken *it*, saith the Lord God.

These "strangers," "the terrible of the nations," are primarily the Chaldeans, whose fearful onslaught and siege of thirteen years' duration brought death to multitudes of her sons and daughters, and ruin over her fair city.——"Against the beauty of thy wisdom," is beauty in the arts, such as manifests peculiar skill, "wisdom."——In v. 8 the sense is, Thou Tyrus, although in the midst of the seas, and therefore supposing thyself safe, shalt yet die the death of those who are pierced through with the sword. "In the midst of the seas," gives, not the manner of being slain, but the reason why she deemed herself secure.——Then and there, in the very presence of those stalwart arms and drawn swords, wilt thou proudly say, I am God? Thy doom shall show that thou art only frail man and not God. "Thou shalt die the death of the uncircumcised"—the profane and impious whom God dooms to perish.

11. Moreover the word of the Lord came unto me, saying,
12. Son of man, take up a lamentation upon the king of Tyrus, and say unto him, Thus saith the Lord God; Thou sealest up the sum, full of wisdom, and perfect in beauty.
13. Thou hast been in Eden the garden of God; every precious stone *was* thy covering, the sardius, topaz, and the diamond, the beryl, the onyx, and the jasper, the sapphire, the emerald, and the carbuncle, and gold: the workmanship of thy tabrets and of thy pipes was prepared in thee in the day that thou wast created.

These verses are not so much God's admission of what is true of Tyre as his representation of what she thinks of herself.——"Thou sealest up the sum," seems to mean; Thou hast filled thine own idea of perfection, as when any required sum is fully made up, it is sealed to indicate that nothing more need be added.——"Eden, the garden of God," man's primeval paradise, fills the conception of beauty. Such in her own esteem was the state of Tyre when she sat proudly, enriched with the wealth of the nations and shining in their concentrated splendor.——This accumulation of terms for gems and precious stones shows at least that a great variety of them were well known and much valued as objects of enduring beauty.——In the last clause of v. 13, the words rendered "tabrets" and "pipes" seem not to refer to musical instruments, but to the *bezel* or cavity into which gems were set. The general idea is, Thou wast ordained to this wealth and splendor from the day when thou wast founded as a city and nation. Tyre had always been a great mart of commerce and a home for its wealth and glory.

14. Thou *art* the anointed cherub that covereth; and I have set thee so: thou wast upon the holy mountain of God; thou hast walked up and down in the midst of the stones of fire.

15. Thou *wast* perfect in thy ways from the day that thou wast created, till iniquity was found in thee.

"Anointed" is probably not the idea, but rather—"the cherub of *expanded* wing"—with allusion to the cherubim in the most holy place, whose wings were extended over the mercy-seat. The original verb represents the two correlated ideas, (1.) of moving the hands outward from the person and from each other as in expanding; and (2.) of *anointing* by a similar use of the hands. Here we have the primary idea.——The allusion to the cherubim in the temple is still further carried out in the phrase, "the holy mountain of God," that on which the temple stood, as in Isa. 11: 9; "in all my holy mountain;" and also Isa. 56: 7; "them will I bring to my holy mountain," etc.——"The stones of fire" are those precious stones, gems, that sparkle and flash as if they were stones of fire. Up and down amid these the king of Tyre had walked. In all his ways this monarch had enjoyed the perfection of earthly glory and splendor from the very foundation of the city and kingdom until iniquity was found in him and the hand of the Almighty came down upon him in righteous judgment.

16. By the multitude of thy merchandise they have filled the midst of thee with violence, and thou hast sinned: therefore I will cast thee as profane out of the mountain of God: and I will destroy thee, O covering cherub, from the midst of the stones of fire.

17. Thy heart was lifted up because of thy beauty; thou hast corrupted thy wisdom by reason of thy brightness: I will cast thee to the ground, I will lay thee before kings, that they may behold thee.

18. Thou hast defiled thy sanctuaries by the multitude of thine iniquities, by the iniquity of thy traffic; therefore will I bring forth a fire from the midst of thee, it shall devour thee; and I will bring thee to ashes upon the earth in the sight of all of them that behold thee.

19. All they that know thee among the people shall be astonished at thee: thou shalt be a terror, and never *shalt* thou *be* any more.

In the midst of this great traffic and by consequence of it, Tyre had become "full of violence"—the usual phrase to denote violations of person, assaults, bloodshed, insecurity of life. "And so," or "and *then* thou didst *sin*," in the emphatic sense; become abandoned and outbreaking in thine immoralities.——The language which describes her doom is transferred from the account of her previous splendor. Once a cherub, sitting in glory in the holy mount of God amid gems sparkling with luster; now the Lord will cast her as a profane thing down from his own holy mount and destroy her. Beauty and wisdom had been her snare, and now become her curse.——"The iniquity of thy traffic (v. 18) I take to be the corrupting influence of thy trade—the moral perversity begotten by the arts of trade. The original implies this. "Therefore I will bring forth a fire from the midst of thee that shall devour thee," intimates that sin works out its own doom—generates the causes that bring retribution upon the sinner. The judgments on Tyre should fill the nations with amazement; should become a terror to the wicked who would fear a like doom for their own sins. ——"And never shalt thou be any more." The full measure of this doom did not come with the siege by Nebuchadnezzar, for Tyre recovered in some degree from this first blow. Another blow fell on her from the hand of Alexander, two hundred and fifty years later. Saracen and Turk have finished the work of her destruction. She has come at last to be only a naked rock on which fishermen dry their nets, as the prophet said.

20. Again the word of the Lord came unto me, saying,

21. Son of man, set thy face against Zidon, and prophesy against it,

22. And say, Thus saith the Lord God; Behold, I *am* against thee, O Zidon; and I will be glorified in the midst of thee: and they shall know that I *am* the Lord, when I shall have executed judgments in her, and shall be sanctified in her.

23. For I will send into her pestilence, and blood into her streets; and the wounded shall be judged in the midst of her by the sword upon her on every side; and they shall know that I *am* the Lord.

24. And there shall be no more a pricking brier unto the house of Israel, nor *any* grieving thorn of all *that are* round about them, that despised them; and they shall know that I *am* the Lord God.

Zidon, the subject of this prophecy, lying but twenty miles north of Tyre; herself like Tyre situated on the Mediterranean, yet never like Tyre distinguished for trade but rather for skill in manufactures—was the more ancient, appearing in Bible history, Gen. 10: 15, 19, and Josh. 11: 8, and 19: 28—in these two latter cases as "Great Zidon." The references to it in Judg. 1: 31, and 18: 28, indicate its military strength.——This prophecy against Zidon is brief; does not specify her sins particularly, but declares that God will be glorified and sanctified in his judgments upon her.*—— These contiguous powers which had been as pricking briers and painful thorns to Israel and which had contemptuously despised her, should be utterly destroyed and be no more. They should be made to know that Jehovah is the living God.

* In v. 23 the verb rendered, "shall be *judged* in the midst of her by the sword," should rather read; *shall fall*—the root of the verb being not בלל, as our translators assumed, but נפל.

25. Thus saith the Lord God; When I shall have gathered the house of Israel from the people among whom they are scattered, and shall be sanctified in them in the sight of the heathen, then shall they dwell in their land that I have given to my servant Jacob.

26. And they shall dwell safely therein, and shall build houses, and plant vineyards; yea, they shall dwell with confidence, when I have executed judgments upon all those that despise them round about them; and they shall know that I *am* the Lord their God.

From these particular cases, the Lord advances to the general truth—"No weapon formed against Zion shall prosper." When the Lord shall gather his people home from their dispersions and shall be sanctified in them before all the heathen, they shall dwell in safety from all their foes. The Lord will surely execute exterminating judgments on all their determined enemies. So true is it that God stands with and for his people, and will surely prove himself their Redeemer and Savior. The world shall yet know his power to save his trusting children, befriend his own cause, and fill all the earth with his glory.

CHAPTER XXIX.

With this chapter commences a series of prophecies against Egypt, filling four chapters. The first begins with the date of "the tenth year, tenth month," etc., one month and eighteen days earlier than the date of the preceding prophecy against Tyre. Both fall within the period of the siege of Jerusalem.——Vs. 17-21 constitute a second part of this chapter, of later date by a fraction over sixteen years. Manifestly this was given to the prophet *after* the thirteen years' siege of Tyre by Nebuchadnezzar had terminated. Since the years of Zedekiah's reign correspond very nearly with the years of Jehoiachin's captivity (the Epoch of Ezekiel) and since the siege of Jerusalem closed in the eleventh year and fourth month of Zedekiah (Jer. 52: 5, 6) the interval between the destruction of Jerusalem and the date of this prophecy is fifteen and two-thirds years. If we may assume that this prophecy (v. 17-21) bears date soon after this "long and hard service" closed, then the famous siege of Tyre must have commenced some two years after the close of the siege of Jerusalem.——The grounds assigned for these judgments upon Pharaoh and Egypt are—(1.) That he had been very proud, had practically disowned God, and put himself in his place:—(2.) That he and his people had been a frail, treacherous staff of help to the Jews—enticing them away from their sworn allegiance to the Chaldeans, to their own ruin; and (3.) To reward Nebuchadnezzar for his unpaid service for the Lord against Tyre.

1. In the tenth year, in the tenth *month*, in the twelfth *day* of the month, the word of the Lord came unto me, saying,

2. Son of man, set thy face against Pharaoh king of Egypt, and prophesy against him, and against all Egypt:

3. Speak, and say, Thus saith the Lord God; Behold, I *am* against thee, Pharaoh king of Egypt, the great dragon that lieth in the midst of his rivers, which hath said, My river *is* mine own, and I have made *it* for myself.

The "great dragon" is the crocodile—almost a speciality to the Nile. But the crocodile of course represents here Egypt's proud king who lies basking in the midst of his rivers, as this animal is wont to do.——It scarcely needs be said that the Nile *makes* Egypt—is the source of all its fertility; the channel for all its commerce; the fountain of all its wealth and subsistence. Without the Nile Egypt were only a desert. Its waters by their annual inundation and by their abundant use in artificial irrigation, beat back the encroaching sands of the desert and insure astonishing fertility. Hence the temptation to Egypt's king to glory in the Nile, and, in the folly of his pride, to claim it as his own, even by creation! Strange folly, and no less strange impiety!——By a striking coincidence Herodotus wrote of this same Pharaoh Hophra (Smith 2: 818) "It is said that Apries," [another form of "Hophra,"] "believed that there was not a god who could cast him down from his eminence, so firmly did he think he had established himself in his kingdom."

4. But I will put hooks in thy jaws, and I will cause the fish of thy rivers to stick unto thy scales; and I will bring thee up out of the midst of thy rivers, and all the fish of thy rivers shall stick unto thy scales.

5. And I will leave thee *thrown* into the wilderness, thee and all the fish of thy rivers: thou shalt fall upon the open fields; thou shalt not be brought together, nor gathered: I have given thee for meat to the beasts of the field and to the fowls of the heaven.

Crocodiles were customarily caught with strong fish-hooks, which being skilfully baited, the animal swallowed. The Lord takes this figure from actual life to indicate how he will seize this proud king and drag him and his princes and the chief of his people who are to stick to his scales, out of his river; cast them abroad upon the dry desert where no fish could live; and there leave them for food to beasts and fowls. This must signify that they are subdued by their enemies, taken captive and brought to a dishonored death. To be left unburied to be devoured by vultures and hyenas fills the oriental and ancient idea of whatever is awful and horrible in death. The classic authors of Greece and Rome are full of this sentiment.

6. And all the inhabitants of Egypt shall know that I *am* the Lord, because they have been a staff of reed to the house of Israel.

7. When they took hold of thee by thy hand, thou didst break, and rend all their shoulder: and when they leaned upon thee, thou brakest, and madest all their loins to be at a stand.

"A staff of reed"—a symbol of what is slender and frail—for a nation to lean upon. When Judah leaned on this staff, it brake; and as they had leaned with their full weight upon it, failing, it rent all their shoulder and made all their loins *to shake*. This seems to be the thought in the last verb, rendered, to "be at a stand."*

8. Therefore thus saith the Lord God; Behold, I will bring a sword upon thee, and cut off man and beast out of thee.

9. And the land of Egypt shall be desolate and waste; and they shall know that I *am* the Lord: because he hath said, The river *is* mine, and I have made *it*.

Of the visible grounds for these fearful judgments, pride was manifestly the chief; here adduced as the only ground; "Because he hath said, The river is mine, and I have made it."——How odious to the Great God must such pride be, and how justly does it evoke judgments such in form and in severity as shall make men, even the proudest of them, *know* that he is God alone!

10. Behold, therefore I *am* against thee, and against thy rivers, and I will make the land of Egypt utterly waste *and* desolate, from the tower of Syene even unto the border of Ethiopia.

11. No foot of man shall pass through it, nor foot of beast shall pass through it, neither shall it be inhabited forty years.

12. And I will make the land of Egypt desolate in the midst of the countries *that are* desolate, and her cities among the cities *that are* laid waste shall be desolate forty years:

---

* The case has its critical difficulties; but the usual sense, *to cause to stand firmly*, is the reverse of what the context requires. Hence there is probably a play upon the word with reference to another verb of the same radical letters but the two first transposed. This other verb has the sense, *to shake*. The change is from עָמֹד *to stand*—to מָעַד *to shake.*

EZEKIEL.—CHAP. XXIX. 165

and I will scatter the Egyptians among the nations, and will disperse them through the countries.

Syene is not (as the reader might suppose) at one extremity of Egypt and "the border of Ethiopia" at the other and opposite; but both are on its southern limit. Syene is on the Nile, on the southern boundary of Egypt. The original reads, "From the tower of Syene, and unto the border of Ethiopia." The enemy came from the north. Of course the northern portion of the country would be laid waste. It was only needful therefore to say that it should be desolated even to its southern border; and to make this border very definite, two points in it are specified. The description shows that this desolation was to be fearful and general.——There can be no reasonable doubt that it was effected by the Chaldean forces under Nebuchadnezzar. See vs. 17-20, and chap. 30: 24, 25, and also Jer. 44: 30, and 46: 25, 26.——Only the most scanty notices of these events have reached us in the channels of profane history. Berosus, the great Chaldean historian, has a fragment which has come down through Josephus (Against Apion 1: 19) to the effect that "Nebuchadnezzar conquered Egypt, Syria, Phenicia, and Arabia, and exceeded in his exploits all that had reigned before him in Babylon and Chaldea."——The duration of this desolate condition ("forty years") would reach forward into the wane of the Chaldean empire, some years later than the death of Nebuchadnezzar, whose reign began with the fourth year of Jehoiakim and continued forty-three years. But this subjugation of Egypt if it followed the fall of Tyre, must have been past the middle point of his reign.

13. Yet thus saith the Lord God; At the end of forty years will I gather the Egyptians from the people whither they were scattered:

14. And I will bring again the captivity of Egypt, and will cause them to return *into* the land of Pathros, into the land of their habitation; and they shall be there a base kingdom.

15. It shall be the basest of the kingdoms; neither shall it exalt itself any more above the nations: for I will diminish them, that they shall no more rule over the nations.

16. And it shall be no more the confidence of the house of Israel, which bringeth *their* iniquity to remembrance, when they shall look after them: but they shall know that I *am* the Lord God.

At the end of forty years, her captivity would cease, and her population return; but her former glory she should never regain. A just doom for her impiety and pride!——"The land of their habitation" is rather (from the original), "the land of their nativity;" the same word used Chap. 16: 3.——V. 16 might be paraphrased, Egypt shall be no more the confidence of the house of Israel which confidence brings to mind their iniquity in their treachery and perjury toward the king of Babylon when they turned from him to the Egyptians' for help, etc.——What is said here of the "baseness of this kingdom" as contrasted with its former greatness and glory, and also in chap. 30: 13; "there shall be no more a prince of the land of Egypt;" has its fulfillment in history in the fact that "from the second Persian conquest, more than two thousand years ago, until our own days, not one native ruler has occupied the throne." See Smith's Bible Dictionary 1: 512. When the prophet wrote, Egypt had been a first-class power from the days of Abraham. Since the fulfillment of this prophecy it has been preëminently "a base kingdom"—for long ages past, scarcely known in the world's history as a kingdom at all. What a testimony is this, not to the *truth* of prophecy alone, but to the fearfulness of God's judgments against kings and nations for their proud impiety in disowning their great Creator and King!

17. And it came to pass in the seven and twentieth year, in the first *month*, in the first *day* of the month, the word of the Lord came unto me, saying,

18. Son of man, Nebuchadrezzar king of Babylon caused his army to serve a great service against Tyrus: every head *was* made bald, and every shoulder *was* peeled: yet had he no wages, nor his army, for Tyrus, for the service that he had served against it:

19. Therefore thus saith the Lord God; Behold, I will give the land of Egypt unto Nebuchadrezzar king of Babylon; and he shall take her multitude, and take her spoil, and take her prey; and it shall be the wages for his army.

20. I have given him the land of Egypt *for* his labor wherewith he served against it, because they wrought for me, saith the Lord God.

The points made here have been mostly discussed in the notes on the prophecies against Tyre, and in the remarks introductory to this chapter.——It is still an unsettled question whether the siege of Tyre closed with its absolute subjugation; or by a capitulation which spared to the people their treasures; or by their removing all their valuables in their ships. The latter is not improbable, and has in its support the testimony (such as it is) of Jerome in his commentary on Ezekiel.——The "hard service" in which "every head was made bald and every shoulder peeled," is accounted for by the manner in which the work was done; viz., by building an immense causeway or road from the main land to the island on which the city stood in order to bring his battering rams and assaulting works close to the city walls. In the state of the arts at that time, the transportation of stone and earth for building this causeway was done on the heads and shoulders of men—reason enough why "every head should be made bald" and the skin of "every shoulder be peeled" and worn.——Remarkably the Lord speaks of this service as being done *for himself*—quite in keeping with those passages in which he calls Nebuchadnezzar "my servant:" see Jer. 25: 9, and 27: 6, and 43: 10. The Lord wished the Jews to understand that he had important ends to answer by this great king of Babylon, as was indeed the case. He was God's instrument for a fearful retribution, not on Judea and Jerusalem alone, but on all the nations of Western Asia and upon Egypt.

21. In that day will I cause the horn of the house of Israel to bud forth, and I will give thee the opening of the mouth in the midst of them; and they shall know that I am the Lord.

"Horn" and "bud" blend two distinct and not altogether homogeneous figures. The "horn" is eminently a symbol of power; while the "budding" and development of vegetables implies growth and beauty. The hopes of Israel would revive, the germ of its nationality would shoot forth afresh at the period here referred to, which would be in the latter years of the captivity in Babylon. As Egypt should go down, Israel should rise. The results of divine discipline would begin to develop themselves in the revived piety of the people, and (we must suppose) in the disappearance of the spirit and practice of idolatry. The passage seems to refer primarily to a period within the lifetime of the prophet, since it is implied that he would be encouraged and emboldened to speak without restraint and with great freedom and, we may hope, unction and success. The captive Jews would see fresh and convincing evidence that their God is truly the Lord Jehovah of Hosts.

CHAPTER XXX.

In this chapter the one theme is judgment on Egypt, yet there are two messages of diverse date; the first comprising vs. 1-19; the second, vs. 20-26. The date of the latter is given definitely (in v. 20); probably that the reader might locate it shortly after the defeat of Pharaoh Hophra when he approached to aid his Jewish friends by an effort to raise the siege of their city, then in progress by the army of Nebuchadnezzar. Critics are not agreed as to the date of the first portion, some connecting it in time with the message chap. 29: 1-16, viz., in the tenth year and tenth month, etc.; others connecting it with the message chap. 29: 17-21, viz., in the twenty-seventh year. I prefer the latter, both because it follows directly with no notice of a different date, and yet more because it represents the final consummation of these fearful judgments as then very near at hand (v. 3). The historical facts are, that the crushing blow from the Chaldean arms fell on Egypt *after* the siege of Tyre had closed, and hence shortly after the prophecy (chap. 29: 17-21) was delivered. Consequently this portion (chap. 30: 1-19) must be assigned to the same date as the five verses next preceding.

1. The word of the Lord came again unto me, saying,
2. Son of man, prophesy and say, Thus saith the Lord God; Howl ye, Wo worth the day!
3. For the day *is* near, even the day of the Lord *is* near, a cloudy day; it shall be the time of the heathen.

The passage in v. 2, "Howl ye," etc., means, Cry aloud in wailing tones, "Wo to the day!" or "Alas, the day!" The former is the literal translation.——"A cloudy day." Darkness is a well-known symbol of calamity.——"The time of the heathen," in the sense of being their day of triumph. The nations hostile to Egypt have their time of vengeance upon her.

4. The sword shall come upon Egypt, and great pain shall be in Ethiopia, when the slain shall fall in Egypt, and they shall take away her multitude, and her foundations shall be broken down.
5. Ethiopia, and Libya, and Lydia, and all the mingled people, and Chub, and the men of the land that is in league, shall fall with them by the sword.

Not Egypt alone but her allies, those powers on the South and West that had been usually associated with her in her great conflicts with the Asiatic powers, now suffer in her fall. Ethiopia on her southern border; Libya and Lydia on her western, are well known as her ancient allies.——Doubt rests on the word "Chub," which occurs in the Scriptures here only. Opinions are divided between Cohen, a part of Ethiopia; Coba or Chobat, a city of Mauritania; and making a slight change in the first letter so as to read it, Nubia. A dearth of the necessary geographical knowledge forbids absolute certainty. The general sense is clear; some city or people of Africa, in alliance with Egypt.

6. Thus saith the Lord; they also that uphold Egypt shall fall; and the pride of her power shall come down: from the tower of Syene shall they fall in it by the sword, saith the Lord God.
7. And they shall be desolate in the midst of the countries *that are* desolate, and her cities shall be in the midst of the cities *that are* wasted.
8. And they shall know that I *am* the Lord, when I have

set a fire in Egypt, and *when* all her helpers shall be destroyed.

Stress is laid on the utter ruin of her helpers, those powerful allies, so long accustomed to make common cause with her against their great and common enemies from the regions of the Euphrates.

9. In that day shall messengers go forth from me in ships to make the careless Ethiopians afraid, and great pain shall come upon them as in the day of Egypt: for lo, it cometh.

The ships referred to were the light-boats that ran far up the Nile to bear the fearful tidings to the Ethiopians, living in fancied security. These tidings would thrill them with terror even as they had the Egyptians when the crash of invasion fell on them.

10. Thus saith the Lord God; I will also make the multitude of Egypt to cease by the hand of Nebuchadrezzar king of Babylon.

11. He and his people with him, the terrible of the nations, shall be brought to destroy the land: and they shall draw their swords against Egypt, and fill the land with the slain.

12. And I will make the rivers dry, and sell the land into the hand of the wicked: and I will make the land waste, and all that is therein, by the hand of strangers: I the Lord have spoken *it*.

The dense population of Egypt would perish by the hand of the king of Babylon. "I will make the rivers dry," is taken by some figuratively in the sense of destroying her resources, which her great river and its numerous canals, cut for irrigation, might well represent. But there is no special objection to taking the words in their literal though modified sense—her rivers becoming so low as to forbid irrigation, and consequently, to insure famine. The Nile is subject to such failures, as *c. g.* in the days of Joseph.

13. Thus saith the Lord God; I will also destroy the idols, and I will cause *their* images to cease out of Noph; and there shall be no more a prince of the land of Egypt: and I will put a fear in the land of Egypt.

14. And I will make Pathros desolate, and will set fire in Zoan, and will execute judgments in No.

15. And I will pour my fury upon Sin, the strength of Egypt; and I will cut off the multitude of No.

16. And I will set fire in Egypt: Sin shall have great pain, and No shall be rent asunder, and Noph *shall have* distresses daily.

17. The young men of Aven, and of Pi-beseth shall fall by the sword: and these *cities* shall go into captivity.

From general statements, the prophet comes to particulars, specifying the several cities that are to feel the weight of this crushing calamity. This is designed and well adapted to strengthen the impression of the fearful facts.——The principal cities of Egypt are here enumerated. They are known by other names also—Greek or Egyptian. These are mostly Hebrew. Hence the following statements may be useful.——"Noph" is also called Memphis; the great city of Lower Egypt, near the Pyramids. "No," or No-Ammon, is Thebes or Diospolis; the great city of Upper Egypt, celebrated for its hundred gates, and even now great in the ruins of its magnificent temples of Luxor, Karnac, etc. "Pathros" is the Egyptian name for Upper Egypt, as Mizraim was sometimes for the lower province. "Zoan" is known in Greek as Tanis, one of the cities of Lower Egypt. "Sin," known by the Greeks as Pelusium, was in the north-eastern extremity of Egypt, the point where their Asiatic enemies would naturally strike first. Hence it was fortified so as to become "the strength of Egypt." Its Hebrew name means a *marsh*, and such it was, and perhaps the stronger therefor. "Aven," doubtless the city "On" of Gen. 41: 45, 50, from which word it differs only in its vowel points, received this form from the Hebrews in contempt for its idols, *nothings*, or vanities—which is the significance of the word thus pronounced. The Greeks called it Heliopolis, city of the sun, which the Hebrews sometimes translated into Bethshemeth, house of the sun. "Pi-beseth," by the Greeks, Bubastis, was on the lower waters of the Nile. Tehaphnehes, the Daphne of the Greeks, was near Pelusium, and seems to have been in these times the residence of the king and his court. See Jer 43: 8–13.——Jeremiah has a prophecy (chap. 46) somewhat analogous to this of Ezekiel.——For the fulfillment of this prophecy, "there shall be no more a prince of the land of Egypt," see notes on chap. 29: 14, 15.——In v. 16, the doom of Noph means, "distress by day," as opposed to the night. Her enemies shall come upon her fearlessly in open day as if perfect masters of their position. Even the proudest cities and the strongest shall be readily subdued with no aid from darkness or surprise.

18. At Tehaphnehes also the day shall be darkened, when I shall break there the yokes of Egypt: and the pomp of her strength shall cease in her: as for her, a cloud shall cover her, and her daughters shall go into captivity.

19. Thus will I execute judgments in Egypt: and they shall know that I *am* the Lord.

The eclipse of Egypt's glory is well represented as falling on the royal city. The darkening of the day and a covering of cloud are analogous figures for extreme calamity. The "pomp of Egypt's strength" would naturally be concentrated about the throne.——

The "yokes of Egypt," if the Hebrew word for yoke is to be retained, must mean her power to enslave her captives, or to hold in subjection foreign tribes or peoples. But the context strongly favors a slight change in the vowels which would make the word mean *rods*, or *scepters*. In this way the sense of the clause would be, the breaking down of regal power in the land. Remarkably the ancient versions give this sense.

20. And it came to pass in the eleventh year, in the first *month*, in the seventh *day* of the month, *that* the word of the Lord came unto me, saying,

21. Son of man, I have broken the arm of Pharaoh king of Egypt; and, lo, it shall not be bound up to be healed, to put a roller to bind it, to make it strong to hold the sword.

22. Therefore thus saith the Lord God; Behold, I *am* against Pharaoh king of Egypt, and will break his arms, the strong, and that which was broken; and I will cause the sword to fall out of his hand.

23. And I will scatter the Egyptians among the nations, and will disperse them through the countries.

24. And I will strengthen the arms of the king of Babylon, and put my sword in his hand: but I will break Pharaoh's arms, and he shall groan before him with the groanings of a deadly wounded *man*.

25. But I will strengthen the arms of the king of Babylon, and the arms of Pharaoh shall fall down; and they shall know that I *am* the Lord, when I shall put my sword into the hand of the king of Babylon, and he shall stretch it out upon the land of Egypt.

26. And I will scatter the Egyptians among the nations, and disperse them among the countries; and they shall know that I *am* the Lord.

As said above in the introduction to this chapter, this prophecy was probably suggested by the defeat of Pharaoh Hophra when he attempted to force Nebuchadnezzar to raise the siege of Jerusalem. See Jer. 44: 30: "I will give Pharaoh Hophra king of Egypt into the hands of his enemies and into the hands of them that seek his life, as I gave Zedekiah into the hands of Nebuchadnezzar," etc. Suggested by this defeat, it probably followed it closely in time. This was only some three months before the fall of the city of Jerusalem—the latter event being in the eleventh year and fourth month and ninth day (Jer. 52: 5, 6), and this, in the eleventh year, first month and seventh day.——The breaking of Pharaoh's sword-arm first, hopelessly past cure; then the breaking of both his arms, and the strengthening of the arms of Nebuchadnezzar and putting the sword into it for the execution of God's judgments—are the leading figures of this passage.——Some critics interpret the two arms of Egypt's king to be two portions of his territory; others, two royal families: but the general sense, his military power, his means of resisting his great Chaldean enemy—is more natural and probable. The sword is the appropriate emblem of military strength.—— Here, as often elsewhere, we have the king of Babylon "the servant of the Lord." The curse of Egypt includes a great slaughter of her people and their dispersion into foreign lands.

CHAPTER XXXI.

This chapter is one distinct and entire message, presenting under the figure of a cedar of Lebanon the case of Assyria, as a lesson of warning to Egypt. If Assyria, so splendid and magnificent in her greatness, yet went down with a crash that astounded the nations, what, O Pharaoh, shall be thy doom? Be not so vain as to imagine that thy greatness and glory, so obviously less than those of Assyria, can insure thee against a like terrible fall!——This message dates only one month and a fraction before the fall of Jerusalem. The fall of Assyria, referred to here as a fact of past history, occurred B. C. 625; *i. e.*, thirty-seven years before the date of this message. Hence it was still fresh in the minds of Ezekiel's readers.——The figure which is finely sustained throughout the chapter is one of exquisite beauty. The Assyrian power was a noble cedar of Lebanon, lofty and fair, of far outspreading magnificent foliage; his roots reaching out to living waters; all the fowls of heaven nestled in his boughs; all the beasts of the field made their homes under his shade;—but he became proud, and God laid him low, and brought him down to the under-world, even as mortals die and go down to the shades beneath.——Art thou, O Egypt, great like this Assyrian cedar? If in thy vanity thou hast compared thyself to proud Assyria, think whether for thy pride thou shalt not suffer an equally terrible fall!——The reader will recall the similar figure (chap. 17) where the king of Judah appears as a young cedar; also in Dan. 4, where a vast, magnificent tree represents the greatness and glory of Nebuchadnezzar. The latter case suffices to show that this figure is Chaldean, and hence entirely appropriate for Ezekiel to use in addressing his brethren residing there.

1. And it came to pass in the eleventh year, in the third *month*, in the first *day* of the month, *that* the word of the Lord came unto me, saying,

2. Son of man, speak unto Pharaoh king of Egypt, and to his multitude; Whom art thou like in thy greatness?

3. Behold, the Assyrian *was* a cedar in Lebanon with fair branches, and with a shadowing shroud, and of an high stature; and his top was among the thick boughs.

"Whom art thou like in thy greatness?" "Behold;" look at this case of the Assyrian power, well known to Egypt; for ages her great rival and military antagonist. Is thy greatness more than hers?——He then proceeds to set forth the splendors of the great Assyrian empire.——In v. 3, "with a shadowing shroud," means with foliage casting a deep shade. In the clause, "his top among the thick boughs," the word for *top* means the woolly *tuft*, crowning the summit of its foliage. Hengstenberg claims that the word rendered "*thick boughs*" means "*the clouds;*" his tuft lay among the clouds. The same clause occurs elsewhere only in vs. 10, 14, and chap. 19: 11. To say only that his top was among the thick boughs implies equality in height with other trees, and not superiority, and consequently does not meet the demands of the context. Hence, "among the clouds," is better.

4. The waters made him great, the deep set him up on high with her rivers running round about his plants, and sent out her little rivers unto all the trees of the field.

5. Therefore his height was exalted above all the trees of the field, and his boughs were multiplied, and his branches became long because of the multitude of waters, when he shot forth.

6. All the fowls of heaven made their nests in his boughs, and under his branches did all the beasts of the field bring forth their young, and under his shadow dwelt all great nations.

7. Thus was he fair in his greatness, in the length of his branches: for his root was by great waters.

A supply of water in that climate insured exuberant fertility. ——In a few instances the prophet drops his figure and gives his thought in literal terms; *e. g.*, "under his shadow dwelt all great nations," *i. e.*, enjoying his military protection and paying him tribute. This was the relation sustained in those ages by the smaller powers to the great central one. Assyria, Chaldea, and Persia, were successively such central powers.

8. The cedars in the garden of God could not hide him: the fir trees were not like his boughs, and the chestnut trees were not like his branches; not any tree in the garden of God was like unto him in his beauty.

9. I have made him fair by the multitude of his branches: so that all the trees of Eden, that *were* in the garden of God, envied him.

The prophet thinks of Eden, the garden of God, as a model of superlative fertility and beauty. This and similar allusions (*e. g.*, chap. 28: 13) show that the Jews of that age had some knowledge of the primeval state of man, doubtless as much as has come down to us in the account given by Moses in Genesis. It is safe to assume that they had this.——"These cedars in the garden of God could not *hide* him," in the sense of overshadowing and surpassing him in their beauty and their shade.——"Chestnut," Gesenius renders—the "plane-tree."

10. Therefore thus saith the Lord God; Because thou hast lifted up thyself in height, and he hath shot up his top among the thick boughs, and his heart is lifted up in his height;

11. I have therefore delivered him into the hand of the mighty one of the heathen; he shall surely deal with him: I have driven him out for his wickedness.

12. And strangers, the terrible of the nations, have cut him off, and have left him: upon the mountains and in all the valleys his branches are fallen, and his boughs are broken by all the rivers of the land; and all the people of the earth are gone down from his shadow, and have left him.

13. Upon his ruin shall all the fowls of the heaven remain, and all the beasts of the field shall be upon his branches:

14. To the end that none of all the trees by the waters exalt themselves for their height, neither shoot up their top among the thick boughs, neither their trees stand up in their height, all that drink water: for they are all delivered unto death, to the nether parts of the earth, in the midst of the children of men, with them that go down to the pit.

Here again the prophet blends literal with figurative language; *e. g.*, "his heart is lifted up in his height," v. 10; also in v. 11, and part of v. 12. The change of person from "thou" to "he" is not uncommon in Hebrew and does not necessarily involve any change in the personage whose pride is here described.——This terrible example of ruin had for its moral purpose to admonish all other great trees of like magnificence that they be not proud and vain, for they are all doomed to die. The greatest and proudest nations must go down, like frail mortal men, to the under-world, the pit. The phrase, "the nether parts of the earth," is more strictly, the "under-world," according to the opinions of the ancients that this was the locality of the dead.

15. Thus saith the Lord God; In the day when he went down to the grave I caused a mourning, I covered the deep

for him, and I restrained the floods thereof, and the great waters were stayed: and I caused Lebanon to mourn for him, and all the trees of the field fainted for him.

This is graphic and beautiful. In the day when this proud cedar fell, I the Lord shrouded the deep in mourning for him (the deep with its great waters had set him up on high, v. 4), and I restrained its waters, and made Lebanon mourn over the loss of her preëminent glory.——The trees of the field were languid, faint of heart, in view of his fall, thinking of their own possible, perhaps probable, doom!

16. I made the nations to shake at the sound of his fall, when I cast him down to hell with them that descend into the pit: and all the trees of Eden, the choice and best of Lebanon, all that drink water, shall be comforted in the nether parts of the earth.

17. They also went down into hell with him unto *them that be* slain with the sword; and *they that were* his arm, *that* dwelt under his shadow in the midst of the heathen.

The trees of Eden are "comforted," probably in the sense of a satisfaction to their envious feelings (v. 9); a sort of revenge upon him for his great pride, like the feeling which Isaiah (14: 9-16) imputes to the kings of the nations in the under-world when they see great Lucifer coming down to their land of weakness and shade; "Art *thou* become weak as we?"——In v. 17, "they that were his arm," his military strength—allied or tributary nations, who had dwelt under his shadow—now go down with him to the pit of destruction.

18. To whom art thou thus like in glory and in greatness among the trees of Eden? yet shalt thou be brought down with the trees of Eden unto the nether parts of the earth: thou shalt lie in the midst of the uncircumcised with *them that be* slain by the sword. This *is* Pharaoh and all his multitude, saith the Lord God.

In this question—"To whom art thou thus like," etc., I understand the prophet to turn from the Assyrian cedar to his Egyptian rival. Art thou as great as this proud Assyrian, or greater? Know thou that if thy pride is great like his, thy doom must needs be fearfully appalling no less than his. The mighty God before whom great Assyria could not stand is equally able to bring down thy greatness, paralyze thy power, and cast thee into that under-world where the silence of death reigns supreme!——So puny are the mightiest nations when they measure arms with the Great God! So vain it is for any of them, even the most magnificent in splendor, to lift themselves up against their Infinite Maker and Lord!

CHAPTER XXXII.

This chapter in two distinct messages, viz., vs. 1–16 and vs. 17–32, with each its distinct date, completes the prophecy concerning the fall of Egypt before the arms of Nebuchadnezzar. The date of the first portion is seven months and a fraction after the fall of Jerusalem; the second portion is still fifteen days later; for the month not being mentioned, we must assume it to be the same as in v. 1.——The danger to Egypt from the Chaldean arms was manifestly greater and more obvious *after* the fall of Jerusalem than at any time before. Whether the Chaldeans invaded Egypt near this time and before their long siege of Tyre, remains in some doubt. Profane history at this period affords only the most scanty records. That they swept over Egypt with terrible devastation *after* their work on Tyre was finished, admits of no doubt. It is not improbable that they made a raid upon their old enemy before they invested Tyre.

1. And it came to pass in the twelfth year, in the twelfth month, in the first *day* of the month, *that* the word of the Lord came unto me, saying,

2. Son of man, take up a lamentation for Pharaoh king of Egypt, and say unto him, Thou art like a young lion of the nations, and thou *art* as a whale in the seas; and thou camest forth with thy rivers, and troubledst the waters with thy feet, and fouledst their rivers.

"Take up a lamentation"—prepare a mourning elegy which may be sung as a dirge over his fall. It was appropriate in such a dirge to celebrate the valor and recount the great deeds of the dead. In the present case the prophet is not excessively eulogistic. God loves truth.——Kings often compare themselves and are compared to a lion—first in power and terror among the beasts of the wilderness. Solomon says, "The king's wrath is as the roaring of a lion (Prov. 19: 12). Isaiah has the same figure (chap. 5: 29, 30).——A second figure makes him "a whale in the sea," as our translators have it; but they have rendered the same Hebrew word (chap. 29: 3) "the great dragon." In both cases, we must think of the crocodile—the speciality of the Nile.——"Thou *camest forth*," has the strong sense, thou didst *rush* forth as an armed host to the battle, breaking out from thy rivers. Pharaoh and his multitude are thought of as *fouling* the Nile and its disparted mouths and numerous canals with their feet—perhaps in the sense of abusing the blessings God had given them in that noble river.

3. Thus saith the Lord God; I will therefore spread out my net over thee with a company of many people; and they shall bring thee up in my net.

4. Then will I leave thee upon the land, I will cast thee forth upon the open field, and will cause all the fowls of the heaven to remain upon thee, and I will fill the beasts of the whole earth with thee.

5. And I will lay thy flesh upon the mountains, and fill the valleys with thy height:

6. I will also water with thy blood the land wherein thou swimmest, *even* to the mountains; and the rivers shall be full of thee.

Consequently, with the aid of many people (the Chaldeans), the Lord will take up this monster crocodile, Pharaoh, in his net, and leave him cast out upon the land in the open field, meat for fowls and beasts.——"Fill the valley with thy *height*," is rather, with the *heaps* of thy dead, for the doom of Pharaoh involves the destruction of his people. Gesenius and Maurer suggest a slight change in the vowels by which the word would mean, *worms* that would feed on the carcasses of the slain Egyptians.——"The land wherein thou swimmest" is literally the *land of thine inundations*—the region inundated by the Nile, which having been the great object of their pride (see chap. 29: 3) should be made prominent in God's judgments. Hence the Lord said, "I will make this whole land even to the mountain-tops drink thy blood," and the river of which thou hast been so proud shall be filled with it.

7. And when I shall put thee out, I will cover the heaven, and make the stars thereof dark ; I will cover the sun with a cloud, and the moon shall not give her light.

8. All the bright lights of heaven will I make dark over thee, and set darkness upon thy land, saith the Lord God.

The figure changes. Calamity is here represented by darkness, perhaps with a tacit reference to the plague of darkness (Ex. 10: 21-23). "When I shall put them out;" meaning, extinguish them from being a light among the nations. Cloud and eclipse combine to shut off the lights of heaven and to doom the land to thick darkness. This figure appears frequently in the poetic portions of the Bible, sometimes in the strong form of "turning the sun into darkness and the moon into blood." See Isa. 13: 10, and Joel 2: 10, 30, 31, and 3: 15. The general sense is the same throughout all these variations of the figure, viz., exceeding great calamity, fearful ruin. Light is a natural emblem of joy and prosperity; darkness, of whatever is fearful and appalling.

9. I will also vex the hearts of many people, when I shall bring thy destruction among the nations, into the countries which thou hast not known.

10. Yea, I will make many people amazed at thee, and their kings shall be horribly afraid for thee, when I shall

brandish my sword before them; and they shall tremble at *every* moment, every man for his own life, in the day of thy fall.

This is the effect of Pharaoh's fall upon other nations, even those whom he had little known, lying out beyond the range of his influence. This reference implies that the fall of Egypt would impress the fear of the Chaldean arms upon remote nations.——" When I shall bring thy destruction among the nations," *i. e.*, shall cause the *report* of it to go forth to them. They shall fear exceedingly for their own lives.

11. For thus saith the Lord God; The sword of the king of Babylon shall come upon thee.

12. By the swords of the mighty will I cause thy multitude to fall, the terrible of the nations, all of them: and they shall spoil the pomp of Egypt, and all the multitude thereof shall be destroyed.

The prophecy is here entirely definite. The conquering, wasting power is the Chaldean. They shall spoil the glory of Egypt, waste her treasures, pillage her cities, break down her national strength, and lay her land for the time quite desolate.

13. I will destroy also all the beasts thereof from beside the great waters; neither shall the foot of man trouble them any more, nor the hoofs of beasts trouble them.

14. Then will I make their waters deep, and cause their rivers to run like oil, saith the Lord God.

15. When I shall make the land of Egypt desolate, and the country shall be destitute of that whereof it was full, when I shall smite all them that dwell therein, then shall they know that I *am* the Lord.

The cattle for which Egypt was celebrated, and of which she thought so much that the cow was the highest object of her worship, came under this sweeping curse. We shall see the force of the language if we consider how their want of water would bring them to the rivers and canals to drink, and how they would poach the banks and foul the waters with their feet. But God would so completely destroy them that no foot of beast or of man should foul those waters any more.——"Then will I" (v. 14) make their waters, not "deep," but *quiet*, causing them to subside and lie undisturbed, so that they would run freely and clear as oil.

16. This *is* the lamentation wherewith they shall lament her; the daughters of the nations shall lament her: they shall lament for her, *even* for Egypt, and for all her multitude, saith the Lord God.

"The daughters of the nations." Women in oriental life were the professional mourners. See Jer. 9: 17-21.

17. It came to pass also in the twelfth year, in the fifteenth *day* of the month, *that* the word of the Lord came unto me, saying,

18. Son of man, wail for the multitude of Egypt, and cast them down, *even* her, and the daughters of the famous nations, unto the nether parts of the earth, with them that go down into the pit.

19. Whom dost thou pass in beauty? go down, and be thou laid with the uncircumcised.

20. They shall fall in the midst of *them that are* slain by the sword: she is delivered to the sword: draw her and all her multitudes.

This entire second message commencing here constitutes another elegy over the fall of Egypt.——In v. 18, "cast them down," means —*predict* their fall; the prophets being said to *do* what they simply predict as to be done. So Jer. 1: 10, and elsewhere.——These allusions to the under-world as in chap. 26: 20, are based on the popular view that the dead go at death to subterranean regions. Nations are thought of here as going to the same under-world when they fall. David thought of his enemies as going there (Ps. 63: 9), and the writer of Ps. 88: 4-6, seems to have used this conception to represent an extreme prostration, yet short of actual death. But the leading passage, specially in the mind of our prophet, is doubtless Isa. 14.——"Whom dost thou pass [surpass] in beauty?" No matter how much thou mayest have surpassed the wealthiest and proudest nations of thy time: thine end is to go down to that under-world of darkness and gloom, to be laid with the uncircumcised heathen nations for whom God has no special favor.——The clause, "She is delivered to the sword," may better be read; "the sword is delivered," *i. e.*, to thine enemies—put into their hand for thy destruction. "Drag her out"—bring her forth from her strong-holds, and slay her utterly.

21. The strong among the mighty shall speak to him out of the midst of hell with them that help him: they are gone down, they lie uncircumcised, slain by the sword.

The sense is, The strongest of his mighty ones shall accost him and his helpers, from the midst of hell. They have already gone down and are lying there, the uncircumcised, slain with the sword. ——The reference here to Isa. 14 is obvious. "Hell from beneath is moved for thee to meet thee at thy coming: it stirreth up the dead for thee, even all the chief ones of the earth; it hath raised up from their thrones all the kings of the nations. All they shall speak and say unto thee, Art thou also become weak as we? Art thou become like unto us? Thy pomp is brought down to the grave, and the noise of thy viols: the worm is spread under thee, and the worms cover thee. How art thou fallen from heaven, O Lucifer, son of the morning! how art thou cut down to the ground, which didst weaken the nations!"

22. Asshur *is* there and all her company: his graves *are* about him: all of them slain, fallen by the sword:

23. Whose graves are set in the sides of the pit, and her company is round about her grave: all of them slain, fallen by the sword, which caused terror in the land of the living.

The general statement, "the strong among the mighty," here becomes specific, and first names Assyria, the ancient rival and enemy of Egypt. She has been destroyed already and lies there with her hosts.——"In the *sides* of the pit;" the deep recesses, the lowest depths. In Jer. 6: 22, "The *sides* of the earth" are the most remote regions. So also Jer. 25: 32. The same word is used for the inner part of a house or a ship, 1 Kings 6: 16, Amos 6: 10, and Jon. 1: 15.——In her day Assyria was mighty on the earth and smote the hearts of the nations with terror. Now "none so poor to do her reverence." Let Egypt take warning!

24. There *is* Elam and all her multitude round about her grave, all of them slain, fallen by the sword, which are gone down uncircumcised into the nether parts of the earth, which caused their terror in the land of the living; yet have they borne their shame with them that go down to the pit.

25. They have set her a bed in the midst of the slain with all her multitude: her graves *are* round about him: all of them uncircumcised, slain by the sword: though their terror was caused in the land of the living, yet have they borne their shame with them that go down to the pit: he is put in the midst of *them that be* slain.

Elam has suffered overthrow: her nationality has been smitten. Let her be added to the list of the great nations in the under-world, ready to meet Egypt when she comes down to the same abode. Elam has had her day of power, a terror to the living nations; but she also bears the shame of those who go down to a dishonored national grave.

26. There *is* Meshech, Tubal, and all her multitude: her graves are round about him: all of them uncircumcised, slain by the sword, though they caused their terror in the land of the living.

27. And they shall not lie with the mighty *that are* fallen of the uncircumcised, that are gone down to hell with their weapons of war: and they have laid their swords under

their heads; but their iniquities shall be upon their bones, though *they were* the terror of the mighty in the land of the living.

28. Yea, thou shalt be broken in the midst of the uncircumcised, and shalt lie down with *them that are* slain by the sword.

For "Meshech and Tubal," see chap. 27: 13.——V. 27 should obviously commence with an interrogation; Shall not all these lie with the mighty? There is no apparent reason why the negative sense should be taken here in opposition to the general strain of the entire context.——It was one of the honors paid to conquerors to bury their weapons of war in the same grave with themselves. So Alexander the Great was buried with his sword. This usage suggests to the prophet that their iniquities also lie upon their bones—those iniquities for which God has doomed them to such an extermination from the land of the living.

29. There *is* Edom, her kings, and all her princes, which with their might are laid by *them that were* slain by the sword: they shall lie with the uncircumcised, and with them that go down to the pit.

30. There *be* the princes of the north, all of them, and all the Zidonians, which are gone down with the slain: with their terror they are ashamed of their might; and they lie uncircumcised with *them that be* slain by the sword, and bear their shame with them that go down to the pit.

Edom, with the nations of the north, including the Zidonians, fill out the catalogue. Essentially the same points are made in regard to each and all. They have been subdued and broken; their nationality eclipsed if not extinguished under the righteous judgments of the Almighty, and they lie in the under-world ready to greet Egypt's proud king, representing her fallen nationality, when he shall come to join them.——In the middle clause of v. 30, "with their terror they are ashamed of their might," I understand to mean that despite of their *terribleness* once among the nations of men, they are now ashamed of their might—thoroughly weak and powerless.

31. Pharaoh shall see them, and shall be comforted over all his multitude, *even* Pharaoh and all his army slain by the sword, saith the Lord God.

32. For I have caused my terror in the land of the living: and he shall be laid in the midst of the uncircumcised with *them that are* slain with the sword, *even* Pharaoh and all his multitude, saith the Lord God.

Pharaoh shall have the comfort of whatever sympathy the fellowship in shame and defeat of such nations as these may afford.——

V. 32 may be translated, "For I have made him a terror [to other nations] in the land of the living; but now [prospectively] he is laid out .[in his narrow bed] in the midst of the uncircumcised," etc. The prophet marks the contrast between the terror he once impressed on the nations, and his utter powerlessness now in his final house in the under-world.——This poetic drapery thrown round the idea of an extinct nationality—a nation itself dying out from among the powers of the earth under the righteous judgments of God—is grand and impressive. Its lessons belong to all time. The nations of our own age who become great in military power, magnificent in their wealth and splendor, and then forget God, disown his authority, and plant their foot upon his higher law and oppress his suffering poor, have ample cause for fear and trembling. Are they mighty against the Great God? Can they evade the search of his eye and cope with the might of his arm? Or can they bring his views of right and justice down to their own? Or will they scoff at the very idea of his rule over the nations of men? Let them ponder the lessons he has given them in his holy word, confirmations of which are written also on all the face of the world's history since nations began to be, to this hour. Can there be a greater madness than to dare Jehovah's wrath?

CHAPTER XXXIII.

This chapter has a manifest unity of purpose throughout, its aim considered as a series of revelations from God to the prophet being first to impress his own mind with a just sense of his responsibility for the souls of the people, and then to give him certain messages which demanded precisely this conscious sense of responsibility, and this true fidelity in their deliverance to the people.——The messages to be borne to the people were, (1.) An earnest rebuke and refutation of the charge against God of crushing the people down under his judgments in a way to crush out all hope from their souls (vs. 10–20.): (2.) A message respecting the survivors in the land of Judah, designed to slay their false hopes and open their eyes both to their own sins and to the certain ruin of their own land; and (3.) A rebuke of the heartless but nicely-critical *hearing* of the people in exile.——In a moral and spiritual point of view, the chapter is one of the highest interest and value, bearing with immense power on the spiritual life of the people among whom Ezekiel labored, and applying with equal force to the spiritual state of multitudes in every gospel land.

1. Again the word of the Lord came unto me, saying,
2. Son of man, speak to the children of thy people, and say unto them, When I bring the sword upon a land, if the people of the land take a man of their coasts, and set him for their watchman:

3. If when he seeth the sword come upon the land, he blow the trumpet, and warn the people;

4. Then, whosoever heareth the sound of the trumpet, and taketh not warning; if the sword come and take him away, his blood shall be upon his own head.

5. He heard the sound of the trumpet, and took not warning; his blood shall be upon him. But he that taketh warning shall deliver his soul.

6. But if the watchman see the sword come, and blow not the trumpet, and the people be not warned; if the sword come, and take *any* person from among them, he is taken away in his iniquity; but his blood will I require at the watchman's hand.

In view of the predatory and nomadic habits of that age and country, the business of the watchman is drawn here to the life. He does not stand on some lofty tower or battlement of the walled city; but he is a scout, far out on the borders of the land, on the mountain tops, where his practiced eye will command a sweep of the great traveled routes which an invading foe must take. Then, trumpet in hand, he is ready to give the shrill and long notes of danger when he sees the sword of some invading foe approaching. ——The received translation of v. 2, "A man of their coasts;" implies that the watchman would be chosen from those who resided on the borders of the land. A slightly different sense of the Hebrew word rendered "coasts" is admissible and preferable, viz., a *man of their whole number*—one of their men. This word is so used in Gen. 47: 2; "He took five out of the whole number of his brethren." Also Num. 22: 41. "Balak brought Balaam up into the high places of Baal that there he might see the *utmost part* of the people"—the whole mass. Literally it means, to the very *end* of them; which implies seeing them all.——The same illustration of the moral duty and responsibility of the Lord's prophets and indeed of all his ministering servants appears chap. 3: 17–21. The case supposed and its application are entirely clear. When it is made a man's special duty to give warning of danger, when the life of a nation depends on his faithfulness, he has but one course to think of; he must be on the alert to mark approaching danger, and must be faithful to make it known to his people. Else the blood of souls will be required of him. If he does this duty faithfully, and the people, duly warned, give no heed to his warnings, their blood will be on their own head. He has done his duty and they die in their folly and under their own righteous curse.——So every minister of the gospel, and indeed every Christian man or woman, each in their own sphere, bear responsibilities for others' souls. If they see others in sin, exposed to perdition, they are solemnly bound to give them warning of this most fearful of all possible dangers. In love to their souls, under the bonds of our broad comprehensive relationship as fellow-travelers onward to a world of eternal retribution, there can be no exemption from this responsibility. Special circumstances may intensify it, but no possible circumstances can exempt any human being, intelligent of obligation, from the duty of warning faithfully whomsoever he may see in this danger. It is a responsibility too solemn to be trifled with; too momentous in its results to be treated with indifference; too positive and pressing to be safely evaded. Alas! that so few are found faithful!

7. So thou, O son of man, I have set thee a watchman unto the house of Israel; therefore thou shalt hear the word at my mouth, and warn them from me.

8. When I say unto the wicked, O wicked *man*, thou shalt surely die; if thou dost not speak to warn the wicked from his way, that wicked *man* shall die in his iniquity; but his blood will I require at thy hand.

9. Nevertheless, if thou warn the wicked of his way to turn from it; if he do not turn from his way, he shall die in his iniquity; but thou hast delivered thy soul.

The Lord himself makes the application of this case of the watchman. It needs no further explanation. The analogy is full of pertinence and force.

10. Therefore, O thou son of man, speak unto the house of Israel; Thus ye speak, saying, If our transgressions and our sins *be* upon us, and we pine away in them, how should we then live?

"Therefore," implies that the prophet's responsibilities come into play at once as a watchman in rebuking this slanderous imputation upon the justice and goodness of God. Since you are such a watchman over my people Israel, note the spirit of this saying of theirs, sift its meaning and its implications to the bottom, and then solemnly warn the people not to delude themselves and not to impugn the goodness and justice of God by this implied charge.——
"If our transgressions and our sins be *upon us*"—made fast and pressing us down hopelessly—"and we pine away in them"— doomed to waste away to utter ruin under their crushing weight— "how should we then live?" Where is the hope for us? What can we do but lie down and die? Doomed to become waste and desolate for the sins of the nation, what hope can we have of life? ——Twice the Lord had used the same word of the doom of the people that is here rendered, "*pine away*," viz., chap. 4: 17—rendered, "consume away for their iniquities;" and chap. 24: 23, in precisely the same words; "Ye shall pine away in your iniquities." Hence the *occasion* (not the justification, but only the occasion) for this plea of a hopeless doom, which assumed that God was heartlessly severe and which ignored his repeated promise of mercy to

EZEKIEL.—CHAP. XXXIII.

the penitent. Hence the Lord replies as one abused and wronged by an unjust implication.

11. Say unto them, *As* I live saith the Lord God, I have no pleasure in the death of the wicked; but that the wicked turn from his way and live: turn ye, turn ye from your evil ways; for why will ye die, O house of Israel?

This implied charge touched the character and the heart of God in a tender point. Nothing could be so cruelly unjust! Had not their own God and Father loved them and borne with them in all long-suffering and with exceedingly great compassion? Had he ever said or done any thing which could with any fairness be construed to imply that he had pleasure in the death of the wicked? Never! On the contrary he had always shown that his heart was with the penitent, and his highest joy in those who turned, sorrowing for their sins, to implore his mercy. Had he not besought them to turn from their wicked ways and live? Had not his heart and hand labored for this result? Had he ever turned coldly away from those who humbly sought his mercy? Never. So he declares here, under the solemnities of his oath, affirming his innocence of the cruel charge which the people had by implication brought against him, and again placing the issue between themselves and him on its true merits—himself entreating them to turn and live, and manifesting his most tender solicitude to secure their obedience and life, so that he shall not be compelled to enforce his fearful judgments in retribution unto their swift destruction.——"Why will ye die?" puts the issue where it truly lies—in the free choice of responsible moral agents. Every exhortation and entreaty from the Lord had fully implied their power as rational and moral beings to see their sins and God's righteous claims, and to yield their heart to the force of his appeals. This question rests the case on their own free purpose and choice. If ye die under my earnest entreaties that ye turn and live, it will be because ye *will die!* It will *not* be because I have doomed you to a hopeless death despite of any efforts you may make toward life. It will *not* be because I have any pleasure in your death and feel no interest in your repentance unto life. It will be only and wholly because, with life and death both before you for your own free choice, you will choose death!

12. Therefore, thou son of man, say unto the children of thy people, The righteousness of the righteous shall not deliver him in the day of his transgression: as for the wickedness of the wicked, he shall not fall thereby in the day that he turneth from his wickedness; neither shall the righteous be able to live for his *righteousness* in the day that he sinneth.

13. When I shall say to the righteous, *that* he shall surely live; if he trust to his own righteousness, and commit iniquity,

all his righteousness shall not be remembered; but for his iniquity that he hath committed, he shall die for it.

14. Again, when I say unto the wicked, Thou shalt surely die; if he turn from his sin, and do that which is lawful and right;

15. *If* the wicked restore the pledge, give again that he had robbed, walk in the statutes of life, without committing iniquity; he shall surely live, he shall not die.

16. None of his sins that he hath committed shall be mentioned unto him: he hath done that which is lawful and right; he shall surely live.

17. Yet the children of thy people say, The way of the Lord is not equal: but as for them, their way is not equal.

18. When the righteous turneth from his righteousness, and committeth iniquity, he shall even die thereby.

19. But if the wicked turn from his wickedness, and do that which is lawful and right, he shall live thereby.

20. Yet ye say, The way of the Lord is not equal. O ye house of Israel, I will judge you every one after his ways.

See chap. 18, where the same points are made with even greater fullness and more ample repetition.——The bearing of these statements to the point now in hand is obvious. The Lord insists that he holds the door most fully open for the repentance of every sinner. If he will turn from his wickedness to cordial obedience, he shall surely live. If he turns from a just and upright life to sin, he shall certainly die. If the people charge their God with injustice in his ways, he denies the charge, and avers that *their* ways are utterly unjust and unequal toward himself. His judgments of them will evermore be precisely according to their ways.

21. And it came to pass in the twelfth year of our captivity, in the tenth *month*, in the fifth *day* of the month, *that* one that had escaped out of Jerusalem came unto me, saying, The city is smitten.

22. Now the hand of the Lord was upon me in the evening, before he that was escaped came; and had opened my mouth, until he came to me in the morning; and my mouth was opened, and I was no more dumb.

The most obvious mode of reckoning makes this period about one and a half years after the fall of the city. Consequently some have supposed there must be an error in the text, since they assume that the news of that event must have reached the prophet and his brethren in Chaldea long ere this. Yet this may possibly have been his first intelligence of the fall of the city, delayed so long by causes unknown to us. It should be noted that the word revealed from the Lord (vs. 24-29) came to meet a feeling among the scattered remnant in Judea which developed itself some time subsequent to the fall of the city. Hence the date as here given is doubtless correct.——V. 22 implies that during the evening and night previous to the arrival of this messenger, the Lord had remarkably opened his mouth to speak—perhaps by impressing his own solemn responsibilities as a prophet-watchman, in the line of the thought in vs. 1–9; and perhaps also in anticipation of the effect of these tidings upon the people. The fall of the city could scarcely fail to make solemn impressions on the exiles. It would create a crisis, demanding the most urgent pressure of truth upon their heart and conscience. Many of their cherished worldly hopes were thereby utterly blasted; could they be brought now to abandon all such hopes and seek their good in the Lord alone?——Such crises occur in the life of communities, and of individuals also, in which if the servants of God are in true communion with him they will find their souls deeply moved with zeal and love, and their mouths opened to press the truth of God upon men for their salvation. The philosophy of revivals of religion turns on this great law of the divine administration in providence and grace.

23. Then the word of the Lord came unto me, saying,

24. Son of man, they that inhabit those wastes of the land of Israel speak, saying, Abraham was one, and he inherited the land: but we *are* many; the land is given us for inheritance.

Those who were then "inhabiting the wastes of the land of Israel" were the small remnant of poor men that survived the fall of the city. Jeremiah has given their history in chaps. 40–44. They are seen here deluding themselves with the hope that the land was given them for their permanent inheritance. Their argument ran thus: Abraham was but one man; yet God gave him this whole land by promise, and all he could use, in fact. We are many; certainly he will give it to us to re-people and to restore to its former greatness.——Ah, how could they overlook the contrast between Abraham's faith in God and their unbelief; Abraham's conscientious, consistent, most exemplary piety, and their persistent, deep-rooted, and unutterably loathsome iniquity! They seem not to have had the slightest sense of the moral grounds on which God gave Abraham the land of Canaan.

25. Wherefore say unto them, Thus saith the Lord God; Ye eat with the blood, and lift up your eyes toward your idols, and shed blood: and shall ye possess the land?

26. Ye stand upon your sword, ye work abomination, and ye defile every one his neighbor's wife: and shall ye possess the land?

27. Say thou thus unto them, Thus saith the Lord God; As I live, surely they that *are* in the wastes shall fall by the sword, and him that *is* in the open field will I give to the beasts to be devoured, and they that *be* in the forts and in the caves shall die of the pestilence.

28. For I will lay the land most desolate, and the pomp of her strength shall cease; and the mountains of Israel shall be desolate, that none shall pass through.

29. Then shall they know that I *am* the Lord, when I have laid the land most desolate because of all their abominations which they have committed.

The Lord's reply is in two parts: (1.) To show them their sin and appeal to their moral sense whether they could or ought to possess the land (vs. 25, 26;) and (2.) To declare most solemnly that he would give them to the sword and the land to utter desolation, until they should know that he is the Lord, the righteous Ruler and Judge of his apostate people (vs. 27–29).——In v. 25, "to eat with the blood" is to eat animal flesh with its own blood—forbidden most explicitly (Gen. 9: 4), and especially in the law by Moses (Lev. 7: 26, and 17: 10, 14, and 19: 26). To "lift up the eyes toward idols" is to regard them with reverence and worship. "Shedding blood" is of course taking human life by violence. "Ye stand upon your sword" means, Ye rely upon it, in place of relying upon God.——Shall men guilty of such crimes inherit the land of the Lord? Sooner would he make it as Sodom.——In v. 27, the word rendered "forts" is strongholds—sometimes artificial, *i. e.*, castles, fortresses; and sometimes places of great natural strength. Coupled here with "caves," the latter is doubtless the sense. In its wild mountain districts, Judea abounded with such caves and fastnesses. The books of Samuel refer to them (*e. g.*, 1 Sam. 13: 6;) so does Josephus.——God will find out these wicked men in those apparently secure retreats, and will smite them with pestilence.—— So vain it must ever be to expect good from the Lord's hand while living in sin, or to hope to escape his threatened judgments otherwise than by turning heartily from one's iniquities. We look with surprise mingled with pity and shame upon the infatuation and delusion of that last remnant of wicked Jews in Judea. How happy if their case did not exemplify a like delusion, and folly equally sad and equally amazing, among myriads of sinners in gospel lands!

30. Also, thou son of man, the children of thy people still are talking against thee by the walls and in the doors of the houses, and speak one to another, every one to his brother, saying, Come, I pray you, and hear what is the word that cometh forth from the Lord.

31. And they come unto thee as the people cometh, and they sit before thee *as* my people, and they hear thy words,

but they will not do them : for with their mouth they shew much love, *but* their heart goeth after their covetousness.

32. And lo, thou *art* unto them as a very lovely song of one that hath a pleasant voice, and can play well on an instrument: for they hear thy words, but they do them not.

33. And when this cometh to pass, (lo, it will come,) then shall they know that a prophet hath been among them.

Here is an inside view of the moral life of the people among whom Ezekiel lived and prophesied in Chaldea, showing how they talked about him between themselves and behind his back; how they sat and heard his messages; how they enjoyed his rich, lively, highly cultivated and finely poetic style, and said very complimentary things about it and about him, but never thought of *doing* the things which the Lord through him enjoined as their duty, and only let their heart press on recklessly after their unrighteous gain. The whole description is beautifully graphic and finely drawn, but in its moral showing is exceedingly painful, revealing among that people an intense depravity, and suggesting the fearful truth that other myriads in gospel lands are using the preaching of the gospel in the same way, for the same ends of amusement, the same gratification of literary taste, and the same pride in displaying their critical skill in making comments on sermons.——Ezekiel was a prophet of rare literary merit. With astonishing variety in his modes of illustration; with great wealth of dramatic representation and of poetic imagery, and with a style always rich and fervid, he must have been eminently *popular* in our modern sense of the term. No wonder the people admired his genius and his culture, and came to hear him as men go to hear a lovely song of one who hath a pleasant voice and can play well on a fine instrument. But they failed to notice that God sent Ezekiel with these engaging qualities and encouraged him in their use, not to amuse their "itching ears," and not even to gratify the universal sensibility to this sort of pleasure, but for objects far higher than these; viz., *to arrest their attention* and *to make on their souls a deeper impression of the great and solemn truths* on which their temporal life and eternal well-being depended. These were the ends that God and his prophet had in view. Alas, that they should fail through the guilty perversion of the hearers! Alas, that these hearers should have sought their own present low gratification, and should not have had the moral sense and the sober thought to say, This tells us of our own sin and peril—of our own God and duty—of our own present responsibility and future doom!——One tear of sympathy for Ezekiel. How he must have felt under this strange and sad revelation of the hearts of his hearers! Ah, (he must have said), Is this the only outcome of all my expostulations and tears ; of all my domestic bereavements, my personal discomforts, my torturing solicitudes, my daily prayers, the agony of my sympathy with a people bent on ruin! Does it all end in this, that they hear me for their own amusement and make my discourses the topics of their keen or their applauding criticism; but not a man of them thinks of saving his own soul; not a man cares to turn from his sins that he may live?——Did not the good man's heart sink within him? Did he not say, Ah me, how can I endure such flattery or such dispraise (all the same), when the only real fruit for the great eventful future is to be the deeper guilt and the more awful doom of these heartless hearers!——It is remarkable that this exposé of the spirit of Ezekiel's hearers should stand in such juxtaposition with the Lord's admonition to him to do his duty faithfully as their spiritual watchman. Let us hope that the quickened sense of this responsibility more than counterbalanced the chilling influence naturally resulting from such disclosures as were made in these last verses. He might still have the joy of feeling that he had sought to please God and to be faithful to their souls.——The manner in which the Lord meets this manifestation in the people should be noticed. When my judgments shall break forth upon them (as they surely must soon), "then shall they know that a prophet has been among them!" a prophet, forewarning them from God of their impending doom, and not a mere poet, stage-actor, or singer; to afford them amusement and help them murder time, stifle conviction of truth, and smooth their way to perdition!

CHAPTER XXXIV.

In this chapter the Lord's people appear as his "*flock.*" The figure of the shepherd and his sheep is maintained throughout. The corrupt priests, false prophets, and wicked princes of Israel and Judah stand here as the shepherds who have long had the care of the Lord's flock. They are denounced; their wicked and ruinous policy is portrayed; and they receive their doom. The Lord himself assumes the care of his flock; will raise up his servant David to be their Shepherd and their Prince; and so the highest prosperity shall ensue.——As to date, it must be assumed that this prophecy follows the period named chap. 33: 21; *i. e.*, follows the arrival of the tidings that the city of Jerusalem is smitten. Probably it was brought out immediately after. Remarkably in both Jeremiah and Ezekiel, the strain of prophecy is that of warning and denunciation *before* the fall of the city, but of consolation and promise *after* that fall. The reason of this is obvious. Before, the people were vainly self-confident: after, they were desponding. Before, they needed stern rebuke; after, the inspirations of promise and of hope. So God is wont to deal with his people.

1. And the word of the Lord came unto me, saying,
2. Son of man, prophesy against the shepherds of Israel, prophesy, and say unto them, Thus saith the Lord God unto

the shepherds; Woe be to the shepherds of Israel that do feed themselves! should not the shepherds feed the flocks?

3. Ye eat the fat, and ye clothe you with the wool, ye kill them that are fed : but ye feed not the flock.

4. The diseased have ye not strengthened, neither have ye healed that which was sick, neither have ye bound up *that which was* broken, neither have ye brought again that which was driven away, neither have ye sought that which was lost; but with force and with cruelty have ye ruled them.

5. And they were scattered, because *there is* no shepherd : and they became meat to all the beasts of the field when they were scattered.

6. My sheep wandered through all the mountains, and upon every high hill : yea, my flock was scattered upon all the face of the earth, and none did search or seek *after them.*

Shepherd life was familiar in all the East. Whole tribes and nations subsisted mainly upon their flocks and herds. No wonder therefore that it appears as a figure to illustrate the spiritual care of the Lord's people.——Jer. 23: 1–4 gives the outlines of this entire chapter of Ezekiel. The reader will readily recall the frequent allusions to the shepherd and his flock in the discourses of our Lord, especially in John 10. Nothing else in human life could furnish illustrations of this thing at once so simple, so beautiful, and so pertinent.——Those men of leading influence in the Jewish State—the priests, the false prophets, and the princes—(for all these are included here) had fed themselves only and never the flock. Selfish men, they had sought only their own aggrandizement and not at all the spiritual good of the people, or the honor of the God of Israel. The case of the flock affords many apposite illustrations of this selfishness. A bad shepherd neglects the feeble, the sick, the maimed, and the wandering; and appropriates the fat and well-conditioned for his personal use. So had these vile men utterly neglected the spiritual culture of the people and sought only their own personal self-indulgence.

7. Therefore, ye shepherds, hear the word of the Lord ;

8. *As* I live, saith the Lord God, surely because my flock became a prey, and my flock became meat to every beast of the field, because *there was* no shepherd, neither did my shepherds search for my flock, but the shepherds fed themselves, and fed not my flock ;

9. Therefore, O ye shepherds, hear the word of the Lord ;

10. Thus saith the Lord God ; Behold, I *am* against the shepherds ; and I will require my flock at their hand, and cause them to cease from feeding the flock ; neither shall

the shepherds feed themselves any more; for I will deliver my flock from their mouth, that they may not be meat for them.

11. For thus saith the Lord God; Behold, I, *even* I, will both search my sheep, and seek them out.

12. As a shepherd seeketh out his flock in the day that he is among his sheep *that are* scattered; so will I seek out my sheep, and will deliver them out of all places where they have been scattered in the cloudy and dark day.

The two great points made here are (1.) That God is *against* those vile shepherds and will hold them to a strict accountability; and (2.) That he will depose them from their place and assume the service himself. He will do this work faithfully. He will seek out the wandering and the lost. Be his name praised for this promise! ——"Scattered in the cloudy and dark day," looks to the scenes of sore calamity through which the nation passed. As sheep would very naturally scatter and become missing in a day of deep eclipse, so the people of the Lord needed to be specially *sought out* after those scenes of great national calamity.

13. And I will bring them out from the people, and gather them from the countries, and will bring to their own land, and feed them upon the mountains of Israel by the rivers, and in all the inhaited places of the country.

14. I will feed them in a good pasture, and upon the high mountains of Israel shall their fold be: there shall they lie in a good fold, and *in* a fat pasture shall they feed upon the mountains of Israel.

15. I will feed my flock, and I will cause them to lie down, saith the Lord God.

16. I will seek that which was lost, and bring again that which was driven away, and will bind up *that which was* broken, and will strengthen that which was sick: but I will destroy the fat and the strong; I will feed them with judgment.

Of course the language and figures used in conveying divine promise to the Jews must be *Jewish*, familiarly known. Scattered now in exile, the first promise is restoration to their land. This is natural. And it was true in its literal sense. The Lord did promise to restore them to their mother-land,—and *fulfilled it*. But he promises here *more* than he fulfilled then and there in the restoration under Zerubbabel. This will appear more fully when we compare other prophecies of Ezekiel parallel with this; *e. g.*, chap. 36: 24–38, and 37: 15–28. See notes on these passages for a more full discussion of the points involved.——In the close of v. 16 a new fact appears—the curse of God upon "the fat and the strong." Fatness of flesh is a Hebrew symbol for hardness of heart. "Jeshurun" [the upright] "waxed fat and kicked: thou art waxen fat, thou art grown thick, thou art covered with fatness: then he forsook God who made him, and lightly esteemed the Rock of his Salvation." (Deut. 32: 15). The "heart waxed gross" [fat] always indicated moral obtuseness. See Ac. 28: 27. Hence these terms refer here to the morally hardened among the people, perhaps including the priests and false prophets, though they appear previously as bad shepherds. The sense is, all the hopelessly wicked.

17. And *as for* you, O my flock, thus saith the Lord God; Behold, I judge between cattle and cattle, between the rams and the he-goats.

This is a discrimination between the morally good and the morally bad. The radical distinction between sheep and goats in their temper and in their habits suggests the discrimination as to moral character which the Lord will bring to light in his judgment.—— Is not this passage the foundation of that remarkable language of our Lord in reference to the final judgment (Mat. 25: 31-33)? "Before him shall be gathered all nations, and he shall separate them one from another as a shepherd divideth his sheep from the goats."

18. *Seemeth it* a small thing unto you to have eaten up the good pasture, but ye must tread down with your feet the residue of your pastures? and to have drunk of the deep waters, but ye must foul the residue with your feet?

19. And *as for* my flock, they eat that which ye have trodden with your feet; and they drink that which ye have fouled with your feet.

Here appears yet another illustration of the spirit and ways of the vile shepherds who are now the he-goats, leaders of the flock, or the fat ones, leading the lean. They not only eat up the good pasture themselves, but trample down all they do not eat, reserving nothing good for the feeble; and they drink of the deep, placid and pure waters, and then foul the rest with their feet—so that they leave for the Lord's flock no grass but what they have trodden down, and no water save what they have made foul. Was this a small thing? Was it not more than merely *mean?* Was it not supremely *wicked?*

20. Therefore thus saith the Lord God unto them; Behold, I, even I, will judge between the fat cattle and between the lean cattle.

21. Because ye have thrust with side and with shoulder, and pushed all the diseased with your horns, till ye have scattered them abroad;

22. Therefore will I save my flock, and they shall no more be a prey; and I will judge between cattle and cattle.

The vile shepherds appear as the fat cattle, thrusting the feeble and diseased with side and shoulder and pushing them with the horn. God will bring them to account and will save his flock from such abuse.

23. And I will set up one Shepherd over them, and he shall feed them, *even* my servant David; he shall feed them, and he shall be their shepherd.

24. And I the Lord will be their God, and my servant David a prince among them; I the Lord have spoken *it*.

This "*one* shepherd, the Lord's "servant David," is the promised Messiah. He can be no other. No other exposition of this promise is possible, in harmony with the scope of the context, and the demands of parallel passages. King David was the great model shepherd-king, walking in the main after the very heart of God, and, therefore, of all the kings of the chosen people, the best representative and model of the great Messiah. This fact stands out with great prominence in numerous prophecies. See 2 Sam. 7: 12–29, Ps. 2 and 110, Isa. 9: 2–7 and 11: 1–10 and 42: 1–4, Jer. 23: 5, 6, and 33: 14–22, Ezek. 37: 21–28, Hos. 3: 5, and Mic. 5: 2, 3. This list does not exhaust the prophecies that refer to the Messiah. It aims only to group together some of those in which he appears as specially related to David:——He is *one* shepherd over *all the people*, with reference to the sad disruption of the nation by Jeroboam. They are all to be united under him, as in chap. 37: 15–28, and Isa. 11: 13.——He is called a "*prince*" among them" rather than a king, perhaps in keeping with the usage of Ezekiel who applies this word "prince" to the Jewish kings; or perhaps with reference to 1 Kings 11: 34; "I will not take the whole kingdom out of his" [Rehoboam's] "hand, but I will make him *prince* all the days of his life," etc. The Lord has solemnly spoken this and will perform it—an indication of the momentous value of this promise.

25. And I will make with them a covenant of peace, and will cause the evil beasts to cease out of the land: and they shall dwell safely in the wilderness, and sleep in the woods.

26. And I will make them and the places round about my hill a blessing; and I will cause the shower to come down in his season; there shall be showers of blessing.

27. And the tree of the field shall yield her fruit, and the earth shall yield her increase, and they shall be safe in their land, and shall know that I *am* the Lord, when I have broken the bands of their yoke, and delivered them out of the hand of those that served themselves of them.

28. And they shall no more be a prey to the heathen, neither shall the beasts of the land devour them; but they shall dwell safely, and none shall make *them* afraid.

The figure of the flock is still kept up with great beauty and force. God will make with them a covenant of peace, binding the wild beasts [outside enemies] to keep the peace with them and do them no harm. So the flock will be safe anywhere, in the wilderness or the forests. "None shall hurt or destroy in all God's holy mountain."——I will make both them and the environs of my hill [Zion] a blessing, causing them not only to enjoy good themselves, but to impart good to others. By the "environs" (the "places round about my hill") are meant the heathen nations, converted to the living God. See the same figure Jer. 31: 38–40, to which Ezekiel may perhaps allude.——The last part of v. 26 should read, "I will bring down the great rain in its time; floods of blessing shall it be." The Hebrew word used here always means a great rain. The figure of rain as a symbol and pledge of all divine blessings appears in full in Lev. 26: 3–6, 19, 20. See also Deut. 11: 14, 15. In Palestine, rain was eminently appropriate to denote the great central blessing on which all other blessings depended inasmuch as in that climate rain stood in precisely this relation to all vegetable growth, animal subsistence, and external beauty. If they had ample and timely rains they had every thing else. If they failed of this, they failed of all.——In vs. 27, 28, the figure is dropped and the literal conception appears. The political bands of the people are broken; the exiles return safely to their country and their homes, no more a prey to the heathen, but dwelling safely in their own loved land.

29. And I will raise up for them a Plant of renown, and they shall be no more consumed with hunger in the land, neither bear the shame of the heathen any more.

Our translators seem to have taken the word rendered "Plant" in the same sense in which we have the word "Branch" (Zech. 3: 8, and 6: 12)—a special name for the Messiah. It is doubtful whether the original can bear this sense. The context does not favor it. The word means a *plantation*. It occurs Ezek. 17: 7, and Isa. 61: 3 and 60: 21, but in none of these cases, in the sense of a plant. The word rendered "raise up" readily bears the sense of establish: made firm and strong. The reference is probably to the Garden of Eden. It promises that the Zion of the Lord shall be a second Eden in beauty, fertility, and glory.——The idea of renown, a good name, stands opposed to "the shame of the heathen" which they shall bear no more. They shall be no more reproached as a broken down nationality, nor shall the name of the Lord be any more blasphemed on their account. The fertility of this plantation will sustain a great people and a strong nation; its splendor and beauty will lift them high above the reproach of the heathen.

30. Thus shall they know that I the Lord their God *am* with them, and *that* they, *even* the house of Israel, *are* my people, saith the Lord God.

31. And ye my flock, the flock of my pasture, *are* men, *and* I *am* your God, saith the Lord God.

This done, they will know that their own God is a glorious Presence among them, and that they themselves are the recognized people of the Lord Jehovah. They will experience the blessedness of being truly his flock, walking themselves in trustful obedience and love, and evermore owned and protected of God, their Great Shepherd and King. Blessed state! Let it be our joy that such a future for the Zion of our God stands fixed in his changeless counsels, never to be forgotten, but to be amply fulfilled in his own time!

CHAPTER XXXV.

This chapter records a prophecy of judgments on Mt. Seir and the people of Edom. Of all the contiguous nations none seem to have cherished more intense and inveterate hatred against Israel than Edom. Hence the prophecy against her, put in brief terms before (chap. 25: 12-14) is resumed and amplified here, manifestly in part for the interesting purpose of bringing into connection with it the greater mercies which God had in store for his own Israel. The next chapter (36) develops the nature and the force of this connection, showing how the jealousy of the Lord was enkindled against the ancient enemies of his people, and how his soul was aroused to great achievements in their behalf out of regard for the glory of his name which Zion's enemies had blasphemed.

1. Moreover the word of the Lord came unto me, saying,
2. Son of man, set thy face against mount Seir, and prophesy against it,
3. And say unto it, Thus saith the Lord God; Behold, O mount Seir, I *am* against thee, and I will stretch out my hand against thee, and I will make thee most desolate.
4. I will lay thy cities waste, and thou shalt be desolate, and thou shalt know that I *am* the Lord.

The fearful word, "I am against thee," forewarns her of the direst possible doom, for what doom can be more terrible than to have God for one's enemy and his infinite resources committed to scourge and destroy!

5. Because thou hast had a perpetual hatred, and hast shed *the blood of* the children of Israel by the force of the sword in the time of their calamity, in the time *that their* iniquity *had* an end:
6. Therefore, *as* I live, saith the Lord God, I will prepare thee unto blood, and blood shall pursue thee: since thou hast not hated blood, even blood shall pursue thee.

The personal ill-feeling of Esau toward his brother Jacob seems to have become the inheritance of his posterity age after age with scarce any perceptible abatement.——The second clause of v. 5, in which the received translation supplies the word "*blood*" would be more close to the original, if rendered thus; "And because thou didst deliver the children of Israel over to the force of the sword in the time of their calamity." It refers to the day when the Chaldeans broke up their city, and the people fled for their lives. Obadiah (vs. 10-15) implies that in this day of chief calamity upon the Jews, Edom was bitter and revengeful as even the proud Chaldeans; looked exultingly upon the fall of his brother as of an old enemy; "spake of them proudly in the day of their distress;" "entered into their gates in that day of their calamity" for pillage and exultant joy; "stood in the crossways to cut off those that were escaping," and "delivered them up" to their Chaldean foes. ——To this great, damning sin the last clause refers as "*the end-sin*"—that crowning iniquity which God could bear no longer, but must punish with exemplary severity—the last sin in the series, and lying next beyond all those which God *could* bear in the sense of long-suffering *delay* to punish. This one he could not "*bear*." The received translation does not give the true sense quite accurately. It is not that iniquity then had an end, but that they had reached the time of their *end-sin*—next beyond the last which God could allow them to commit, and yet delay its punishment.——In v. 6 "I will prepare thee unto blood," is better read; "I will appoint or destine thee for blood." Edom had not been averse to blood in the day of his brother's calamity: now let him have his fill of it. Let it pursue him, even as *his* greedy sword thirsted for the blood of his Jewish brother, and chased him down to drink it!

7. Thus will I make mount Seir most desolate, and cut off from it him that passeth out and him that returneth.

8. And I will fill his mountains with his slain *men:* in thy hills, and in thy valleys, and in all thy rivers, shall they fall that are slain with the sword.

9. I will make thee perpetual desolations, and thy cities shall not return: and ye shall know that I *am* the Lord.

"Him that passeth out and him that returneth," is the usual Hebrew phrase for the travel incident to traffic in those ages. This prophecy is the more noticeable because Edom, and its great capital, Petra, had been for ages the great thoroughfare of commercial travel between Central and Southern Asia on the East, and Egypt and North Africa on the South-west. Her capital had amassed great wealth and had risen to splendor by means of trade and travel; yet under the curse denounced in this prophecy, no spot on this wide earth ever trod by human foot is less frequented to-day than this same Petra! Desolation has made her deepest imprints of ruin there. The sparse Arab population that assume to control the country is of the most savage, ferocious character, so that only a very few travelers are willing to confront at once the utter desolation of the land and the savage barbarity of the people for the sake of exploring those truly grand and magnificent ruins.

10. Because thou hast said, These two nations and these two countries shall be mine, and we will possess it; whereas the Lord was there:

11. Therefore, *as* I live, saith the Lord God, I will even do according to thine anger, and according to thine envy which thou hast used out of thy hatred against them; and I will make myself known among them, when I have judged thee.

12. And thou shalt know that I *am* the Lord, *and that* I have heard all thy blasphemies which thou hast spoken against the mountains of Israel, saying, They are laid desolate, and they are given us to consume.

13. Thus with your mouth ye have boasted against me, and have multiplied your words against me: I have heard *them*.

"Two nations and countries;" Judah and Israel. When these were successively smitten in war, and the people taken into captivity, Edom gloated in the selfish confidence of having those countries as her own. Ah, she did not take into her view that *God was there!* Therefore God will visit upon Edom according to her hatred and anger against his people.——"I will make myself known among them" (my ancient people) "when I shall have judged thee" (Edom).

14. Thus saith the Lord God; When the whole earth rejoiceth, I will make thee desolate.

15. As thou didst rejoice at the inheritance of the house of Israel, because it was desolate, so will I do unto thee: thou shalt be desolate, O mount Seir, and all Idumea, *even* all of it: and they shall know that I *am* the Lord.

It would be a double calamity on Edom to be made desolate precisely when the whole earth should be joyful in its prosperity. The primary reference here is probably to the period when the Chaldean supremacy in Western Asia should be broken, and many of those nations whom they had subjugated should regain their former prosperity. Then Edom should be an exception.——A still further installment of the same doom came on Edom near the Christian Era—a time of general prosperity to the nations of that region, but of almost utter national extinction to Edom.——Because she had rejoiced with proud and selfish exultation over the captivity of the house of Israel, God would lay her desolate. Such national sins demand of the Great Ruler of nations condign and exemplary punishment. The nations of men must be made to know that Jehovah is Ruler and Lord of all, evermore administering his rule over nations with a just and righteous retribution.

CHAPTER XXXVI.

The central idea of this chapter is that God's people having brought reproach on his name before the heathen, he will retrieve it from this disgrace. For the sake of his own glory he will restore his people to their land, renew the fertility of its soil, rebuild its long-time wasted cities, and (more and better than all) will *renew the hearts* of his people, taking away the stone and giving flesh instead; "putting his own Spirit within them, and causing them henceforth to walk in his statutes and do them."——Yet lying back of this idea of interposing to retrieve his name from reproach before the heathen is doubtless the more fundamental one—*the divine purpose and promise of salvation to his people;*—that in his own eternal counsels he had purposed to have a people saved unto holiness, and therefore could not and would not be frustrated in his purpose by their waywardness and sin, but would press the agencies of discipline and the yet mightier agencies of his Spirit to reclaim, renew, and save. Thus he would show his people that he is really the very God, ever faithful to his promise, ever abiding in his love for his people.——The honor of the divine name before the heathen is fully seen only when we take into view the current sentiment of all heathen nations respecting their national divinities, viz., that those divinities were essentially the patrons and protectors of the people who accepted and worshiped them in that capacity. Now, it was well known among them that Israel claimed to be the people of Jehovah, the Lord God of Hosts. He was known as the God of Israel. Hence when their nationality was broken down, their king slain or taken captive, their great city and the Lord's temple destroyed, and the people who survived were all in exile, the heathen would say that either their God was unfaithful to his promises and therefore untruthful and unreliable; or was short of power to save and therefore unfit to be trusted as the patron God of any nation. It is in this point of view that God's jealousy for his holy name becomes so prominent as a reason or occasion for his interposition to restore and save his people.——Remarkably in the first portion of this chapter, (vs. 1-15) the Lord addresses "the mountains of Israel;" while in the second portion, (vs. 16-38) he addresses the prophet, yet announcing great truths especially for the people then in exile, but richly applicable to God's people in all ages.

1. Also, thou son of man, prophesy unto the mountains

of Israel, and say, Ye mountains of Israel, hear the word of the Lord:

2. Thus saith the Lord God; Because the enemy hath said against you, Aha, even the ancient high places are ours in possession:

3. Therefore prophesy and say, Thus saith the Lord God; Because they have made *you* desolate, and swallowed you up on every side, that ye might be a possession unto the residue of the heathen, and ye are taken up in the lips of talkers, and *are* an infamy of the people:

4. Therefore, ye mountains of Israel, hear the word of the Lord God; Thus saith the Lord God to the mountains, and to the hills, to the rivers, and to the valleys, to the desolate wastes, and to the cities that are forsaken, which became a prey and derision to the residue of the heathen that *are* round about;

5. Therefore thus saith the Lord God; Surely in the fire of my jealousy have I spoken against the residue of the heathen, and against all Idumea, which have appointed my land into their possession with the joy of all *their* heart, with despiteful minds to cast it out for a prey.

The reader will notice the bold personification by which this prophecy addresses "the mountains of Israel." The very land itself is thought of as intelligent and conscious, sensible of the reproach under which it has lain, and sympathizing with the grief and shame under which its exiled population are now suffering. ——In the previous chapter (vs. 10, 12, 15) we saw that the Edomites had fixed their covetous eyes on Palestine, hoping to secure it to themselves for a permanent possession. This thought leads the course of remark here. Edom "is the enemy who has said against you," ye mountains, "Aha! even those ancient high places are ours in possession."——In v. 3 the relation of cause or occasion is made emphatic in the original by repetition; "Because, yea *because* they have made you desolate," etc.——V. 5 shows that while other heathen nations were implicated, Idumea (Edom) is prominent. ——"Appointed my land into their possession," is in Hebrew, *given* or *assigned my land to themselves for a possession*"—"with the joy of their whole heart and with soul-pantings;" *i. e.*, with a most eager desire, longing to clutch it as their prey. "Despiteful mind," does not exactly express the original.——"To cast it out," should rather be, to *spoil* it as their prey; to pillage it at their pleasure.

6. Prophesy therefore concerning the land of Israel, and say unto the mountains, and to the hills, to the rivers, and to the valleys, Thus saith the Lord God; Behold, I have spoken in my jealousy and in my fury, because ye have borne the shame of the heathen:

7. Therefore thus saith the Lord God; I have lifted up my hand: surely the heathen that *are* about you, they shall bear their shame.

8. But ye, O mountains of Israel, ye shall shoot forth your branches, and yield your fruit to my people of Israel; for they are at hand to come.

9. For behold, I *am* for you, and I will turn unto you, and ye shall be tilled and sown:

10. And I will multiply men upon you, all the house of Israel, *even* all of it: and the cities shall be inhabited, and the wastes shall be builded:

11. And I will multiply upon you man and beast: and they shall increase and bring fruit: and I will settle you after your old estates, and will do better *unto you* than at your beginnings: and ye shall know that I *am* the Lord.

Ye mountains and hills that have borne shame from the heathen, shall bear it no longer. The heathen shall bear their own shame; *i. e.*, shall themselves be ashamed and confounded before the mighty God of Israel. Ye mountains shall again become productive, bearing fruit for my people Israel, for they are coming back soon; ("they are at hand to come.")——In v. 11 "settle you after your old estates" does not mean that the family estates should return to the heirs of their former owners, but only in general; "I will cause you, ye mountains, to be inhabited as of old and I will do you good more than in your beginning"—first settlement.——"And ye shall know that I am the Lord," still keeps up the conception of conscious intelligence in these mountains of Israel. They would themselves have the evidence that the Lord is truly God.

12. Yea, I will cause men to walk upon you, *even* my people Israel; and they shall possess thee, and thou shalt be their inheritance, and thou shalt no more henceforth bereave them *of men*.

13. Thus saith the Lord God; Because they say unto you, Thou *land* devourest up men, and hast bereaved thy nations;

14. Therefore, thou shalt devour men no more, neither bereave thy nations any more, saith the Lord God.

15. Neither will I cause *men* to hear in thee the shame of the heathen any more, neither shalt thou bear the reproach of the people any more, neither shalt thou cause thy nations to fall any more, saith the Lord God.

In the current sentiment of the Jewish people, no calamity to a family was so great as being bereaved of children. They would have the same view of a state, bereaved of its population. "In the multitude of people is the king's honor; but in the want of people is the destruction of the prince" (Prov. 14: 28). It seems to be tacitly assumed here that the mountains and the hills, the country itself, might inflict this calamity, i. e., might itself bereave the state of its sons and daughters—might eat up its own population. But God promises that the mountains of Israel shall no more bereave the state of its loved people.——In these four verses, two verbs are used for this leading idea, viz., the common word for being bereaved of children and another with the same radicals, yet with the first two transposed, meaning in the form here used, to cause to fall. This is so rendered in the last clause of v. 15. This play upon these two words is one of the nicer beauties of style. The general thought is that the land will be depopulated no more. ——But the real *fulfillment* of this promise appears only in its spiritual significance as relating to the true Zion of the living God. For Palestine has long been forsaken of the seed of Abraham and has long since ceased to be the local home of the organized people, worship, and institutions of God. But God's true Zion lives; has not been depopulated, but has been exceedingly multiplied even already, and doubtless is yet to be far more. Compare Isa. 54: 1–8.

16. Moreover, the word of the Lord came unto me, saying,

17. Son of man, when the house of Israel dwelt in their own land, they defiled it by their own way and by their doings: their way was before me as the uncleanness of a removed woman.

18. Wherefore, I poured my fury upon them for the blood that they had shed upon the land, and for their idols *wherewith* they had polluted it:

19. And I scattered them among the heathen, and they were dispersed through the countries: according to their way and according to their doings I judged them.

Here the Lord addresses the prophet, and through him his own people.——By the worship of idols and by all the abominations of murder and lust and of dishonor cast on God which are involved in such idolatry, the people had utterly defiled their own land. Therefore the Lord poured out his fury upon them, scattered them among the heathen, and judged them thoroughly according to their ways.

20. And when they entered unto the heathen, whither they went, they profaned my holy name, when they said to them, These *are* the people of the Lord, and are gone forth out of his land.

21. But I had pity for mine holy name, which the house

of Israel had profaned among the heathen, whither they went.

The remarks introductory to this chapter will show the significance of these ideas of profaning God's name before the heathen. It was currently said among them, "These are the people of Jehovah, God of Israel, and they are set adrift, borne away captive from his land. What can this signify? Either that God is weak or is untrue. So in either case their conclusion was reproachful to the God of Israel. Therefore the Lord had pity for his holy name's sake. It would be only disastrous to his reputation before the world to leave such inferences to be drawn and to stand without refutation.——Cases illustrating the same holy and jealous regard for his own great name may be seen in the early history of the nation, Exod. 32—the sin of the golden calf—and in Num. 14,—the sin of unbelief; and in Deut. 9—a sort of resumé of these cases.

22. Therefore, say unto the house of Israel, Thus saith the Lord God; I do not *this* for your sakes, O house of Israel, but for my holy name's sake, which ye have profaned among the heathen, whither ye went.

23. And I will sanctify my great name, which was profaned among the heathen, which ye have profaned in the midst of them; and the heathen shall know that I *am* the Lord, saith the Lord God, when I shall be sanctified in you before their eyes.

It was vital to the best moral impression upon the people that they should see that this interposition of God to deliver them from their captivity and restore them to their land was not done for *their sake*—had none of its causes or grounds in their goodness or merits: but was done entirely for his own holy name's sake, to redeem his character and throne from dishonor before the nations. These statements uniformly rest the case here, although (as suggested above) we may well go deeper, even to the eternal love of God for lost men and to his glorious purpose of redeeming a people unto himself. It was for the sake of these highest ends that he deemed it so important to retrieve his name before the heathen, for his great thoughts of salvation embraced the gathering yet of myriads from among the heathen to fear, love, and adore their own Maker and Father.——"When I shall be sanctified *in you* before their eyes," develops the morally vital idea that God's glory before the heathen turns on the holiness of his people. When he shall have made them radically holy in heart, then the nations will see in them an illustration of what holiness is in God. God will stand forth before the heathen as the Holy One, his holiness being illustrated and reflected in the holiness of his people.

24. For I will take you from among the heathen, and

gather you out of all countries, and will bring you into your own land.

Then and there, under those circumstances, the honor of God demanded that his people should be brought back to their own land of covenant promise. Hence a literal restoration was then a necessity. Consequently the Lord met this necessity by causing them to return literally and rebuild the temple and restore the institutions of Moses.——But this by no means implies that the same sort of restoration must be reënacted, either now or at any time yet future. The necessity of a literal return ceased when the people had once been literally restored. Besides, if a literal restoration were to take place at any point during the Christian age in order to fulfill the legitimate sense of this and subsequent prophecies of Ezekiel, then certainly *Judaism must be restored as well.* The Christian system must give way and disappear, and the Mosaic system take its place.——But this whole subject will be resumed and fully discussed when we come to the closing chapters (40–48).

25. Then will I sprinkle clean water upon you, and ye shall be clean: from all your filthiness, and from all your idols, will I cleanse you.

The conception of cleansing by sprinkling clean water comes from the Mosaic ceremonial system. See especially Num. 19: 17–19, and also Ps. 51: 9. The former passage—the case of a man rendered unclean by contact with a dead body—is forcibly translated by Hengstenberg, thus:—"And they take for the unclean from the ashes of the burnt sin-offering and put thereon living water in a vessel, and they take hyssop, and a clean man dips it in the water, sprinkles the tent and all the vessels and the souls which are there, and the clean sprinkles it upon the unclean and sanctifies him."——In every age and among all nations, water is both the prime agent for cleansing, and the first and main symbol to denote it. Hence it is used here with equal beauty, fitness, and force of the moral cleansing which the Lord was to effect in the hearts of his people. As looking to the case (then present) of the Jewish exiles in Chaldea, to be restored to Canaan, it makes prominent the filthiness and abominations of idolatry. From these the Lord would effectually cleanse them. This became a great historic fact. The nation as such were cured of idolatry, at least during several generations.——But this promise is good against all the filthiness and all the abominations of human hearts. The gracious promise of the Lord covers all. And there is a wealth of blessedness in this broad, magnificent promise! By what power performed and how applied, the Lord proceeds to show.

26. A new heart also will I give you, and a new spirit will I put within you: and I will take away the stony heart out of your flesh, and I will give you a heart of flesh.

27. And I will put my Spirit within you, and cause you

to walk in my statutes, and ye shall keep my judgments, and do *them*.

Compare chap. 11: 17-20, where in briefer statements, the same general ideas appear.——The "heart" and the "spirit" represent what is most radical in human character—what is farthest removed from hypocrisy or from the merely external life. Comprehensively they embody man's deepest purposes and intentions—the governing will that animates his whole activities, and morally constitutes the man. To make these wholly new is to breathe into the soul of man a new moral life. It changes the great drift and aim of his endeavors; gives him a new object to live for; inspires his soul with new motives, and brings him under new influences. It is made prominent here that this change is wrought by the Spirit of God; "I will put my Spirit within you, and (so) will cause you to walk in my statutes," etc. God himself becomes a controlling power in the hearts of men unto a holy life.——This is the great doctrine of the New Testament, taught forcibly by our Lord himself in his statements respecting the new birth (Jn. 3: 3-8), and every-where presented as preëminently the work of the Spirit of God.——The heart of stone, contrasted with the heart of flesh, is forcible imagery, yet wonderfully true to human consciousness. Its significance applies appositely to the sensibilities—cold and dead, apart from the living, quickening power of God in the soul—but tender, flowing and free when the Spirit touches the soul and even makes his abode there. And yet we must not restrict the Spirit's work to the sensibilities. The intellect also—the mind's apprehension of divine truth—is by no means unaffected in this great change from stone to flesh. The dullness of apprehension, the resistance to truth, which appears where God is not in the heart, may fitly be called "*stony;*" while the sharpened thought, the quick apprehension, and the genial welcome of truth, attach the qualities of living flesh even to the intellect.——Yet these terms were never intended to be acutely metaphysical. They address the popular mind. Considered as so addressed, they are exceedingly forcible and happy.——I can not forbear to add that they reveal a most blessed, glorious truth, viz., *that God himself becomes an effective power in the souls of men unto real holiness.* While all merely external agencies forever fail, this divine agency is forever efficacious. It does for man the very thing he needs. His own unaided endeavors, his firmest resolutions, prove unavailing. Under his bitter experience of their failure, this promise comes to his soul as the dawn of day upon the thickest darkness. When God says, "I will put my Spirit within you and will cause you to walk in my statutes," his heart responds, That meets my soul's great want. It is enough. If God will grant me that effective spiritual aid under which I shall wholly obey and please him, I can ask nothing better; I aspire to nothing higher and nobler.——As already suggested, this is the gospel. These are the provisions of gospel grace for the regeneration and sanctification of unholy men. They are large promises. Nothing larger, broader, or richer, appears in the whole New Testament. In their comprehensive reach and scope they must be taken to embrace the gospel scheme and the gospel age. Hence we can not think of their fulfillment as being exhausted in the time of Zerubbabel, or at any period anterior to the coming of Christ. In fact, since our Lord represents the Spirit as coming with preëminent fullness only after his own ascension, we must assign the more ample fulfillment of this great promise to the Christian age. No doubt its richest and most glorious fulfillment is reserved for the latter days of even this Christian age—the era when "all shall know the Lord from the least to the greatest." See Jer. 31: 34, and Isa. 11: 9.

28. And ye shall dwell in the land that I gave to your fathers; and ye shall be my people, and I will be your God.

That they should "dwell in the land promised to their fathers," applied specially to the exiles in captivity. The primary bearing of these promises was for them. What was in the letter as distinct from the spirit—what related to the very land of Palestine in distinction from what belongs to God's spiritual Zion, we naturally and fitly assign to the exiles to whom these words were first spoken.

29. I will also save you from all your uncleannesses: and I will call for the corn, and will increase it, and lay no famine upon you.

30. And I will multiply the fruit of the tree, and the increase of the field, that ye shall receive no more reproach of famine among the heathen.

The land would become fertile again, and abundant prosperity would wipe away the scandal and reproach resting on the name and the land of the Lord their God.

31. Then shall ye remember your own evil ways, and your doings that *were* not good, and shall loathe yourselves in your own sight for your iniquities, and for your abominations.

32. Not for your sakes do I *this*, saith the Lord God, be it known unto you: be ashamed and confounded for your own ways, O house of Israel.

The restored people would indeed have most ample reason to be ashamed and confounded as they should think of their moral abominations, and of the exceeding great compassion and loving kindness of the Lord their God. They must see and deeply feel that they owed every thing to the self-moved interposition of their own God to save; nothing to themselves as having wrought out, or in any way deserved, their own salvation.

33. Thus saith the Lord God; In the day that I shall

have cleansed you from all your iniquities I will also cause *you* to dwell in the cities, and the wastes shall be builded.

34. And the desolate land shall be tilled, whereas it lay desolate in the sight of all that passed by.

35. And they shall say, This land that was desolate is become like the garden of Eden ; and the waste and desolate and ruined cities *are become* fenced, *and* are inhabited.

36. Then the heathen that are left round about you shall know that I the Lord build the ruined *places, and* plant that that was desolate : I the Lord have spoken *it*, and I will do *it*.

In these verses, the temporal side (so to speak) of these promises stands forth prominently. They needed to have a temporal side for the special encouragement of the exiles in Chaldea, and perhaps I might add, for the verification of the promises themselves. But the spiritual side furnishes the richer installments and stands guaranteed to us by the fulfillment, already past, of the temporal part in the restoration from Babylon, and in the external prosperity which succeeded that great event.

37. Thus saith the Lord God; I will yet *for* this be inquired of by the house of Israel, to do *it* for them ; I will increase them with men like a flock.

38. As the holy flock, as the flock of Jerusalem in her solemn feasts ; so shall the waste cities be filled with flocks of men : and they shall know that I *am* the Lord.

In the clause, "I will yet for this be inquired of," etc., the precise force of the word rendered "*yet*" becomes an important question. Does it mean that *although* I have made this full promise, *yet* I will be inquired of in prayer before I shall do it for them ? Or does it mean that having previously declared that I would *not* be inquired of by this people, I now announce that I will *yet again* be inquired of—opening again the long-closed door for prevailing intercession, and inviting the people again to seek their God in prayer?——The proper sense of the original word, as well as the historical facts, seem to decide in favor of the latter view.——The normal sense of the Hebrew word is *yet again*, said properly of that which *comes round* a second time.——Historically, the fact that God had closed the door against prayer was of immense significance. See chap. 14: 3, and 20: 3, 31, and Jer. 14: 11, and 7: 16, and 11 : 14. It was altogether pertinent for the Lord to apprise the people that the day of mercy had opened upon them once more and that prayer would be accepted yet again.——No doubt it is fully implied in this passage that the people were to pray for the great blessing just now promised, and none the less because it was promised so implicitly. This point is one of great moral significance. Definite promise should encourage prayer and never supersede it—never be held to relieve God's people from the duty, or exclude them from the privilege. But while this is *implied* here as often elsewhere, the precise thing affirmed in the text is that the previous prohibition of prayer for Jerusalem is now removed, and God is again accessible "to be inquired of by the house of Israel."——In the words that follow stress is laid upon the great increase of population as being the central thing. It was central among the temporal blessings here promised.——The word "flock" comes from the previous figure which accounts the people as the Lord's sheep and himself as their shepherd. The population would crowd the cities densely, as the throng filled Jerusalem in the great national feasts.

The question will arise; Are not the temporal blessings promised in this passage, especially in vs. 29, 35, 38, too great to have received their fulfillment in the time of Zerubbabel, or indeed at any period before Christ? I answer, doubtless they are too great to have been received both *in kind* and in their *full measure*. But we may assume that in this and in other similar prophecies, the distinction between the temporal and the spiritual is not sharply drawn; that the corn, the wine, and the oil as here put, are (like Canaan itself) to some extent *representative* blessings, named rather as indications of the divine favor than as defining precisely the *form* which that favor would assume. They may be taken as pledges of good, put in this form in order that the people may appreciate them as a great good; and yet it may not have been the thought of God to tie himself down to corn and wine, or even to a dense "flock of men" as filling out and exhausting the good here promised. The general import is; You may rest assured it is in the heart of your God to do great and glorious things for his cause and people. If he names Canaan and corn and hosts of men, let it be that he thereby condescends to an earthly condition of things then present—to a style of wants then pressing and uppermost but really means not these things alone, but things far purer, higher and better. See also Amos 9: 13-15.

CHAPTER XXXVII.

The strain of rich and glorious promise still continues, looking primarily to the immediate case of the exiles to whom the message first came, but stretching its view far onward into the great sublime future of the Zion of the Lord our God.——As to its figures and symbols, the chapter is in two parts. The first (vs. 1-14) is a vision of dry bones brought back to life, vigor, and beauty—to represent the restored nationality of the captive, dispirited Jews and their renewed spiritual life: while the second part (vs. 15-20) gives us by a figure the enduring union of the two kingdoms, Israel and Judah. Then vs. 21-28 expand into a rich promise of the future peace and purity of Messiah's kingdom.——The first section is prophetic vision and not symbolic transaction in real life. But the second section is manifestly a real transaction, of a symbolic character.

1. The hand of the Lord was upon me, and carried me out in the Spirit of the Lord, and set me down in the midst of the valley which *was* full of bones,

"The hand of the Lord upon me;" "bearing me out abroad in the Spirit of the Lord;" "setting me down," etc., all indicate most conclusively that this is purely a prophetic vision.——" *The* valley," with the definite article, must refer to the well-known valley in which other prophetic visions had been located; *c. g.*, chap. 3; 22, 23, where the Hebrew word is the same though rendered in our received version, "the plain."——This valley was seen to be full of bones.

2. And caused me to pass by them round about: and, behold, *there were* very many in the open valley; and, lo, *they were* very dry.

"In the open valley," is in the Hebrew *on the face of the valley*, the sense being, on the surface of the ground, and not covered with earth as bones should be.

3. And he said unto me, Son of man, can these bones live? And I answered, O Lord God, thou knowest.

The prophet's answer seems to say, How can I tell? How can I understand the import of this scene until thou shalt reveal it? O Lord, thou *only* knowest.

4. Again he said unto me, Prophesy upon these bones, and say unto them, O ye dry bones, hear the word of the Lord.

5. Thus saith the Lord God unto these bones; Behold, I will cause breath to enter into you, and ye shall live.

6. And I will lay sinews upon you, and will bring up flesh upon you, and cover you with skin, and put breath in you, and ye shall live: and ye shall know that I *am* the Lord.

The pertinence of prophesying to dry bones becomes fully apparent when we get the true idea of their significance in this vision. These dead and dry bones, according to the Lord's own interpretation (v. 11), "are the whole house of Israel," as they lay in their captivity. They were saying, "Our bones are dried and our hope is lost; as for us, we are utterly cut off," *i. e.*, from being a nation; we are nationally annihilated. So the hearts of the exiles had sunk into despair of ever returning to their native land and becoming again a nation enjoying the favor of God there.——Now, despondency does not preclude reasoning, although real death does. Despondency does not shut off preaching—does not make it absurd to proclaim the word of the Lord. These exiled Jews were dead only in figure; they were dry bones only in the sense of being utterly discouraged, and of having lost heart and hope in their nation's future. Preaching and prophesying to them the word of the Lord was the legitimate remedy. It might perhaps have the aspect of an absurdity while they are thought of only as dead and dry bones. The absurdity comes of forcing the figure, not of understanding the fact it represents.——A special interpretation has been sometimes put upon this entire vision whereby these bones are spiritually dead sinners, and their resurrection is regeneration by the Spirit of the Lord. In this view of it, the prophet (gospel minister) prophesies (preaches) to sinners void of spiritual life, only because he is commanded to do so, and not because there is any natural adaptation of the means to the end proposed—their resuscitation to life.——When this view of the sinner's death is pushed to the extreme of denying to him intelligence to understand God's truth and conscience to feel its force, the absurdity becomes glaring.——Yet the thing to be said here of these views is that whatever may or may not be true in regard to them, they are entirely foreign from the doctrine of this vision. Any effort to make this passage teach the laws of regeneration is altogether gratuitous. The Lord should be allowed to put his own interpretation upon the visions which he gives. When he has done this, we have but one duty; viz., to abide by it, and resist all abuse and perversion of God's word.

7. So I prophesied as I was commanded: and as I prophesied there was a noise, and behold a shaking, and the bones came together, bone to his bone.

8. And when I beheld, lo, the sinews and the flesh came up upon them, and the skin covered them above: but *there was* no breath in them.

9. Then said he unto me, Prophesy unto the wind, prophesy, son of man, and say to the wind, Thus saith the Lord God; Come from the four winds, O breath, and breathe upon these slain, that they may live.

10. So I prophesied as he commanded me, and the breath came into them, and they lived, and stood up upon their feet, an exceeding great army.

In v. 9, the Hebrew reader would notice that the original words rendered "wind" and "breath" are the same. This fact looks toward the ancient notion that the living animal soul inheres in the breath—comes into the body and goes forth from the body, with and in the breath. Virgil's account of the death of Dido (Æneid Bk. IV) assumes this doctrine.

11. Then he said unto me, Son of man, these bones are

the whole house of Israel: behold they say, Our bones are dried, and our hope is lost: we are cut off for our parts.

12. Therefore prophesy and say unto them, Thus saith the Lord God; Behold, O my people, I will open your graves, and cause you to come up out of your graves, and bring you into the land of Israel.

13. And ye shall know that I *am* the Lord, when I have opened your graves, O my people, and brought you up out of your graves,

14. And shall put my Spirit in you, and ye shall live, and I shall place you in your own land: then shall ye know that I the Lord have spoken *it*, and performed *it*, saith the Lord.

We have real occasion for gratitude to our divine Teacher that he explains his visions whenever their significance might otherwise be unintelligible or even uncertain. The first concern of those who find dark or doubtful passages in the Word of God should be, to mark God's own interpretation of them and regard that as absolutely decisive; discarding all speculations of their own at variance with God's explanations.——"O *my* people," breathes the tone of kind, parental recognition. Compare chap. 13: 17, where, as if God would disown them, he calls them, not *my* people, but "*thy* people." The change from *thy* to *my* betokens the tenderness of returning love. It indicates that deep spiritual blessings are involved in this promised revivification and restoration of their own land.——The reader will notice with interest that this vision assumes the doctrine of a resurrection of the dead from their graves. It is based precisely on this great idea. The figure is drawn from the fact of a resurrection, and of course assumes not merely that the resurrection of the body is a truth, yet to become reality, but that this doctrine was currently known by the Jews of Ezekiel's time. Figures, legitimately used, always draw their analogies from *things known.* Else they would only make darkness yet more dark. There is no law of language more rational, universal, and fixed than this; that figures of speech are legitimate and useful only when drawn from things palpable and visible, or from facts understood and believed. The thing we would explain or set in yet stronger light, we compare with something better known than itself; else our figures and analogies avail nothing.——In the case before us, it should be borne in mind that the resurrection is not a doctrine of nature. Nature never has taught it, and it never can. It comes to men only through revelation. The Jews had this revelation; else Ezekiel in these allusions to it would have been as one who speaks in an unknown tongue. Suppose that, instead of this allusion to the resurrection, he had represented the reanimated, encouraged people as mounting upward and flying to the moon. The people would have thought him insane, just because they had no faith in such flying.——On the other hand, if he had compared the attractive force of their faith and love toward God, to the law of gravitation, holding the planets in their orbits round the sun, and had clearly shown that he regarded this influence of gravitation as the same which brings to the ground the apple detached from its bough, this illustration would be accepted by all as proof that he and his readers were familiar with the law of gravitation. Hence this reference to the resurrection irresistibly implies the general belief in that doctrine among the Jews at that time.——A similar use of this figure appears in Isaiah (chap. 26: 14, 19), applied first to the godless nations; "They are dead; they shall not live; deceased; they shall not rise; because thou hast visited and destroyed them and made all their memory to perish." Next he applies it to the penitent and trustful nation;. " *Thy* dead shall live; being my own dead body, they shall arise: awake and sing, ye dwellers in dust, for thy dew is the dew of herbs" (fertilizing and life-inspiring), "and on the earth, on the dead, Thou wilt cause it to fall."—— Hence the doctrine of the resurrection was certainly current among the Jews in the time of Isaiah.——The great point revealed to the exiled Jews in this prophecy was that God would burst the bars of their captivity, and despite of their present despondency, bring them forth, restore them to their land, call back to life their apparently extinct nationality, and bring their hearts back to a living trust and to an earnest love toward the Lord their God. Then they would know that he is the *Lord*, the real Jehovah, immutable, faithful, never failing to fulfill his words of promise.

15. The word of the Lord came again unto me, saying,

16. Moreover, thou son of man, take thee one stick, and write upon it, For Judah, and for the children of Israel his companions: then take another stick, and write upon it, For Joseph, the stick of Ephraim, and *for* all the house of Israel his companions:

17. And join them one to another into one stick; and they shall become one in thy hand.

18. And when the children of thy people shall speak unto thee, saying, Wilt thou not shew us what thou *meanest* by these?

19. Say unto them, Thus saith the Lord God; Behold, I will take the stick of Joseph, which *is* in the hand of Ephraim, and the tribes of Israel his fellows, and will put them with him, *even* with the stick of Judah, and make them one stick, and they shall be one in my hand.

20. And the sticks whereon thou writest shall be in thy hand before their eyes.

21. And say unto them, Thus saith the Lord God; Behold, I will take the children of Israel from among the

heathen, whither they be gone, and will gather them on every side, and bring them into their own land:

22. And I will make them one nation in the land upon the mountains of Israel; and one king shall be king to them all; and they shall be no more two nations, neither shall they be divided into two kingdoms any more at all:

As said above, this scene is a real transaction.——These "sticks" were rather rods than tablets,·yet such rods that a name might be written upon them. This use of rods may have a tacit reference to the scenes described Num. 17, where, twelve rods being taken, the names of the tribes were written severally upon them, and Aaron's rod alone budded, to show the Lord's choice of him for the priesthood.——The import of this transaction is fully explained in vs. 21, 22, viz., the perfect and enduring union of the two kingdoms, Ephraim and Judah, in one. The revolt under Jeroboam was one of the saddest facts of Hebrew history. It occasioned terrible and destructive wars; it mainly severed the ten tribes from the sanctuary and from the entire Mosaic institutions, and precipitated first that northern kingdom, and ultimately the southern as well, into the depths of a most guilty and debasing idolatry. It then led on by natural result and rapid step to the national ruin of both kingdoms, and to the captivity of the masses who survived the shock under which the nations fell. Hence most naturally that rending asunder became a symbol of the sorest calamity; and in like manner the reunion of the two kingdoms into one became the symbol of the best, the largest, most enduring prosperity. So the figure is to be taken here—not so much a prediction of the gathering up of the scattered ten tribes, their literal restoration and actual reunion with Judah, as a general symbol of the greatest and best prosperity. History gives but meager evidence of any restoration of the ten tribes ever, after they were taken off by the Assyrians into their remote colonies. There is nothing in the history of the restoration under Zerubbabel to prove that the ten tribes in any appreciable numbers were there. On the contrary the showing is all the other way. The genealogies in the record (*e. g.*) prove that the returning exiles were of the tribe and kingdom of Judah. Hence we are shut up to the general in distinction from the closely specific sense of this prophecy.——In v. 16 the phrase, "his companions," means *his associates;* in the first case, "for Judah and for the sons of Israel who have been associated with him," *i. e.*, who, through their love for the God and the institutions of their fathers, chose to cast in their lot with Judah: and in the second case, for all out of the various ten tribes who had affiliated with Ephraim in her distinct nationality.——The "one king to them all"—the best part of the promise—looks onward to their great King and Messiah, as the context clearly shows.

23. Neither shall they defile themselves any more with their idols, nor with their detestable things, nor with any

of their transgressions: but I will save them out of all their dwelling-places, wherein they have sinned, and will cleanse them: so shall they be my people, and I will be their God.

24. And David my servant *shall be* king over them; and they all shall have one shepherd: they shall also walk in my judgments, and observe my statutes, and do them.

25. And they shall dwell in the land that I have given unto Jacob my servant, wherein your fathers have dwelt, and they shall dwell therein, *even* they, and their children, and their children's children forever: and my servant David *shall be* their prince forever.

26. Moreover I will make a covenant of peace with them; it shall be an everlasting covenant with them: and I will place them, and multiply them, and will set my sanctuary in the midst of them for evermore.

27. My tabernacle also shall be with them: yea, I will be their God, and they shall be my people.

28. And the heathen shall know that I the Lord do sanctify Israel, when my sanctuary shall be in the midst of them for evermore.

That this passage is Messianic, looking far down, not only *to* but *into* the Gospel age, can admit of no question.——"David my servant," is here, as in chap. 34: 23, 24, and Jer. 30: 9, and Hos. 3: 5, the greater Son of David to whom "the Lord God will give the throne of his father David." So the inspired angel explained and applied these prophecies in Luke 1: 32, 33. The designation, "my servant," identifies him fully and beautifully. Compare Isa. 42: 1, and 49: 3, 6, and 52: 13, and 53: 11.——The most precious fact of his reign is the moral purity of his people under his redeeming, sanctifying power. They shall defile themselves no more with their idols, nor with any of their transgressions! Blessed fruition! How glorious this state of moral purity shall be can be best appreciated by those who have most deeply deplored their own proclivities to sin and their agonizing relapses under the power of temptation, and who have most fervently and with most irrepressible longings sought for a pure and perfect heart toward the Lord their God.——Let us not fail to notice the forceful repetition of the idea that *God dwells among his people* in these latter days. "I will set my sanctuary in the midst of them for evermore;" "my tabernacle also shall be with them;" "the heathen shall know that I the Lord do sanctify Israel when my sanctuary shall be in the midst of them for evermore."——Ezekiel had seen the visible glory of God go up from the midst of the city as if to depart from the temple (chap. 11: 23). With the fall of that temple, this symbol of his presence had of course disappeared from among them. But here the Lord pledges himself to return and indeed to dwell with his people in forms and manifestations far more rich, effective and perfect than ever before. The ancient Shekinah was rather a symbol than itself a power. It prophesied of the glorious presence of God by his Spirit in the future days of Zion. But here those days are drawn up near the eye for a more distinct and impressive view. Christian hearts become the temple of the living God. Here are the germs of those precious thoughts which our Lord unfolded so richly when he opened his mouth to speak of the Comforter (Jn. chaps. 12–16), and which Paul grasped with so clear a view of their spiritual power in his letter to the brethren at Corinth (2 Cor. 6: 16–18, and 7: 1). "For ye are the temple of the living God; as God hath said; I will dwell in them and walk in them, and I will be their God, and they shall be my people," etc.——The reader should not fail to notice that this very blessing—God dwelling with and in his people, making his presence manifest as a power unto their holiness and blessedness—is the great comprehensive promise of both the Old Testament dispensation and the New. It had the Shekinah in the most holy place as its symbol under the Old Dispensation: it was embodied in the promise and gift of the Holy Ghost in the Gospel age. To Moses the Lord said (Ex. 29: 45, 46) "I will dwell among the children of Israel and will be their God; and they shall know that I am the Lord their God who brought them forth out of the land of Egypt that I may dwell among them: I am the Lord their God." And again (Lev. 26: 3, 11, 12); "If ye walk in my statutes and keep my commandments and do them . . . . . I will set my tabernacle among you, and my soul shall not abhor you, and I will walk among you, and will be your God, and ye shall be my people." These are specimen passages from the records of the ancient economy. As to the Gospel age it may suffice to refer to the promises of our Lord; "He that loveth me shall be loved of my Father, and I will love him and *will manifest myself unto him.*" "If a man love me, he will keep my words, and my Father will love him, and we *will come unto him* and *make our abode with him.*" "It is expedient for you that I go away, for if I go not away, the Comforter will not come; but if I depart, I will send him unto you." "He shall teach you all things, and bring all things to your remembrance whatsoever I have said unto you." "He shall testify of me." "He will guide you into all truth. He shall take of mine and shall show it unto you," etc. John 14: 21, 23, 26, and 15: 26, and 16: 7–15.—— From Paul come these expressive words. "Know ye not that ye are the temple of God, and that the Spirit of God dwelleth in you?" "Know ye not that your body is the temple of the Holy Ghost which is in you which ye have of God, and ye are not your own?" "And what agreement hath the temple of God with idols? For ye are the temple of the living God," etc. 1 Cor. 3: 16, and 6: 19, and 2 Cor. 6: 16. "In whom (Christ) ye are builded together for an habitation of God through the Spirit" (Eph. 2: 22). Paul speaks of this doctrine as specially *well known*—one of the obvious and fundamental truths of the Gospel system. In its very nature it must be.——The exiles needed precisely the encouragement and the inspiration which such promises bore to their hearts. The time then present was the great crisis in their moral renovation. The fierce judgments of the Almighty had smitten down the city and temple of their fathers. Would they, the children, now turn from their idol-worship; open their eyes to the spiritual mercies which the Lord was so gloriously revealing; abandon all their carnal trust in the external things of Judaism, and seek the new heart and the new spirit which the Lord so kindly promised? If so, this revelation of a glorious future for the true Israel and Zion would be most pertinent and most welcome.——"Save them out of all their dwelling-places wherein they have sinned," is a remarkable expression, tacitly implying that the very localities of their sin had become a power, under the laws of association, toward continued sinning, from which they needed to be saved. Was it for this reason that the Lord sent off the better and hopeful portion of the people into exile till he could burn the land over with the fires of war and desolation, and efface the last vestige of its old pollutions, and break up forever those impure associations which ages of idol-worship had impressed on its hills and groves and its valley of Hinnom?——And is there any thing analogous to this in the Christian life of God's people whereby he crucifies the power of old sins, and smites down the influence of their mental associations so as to undo effectually the mischief which years of sin have wrought?——Other questions, somewhat less vital intrinsically, yet important and variously held, demand notice; *e. g.*, *When* are these prophecies to be fulfilled? Do they not assume the yet future restoration of the Jews to Canaan and make that land the locality, the *place*, of their fulfillment?——Briefly, my views of these chapters of Ezekiel (34, 36, 37) are these: They are general, not specific; comprehensive rather than minute. Their central thought is *promise*—the assurance of God's love and faithfulness to his Zion, especially in his pledge of his presence as a power unto her sanctification. "I will be with you to sanctify and to save you from all your sins," is the elementary and precious truth which they bear. Now let it be carefully noted:—*This great central truth applied under the old dispensation while it lasted, in harmony with the genius of that dispensation. It applies under the new, in harmony with its genius and spirit.* Under the old, it promised restoration to the literal Canaan and the reëstablishment of the Mosaic ritual system. It came to the exiles with these cheering promises and hopes, in terms which they could not misunderstand. To them these promises in this sense were the very thing they needed, for the Zion and kingdom of God had not yet cast off the forms of the Mosaic system.——But for the gospel age, under the New Testament dispensation, these same promises had a new and different specific sense. Their general sense was and is still the same; but their external, specific sense has changed. To explain this change and to bring the practical views and the actual Christian life of the church into harmony with it were the great struggle and labor of the Apostolic age. To induce converted Jews to let go the ritual and joyfully accept the spiritual; to forego what was exclusive and national in Judaism, and still retain all that its symbols signified and its promises pledged, cost the Apostles whole years of intensest labor. That labor should suffice to give us the clew to the interpretation of these prophecies *as applied to the Gospel age*. That part of their significance which yet remained to be fulfilled after the death of Christ—no small part surely—must be seen in the light of New Testament ideas. It would be the greatest and grossest of mistakes to ignore the immense work wrought by Christ and his Apostles toward the just interpretation of the Mosaic ritual system and of the whole Hebrew economy, with all its gospel promise and gospel prophecy, in their application to the Christian age.——We have this gospel idea in a nutshell in the passages already quoted from Paul. Comparing Paul (2 Cor. 6: 16) with Ezekiel in the passage before us, we shall see it. Ezekiel reads, "I will set my sanctuary in the midst of them forever more;" "My tabernacle shall be with them; yea, I will be their God and they shall be my people," etc. Now, in the old dispensation, this sanctuary was God's temple of wood and stone; his residence in it was through the visible glory over the ark of the covenant.——What form does his presence assume in the new dispensation? Let Paul answer. "*Ye* are the temple of the living God; as God hath said (*e. g.*, Ezek. 37: 26, 28 and elsewhere) "I will dwell in them and walk in them, and I will be their God, and they shall be my people." Every Christian becomes "a *temple* of the living God;" "an habitation of God through the Spirit." Consequently in the Christian age we look no longer for the restriction of worship to the one place, the holy temple at Jerusalem. Our Lord decided this very question in his discourse with the woman of Samaria (Jn. 4: 20–24). Hence we look for no reoccupancy of Canaan by the covenant people, for the covenant people are now the Christian men and women of every nation under the whole heaven, and the Canaan where they offer accepted worship is any place whatever in the wide world where they please to worship God in spirit and in truth.——To bring back the Jews to Palestine in times yet future under this promise carries with it the return to Judaism and the rebuilding of the material temple, and goes back from the accepted worship every-where of all pious hearts through faith in the Redeemer's blood—goes back from the glorious gospel idea that the Holy Ghost makes every Christian heart his temple;—goes back to reëstablish that ancient system which in the age of Paul had already "waxed old and was vanishing away." (Heb. 8: 13).—— The position to which I adhere is that the church is now and henceforward in the Christian age and not in the Jewish; that she has passed by the Jewish, and that God does not intend she shall return to it again; that the Jewish in its peculiar form and symbolic significance has done its work and will never do it over again; and that it behooves us to be satisfied with the Christian system, make the most of it, develop its inherent energies to their utmost extent, and thus, through the resources of the Spirit's power, cause it to become mighty through God to convert the nations to Christ and regenerate the world.

CHAPTERS XXXVIII AND XXXIX.

These two chapters are essentially one in their subject-matter and aim, and are closely connected with chaps. 34, 36, and 37 preceding, and with chaps. 40–48 following. They are manifestly part of the series of prophecies recorded in the three preceding chapters—refer to the same great future of Zion, and are in the same sense general rather than specific in their ultimate meaning. The one great truth which they teach is expressed forcibly by Isaiah (54: 17, 15). "No weapon that is formed against thee shall prosper." "Behold, they shall gather together (*i. e.*, against thee) but not *by me*; whosoever shall gather together against thee shall fall for thy sake."——The manner of presenting this great truth—the costume of the prophecy—sets forth that in the remote future, after Israel had been a long time at rest and in peace in their own land, and had become wealthy, a vast horde of northern barbarians should fall upon their land for purposes of plunder; but God calls for a sword against them. Indignant at this outrage, and jealous for his holy name, he interposes with terrific judgments upon them, cuts them off with immense slaughter, and forever exalts his name before all the heathen as the Deliverer and Savior of his people.——It is assumed with a fair degree of probability that Ezekiel names these supposed enemies of Israel with his eye on a vast marauding expedition of Scythians, in which they swept over Western Asia about the time of the fall of Nineveh (*i. e.*, B. C. 625), and were not thoroughly driven back short of about twenty-eight years. Gesenius (in his Thesaurus) says; "There is scarcely a doubt that for the most part those nations are meant here whom the Greeks comprehended under the name Scythians, whose vast expedition against Egypt in the very age of Ezekiel seems to have given that prophet the occasion for this reference—the handle for such a prophecy." The writer of the article on Magog in Smith's Bible Dictionary represents them as at this time a formidable power throughout Western Asia; as having been crowded from their original homes, north of the Caucasian mountains, by the inroads of the Massagetae; as then forcing their way into Asia Minor in war against Lydia, and later, against Media; then into Egypt; whence they were finally ejected (B. C. 596) after having made their name a terror to the whole Eastern world. They are described by classic writers as expert with the bow, famous as mounted bowmen, and notorious for their rapacious and cruel habits.——The memory of these events being yet fresh in the minds of his readers, Ezekiel (*i. e.*, God *through* him) selected these Scythians as the symbol of earthly violence arrayed against the people of God, but meeting a signal and utter overthrow.

1. And the word of the Lord came unto me, saying,
2. Son of man, set thy face against Gog, the land of Magog, the chief prince of Meshech and Tubal, and prophesy against him,
3. And say, Thus saith the Lord God; Behold, I *am* against thee, O Gog, the chief prince of Meshech and Tubal:
4. And I will turn thee back, and put hooks into thy jaws, and I will bring thee forth, and all thine army, horses and horsemen, all of them clothed with all sorts *of armor, even* a great company *with* bucklers and shields, all of them handling swords:
5. Persia, Ethiopia, and Libya with them; all of them with shield and helmet:
6. Gomer, and all his bands; the house of Togarmah of the north quarters, and all his bands: *and* many people with thee.

"Magog" is here the name of the king; "Gog" the name of his country.——The word rendered "chief," in the clause, "chief prince," etc., is not an adjective as our translators supposed, but a proper noun. The word is *Rosch*, and is supposed to be the earliest historical allusion to the people afterward known as the Russians.——"Meshech and Tubal," the countries of the Moschi and the Tibareni, lay on the south of the Caspian, the home of the people known by the ancient Greeks as the Scythians. Josephus, (Antiquities 1: 6: 1) says that "Magog, second son of Japheth, (Gen. 10: 2) founded those who were called by the Greeks Scythians."——"Gomer," named first of the sons of Japheth (Gen. 10: 2), probably the father and founder of the Cimmerians, helped to swell the great Scythian horde. "Togarmah" was a kindred tribe, thought by some to be the Armenians.——Persia, Ethiopia, and Libya are named here with them to fill out the representation of an immense and countless horde. These names do not occur again.——In v. 4 the original phrase rendered, "clothed with all sorts of armor," seems not to refer to military *armor*, but to gorgeous apparel. Their armor, offensive and defensive, is spoken of subsequently.

7. Be thou prepared, and prepare for thyself, thou, and all thy company that are assembled unto thee, and be thou a guard unto them.
8. After many days thou shalt be visited: in the latter years thou shalt come into the land *that is* brought back

from the sword, *and is* gathered out of many people, against the mountains of Israel, which have been always waste: but it is brought forth out of the nations, and they shall dwell safely all of them.

9. Thou shalt ascend and come like a storm, thou shalt be like a cloud to cover the land, thou, and all thy bands, and many people with thee.

"Be thou prepared;" "prepare for thyself;" are not to be taken as commanding in serious earnest, but as daring and challenging in irony. Since so you will, do it if you dare! So through Isaiah, (chap. 8: 9, 10) the Lord accosts the proud Assyrians and others; "Associate yourselves, O ye nations, and ye shall be broken to pieces; gird yourselves, and ye shall be broken to pieces. Take counsel together, and it shall come to naught," etc.——"Be thou a guard unto them," means rather, *Take the lead of them;* head the grand enterprise, O Gog!——In v. 8, "Thou shalt be visited," means— not, thou shalt be *punished*, but thou shalt *muster* thy forces and become their leader, making all ready for the great expedition against Israel. The prediction of his punishment comes in later, in v. 18.——This verse describes the land of Israel as having passed through the scenes of the Chaldean captivity and desolation; as having been long waste, but as repeopled, reclaimed from its waste condition, and now for a long time prosperous. I paraphrase the latter part of the verse thus: "The mountains of Israel which have long lain waste—the same which have been resettled by returning exiles brought forth from the nations, and who have now long dwelt in safety and prosperity." Against this people, Gog and his hosts came down like a storm to sweep and a cloud to cover the land.

10. Thus saith the Lord God; It shall also come to pass, *that* at the same time shall things come into thy mind, and thou shalt think an evil thought:

11. And thou shalt say, I will go up to the land of unwalled villages; I will go to them that are at rest, that dwell safely, all of them dwelling without walls, and having neither bars nor gates,

12. To take a spoil, and to take a prey; to turn thy hand upon the desolate places *that are now* inhabited, and upon the people *that are* gathered out of the nations, which have gotten cattle and goods, that dwell in the midst of the land.

God knew and here describes how the thought of plundering a people, unprotected and off their guard, excited his rapacity and put him upon this expedition.——The last clause of v. 12 means not precisely "in the *midst* of the land," but on the *height* of the land. The Jews thought of their country, Palestine, as not only the glory of all lands, but also as the crown, the *height* of the world. This is the sense of the rare word here used by the prophet.

It occurs elsewhere, Judg. 9: 37; there rendered, "the middle of the land," but better, "down from the *height* of the land."

13. Sheba, and Dedan, and the merchants of Tarshish, with all the young lions thereof, shall say unto thee, Art thou come to take a spoil? hast thou gathered thy company to take a prey? to carry away silver and gold, to take away cattle and goods, to take a great spoil?

Sheba and Dedan, prominent districts of Arabia, and Tarshish of Spain, famed for its trade with the Phenician cities, appear suddenly and for the moment only in this drama. Their question might under some circumstances be taken as a rebuke; but in this case probably it is one of sympathy, as much as to say, You are in, it seems, for a grand scene of plunder: let us have a share! For these people also are to be thought of as enemies of God's children, and as introduced here to amplify the description and set forth that *all the nations* of the earth, outside of Palestine, are in arms against her for one combined and fearful onslaught.

14. Therefore, son of man, prophesy and say unto Gog, Thus saith the Lord God; In that day when my people of Israel dwelleth safely, shalt thou not know *it?*

15. And thou shalt come from thy place out of the north parts, thou, and many people with thee, all of them riding upon horses, a great company, and a mighty army:

16. And thou shalt come up against my people of Israel, as a cloud to cover the land; it shall be in the latter days, and I will bring thee against my land, that the heathen may know me, when I shall be sanctified in thee, O Gog, before their eyes.

17. Thus saith the Lord God; *Art* thou he of whom I have spoken in old time by my servants the prophets of Israel, which prophesied in those days *many* years, that I would bring thee against them?

The points made here are not intricate. Shall not these combined nations know their time for assault on my defenseless people? They will. They are to come from the northern parts, analogous to the avalanche from northern Europe that overran the old and effete Roman empire; or in later times, the sweep of the Tartar hordes under Tamerlane.——It should be "in the latter days"— here quite indefinite and very probably referring in part, perhaps in large part, to events yet future.——V. 17 intimates that this onslaught upon the kingdom and people of God is the same which his prophets had predicted in years then past. Since no prophet up to that time had named precisely these enemies, we are compelled (as above indicated) to give these names a general and not specific sense, accounting them to represent not those nations in particular, but any and every form of hostility to the kingdom of God. Only in this sense could it be said to have been the burden of previous prophecy.——In the clause, "In those days *many* years," the word "*many*" is superfluous, the sense being, "in those days and years."

18. And it shall come to pass at the same time when Gog shall come against the land of Israel, saith the Lord God, *that* my fury shall come up in my face.

19. For in my jealousy *and* in the fire of my wrath have I spoken, Surely in that day there shall be a great shaking in the land of Israel;

20. So that the fishes of the sea, and the fowls of the heaven, and the beasts of the field, and all creeping things that creep upon the earth, and all the men that *are* upon the face of the earth, shall shake at my presence, and the mountains shall be thrown down, and the steep places shall fall, and every wall shall fall to the ground.

21. And I will call for a sword against him throughout all my mountains, saith the Lord God: every man's sword shall be against his brother.

22. And I will plead against him with pestilence and with blood; and I will rain upon him and upon his bands, and upon the many people that *are* with him, an overflowing rain, and great hailstones, fire, and brimstone.

23. Thus will I magnify myself, and sanctify myself; and I will be known in the eyes of many nations, and they shall know that I *am* the Lord.

"My fury shall come up in my face," refers to the usual manifestations of intense excitement—a flushed countenance, the blood rushing to the head and imprinting the marks of strong feeling upon the face. The indignation of the Almighty is intensely aroused against these heathen hosts who are combined to pillage and destroy his people. A great shaking follows, a terrible earthquake, felt by all who dwell in the vast deep, by every fowl of the heavens and every beast of the field, before which the mountains are thrown down, and every wall built of man, however deep-laid its foundations, shall fall to the ground. The mighty God calls for a sword against this huge host throughout all his mountains; every man's sword is against his brother. These enemies of God's people become their own destroyers. Ah truly, evermore the Lord knows how to make the wrath of man praise himself and to gird about him the extremest wrath of men as his own sword for their destruction. The last clause of this significant passage (Ps. 76: 10) announces the very principle or law developed in this predicted slaughter. The Almighty God girds on the extremest wrath of these wicked men and makes it his own sword for their universal destruction.——The description here is graphic and fearful. "I will plead against him with pestilence and with blood"—the plague combining with the sword to cut short the lives of myriads and strew the land with mountain heaps of the slain.——"I will rain upon him and upon his bands and upon the many people that are with him, an overflowing rain and great hailstones, fire and brimstone"—in which description all the great and destructive agencies of the physical world combine to fill out the picture and make up a scene of appalling slaughter. So the Psalmist; "Upon the wicked, God will rain snares, fire and brimstone and an horrible tempest; this shall be the portion of their cup (Ps. 11: 6). The fire on Sodom (Gen. 19: 24, 25) and Isaiah's smitten Idumea (chap. 34) are in the same strain of appalling grandeur and of fearful destruction!——The exalted purpose of God in these judgments is shown, viz., to magnify his power; to make his name great; to vindicate his holiness and his righteous justice, and to make all the nations know that he is the Lord, the glorious Ruler of all kingdoms, and the no less glorious Deliverer of his people.

CHAPTER XXXIX.

This chapter continues and closes the subject of the preceding one, expanding its descriptions and reiterating its momentous truths.

1. Therefore, thou son of man, prophesy against Gog, and say, Thus saith the Lord God; Behold, I *am* against thee, O Gog, the chief prince of Meshech and Tubal:

2. And I will turn thee back, and leave but the sixth part of thee, and will cause thee to come up from the north parts, and will bring thee upon the mountains of Israel:

3. And I will smite thy bow out of thy left hand, and will cause thine arrows to fall out of thy right hand.

4. Thou shalt fall upon the mountains of Israel, thou, and all thy bands, and the people that *is* with thee: I will give thee unto the ravenous birds of every sort, and *to* the beasts of the field, to be devoured.

5. Thou shalt fall upon the open field: for I have spoken *it*, saith the Lord God.

6. And I will send a fire on Magog, and among them that dwell carelessly in the isles: and they shall know that I *am* the Lord.

7. So will I make my holy name known in the midst of my people Israel; and I will not *let them* pollute my holy

name any more: and the heathen shall know that I *am* the Lord, the Holy One in Israel.

In the first clause of v. 2 the ablest modern critics read, not "I will leave but a sixth part of thee;" but, "I will bring thee out, *and lead or urge thee on*," etc.—in harmony with the latter part of the verse and describing yet further God's permissive agency in suffering this vast combination of his enemies. The prophet proceeds soon to speak of their destruction; but does not touch that subject in this second verse.——In general these verses repeat the points made in the previous chapter, and in the subsequent parts of this.

8. Behold, it is come, and it is done, saith the Lord God; this *is* the day whereof I have spoken.

This verse corresponds with chap. 38: 17, to the point that this invasion represents the hostility of God's enemies against his cause and people, and had even then been already spoken of by the prophets.

9. And they that dwell in the cities of Israel shall go forth, and shall set on fire and burn the weapons, both the shields and the bucklers, the bows and the arrows, and the hand-staves, and the spears, and they shall burn them with fire seven years:

10. So that they shall take no wood out of the field, neither cut down *any* out of the forests; for they shall burn the weapons with fire: and they shall spoil those that spoiled them, and rob those that robbed them, saith the Lord God.

To measure the vastness of this grand armament and give the reader some conception of its magnitude, their weapons of war are said to have supplied fuel for all Israel seven years.——Now is the time for Israel to rob and plunder those who have long robbed and plundered her.——These "*weapons*" made thus prominent remind us of Isaiah's words; "No *weapon* that is formed against thee shall prosper."

11. And it shall come to pass in that day, *that* I will give unto Gog a place there of graves in Israel, the valley of the passengers on the east of the sea: and it shall stop the *noses* of the passengers: and there shall they bury Gog and all his multitude: and they shall call *it* The valley of Hamon-gog.

12. And seven months shall the house of Israel be burying of them, that they may cleanse the land.

13. Yea, all the people of the land shall bury *them*: and

it shall be to them a renown the day that I shall be glorified, saith the Lord God.

14. And they shall sever out men of continual employment passing through the land to bury with the passengers those that remain upon the face of the earth, to cleanse it: after the end of seven months shall they search.

15. And the passengers *that* pass through the land, when *any* seeth a man's bone, then shall he set up a sign by it, till the buriers have buried it in the valley of Hamon-gog.

16. And also the name of the city *shall be* Hamonah. Thus shall they cleanse the land.

Still further to aid the mind to conceive the vastness of this slaughter, the prophet describes the burial of their dead. It occupied seven months—seven, the round number occurring here again in its long, indefinite sense. At first all the people of the land seem to have been engaged in this work. Ultimately they set apart "men of continual employment" to prosecute the work as their regular and constant business. Even they had the aid of all travelers who were passing through the land. If any of these saw an unburied body or bone, they set a pillar to mark the spot, till the force detailed for this purpose had buried all.——In v. 11 the word "*noses*," in italics, should be omitted and the passage be read; "It" (the place of graves for Gog) "shall stop the way of passengers"— shall block their passage. Located in a great thoroughfare along the eastern shore of the sea, it would obstruct travel by its masses of slaughtered dead.——In v. 14, "bury with the passengers," is *with the aid* of the passengers, as the next verse explains, and does not imply that the passengers are buried with the slain enemies of God.——The valley of Hamon-gog is the valley of the multitude or *hosts* of Gog.——In v. 14, "shall they search," means they shall glean thoroughly; shall make a very special and final exploration. The kingdom of God must be purified with the utmost care. The Mosaic law accounted defilement by a dead body more·polluting than any other. And of all dead bodies, those of their heathen foes would be most polluting.

17. And, thou son of man, thus saith the Lord God; Speak unto every feathered fowl, and to every beast of the field, Assemble yourselves, and come; gather yourselves on every side to my sacrifice that I do sacrifice for you, *even a* great sacrifice upon the mountains of Israel, that ye may eat flesh, and drink blood.

18. Ye shall eat the flesh of the mighty, and drink the blood of the princes of the earth, of rams, of lambs, and of goats, of bullocks, all of them fatlings of Bashan.

19. And ye shall eat fat till ye be full, and drink blood

till ye be drunken, of my sacrifice which I have sacrificed for you.

20. Thus ye shall be filled at my table with horses and chariots, with mighty men, and with all men of war, saith the Lord God.

Here is another of the usual features in a description of great slaughter—a summons to every beast and fowl; to the hyenas and vultures that delight in human flesh; to gather to this great feast prepared of God for them. Of course, this aims to fill out and heighten the description of an immense slaughter.

21. And I will set my glory among the heathen, and all the heathen shall see my judgment that I have executed, and my hand that I have laid upon them.

22. So the house of Israel shall know that I *am* the Lord their God from that day and forward.

Sublimely will the Lord Jehovah "set his glory before all the heathen" by means of this appalling destruction of their armed hosts. They shall know that this is the work of his hand, and shall see that indeed he is mighty to save his people and to avenge them on their proudest foes.——The house of Israel too shall see and know God's hand. This grand display of it will suffice from this time forward and for evermore! They will never again have occasion to doubt whether God loves Zion and will defend her against whatever may assail.

23. And the heathen shall know that the house of Israel went into captivity for their iniquity: because they trespassed against me, therefore hid I my face from them, and gave them into the hand of their enemies: so fell they all by the sword.

24. According to their uncleanness, and according to their transgressions have I done unto them, and hid my face from them.

Most pertinently the Lord declares that now the heathen shall understand why he seemed to abandon his people and leave them to go into captivity. It was not (as they would fain suppose) because his arm was too short to save them; neither was it that he had utterly forsaken them and given them over to hopeless ruin: but it was because of their apostasy and transgression, and hence as a discipline to reclaim, and not as a judgment that should exterminate.

25. Therefore thus saith the Lord God; Now will I bring again the captivity of Jacob, and have mercy upon the whole house of Israel, and will be jealous for my holy name;

26. After that they have borne their shame, and all their trespasses whereby they have trespassed against me, when they dwelt safely in their land, and none made *them* afraid.

27. When I have brought them again from the people, and gathered them out of their enemies' lands, and am sanctified in them in the sight of many nations;

28. Then shall they know that I *am* the Lord their God, which caused them to be led into captivity among the heathen: but I have gathered them unto their own land, and have left none of them any more there.

29. Neither will I hide my face any more from them: for I have poured out my Spirit upon the house of Israel, saith the Lord God.

The nearer fulfillment of vs. 25, 26—the first installment of blessings—came in the restoration from Babylon under Zerubbabel. Its subsequent installments belong chiefly or wholly to the gospel age, and take the form peculiar to this age—gospel blessings. That great restoration was a pledge and symbol of all future deliverances that God would achieve for his people. In its light they might see that their own God is almighty to save, and will certainly fulfill every good word he has spoken.——The perpetuity of his favor and love is insured by the mission and work of his Spirit; for the prosperity of God's people is forever sure, provided only that their hearts are kept pure before the Lord. Given, a sanctified people, and there will also be a prosperous and happy people. Zion has nothing to fear, provided only that she walks humbly and softly before God. "*For* I have poured out my Spirit upon the house of Israel," is therefore the unfailing guaranty and pledge of abiding and glorious prosperity to Zion.——Of course this promise looks down into the gospel age, of which age the mission of the Comforter is the grand, distinctive characteristic. Jesus spake by anticipation of this mission and of its fruits when "in the last day, that great day of the feast" (Jn. 7: 37–39) "he stood and cried, 'If any man thirst let him come unto me and drink.' He that believeth on me, as the scripture hath said, out of his belly shall flow rivers of living water;—for he spake this of the Spirit which they that believe on him should receive when the Holy Ghost should be given"—which time then was not yet because that Jesus was not yet glorified.

As to the general scope of these two chapters, treating of a great invasion of Israel by the hosts of Gog, there can be no reasonable doubt. They depict the intense antagonism of the powers of sin and hell in this world against the church and kingdom of God. In costume Jewish, to make it readily intelligible to the people for whom Ezekiel wrote, it is yet in thought and bearing, mainly Christian, belonging to the latter days of the reign of Satan. It does not show that the land of Israel (Palestine proper) shall be the battle-ground; it does not teach that this malign onset shall be with bows and spears and horsemen; it does not even show that Zion's enemies shall come out of "the north parts:"—all these are features of costume, drapery, representation. The real truth lies under all these features and should be carefully kept distinct from them all. This truth is that sin and Satan will assail God in the form of an assault upon his truth and his people. The conflict will be terrible. What precise form it shall assume, this passage did not aim to show. The forms of Satan's onsets change from age to age. Their name is legion. It is quite in vain to speculate beforehand as to the form they will assume in any given age, present or future. It rather behooves us to study all his wiles and never be ignorant of his devices; but especially, to rally round the banner of our King and accept his leadership in the mighty conflict. So fighting and so trusting, victory is sure to Zion, for the mouth of the Lord hath spoken it!

CHAPTER XL.

The remaining nine chapters constitute one vision, given to the prophet in the twenty-fifth year of the captivity, *i. e.*, about fourteen years after the fall of Jerusalem. It is entirely unique in its character, yet closely connected in its leading thought and purpose with chapters 36–39, immediately preceding.——I propose to state first in general and briefly, my view of its meaning and purpose; then pass over the whole with explanations of special passages; and then finally, give my reasons for my system of interpretation.

I. I regard this vision as an ideal representation of the glorious future of Messiah's kingdom. The *mode* of representing it corresponds with the external character of Christ's church and kingdom under the Mosaic economy. This correspondence is natural and should be expected. Ezekiel and his people, the exiles in Chaldea, were familiar with no other form of divine worship and with no other organization—no other external life, for the people of God. Hence there was the same reason for using this class of symbols to represent the future kingdom of Christ as for using the Hebrew language in speaking to them, rather than the Greek, the Latin, or the English—viz,, the fitness of using figures and symbols as well as words which the prophet and his people would readily understand.——Let it be borne in mind that Ezekiel was by birth, training and profession, a *priest*. Of course he was perfectly at home in all that pertained to the temple, the priesthood, and the prescribed forms of Mosaic worship. In the world of symbols, therefore, this was his vernacular tongue. Approximately and in general, the same may be said of the Jews of his time, his captive brethren.——In the next place let it be remembered that the people had now been in exile twenty-five years, and their beloved city in ruins fourteen;—long enough to awaken anxious fears lest their people should never return, the temple never be rebuilt, and lest the Zion of their God should never rise again from its ruins. These fears are amply indicated in chap. 37: 11. To meet precisely this great fear and to inspire a precious confidence in a future for Zion far more glorious than its past had ever been, this vision came. It describes with great minuteness (chaps. 40–43) the new temple yet to be; then the return of the glorious Shekinah to fix his abode once more in this temple, henceforward to be there perpetually (chap. 43); next the altar and its laws of worship; then, regulations for the prince and for the priests (chap. 44); then the assignment of territory for the temple, the priests, the Levites, and the adjacent city (chap. 45). Next, various ordinances for the people, and for the prince (chap. 46); then a vision of holy waters issuing from the sanctuary, and of the blessings they bear where they go; then the boundaries of their land (chap. 47); and finally the apportionment of territory to the several tribes, together with a great reservation for sacred purposes—for the temple, the priests, the Levites, and the prince—all culminating in the one comprehensive fact, embodied in the name of the city, "*Jehovah Shammah;*" "*the Lord is there.*"

As to the meaning of this very full and minute vision, I reject the literal sense most decidedly. It may be understood to *assume* a restoration from their then present captivity, but certainly it does not relate specially to this nearer restoration under Zerubbabel and does not minutely describe it. Nor does it teach that at some period in the Christian age the Jews shall be restored to their former land, and then their temple be rebuilt, their ceremonial worship be restored, and this modified form of the Mosaic system be developed into actual life.——As already indicated, I shall reserve my argument against this view till the whole passage is before us. Then it will be more in place and better understood. At this stage it may suffice to say that I regard this vision as a magnificent panorama, thoroughly symbolical, and setting forth in Jewish costume and drapery the future prosperity, the order, beauty, and moral power of the church in those days when God shall dwell forever with his people by his Holy Spirit, a power unto holiness in their hearts and lives, making the institutions and agencies of the gospel exceedingly effective for evangelizing the world and bringing the nations to know the Lord.

1. In the five and twentieth year of our captivity, in the beginning of the year, in the tenth *day* of the month, in the fourteenth year after that the city was smitten, in the selfsame day the hand of the Lord was upon me, and brought me thither.

2. In the visions of God brought he me into the land of Israel, and set me upon a very high mountain, by which *was* as the frame of a city on the south.

3. And he brought me thither, and behold, *there was* a

man, whose appearance was like the appearance of brass, with a line of flax in his hand, and a measuring reed; and he stood in the gate,

4. And the man said unto me, Son of man, behold with thine eyes, and hear with thine ears, and set thy heart upon all that I shall shew thee; for to the intent that I might shew *them* unto thee *art* thou brought hither: declare all that thou seest to the house of Israel.

In these verses we have the *date* of this vision, as already explained in my introduction to these chapters. Then the account proceeds to show that this was truly a *vision*, the prophet being transported to the land of Israel and there shown the frame of a city and a man bearing the instruments for its measurement. The prophet is directed to note with very special care all he shall see, that he may declare it to his people.

5. And behold a wall on the outside of the house round about, and in the man's hand a measuring reed of six cubits *long* by the cubit and a hand-breadth: so he measured the breadth of the building, one reed: and the height, one reed.

6. Then came he unto the gate which looketh toward the east, and went up the stairs thereof, and measured the threshold of the gate, *which was* one reed broad; and the other threshold *of the gate, which was* one reed broad.

7. And *every* little chamber *was* one reed long, and one reed broad; and between the little chambers *were* five cubits; and the threshold of the gate by the porch of the gate within *was* one reed.

8. He measured also the porch of the gate within, one reed.

9. Then measured he the porch of the gate, eight cubits; and the posts thereof, two cubits; and the porch of the gate *was* inward.

10. And the little chambers of the gate eastward *were* three on this side, and three on that side; they three *were* of one measure: and the posts had one measure on this side and on that side.

11. And he measured the breadth of the entry of the gate, ten cubits; *and* the entry of the gate, thirteen cubits.

12. The space also before the little chambers *was* one cubit *on this side*, and the space *was* one cubit on that side: and the little chambers *were* six cubits on this side, and six cubits on that side.

13. He measured then the gate from the roof of *one* little chamber to the roof of another: the breadth *was* five and twenty cubits, door against door.

14. He made also posts of threescore cubits, even unto the post of the court round about the gate.

15. And from the face of the gate of the entrance unto the face of the porch of the inner gate *were* fifty cubits.

16. And *there were* narrow windows to the little chambers, and to their posts within the gate round about, and likewise to the arches: and windows *were* round about inward: and upon *each* post *were* palm-trees.

17. Then brought he me into the outward court, and lo, *there were* chambers, and a pavement made for the court round about: thirty chambers *were* upon the pavement.

18. And the pavement by the side of the gates, over against the length of the gates *was* the lower pavement.

19. Then he measured the breadth from the forefront of the lower gate unto the forefront of the inner court without, a hundred cubits eastward and northward.

20. And the gate of the outward court that looked toward the north, he measured the length thereof, and the breadth thereof.

21. And the little chambers thereof *were* three on this side and three on that side; and the posts thereof and the arches thereof were after the measure of the first gate: the length thereof *was* fifty cubits, and the breadth five and twenty cubits.

22. And their windows, and their arches, and their palm-trees, *were* after the measure of the gate that looketh toward the east: and they went up unto it by seven steps; and the arches thereof *were* before them.

23. And the gate of the inner court *was* over against the gate toward the north, and toward the east; and he measured from gate to gate a hundred cubits.

24. After that he brought me toward the south, and behold a gate toward the south: and he measured the posts thereof and the arches thereof according to these measures.

25. And *there were* windows in it and in the arches thereof round about, like those windows: the length *was* fifty cubits, and the breadth five and twenty cubits.

26. And *there were* seven steps to go up to it, and the arches thereof *were* before them: and it had palm-trees, one on this side, and another on that side, upon the posts thereof.

27. And *there was* a gate in the inner court toward the south: and he measured from gate to gate toward the south a hundred cubits.

28. And he brought me to the inner court by the south-

gate: and he measured the south-gate according to these measures:

29. And the little chambers thereof, and the posts thereof, and the arches thereof, according to these measures: and *there were* windows in it and in the arches round about: *it was* fifty cubits long and five and twenty cubits broad.

30. And the arches round about *were* five and twenty cubits long, and five cubits broad.

31. And the arches thereof *were* toward the outer court; and palm-trees *were* upon the posts thereof, and the going up to it *had* eight steps.

32. And he brought me into the inner court toward the the east: and he measured the gate according to these measures.

33. And the little chambers thereof, and the posts thereof, and the arches thereof, *were* according to these measures: and *there were* windows therein and in the arches thereof round about: *it was* fifty cubits long, and five and twenty cubits broad.

34. And the arches thereof *were* toward the outward court; and palm-trees *were* upon the posts thereof, on this side, and on that side: and the going up to it *had* eight steps.

35. And he brought me to the north gate, and measured *it* according to these measures;

36. The little chambers thereof, the posts thereof, and the arches thereof, and the windows to it round about: the length *was* fifty cubits, and the breadth five and twenty cubits.

37. And the posts thereof *were* toward the outer court; and palm-trees *were* upon the posts thereof, on this side, and on that side: and the going up to it *had* eight steps.

38. And the chambers and the entries thereof *were* by the posts of the gates, where they washed the burnt-offering.

39. And in the porch of the gate *were* two tables on this side, and two tables on that side, to slay thereon the burnt-offering, and the sin-offering, and the trespass-offering.

40. And at the side without, as one goeth up to the entry of the north gate, *were* two tables; and on the other side, which *was* at the porch of the gate, *were* two tables.

41. Four tables *were* on this side, and four tables on that side, by the side of the gate; eight tables, whereupon they slew *their sacrifices.*

42. And the four tables *were* of hewn stone for the burnt-offering, of a cubit and a half long, and a cubit and a half broad, and one cubit high: whereupon also they laid the

instruments wherewith they slew the burnt-offering and the sacrifice.

43. And within *were* hooks, a hand broad, fastened round about: and upon the tables *was* the flesh of the offering.

44. And without the inner gate *were* the chambers of the singers in the inner court, which *was* at the side of the north gate; and their prospect *was* toward the south: one at the side of the east gate *having* the prospect toward the north.

45. And he said unto me, This chamber, whose prospect *is* toward the south, *is* for the priests, the keepers of the charge of the house.

46. And the chamber whose prospect *is* toward the north *is* for the priests, the keepers of the charge of the altar: these *are* the sons of Zadok among the sons of Levi, which come near to the Lord to minister unto him.

47. So he measured the court, a hundred cubits long, and a hundred cubits broad, four-square; and the altar *that was* before the house.

48. And he brought me to the porch of the house, and measured *each* post of the porch, five cubits on this side, and five cubits on that side: and the breadth of the gate *was* three cubits on this side, and three cubits on that side.

49. The length of the porch *was* twenty cubits, and the breadth eleven cubits; and *he brought me* by the steps whereby they went up to it: and *there were* pillars by the posts, one on this side, and another on that side.

There seems to be no occasion for extended comments on this description of the temple. Let it suffice to suggest to the reader the remarkable regularity and uniformity of dimensions that prevailed throughout, indicating, we must suppose, the beautiful *order* that shall prevail under the final triumph of the gospel in our world. Then every thing will be in its place: whatever is shapeless, rude, uncouth, will be discarded; all will be morally right, and the whole external world will be in beautiful harmony with the perfect moral order and purity that will then rule in human hearts and in all society.

CHAPTER XLI.

This continued description embraces the most holy place; the chambers also, and the altar, pointed out to the prophet particularly as the table of the Lord, with frequent allusions to the ornamentation of these apartments and walls by means of engraving upon them figures of palm-trees and cherubim.——The same wonderful regularity obtains here as in the previous chapter, and with the same significance.

1. Afterward he brought me to the temple, and measured the posts, six cubits broad on the one side, and six cubits broad on the other side, *which was* the breadth of the tabernacle.

2. And the breadth of the door *was* ten cubits; and the sides of the door *were* five cubits on the one side, and five cubits on the other side: and he measured the length thereof, forty cubits: and the breadth, twenty cubits.

3. Then went he inward, and measured the post of the door, two cubits; and the door, six cubits; and the breadth of the door, seven cubits.

4. So he measured the length thereof, twenty cubits; and the breadth, twenty cubits, before the temple: and he said unto me, This *is* the most holy *place*.

5. After, he measured the wall of the house six cubits; and the breadth of *every* side-chamber, four cubits, round about the house on every side.

6. And the side-chambers *were* three, one over another, and thirty in order; and they entered into the wall, which *was* of the house for the side-chambers round about, that they might have hold, but they had not hold in the wall of the house.

7. And *there was* an enlarging and winding about still upward to the side-chambers: for the winding about of the house went still upward round about the house; therefore the breadth of the house *was still* upward, and so increased *from* the lowest *chamber* to the highest by the midst.

8. I saw also the height of the house round about: the foundations of the side-chambers *were* a full reed of six great cubits.

9. The thickness of the wall, which *was* for the side-chamber without, *was* five cubits: and *that* which *was* left *was* the place of the side-chambers that *were* within.

10. And between the chambers *was* the wideness of twenty cubits round about the house on every side.

11. And the doors of the side-chambers *were* toward *the place that was* left, one door toward the north, and another door toward the south: and the breadth of the place that was left *was* five cubits round about.

12. Now the building that *was* before the separate place at the end toward the west, *was* seventy cubits broad; and

the wall of the building *was* five cubits thick round about, and the length thereof ninety cubits.

13. So he measured the house, a hundred cubits long; and the separate place, and the building, with the walls thereof, a hundred cubits long;

14. Also the breadth of the face of the house, and of the separate place toward the east, a hundred cubits.

15. And he measured the length of the building over against the separate place which *was* behind it, and the galleries thereof on the one side and on the other side, a hundred cubits, with the inner temple, and the porches of the court;

16. The door posts, and the narrow windows, and the galleries round about on their three stories, over against the door, ceiled with wood round about, and from the ground up to the windows, and the windows *were* covered;

17. To that above the door, even unto the inner house and without, and by all the wall round about within and without, by measure.

18. And *it was* made with cherubims and palm-trees, so that a palm-tree was between a cherub and a cherub; and *every* cherub had two faces;

19. So that the face of a man *was* toward the palm-tree on the one side, and the face of a young lion toward the palm-tree on the other side: *it was* made through all the house round about.

20. From the ground unto above the door *were* cherubims and palm-trees made, and *on* the wall of the temple.

21. The posts of the temple *were* squared, *and* the face of the sanctuary; the appearance *of the one* as the appearance *of the other*.

22. The altar of wood *was* three cubits high, and the length thereof two cubits; and the corners thereof, and the length thereof, and the walls thereof, *were* of wood: and he said unto me, This *is* the table that *is* before the Lord.

23. And the temple and the sanctuary had two doors.

24. And the doors had two leaves *apiece*, two turning leaves; two *leaves* for the one door, and two leaves for the other *door*.

25. And *there were* made on them, on the doors of the temple, cherubims and palm-trees, like as *were* made upon the walls; and *there were* thick planks upon the face of the porch without.

26. And *there were* narrow windows and palm-trees on

the one side and on the other side, on the sides of the porch, and *upon* the side chambers of the house, and thick planks.

In many respects this temple resembles that built by Solomon. These respects might be indicated, but could not be specially interesting or profitable to the reader.

CHAPTER XLII.

This chapter closes the description of the temple proper.

1. Then he brought me forth into the outer court, the way toward the north: and he brought me into the chamber that *was* over against the separate place, and which *was* before the building toward the north.

2. Before the length of a hundred cubits was the north door, and the breadth *was* fifty cubits.

3. Over against the twenty *cubits* which *were* for the inner court, and over against the pavement which *was* for the outer court, was gallery against gallery in three *stories*.

4. And before the chambers *was* a walk of ten cubits breadth inward, a way of one cubit; and their doors toward the north.

5. Now the upper chambers *were* shorter; for the galleries were higher than these, than the lower, and than the middlemost of the building.

6. For they *were* in three *stories*, but had not pillars as the pillars of the courts: therefore *the building* was straitened more than the lowest and the middlemost from the ground.

7. And the wall that *was* without over against the chambers, toward the outer court on the forepart of the chambers, the length thereof *was* fifty cubits.

8. For the length of the chambers that *were* in the outer court *was* fifty cubits: and lo, before the temple *were* a hundred cubits.

9. And from under these chambers *was* the entry on the east side, as one goeth into them from the outer court.

10. The chambers *were* in the thickness of the wall of the court toward the east, over against the separate place, and over against the building.

11. And the way before them *was* like the appearance

of the chambers which *were* toward the north, as long as they, *and* as broad as they: and all their goings out *were* both according to their fashions, and according to their doors.

12. And according to the doors of the chambers that *were* toward the south *was* a door in the head of the way, *even* the way directly before the wall toward the east, as one entereth into them.

13. Then said he unto me, The north chambers *and* the south chambers which *are* before the separate place, they *be* holy chambers, where the priests that approach unto the Lord shall eat the most holy things, and the meat-offering, and the sin-offering, and the trespass-offering; for the place *is* holy.

14. When the priests enter therein, then shall they not go out of the holy *place* into the outer court, but there they shall lay their garments wherein they minister; for they *are* holy; and shall put on other garments, and shall approach to *those things* which *are* for the people.

15. Now when he had made an end of measuring the inner house, he brought me forth toward the gate whose prospect *is* toward the east, and measured it round about.

16. He measured the east side with the measuring reed, five hundred reeds, with the measuring reed round about.

17. He measured the north side, five hundred reeds, with the measuring reed round about.

18. He measured the south side, five hundred reeds, with the measuring reed.

19. He turned about to the west side, *and* measured five hundred reeds, with the measuring reed.

20. He measured it by the four sides: it had a wall round about, five hundred *reeds* long, and five hundred broad, to make a separation between the sanctuary and the profane place.

The point of chief and special interest in this part of the description is the manifest care taken and the arrangements made to isolate holy things from profane, as if to guard henceforward forever against debasing the worship of God and against all contamination of God's people by contact with sin and its temptations. Thus (vs. 13, 14) the priests have special chambers where none but themselves may eat the most holy things. Their sacred ministrations are to be performed in holy garments, to be laid off when they come before the people.——Vs. 15–20 describe an area outside the holy place inclosed by a wall designed to "make a separation between the sanctuary and the profane place."——It may fitly be noticed that while the temple proper corresponded precisely in dimensions with that built by Solomon, this wall-inclosed area was vastly larger, viz., a square of *five hundred* reeds or nearly one English mile on each side;—"considerably larger than the whole area of the city of Jerusalem, its temple included!"——This fact goes far to show that this temple and its surroundings were simply *ideal;* seen in vision only, and never designed to be developed into actual reality. Taken ideally, its significance is obvious and pertinent, and is forcibly expressed.——So carefully and jealously will God guard his church in the future days against being contaminated with sin. Once redeemed and sanctified unto Christ and holiness, they will be "kept by the power of God through faith unto salvation." Blessed truth! Obviously in the nature of the case, this must be one of the grand features of the Millennial age—*the church preserved from relapsing into worldliness and kept near to God.* What is indispensable in the nature of the case to a glorious millennial state, it is pleasant to find specially indicated here in this figurative vision.

CHAPTER XLIII.

The visible glory of God returns to dwell in this new temple (vs. 1–4); the Lord states to the people the conditions on which he will dwell with them (vs. 5–11); the altar is measured and its ordinances of worship described (vs. 12–27).

1. Afterward he brought me to the gate, *even* the gate that looketh toward the east:

2. And behold, the glory of the God of Israel came from the way of the east: and his voice *was* like a noise of many waters: and the earth shined with his glory.

3. And *it was* according to the appearance of the vision which I saw, *even* according to the vision that I saw when I came to destroy the city: and the visions *were* like the vision that I saw by the river Chebar; and I fell upon my face.

4. And the glory of the Lord came into the house by the way of the gate whose prospect *is* toward the east.

The prophet is careful to say that this is the same Shekinah, the same visible glory of the Lord, which he had seen before, both in the temple and also withdrawing from it. Compare chap. 1: 1, and 3: 23, and 10: 4, and especially 11: 22, 23.——In v. 3, "when I came to destroy the city," means, when I came to *announce* its destruction, as (*e. g.,*) in chaps. 8–11. The prophets are often said to *do* what they only predict as to *be done.* Thus in chap. 32: 18 the Lord directs the prophet not only to "wail for the multitude of Egypt," but to "cast them down unto the nether parts of the earth," although his hand had never reached them, and he only predicted their fall. Jacob, predicting the future life of Simeon and Levi (Gen. 49: 7), said, "I will divide them in Jacob and scatter them in Israel;" yet he did this only in the sense of *predicting* it. See also Isa. 6: 10, and Jer. 1: 10.

5. So the spirit took me up, and brought me into the inner court; and behold, the glory of the Lord filled the house.

6. And I heard *him* speaking unto me out of the house; and the man stood by me.

7. And he said unto me, Son of man, the place of my throne, and the place of the soles of my feet, where I will dwell in the midst of the children of Israel forever, and my holy name, shall the house of Israel no more defile, *neither* they, nor their kings, by their whoredoms, nor by the carcasses of their kings in their high places.

8. In their setting of their threshold by my thresholds, and their post by my posts, and the wall between me and them, they have even defiled my holy name by their abominations that they have committed: wherefore I have consumed them in mine anger.

9. Now, let them put away their whoredom, and the carcasses of their kings, far from me, and I will dwell in the midst of them forever.

10. Thou son of man, shew the house to the house of Israel, that they may be ashamed of their iniquities: and let them measure the pattern.

11. And if they be ashamed of all that they have done, shew them the form of the house, and the fashion thereof, and the goings out thereof, and the comings in thereof, and all the forms thereof, and all the ordinances thereof, and all the forms thereof, and all the laws thereof: and write *it* in their sight, that they may keep the whole form thereof, and all the ordinances thereof, and do them.

The allusion to the "place of his throne" (vs. 7, 8) and to their kings as having defiled God's sanctuary by setting up idol gods there looks to Manasseh. See 2 Kings 21: 4–7.——These verses are specially valuable as revealing the conditions on which alone the Lord would return and continue to dwell among his people. They *must*—absolutely MUST put away their sins and be ashamed of their iniquities. If they consented heartily to these conditions, the prophet was to show them the form of the house, and all that the Lord had revealed of this new temple, and of its ordinances of worship as a pledge of his own restoring mercy and his return to dwell among them.——This was specially pertinent to the exiles among whom the prophet lived, and shows that the Lord designed this vision to bear vigorously upon the hearts of that people then and there.

12. This *is* the law of the house; Upon the top of the mountain, the whole limit thereof round about *shall be* most holy. Behold, this *is* the law of the house.

This temple stood on a mountain. So did that of Solomon, though this appears to have been the loftier one. The whole area of this mountain top was most holy as being the place where the Lord Jehovah truly dwelt.——The subsequent verses of this chapter describe the great altar, and give the ordinances to regulate the sacrifices upon it.

13. And these *are* the measures of the altar after the cubits: The cubit *is* a cubit and a hand-breadth; even the bottom *shall be* a cubit, and the breadth a cubit, and the border thereof by the edge thereof round about *shall be* a span: and this *shall be* the higher place of the altar.

14. And from the bottom *upon* the ground *even* to the lower settle *shall be* two cubits, and the breadth one cubit; and from the lesser settle *even* to the greater settle *shall be* four cubits, and the breadth *one* cubit.

15. So the altar *shall be* four cubits; and from the altar and upward *shall be* four horns.

16. And the altar *shall be* twelve *cubits* long, twelve broad, square in the four squares thereof.

17. And the settle *shall be* fourteen *cubits* long and fourteen broad in the four squares thereof; and the border about it *shall be* half a cubit; and the bottom thereof *shall be* a cubit about; and the stairs shall look toward the east.

18. And he said unto me, Son of man, thus saith the Lord God; These *are* the ordinances of the altar in the day when they shall make it, to offer burnt-offerings thereon, and to sprinkle blood thereon.

19. And thou shalt give to the priests the Levites that be of the seed of Zadok, which approach unto me, to minister unto me, saith the Lord God, a young bullock for a sin-offering.

20. And thou shalt take of the blood thereof, and put *it* on the four horns of it, and on the four corners of the settle,

and upon the border round about: thus shalt thou cleanse and purge it.

21. Thou shalt take the bullock also of the sin-offering, and he shall burn it in the appointed place of the house, without the sanctuary.

22. And on the second day thou shalt offer a kid of the goats without blemish for a sin-offering; and they shall cleanse the altar, as they did cleanse *it* with the bullock.

23. When thou hast made an end of cleansing *it*, thou shalt offer a young bullock without blemish, and a ram of the flock without blemish.

24. And thou shalt offer them before the Lord, and the priests shalt cast salt upon them, and they shall offer them up *for* a burnt-offering unto the Lord.

25. Seven days shalt thou prepare every day a goat *for* a sin-offering: they shall also prepare a young bullock, and a ram out of the flock, without blemish.

26. Seven days shall they purge the altar and purify it; and they shall consecrate themselves.

27. And when these days are expired, it shall be, *that* upon the eighth day, and *so* forward, the priests shall make your burnt-offerings upon the altar, and your peace-offerings: and I will accept you, saith the Lord God.

CHAPTER XLIV.

After a single direction for the prince, briefly stated (vs. 1–3), this chapter proceeds to define the ceremonial laws and regulations for the priests.

1. Then he brought me back the way of the gate of the outward sanctuary which looketh toward the east; and it *was* shut.

2. Then said the Lord unto me: This gate shall be shut, it shall not be opened, and no man shall enter in by it; because the Lord the God of Israel hath entered in by it, therefore it shall be shut.

3. *It is* for the prince; the prince, he shall sit in it to eat bread before the Lord; he shall enter by the way of the porch of *that* gate, and shall go out by the way of the same.

Through this eastern gate, now seen shut, the visible glory of Jehovah had passed when he entered this temple. (See chap. 43:

1–4). Consequently no man might enter by this gate save the prince. In chap. 46: 2, 12, is a renewed allusion to this special rule, opening this gate to the prince for his entrance to worship, but to none other. The case indicates that an extraordinary sanctity attached to the *prince.* Does not this look toward the exalted character of the future Prince of the Lord's people—the *Great Immanuel?*

4. Then brought he me the way of the north-gate before the house: and I looked, and behold, the glory of the Lord filled the house of the Lord: and I fell upon my face.

5. And the Lord said unto me, Son of man, mark well, and behold with thine eyes, and hear with thine ears all that I say unto thee concerning all the ordinances of the house of the Lord, and all the laws thereof; and mark well the entering in of the house, with every going forth of the sanctuary;

Again, approaching from the north, the prophet in vision is impressed with a sense of the glory of Jehovah as filling his temple, and he falls upon his face in profound adoration. This case anticipates the great truth brought out so distinctively at the close of this entire vision, which indeed is the central thought throughout, viz., *that God dwells among his people by his spiritual presence and glory.* The name of the whole city shall be, " *The Lord is there.*" This being chief in importance gave name to the city.——Now the Lord solemnly charges the prophet to mark well ("set his heart upon") all he was about to say in respect to the modes of worship in this temple and in respect to entering and leaving it.

6. And thou shalt say to the rebellious, *even* to the house of Israel, Thus saith the Lord God; O ye house of Israel, let it suffice you of all your abominations;

7. In that ye have brought *into my sanctuary* strangers, uncircumcised in heart, and uncircumcised in flesh, to be in my sanctuary, to pollute it, *even* my house, when ye offer my bread, the fat and the blood, and they have broken my covenant because of all your abominations.

8. And ye have not kept the charge of my holy things: but ye have set keepers of my charge in my sanctuary for yourselves.

Let your past abominations suffice; let them be deemed enough; let there be no more! Ye have brought into my temple to officiate there, men of impure heart—a thing that God can not endure! Ye have pleased yourselves and not me; ye have made your own laws and have not kept mine in your choice of priests and in your rules for their service. This, which I take to be the sense of v. 8, may look historically to Jeroboam, who (1 Kings 12: 31–33) "made priests of the lowest of the people who were not of the sons of Levi."——The case admonishes the people of God to guard most vigilantly against the introduction of ungodly men into the sacred office of the gospel ministry. The future prosperity and purity of Zion turn upon this to an extent not easily overestimated.

9. Thus saith the Lord God; No stranger, uncircumcised in heart, nor uncircumcised in flesh, shall enter into my sanctuary, of any stranger that *is* among the children of Israel.

10. And the Levites that are gone away far from me, when Israel went astray, which went astray away from me after their idols; they shall even bear their iniquity.

11. Yet they shall be ministers in my sanctuary, *having* charge at the gates of the house, and ministering to the house: they shall slay the burnt-offering and the sacrifice for the people, and they shall stand before them to minister unto them.

12. Because they ministered unto them before their idols, and caused the house of Israel to fall into iniquity; therefore have I lifted up my hand against them, saith the Lord God, and they shall bear their iniquity.

13. And they shall not come near unto me, to do the office of a priest unto me, nor to come near to any of my holy things, in the most holy *place:* but they shall bear their shame, and their abominations which they have committed.

14. But I will make them keepers of the charge of the house, for all the service thereof, and for all that shall be done therein.

15. But the priests the Levites, the sons of Zadok, that kept the charge of my sanctuary when the children of Israel went astray from me, they shall come near to me to minister unto me, and they shall stand before me to offer unto me the fat and the blood, saith the Lord God:

16. They shall enter into my sanctuary, and they shall come near to my table, to minister unto me, and they shall keep my charge.

Strangers residing in Israel, but of uncircumcised heart, must by no means be permitted to enter the Lord's sanctuary. The Levites who had apostatized into idolatry must bear the punishment of this great iniquity. They were forbidden to come near before the Lord, but were assigned to the more remote and less hallowed and honored services of the sanctuary. They were to minister in the presence of their more favored brethren, the priests, as their servants;

but might not come specially near to the Lord. To the sons of Zadok who had not thus apostatized was assigned the distinguished honor of coming near to minister before the very presence of the divine majesty. This discrimination had a most significant and earnest moral bearing. "Holiness becometh God's house forever." The favored ones there are the men of lowly heart who live near to God, walking softly before him.

17. And it shall come to pass, *that* when they enter in at the gates of the inner court, they shall be clothed with linen garments; and no wool shall come upon them, while they minister in the gates of the inner court, and within.

18. They shall have linen bonnets upon their heads, and shall have linen breeches upon their loins; they shall not gird *themselves* with any thing that causeth sweat.

19. And when they go forth into the outer court, *even* into the outer court to the people, they shall put off their garments wherein they ministered, and lay them in the holy chambers, and they shall put on other garments; and they shall not sanctify the people with their garments.

Outward purity symbolizes inward; the purity of the person, that of the heart. Hence linen rather than woolen garments were prescribed. Sweat as indicating impurity must be avoided. Special garments were assigned to be worn exclusively before the Lord, to be exchanged for others when they came before the people. The last clause of v. 19 means, they shall not sanctify the people ministering *in* their ordinary garments, but only while wearing their sacred vestments.

20. Neither shall they shave their heads, nor suffer their locks to grow long; they shall only poll their heads.

In respect to the hair of their head, they must take a medium course, not shaving it close, nor wearing it long and dishevelled without cutting. A decent propriety befits God's house.

21. Neither shall any priest drink wine, when they enter into the inner court.

The priest must not drink wine when about to enter into the inner court of the temple. The excitement of wine, even though falling much short of intoxication, ministers often to manifold improprieties which are by no means becoming in the near presence of Jehovah.——The case should solemnly admonish gospel ministers to abjure even the least alcoholic stimulus, both when they are preparing to preach and when they are preaching in the name of the Lord. No doubt it is wise for them *never* to drink wine as a beverage, and never at all unless in rare cases of sickness.

22. Neither shall they take for their wives a widow, nor her that is put away: but they shall take maidens of the

seed of the house of Israel, or a widow that had a priest before.

Under the law of Moses (Lev. 21: 13, 14) similar restrictions—the same excepting that in the last clause—were applied to the high-priest. Here they apply to all priests. The difference indicates the increased care and caution to be used under the great Messiah's reign to keep his servants morally pure.

23. And they shall teach my people the *difference* between the holy and profane, and cause them to discern between the unclean and the clean.

Under the ancient economy, the ceremonial distinction between the holy and the profane, the clean and the unclean, had the high moral purpose of training the mind to recognize the distinction between holiness and sin. This same distinction it must be the great duty of God's servants in the millennial age to teach and to enforce.

24. And in controversy they shall stand in judgment; *and* they shall judge it according to my judgments: and they shall keep my laws and my statutes in all mine assemblies; and they shall hallow my sabbaths.

Under the law given through Moses, the distinction recognized in modern times between civil and religious statutes was scarcely known. The priests and Levites were then judges of civil cases. See Deut. 17: 8-13, and 2 Chron. 19: 8-11. Hence naturally the same system obtains here.——"In controversy," means not a verbal dispute but a legal prosecution—a case in court. I translate; "In cases of trial at law, they (the priests) shall stand for judgment" (*i. e.*, shall perform the functions of judge), "and they shall judge them (the people) according to my statutes," etc.

25. And they shall come at no dead person to defile themselves: but for father, or for mother, or for son, or for daughter, for brother, or for sister that hath had no husband, they may defile themselves.

26. And after he is cleansed, they shall reckon unto him seven days.

27. And in the day that he goeth into the sanctuary, unto the inner court, to minister in the sanctuary, he shall offer his sin-offering, saith the Lord God.

No form of ceremonial uncleanness was accounted more flagrant than that which comes from contact with a dead body or near approach to one. Hence promiscuous mourning for the dead and attendance upon these funeral solemnities were strictly forbidden to the priests, the law defining by name the near relatives for whom they might mourn. The same reason is here, to indicate the moral purity which will characterize the future kingdom of the Messiah.

28. And it shall be unto them for an inheritance: I *am* their inheritance: and ye shall give them no possession in Israel: I *am* their possession.

29. They shall eat the meat-offering, and the sin-offering, and the trespass-offering; and every dedicated thing in Israel shall be theirs.

30. And the first of all the first-fruits of all *things*, and every oblation of all, of every *sort* of your oblations, shall be the priest's: ye shall also give unto the priest the first of your dough, that he may cause the blessing to rest in thy house.

31. The priests shall not eat of any thing that is dead of itself, or torn, whether it be fowl or beast.

In v. 28, "*it* shall be to' them for an inheritance," means that their service in the temple of God and in his institutions shall be their portion, their estate, their living and their wealth. They were to have subsistence from the altar and from the tithes which the law prescribed. Beyond this they had no inheritance. From landed estates the Lord purposely debarred them. This was also the doctrine of the ancient Mosaic system.

CHAPTER XLV.

The Lord sets apart a large and well-defined portion of the land for specially sacred uses (vs. 1–8); admonishes the princes against unjust exactions from the people and provides a system of weights and measures (vs. 9–12); and specifies certain religious ceremonial observances (vs. 13–25).

1. Moreover, when ye shall divide by lot the land for inheritance, ye shall offer an oblation unto the Lord, a holy portion of the land: the length *shall be* the length of five and twenty thousand *reeds*, and the breadth *shall be* ten thousand. This *shall be* holy in all the borders thereof round about.

2. Of this there shall be for the sanctuary five hundred *in length*, with five hundred *in breadth*, square round about; and fifty cubits round about for the suburbs thereof.

3. And of this measure shalt thou measure the length of five and twenty thousand, and the breadth of ten thousand: and in it shall be the sanctuary *and* the most holy *place*.

4. The holy *portion* of the land shall be for the priests,

the ministers of the sanctuary, which shall come near to minister unto the Lord: and it shall be a place for their houses, and a holy place for the sanctuary.

5. And the five and twenty thousand of length, and the ten thousand of breadth, shall also the Levites, the ministers of the house, have for themselves, for a possession for twenty chambers.

6. And ye shall appoint the possession of the city five thousand broad, and five and twenty thousand long, over against the oblation of the holy *portion:* it shall be for the whole house of Israel.

7. And *a portion shall be* for the prince on the one side and on the other side of the oblation of the holy *portion,* and of the possession of the city, before the oblation of the holy *portion,* and before the possession of the city, from the west side westward, and from the east side eastward: and the length *shall be* over against one of the portions, from the west border unto the east border.

8. In the land shall be his possession in Israel: and my princes shall no more oppress my people; and *the rest of* the land shall they give to the house of Israel according to their tribes.

In full harmony with the genius though varying from the forms of the Mosaic system, we have here the extraordinary feature of a very large portion of the whole land, a little less than half of it, set apart for public uses, more or less sacred, the object apparently being to wall in the sacred institutions of religion so effectually as to shut off from the church the corrupting influences of the world. ——As to the dimensions of this vast reserved square of twenty-five thousand reeds in length and breadth, I shall assume, in the absence of any Hebrew term for it, that this "*reed*" (v. 1) corresponds with that defined in chap. 40: 5; viz., six cubits and a hand breadth; *i. e.*, proximately ten and a half feet in length. This may be assumed with the greater confidence because both the measuring reed and the man who bore it are made very prominent in the opening of this vision (chap. 40: 3, 5). There can scarcely be a doubt that the same standard of measure obtains throughout this entire vision. By this standard, the "oblation" will be a square of forty-nine and seventy-one hundredths miles on each side, varying only a small fraction from the average breadth of Palestine proper from the Mediterranean sea to the Jordan valley. Anticipating here from chapter 48 the geographical location of the tribes, the entire allotment of the territory may be readily seen from the following diagram copied from Rosenmueller and supposed to be proximately correct.——The reader will be struck with the perfect regularity which rules throughout. The entire territory is sup-

DIAGRAM
OF THE
HOLY LAND AND THE SACRED PLACES,
ACCORDING TO EZEKIEL.
(FROM ROSENMUELLER.)

NORTH.

| Dan. |
| Asher. |
| Naphtali. |
| Manasseh. |
| Ephraim. |
| Reuben. |
| Judah. |

WEST. — Portion of the Prince. | Levites. / Priests. Temple. Priests. / Laborers of City. the city. | Portion of the Prince. — EAST

| Benjamin. |
| Simeon. |
| Issachar. |
| Zebulon. |
| Gad. |

SOUTH.

posed to be of uniform width; twenty-five thousand reeds (about fifty miles); each tribe has its own narrow belt, stretching across the entire width. Beginning at the north end, seven tribes have their portion north of the "holy oblation" or reserve; then the Levites have a very ample territory twenty miles wide on the northern part of this reserve; and the city with its laboring population, half as much—ten miles wide—on its southern border; inclosing between them the territory of the priests, twenty miles wide, in the middle of which stood the temple. Spacious territory is assigned to the prince at each end of this sacred reserve.—— Under the Mosaic economy and in the distribution of the land of Canaan by Joshua, no provision whatever was specially made for the king or "prince." It would then have been premature. Here it is timely and is made prominent. The "prince" is a prominent character in this new regime. The prophecies of Zechariah also foreshadow this prominence. With him, however, royalty and priesthood reside in the same glorious personage. He shall not only build the temple of the Lord, but "shall bear glory" (preëminent glory), and shall sit and rule upon his throne, and shall be a priest on his throne, and be crowned as both king and priest (Zech. 6: 12, 13). This millennial state being the result of the glorious reign of the Messiah, the *Prince* of Peace, its strong points could not be presented without giving great prominence to "the *prince.*"

9. Thus saith the Lord God; Let it suffice you, O princes of Israel: remove violence and spoil, and execute judgment and justice, take away your exactions from my people, saith the Lord God.

10. Ye shall have just balances, and a just ephah, and a just bath.

11. The ephah and the bath shall be of one measure, that the bath may contain the tenth part of a homer, and the ephah the tenth part of a homer: the measure thereof shall be after the homer.

12. And the shekel *shall be* twenty gerahs: twenty shekels, five and twenty shekels, fifteen shekels, shall be your maneh.

* With an eye to the human relations of this prince and as if mindful of such oppressive exactions as that of Ahab from Naboth, and of Jehoiakim from his people (Jer. 22: 13–19) and to forestall the temptations to this sin, the Lord specially provides for the prince an ample territory and solemnly admonishes him against exacting from the people their land. See also chap. 48: 18. A complete system of standard weights and measures is exceedingly valuable as a check on human selfishness and a means of securing exact justice in trade and exchange. It is not specially important that we should be able to compare these weights and measures with our own, or know their absolute quantities. It is both the less important and

the more difficult to settle these points because we can not assume that this system was the same as the ancient Jewish one. Probably it is purely ideal, never to be actual; hence I pass it. Let it suffice us to learn from this passage that in the better times of the gospel age, religion will not be in anywise divorced from morality, but Christians, however high in power, will hold themselves closely and conscientiously to fair and just dealings in business with all men. No man will be accounted religious who is not *just*. No amount of pious feeling or religious profession will atone for the lack of intrinsic honesty.

13. This *is* the oblation that ye shall offer; the sixth part of an ephah of a homer of wheat, and ye shall give the sixth part of an ephah of a homer of barley;

14. Concerning the ordinance of oil, the bath of oil, *ye shall offer* the tenth part of a bath out of the cor, *which is* a homer of ten baths: for ten baths *are* a homer:

15. And one lamb out of the flock, out of two hundred, out of the fat pastures of Israel; for a meat-offering, and for a burnt-offering, and for peace-offerings, to make reconciliation for them, saith the Lord God.

16. All the people of the land shall give this oblation for the prince in Israel.

17. And it shall be the prince's part *to give* burnt-offerings, and meat-offerings, and drink-offerings, in the feasts, and in the new-moons, and in the sabbaths, in all solemnities of the house of Israel: he shall prepare the sin-offering, and the meat-offering, and the burnt offering, and the peace-offerings, to make reconciliation for the house of Israel.

18. Thus saith the Lord God; In the first *month*, in the first *day* of the month, thou shalt take a young bullock without blemish, and cleanse the sanctuary:

19. And the priest shall take of the blood of the sin-offering, and put *it* upon the posts of the house, and upon the four corners of the settle of the altar, and upon the posts of the gate of the inner court.

20. And so thou shalt do the seventh *day* of the month for every one that erreth, and for *him that is* simple: so shall ye reconcile the house.

21. In the first *month* in the fourteenth day of the month, ye shall have the passover, a feast of seven days; unleavened bread shall be eaten.

22. And upon that day shall the prince prepare for himself and for all the people of the land a bullock *for* a sin-offering.

23. And seven days of the feast he shall prepare a burnt-offering to the Lord, seven bullocks and seven rams without blemish daily the seven days; and a kid of the goats daily *for* a sin-offering.

24. And he shall prepare a meat-offering of an ephah for a bullock, and an ephah for a ram, and an hin of oil for an ephah.

25. In the seventh *month*, in the fifteenth day of the month, shall he do the like in the feast of the seven days, according to the sin-offering, according to the burnt-offering, and according to the meat-offering, and according to the oil.

The "meat-offerings" (so called) were of flour, not of flesh. "Meat" is one of those words which time has changed so that the "meat-offering" of ancient times had no *meat* in our modern sense in it.——In vs. 17, 20, the word rendered, "to make reconciliation;" "to reconcile the house;" is the precise word most used for making atonement for sin—*covering* it from the view, the reprobation and the curse, of a just God.——The prince is to be specially active in the religious sacrifices of these times; a leader of the people in their public worship.——Isaiah had already said in the same strain; "Kings shall be thy nursing fathers, and their queens thy nursing mothers;" also; "I will make thy officers peace and thine exactors righteousness" (chap. 49: 23 and 60: 17.)——Among these specially sacred seasons the reader will recognise the "new moon" (vs. 18, 19), the Passover (vs. 21–24) and the feast of tabernacles (vs. 25).

CHAPTER XLVI.

Here are special ordinances prescribing who may pass through the glorious eastern gate, through which the Shekinah had passed; also *when* and *how* (vs. 1–3, 12); how the people may enter the temple (vs. 9, 10); various ordinances in respect to "meat-offerings" to accompany the bloody sacrifices; how the prince may entail his real estate (vs. 16–18); and the provision of apartments for cooking (vs. 19–24).

1. Thus saith the Lord God; The gate of the inner court that looketh toward the east, shall be shut the six working days; but on the sabbath it shall be opened, and in the day of the new-moon it shall be opened.

2. And the prince shall enter by the way of the porch of *that* gate without, and shall stand by the post of the gate, and the priests shall prepare his burnt-offering and his peace-offerings, and he shall worship at the threshold of the

gate: then he shall go forth; but the gate shall not be shut until the evening.

3. Likewise the people of the land shall worship at the door of this gate before the Lord in the sabbaths and in the new-moons.

Very special sacredness attached to this eastern gate since through this gate the visible glory of the Lord entered into the most holy place. See chap. 44: 1–4. Through this gate the prince and he only might enter (vs. 2, 12). It was to be opened only on the Sabbath; on the days of new moon; and when the prince had occasion to present a voluntary (not specially prescribed) offering (v. 12).—— The significance of these points looks toward the special sacredness of the prince as one near to God, and was also intended to impress the people with the great central truth of this entire vision, viz., that in this new, holy and beautiful state of the church, the Lord God would dwell among his people with preëminent manifestations of his presence. The place of his feet would be sublimely glorious.

4. And the burnt-offering that the prince shall offer unto the Lord in the sabbath day *shall be* six lambs without blemish, and a ram without blemish.

5. And the meat-offering *shall be* an ephah for a ram, and the meat-offering for the lambs as he shall be able to give, and a hin of oil to an ephah.

6. And in the day of the new-moon *it shall be* a young bullock without blemish, and six lambs, and a ram: they shall be without blemish.

7. And he shall prepare a meat-offering, an ephah for a bullock, and an ephah for a ram, and for the lambs according as his hand shall attain unto, and a hin of oil to an ephah.

These special directions for the offerings made by the prince do not appear in the old Levitical law, and hence have a special significance here in respect to the sacredness of his person and relations. As already suggested, the prince is a new character, appearing first in this special economy.

8. And when the prince shall enter, he shall go in by the way of the porch of *that* gate, and he shall go forth by the way thereof.

9. But when the people of the land shall come before the Lord in the solemn feasts, he that entereth in by the way of the north gate to worship shall go out by the way of the south gate; and he that entereth by the way of the south gate shall go forth by the way of the north gate: he shall

not return by the way of the gate whereby he came in, but shall go forth over against it.

10. And the prince in the midst of them, when they go in, shall go in; and when they go forth, shall go forth.

The prince having but one gate for himself might enter by it; then turn about and retire through the same eastern gate. But the people were not permitted to turn about to go out by the same gate through which they entered. If they came in by the north gate, they must go out by the south one, and vice versa.——The reason of this rule is not stated. We may suppose it to have been analogous to the law of movement which obtained respecting "the living creature," as given chap. 1, viz.: that turning about is associated with moral obliquity—with turning away from God. No other reason suggests itself to my mind.——Remarkably the prince was to enter the temple when the people did, and withdraw from it when they did—an ever attending presence with the people, reminding us of the promise, "Lo, I am with you always, even to the end of the world." Since in certain aspects of his character and relations this "prince" was a foreshadowing type of the Messiah, we may accept this law of his attendance with the people as implying that they should approach God's holy presence only *with* and *in* and *through* their great mediator, Christ Jesus.

11. And in the feasts, and in the solemnities, the meat-offering shall be an ephah to a bullock, and an ephah to a ram, and to the lambs as he is able to give, and a hin of oil to an ephah.

12. Now, when the prince shall prepare a voluntary burnt-offering or peace-offerings voluntarily unto the Lord, *one* shall then open him the gate that looketh toward the east, and he shall prepare his burnt-offering and his peace-offerings as he did on the sabbath day: then he shall go forth; and after his going forth *one* shall shut the gate.

This remarkable law for the prince when he made a free-will offering and passed through the eastern gate, has been noticed already.

13. Thou shalt daily prepare a burnt-offering unto the Lord *of* a lamb of the first year without blemish: thou shalt prepare it every morning.

14. And thou shall prepare a meat-offering for it every morning, the sixth part of an ephah, and the third part of a hin of oil, to temper with the fine flour; a meat-offering continually by a perpetual ordinance unto the Lord.

15. Thus shall they prepare the lamb, and the meat-offering, and the oil, every morning, *for* a continual burnt-offering.

These rules for the daily offerings differ slightly from those given through Moses (Num. 28: 3–8). By the ancient law there were two lambs offered daily, one in the morning and the other in the evening. Here is but one, offered each morning. May it be supposed that this looks especially to the one Lamb that was slain for us—the "*one* offering whereby he hath perfected forever them that are sanctified" (Heb. 10: 14)? The meat-offering to accompany it was, in Moses, the tenth part of an ephah of flour with the fourth part of a hin of oil; while here in Ezekiel the quantities are the sixth part of an ephah and the third part of a hin. The diversity shows that this new system is not an exact copy of the old; while yet in its general features it is quite analogous.

16. Thus saith the Lord God; If the prince give a gift unto any of his sons, the inheritance thereof shall be his sons'; it *shall be* their possession by inheritance.

17. But if he give a gift of his inheritance to one of his servants, then it shall be his to the year of liberty; after, it shall return to the prince: but his inheritance shall be his sons' for them.

18. Moreover, the prince shall not take of the people's inheritance by oppression, to thrust them out of their possession; *but* he shall give his sons inheritance out of his own possession: that my people be not scattered every man from his possession.

For the thought in v. 18, compare chap. 45: 8, 9. The prince must not abuse his power to thrust his people from their estates. Nor might he alienate his lands from his own family. His sons may inherit it permanently, but his servants only till the next Jubilee, here called "the year of liberty," as that in which landed estates reverted back to their lineal owners. See Lev. 25: 10.

19. After, he brought me through the entry, which *was* at the side of the gate, into the holy chambers of the priests, which looked toward the north: and behold, there *was* a place on the two sides westward.

20. Then said he unto me, This *is* the place where the priests shall boil the trespass-offering and the sin-offering, where they shall bake the meat-offering; that they bear *them* not out into the outer court, to sanctify the people.

21. Then he brought me forth into the outer court, and caused me to pass by the four corners of the court; and behold, in every corner of the court *there was* a court.

22. In the four corners of the court *there were* courts joined of forty *cubits* long and thirty broad: these four corners *were* of one measure.

23. And *there was* a row *of building* round about in them, round about them four, and *it was* made with boiling places under the rows round about.

24. Then said he unto me, These *are* the places of them that boil, where the ministers of the house shall boil the sacrifice of the people.

To impress more deeply the idea of sanctity in this temple, and all its surroundings, special provision is made for the culinary operations. The cooking is all to be done in special apartments provided for that purpose.——So carefully does the Lord guard in this new representative dispensation against whatever might lessen the sacredness of divine service and worship.

CHAPTER XLVII.

In this chapter vs. 1–12 record a precious vision of waters coming forth from under the temple: vs. 13–20 give the boundaries of the land; and vs. 21–23 provide for strangers who would fain affiliate with the people of God.——In commenting upon the first portion, I propose first to explain the words and phrases that seem to need explanation, and then speak of its general significance.

1. Afterward he brought me again unto the door of the house; and behold, waters issued out from under the threshold of the house eastward: for the forefront of the house *stood toward* the east, and the waters came down from under from the right side of the house, at the south *side* of the altar.

"Brought me again," etc., *i. e.*, from the outer court where we left him in the previous chapter.——"The house" is of course the temple.——The waters issue forth from under the temple as if the temple itself had become a living fountain.

2. Then brought he me out of the way of the gate northward, and led me about the way without unto the outer gate by the way that looketh eastward; and behold, there ran out waters on the right side.

His angel-guide now leads him to the outer gate—*i. e.*, of the wall which inclosed the court of the temple. Here the same waters appear issuing forth on the right side of the eastern gate. The Hebrew word in the last clause, rendered "ran out," means—they *distilled*, came in drops, oozed forth. The amount of water at this point—the distance of the first half-mile—seems therefore to have appeared small.

3. And when the man that had the line in his hand went forth eastward, he measured a thousand cubits, and he brought me through the waters; the waters *were* to the ankles.

4. Again he measured a thousand, and brought me through the waters; and the waters *were* to the knees. Again he measured a thousand, and brought me through; the waters *were* to the loins.

5. Afterward he measured a thousand; *and it was* a river that I could not pass over: for the waters were risen, waters to swim in, a river that could not be passed over.

The remarkable fact shown here is the rapid increase in the volume of these waters. At the distance of one thousand cubits by measure, the prophet is led through the waters and finds them only to the *soles of his feet*, which is the sense of the word rendered "ankles;" at the distance of the second thousand cubits, they have risen to his knees; at the third thousand, to his loins; and at the fourth, they have become a great river—waters to swim in—which he can not ford.

6. And he said unto me, Son of man, hast thou seen *this?* Then he brought me, and caused me to return to the brink of the river.

7. Now, when I had returned, behold, at the bank of the river *were* very many trees on the one side and on the other.

The angel-guide says, Hast thou carefully noted the wonderful increase of these waters? Do not lose sight of this fact while we pass on to other scenes. Then he returns to observe that all along the bank of the river on either side were very many trees, flourishing in verdure and beauty, being fertilized by these living waters. ——The Revelator John has the same symbols of surpassing beauty and verdure in his paradise (Rev. 22: 1, 2).

8. Then said he unto me, These waters issue out toward the east country, and go down into the desert, and go into the sea: *which being* brought forth into the sea, the waters shall be healed.

9. And it shall come to pass, *that* every thing that liveth, which moveth whithersoever the rivers shall come, shall live: and there shall be a very great multitude of fish, because these waters shall come thither: for they shall be healed; and every thing shall live whither the river cometh.

10. And it shall come to pass *that* the fishers shall stand upon it from En-gedi even unto En-eglaim; they shall be a *place* to spread forth nets: their fish shall be according to their kinds, as the fish of the great sea, exceeding many.

The next special feature is that these waters flow off eastward "toward the east country and go down into the desert"—more properly the great *valley* of the Jordan and its continuation in the Dead Sea. Falling into the Dead Sea, where ordinarily no fish or other animal can live, those waters are healed—made salubrious and healthful, so that the sea becomes full of fish, even like the Mediterranean, "the great sea" of v. 10. The passage 2 Kings 2: 20-22, uses the same words to describe the change whereby water from being poisonous, or at least, insalubrious, becomes salubrious.—— Fishermen line the whole shore from En-gedi to En-eglaim—its northern to its southern extremity. Every thing betokens life, prosperity and abundance. The Dead Sea is full of animal life.

11. But the miry places thereof and the marshes thereof shall not be healed; they shall be given to salt.

But there are still marshy, miry places, given up to salt—doomed to sterility.

12. And by the river upon the bank thereof, on this side and on that side, shall grow all trees for meat, whose leaf shall not fade, neither shall the fruit thereof be consumed: it shall bring forth new fruit according to his months, because their waters they issued out of the sanctuary: and the fruit thereof shall be for meat, and the leaf thereof for medicine.

Returning to note again the trees on either bank, he sees them in great variety—"all trees for food"—*i. e.*, fruit-trees of every sort; their leaves never fade, but are sustained in perpetual verdure; and their fruit never *fails*. This is the sense of the word rendered "consumed," which does not mean that this fruit is not *used*, but that the trees never fail to bear; never fail to yield an abundant supply. In fact they ripen their fruit promptly every month because the waters that feed their fertility issue from under the sanctuary. The fruit affords not only delicious food, but restoring medicine. What symbols are these of ever-varied and untold blessings!——Now as to the general significance of these symbols as seen in this vision, there can be no ground for reasonable doubt. Water is the well-established symbol for the cleansing, life-renewing work of the Spirit of God on human hearts. Even David has it; "Wash me, and I shall be whiter than snow; renew a right spirit within me; take not thy Holy Spirit from me" (Ps. 51: 7, 11). Isaiah also; "Fear not, O Jacob my servant, for I will pour water on him that is thirsty and floods upon the dry ground: I will pour my Spirit upon thy seed and my blessing upon thine offspring" (chap. 44: 2, 3). Joel also; "I will *pour out* my Spirit (as if it were water) upon all flesh," and "all the rivers of Judah shall flow with water and a fountain shall come forth from the house of the Lord, and shall water the valley of Shittim," or of the *acacias* (a plant at home in the sterile desert),"for I will cleanse their blood that I have not cleansed; for the Lord dwelleth in Zion."——The reader will notice the striking analogy between this passage of Joel and Ezekiel as in our text. In both, waters are the symbol of God's gift of his Spirit; in both, the fountain is in the temple where God of old dwelt among his people; in both, these waters are freighted with blessings wherever they go. As we have already seen, Ezekiel himself has the same figure in chap. 36: 25–27, a case the more in point because in the same writer. And finally, Zechariah (14: 8) has a passage closely analagous; "And it shall be in that day that living waters shall go out from Jerusalem, half of them toward the former" (front) "sea, and half of them toward the hinder sea" (the Mediterranean); "in summer and in winter shall it be."——The peculiar feature here of a division in these waters, making two rivers; one running eastward to the Dead Sea; the other westward to the Mediterranean; serves to show that these rivers are only symbols, and were never thought of as actual rivers in real life. As symbols, it matters not whether they run in both directions or only in one.——Some of the ancient Jewish interpreters (*e. g.*, the Chaldee paraphrast) supposed that Ezekiel's language implies two rivers; but obviously it does not. The whole description shows that his river falls into the Dead Sea only.——It scarcely needs to be said that this symbol of water to represent the agencies of the Spirit appears throughout the New Testament, especially in such passages as Jn. 3: 5, "Born of water and of the Spirit;" and Jn. 7: 37–39, and Ac. 2: 17, 33; also in the Christian rite of baptism.——I hold therefore most fully that this vision looks to the glorious effusions of the Spirit in the latter days. That these waters proceed from under the temple develops a great central truth in the Christian economy, viz., that the divine Spirit attends and blesses human agencies when these agencies work in the line of his appointed gospel institutions and instrumentalities. Human hands build God's temples; God himself fills them with his presence and makes them living fountains of water to fertilize the great deserts long wasted by sin; to restore life and life-giving qualities to the dead seas of human depravity, and so to cleanse and clothe with beauty the moral face of all the earth.——The figures here are exceedingly beautiful and expressive. There, almost within sight of Jerusalem, lay the dark, black, lurid Sea of Death. There it had lain for ages, covering the smoking, seething ruins of the doomed cities of the plain—a sad and solemn memorial of God's wrath against sin and of the remediless doom of fatally hardened sinners—"set forth as an example, suffering the vengeance of eternal fire" (Jude 7).——Will the gospel ever avail to regenerate this sin-cursed earth? If so, no symbol of this fact could be more in point than this—waters from under the temple where God dwells present among his people, flowing forth, a growing, mighty river, and reclaiming to life that Sea of Death—clothing with beauty, health and glory that long desolate and dismal vale.——Here let us note more particularly the significance of the rapid increase of these waters. The manner of the statement does not properly indicate that the stream as it came from the temple enlarged in volume with the lapse of time—the temple itself sending forth a rapidly increasing supply. It is rather that the river *grew as it ran*—became broader and deeper as it progressed outward from the fountain. This is certainly a very remarkable feature, and (it would seem) should have some special and noteworthy significance. For, rivers in Palestine are wont often to *lessen as they run*, rather than increase in volume, being made up mainly or wholly from one fountain in the dry season, and then losing their waters in the sands, or the fissures of the rocks. Hence this feature is the more striking.——Furthermore, under the ancient Jewish regime, religious influences, emanating from a common center at the temple, naturally lessened as the distance from that center increased. Their normal law would be; strongest at the center, and strength elsewhere inversely as the distance from that center. In remote lands their power would become inappreciable. The stream from the temple would be absorbed in the desert sands and be lost. Now bearing in mind this law of the old economy, what could the Lord mean here less or other than that this new economy should precisely reverse the law of the old? Under the gospel system the moral power of the cross would grow as it traveled outward; diffusion and expansion, involving an intensified activity, become the law of its growth; that the divine purpose is to develop in the Christian system a moral power that will really pervade the wide earth, not only with no waste as it diffuses itself abroad, but actually with ever-increasing force—in this respect precisely reversing the law of the ancient Jewish economy! Has not our Lord a kindred truth in his eye in his parable of the mustard-seed? This is indeed "the least of all seeds, yet it becomes a great tree, so that the fowls of the air lodge in the branches thereof." So is to be the gospel kingdom in its law of unparalleled growth and glorious expansion! See Matt. 13: 31, 32.——A blessed truth is this; and yet no truth could well be put in clearer symbol or in stronger form. Let our hearts hail it with befitting joy and gratitude! Blessed be the God of all grace and love for such great thoughts of mercy for our lost world! ——One other feature remains to be noticed. There were some marshy, miry districts that no waters could restore. They are doomed to miasms, sterility, and death. So there will be some human souls, possibly some localities, never blessed by the gospel. Having ears to hear, they hear not; having the gospel brought to their door and pressed on their heart, they repel it and doom themselves to eternal reprobation!——A few isolated spots of this sort enforce the moral lessons of human responsibility, and serve to reaffirm the freedom of man in all his voluntary activities, even under the most powerful agencies of God's Spirit.——Let sinners beware how they trifle with the offered grace of the gospel. Let them see to it that in whatever day the Lord comes near to bless them, they spurn not his call to life lest he turn himself away and leave them to their own infatuation!

13. Thus saith the Lord God; This *shall be* the border, whereby ye shall inherit the land according to the twelve tribes of Israel: Joseph *shall have* two portions.

14. And ye shall inherit it one as well as another: concerning the which I lifted up my hand to give it unto your fathers: and this land shall fall unto you for inheritance.

Before proceeding to define the boundaries of the land geographically, the revealing angel premises these points; viz., that they were to inherit as the original twelve tribes; that since Levi had his portion in the sacred reserve, adjacent to the great section which inclosed the temple, Joseph should count two (Ephraim and Manasseh) to fill out the twelve; that the portions for each several tribe should be equal, this being the precise sense of the first clause in v. 14; "Ye shall inherit it" (the land) "*each one as his brother;*" and finally that this is the land which the Lord bound himself by oath to the tribes to give them for their inheritance.——Remarkably the uniform law of Messianic prophecy is to promise the future Canaan not to Judah alone, but to the twelve tribes—to Ephraim and the lost ten tribes as truly as to Judah and Benjamin, the two tribes which so long constituted the southern kingdom. It would seem that the Spirit of inspiration overlooked the fact of the revolt under Jeroboam; started at a point much farther back, even with the promise made to the patriarchs and specially renewed to David, and built upon that basis the whole structure of their glorious future. We may notice this remarkable feature of Messianic prophecy in both Jeremiah (chap. 3: 12, 18, and 23: 2, 6–8, and 31: 1, 9, 23, 33) and in Ezekiel (chap. 36: 1, 8, 12, 32, 37, and 37: 11, 12, 28, and 39: 25).——The question whether the ten tribes did in fact return in any considerable numbers under Zerubbabel has been much mooted, and with various conclusions. I have had occasion heretofore to say that the evidence for the affirmative from the records in Ezra and Nehemiah is exceedingly weak. Indeed the inquirer who has no foregone conclusion to sustain would not suspect that those records refer to the ten tribes at all. The historian who notes the captivity of the two and a half tribes on the east of Jordan (1 Chron. 5: 26) explicitly denies their restoration at any period prior to his own times.——The question whether the ten tribes (Ephraim) or the two tribes (Judah and Benjamin) will in any future day return to Palestine to rebuild their old nationality, will be in place for consideration soon, *i. e.*, at the close of my special explanation of the words and phrases throughout chapters 40–48.

15. And this *shall be* the border of the land toward the north side, from the great sea, the way of Hethlon, as men go to Zedad:

16. Hamath, Berothah, Sibraim, which *is* between the

border of Damascus and the border of Hamath; Hazar-hatticon, which *is* by the coast of Hauran.

17. And the border from the sea shall be Hazar-enan, the border of Damascus, and the north northward, and the border of Hamath. And *this is* the north side.

18. And the east side ye shall measure from Hauran, and from Damascus, and from Gilead, and from the land of Israel *by* Jordan, from the border unto the east sea. And *this is* the east side.

19. And the south side southward, from Tamar *even* to the waters of strife *in* Kadesh, the river to the great sea. And *this is* the south side southward.

20. The west side also *shall be* the great sea from the border, till a man come over against Hamath. This *is* the west side.

21. So shall ye divide this land unto you according to the tribes of Israel.

These boundaries differ in no important respect from the ancient boundaries of the land as given by the Lord through Moses, Num. 34: 1–12. This passage is not a copy of that. The description commences in each at different points; that in Numbers with the southern border, and this in Ezekiel with the northern. As we shall see in the next chapter, the location of the several tribes differs widely from that made by Joshua, and assumes a very differently shaped territory to be divided.

22. And it shall come to pass, *that* ye shall divide it by lot for an inheritance unto you, and to the strangers that sojourn among you, which shall beget children among you: and they shall be unto you as born in the country among the children of Israel: they shall have inheritance with you among the tribes of Israel.

23. And it shall come to pass, *that* in what tribe the stranger sojourneth, there shall ye give *him* his inheritance, saith the Lord God.

Inasmuch as enlargement by the accession of Gentiles proselyted to the Jewish faith was a cherished feature of the ancient economy and afforded a choice symbol of the great and glorious ingathering of the Gentiles in the Christian age, it was every way fitting that special provision should be made here for the location and naturalization of strangers who might choose to cast in their lot with Israel. Here it stands.

CHAPTER XLVIII.

This vision closes legitimately with a definite geographical location of the several tribes (vs. 1–7, 23–28); a more expanded description of the sacred reserve (vs. 8–22) resumed from chap. 45: 1–7; and a description of the gates of the great city (vs. 29–35).

1. Now these *are* the names of the tribes. From the north end to the coast of the way of Hethlon, as one goeth to Hamath, Hazar-enan, the border of Damascus northward, to the coast of Hamath; for these are his sides east *and* west; a *portion for* Dan.

2. And by the border of Dan, from the east side unto the west side, a *portion for* Asher.

3. And by the border of Asher, from the east side even unto the west side, a *portion for* Naphtali.

4. And by the border of Naphtali, from the east side unto the west side, a *portion for* Manasseh.

5. And by the border of Manasseh, from the east side unto the west side, a *portion for* Ephraim.

6. And by the border of Ephraim, from the east side even unto the west side, a *portion for* Reuben.

7. And by the border of Reuben, from the east side unto the west side, a *portion for* Judah.

The best view of this assignment of the tribes will be obtained from the diagram, page 248. It will be seen there at a glance that the territory of each tribe extended entirely across the country from west to east, and of equal width. The actual sinuosities and irregularities of the western border and of the eastern also, are overlooked, as well as the narrowing of the real Palestine from its greatest width at its southern extremity to its least at the northern. The location of the tribes differs in other respects widely from that made by Joshua. The latter was every way irregular; the former is a model of perfect mathematical regularity. Doubtless the consideration of *order* ruled in this arrangement. Every thing about it indicates that it was and is only *ideal*—a thing of vision only, and never to be a thing of fact; shaped for its suggestive and symbolic bearings rather than with any reference to the territory to be divided or the adaptation of its parts to the several tribes.

8. And by the border of Judah, from the east side unto the west side, shall be the offering which ye shall offer of five and twenty thousand *reeds in* breadth, and *in* length as one of the *other* parts, from the east side unto the west side: and the sanctuary shall be in the midst of it.

9. The oblation that ye shall offer unto the Lord *shall be*

of five and twenty thousand in length, and of ten thousand in breadth.

10. And for them, *even* for the priests, shall be *this* holy oblation; toward the north five and twenty thousand *in length*, and toward the west ten thousand in breadth, and toward the east ten thousand in breadth, and toward the south five and twenty thousand in length: and the sanctuary of the Lord shall be in the midst thereof.

11. *It shall be* for the priests that are sanctified of the sons of Zadok; which have kept my charge, which went not astray when the children of Israel went astray, as the Levites went astray.

12. And *this* oblation of the land that is offered shall be unto them a thing most holy by the border of the Levites.

13. And over against the border of the priests the Levites *shall have* five and twenty thousand in length, and ten thousand in breadth: all the length *shall be* five and twenty thousand, and the breadth ten thousand.

14. And they shall not sell of it, neither exchange, nor alienate the first fruits of the land: for *it is* holy unto the Lord.

15. And the five thousand, that are left in the breadth over against the five and twenty thousand, shall be a profane *place* for the city, for dwelling, and for suburbs, and the city shall be in the midst thereof.

16. And these *shall be* the measures thereof; the north side four thousand and five hundred, and the south side four thousand and five hundred, and on the east side four thousand and five hundred, and the west side four thousand and five hundred.

17. And the suburbs of the city shall be toward the north two hundred and fifty, and toward the south two hundred and fifty, and toward the east two hundred and fifty, and toward the west two hundred and fifty.

18. And the residue in length over against the oblation of the holy *portion shall be* ten thousand eastward, and ten thousand westward; and it shall be over against the oblation of the holy *portion;* and the increase thereof shall be for food unto them that serve the city.

19. And they that serve the city shall serve it out of all the tribes of Israel.

20. All the oblation *shall be* five and twenty thousand by five and twenty thousand: ye shall offer the holy oblation four-square, with the possession of the city.

21. And the residue *shall be* for the prince, on the one side and on the other of the holy oblation, and of the possession of the city, over against the five and twenty thousand of the oblation toward the east border, and westward over against the five and twenty thousand toward the west border, over against the portions for the prince: and it shall be the holy oblation; and the sanctuary of the house *shall be* in the midst thereof.

22. Moreover, from the possession of the Levites, and from the possession of the city, *being* in the midst *of that* which is the prince's, between the border of Judah and the border of Benjamin, shall be for the prince.

This is the sacred reserve, "the holy oblation," first brought to view chap. 45: 1–7; but here taken up again, repeated, and somewhat expanded. The diagram (p. 248) will give the best view of these apportionments. As said in the notes on chap. 45: 1–7, the purpose of this reserve is obviously to carry out the great idea of the ancient economy in its extreme form—seclusion of the holy from the profane and earthly—the broadest possible distinction between things sacred and things common every-where kept up in order to cultivate a critical habit of moral discrimination between holiness and sin, and to impress a sense of the obligation of moral purity. This moral discipline is above all price in value. But we should quite mistake the genius of the gospel dispensation if we were to assume that God proposes to develop its future and higher stages by returning to the modes and forms of Judaism. No; his thought is rather to carry the culture obtained by the aid of that ancient regime, out into the world-wide fields of human society, and train men to "live holily, justly, and unblamably *in this present world;*" not to shut themselves out of it for the sake of the holiness of the cloister.——We may fitly notice that the Lord makes ample provision for the support of his Levite servants as well as for the priests and for those who serve in the city, taken from all the tribes of Israel. The ministers who labor and serve under this new regime are thoughtfully provided for as if specially worthy of their hire. The implication is that only *with such provision* can they be expected to hold on, true to their work, kept above the torturing power of poverty to seduce them from their sacred functions.

23. As for the rest of the tribes, from the east side unto the west side, Benjamin *shall have* a *portion*.

24. And by the border of Benjamin, from the east side unto the west side, Simeon *shall have* a *portion*.

25. And by the border of Simeon, from the east side unto the west side, Issachar a *portion*.

26. And by the border of Issachar, from the east side unto the west side, Zebulun a *portion*.

27. And by the border of Zebulun, from the east side unto the west side, Gad a *portion*.

28. And by the border of Gad, at the south side southward, the border shall be even from Tamar *unto* the waters of strife *in* Kadesh, *and* to the river toward the great sea.

29. This *is* the land which ye shall divide by lot unto the tribes of Israel for inheritance, and these *are* their portions, saith the Lord God.

30. And these *are* the goings out of the city on the north side, four thousand and five hundred measures.

31. And the gates of the city *shall be* after the names of the tribes of Israel: three gates northward; one gate of Reuben, one gate of Judah, one gate of Levi.

32. And at the east side four thousand and five hundred: and three gates; and one gate of Joseph, one gate of Benjamin, one gate of Dan.

33. And at the south side four thousand and five hundred measures: and three gates; one gate of Simeon, one gate of Issachar, one gate of Zebulun.

34. At the west side four thousand and five hundred, *with* their three gates; one gate of Gad, one gate of Asher, one gate of Naphtali.

35. *It was* round about eighteen thousand *measures:* and the name of the city from *that* day *shall be*, The Lord *is* there.

This great city, a model of method and order—each tribe represented in its twelve gates—is imitated by the Revelator John in his city of the New Jerusalem (Rev. 21: 10–21). John however was farther advanced in the light of the new dispensation, for in his city is "no temple," while here the temple is the central fact. But the glory of the whole scene is brought out here in the significant name of the city which was to stand from that day onward; "Jehovah Shammah;" *The Lord is there!!* It is the place of Jehovah's dwelling in the midst of his people. Every thing is shaped according to Mosaic ideas, for the perpetual dwelling of Jehovah among his people. The entire arrangements, including the sacred reserve, its special localities for the Levites, for the priests, for the more menial servants of the sanctuary; for the prince also and for all the tribes; all, every several thing, provides for the great central fact, and adjusts itself around that living truth—Jehovah dwelling forever, and forever manifesting himself among his chosen; he their God, and they, his people. Prophetically, it looks down into the Christian age to its great central truth—the Lord by his divine Spirit making his abode through all ages in the hearts of his children. "Lo, I am with you always, even to the end of the world." "I will send you the Comforter;" he will guide you into all truth;"

"he shall glorify me; for he shall take of mine and shall show it unto you."

It now remains to present with somewhat more method and fullness than heretofore my reasons for the general system of interpretation which I have applied to these closing chapters of Ezekiel (40–48).——Let it then be premised that they refer mainly and properly to the Messianic times—to the Christian age of the world. It might be claimed with reason that these chapters would naturally inspire in the hearts of the pious Jews then around the prophet, the hope of returning to their own land and of rebuilding their city and temple. Granted. This may have been an incidental and minor purpose of these visions. But they *assume* rather than *assert* this. Or perhaps there would be no objection to saying that this nearer restoration under Zerubbabel was a first installment—a sort of earnest and pledge of the far greater blessings yet in the remote future. But no sound interpreter would venture to say that the significance of these chapters is exhausted in the events of that first restoration, or at any time before Christ. Let this be considered as settled. They look onward into the gospel age for their main fulfillment. This point is so clear as to call for no argument.

——Hence the question now at issue becomes simple and definite. The choice lies between two systems of interpretation; the literal, and the figurative—otherwise called the *symbolic*. The literal interpretation would teach that the Jews at some time yet future are to be restored to their own native land; that this land is to be divided among them as here directed; the "holy oblation" or sacred reserve, set off as here described; the temple and city rebuilt; the Mosaic ritual with feasts, bloody sacrifices and attendant meat-offerings, all restored in manner and form as here detailed. The holy waters from under the sanctuary are real waters, and flowing into the actual Dead Sea, will purify it and thus supply fish in abundance for the restored people;—while along its banks will cluster beautiful trees for shade and fruit and for medicine.—— The literal interpretation is exceedingly easy because the statements are entirely plain and definite, so that if this system is the right one, the significance of the entire vision is as plain as the English alphabet.——Let it be said also that on every just principle of construction, if the literal system is adopted, it should be carried honestly through. There is as much reason for making *every part* of this vision literal as for making *any* part of it so. There can be no valid reason for mixing up the literal and the figurative methods, making one line or verse in the same passage literal and the next figurative. Such changes can be nothing else than purely capricious. They can never be justified on any sound law of interpretation. If the return of the Jews to Palestine to restore their nationality there be literal, then the ritual worship described here is literal also; for it is part of the same vision—part of the same state of things, and should therefore be interpreted by the same laws of language.

I plead *for* the figurative interpretation and *against* the literal, and draw my arguments,
1. *From the New Testament;*
2. From the Old, and especially from these prophecies themselves in their relation to the writer and his first readers.
3. From the nature of the case—especially as creating an intensely strong probability against the literal and in favor of the figurative interpretation.

1. The literal system of interpretation must be rejected because it is absolutely precluded and forbidden by the New Testament. The entire spirit and genius of the gospel dispensation as unfolded by Christ and his inspired apostles is utterly, squarely, fatally against it. For, the literal system must hold that according to this vision, Judaism will yet be fully restored—restored with more than all its ancient surroundings, and in more than its ancient fullness. But according to the New Testament, *Judaism is dead.* It had done its great work when Jesus died as the Lamb of God and thenceforth it ceased to exist under divine authority. In the age of the epistle to the Hebrews, it had already "decayed, waxed old, and was ready to vanish away." Paul declared repeatedly and in many various forms that Christ had "broken down the middle wall" of partition between Jews and Gentiles" by setting aside whatever was peculiar to the Jew; that he "had abolished in his flesh the enmity, even the law of commandments contained in ordinances," etc. (Eph. 2: 14, 15); that he had "blotted out the handwriting of ordinances that was against us" (Gentiles), "which was contrary to us, and took it out of the way, nailing it to his cross" (Col. 2: 14). This was the end of the Mosaic system. And yet more if possible to this point, the burden of Paul's epistle to the Galatians is, that relapsing from Christianity to Judaism is not only a folly (chap. 3: 1, 3) but a sin, and essentially an apostasy from Christ. He declares, " There is neither Jew nor Greek" (Judaism being defunct), "for ye are all one in Christ Jesus." "But now, after that ye have known God, how turn ye again to the weak and beggarly elements, whereunto ye desire again to be in bondage?" "Ye observe [Jewish] days and months and times and years. I am afraid of you lest I have bestowed upon you labor in vain" (Gal. 4: 9–11). "I, Paul, say unto you that if ye be circumcised, Christ shall profit you nothing; for I testify again to every man that is circumcised that he is a debtor to do the whole law. Christ is become of no effect unto you, whosoever of you are justified by the law: ye are fallen from grace" (Gal. 5: 2–4). That is; circumcision and the whole ritual system has no farther mission, has no longer any binding force. Before Christ came, it led *toward* and *unto* Christ; after his coming, it leads *away from* Christ; forces itself in as a substitute for Christ, and therefore must be rejected and denounced as ruinous to souls.——With admirable and wise forbearance the Lord allowed the converted Jews time on this great change from Judaism to a pure Christianity; but yet gave unmistakable indications of his will to rule Judaism

proper out of existence as a thing that had done its work and could never be used in his kingdom any more.——And now is it credible that this wall of partition is going up again? that "ordinances," bloody sacrifices, all and more than all that the Mosaic system ever had, shall be restored? If it were to be restored according to the literal construction of Ezekiel 40–48 chapters, what would it mean? Would it point to *another* Christ, *another* atoning Lamb, *another* great High Priest to make intercession for us? If our present New Testament be accepted as authority, a return to Judaism is forever foreclosed. The testimony of Jesus and his apostles on this point could not be made stronger than it is.——Our Lord spake on this vital question in decisive terms. Standing in view of Mt. Gerizim, with the long mooted question before him whether that mount or Jerusalem were the one prescribed locality for all acceptable worship, he plainly signified that this question had ceased to be a practical one; that the whole system of restricting special forms of worship to one place was now passing by. To the woman of Samaria he solemnly averred (Jn. 4: 21-24); "Woman, believe me; the hour cometh when ye shall neither in this mountain nor yet at Jerusalem, worship the Father. The hour cometh and now is when the true worshipers shall worship the Father in spirit and in truth," implying that nothing else should be requisite for acceptance with God. So long as sacrifices, altars, and a visible glory in the most holy place were of divine appointment, some *one place* for this worship would be a necessity. If these prophecies of Ezekiel are literal, that necessity must return again, and the words of our Lord to the woman of Samaria must cease to have force. The hour must arrive—with the literal fulfillment of Ezekiel—when men must worship God as of old in the one prescribed place, and not merely in spirit and in truth, but in all the forms of ancient Judaism as well.——Did Christ anticipate this supposed change back to Judaism? Had he himself inspired Ezekiel to predict it? The question is its own answer! There can be no return to the old regime of one only place of acceptable worship; and that, in the forms of a dead Judaism! Under the gospel economy, every pious heart is God's temple, and the wide world is open to the offering of each heart's truthful homage to God. This gospel economy can never in any future age give place to Judaism.——Yet again. The inspired apostles were in all vital points inspired interpreters of Old Testament prophecy. In all that affects the great elementary features of the old system and of the new, this position must be valid, else their inspiration becomes practically of no account.——Inquiring now for their inspired interpretation of those prophecies which speak of the Christian age, we may fitly begin with asking what place and what significance they assign to the *temple of God* in these gospel days. Prophecy speaks of a temple of God in the Messiah's age; what do the apostles understand it to mean?——They answer that in this age Christians are *themselves the temple of the living God*, and that "God dwells in them and walks in them." "Know ye not," (said Paul, 1 Cor. 3·

16,) "that ye are the temple of God and that the Spirit of God dwelleth in you?" "What! know ye not that your body is the temple of the Holy Ghost which is in you?" (1 Cor. 6: 19.) And then as if to clinch this argument, Paul cites the Old Testament prophecy in which God said, "I will dwell in them and walk in them," and finds its fulfillment in the new gospel fact; "Ye are the temple of the living God." See 2 Cor. 6: 16.——Further, ask the apostle James how he understands the prophecy of Amos (chap. 9: 11, 12) about rebuilding the fallen tabernacle of David. He replies that it refers to the conversion of the Gentiles, and to their being gathered into the Christian Church. He gives not a hint of the literal rebuilding of the old temple. See Acts 15: 13-18. And this was the doctrine of the whole Church in council assembled then and there.——Or ask the Apostle Paul whether he connects the future conversion of the Jews with their restoration to their own land. Ask him if he assumes that these two events will be coincident, and their restoration a necessary means to their conversion. He answers that he knows nothing about such restoration. Their conversion to Christ he believes in, rejoices in exultingly; but he has not the first hint of their returning to their own land—much less of their rebuilding the temple of wood and stone. Examine his words, Rom. 11: 11-36.——Finally the old system and the new have too many vital points of dissimilarity, not to say antagonism, to admit of being amalgamated, or in any way compounded together. The genius of the old was restrictive, exclusive, and put itself on the defensive. The genius of the new is expansive, aggressive, framed to grasp the whole world. The former walls itself in to shut off idolatry and all contamination from the world without: the latter faces and assails the idolatry and sin of the world every-where under the one grand behest; "Go ye into all the world, and preach the Gospel to every creature." How can these two systems amalgamate? And how can it be supposed that the world is to be converted by going back to the centralized forms of Judaism?

2. The evidence from the Old Testament, *i. e.*, from these prophecies themselves, considered in view of the circumstances of their authors and first readers, has been frequently referred to in these notes, and hence may be presented with the more brevity here. ——In a word, then, these prophets were *Jews*, of Jewish education, with only Jewish conceptions of the kingdom of God, and with only Jewish terms, phrases, figures and symbols for expressing these conceptions. The same is true of their first readers, to whom of necessity they must adapt their writings. If any should suggest here that the Lord himself is the speaker and revealer, still the case remains the same; for the Lord speaks *to Jews*, whether prophets or people, and only in Jewish language and figures. Hence the future kingdom of Christ *must be revealed* to the prophets and to the Jewish people in words and symbols drawn from the existing economy. This necessity is absolute, *if* the Lord aimed to *reveal* any thing—if he aimed to speak so as to be understood.——This principle is introduced here, not precisely to prove that these prophecies

reveal gospel blessings, but to *account for* their phraseology and their symbols. The proof that they teach the gloriously converting power of the Gospel and of the Spirit of God in the latter days comes from the facts, (1.) That they refer to gospel times. (2.) That they must therefore be construed of gospel blessings, and not of Mosaic forms and ritualities: and (3.) That the nature and magnitude of these symbols demand a most magnificent fulfillment and can be satisfied with nothing less.*

3. It remains to show in a few closing words that in the nature of the case the literal system is for every reason intensely improbable. Thus; That the ten tribes, thoroughly lost to all reliable history since their captivity two thousand five hundred and eighty-seven years ago, should appear again; produce their unbroken and distinct genealogies; prove their identity, and file into their places in the allotment of tribes as given in Ezek. 48, is violently improbable. †—— That the natural boundaries of Palestine should be miraculously changed so as to make it a perfect rectangle; that the great river from the sanctuary should flow, with a growth so unprecedented, into the Dead Sea, and make its waters salubrious, fill them with fish, etc., all in the literal sense, is very improbable. That the better times of the gospel age; its one period of most perfect beauty, purity and glory, should be brought about by receding from the genius of

---

* This subject is discussed somewhat fully in my notes on Zech. 12.

† The restoration of the lost ten tribes should be considered in the light of Bible history. Thus: 2 Kings 17 shows that the ten tribes had forsaken the God of Israel, and were therefore utterly rejected with no qualifying promise of restoration (vs. 17-20); that their captivity, so far as known to the sacred historian, was *final* (vs. 23, 34, 41); that the change of population then made was *entire*, the Assyrian king taking away all the Hebrew people, and filling their homes and country with colonists from Assyria, sending back only one priest to teach them the worship of the former God of the land. The Samaritan community had scarcely the least tinge of Israelite blood.——Next, note that 1 Chron. 5: 25, 26 certifies respecting the two and a half tribes that they were carried away captive "*unto this day*;" *i. e.*, up to the date of the last finishing touch of this genealogical history, which, as the reader will see by comparing 1 Chron. 9 with Neh. 11, comes down to a period many (130) years later than the first return of the Jews with Zerubbabel. Nehemiah's latest date is B. C. 400, and his genealogies correspond with those of 1 Chron. 9, so that the testimony which precludes the restoration of the two and a half tribes "down to this day" reaches long after the return of the Jews to Palestine in B. C. 536-444.——And finally the book of Ezra shows (chap. 1: 5) that the returning captives were "the fathers of Judah and Benjamin;" in chap. 2, that special regard was had to the point of genealogy, since those are named who could not make out their record (vs. 59-63); that Ezra gives his own record carefully (7: 1-5), and also that of his company (8: 1-14), and of the Levites (8: 16-20); but gives not the least hint of the ten tribes.——Further, his book shows that the taking of strange [heathen] wives was the besetting sin of the people (chaps. 9 and 10), which the testimony of Nehemiah confirms (chap. 13: 23-30). If this sin needed such stringent measures to withstand it among the Jews proper, even while residing in their own land, how much more must the ten tribes have lost their distinct nationality by its power over them in that remote land of Assyria?——Thus stands the historical evidence of Scripture in reference to the restoration of the ten tribes—utterly and strongly *against* it. In the light of Scripture, the supposition is unhistorical, every way improbable, and in nowise credible.——Hence the restoration of these lost tribes, in any yet future age, becomes intensely improbable—virtually impossible.

New Testament Christianity to the genius of Judaism, is preëminently improbable. That the Lord should subject his Gentile churches to the same terrible contest with Judaism which cost so much martyr-blood in the first and second centuries, is improbable. That he should subject the Jews themselves to those temptations to bigotry, exclusiveness, and uncharitableness, which in the first Christian age often proved too stubborn for even the grace of the gospel, is improbable. That he should expose them to the power of the old national spirit of reliance upon ritual forms and ceremonies, or to the national pride in which they accounted themselves the only favored people of God, is utterly improbable. And finally, that the Lord should give his Church in the future age a system in which the spirit of love, purity and peace is lost in the letter of forms and ceremonies; in which (as *e. g.* in Ezek. 47: 1–12) you have, instead of the unexampled glory and power of the Divine Spirit, only a beautiful river and plenty of good fish, and fruit-trees in abundance for sensual delights; in short, that God should lead the church and the world backward from a spiritual gospel to a sensual paradise—is utterly improbable and even incredible.——For one, I rejoice that it is. I rejoice that the instincts of our Christian nature revolt against this view of these prophecies. I rejoice that there is no trustworthy evidence to sustain the literal interpretation, and that the figurative view is amply supported by evidence, unfolding glorious truth in harmony with the whole tenor of Old Testament prophecy and of New Testament interpretation of it, and revealing a sublimely grand and auspicious future for the kingdom of our divine Redeemer. AMEN.

DANIEL.

PREFACE.

THE best of commentators have interpreted the prophecies of Daniel variously. It is only natural that people who read commentaries should think as variously, save that some may lose confidence in any of the proposed systems of interpretation—not to say, confidence that any reliable system can be found. Consequently a new commentary on Daniel, by whomsoever put forth, or however able, must fail to meet the previous views of all its possible readers.

——In the outset, therefore, let me say that in this book I dissent from some worthy critics, not through any lack of deference or respect for them, but through the force of my own convictions. I have labored upon these prophecies—not to harmonize the conflicting opinions of others; not to select the most worthy and follow them; not to meet some foregone and favorite scheme of fulfillment;—but simply and only to apply what I deem just principles of interpretation, and thus arrive at the truth. I have sought to apply to these prophetic words and symbols those great principles of interpretation which legitimately determine the sense of all language. These principles, as they should apply to Daniel, I have briefly presented near the close of my General Introduction. I submit that this method of reaching the truth and this only is entitled to confidence.

——My earliest views of these prophecies were taken from Dr. Scott and Bishop Newton—accepted without dissent, and indeed, without rigorous questioning. But being called (some twenty-eight years since) to the responsibility of conducting theological students through these prophecies, I was put upon a rigorous investigation of their meaning. It was in the study of the eleventh chapter that I first saw that their system palpably violated the laws of philology. It was impossible to break the bonds of connection which held the entire passage (chap. 11: 21–45) to one individual, and this one a king—the well-known "king of the north," Antiochus Epiphanes. In chap. 8, the force of God's own interpretation compelled me to discard the Roman theory, and apply what is said of the "little horn" to Antiochus. In the same way, the interpretation given by God himself, coupled with the metes and bounds within which the fulfillment is located, constrained me to recast my former system of Dan. 7. Then the proofs of general parallelism throughout his four great prophecies attracted my attention, and being found invincible, could not be ignored. Thus through repeated investigations, renewed from time to time during twenty-five years, laboring to get the full and exact sense of all that Daniel had seen and said—laboring also to make myself master of his stand-point of view, and to enter as fully as possible into his relations both of sympathy and of personal and public ministry for his people, the Jews; I have gradually matured the system herein presented. Each successive examination has contributed to clear up difficult points; to bring out new aspects of these visions; to suggest new views of their fitness and force; and to settle more firmly my conviction that in the main the interpretation here presented will stand the test of candid scrutiny, however searching, and approve itself as based upon sound principles of interpreting prophecy.——Somewhat early in the course of these studies, a fresh impulse was given them by the appearance (1841–43) of the views of Mr. William Miller on the Second Advent. It is only on rare occasions that such a stimulus comes to quicken prophetic investigation. The student of prophecy can afford to express his obligation (on the score solely of stimulus and suggestion) to the very crude and wild sentiments but very quickening impulses of that extraordinary movement. Mr. Miller and his associates made a vigorous but not legitimate use of various errors which had been admitted into the interpretation of this book. See a brief Dissertation upon his system at the close of this volume.

These words, personal to myself, reluctantly admitted here, will show how I have reached my present views and why I hold and express them so strongly. I have made these allusions to the rise and growth of the scheme of interpreting Daniel herein presented, with no wish to influence any reader's mind, save by the force of argument, yet as a sort of apology for inviting all readers, of every shade of opinion, to give these pages a candid and careful examination.

OBERLIN, O., Aug., 1867.

DANIEL.

GENERAL INTRODUCTION.

1. The questions of personal history appropriate to an introduction are, for the most part, readily answered from the book itself.

Daniel comes first to view, a Jewish youth of the royal family,* taken captive to Babylon in the first deportation of captives, in the third year of Jehoiakim, B. C. 606 or 607; and is soon after selected with others for his wisdom, efficiency and agreeable person, to be trained in the learning and the tongue of the Chaldeans, for service under the king. This custom of taking young men of the finest parts from a captive or subject race to fill responsible positions about the king, has prevailed in many despotic governments, and is essentially the usage of the Turkish empire to this day. It finds its motives, (1.) In the fact that such monarchs need men about them of the very first abilities; (2.) In the difficulty they would experience in getting young men of such ability from among their own people who might not, by virtue of their social position or connections, become dangerous to the throne. We are then to think of Daniel as educated thoroughly in the language, literature, and general culture of the Chaldeans (this term being used here for the learned, sacerdotal and scientific class, and not for the mass of the people), but yet as adhering with noble firmness to the religious faith of his fathers. In this position, he developed extraordinary capacities in the line of wisdom, fidelity and efficiency, and consequently rose to the rank of prime minister under the Chaldean sovereigns, Nebuchadnezzar and Belshazzar, and remarkably, attained and held an equally exalted position in the succeeding dynasty, the Medo-Persian, under Darius the Median and Cyrus.

Daniel must have lived and retained his vigor to a great age. The period during which he appears before us in this book, from the beginning of the captivity to the very end of it, was seventy years, and we may reasonably suppose him from sixteen to twenty years of age at the beginning of this period, and of course almost ninety at its close. Yet his heart appears full of earnest life and power in his memorable prayer for his people, given us in chap. 9, just on the eve of the restoration. Tradition holds that he was the special instrument under God of obtaining from Cyrus the decree

---

* Josephus says that Daniel was of the seed of Zedekiah. Ant. Jud. X: 10. The text says only "of the king's seed and of the princes." Chap 1: 3.

for the restoration of his people to their own land—no small achievement for the physical stamina of a patriarch of ninety! Temperate habits through the whole of life, and a soul evermore steadfastly stayed on God, are eminently congenial to length of days and to freshness and vigor of days as well.

II. The reader will recall some points of close analogy between Daniel and Joseph. Both were captives; each rose in a foreign kingdom to the same rank of prime minister, by the same qualities of personal character—sterling integrity, unselfish devotion to their work, great business capacity, and unfaltering faith in God. Each became, under God, a patron and protector to his suffering people. To each was given of God extraordinary prophetic powers which served to raise him to general notice and confidence, and manifestly in the case of Daniel, served to exalt the God of the Hebrew race highly in the convictions of the monarchs under whom he served. Each was able to distance and confound all the pretenders to supernatural knowledge, of whom there were many both in Egypt and in Babylon.

III. Here it may be well to notice carefully the critical objections made in modern times against the entire book by those *who deny its genuineness* and *impugn its historic veracity*.——First in time by Porphyry, a prominent infidel of the third century, but most ably by a considerable body of recent German critics, it has been gravely and confidently denied that the book was written by that Daniel whose name it bears, whose history it gives, and who is referred to by Ezekiel (chap. 14: 14, 20, and 28: 3) and also by our Lord himself (Mat. 24: 15, 16). They also impugn the general veracity of its historical accounts, and attempt to sustain their main position by a variety of critical objections. They claim that the book was not written until after the death of Antiochus Epiphanes (B. C. 163); that it was written shortly after that event; and of course that it is a forgery and contains no prophecy whatever, being written *after* the minute events which its pretended visions of an assumed early date gave forth as prophecy.——Their central point is the denial of its genuineness and date; *i. e.*, they deny that it was written by that Daniel who lived during the captivity, or by any one else at that time.——As collateral, yet altogether minor points, they say that the book contains some Greek and some Persian words, which evince a date later than the captivity; that part of it is written in Chaldee and part in Hebrew; that the tone of the composition is peculiar, unlike that of the other prophets; that its miracles are grotesque; that its doctrines respecting angels, the Messiah, and an ascetic life, indicate a later age; and finally that Daniel speaks too well of himself and was too young to stand so high as he appears in Ezekiel.——These minor points shall receive due attention in their place; the main one should come first in order. To meet their central and main dogma somewhat fundamentally, I maintain—1. That the Daniel of the age of the captivity was a very prominent man in Jewish history. Even King David was scarcely more so. He was a city set on a hill, known to all intelligent Jews of that age and onward into later times. Far above all other Jews of his time, he was *the distinguished* man—prime minister in the courts successively of Nebuchadnezzar and Darius, and promoted to the very highest rank by Belshazzar just on the eve of his final fall. Obviously not the doings only of such a man but his writings must be matters of public notoriety. By how much the more prominent the man, and by how much the more highly esteemed among his countrymen, by so much the greater would be the difficulty of putting forth forgeries in his name successfully during his lifetime, or at any period while his name would be worth using in a forged production; and hence by so much the greater would be the certainty that written documents purporting to be from him would be genuine.

2. This book of Daniel, in both its historic and prophetic parts, is closely interwoven with his actual life. It is not easy to conceive how any book could be more so. Both the outer and the inner life of the man stand out in his writings with remarkable distinctness. There is not a word in the whole book that does not fit naturally and closely to the life, to the heart, and to the whole character of this prominent man—Daniel of the captivity. Hence the assumption that this book is a forgery, gotten up three hundred and seventy years after the latest record of his life, is violently improbable—not to say, utterly incredible.

3. The languages in which the book is written determine its age, proving that it must have been written during, or very near, the captivity, and completely disproving the fiction of Porphyry. The facts are that the portion, chaps. 2: 4–7: 28, is in Chaldee; all the rest in Hebrew. Now the period of the captivity is the only one during the whole range of Jewish history in which one of the Jewish sacred books could have been written thus, a part in each tongue. For, all scripture was written for the common people and primarily for the people then living. This was the only period in the entire national history of the Jews in which *they* understood both these languages.——Again, this was the only period in which the Chaldee portion could have been reasonably written, for the benefit of the Chaldean people. Let any man intelligent in history, think of the Chaldee portion of Daniel as written for the Chaldean people in the age of Antiochus Epiphanes! The idea is simply absurd. Babylon had then almost ceased to be. Its relations to Nebuchadnezzar were all forgotten by its population.——In the book of Ezra, chap. 5 throughout, portions of chaps. 4, 6, and 7, are in Chaldee, and a verse or too in Jeremiah; but these prophets were substantially in the same age with Daniel.

4. Some of the salient points in the history found in this book are referred to in subsequent Jewish history, prior to the death of Antiochus Epiphanes, in a way which renders it nearly certain that the book itself was then extant. In 1 Mac. 2: 51–60, the venerable Mattathias of Moden, himself then near death, exhorts his sons to "call to remembrance what acts their fathers did in their time;" alludes successively to Abraham, Joseph, Phineas, Joshua, Caleb, David and Elijah; and then adds: "Ananias, Azarias and Misael, by be-

lieving, were saved out of the flame. Daniel, for his innocency was saved from the mouth of lions." These words were spoken by Mattathias *before* the date fixed by these German critics for the writing of the book of Daniel. I maintain that there is the strongest presumption for the existence of this book long before the death of Epiphanes, even as there is of the other histories drawn from in this same speech.——Furthermore, the second book of Maccabees (chap. 7: 9, 14, 36) speaks of the resurrection in a way not easily accounted for otherwise than as an allusion to Dan. 12: 2, 3. The presumption is certainly very strong that the dying martyrs whose words are there quoted must have had this twelfth chapter in their hands. Compare what Daniel says with what they say. Daniel thus: "Many of them that sleep in the dust of the earth shall awake; some to everlasting life, and some to shame and everlasting contempt: and they that be wise shall shine as the brightness of the firmament, and they that turn many to righteousness as the stars forever and ever." The martyrs referred to say; "Thou like a fury takest us out of the present life, but the King of the world shall raise up us who have died for his laws, unto everlasting life." "It is good being put to death by men, to look for the hopes that are of God, to be raised up again by him; but for thee there shall be no resurrection unto life." "For now our brethren, after enduring brief pain, have fallen under God's covenant of everlasting life; but thou, under God's judgment, shall receive the just punishment for thy pride." And yet further, there can scarcely be a doubt that these visions of Daniel, especially the last (chaps. 10-12) inspired the faith, zeal, and hope of the heroic Maccabees through their terrific struggle. Their words and deeds evince the power of such inspirations; the truths taught in Daniel were adapted (must we not say *designed*) of God for such results.

5. Josephus is a valuable Jewish witness. A man of eminent learning, in very high repute among his countrymen, the author of a full and very elaborate history of the Jewish nation from Abraham down to the destruction of their city by the Romans (A. D. 70); born A. D. 37 and publishing his works in the latter part of the first century; his testimony to the current opinions of his nation can not be impeached. He speaks (Ant. XII: 7: 6) of the prophecies of Daniel as being "uttered four hundred and eight years before;" *i. e.* before the events in the time of Antiochus Epiphanes. He also says (Ant. X: 11: 7), "All these things, he (Daniel) left in writing, God exhibiting them to him, so that those who read, observant of the events, must needs look on Daniel with wonder on account of the honor done to him by God."——The fiction of these modern German critics is squarely confronted by this testimony of Josephus. They say Daniel did not write the book which bears his name; Josephus says he did. They deny the fact of any real prophecy in this book; Josephus specially affirms it, and declares it to be of the most extraordinary and unquestionable character.

6. Yet again, we have the testimony of Josephus that this very book of Daniel was shown by the High Priest Jaddua to Alexander

the Great in the year B. C. 332. The circumstances strongly confirm this statement, to this extent at least; for Alexander certainly spared the Jews and their city; took them into favor, and exempted them from the tribute which it was his custom to impose on subject nations. This was sixty-six years before the earliest date allowed by these critics for the existence of this book of Daniel.

7. There can be scarcely a doubt that the book of Daniel was translated into the Septuagint one hundred years before the German skeptics admit it to have existed. Some points in respect to the authors of this celebrated version and to its production remain considerably obscure; but there is no ground for doubt that it was made within the reigns of the first two Ptolemies in the Greek Egyptian dynasty, and at the request and with the aid of these two kings. Their reigns fill the period B. C. 323-246. The Pentateuch was brought out first, and about B. C. 285. It might be difficult to show when the whole work was completed, or when the translation of Daniel was made. But the whole was manifestly carried through in the same general movement, for the same common purposes and objects, and hence, in all probability, without unnecessary delay. *The book of Daniel was in that version.* It must, therefore, with the highest probability, have been translated before A. D. 163. It is not conceivable that one hundred and twenty years could have been occupied in completing this work.

8. The book of Daniel was brought into the accepted canon of the Old Testament scriptures not later than the close of the reign of Artaxerxes Longimanus (B. C. 474-424); *i. e.*, not far from three hundred years before the death of Epiphanes. Here Josephus is a competent witness. He says: "We have not a countless number of books, discordant and arrayed against each other, but only twenty-two books; which are justly accredited as divine." Of these, five are the books of Moses: "four contain hymns to God and rules of life for men." [This leaves thirteen which were historical and prophetical. In our modern arrangement as compared with that given by Josephus, several are subdivided. The thirteen included all the Old Testament, not embraced in the two other portions.] Of this body of thirteen, Josephus says; "From the death of Moses to the reign of Artaxerxes, king of Persia after Xerxes, the prophets who followed Moses have described the things which were done during the age of each one respectively. From the time of Artaxerxes until our present period, all occurrences have been written down, *but they are not regarded as entitled to the like credit with those which preceded them because there was no certain succession of prophets.*" Hence the canon of books accepted as inspired comes down through the reign of Artaxerxes but no further. The twenty-two books of our accepted Old Testament—Daniel included—were all written, according to Josephus, before that reign closed; *i. e.*, say at least before B. C. 400.

9. It is remarkable that the time assigned by these German critics for the writing of this book of Daniel was one in which the leading Jews knew they had no prophet among them—knew they had not

had one for many years past—and could not expect one for many years to come. That is, the existing state of opinion was thoroughly adverse both to the writing and to the reception of such a forgery as they claim this book to be. But it requires a peculiarly facile state of public feeling toward the main purpose and scope of a forgery to admit of its success. Against strong public convictions, it never could succeed.——What was the state of the public mind here?——The author of the first book of Maccabees (writing about B. C. 135), describing the calamities that came upon Judea in consequence of the death of Judas Maccabeus (B. C. 161), says, "that there was great affliction in Israel, such as had not been since the last prophet appeared among them." He manifestly implies that this had been a long time. It was then about two hundred and seventy years since the latest reliable date for the prophet Malachi.——Again, according to 1 Mac. 4: 16, the Jews laid away the polluted stones of the altar set up by Antiochus Epiphanes in their holy temple, "until the coming of some prophet to decide respecting them."——And further according to 1 Mac. 14: 41, "Simon was constituted leader and high priest forever ['eis ton aiona'] until some faithful prophet should arise"—a passage which manifestly looks to the Messiah, and indicates that they expected no prophet till he should come.——These indications of current public sentiment existing among the Jews both at the period shortly after the death of Antiochus (just when these critics would bring out this prophecy of Daniel) and also at the time when the first book of Maccabees was written (full thirty years later), go far to show that their theory paid not the least regard to the existing state of the public mind at the time fixed for its appearance. They did not look to see whether it could have been written then, or whether, if written, it could have been imposed upon and wrought into the confidence of the people. Were ever great critics so uncritical!

The arguments thus far adduced against the great central position of the critics in question have designedly been of that historical and critical sort which those who impugn Daniel usually delight to honor. It seemed well first of all to meet them on their own ground.——It remains to adduce yet one argument which those who recognize the divine mission of Jesus Christ as the great Teacher sent from God, will surely honor. Our divine Lord himself refers (Mat. 24: 15, 16) to Daniel and to this book of his, in these words; "When ye shall see the abomination of desolation, spoken of by Daniel the prophet, stand in the holy place (whoso readeth let him understand); Then let them which be in Judea flee into the mountains."——Here note distinctly,—(1.) That our Lord recognizes Daniel as "a prophet." (2.) Quotes some of his written prophecies; *i. e.*, from Dan. 9: 27. (3.) Hence he witnesses that Daniel wrote his own prophecies—specially this book that bears his name; (4.) And finally that this book of his should be read and accepted as a part of the inspired Jewish sacred scriptures.——In view of such testimony, those who honor Jesus Christ will regard the question of the genuineness and veracity of this

DANIEL.—GENERAL INTRODUCTION. 281

book of Daniel as settled.——But it will be asked, What do these skeptical critics say in support of their positions?——1. To support their main, central position, they begin with denying the fact of any inspired prophecy either here or elsewhere, and resolving all predictions of future events into human sagacity or unfounded anticipations. But inasmuch as this book of Daniel records as prophecy a long series of very minute historic events far in the future (*e. g.*, in chaps. 11 and 8), as well as the general succession of great dynasties—too much to be attributed to human sagacity—they insist that the book must have been written *after* these events took place. This they maintain is the common law of historical criticism. If an ancient book of history should come to light, all critics would settle the question of its date on the assumption that it was written later than the events it records.

I reply, This is very true of what is merely human history; not at all true of divinely-inspired prophecy. The fact of a really divine inspiration constitutes a bold exception. The plausibility of this modern plea against Daniel lies in its tacitly ignoring this distinction.

(2.) All the other points made in the attack upon Daniel are trivial; *e. g.*, as above stated, that the book contains some Greek words and some Persian; that part of it is written in Chaldee and part in Hebrew; that the tone of the composition is peculiar—unlike that of the other prophets; that its miracles are grotesque, and its ideas respecting angels, the Messiah, and an ascetic life, indicate unmistakably a late age; and finally that Daniel speaks too well of himself, and was too young to stand so high as he appears in Ezekiel.

The candid and intelligent reader will readily see that these points are trivial. For there are not more Greek or Persian words here than ought to be expected in an author living and writing in the great commercial and political center of the known world. For this known world at that time practically embraced both Greece and Persia.——There were the best of reasons for writing some portions in Chaldee; viz., the special benefit of the Chaldean people. If the book had been written wholly in Hebrew, a much stronger objection could be raised against it, as scarcely credible in view of the author's relations to the Chaldean people, government, and language. On the other hand there were some good reasons for writing some of it in Hebrew.——Further, the cast of the book is unobjectionable. True, it is part history and part prophecy; but it is all the more useful for this; was all needed at the time, and needed from this author.——True, he uses *symbols;* but so did Ezekiel and Zechariah—prophets nearest his age and of most similar surroundings: and (what is not less worthy of note) his symbols are remarkably *Chaldean,* as recent discoveries most abundantly attest.——Yet further, its miracles, so far from being "grotesque," are morally grand and solemnly impressive. Note how the salvation of those three men in the furnace and of Daniel in the den of lions affected in each case the king on his throne.——As to its doctrines respecting angels and the Messiah, why should there not be some advance in ideas on these points, as compared with those of previous prophets? And who can say that the advance manifest in Daniel is too great for the period of the captivity and for the extraordinary piety and prominence of the man?——The charge of being prematurely ascetic looks toward Daniel's refusing the dainties of the king's table—for which, however, ample reasons may be supposed, entirely apart from asceticism. Or, perhaps, toward a special case in which he "ate no pleasant bread, flesh or wine, for three weeks" (chap. 10: 2, 3)— a form and degree of abstinence due to his extraordinary state of mind at a time when God came ineffably near to reveal to him "what should befall his people in the latter days."——As to Daniel's speaking of his own wisdom and being too young to have attained such a reputation as Ezekiel's references to him imply, let it be noted that in the main passage in question (chap. 1: 17, 19, 20) Daniel speaks not of himself alone but of all the four Jewish youth, saying only what was doubtless true; and that he specifies of himself in particular only that he had "understanding in all visions and dreams." This is one of the most prominent facts of the history, and for this reason deserved mention. In the detailed record, Daniel bears himself with extraordinary modesty and Christian humility.——Daniel may have been young when God by Ezekiel spake in high terms of his wisdom. If the history in the book is true, Daniel rose to distinction, not slowly, but by one bound, in the second year of the king and of his own captivity. He was therefore very great while very young. Why should not God speak of men according to truth? Such great capacity so early in life is not altogether without precedent. Though rare, it is possible, and therefore not incredible. William Pitt became prime minister of England at the age of twenty-four. Charles XII and Napoleon evinced their transcendent military genius at a yet earlier age.

That Daniel was so young yet so exalted in position and in reputation at the court, served to make his name the more notable among both Jews and Chaldeans.——It will be found that the more thoroughly all these critical objections against the book of Daniel are examined, the more they serve to bring out and brighten the evidence of its being written at the time, and by the veritable Daniel of that age.

Having indicated thus very briefly the special points of these critical objections, and alluded in few words to their uncritical nature and to their entire lack of force, I proceed to strengthen the whole argument for the genuineness of this book and for its historic credibility by adducing collateral evidence that the historical notices found here are strictly correct; that they evince a most accurate acquaintance with Chaldean life, and are verified most abundantly by all that is known of those times through profane sources ancient or recent; and therefore *can not have been written* (as is claimed) *four hundred years after the age of the captivity*.—— This argument from collateral history, coming up from entirely independent sources, embraces a considerable number of distinct points.

(*a*.) The captivity and deportation of the Jews to Babylon underlies the entire history of this book. Now, this great fact in the history of that people is not only confirmed by the prophecies of Isaiah, Jeremiah, and many of the minor prophets; by the histories of the books of Kings and Chronicles; of Ezra and of Nehemiah; but also by ample heathen testimonies. Indeed it was a permanent feature in the policy of the Assyrian, Chaldean, and Persian governments for the subjugation of conquered countries, especially the restive and refractory, to remove them from their own to other and remote lands, and thus uproot the love of home and country, and sever the social bonds that might else make them dangerous to the great central power. In addition to the ample evidence to this general feature of their policy, there is the special testimony of Berosus, the great Chaldean historian, who wrote in the age of Alexander the Great. In a passage which describes the expedition of Nebuchadnezzar, then crown prince and general of the army, against the Egyptians, Syrians and Phenicians in revolt, in which he fought and won the great battle of Carchemish, he says; "Not long after, Nebuchadnezzar, having heard of the death of his father (the king) when he had settled the affairs of Egypt and the adjacent regions, and had arranged with certain of his friends *to bring to Babylon the captives of the Jews...* came himself with great haste and with a small company through the wilderness to Babylon. There, assuming the administration of affairs... he succeeded to all his father's dominions; and when the captives arrived, he appointed colonies for them in the most suitable parts of Babylonia."

(*b*.) The personal history, character and achievements of Nebuchadnezzar stand out prominently in this book of Daniel. He is here a monarch of great energy, of indomitable will, ruling a vast empire, and especially building, or more strictly, *re*-building and greatly enlarging, Babylon. His insanity for seven years; his removal from the management of public affairs during this period, and his restoration again first to reason and then to power, constitute very peculiar features of his history as it appears in this book. That he was an idolater and that he worshiped some one god in particular is also manifest. See for the latter point chap. 1: 2; " to the house of *his* god;" "into the treasure-house of his god;" and chap. 4: 8, " according to the name of my god." Moreover, we read much of images of *gold*.——The length of his reign is not definitely given in Daniel, but the general cast of the history implies that it was long. The books of Kings, Chronicles, and Jeremiah give the desired data. Jehoiakim reigned about eleven years; in his fourth year, the first large deportation of captives took place. Daniel was among them. Nebuchadnezzar was then just ascending his throne. Jehoiachin, the son, succeeded; reigned three months, was then carried captive to Babylon, kept there in prison at least thirty-six full years, and in his thirty-seventh was taken out of prison by Evil-Merodach, the immediate successor of Nebuchadnezzar, and in the first year of his reign. Hence, Nebuchadnezzar's reign is measured thus; about seven years contemporary with Jehoiakim, one-fourth of a year with Jehoiachin reigning; thirty-six with Jehoiachin a prisoner, equal to forty-three.

Let us now turn to confirmations from profane history. And first on this last mentioned point; profane history makes his reign precisely forty three years. This is the language of Berosus: "Now Nebuchadnezzar, just as he began to build the aforesaid wall, fell sick and died, after having reigned forty-three years." The celebrated canon of Ptolemy (an official register of the kings of Assyria and Babylon) assigns him forty-three years; viz., from B. C. 604 to B. C. 561. A clay tablet, discovered recently, almost proves the same thing. These tablets are mostly orders on the imperial treasury, dated in the current year of the reigning monarch. The one referred to dates in his *forty-second year*. Of course his reign can not have been less than this; may have been more.——That all profane history makes him a great king, great in war, but greater in peace, is well known. That he was the great rebuilder of Babylon is affirmed by Berosus thus; "Nebuchadnezzar repaired the city which had existed from the first, and added another to it; and in order that besiegers might not again be able, by turning aside the course of the river, to get possession of the city, he built three courses of walls around the inner city and as many around the outer.' But the most remarkably confirming fact is of recent development, viz., that nine-tenths of the inscribed bricks from the site of ancient Babylon are stamped with the name of Nebuchadnezzar!——Concerning the extraordinary fact of his temporary insanity and removal from his throne, we might naturally be inquisitive to see what the public records of the realm would say and what version of it would pass into current and future history. Bearing in mind that the strong moral impression which extorted such an acknowledgment of the one true God as we find in chap. 4: 34-37, was obviously not abiding; at least was not, in the Christian sense, converting; and considering also that he lived to modify the public records at his own pleasure, we can not expect a very frank confession of the whole case.——Now as to the facts: Berosus makes no decisive allusion to this event. But on what is known as "the Standard Inscription of Nebuchadnezzar," the following passage occurs. The first clause is defective, some words being illegible; but the statements as a whole are remarkably *negative*, and silent as to the causes.——"Four years ... the seat of my kingdom in the city ... which ... did not rejoice my heart. In all my dominions, I did not build a high place of power; the precious treasures of my kingdom I did not lay up. In Babylon, buildings for myself and for the honor of my kingdom, I did not lay out. In the worship of Merodach, my lord, the joy of my heart, in Babylon, the city of his sovereignty and the seat of my empire, I did not sing his praises and I did not furnish his altars [with victims], nor did I clear out the canals."——So much could not well be ignored on the

DANIEL.—GENERAL INTRODUCTION.   285

public records. What was more than this, human pride prevailed against unwelcome truth to suppress.——Mr. Rawlinson remarks that "the whole range of cuneiform literature presents no similar instance of a king putting on record his own inaction." It is in human nature that kings should chronicle and send down to future ages what they have *done*, not what they have *left undone*.

Yet further; according to the Scriptures Nebuchadnezzar only of all the heathen monarchs there referred to, had revelations of the future in visions. Correspondingly, this remarkable record comes down to us from the ancient historian Abydenus, as quoted by Eusebius; somewhat inaccurate as to the facts and apparently ascribing to Nebuchadnezzar in part what pertains to Belshazzar.
——"Afterward, as is said by the Chaldeans, he went up into his palace, when he was seized by some divine influence, and uttered these words;—'O Babylonians, I, Nebuchadnezzar, announce to you this future calamity. There shall come a Persian mule, using our divinities as allies: he shall bring us into bondage: leagued with him shall be the Mede, the boast of Assyria.' Having uttered these predictions, he immediately disappeared."——His devotion to his own god Merodach, (akin to the planet Jupiter) may be noticed in the extract above given from his standard inscription. It appears every-where in the monumental records of Nebuchadnezzar. Rawlinson states that "the inscriptions (of this king) always terminate with a prayer to Merodach, invoking the favor of the god for the protection of the king's throne and empire, and for its continuance through all ages to the end of time." Remarkably, Nebuchadnezzar, though living in an age of polytheism, seems to have concentrated his reverence, worship, and trust, mainly upon this one god. His language on his inscriptions runs thus; "Merodach, the great lord, has appointed me to the empire of the world, and has confided to my care the far-spread people of the earth;" "Merodach, the great lord, the senior of the gods, the most ancient, has given all nations and people to my care:" "Merodach, the great lord, has established me in strength."——This, it will be seen harmonizes with the repeated references in Daniel, to "his own god."——It should be noted that the full name of this god is Bel-Merodach; that it was originally Bel; and hence probably Merodach was first appended, and then came to be used often alone. Of Daniel, Nebuchadnezzar remarks (chap. 4: 18), "whose name was Belteshazzar, according to the name of my god"—said with reference to the leading syllable, "*Bel*."——Again, Daniel represents "gods of gold" as common in Babylon. See chap. 3: 1, and 5: 4. The historic facts are that Nebuchadnezzar made some extensive conquests immediately before he ascended the throne and others shortly afterward; that plunder of all most valuable things, or enormous tribute, was the law of conquest in that age; and that gold was especially devoted to the service of the gods and wrought into their images. Rawlinson considers it proven that "the statue of Jupiter Belus, described by Herodotus, is the same as the great idol of Merodach, which was made of silver by an earlier king, but was overlaid with

plates of gold by Nebuchadnezzar."——These points of correspondence between sacred history and profane, out of the life of Nebuchadnezzar, must suffice.

(c.) The history of Belshazzar affords another point of striking confirmation.——Until recently, critics have been greatly perplexed with the question—Who was the Belshazzar of Daniel? The canon of Ptolemy fails to give his name among the kings in the line between Nebuchadnezzar and the subversion of the empire by Cyrus. Of the three who fill this chasm in the canon of Ptolemy—usually known by the names of Evil-Merodach, Nergal-sharezer, and Nabonned, alias Labynetus, each one in his turn has been supposed to be the Belshazzar of Daniel. But no satisfactory explanation could be given of the diversity in name. Besides, Berosus had said that the last king of Babylon, instead of being slain in the capture of the city, had previously retired to Borsippa, was besieged there, surrendered, was treated with clemency, and had estates assigned him by Cyrus in Carmania, where he lived till his natural death. ——These apparent discrepancies between the sacred records and the profane were (as usual) put to their utmost account by skeptical critics. A slight circumstance has relieved all these difficulties. In the year 1854, Sir Henry Rawlinson deciphered the inscriptions found on some ancient cylinders among the ruins of Um Queer, (the ancient "Ur of the Chaldees") where he found it stated that Nabonned admitted his son Belsharezer (Belshazzar) to share the government with him, with the title of king. This son, the prince royal, was obviously left in charge of the city while his father took the field. The son was slain.

(d.) The subversion of the dynasty and kingdom by a Medo-Persian army is another boldly outstanding point in the history of this book. It is not less prominent in profane history. Greek historians have long since wrought the leading facts of this subversion into the warp of universal history.

(e.) I close this series of coincidences with the duration of the captivity and the date of the restoration ——Daniel 9: 1, 2, shows that he estimated the seventy years of Jeremiah's prophecy (chap. 25: 11, 12) to be near their close in the first year of Darius the Mede. Of course he would count from the first great deportation of captives among whom he himself came, which mostly fell within the year before Nebuchadnezzar ascended the throne. Then at least three ancient historians (Berosus, Polyhistor and Ptolemy) make the reign of Nebuchadnezzar forty-three years. His four Chaldean successors reigned respectively 2; 3½; ¾; and 17 years. Then counting one for Darius, we have about sixty-eight—which brings us near to the determined number in Jeremiah's prophecy.*

——The thoughtful reader will appreciate the importance of these points of historic criticism, and hence will not account this inves-

---

* For most of these points of more recent investigation, I am indebted to the "Historical Evidences" of George Rawlinson; to his Herodotus; and to various articles in Smith's Bible Dictionary, all which evince learning, research and sound judgment on the archeology of Assyria and Chaldea.

tigation excessively minute or protracted. For, evidently, if this book is not reliably accurate as history, there is a somewhat strong presumption in favor of its being written at a later date. If it be a forgery of later date, written by some unknown hand and *after* the fulfillment of its apparent prophecies, its religious value to us becomes nothing, and painful doubts are thrown upon the reliability of other canonical scriptures.——But if this book is historically true, then it was no doubt written by the Daniel of the captivity. If written by him, it contains most wonderful prophecy and becomes its own witness to its divine inspiration. Thus the general truth of its history confirms its genuineness and authenticity, rescues it from the ruthless hands of mistaken critics, and gives it back to the church and to mankind, its proofs brightened and its reliability confirmed by the ordeal of this fiery furnace of hypercriticism.—— When this book of Daniel becomes fully and justly known, it will appear that in respect to both its history and its prophecy it interlaces itself so perfectly, not only with the scriptures of the Old Testament and the New, but with all contemporary and subsequent history at least down to the Christian era, that no violence can wrench it away. Its position is such among the pillars of the great temple of truth that none can pluck it down without laying the temple itself in ruins. If there be any reliable history of the ages, then is this book reliable. Its prophecies have mostly become history: itself came forth from the Spirit of God.——I must advance now to other points appropriate to an introduction.

IV. Let us note with care the peculiar position of Daniel as a prophet of the Lord with reference both to the covenant people and to the heathen kings and courts with whom he lived.

(1.) The providence of God raised him to a station of great responsibility and influence. The jealousy manifested toward him in the Medo-Persian court testifies to his high standing and influence. ——(2.) He used his influence most wisely and devotedly for God and righteousness. Of this the record gives us several noble examples.——(3.) As he testified for God fearlessly, even at the risk of the greatest personal peril, so God testified for him in forms of surpassing grandeur and in a way that illustrates God's loving care of his people, and that must have made strong impressions upon the heathen minds about him.——(4.) He was therefore in a situation to act as the Patron and Guardian of his people. A measure of the esteem accorded to him would naturally pass over to his countrymen, and serve to ameliorate their condition as captives. It can scarcely be questioned that he obtained for them some favors from Nebuchadnezzar. Tradition affirms that shortly after the accession of Cyrus to the throne, Daniel obtained from him the decree for the restoration of his people, and that for this purpose he brought to his notice the prophecies of Isaiah (chap. 44: 23-28, and 45: 1-4) in which Cyrus is mentioned by name. The decree itself which comes down to us in Ezra 1: 1-4, and 2 Chron. 36: 22, 23, is such as at least to favor the credibility of this tradition.——(5.) It is pleasant to note that his influence was great, not only in the courts of Nebuchadnezzar and Cyrus, but in the court of Heaven. His prayers to God for mercy to his people and for their restoration to their own land, as they stand recorded in chap. 9, are among the most signal examples on record of prevailing intercession.——(6.) His religious influence with his people, the Jews, must have been very great, especially in the line of withstanding firmly all temptations to idolatry and heathen superstitions, and also of waiting on God in assured hope for the day of national deliverance. Nor was his influence small toward the requisite antecedent repentance, confession, humiliation and prayer.——(7.) These points bring us to one conclusion of prime importance in the interpretation of Daniel's prophecies, viz., *that they may safely be presumed to bear very directly upon the religious condition of his countrymen in the age then present and in the nearer future.* In behalf of those generations Daniel felt most intensely; for these he lived, prayed, planned and labored; upon these generations therefore his prophecies must be presumed especially to bear.——This is the common law of prophetic life and labor. The prophets devoted their lives, delivering their messages orally, or in writing as the Lord might lead them, but always with reference more or less to the moral and religious welfare of the generation then living. The higher their responsibilities for their own people, the more direct and exclusive, other things being equal, would be the reference of their messages *to* the case of those people. Daniel bore preëminent responsibilities for the Jewish nation: they lay heavily both on his hands and on his heart; and hence with the greater force is it inferred that his prophecies will respect the present and the nearer future of the Jews.——And here it should be distinctly noted as greatly confirming this opinion, that Daniel accounts the Jews to be *his own people;* that God repeatedly recognizes them as such; and in the last prophecy (chapters 10–12) he explicitly declares, "I am come to make you understand *what shall befall thy people* in the latter days" (chap. 10: 14). That they are Daniel's own people, may be seen also in his prayer for them (chap. 9: 20): "I was confessing the sin of *my* people Israel;" and in the answer of the Lord; "Seventy weeks are determined upon *thy people:*" and in chap. 12: 1; "for the children of *thy people;*" "at that time *thy people* shall be delivered," etc.——Thus manifest is it, both from the tenor of the book and from the known position of Daniel, that he was the father and patron of the captive Jews during their captivity, ministering to their faith in God, and sustaining their hope and spirit, despite of their subjection to a foreign yoke. It was no small part of his mission to assure them that the Lord could easily break this yoke; that the scepters and thrones of all earthly kings were in his hand; and *that he had fully purposed to control the course of empire,* casting down one, and setting up another in its stead, and making all these revolutions subserve the present good of his people, and hasten the coming reign of their own Messiah. This great idea is central in the prophecies of Daniel and gives the clew to their interpretation. No greater violence was ever done to the genius of prophecy than

has been inflicted upon Daniel by the assumption that he occupied himself with the minute details of European or Asiatic history during the eighteenth and nineteenth centuries of the Christian era!
V. It is well here to note the points of difference between Daniel and other Jewish prophets in regard to his general course of thought and manner of presenting it.——(1.) In his prophetic portions he makes but few allusions to Jerusalem; none to the great national sin of the Jews, idolatry. He never employs that peculiar Jewish costume under which Isaiah, Zechariah, and others represent all the Gentile nations as coming up to Jerusalem to build in her temple, etc. This is as we should naturally expect in one who flourished during the captivity, who lived remote from Judea, and came but very little in contact with the elements out of which those Jewish conceptions were formed. His education and training were never thoroughly Jewish.——(2.) On the other hand, he deals almost exclusively with the rise and fall of the great kingdoms of the earth within a given period. The grand succession of supreme dominion from hand to hand, and the bearing of these changes upon the planting, growth, and triumph of Messiah's kingdom, are his great themes.——It is easy to see that this grows out of his surroundings. These were precisely the things with which his whole public life was most familiar. No other Jewish prophet is like him in this respect. The course of divine providence schooled him in courts and cabinets, and kept before his mind the rise and fall of dynasties. Both his education and his long and active life were full of this theme.——This correspondence between the cast of his life and the cast of his prophetic themes, symbols, and phraseology, constitutes a strong point of internal evidence of genuineness. The man who should do what modern German skeptics claim for the pseudo-Daniel in the Maccabean age must have been specially inspired, to have thought of this and then to have carried it out so perfectly!——(3.) In this line of thought, let it be noted that the New Testament phrases, "kingdom of God," and "kingdom of heaven," are specially taken from Daniel. In his first prophetic vision, the series of world-wide kingdoms closes thus: "In the days of these kings shall the God of heaven set up a kingdom which shall never be destroyed" (chap. 2: 44). Being set up by the God of heaven, it is called interchangeably, "The kingdom of God," and "The kingdom of heaven." The second vision (chap. 7: 13, 14, 27) gives the inauguration of its king, and also the extent and duration of his reign. This, for Daniel, is a perfectly natural conception of the cause and interest, of the work and sway of the Messiah upon this earth. He, more exclusively than any other Jewish prophet, would think of the Messiah as a king, and more still, as supplanting and succeeding those universal world-monarchs with whom he was so intimately conversant.——David, being himself a king, sees in the Messiah his successor in royalty and dominion, and even grasps the idea of his supreme dominion: "I have set my king upon my holy hill of Zion." "I will give thee the heathen for thine inheritance, and the uttermost parts of the earth for thy pos-

session." Ps. 2: 6, 8.——But the Messiah's succession in the series of universal empires stands out much more distinctly in Daniel than in David.——The same idea of Christ as king may be found in yet other prophets, but less prominently and by no means so exclusively. Remarkably the prophetic spirit falls in with the cast of each prophet's mind, and uses those illustrations with which each was most familiar. To Ezekiel, a priest, though like Daniel a captive in Chaldea, the future of the Messiah's work on earth is presented in a costume that is intensely Mosaic and Levitical. The land of Judea is repeopled; the temple rebuilt and refurnished; all and more than all its old rituals are reëstablished. The whole presentation is wonderfully full, minute, and graphic, culminating in this one thought; "The name of the city from that day shall be, *The Lord is there!*" We should look in vain to find such a passage as Ezek. (chaps. 40–48) in any prophet not himself a priest. So, to the mind of Amos, called out from the herdmen of Tekoa and at home among plowmen, reapers, and vineyards, the glories of the Messianic age stand out in yet other symbols. "The plowman shall overtake the reaper, and the trader of grapes him that soweth seed; the mountains shall drop new wine," etc. (chap. 9: 13). But Daniel sees the Messiah succeeding and gloriously eclipsing those great, overshadowing monarchies in the midst of which his life-experiences were cast. This fact is one of no trivial importance in the interpretation of his prophecies.——(4.) In the point of symbolic vision, Daniel resembles the other prophets of his age—*i. e.*, during and after the captivity, especially Ezekiel and Zechariah; but he is very unlike all the rest. This is traceable to his Chaldean education. During the last half century, the ruins of Nineveh have disclosed the same general modes of thought and forms of imaginative pictorial representation. Indeed they are shown to belong specially to that age and people. It is safe to assume that in points of this sort Nineveh well represents the Babylon of Daniel's time. Indeed, Babylon was only a new edition of Nineveh.——(5.) Daniel is remarkable for the repetition of his leading themes—his four great prophecies being manifestly, in the main, parallel in their general scope and purpose. This point will be examined more fully in its proper place.

VI. The deep interest that has been felt in Daniel's prophecies, especially at particular periods; the great abuse to which they have been subjected; the strange, wild, visionary interpretations often put upon them—render it proper for me here to state briefly the principles of interpretation that will guide me in my exposition of his prophecies, and especially of his four great parallel visions, viz., chap. 2: 31–45; chap. 7; chap. 8, and chapters 10–12.

(1.) God's own interpretation of the symbols must be accepted as of supreme authority. So far as it applies directly, every candid mind must and will admit this principle. Its indirect application has also important uses.

(2.) The fact of parallelism in these four visions above named having been substantiated, an interpretation given on divine authority in any one of them must be admitted to have great influence over the interpretation of analogous points in either of the others.

(3.) The same general principles and methods of interpretation should be carried through the same vision. There should be a close analogy between the portions that are explained by the Lord himself, and other portions not so explained. It may be safely assumed that the same general cast of thought and representation will obtain through the latter as through the former portions of the same vision. If the former part be explained and not the latter, the Lord would certainly expect us to learn from the part explained how to explain the rest.

(4.) Important use may be made of the *limits*—the termini—within which the events predicted must fall;—*i. e.*, the point of time where they begin and the point where they must close. Wherever these points can be ascertained on substantial authority, they must have an influence upon the interpretation, always great and indeed decisive.

(5.) Regard should be had to Daniel's known circumstances and relations to his people. From these relations it may safely be inferred that his prophecies had at the time, a present moral bearing upon their religious life; their hopes and fears, their faith and piety. Apart from any direct statement to this effect, it should be presumed that his prophecies would have special relation to the future history of that people. How much more must this be assumed now, since we have this explicit affirmation in respect to the last of the four great parallel visions—one which certainly comes down as far into the period then future as any one of the four;—"I am come to make thee understand *what shall befall thy people* in the latter days" (chap. 10: 14). Moreover, Daniel's personal relations to the great monarchies of Chaldea and Medo-Persia would naturally insure some predictions of the rise and growth of Messiah's kingdom as the only real *world-monarchy*. We might expect him to show his people that their own king Messiah would surely supplant and then immeasurably surpass in glory all human kingdoms. What could minister more effectively than this to their faith and courage?——On the other hand, it must be very unreasonable to look here for minute prophecies respecting the political events of our own times which it could scarcely be of the least imaginable consequence for the Jews of that age to understand. Is it probable that the Lord would press on Daniel's attention the history of the Papal power in the nineteenth century of the Christian era when Daniel might so pertinently reply: "Lord, I have a whole nation on my heart already. My soul is burdened with their case and with their destinies. Why should I turn my mind from these things and try to understand those remote events which are so foreign from my responsibilities, from my heart, and from the case of my people?"

(6.) Fulfillment, after it has taken place, may be legitimately used to verify the interpretation given, provided always that it be done judiciously, with good common sense. But it has been the besetting sin of interpreters of Daniel to make this the chief and almost the only criterion for determining his meaning. Consequently, there has been no limit to the fancies and vagaries that have been put forth as commentary and interpretation of this book. Disregarding the great principles of interpretation above suggested, and throwing a loose rein upon their imagination, and moreover straining the facts of history often rudely, commentators would seem to have exhausted the possibilities of human fancy, not to say of absurdity, in their speculations upon the prophecies of Daniel.

(7.) It is of the utmost consequence that interpreters of this book should relieve their minds of all prejudice, in the sense of preconceived opinions, and especially of that most fruitful source of mischief—the passion for finding here the *great events of one's own time*. During the last hundred years there have been numerous efforts to find European history anticipated in Daniel—to trace out in his prophecies the latest moves on the chess-board of European politics—the career of Napoleon the Great, or of Napoleon the less; of the Turk or Pasha; or of the Emperor of all the Russians. No author was ever stretched or cut to a Procrustean bed with more recklessness than this same sensible and excellent Daniel. The sad record of his experiences at the hands of expositors of prophecy should admonish us to approach his writings with a docile spirit, to ask *him* what he meant to say, and not to bring to him a set of ideas, and then torture him and his words till they can be made to indorse them. And finally, in view of the solemn responsibility of interpreting these immortal words of Daniel in harmony with the mind of the inditing Spirit, let us reverently bow at his feet, and implore his guiding hand to lead our thought and to shape our judgment evermore in all our inquiries after the great and blessed truths borne to us in this book of Daniel the prophet.

CHAPTER I.

This chapter introduces Daniel; gives his early personal history and that of his three young friends. They refuse the delicacies of the king's table, and at their own request are proved on purely vegetable food—successfully (vs. 8–16). They appear before the Chaldean king and are approved (vs. 17–21).

1. In the third year of the reign of Jehoiakim king of Judah came Nebuchadnezzar king of Babylon unto Jerusalem, and besieged it.

This first attack upon Jerusalem by Nebuchadnezzar, said here to have been in the third year of Jehoiakim, appears to be assigned by Jeremiah (chap. 25: 1, and 46: 2) to his fourth year. For he makes the fourth year of Jehoiakim coincide (at least in part) with the first year of Nebuchadnezzar.——In the introduction (p. 283) it was shown on the authority of Berosus that Nebuchadnezzar smote Pharaoh Necho and his army of Egyptians and allies at Carchemish, and wrested from their hand Judah and the sovereignty of Judah immediately *before* he ascended the throne. Probably the latter part of this series of events occurred in the fourth year of Jehoiakim and the former part in his third. The Jewish captives might have left Jerusalem before the close of Jehoiakim's third year, and have arrived in Babylon in the early part of his fourth. Often such small discrepancies may be explained by reference to the Jewish usage of counting a fraction of a year in the number of years. Moreover Daniel may have followed Chaldean usage as to the time of beginning his year, while Jeremiah followed the Jewish.——A discrepancy of this sort would scarcely call for explanation were it not that captious critics have sought by means of it to impeach the historical accuracy of Daniel.

2. And the Lord gave Jehoiakim king of Judah into his hand, with part of the vessels of the house of God, which he carried into the land of Shinar to the house of his god; and he brought the vessels into the treasure-house of his god.

Daniel is careful to say (with historical accuracy) that at this time the king of Babylon took away only a part of the vessels of the temple. Many more were taken during the short reign of Jeconiah (see 2 Kings 24: 13) and yet some were left behind then, to be taken at the final destruction of the city in the reign of Zedekiah. Of the latter, special mention is made by Jeremiah (chap. 27: 19–22).——This matter of the sacred vessels of the temple was to the Jews of the utmost moment.——This heathen king carried these sacred vessels into the house of his god as trophies of victory gained by the favor of his idol over the God of Israel. It was common for heathen kings to honor their own gods in this way.

3. And the king spake unto Ashpenaz the master of his eunuchs, that he should bring *certain* of the children of Israel, and of the king's seed, and of the princes;

4. Children in whom *was* no blemish, but well favored, and skillful in all wisdom, and cunning in knowledge, and understanding science, and such as *had* ability in them to stand in the king's palace, and whom they might teach the learning and the tongue of the Chaldeans.

In respect to this custom of training executive officers for the king's service, see the Introduction to Daniel. They were taught the literature as well as the language of the Chaldeans. The original word rendered "learning" means "book."

5. And the king appointed them a daily provision of the king's meat, and of the wine which he drank: so nourishing them three years, that at the end thereof they might stand before the king.

The king assigned them a daily allowance from his own table. The word rendered "king's-meat," implies, his delicacies, his choice and rich diet.

6. Now, among these were of the children of Judah, Daniel, Hananiah, Mishael, and Azariah;

7. Unto whom the prince of the eunuchs gave names: for he gave unto Daniel *the name* of Belteshazzar; and to Hananiah, of Shadrach; and to Mishael, of Meshach; and to Azariah, of Abed-nego.

Of these four Jewish names it may be noted that they are all compounded with the names of the true God; *El* being wrought into Daniel, (meaning judge for God) and into Mishael (who is what God is?), while the last syllable of Jehovah appears in Hananiah (whom Jehovah has graciously given) and Azariah (one helped of God). The new names expunge all recognition of the true God, and honor the Chaldean gods instead; Daniel having Bel wrought into his, Belteshazzar, which means *a prince of Bel.* This change of name must have been to them a sore trial.

8. But Daniel purposed in his heart that he would not defile himself with the portion of the king's meat, nor with the wine which he drank: therefore he requested of the prince of the eunuchs that he might not defile himself.

Plainly one of Daniel's objects was to avoid ceremonial defilement, as determined by the Mosaic law. At the same time it appears from what follows that on physiological grounds he was sure of better health on a simple, plain diet. The case evinces both his conscientiousness in reference to the law of his God, and his noble self-control in the matter of appetite. He held his appetite in firm subjection to the dictates of enlightened judgment and experience as to what was best for his health and physical vigor. These are among the first and most vital elements in the formation of a character of the highest promise for efficiency and usefulness.

9. Now God had brought Daniel into favor and tender love with the prince of the eunuchs.

10. And the prince of the eunuchs said unto Daniel, I fear my lord the king, who hath appointed your meat and your drink: for why should he see your faces worse liking than the children which *are* of your sort? then shall ye make *me* endanger my head to the king.

"Why should he see your faces worse liking?" etc., means practically, "*worse looking.*" The original means "more depressed," as by sadness or low spirits. "Than the children of your sort" means, those of your *circle;* of your age and circumstances. This prince assumed that high living is quite essential to fair flesh and fine health—a capital though not uncommon mistake.

11. Then said Daniel to Melzar, whom the prince of the eunuchs had set over Daniel, Hananiah, Mishael, and Azariah,

12. Prove thy servants, I beseech thee, ten days; and let them give us pulse to eat, and water to drink.

13. Then let our countenances be looked upon before thee, and the countenance of the children that eat of the portion of the king's meat: and as thou seest, deal with thy servants.

Melzar, having the article in the original (*the* Melzar) is not a proper name, but means "the chief butler."——Daniel had a safe proposal ready. Let them try us on our vegetable diet and pure water, ten days.——"Pulse" means vegetables in general, plants grown from seed-sowing.

14. So he consented to them in this matter, and proved them ten days.

15. And at the end of ten days their countenances appeared fairer and fatter in flesh than all the children which did eat the portion of the king's meat.

16. Thus Melzar took away the portion of their meat, and the wine that they should drink; and gave them pulse.

The experiment being triumphantly successful, Daniel and his friends are relieved of both the ceremonial defilement and the physical mischiefs incidental to the king's diet.

17. As for these four children, God gave them knowledge

and skill in all learning and wisdom: and Daniel had understanding in all visions and dreams.

While wisdom and learning were common to all the four, Daniel had special "understanding in all visions and dreams." The divine purpose in this gift to Daniel was to qualify him for transcendent influence in that heathen court and country, and to make him a prophet of high order among his own people.

18. Now at the end of the days that the king had said he should bring them in, then the prince of the eunuchs brought them in before Nebuchadnezzar.

19. And the king communed with them: and among them all was found none like Daniel, Hananiah, Mishael, and Azariah: therefore stood they before the king.

20. And in all matters of wisdom *and* understanding, that the king inquired of them, he found them ten times better than all the magicians *and* astrologers that *were* in all his realm.

"The end of days" is the expiration of the three years fixed by the king and referred to v. 5.——The king "communed with them" for the purpose of sounding their depth and testing their adaptation to his wants. He became abundantly satisfied. Hence they took their position; they "stood before the king," awaiting orders and ready for his service. This is the usual phrase for servants in attendance upon their superiors. So angels are said to "stand before God."——"Ten times better," is a definite phrase in the sense of an indefinite.

21. And Daniel continued *even* unto the first year of king Cyrus.

It is not said that Daniel continued no longer, but only that he continued to that time. Probably this closed his official life. This book gives no notice of the time or the circumstances of his death.

CHAPTER II.

Nebuchadnezzar is greatly troubled by a dream which he can not recall: his Chaldean Magi can not help him to it; but Daniel reveals to the king his dream and its interpretation. Thereupon the king acknowledges the great superiority of the God of Daniel, and promotes him and his three friends to high positions of trust in the state.——This dream or vision is the first in a series of four to which very special attention must be given in the proper place.

1. And in the second year of the reign of Nebuchadnez-

zar, Nebuchadnezzar dreamed dreams, wherewith his spirit was troubled, and his sleep brake from him.

Dreams are usually the mere fancies of the mind during sleep, and of no account as indicating future events. But the God who made us is able to reach our minds no less while we sleep than while we are awake; and hence can determine our dreams as truly and perfectly as the succession and character of our waking thoughts. Hence he was wont in ancient times to manifest himself to men in their dreams—as here in the case of this Chaldean king.——This dream troubled him and made sleep impossible. It left his mind painfully anxious as if it foreboded some great calamity; while yet he could not recall the particular points of the dream. Much less could he reach its prophetic significance.

2. Then the king commanded to call the magicians, and the astrologers, and the sorcerers, and the Chaldeans, for to shew the king his dreams. So they came and stood before the king.

In this emergency, the king called in the aid of those classes of men who professed skill in the occult sciences and in auguries of future events. Most if not all of the unevangelized nations of all history have had such men, often known as a special class, under some distinctive name.——Here are four different terms of designation. The word rendered "magicians" means sacred scribes—priests of religion. The original Hebrew word from which it is derived means a graving tool—the very instrument used in that age for writing on stone, and probably too on bricks while in their plastic state. Babylonian documents are found in immense numbers written on both these sorts of material.——The next term rendered "astrologers," is several times translated "magoi," (magi) in the Septuagint. The magoi are the "wise men" who came from the east (Mat. 2: 1) to inquire for the new-born Messiah whose star they had seen, and therefore came to worship him.——The second and the third terms imply in the original Hebrew, the use of occult arts, secret practices, by which their authors pretended to have communication with invisible powers or agencies, and to learn from them what no unaided human mind could attain.——The term Chaldean as used in this connection can not denote the whole people of the country, Chaldea, but a learned class, who retained the language and the wisdom of the ancient Kaldi people. The latter were of the Cushite family, allied to the Ethiopians. While the great body of the people inhabiting Chaldea used a Semitic language, closely related to the Hebrew, and known variously as Syriac, Aramaic, Chaldee; this learned class retained for their religious and probably scientific purposes another language which testifies to their connection with the ancient Cushite or Ethiopian family. They are sometimes spoken of also as a Scythic race. The authority for these views of their ethnic relations is found in the language used in ancient inscriptions.——These brief explanations may suffice to show in general that these classes combined with much real learning and science, more or less claim to communion with superhuman beings or agencies by which they sought to interpret dreams and to foretell future events.——They came at the king's call and stood before him.

3. *And the king said unto them, I have dreamed a dream, and my spirit was troubled to know the dream.*

The king is specially anxious to know, not the dream only, but its interpretation—its true significance.

4. *Then spake the Chaldeans to the king in Syriac, O king, live forever: tell thy servants the dream, and we will shew the interpretation.*

The Chaldeans spoke to the king "in Syriac"—the usual language of the country. From this point to the end of chap. 7, the author of this book wrote in this dialect, here called "Syriac;" but in the original, "Aramaic;" and more generally known as the Chaldee language. It differs altogether in the forms of its letters and somewhat in its grammatical forms and words, from the Syriac of the earlier ages of the Christian era.——Daniel's reasons for this use of the Chaldee tongue are obvious. The subject-matter of these chapters was of the utmost interest and moment to the Chaldean people. It related to their own monarchs and to great events of their own national history. It bore repeated testimonies to the supreme power, wisdom and glory, of the Great God—testimonies that came from their own monarchs. Wisely therefore did Daniel afford them the requisite facilities for reading these testimonies in their own tongue. This dialect would be readily understood by the captive Jews.

5. *The king answered and said to the Chaldeans, The thing is gone from me: if ye will not make known unto me the dream, with the interpretation thereof, ye shall be cut in pieces, and your houses shall be made a dunghill:*

6. *But if ye shew the dream, and the interpretation thereof, ye shall receive of me gifts and rewards and great honor: therefore shew me the dream, and the interpretation thereof.*

The Chaldean wise men steadily demand that the king shall tell his dream. The king has lost it, and hence demands no less persistently that they shall give him both his dream and its interpretation. Feeling intensely anxious to know it, he resorts to the utmost terror of his supreme power of life and death over his subjects, and threatens them the most terrible and disgraceful death if they fail, backing up this penalty by the promise of immense rewards if they are successful. It is plain that God is shaping this matter to test the intrinsic futility of their pretensions to superhuman knowledge, and to bring out in the most public manner his own infinite superiority over them all.

7. They answered again and said, Let the king tell his servants the dream, and we will shew the interpretation of it.

8. The king answered and said, I know of certainty that ye would gain the time, because ye see the thing is gone from me.

9. But if ye will not make known unto me the dream, *there is but* one decree for you: for ye have prepared lying and corrupt words to speak before me, till the time be changed: therefore tell me the dream, and I shall know that ye can shew me the interpretation thereof.

To their renewed request for the dream, the king, yet more excited, replies, charging them with seeking to stave off this professional duty of theirs (as he deems it) by delay. The king seems to assume that in their view, lapse of time will divert his attention, or lessen his interest in the matter, so that he would at least relax the severity of his decree, if not, indeed, forget, or reverse it. Hence he meets this point with characteristic rigor and sternness. The whole bearing of the king in this case shows what an earnest, self-reliant man becomes under the reacting influence of absolute power over the destiny and life of his fellow-beings.

10. The Chaldeans answered before the king, and said, There is not a man upon the earth that can shew the king's matter: therefore *there is* no king, lord, nor ruler *that* asked such things at any magician, or astrologer, or Chaldean.

11. And *it is* a rare thing that the king requireth, and there is none other that can shew it before the king, except the gods, whose dwelling is not with flesh.

Forced upon impossibilities as the sole condition of life, the Chaldeans are emboldened to speak out plainly even before this absolute and terribly stern monarch. They assure him that the thing he demands is beyond all human skill, and that no reasonable king ever before made such demands as this upon men of their profession.——The word rendered "rare" in the phrase, "it is a *rare* thing," means usually, "hard," "difficult;" and here, manifestly, "impossible"—a thing entirely above the range of mortal knowledge; such a thing as none can reveal but the gods who dwell not in human flesh. This admission was of the utmost importance in its bearing upon Daniel and Daniel's God. It shows moreover that they had a distinct conception of a higher Intelligence—some Great Mind or Minds, possessed of knowledge and forecast far beyond that of men.

12. For this cause the king was angry and very furious, and commanded to destroy all the wise *men* of Babylon.

13. And the decree went forth that the wise *men* should be slain; and they sought Daniel and his fellows to be slain.

Here is absolutism, under inflamed passion. The king will bear no implication that he is unreasonable, and will not consent to be baffled in his cherished purpose to get back the lost dream and find its meaning.——Daniel and his three associates, ("fellows") seem not to have been present among the magicians, astrologers, etc., who were summoned before the king, and hence knew nothing of this transaction. But now that death is the doom of all the wise men, they are less disposed to count out Daniel and his three friends. All this, whether well or ill intended on their part, was of the Lord, who is wont to make the wrath of man work out his own praise.

14. Then Daniel answered with counsel and wisdom to Arioch the captain of the king's guard, which was gone forth to slay the wise *men* of Babylon:

15. He answered and said to Arioch the king's captain, Why *is* the decree *so* hasty from the king? Then Arioch made the thing known to Daniel.

Arioch, captain of the king's guard, was really, as the margin intimates, "chief of the executioners"—the two sorts of service, viz., commanding the body-guard of the king and serving as public executioner to take the life of persons condemned by the king to death—being naturally performed by the same officer.——Daniel spoke prudently to this officer: and yet the original word he used, rendered "hasty" ("why is the decree of the king so *hasty?*") means "stern," "severe,"—standing related to justice and common humanity, and not merely to *time*.

16. Then Daniel went in, and desired of the king that he would give him time, and that he would shew the king the interpretation.

It is noticeable that the king does not object to giving Daniel reasonable time, though he had been so violent against his magicians when he thought they meant to evade his demands by gaining time. He saw in Daniel the marks of an honest man. Moreover, we need not be slow to recognize a divine hand, giving Daniel favor before the king.

17. Then Daniel went to his house, and made the thing known to Hananiah, Mishael, and Azariah, his companions:

18. That they would desire mercies of the God of heaven

concerning this secret; that Daniel and his fellows should not perish with the rest of the wise *men* of Babylon.

It was eminently fitting that this case should be borne to God in special prayer, and that Daniel should invite the sympathy and help of his three friends in supplication before God. The results purposed of God are to be signally honorable to all these men. First, then, let them humbly and earnestly seek God in prayer. This is the order of both providence and grace. Asking comes before receiving. Moreover, the results are to be momentous upon the political condition of the captive Jews and upon their faith in the God of their fathers. How appropriate then, for every reason, that this divine mercy needed by Daniel should be earnestly sought in prayer by all his pious friends!

19. Then was the secret revealed unto Daniel in a night vision. Then Daniel blessed the God of heaven.

20. Daniel answered and said, Blessed be the name of God forever and ever: for wisdom and might are his:

21. And he changeth the times and the seasons; he removeth kings, and setteth up kings; he giveth wisdom unto the wise, and knowledge to them that know understanding:

22. He revealeth the deep and secret things: he knoweth what *is* in the darkness, and the light dwelleth with him.

23. I thank thee, and praise thee, O thou God of my fathers, who hast given me wisdom and might, and hast made known unto me now what we desired of thee: for thou hast *now* made known unto us the king's matter.

The revelation was made to Daniel forthwith, in the manner of a vision by night. He is at once conscious that God has given him the secret prayed for and so much desired, and hence he breaks out in grateful praise for this blessing.——The expressions, "wisdom and might are his;" "he changeth the times and the seasons;" "he removeth kings and setteth up kings;" are evidently suggested by the subject-matter of the king's dream which is now both revealed and expounded to Daniel. The central idea of that dream is (as we shall see), the changing course of empire and the divine agency in casting down one great world-ruling dynasty and setting up another in its stead. In most sublime strains, Daniel celebrates also the omniscience and foreknowledge of Jehovah: "He revealeth the deep and secret things," such as no mortal eye can reach; "He knoweth what is in the darkness, and the light dwelleth with him." Dwelling himself in light unapproachable and full of glory, nothing present, past, or future, can be dark to his all-searching eye.

24. Therefore Daniel went in unto Arioch, whom the king had ordained to destroy the wise *men* of Babylon: he went and said thus unto him: Destroy not the wise *men* of

Babylon: bring me in before the king, and I will shew unto the king the interpretation.

25. Then Arioch brought in Daniel before the king in haste, and said thus unto him, I have found a man of the captives of Judah,* that will make known unto the king the interpretation.

No time is to be lost. Daniel reports himself as ready now to meet the king and is accordingly brought into his presence.

26. The king answered and said to Daniel, whose name *was* Belteshazzar, Art thou able to make known unto me the dream which I have seen, and the interpretation thereof?

27. Daniel answered in the presence of the king, and said, The secret which the king hath demanded can not the wise *men*, the astrologers, the magicians, the sooth-sayers, shew unto the king;

28. But there is a God in heaven that revealeth secrets, and maketh known to the king Nebuchadnezzar what shall be in the latter days. Thy dream, and the visions of thy head upon thy bed, are these;

29. As for thee, O king, thy thoughts came *into thy mind* upon thy bed, what should come to pass hereafter: and he that revealeth secrets maketh known to thee what shall come to pass.

30. But as for me, this secret is not revealed to me for *any* wisdom that I have more than any living, but for *their* sakes that shall make known the interpretation to the king, and that thou mightest know the thoughts of thy heart.

The king's question, "Art *thou* able?" etc., brings out Daniel's genuine humility and his hearty recognition of all his special power in this line as from the Great God of heaven. He therefore remarks first (v. 27) that none of the wise men of Babylon, and by implication, no wise men on the face of the earth, can reveal this secret; and then that the God of heaven, and he alone and only, has made this revelation. Remarkably, he begins (v. 28) as if he would go on at once to recite the dream; but checks himself and returns to say again, as to the king, that, through the hand of God, his thoughts upon his bed were of what should take place thereafter; and as to himself, that this secret was not revealed to him because of any special wisdom of his above other men, but for the sake of making the interpretation known to the king. In this latter clause, the marginal reading gives the sense more accurately than the text. It should not read, "for their sakes who should make this thing known," as if there were certain other parties to be used in revealing this matter to the king, and it was revealed to Daniel *for their sakes*. This is not the sense, but rather simply, that God revealed it to Daniel in order that it might be made known to the king.——Daniel's humble disclaimer of personal merit may remind us of the same thing in Joseph; "Do not interpretations belong to God?" Gen. 40: 8; also, "Joseph answered Pharaoh, saying, "It is not in me; God shall give Pharaoh an answer of peace" (Gen. 41: 16). Also, of the divine law, "Them that honor me, I will honor" (1 Sam. 2: 30).——The reference made here and elsewhere to the time when the events signified by this dream should take place are altogether indefinite. Thus, "what shall be in the latter days" (v. 28); "what shall come to pass" (v. 29), and "what shall come to pass hereafter" (v. 45), give us no certain clue to the precise period. So far as these phrases are concerned, the events might come sooner or later; might spread over the centuries before the Christian era, or lie in the future beyond it. We look in vain to these phrases to find definite marks of future time.

31. Thou, O king, sawest, and behold a great image. This great image, whose brightness *was* excellent, stood before thee; and the form thereof *was* terrible.

32. This image's head *was* of fine gold, his breast and his arms of silver, his belly and his thighs of brass,

33. His legs of iron, his feet part of iron and part of clay.

34. Thou sawest till that a stone was cut out without hands, which smote the image upon his feet *that were* of iron and clay, and brake them to pieces.

35. Then was the iron, the clay, the brass, the silver, and the gold, broken to pieces together, and became like the chaff of the summer threshing-floors; and the wind carried them away, that no place was found for them: and the stone that smote the image became a great mountain, and filled the whole earth.

36. This *is* the dream; and we will tell the interpretation thereof before the king.

37. Thou, O king, *art* a king of kings: for the God of heaven hath given thee a kingdom, power, and strength, and glory.

38. And wheresoever the children of men dwell, the beasts of the field and the fowls of the heaven hath he given into thy hand, and hath made thee ruler over them all. Thou *art* this head of gold.

39. And after thee shall rise another kingdom inferior to thee, and another third kingdom of brass, which shall bear rule over all the earth.

40. And the fourth kingdom shall be strong as iron: for-

asmuch as iron breaketh in pieces and subdueth all *things:* and as iron that breaketh all these, shall it break in pieces and bruise.

41. And whereas thou sawest the feet and toes, part of potters' clay, and part of iron, the kingdom shall be divided; but there shall be in it of the strength of the iron, forasmuch as thou sawest the iron mixed with the miry clay.

42. And *as* the toes of the feet *were* part of iron, and part of clay, *so* the kingdom shall be partly strong, and partly broken.

43. And whereas thou sawest iron mixed with miry clay, they shall mingle themselves with the seed of men: but they shall not cleave one to another, even as iron is not mixed with clay.

44. And in the days of these kings shall the God of heaven set up a kingdom, which shall never be destroyed: and the kingdom shall not be left to other people, *but* it shall break in pieces and consume all these kingdoms, and it shall stand forever.

45. Forasmuch as thou sawest that the stone was cut out of the mountain without hands, and that it brake in pieces the iron, the brass, the clay, the silver, and the gold; the great God hath made known to the king what shall come to pass hereafter: and the dream *is* certain, and the interpretation thereof sure.

This passage is in two parts;—the dream (vs. 31–35); and its interpretation (vs. 37–45). The dream is symbolic;—one connected, compact series of symbols;—the interpretation renders these symbols into literal language.——The symbols scarcely need any comment. The language itself is plain. Here is one huge image of the human form, the head of gold being the first part; the breast and arms of silver, the second; the belly and thighs of brass, the third; the legs, feet and toes, part iron and part clay, the fourth. Then a stone cut from the mountain without hands, smites the image upon its feet, but breaks in pieces the whole image and scatters it to the winds of heaven; and then itself becomes a great mountain and fills the whole earth. A stone is a proper symbol of an agency that comes to break a huge metal image. That it is "cut from the mountain without hands" indicates that the Messiah was born and brought forth before the world as King of nations by divine rather than human agencies; while his smiting the great image to its destruction denotes the power of God in his providential government, overturning guilty nations.——The interpretation shows that the central idea of the dream is *the course of empire;* the rapid succession of great world-monarchies. The reader should not fail to note that while these symbols, standing unexplained, would be obscure and might greatly perplex all commentators, yet the interpretation makes their meaning definite and certain. For in the first place an inspired interpretation is perfect authority. When God himself interprets, and we get his meaning, it is the end of all uncertainty, and should be the end of all doubt. And as to the problem of getting his meaning, it is safe to infer that if God professes to interpret, he intends to make himself understood. Hence he will use plain language and use it according to the laws of human speech, so that due candor, care and diligence, with the divine blessing, will surely lead men into all the important truth that God has sought to teach.——Guided especially by this inspired interpretation, let us now search out the truth taught by this vision.——As above suggested, the central idea is the *course of empire*—the succession of great, universal monarchies. Of these the first four are of the earth, earthly—mere human kingdoms. The fifth is in some respects peculiar, being "set up by the God of heaven." The points affirmed here of this fifth kingdom are that it first destroys and then supersedes all the other kingdoms; that it shall not pass over into the hands of other races and people, as those that preceded it had done; that it shall not be transient, like them, but enduring; and finally it shall be in a higher sense than they, universal in extent, filling all the earth.——As to the first four, the interpretation makes it absolutely certain that the head of gold representing the first kingdom is the Chaldean empire, specially embodied in its one great monarch—the author mainly of its splendor and greatness—Nebuchadnezzar. "Thou art this head of gold."——It is scarcely less certain that the second—the silver breast and arms—is the kingdom actually next in the order of time. "Arising after thee and inferior to thee," it must be the Medo-Persian, of which Cyrus was the great central representative. On this point interpreters agree. Equally clear is it that the third—the belly and thighs of brass; that "shall bear rule over all the earth;" is the Grecian empire whose one sole representative was Alexander. His place in the series is so well defined by the description and by the historic facts, as to leave no room for rational doubt.——The identity of the fourth kingdom is the great question of this prophecy. The two conflicting opinions between which commentators have been divided for ages are; (1) That it is the Roman power; (2) That it is the broken, divided empire that in fact next succeeded Alexander, known in history as the "Empire of Alexander's successors." The portions with which the Jews came specially in contact were the Syrian kingdom, founded by Seleucus Nicator, and the Egyptian, founded by Ptolemy Lagus. In point of time, these powers fill the two or three centuries that immediately followed the death of Alexander, B. C. 323.——It is impossible to do justice to the prophecies of Daniel without a very careful and thorough investigation of this radical question. Let it be our aim to advance cautiously, with candor and patience, endeavoring to embrace all the elements that bear upon this question and giving to each its due weight in the final decision.

In regard to this fifth kingdom, specially described in v. 44, observe that in the opinion of all intelligent commentators, our divine Lord and his forerunner John the Baptist take their current and oft-used phrases, "Kingdom of God," and "Kingdom of heaven," from this passage. Daniel says, "The God of heaven shall set up a kingdom." Hence it might be called either, "The kingdom of God," or, "The kingdom of heaven." In fact both these designations are used frequently. John began his preaching, saying, "Repent ye, for the kingdom of heaven is at hand". (Mat. 3: 2). Jesus began with the same text (see Mat. 4: 17). According to Mark (chap. 1: 15) Jesus came into Galilee preaching the gospel of the kingdom of God and saying, "The *time is fulfilled* and the kingdom of God is at hand." Luke has it, "The kingdom of God" (chap. 4: 43, and 8: 1). "I must preach the kingdom of God to other cities also." "Showing the glad tidings of the kingdom of God."——I quote only a part of these numerous cases, yet enough to show (1.) that Daniel's fifth kingdom is precisely the gospel kingdom of the New Testament, our divine Lord himself being the highest authority for this identity; and (2.) that its time was then "fulfilled;" it was "at hand" and was set up during that generation. (The proof of this last point will be adduced more fully in my notes on Dan. 7.) This identification of the fifth kingdom is a point of the greatest importance. Especially should it be noted that both Jesus Christ and his inspired apostles, by taking up these words of Daniel and applying them to the reign of Christ, become themselves so far forth the interpreters of Daniel's prophecy, certifying to us that in their view the Spirit who spake by Daniel meant by this fifth kingdom that of the gospel age whose king was Jesus the Messiah.——Let it be borne in mind that of these five kingdoms, four are in point of origin earthly; the fifth heavenly: four are of this world; the fifth is "not of this world:" four are of the sort well known to profane history; the fifth is of the sort little known, except in sacred history—a kingdom whose defined purpose is "righteousness, peace and joy in the Holy Ghost." Though eminently spiritual, it yet none the less controls the external life— unto universal righteousness.

I call special attention to yet another point. In a definite series of prophetic events—a series which has a well-defined commencement and a well-defined close—it is of the utmost consequence to note well *where* it begins and where it closes. What are technically called the termini—the "terminus a quo," the starting-point from which the series begins: and the "terminus ad quem," the closing point down *to which* it comes but no farther—are beyond measure important to be carefully ascertained. They are the great landmarks of prophetic interpretation. For these symbols do not mean every thing. They must not be wrested to mean any and every sort of thing that the fancy of any interpreter or any reader may suggest. Their meaning is shut up within these ascertained termini;

between the point where the series begins and the point where it closes.——In the present case, the series begins with Nebuchadnezzar. "Thou art this head of gold." The fourth kingdom ends not later than the point where the fifth begins; for plainly the fifth succeeds the fourth as the second does the first, and the third the second, and the fourth the third. So the symbols imply. The stone while yet a stone, and before it has grown into a mountain, smites the whole image—legs, feet, and toes, as truly as head, breast, belly and thighs—and breaks all in pieces. In fact, the smiting blow is specially said to have been upon the feet. Hence the natural sense of the symbol is that the fourth kingdom (as really as the first three) is demolished before the fifth is inaugurated as a visible kingdom among men.——But here special attention should be given to the corresponding interpretation (v. 44). "In the days of these kings shall the God of heaven set up a kingdom." On this passage two important questions arise; (a.) What kings are meant? (b.) In what sense does the God of heaven set up his kingdom in their days?——(a.) As to the first point, some interpreters assume that the kings referred to are the toes of the image. But this view can not be sustained. The language, "these kings," implies that they have been distinctly brought to view already. But there has been no hint that the toes are kings. Other kings have been before the mind; Nebuchadnezzar especially and first—leading the analogy of the vision. The next kingdom had its equally prominent representative king—Cyrus. The third was embodied in its one great monarch—practically its first and its last—Alexander. Analogy would suggest that the fourth had also its great kings, one or more. To these, then, we must suppose reference is made in the phrase, "In the days of these kings," and not to the toes of the image specially, and much less exclusively. (b.) To the question, In what sense was Messiah's kingdom set up in the days of those kings? I answer: Only in the sense of preparatory work, done by the agencies of divine providence. The demolition of those kingdoms prepared the way for the formal, visible inauguration of Messiah's kingdom. This visible inauguration and setting up followed that demolition, and was not strictly simultaneous. The language which is very general, certainly admits this construction; the sense of the symbols seems to require it; and yet further, the genius of the entire vision sustains it—this genius or scope being, in the words of Ezekiel (chap. 21: 27), "I will overturn, overturn, overturn it; and it shall be no more, until he come whose right it is: and I will give it him."——But a more thorough and extended investigation of this point, and indeed of many other points, will be due when we reach the seventh chapter. That vision of successive beasts is beyond all question parallel to this vision of the great image. It goes over the same line of thought; gives the same series of four great empires, followed by the fifth—that of Messiah and of his people; and scarcely differs from this in any respect, save that it presents a new set of symbols and gives much more detail on two important points; viz., (I.) The work and the doom of the fourth beast and of his little horn: and (2.) The precise order of succession between the fourth and the fifth kingdoms; the destruction of the fourth beast and all his horns, preceding and followed by the inauguration both in heaven and in earth of this fifth king and kingdom. I propose therefore to defer the full and exhaustive discussion of the significance of the fourth kingdom till we come to chap. 7.—— Enough has been adduced however already to show that the fourth kingdom must be that of Alexander's successors and not the Roman empire.——For, consider the *field* where we are to look for this fourth kingdom.——*Chronologically*, its whole history must lie between the death of Alexander, B. C. 323, and the birth of Christ. Rome is *not* there: the fragments of Alexander's empire under his successors are there.——*Territorially*, it should be sought in Western Asia, not in Europe; in general, on the same territory where the first, second, and third kingdoms stood.——*Politically*, it should be the immediate successor of Alexander's empire, recasting much of the same materials; in general, changing the dynasty, but not the nations and tribes composing the elements of its population and power. This law obtains in respect to the first three kingdoms; why should it not in respect to the fourth as well? Analogy requires it. In this point, therefore, analogy shuts off Rome and points to the kingdoms of Alexander's successors.——Yet again, as to general character; this fourth kingdom, according to the symbol and its interpretation, is mixed, composite, brittle, inadhesive, not unified and consolidated into one firm power. These are strong points of its character.——In all these points the description fits the fragmentary empire that immediately follows Alexander; while *for this period* (B. C. 332–0) it does not fit Rome at all. No human kingdom was ever more unlike this description than Rome was in the early ages of history; or say during two centuries after the death of Alexander.——Finally, the first three kingdoms were of special interest to the Jews, because their own nation bore the closest political relations to each of them; either in captive subjection or under friendly protection, or exposed more or less to hostile collision.——The powers that next succeeded Alexander, filling these relations to the Jews, were first and most, the Greek-Syrian; and next the Greek-Egyptian. It was not till very near the close of this period that the Romans came into any political relations whatever toward the Jews.——Or, to put this thought in another form: These four kingdoms have a place in Jewish prophecy because of their relations to the Jewish state and to the kingdom of God as embosomed in its undeveloped germ among that people. It was really for the sake of revealing to Daniel and to Daniel's people what should "befall them in the latter days" (chap. 10: 14), all along down to the coming of their Messiah, that these prophecies were revealed. They touch the political history of the kingdoms of this world only because those particular kingdoms sustained very special relations to the great kingdom that is not of this world, which lay in embryo in the Jewish state, yet nursed and guarded there under the perfect eye of God, till the time was fulfilled and the kingdom of God truly came—*i. e.*, came forth visibly before all the world. That is to say, it is not the genius of Daniel's prophecy to teach universal history, nor to teach profane history at all, apart from its relations to Christ's kingdom before his coming and down to that coming. His great central idea is—The invisible arm of King Messiah, defending his unborn kingdom (lying in embryo in the Jewish state) against four great worldly powers in succession, overturning one, and another, and yet another, and thus giving visible birth and development to Messiah's kingdom, to supercede them all, and surpass them all in its world-wide sway.—— Rome has no place in this programme. Universal history, in its scientific point of view, or as related to what we are wont to account the march of the great civilizations of mankind, was never the governing purpose of Daniel's prophecy.——If it be yet maintained that the fourth kingdom must be the Roman because of its iron strength, I answer, (1.) Here was strength and weakness blended—a fact which harmonizes with the brittle character of the kingdoms of Alexander's successors, but does not by any means harmonize with the Roman power *of this age;*—and (2.) Daniel could not fail to see and measure the strength of these kingdoms from his stand-point of paternal care for his own people. Those powers would be seen strong and terrible; which were in fact formidable or destructive to the Jews. Of this more will be said in the notes upon chap. 7.——These points of reply by no means include all the objections to the Roman theory. They only touch the special plea for it, on the score of its assumed iron strength.

46. Then the king Nebuchadnezzar fell upon his face, and worshiped Daniel, and commanded that they should offer an oblation and sweet odors unto him.

47. The king answered unto Daniel, and said, Of a truth *it is*, that your God *is* a God of gods, and a Lord of kings, and a revealer of secrets, seeing thou couldest reveal this secret.

Profoundly impressed with the greatness of Daniel and of Daniel's God, and quite too oblivious of Daniel's personal disclaimer ("not for any wisdom that I have more than any living,") the king fell prostrate before him and gave command that an oblation and sweet odors should be offered to him. This must be ascribed to his heathen ideas. Still it did not preclude from his mind a strong conviction of the supremacy of the God of Daniel. His profession of faith on this point is (for the time) very strong. We have to deplore that it was so transient, or, at least, so inefficacious in the line of its proper antagonism to his notions of idol gods and of image worship.

48. Then the king made Daniel a great man, and gave him many great gifts, and made him ruler over the whole province of Babylon, and chief of the governors over all the wise *men* of Babylon.

49. Then Daniel requested of the king, and he set Shadrach, Meshach, and Abed-nego, over the affairs of the province of Babylon: but Daniel *sat* in the gate of the king.

Promotion followed, and Daniel is advanced to the position of prime minister for the province of Babylon and head-man over the whole fraternity of magicians, soothsayers, priests of religion and of science. At his request his three friends also are promoted to important trusts. Daniel's place in the gate of the king put him next the royal person as his first counsellor—a position of the very highest trust and influence.——Such were the first and immediate results of the divine favor to Daniel in revealing the secret of the king's dream.

CHAPTER III.

The king makes a huge golden image, sets it up, and convenes the officers of every grade in his kingdom to attend its dedication and join in its worship. Daniel's three friends refuse, and are cast into a furnace of fire: God preserves them from all harm, and the king by decree dooms to death all who shall speak against their God.

1. Nebuchadnezzar the king made an image of gold, whose height *was* threescore cubits, *and* the breadth thereof six cubits: he set it up in the plain of Dura, in the province of Babylon.

Assuming the cubit to be about eighteen inches in length, this image of gold was ninety feet high and nine broad.——In view of the facts adduced in the general introduction respecting this king's devotion to his own God, Bel-Merodach, there can be no rational doubt that he intended this image to represent the great power, majesty, and excellence of this god.——Was the idea of it suggested by his wonderful dream of a great image? That image was "great," "its brightness was excellent," and "the form thereof was terrible." It is not specially surprising, therefore, that in a mind thoroughly imbued with the notions of idol and image worship, the huge image seen in his dream should suggest the construction of this great image of gold to represent his view of the greatness and excellent glory of his god. The consummate art of Satan's master-mind was in it also, the managing spirit in the whole realm of idolatry. He held and led the mind of this heathen king.——Alas, that a mind of such decision and energy should so utterly lack the just idea of the spiritual being of the Great God, and of his transcendant moral perfections!

2. Then Nebuchadnezzar the king sent to gather together

the princes, the governors, and the captains, the judges, the treasurers, the counsellors, the sheriffs, and all the rulers of the provinces, to come to the dedication of the image which Nebuchadnezzar the king had set up.

3. Then the princes, the governors, and captains, the judges, the treasurers, the counsellors, the sheriffs, and all the rulers of the provinces, were gathered together unto the dedication of the image that Nebuchadnezzar the king had set up: and they stood before the image that Nebuchadnezzar had set up.

The king could not convene all the people of his vast dominions. The next thing to it was to convene all the officers of every name and grade. These would be the strong and influential men of his realm. Hence this convocation would send its influence for idolatry down through the whole political frame-work of his kingdom and reach its entire population.——The great number of grades of officers indicates a high degree of system and order in the constitution of this government. Of the eight several officers grouped in this summons, the first is the highest grade, a sort of viceroy. The second is the class of deputies. The third is commonly rendered "governor," and is used repeatedly by Ezra, Nehemiah, and others; indeed, it is identically the Pasha. The fourth class are the chief judges; the fifth the royal treasurers; the sixth were persons skilled in the law and might be either counsellors or judges; the seventh term seems to be essentially the same as the sixth, lawyers; and the last comprehends all other officers in the province. All these were summoned to come to the dedication of the great image.

4. Then an herald cried aloud, To you it is commanded, O people, nations, and languages,

5. *That* at what time ye hear the sound of the cornet, flute, harp, sackbut, psaltery, dulcimer, and all kinds of music, ye fall down and worship the golden image that Nebudchadnezzar the king hath set up.

6. And whoso falleth not down and worshipeth, shall the same hour be cast into the midst of a burning fiery furnace.

7. Therefore, at that time, when all the people heard the sound of the cornet, flute, harp, sackbut, psaltery, and all kinds of music, all the people, the nations, and the languages, fell down *and* worshiped the golden image that Nebuchadnezzar the king had set up.

The signal for simultaneous worship by prostration of the body before the great image was to be given by this grand orchestra, which seems to have combined all sorts of musical instruments known in that age—another case in proof that the controlling spirit in all systems of idolatry seizes on every attraction of art, and not least, upon external beauty and upon music as important auxiliaries of power.——The precise character of these various instruments can be reached in this age only proximately. The first was a horn. The third is the word "cithera" in Hebrew letters. The "sackbut" is thought to have been a trombone—an instrument which secures a wide range of tone by being constructed with a slide by which its length and volume may be changed at pleasure. The word "psaltery" is the same in Hebrew and in Greek. The last specified kind is in the Chaldee, "symphony;" perhaps resembling our keyed instruments which perform two or more parts in harmony.——Burning to death in a furnace of fire was one mode of capital punishment. Its horrid cruelty testifies that the age had scarcely begun to emerge from barbarism.

8. Wherefore at that time certain Chaldeans came near, and accused the Jews.

9. They spake and said to the king Nebuchadnezzar, O king, live forever.

10. Thou, O king, hast made a decree, that every man that shall hear the sound of the cornet, flute, harp, sackbut, psaltery, and dulcimer, and all kinds of music, shall fall down and worship the golden image:

11. And whoso falleth not down and worshipeth, *that* he should be cast into the midst of a burning fiery furnace.

12. There are certain Jews whom thou hast set over the affairs of the province of Babylon, Shadrach, Meshach, and Abed-nego: these men, O king, have not regarded thee: they serve not thy gods, nor worship the golden image which thou hast set up.

This accusation might be due to their jealousy of the high honor enjoyed by those Jews, or to their zeal for idol-worship and for universal obedience to the king—in the present case mostly to the former. They put the case as one involving both contempt of the king and of his gods. The original words rendered "accused" are singularly expressive; "They ate up the pieces of the Jews"— ate them up piecemeal—indicating savage and even cannibal ferocity. In more than one oriental language this is a current conception of slander and the way of expressing it.

13. Then Nebuchadnezzar in *his* rage and fury commanded to bring Shadrach, Meshach, and Abed-nego. Then they brought these men before the king.

14. Nebuchadnezzar spake and said unto them, *Is it* true, O Shadrach, Meshach, and Abed-nego, do not ye serve my gods, nor worship the golden image which I have set up?

15. Now if ye be ready that at what time ye hear the sound of the cornet, flute, harp, sackbut, psaltery, and dulcimer, and all kinds of music, ye fall down and worship the image which I have made, *well:* but if ye worship not, ye shall be cast the same hour into the midst of a burning fiery furnace; and who *is* that God that shall deliver you out of my hands?

The king orders these offenders before him; states the case; and gives them one more trial to test their obedience. His last words, "Who is that God that shall deliver you out of my hand?" shows that as yet he has practically no just sense of the power of the Supreme Being, or indeed of any god higher than mortal man.

16. Shadrach, Meshach, and Abed-nego, answered and said to the king, O Nebuchadnezzar, we *are* not careful to answer thee in this matter.

17. If it be *so,* our God whom we serve is able to deliver us from the burning fiery furnace, and he will deliver *us* out of thy hand, O king.

18. But if not, be it known unto thee, O king, that we will not serve thy gods, nor worship the golden image which thou hast set up.

The original word rendered "careful," in the phrase, "We are not careful to answer thee," is specially forcible. It means, "We have no *need* to answer thee," we are in no straits; are not pressed by any stringent necessity as men who tremble in fear for their lives; for if thou shouldest do thy worst—cast us into the fiery furnace—our God is able to deliver us; and if he should not, we are ready for the result, let come what may. Be it known to thee, therefore, we *will not* serve thy gods nor worship thy golden image! This was moral heroism and devoted piety, both of the highest order.

19. Then was Nebuchadnezzar full of fury, and the form of his visage was changed against Shadrach, Meshach, and Abed-nego: *therefore* he spake, and commanded that they should heat the furnace one seven times more than it was wont to be heated.

20. And he commanded the most mighty men that *were* in the army to bind Shadrach, Meshach, and Abed-nego, *and* to cast *them* into the burning fiery furnace.

21. Then these men were bound in their coats, their hosen, and their hats, and their *other* garments, and were cast into the midst of the burning fiery furnace.

22. Therefore because the king's commandment was ur-

gent, and the furnace exceeding hot, the flame of the fire slew those men that took up Shadrach, Meshach, and Abednego.

23. And these three men, Shadrach, Meshach, and Abednego, fell down bound into the midst of the burning fiery furnace.

The king of Babylon had never met such heroic men before. His will had perhaps never been so squarely resisted. Hence his wrath is wrought up intensely. His order to heat the furnace sevenfold above its usual point only evinced his own heated and almost maddening passion, for no man in his cool reason would think the killing any more sure with sevenfold heat than with the usual amount. Such wrath of man, however, is very sure to work out God's praise, as it did here. The miracle of protection was the more signal; the rebuke to the king was the more pungent and the more widely known; and the reaction from the death of the executioners served still to heighten the good moral impression.——The writer states carefully that the men were bound with all their usual clothing on. The special reason for noting this with care was to show that the fire was restrained from harming not their persons only, but their clothes also.——The precise sense of the words rendered, "Their coats, their hosen, and their hats," is of relatively small consequence to us; yet it may be worth the space required to say briefly, that in the original the first word means (probably) their mantles, the usual outer garment; the second, either the tunic, the usual undergarment coming down to the knees, or as some suppose, wide and loose trowsers. The latter was the view of our English translators in the word "hosen," which at that time was used to denote trowsers and not stockings. The last word seems to mean a garment girded on about the person, and not a "hat."

24. Then Nebuchadnezzar the king was astonished, and rose up in haste, *and* spake, and said unto his counsellors, Did not we cast three men bound into the midst of the fire? They answered and said unto the king, True, O king.

25. He answered and said, Lo, I see four men loose, walking in the midst of the fire, and they have no hurt: and the form of the fourth is like the Son of God.

Then, when the king heard the result, he became greatly excited with new and strange emotions, far unlike those of his previous passion. The thought flashes upon him that he has come into conflict here with a new and unknown Power! He has cast three men into his furnace of fire sevenfold heated, and lo, the fire does not touch them! And more fearful, if possible, than even this—there is a fourth personage there, and the glory of his form strikes him as that of a Son of God! It is altogether unearthly!——The word

"Son" in the phrase "Son of God' is without the article. The expression therefore does not imply any knowledge of the Son of God in the New Testament sense, but only indicates that he thought this personage divine.

26. Then Nebuchadnezzar came near to the mouth of the burning fiery furnace, *and* spake, and said, Shadrach, Meshach, and Abed-nego, ye servants of the most high God, come forth, and come *hither*. Then Shadrach, Meshach, and Abed-nego, came forth of the midst of the fire.

27. And the princes, governors, and captains, and the king's counsellors, being gathered together, saw these men, upon whose bodies the fire had no power, nor was a hair of their head singed, neither were their coats changed, nor the smell of fire had passed on them.

The king knows now that the great God is with those men and that they are his servants. So he accosts them; "Ye servants of the most High God, come forth and come hither." He does not question their power though bound, to come forth at their own option.——The miracle was wrought in the most public manner. The king's high officers were called together. They could see the sevenfold heated furnace. They knew those three men were cast in there, bound; they saw them come out unharmed—not a hair singed—not even the smell of fire on their clothing. Verily, this was the finger of God and they all were witnesses.

28. *Then* Nebuchadnezzar spake, and said, Blessed *be* the God of Shadrach, Meshach, and Abed-nego, who hath sent his angel, and delivered his servants that trusted in him, and have changed the king's word, and yielded their bodies, that they might not serve nor worship any god, except their own God.

It is worthy of notice that the king began now to appreciate the consistency and moral heroism of these men who so firmly refused to worship any other God than their own. The very qualities which so stirred his wrath before, command his profoundest admiration now. He really finds that the God of these Hebrew youth is able to protect them in the midst of the hottest furnace, and hence he concludes that the exclusive worship of such a God will pay. The things he specially notes as done by them are—that they "trusted in their God" (he had never seen such trust before!); that they "*changed*" in the sense of disregarding and finally reversing the king's mandate; and that they "yielded their bodies" to be burned if the Lord should not be pleased to protect them. These were new developments for Babylon! When in all the foregone ages had such things been seen in that proud city?

29. Therefore I make a decree, that every people, nation, and language, which speak any thing amiss against the God of Shadrach, Meshach, and Abed-nego, shall be cut in pieces, and their houses shall be made a dunghill: because there is no other god that can deliver after this sort.

One important result of these events is a special decree, forbidding the people of his entire realm to say aught amiss against the God of these Hebrews. Apparently, the reason assigned went forth with the decree—viz., "Because there is no other God that can deliver after this sort"—a distinct recognition of the God of Israel as higher and mightier than all the gods of the heathen. This decree went over all his realm, a grand manifesto, setting forth the conviction of this autocrat on his throne in favor of the great Jehovah. Naturally it would carry with it an account more or less full of the circumstances which had called it forth. Officers of government from his whole realm were its witnesses. Hence these events must have sown broadcast some ideas of the true God among the thousands and probably millions of his subjects. Verily the hand of God was gloriously manifested in this!——Its moral effect must have been all the greater because this was the final outcome of a public conflict between the king's heathen god and Jehovah of Hosts. Nor let us fail to note that here as usual, an unseen hand made the wrath of man work out the praise of God. By how much the more the proud king manifested his wrath against those Hebrew youth, by so much the more signally did God bring forth his own glory in protecting them and confounding all those idol-worshipers! In what emergency never so difficult have the resources of the Almighty failed to overmaster the wit and the might of mortals and make his own glory shine the more by reason of their most fierce and mad endeavors!

30. Then the king promoted Shadrach, Meshach, and Abed-nego, in the province of Babylon.

The word rendered "promoted," means to put forward rapidly to higher positions of trust.——Why Daniel was not a party with his three brethren, both in their noble resistance to this wicked mandate, and in their furnace experience, does not appear. We may be very sure he never obeyed that mandate! Very probably his position shielded him from prosecution. His sympathies would be wholly with his brethren.

CHAPTER IV.

Nebuchednezzar has a second dream, predicting his own insanity; his magicians and Chaldeans can not give him its interpretation. Daniel gives it; it takes place at the end of twelve months. The king is deposed from his throne and continues insane seven years. His reason then returns; he resumes his scepter, and ascribes honor and glory to the Most High God.

1. Nebuchadnezzar the king, unto all people, nations, and languages, that dwell in all the earth; Peace be multiplied unto you.
2. I thought it good to shew the signs and wonders that the high God hath wrought toward me.
3. How great *are* his signs! and how mighty *are* his wonders! his kingdom *is* an everlasting kingdom, and his dominion *is* from generation to generation.

This entire chapter is in its nature a royal manifesto or proclamation, announcing to all the world the extraordinary ways of the great God in his providences toward the king. By "signs and wonders" he means the supernatural dreams; the predicted insanity; the moral ends which the Lord sought to gain by it; and the actual results. These terms are usually employed in the scriptures to denote the supernatural works of God—those which are unlike the common course of natural events, and such as men are wont to conceive of therefore as *above* nature—supernatural.——It is noticeable that the introduction to this manifesto recognizes "the High God" as the Supreme and Eternal Ruler, at the head of a kingdom which endures forever, and swaying a dominion which does not, like those of mortal men, pass away with the lapse of human generations, but holds on, unaffected by time, from generation to generation.——This manifesto is addressed, not to the people of his own vast realm alone, but to "all people, nations and languages that dwell in all the earth." This universality, coupled with the moral fitness and force of the document, render it truly magnificent and sublime. Think of it as translated into every spoken language throughout all the tribes of earth's entire population and sent to them from the once proud king of great Babylon and of the vast Chaldean empire!——A humble testimony that, great as this monarch of Babylon had been, the most High God is immeasurably greater; that glorious and powerful as his empire had been in the eyes of men, the kingdom of the great God is mightier far and exalted in far higher glory!

4. I Nebuchadnezzar was at rest in my house, and flourishing in my palace:

5. I saw a dream which made me afraid, and the thoughts upon my bed and the visions of my head troubled me.

It was while he was at rest in his magnificent palace and at the height of his prosperity that suddenly this dream befel him, and rudely broke up his peace and rest. When did it ever happen that a stream of mere earthly pleasure ran long without disturbance or waning? The joys of those that forget God have no living fountain.

6. Therefore made I a decree to bring in all the wise *men* of Babylon before me, that they might make known unto me the interpretation of the dream.

7. Then came in the magicians, the astrologers, the Chaldeans, and the soothsayers: and I told the dream before them; but they did not make known unto me the interpretation thereof.

As usual, and as before (chap. 2: 2), the king calls in the wise men of Babylon—the professional interpreters of dreams—to make known to him the significance of this dream. In the present case (unlike the former) he had retained the dream, and could readily relate it; but even so, the magicians could not give its interpretation. The failure was for this reason the more humiliating. Before they could say, Give us the dream and we will interpret. Now they can not say this. Their extraordinary pretensions react upon them to their deep disgrace.

8. But at the last Daniel came in before me, whose name *was* Belteshazzar, according to the name of my god, and in whom *is* the spirit of the holy gods: and before him I told the dream, *saying,*

9. O Belteshazzar, master of the magicians, because I know that the spirit of the holy gods *is* in thee, and no secret troubleth thee, tell me the visions of my dream that I have seen, and the interpretation thereof.

Here the king's manifesto introduces Daniel, properly referring to his now Chaldean name, Belteshazzar, by which he seems to have been known in the king's court, and probably to foreign powers as well. It specially recognizes him as having in himself "the spirit of the holy gods," and as obtaining his surpassing skill from this truly divine source. No distinctive feature, not even that of almighty power, more fitly discriminates between Jehovah and all the false gods of the heathen, than this quality of infinite holiness. For those gods are utterly impure and vile; are recognized by their worshipers as sharing in common with men the basest passions of depraved human nature; as quarrelsome, envious, and jealous; as sensual and utterly selfish—infinitely unlike the holy God above, in every moral quality of character.——The king well understands that no secret troubles Daniel, for his God is omniscient, and omniscience is never perplexed with any thing, however deep and dark to mortal vision. He therefore came with confidence to Daniel for the interpretation of his dream.

10. Thus *were* the visions of my head in my bed; I saw, and behold a tree in the midst of the earth, and the height thereof was great.

11. The tree grew, and was strong, and the height thereof reached unto heaven, and the sight thereof to the end of all the earth:

12. The leaves thereof *were* fair, and the fruit thereof much, and in it *was* meat for all: the beasts of the field had shadow under it, and the fowls of the heaven dwelt in the boughs thereof, and all flesh was fed of it.

13. I saw in the visions of my head upon my bed, and behold, a watcher and a holy one came down from heaven;

14. He cried aloud, and said thus, Hew down the tree, and cut off his branches, shake off his leaves, and scatter his fruit: let the beasts get away from under it, and the fowls from his branches.

15. Nevertheless, leave the stump of his roots in the earth, even with a band of iron and brass, in the tender grass of the field; and let it be wet with the dew of heaven, and *let* his portion *be* with the beasts in the grass of the earth.

16. Let his heart be changed from man's, and let a beast's heart be given unto him; and let seven times pass over him.

17. This matter *is* by the decree of the watchers, and the demand by the word of the holy ones: to the intent that the living may know that the Most High ruleth in the kingdom of men, and giveth it to whomsoever he will, and setteth up over it the basest of men.

The dream is really in two parts: one part presented to the *eye;* the other to the ear: the first part a great tree which the king saw; the second, an oral declaration made by an angel from heaven, which he heard. The first part (vs. 10–12) describes the tree—exceeding great, tall, strong, visible to the ends of the earth; of immense foliage and most abundant fruit. The beasts repose under its shade; the fowls of heaven dwell amid its branches, and all flesh is fed from its stores of fruit.——The second part (vs. 13–17) recites the audible proclamation. The king sees a glorious personage, here described as "a watcher, even a holy one, coming down from heaven." He is a watcher, one of God's unsleeping angels whom he puts in charge over portions of the vast providential agencies of his universe. The term angel, contemplates this order of beings as *sent forth* on some mission, "angel" meaning a messenger. But the term "watcher" expresses their work equally well. "Are they not all ministering spirits?" (Heb. 1:14). Some are sent specially to minister to the heirs of salvation: others, as the book of Daniel teaches (see chap. 10: and 11: 1, and 12: 1), are put in charge over the kingdoms of men—the great agents of the Most High in the execution of his providential purposes and government.——In this case, "the watcher, an holy one," came down to finish out the dream by announcing the destiny of the tree. This he proclaims with a loud voice; "Hew down the tree, cut off its branches," etc., but leave the stump of its roots in the earth, firmly fixed there as if bound with a band of iron and brass.—— From this point, the description slides insensibly from the figure to the reality—from the stump of the tree to the king himself, shorn of his glory. "Let it be wet with the dew of heaven," looks toward the insane king, outcast from human society and from the homes of men, taking his portion with the beasts of the earth. His heart changed from man's and a beast's heart given to him, indicate the utter loss for the time of his understanding and reason. He has dropped down from the grade of thinking, reasoning man to that of the unthinking, unreasoning beast. And this is to continue "until seven times have passed over him." The word "times" refers to the best known division of time, the year. It is (perhaps) a definite number for an indefinite—the real duration being possibly somewhat less than seven full years. The manifest allusion to the same event in the fragmentary record quoted in the General Introduction, speaks of it as four years. This part of the inscription, however, is so imperfect that no considerable reliance can be reposed upon it as defining the exact duration.——In v. 17, "This matter is by the decree of the watchers," etc., the preposition "*by*" indicates rather the agents than the author; the agents by whom the decree is announced and executed, rather than the author of it from whom it came and whose purpose it is commissioned to execute. (See v. 24.) God himself has ordained this infliction upon the great king. He has done it for a special purpose here assigned, viz., that the living may know that the Most High ruleth in the kingdoms of men, giving regal power to whom he will, and often setting upon earthly thrones the basest of men. This last fact should take down the pride of kings, since to be a king is to be one of a class which has certainly included many of the meanest, wickedest men that have ever cursed and disgraced our world.——The great purpose of this insanity brought upon Nebuchadnezzar was to humble his pride; to teach him impressively that the Most High ruleth over all earthly kings; and to make him and all others feel that reason is his gift, and should be used in grateful recognition of the Supreme Author of this and all other blessings.

18. This dream I king Nebuchadnezzar have seen. Now

thou, O Belteshazzar, declare the interpretation thereof, forasmuch as all the wise *men* of my kingdom are not able to make known unto me the interpretation: but thou *art* able; for the spirit of the holy gods *is* in thee.

The king submits this dream to Daniel for him to interpret. He is confident Daniel can do it, because "the spirit of the holy gods is in him." This recognition of the great doctrine that God's spiritual presence and power are with his people, that he can and sometimes does reveal to them his own exclusively divine foreknowledge of events, is a remarkable testimony from the greatest king and the master-mind of the age.

19. Then Daniel, (whose name *was* Belteshazzar,) was astonished for one hour, and his thoughts troubled him. The king spake and said, Belteshazzar, let not the dream, or the interpretation thereof, trouble thee. Belteshazzar answered and said, My lord, the dream *be* to them that hate thee, and the interpretation thereof to thine enemies.

Daniel sees at once the significance of this dream, and feels both personally afflicted and sorely tried. It is plain that he both respected and loved his king, and hence felt this infliction upon him as if it were a personal calamity on himself. He might also have thought of the perils incident to the kingdom and hence to the people, consequent upon the insanity of the king. We do not need to place among the causes of his distress any personal fear for his own safety as affected by his giving such an interpretation. We should do him injustice if we were to assume that he could be capable of such fear. The other causes of grief and anxiety are all-sufficient to account for his manifest sorrow and perturbation. ——The king quickly observes that he is troubled and begs him to relieve his mind of all solicitude. Daniel nobly replies; Would to God the calamity it portends were for those only that hate thee, its terrible significance only for thine enemies!

20. The tree that thou sawest, which grew, and was strong, whose height reached unto the heaven, and the sight thereof to all the earth;

21. Whose leaves *were* fair, and the fruit thereof much, and in it *was* meat for all; under which the beasts of the field dwelt, and upon whose branches the fowls of the heaven had their habitation;

22. It *is* thou, O king, that art grown and become strong: for thy greatness is grown, and reacheth unto heaven, and thy dominion to the end of the earth.

23. And whereas the king saw a watcher and a holy one coming down from heaven, and saying, Hew the tree down, and destroy it; yet leave the stump of the roots thereof in

the earth, even with a band of iron and brass, in the tender grass of the field; and let it be wet with the dew of heaven, and *let* his portion *be* with the beasts of the field, till seven times pass over him;

24. This *is* the interpretation, O king, and this *is* the decree of the Most High, which is come upon my lord the king:

25. That they shall drive thee from men, and thy dwelling shall be with the beasts of the field, and they shall make thee to eat grass as oxen, and they shall wet thee with the dew of heaven, and seven times shall pass over thee, till thou know that the Most High ruleth in the kingdom of men, and giveth it to whomsoever he will.

26. And whereas they commanded to leave the stump of the tree roots; thy kingdom shall be sure unto thee, after that thou shalt have known that the heavens do rule.

Here is the interpretation. The great tree is no other than the great king. This description corresponds in most respects with that given above (vs. 10–17) save only that here it is applied to the king, and remarkably, the clause which referred most plainly to his insanity, "Let his heart be changed from man's and let a beast's heart be given him," is here omitted. In verses 25, 26, the agents referred to, "*they* shall drive thee from men;" "*they* shall make thee eat grass;" "*they* shall wet thee with the dew of heaven;" are apparently those angelic beings whom God employs in his providential administration, controlling the activities of men and bringing about the course of events in harmony with the divine will.——That the stump and roots are left living and strong in the earth denoted that his kingdom should still remain sure to him and should return to his hand after he should have fully seen and heartily admitted that the God of heaven (for brevity's sake here "the heavens") does rule.——This preservation of the kingdom to him by preventing any successor from obtruding himself upon the throne, may, not improbably, have been due to this known prediction and to Daniel's personal influence. Daniel was in a position to have almost unlimited control in this thing.

27. Wherefore, O king, let my counsel be acceptable unto thee, and break off thy sins by righteousness, and thine iniquities by shewing mercy to the poor; if it may be a lengthening of thy tranquillity.

As the time of this calamity was not fixed, it might be postponed by the king's repentance; indeed it might have been altogether prevented if he had become truly penitent. Why not as really as the destruction of Nineveh foretold by Jonah, the precise date of which moreover was set to ninety days. Hence the way is open for Daniel to exhort his sovereign in all fidelity and love to "break off his sins by righteousness, and his iniquities by showing mercy to the poor," since thus he might, nay would, prolong this present peace and prosperity.——This noble example of manly and Christian fidelity to his sovereign is worthy of all admiration, and of course *imitation*. Prompted by such manifest love and in manner so respectful to the king, and yet with so much personal dignity, it must have fallen upon the king's mind with great force.——The sin specially indicated here, unrighteous oppression of the poor, looks very probably toward the terrible exactions of labor imposed upon his defenceless subjects (some of them captives of war) in those immense public works which were in the eyes of men, the glory of his reign. The eye of man, dazzled with so much architectural splendor, commonly fails to look down through to the crushed bodies and broken hearts, and to the hopeless, never-lifted pressure of woe which such a mass of coerced labor always signifies. Human eyes rarely see it; still more rarely make any account of it; but the Great Father sees it and can never fail to take it into most solemn account.

28. All this came upon the king Nebuchadnezzar.
29. At the end of twelve months he walked in the palace of the kingdom of Babylon.
30. The king spake, and said, Is not this great Babylon, that I have built for the house of the kingdom by the might of my power, and for the honor of my majesty?
31. While the word *was* in the king's mouth, there fell a voice from heaven, *saying*, O king Nebuchadnezzar, to thee it is spoken; The kingdom is departed from thee.
32. And they shall drive thee from men, and thy dwelling *shall be* with the beasts of the field: they shall make thee to eat grass as oxen, and seven times shall pass over thee, until thou knowest that the Most High ruleth in the kingdom of men, and giveth it to whomsoever he will.
33. The same hour was the thing fulfilled upon Nebuchadnezzar: and he was driven from men, and did eat grass as oxen, and his body was wet with the dew of heaven, till his hairs were grown like eagles' *feathers*, and his nails like birds' *claws*.

It may be supposed that Daniel's faithful exhortation had some good moral influence on the king for a season. The impending calamity was deferred twelve months. But his goodness was as the morning cloud. When his pride resumed its sway over his heart, just while he was walking on the flat roof of his lofty palace, overlooking the splendor of that most splendid city, and saying, "Is not this great Babylon that I have built for the house of the kingdom by the might of my power and for the honor of my majesty"—at that moment there came another voice; it fell from heaven: it made its pointed address to Chaldea's proud king by name, and said, "The kingdom is departed from thee!" The dream is to be fulfilled! It was!——That the execution of this long impending decree should wait to smite the king at last in precisely this juncture was of set divine purpose, to indicate the more unmistakably the sin for which this was the destined scourge. So God is often wont to make the connection between the sin and the infliction of chastisement or judgment for it, so palpable that there shall need be no mistake in tracing it out.

34. And at the end of the days I Nebuchadnezzar lifted up mine eyes unto heaven, and mine understanding returned unto me, and I blessed the Most High, and I praised and honored him that liveth forever, whose dominion *is* an everlasting dominion, and his kingdom *is* from generation to generation:

35. And all the inhabitants of the earth *are* reputed as nothing: and he doeth according to his will in the army of heaven, and *among* the inhabitants of the earth: and none can stay his hand, or say unto him, What doest thou?

36. At the same time my reason returned unto me; and for the glory of my kingdom, mine honor and brightness returned unto me: and my counsellors and my lords sought unto me; and I was established in my kingdom, and excellent majesty was added unto me.

37. Now I Nebuchadnezzar praise and extol and honor the King of heaven, all whose works *are* truth, and his ways judgment: and those that walk in pride he is able to abase.

His understanding seems now to return to him as a new-born gift, fresh from the God of heaven. With the utmost propriety he makes his first use of it in this devout recognition of the glory and majesty, the justice and righteousness too, of the Most High God. It is a sublime testimony. In thought most appropriate; in choice of terms unexceptionable; in its whole expression majestic and eloquent, it is one of the grandest passages in English literature. If we may suppose it to have gone forth from the throne of the restored monarch to the millions of his people and to foreign lands also, it must have produced a profound sensation. Its influence may have been mostly evanescent; yet it was for the time a grand testimony to the glory and majesty of the one Supreme God, and a witness against the folly of paying even the least regard to the gods of the heathen.——How long or how deeply it affected the heart of Nebuchadnezzar, we have no positive data for determining. The sacred record leaves him here. It would be grateful to every feeling of the heart to know that this king became under such influences a humble child and faithful servant of that Great God to whose glories he bears witness in strains so sublime. But we lack the evidence to justify such a belief. Something more decisive to this effect might be expected in the sacred record if such had been the fact. The fragmentary record that has come down to our times on "the Standard Inscription" of this king (quoted in the General Introduction, p. 284) shuts us up to the conclusion that the temptations of royalty were too strong for his moral nature to overcome. Great men, as well as men not great, may come very near the gate of heaven's kingdom, and yet never enter therein. When King Herod heard John Baptist, "he did many things and heard him gladly;" but alas! Herod never turned heartily from all his sins to God. His record stands, like this of Nebuchadnezzar, a solemn admonition against coming short of doing one's whole duty when God reveals it plainly, and conscience presses its demand, and the Divine Spirit comes near for one last effort to save the soul.—— The Lord had great purposes to answer by this Chaldean king, and he accomplished those purposes, even though that king would not bow his whole heart to truth and to God. He made all that king's frailties as well as his nobler qualities of character subserve his own glory and praise; drew from him reiterated testimonials to the majesty, justice and glory of Jehovah, and gave them to the kings and princes of all the earth to whom this revelation should ever come, for their admonition and instruction. Here we leave this greatest and perhaps best of all the sovereigns of the Chaldean empire.

CHAPTER V.

This chapter presents Belshazzar in his revelries and blasphemy; the awful hand that wrote his doom upon the palace-wall; the utter failure of his astrologers to read and interpret the writing; how Daniel read and interpreted, and how it was fulfilled in that eventful night.

1. Belshazzar the king made a great feast to a thousand of his lords, and drank wine before the thousand.

2. Belshazzar, while he tasted the wine, commanded to bring the gold and silver vessels which his father Nebuchadnezzar had taken out of the temple which *was* in Jerusalem; that the king, and his princes, his wives, and his concubines, might drink therein.

3. Then they brought the golden vessels that were taken out of the temple of the house of God which *was* at Jerusalem; and the king, and his princes, his wives, and his concubines, drank in them.

4. They drank wine, and praised the gods of gold, and of silver, of brass, of iron, of wood, and of stone.

On the question, Who was Belshazzar? see the general introduction to Daniel (page 286).——Nebuchadnezzar is supposed to have been the grandfather of Belshazzar on his mother's side. This latitude in the use of the word "father" was not uncommon with the Hebrews.——As the city was already besieged, and the real king Nabonned had gone into the field against the armies of the Medes and Persians under Cyrus, the sense of security which this feast implied must be accounted for by their confidence in the assumed strength of the city. Plainly it was supposed to be absolutely impregnable.——It may be added that God had given up the king and his princes to a blind infatuation, of such sort as usually precedes destruction.——Drinking wine from the vessels taken out of Jehovah's temple in Jerusalem was intended as an insult to his majesty. In the current notions of the age, each nation's gods were its patrons and defenders, so that victory over a nation was a triumph over its gods. Chaldea, in the person of Belshazzar and his lords, is now exulting over Jehovah as unable to protect his people against the superior power of their idols. As they drank, "they praised the gods of gold and of silver," as being mightier than the God of the Hebrew people. Hence the time had fully come for the Lord to vindicate his own glory and crush out this proud and blasphemous dynasty.

5. In the same hour came forth fingers of a man's hand, and wrote over against the candlestick upon the plaster of the wall of the king's palace: and the king saw the part of the hand that wrote.

6. Then the king's countenance was changed, and his thoughts troubled him, so that the joints of his loins were loosed, and his knees smote one against another.

The precise location of this writing on the wall "over against the candlestick," would make it very conspicuous amid the revelries of those banqueting halls.——It is an appalling scene when a sinning mortal knows that the Great God has come to meet him in the very midst of his sins! Belshazzar might well stand aghast to find himself thus confronted face to face with the dread Jehovah whom he is purposely insulting! He has a sense of a present Power, more than human, in that strange *hand*, writing unknown words on his palace-wall, and a guilty conscience helps him to forecast some fearful doom! The brightness of his countenance is gone (so the original imports); his mind is fearfully agitated; his knees smite against each other.——How changed the scene from the glee of his blasphemous revelry to this paleness of cheek, convulsion of frame, remorse of conscience, and dread foreboding of doom! Many a sinner has had a like experience, and other thousands must have it!

7. The king cried aloud to bring in the astrologers, the Chaldeans, and the soothsayers. *And* the king spake and said to the wise *men* of Babylon, Whosoever shall read this

writing, and shew me the interpretation thereof, shall be clothed with scarlet, and *have* a chain of gold about his neck, and be the third ruler in the kingdom.

8. Then came in all the king's wise *men:* but they could not read the writing, nor make known to the king the interpretation thereof.

9. Then was king Belshazzar greatly troubled, and his countenance was changed in him, and his lords were astonished.

His first resort is to his professional expounders of all mysterious things. He summons them to his aid, and presses them, by the most winning promises, to expound this mysterious handwriting. They fail him utterly, and he is only the more alarmed.

10. *Now* the queen, by reason of the words of the king and his lords, came into the banquet-house: *and* the queen spake and said, O king, live forever: let not thy thoughts trouble thee, nor let thy countenance be changed:

11. There is a man in thy kingdom, in whom *is* the spirit of the holy gods; and in the days of thy father, light and understanding and wisdom, like the wisdom of the gods, was found in him; whom the king Nebuchadnezzar thy father, the king, *I say*, thy father, made master of the magicians, astrologers, Chaldeans, *and* soothsayers;

12. Forasmuch as an excellent spirit, and knowledge, and understanding, interpreting of dreams, and shewing of hard sentences, and dissolving of doubts, were found in the same Daniel, whom the king named Belteshazzar: now let Daniel be called, and he will shew the interpretation.

The "queen" in this passage is the queen-mother, as may be inferred from the fact that the king's wives and concubines are with him in his carousals while this woman was not; and also from her intimate acquaintance with Daniel and with the incidents of Nebuchadnezzar's life. She was probably the daughter of Nebuchadnezzar and the mother of Belshazzar.

13. Then was Daniel brought in before the king. *And* the king spake and said unto Daniel, *Art* thou that Daniel, which *art* of the children of the captivity of Judah, whom the king my father brought out of Jewry?

14. I have even heard of thee, that the spirit of the gods *is* in thee, and *that* light and understanding and excellent wisdom is found in thee.

15. And now the wise *men*, the astrologers, have been brought in before me, that they should read this writing,

and make known unto me the interpretation thereof; but they could not shew the interpretation of the thing:

16. And I have heard of thee, that thou canst make interpretations, and dissolve doubts: now if thou canst read the writing, and make known to me the interpretation thereof, thou shalt be clothed with scarlet, and *have a chain of gold about thy neck*, and shalt be the third ruler in the kingdom.

The sacred record throws no light on the history of Daniel during the period since the death of Nebuchadnezzar. The fact that Belshazzar knows him only by report and tradition implies that he had retired from public office some years before; very probably at the death of Nebuchadnezzar. Evil-Merodach, his son and successor, changed the policy of his father in some respects certainly; *e. g.*, in taking Jehoiachin from prison to his favor and table. (See 2 Kings 25: 27–30, and Jer. 52: 31–34.) Berosus says of him, "This man, having used his authority in a lawless and dissolute manner, was slain by conspirators." He reigned but two years. Such revolutions in government would naturally have the effect of displacing Daniel.

17. Then Daniel answered and said before the king, Let thy gifts be to thyself, and give thy rewards to another; yet I will read the writing unto the king, and make known to him the interpretation.

So far from having any sympathy with Belshazzar, Daniel could feel only abhorrence and detestation of his revelry and blasphemous insult of Jehovah. Hence he will not look at the king's promised rewards, but repels them with disdain. He seems to have had much sincere respect for Nebuchadnezzar, but not the least for his degenerate grandson. Yet for his satisfaction, and, withal, his rebuke, he will read the writing and give the interpretation.

18. O thou king, the most high God gave Nebuchanezzar thy father a kingdom, and majesty, and glory, and honor:

19. And for the majesty that he gave him, all people, nations, and languages, trembled and feared before him: whom he would he slew; and whom he would he kept alive; and whom he would he set up; and whom he would he put down.

20. But when his heart was lifted up, and his mind hardened in pride, he was deposed from his kingly throne, and they took his glory from him:

21. And he was driven from the sons of men; and his heart was made like the beasts, and his dwelling *was* with

the wild asses: they fed him with grass like oxen, and his body was wet with the dew of heaven; till he knew that the most high God ruled in the kingdom of men, and *that* he appointeth over it whomsoever he will.

The language which describes the sin of Nebuchadnezzar is specially pertinent and forcible. "When his heart was lifted up and his mind hardened in pride," etc. The terrible influence of power in the hands of depraved men, reacting on the heart, has rarely been portrayed more justly. The perpetual incense of flattery, coupled with the daily experience of being dependent on no one and of having every one dependent on himself, tempts an absolute monarch to feel himself almost a god. Under such influences, the moral sensibilities become fearfully hardened against all sense of obligation whether to God or to man. When any man has reached this moral state, what can remain for him but a fall? It is fully time for Almighty God to hurl such a hardened sinner down! Such "pride goeth before destruction."——In the clause which states that his insanity continued "*till he knew* that the Most High rules in the kingdoms of men, and appoints to this power whomsoever he will," the word "knew" should be taken in the sense of freely recognizing and of adjusting himself morally to this knowledge, rather than in the closely intellectual sense of having then first obtained this knowledge. For, his sin did not lie in not *knowing* but in not duly regarding, and in not rightly using the knowledge he actually had. "To him that knoweth to do good and doeth it not, to him it is sin."

22. And thou his son, O Belshazzar, hast not humbled thy heart, though thou knewest all this;

23. But hast lifted up thyself against the Lord of heaven; and they have brought the vessels of his house before thee, and thou, and thy lords, thy wives, and thy concubines, have drunk wine in them; and thou hast praised the gods of silver, and gold, of brass, iron, wood, and stone, which see not, nor hear, nor know: and the God in whose hand thy breath *is*, and whose *are* all thy ways, hast thou not glorified.

Having set before this recreant son the dealings of the Great God with his father which the king had known and ought to have regarded, Daniel now turns pointedly to him and sets his sins in order before his eyes in the plainest style of honest and fearless rebuke. He charges home upon his conscience his pride, although he had well known how God afflicted his father for this very sin; also, his defiant bearing toward the God of heaven in the matter of desecrating the sacred vessels of his temple and honoring the gods of gold, "which see not, nor hear, nor know," adding, with unsurpassed fitness and force—"And the God in whose hand thy breath is and whose are all thy ways, hast thou not glorified."—— The clause, "whose are all thy ways," follows in the same line of thought with the preceding, "in whose hand thy breath is," and affirms that all his goings, all that made up his life and destiny, were dependent on God—a truth which this king had most wickedly ignored.——*Not* to glorify, is here to be taken with a strong emphasis on the negative, giving the clause the opposite sense; whom thou hast contemned and despised. Precisely this the king was then doing. This usage of the negative is by no means uncommon.

24. Then was the part of the hand sent from him; and this writing was written.

25. And this *is* the writing, that was written; MENE, MENE, TEKEL, UPHARSIN.

26. This *is* the interpretation of the thing: MENE; God hath numbered thy kingdom and finished it.

27. TEKEL; Thou art weighed in the balances, and art found wanting.

28. PERES; Thy kingdom is divided, and given to the Medes and Persians.

"Then," is not here a particle of time, but of consequence. *Consequently*, because of this insult offered by the king to the great God, was that part of a hand sent forth from him (*i. e.*, from God) which wrote upon the wall (v. 5). The writing was done some considerable time before Daniel uttered these words, interpreting the writing and announcing to the king his righteous doom.——The literal rendering of the words written on the wall is, "*Numbered; numbered; weighed; and divided.*" Remarkably the last word is plural as it stands in v. 25, but appears in its singular form in v. 28. It is not clear that any special sense attaches to the plural. If so, it should have been in the plural when repeated for the purpose of being interpreted.——The English reader would not readily see that *Upharsin* is nearly identical with *Peres*. It is so, however. The letter U translates the Chaldee prefix for *and*, which, dropped off, leaves Pharsin. Then "*in*" is the plural termination, and the rest of the difference is due to the change of vowels consequent upon this plural termination. Pharsin is simply the plural form of Peres.——"*Mene*" is repeated, apparently for the sake of intensity. The days of thy kingdom are certainly and precisely numbered, and having now all past, the end has come.——Tekel, the first letter being the character for *th*, which is used in Chaldee for the Hebrew *sh*, is identical with *shekel*, which as a noun is a well known standard weight; and as a verb, means to weigh. In the moral sense, weighing puts one to the test, tries him by the divine standard. So Job said (chap. 31: 6), "Let me be *weighed* in an even balance that God may know mine integrity." God had thrown Belshazzar upon his great scales of justice and righteousness and found him utterly wanting. He was not fit to reign longer.——The "kingdom divided and given to the Medes and Persians" predicted one of the great historic facts of the age—the fall of Babylon, and the subversion of the Chaldean dynasty. It fell before Cyrus, at the head of the combined armies of the Medes and Persians. Herodotus and Xenophon, the great Greek historians of their time, have left detailed accounts of this transaction. Cyrus invested the city, turned the current of the Euphrates, and marched his army into the city by way of the river-channel.——Jeremiah had foretold this event with extraordinary minuteness (chaps. 50 and 51), giving, among many other things, the names of their conquerors; "Prepare against her the nations, the kings of the Medes" (chap. 51: 28); the drying up of her waters (51: 36); and the drunken condition of her princes at the time (chap. 51: 39, 57). "In their heat, I will make their feasts and I will make them drunken, that they may rejoice, and sleep a perpetual sleep and not wake, saith the Lord."

29. Then commanded Belshazzar and they clothed Daniel with scarlet, and *put* a chain of gold about his neck, and made a proclamation concerning him, that he should be the third ruler in the kingdom.

Belshazzar lived only long enough to fulfill this promise and give Daniel these honors. But Daniel cared little for honors under such a monarch at any time, and least of all, now, in these last hours of the kingdom. These circumstances however may have been his stepping-stone to an equally high position under the next dynasty, and this seems to have been a part of the divine purpose. Remarkably, under God's all-wise plans, single events have multiform results—bearings that ramify outward indefinitely.

The reader is referred to the introduction for an attempt to harmonize the statements of Berosus respecting the last king of Babylon with what is said here of Belshazzar. I can not say it is entirely satisfactory, the main difficulty being that Belshazzar appears in the Bible record as sole king, and not merely as crown prince with the title of king. Yet this appearance is not such as to exclude the possibility of the facts stated by that ancient and standard historian.

30. In that night was Belshazzar the king of the Chaldeans slain.

31. And Darius the Median took the kingdom, *being* about threescore and two years old.

The effort to identify this Darius the Mede with certainty in the various records of profane history has been thus far unsuccessful. George Rawlinson remarks: "There still remains one historical difficulty in the book of Daniel which modern research has not yet solved, but of which Time, the Great Discoverer, will, perhaps, one day bring the solution. At present we can only indulge conjectures concerning Darius the Mede," etc.——The opinions of critics have been divided between (1.) Astyages, the grandfather of Cyrus; (2.) Cyaxares, a supposed son of this Astyages; and (3.) Some deputy bearing this name, unknown to profane history, whom Cyrus put in charge over Babylonia. That he "*took* the kingdom" in the sense of being a deputy and not a king in his own right, is involved in the usage of the verb. In chap. 2: 6, it is used for *receiving* great gifts; and in chap. 7: 18, of the saints of the Most High *receiving* the kingdom." A renewed mention of Darius (chap. 9: 1) speaks of him as "made king over the realm of the Chaldeans."——The difficulties in identifying this Darius lie mainly if not entirely with the profane historians themselves.

CHAPTER VI.

This chapter treats of the administration of Darius. Daniel is promoted to the highest position next to the king; the other presidents and all the princes, through envy, plot his destruction by procuring a law making it a capital crime to offer any petition to any god or man, save unto the king, for thirty days: Daniel continues to pray as aforetime; is therefore cast into the lion's den, but comes forth unharmed; whereupon the king by public decree calls on all men to fear the God of Daniel.

1. It pleased Darius to set over the kingdom a hundred and twenty princes, which should be over the whole kingdom;

2. And over these three presidents; of whom Daniel *was* first: that the princes might give accounts unto them, and the king should have no damage.

The kingdom as here spoken of is Babylonia proper, and not the whole of that vast realm, embracing several distinct nationalities, which was brought under the sway of Nebudchadnezzar. Darius himself was a sort of deputy or viceroy under Cyrus, and Babylonia was virtually a province in the great Medo-Persian empire. These verses show how the executive department of the government was organized.

3. Then this Daniel was preferred above the presidents and princes, because an excellent spirit *was* in him; and the king thought to set him over the whole realm.

Daniel was preëminent, not only in wisdom and executive ability, but in his disinterested devotion to the public weal. While the other high officers were selfish and corrupt men (as is usual), the king could not but see that Daniel was thoroughly a good man, devoted to the welfare of his country, and unselfishly true to the interests of his king. Hence the king put him above all his other officers, and had even thought to intrust the whole executive management of the kingdom in his hands, i. e., by making him sole president instead of being simply the head man of the three.

4. Then the presidents and princes sought to find occasion against Daniel concerning the kingdom; but they could find none occasion nor fault; forasmuch as he *was* faithful, neither was there any error or fault found in him.

Such a model of excellence, so far surpassing and so uncomfortably eclipsing themselves, was keenly cutting to those corrupt officers, and aroused their bitterest hostility. So they sought to find some fault in his official life, but they sought there in vain. He was both wise and faithful, and hence left them no ground of accusation there.

5. Then said these men, We shall not find any occasion against this Daniel, except we find *it* concerning the law of his God.

Abandoning all hope of finding any occasion even for slander against Daniel in the line of his official conduct, they set themselves to make an occasion in the line of his religion. This is avowedly their only hope. They know he is not an idolator, but is a conscientious worshiper of the true God. They know him to be a praying man.

6. Then these presidents and princes assembled together to the king, and said thus unto him, King Darius, live forever.

7. All the presidents of the kingdom, the governors and the princes, the counsellors and the captains, have consulted together to establish a royal statute, and to make a firm decree, that whosoever shall ask a petition of any God or man for thirty days, save of thee, O king, he shall be cast into the den of lions.

8. Now, O king, establish the decree, and sign the writing, that it be not changed, according to the law of the Medes and Persians, which altereth not.

9. Wherefore king Darius signed the writing and the decree.

With satanic cunning, they shaped this proposed law to take with the king by a bait for his low vanity, and to entrap Daniel through his known decision and firmness in the worship of his God. It was the best compliment they could pay to Daniel that they assumed so confidently that he would pray to God none the less for this monstrous law. It was the keenest reproach to their king that they should anticipate his ready assent to such a law under the impulses of his excessive vanity. Darius was a weak and vain king, utterly unfit to wear a crown, else he would have asked, What can be the motive of these men in proposing such a law? What! must no child ask bread of his father for thirty days save under pain of being cast to the lions? Must no friend ask favor of friend save under such a penalty? What can this proposal mean? Who can be the better for such a law?——Plainly, the appended exception, "Save of thee, O king," was so grateful to his vanity that it blinded his dull eye to the monstrous nature and possible bearings of this law.——This point in the fundamental law of the Medo-Persian realm, that no royal decree, once duly signed and sealed, should ever be changed, was probably adopted for the purpose of forestalling the caprice of monarchs and guarding against sudden and rash changes. It was probably hoped that it would operate to lessen the evils incident to arbitrary and absolute power. It was, however, a radically vicious principle. For why should not every man be wiser to-day than he was yesterday? Why should not the windows be always kept open to admit new light on all subjects; and if so, then, also, to adjust our activities to the demands of this new light? The present case shows that the original law, not less than any proposed amendment, may be capricious and wicked, and therefore may need to be changed. But the Medo-Persian constitution seemed to pique itself upon this peculiarity.

10. Now when Daniel knew that the writing was signed, he went into his house; and his windows being open in his chamber toward Jerusalem, he kneeled upon his knees three times a day, and prayed, and gave thanks before his God, as he did aforetime.

Daniel saw in an instant that this law was planned for his destruction, yet without one moment's debate with his love of life, or fear of lions, he said, I shall pray to God none the less but all the more for that, and none the less openly. With the God whom I serve I leave the whole question of my living or dying. I know it is my duty and my right to pray. I can not know that it is my duty to live. If the Lord sees fit to protect my life, he can readily do so. I bear my case to him, and leave it in his hand. With his heart thus full of firmness, prayer, and trust, he hastened home to his house and to his accustomed chamber of prayer, and there—his window open—not closed as if he would conceal his devotions—but open and toward Jerusalem as the place of God's visible glory and the locality of his earthly mercy-seat, he kneeled three times a day with prayer and thanksgiving as aforetime.——Blessed man! How quietly, how calmly, and how peacefully did thy heart repose on the enduring love and faithfulness and the never-failing power of thy fathers' God! We love thee for thy firmness, and yet more for thy precious faith in Him who is both thy God and ours. And we thank the God of our fathers that he sustained thee so graciously and made thy faith and firmness in duty an example so inspiring to all who come after thee even down to the end of time!

11. Then these men assembled, and found Daniel praying and making supplication before his God.

These men assembled, all intensely eager to see if their scheme was working well, and moreover apparently aware of his accustomed hours of devotion. They find him praying; and now they feel sure of his ruin.

12. Then they came near, and spake before the king concerning the king's decree; Hast thou not signed a decree, that every man that shall ask *a petition* of any god or man within thirty days, save of thee, O king, shall be cast into the den of lions? The king answered and said, The thing *is* true, according to the law of the Medes and Persians, which altereth not.

13. Then answered they and said before the king, That Daniel, which *is* of the children of the captivity of Judah, regardeth not thee, O king, nor the decree that thou hast signed, but maketh his petition three times a day.

They hasten to the king, and artfully begin with referring to the decree, the standing law of the realm, for these thirty days. When the king had recognized it, they bring out the fact that Daniel has broken it, putting this in the most offensive light possible even for slander; "regardeth not thee, nor the decree which thou hast signed." That same Daniel whom thou hast promoted so excessively and so unwisely, has no proper regard for thee, O king! He prays to others as much as he pleases, despite of thine own law.

14. Then the king, when he heard *these* words, was sore displeased with himself, and set *his* heart on Daniel to deliver him: and he labored till the going down of the sun to deliver him.

The king is chagrined and ashamed of himself that he allowed himself to be caught in this snare. Now for the first time he sees the envious and mean spirit of his officers in obtaining from him that decree, and bites his lips in shame that he could have been so beguiled and entrapped. He labored to save Daniel till the going down of the sun. No doubt he heartily esteemed Daniel and probably loved him, and felt therefore the bitterest grief and shame that he should be made unwittingly the author of his destruction.

15. Then these men assembled unto the king, and said unto the king, Know, O king, that the law of the Medes and Persians *is*, That no decree nor statute which the king establisheth may be changed.

All his efforts are unavailing. Those men come *en masse* and press him with the great doctrine of their national constitution, that by the laws of the Medes and Persians, no decree or statute, once established by the king, can be changed.

16. Then the king commanded, and they brought Daniel, and cast *him* into the den of lions. *Now* the king spake and said unto Daniel, Thy God whom thou servest continually, he will deliver thee.

The king at length yields and gives command that Daniel be cast into the den of lions. He had however known enough of the one Jehovah to feel assured that he would deliver his own servant from the lions, and said this to Daniel.

17. And a stone was brought, and laid upon the mouth of the den; and the king sealed it with his own signet, and with the signet of his lords; that the purpose might not be changed concerning Daniel.

By this arrangement the miracle of divine protection was put beyond any suspicion of collusion and fraud.

18. Then the king went to his palace, and passed the night fasting: neither were instruments of music brought before him: and his sleep went from him.

The king's heart is heavy with both grief and shame; he eats not, sleeps not. The word rendered "instruments of music," is supposed by the ablest critics to mean concubines. Hence the clause states that they were not admitted to his society.

19. Then the king arose very early in the morning, and went in haste unto the den of lions.

20. And when he came to the den, he cried with a lamentable voice unto Daniel: *and* the king spake and said to Daniel, O Daniel, servant of the living God, is thy God, whom thou servest continually, able to deliver thee from the lions?

With the dawn, in the first light, the king came to the den, with trepidation as well as haste (so the word implies) and cries out with a sad voice, indicating his grief and anxiety. Though he had expressed to Daniel his confidence that God would deliver him, yet he still asks the question as one who would feel better assured by the evidence of his senses.

21. Then said Daniel unto the king, O king, live forever.

22. My God hath sent his angel, and hath shut the lions'

mouths, that they have not hurt me; forasmuch as before him innocency was found in me; and also before thee, O king, have I done no hurt.

Daniel casts no severe reproach upon the king. Indeed, the original rather expresses a genial and kindly feeling; Daniel "talked with the king." With beautiful modesty, he ascribes his deliverance to God's own hand alone through his angel, and very properly asserts his innocence of any wrong in this matter, either toward God or toward his king. He could not admit that he had done any harm toward the king by offering his prayer to the God of heaven. A law so intrinsically wicked he could not obey—*ought not* to obey—and was consciously guilty of no wrong against the law-making power in disobeying.——We may suppose Daniel to have had a sweet sense of the presence of God by his angel while spending the night in the den with those hungry lions. There they were, their savage nature and clamoring appetites held in firm subjection, and God's own hand in it visibly present to his eye and consciously to his innermost soul. That was a night of mingled prayer and praise.——Is it not safe for all men to trust God in the path of known duty, though it lead into a lion's den? Nay, is it not more than safe—even gloriously blessed, to live so near to God and to see his angels present in such forms of power and glory for the protection of his trusting people? Who would not welcome such an experience as that of Daniel, and rejoice to make it his own?

23. Then was the king exceeding glad for him, and commanded that they should take Daniel up out of the den. So Daniel was taken up out of the den, and no manner of hurt was found upon him, because he believed in his God.

The king is relieved and joyous to find that his valued friend is safe and that no serious consequences have come from his wicked law. The demands of the law having now been met, he orders Daniel brought forth from the den. Not a scratch is on him, and those heathen men know that this comes of his believing in his God. They are witnesses to the saving power of Jehovah, God of Israel.

24. And the king commanded, and they brought those men which had accused Daniel, and they cast *them* into the den of lions, them, their children, and their wives; and the lions had the mastery of them, and brake all their bones in pieces or ever they came at the bottom of the den.

The great crime of Daniel's accusers now meets its righteous punishment. They had plotted his death; and though they had sought to effect it by the forms of law, yet their malice and hence their guilt were none the less for this reason. It was right and just that they should be made a public example, and the king was fully prepared to do it.

25. Then king Darius wrote unto all people, nations, and languages, that dwell in all the earth; Peace be multiplied unto you.

26. I make a decree, That in every dominion of my kingdom men tremble and fear before the God of Daniel: for he *is* the living God, and steadfast forever, and his kingdom *that* which shall not be destroyed, and his dominion *shall be even* unto the end.

27. He delivereth and rescueth, and he worketh signs and wonders in heaven and in earth, who hath delivered Daniel from the power of the lions.

These proceedings culminate in a royal decree after the manner of Nebuchadnezzar (chap. 3: 29), calling on all men of every tribe and language in all the earth, to tremble and fear before the God of Daniel. The logic of this decree is simple. God delivered Daniel from the lions by his supernatural power. He whose power is so manifestly above nature must be the God of nature—the Maker and Lord of all. He alone is the object of all rightful worship and of true reverence, homage, love and trust.

28. So this Daniel prospered in the reign of Darius, and in the reign of Cyrus the Persian.

Daniel's prosperity, his high position and commanding influence in public affairs, continued throughout the reign of Darius and into the reign of Cyrus:—how far into the latter is not said. His last recorded vision was in the third year of Cyrus.——The reader will scarcely need the suggestion that the character of Daniel, thus far brought out fully under various and most trying circumstances, shines only the more brilliantly by how much the fiercer the ordeal through which it passes. He evinces the docility and modesty of a child, coupled with superlative wisdom, great executive ability, unswerving fidelity, and a firmness of principle that is above all praise. His case presents the highest order of human qualities of character, ennobled and exalted by the best type of true piety. Behold in Daniel what the rich gifts of God's grace can make of the noblest of men! Let all who look toward office or any public trust take note of Daniel, and account him one of the best models of character for those who would hold well the trusts to which they aspire.

CHAPTER VII.

This chapter gives the second of the four great prophecies of Daniel—a vision obviously in very close analogy with that of chap. 2: 31–45, and in general parallel with that of chap. 8, and also that of chaps. 10–12.——The prophet sees in succession four great beasts, the last of which has ten horns and ultimately an eleventh (vs. 2–8); he then sees the fourth beast judged and slain (vs. 9–11); next "one like a Son of man," receiving his eternal kingdom (vs. 13, 14); finally, he asks and obtains an interpretation of this vision, especially of the fourth beast and his horns (vs. 15–28).

In commenting upon this chapter, I propose to give, first, such special expositions as the several clauses may seem to require, and then discuss the great question at issue here—the real significance of the fourth beast and his horns. This latter is the point on which commentators differ; in all else, they mostly agree.

1. In the first year of Belshazzar king of Babylonia Daniel had a dream and visions of his head upon his bed: then he wrote the dream, *and* told the sum of the matters.

Any attempt to fix the date of this vision involves the identification of Belshazzar with some one of the monarchs of Babylon. (On this subject, see the general introduction to Daniel, p. 286.)——I do not find him in Evil-Merodach who reigned after the death of his father Nebuchadnezzar, two years, B. C. 561–559; nor in Neriglissar, his successor, reigning four years, B. C. 559–555; nor in his son, Laborosoarchod who reigned but nine months, and whose name therefore does not appear on the canon of Ptolemy; nor in Nabonidus (shortened into Nabonned), known by the Greeks as Labynetus, who reigned seventeen years, B. C. 555–538, which brings us down to the subversion of the Chaldean empire by Cyrus. But I do find him coincident with the last years of Nabonidus, his .father, who took him into partnership with the title of king, as is shown by an inscription recently discovered. How long he stood in this relation, bearing the title of king, is not known. The sacred record speaks (chap. 8: 1) of his third year. His death occurred B. C. 538.——In his first year Daniel had this vision, and immediately committed to writing its main points, as revealing matters of high moment.

2. Daniel spake and said, I saw in my vision by night, and, behold, the four winds of the heaven strove upon the great sea.

3. And four great beasts came up from the sea, diverse one from another.

The elements of nature are in great commotion, symbolizing convulsions in the political elements. These four great beasts come forth from the agitated sea, manifestly *in succession*, to denote succession in the order of time in the great empires of which they are the symbols.

4. The first *was* like a lion, and had eagle's wings: I beheld till the wings thereof were plucked, and it was lifted up from the earth, and made to stand upon the feet as a man, and a man's heart was given to it.

This lion with eagle's wings is thoroughly a Chaldean conception. Layard's late work, entitled, "Discoveries in Nineveh," abounds with cases of this mongrel type, putting an eagle's wings upon a lion, or, as the case may be, upon a bull. "Winged lions," "winged bulls," and even human figures, with wings extending from the shoulders, have been disinterred in considerable numbers from the ruins of Nineveh within the present century, affording remarkable proof that these conceptions in this vision of Daniel, and also in Ezekiel chap. 1, and elsewhere, are fully in keeping with the popular ideas and the artistic usages of the people living in the valley of the Euphrates during the age of these prophets.—— Moreover, the lion and the eagle were then as now, symbols of royalty, figuring conspicuously in the memorial arms of sovereigns. Layard speaks of the name and title of the Khorsabad kings, accompanied by the figure of a lion. The reader will recall "the British lion," and "the American eagle." So this first beast is a lion with eagle's wings.——As Daniel continued to study this beast, lo, a change comes over him. His wings are plucked; he is lifted up to stand erect as a man, and a man's heart is given him. This change is not from brutal to human intelligence, but from the brute force and resistless ferocity of the lion and the eagle, to the comparative physical weakness of the man. The Chaldean empire is fast waning to its fall. Its glory has departed; its pristine vigor has gone.——In saying Chaldea, I have of course assumed this to be the meaning of the lion with eagle's wings. On this point all commentators agree. There is no room for doubt or difference of opinion. The series of great empires begins at the point of time then present, even as it did in the great image, chap. 2: 31–45.——Let it be distinctly noted also that Daniel asks no explanation whatever of the first three of these symbols; the lion, the bear, and the leopard. They correspond so perfectly with the first three divisions of the great image— the head; the breast and arms; and the belly and thighs; that he has no occasion to raise any question for further explanation.—— Moreover it is not distinctly affirmed here that these beasts come forward *in succession*, each supplanting its predecessor. The idea of succession and the manner of it, are not made so clear in this chapter as in chap. 8, where the he-goat overpowers the ram, and then succeeds to his empire. Yet it is very manifest that these beasts do follow each other in regular succession. The first has had great power, but is now seen shorn of it and ready to be vanquished. The second in its time is a devourer of nations; to the third, "dominion is given." No other view can reasonably be taken of these beasts considered as great national powers, except that they sway the empire of the world *successively*—each being for his time supreme on the field of their location.

5. And behold another beast, a second, like to a bear, and it raised up itself on one side, and *it had* three ribs in the mouth of it between the teeth of it: and they said thus unto it, Arise, devour much flesh.

Of this second beast like a bear, our translation states that "it raised up itself on one side." The original gives no sanction to this reciprocal sense, raising *one's-self* up, but rather means that it was *made to stand,* or simply arose and stood. Its "*standing on one side*" should mean, either, on one side of the lion-power of v. 4, viz., on the North, or more closely N. N. E.; or that it put forth its aggressions *in one direction, i. e.,* toward Chaldea, and the tribes of Western Asia. Either sense is admissible in view both of the original language and of the historic facts.——Its "three ribs in the mouth" indicate that it has been devouring flesh and still has these three ribs not yet cranched and swallowed. I doubt if any special significance attaches to the *number* of these ribs. The beast is commissioned to devour yet more. Of course this denotes the subjugation of yet other nationalities, and absorbing them into its own—an accurate history so far of the Medo-Persian power.

6. After this, I beheld, and lo, another, like a leopard, which had upon the back of it four wings of a fowl: the beast had also four heads; and dominion was given to it.

This beast, all commentators agree, is the Grecian empire of Alexander—winged to denote the velocity of its armies and the rapidity of its conquests. "Dominion given to it," almost drops the figure of a beast, to give us in literal phrase the history of this power. Correspondingly the passage (chap. 2: 39), has it, "Another third kingdom of brass which shall bear rule over all the earth."——Its having four heads is altogether in harmony with the peculiar style of composite and compound forms which abounds in the ruins of ancient Nineveh and Babylon. I doubt if any special significance pertains to it; but, if any, it may be this—that the Grecian empire of Alexander was distinguished (as was Greece herself) more by the power of *thought* than the power of brute force. Among the great kingdoms of that ancient world, this was the empire of brains.

7. After this I saw in the night visions, and behold a fourth beast, dreadful and terrible, and strong exceedingly; and it had great iron teeth: it devoured and brake in pieces, and stamped the residue with the feet of it: and it *was* di-

verse from all the beasts that *were* before it; and it had ten horns.

8. I considered the horns, and behold, there came up among them another little horn, before whom there were three of the first horns plucked up by the roots: and behold in this horn *were* eyes like the eyes of man, and a mouth speaking great things.

Postponing my full discussion of the identity of this fourth beast until other points in the chapter shall have been considered, I wish the reader to notice now——(1.) That this beast is specially described as strong, dreadful and terrible.——(2). That according to the interpretation (vs. 23, 24), this beast stands for the fourth kingdom; and his ten horns are ten kings in this kingdom, and the little horn is also a king in the same line.——(3.) Apparently, the terribleness of this fourth kingdom lies specially (though not solely) in this little horn-king. In proof of this, I adduce two facts: (*a*) that the detailed account of the devastations wrought by this entire power ascribes them to the little horn (see vs. 21, 22): and (*b*) that the judgment which comes down from God upon this fourth beast is represented as invoked specially by the spirit and the deeds of this little horn, (see vs. 11 and 26). It was "*because* of the voice of the great words which the horn spake," that "the beast was slain." And v. 26, also implies that the court for judgment sat upon the case of the little horn, and took away his dominion, to consume and destroy it utterly. That is, *he* was king of the fourth kingdom at the time of this consuming judgment.——(4.) The terrible devastations effected by this little horn manifestly fall upon the recognized people of God, his visible church; and at a period when that church was *Jewish*, as is indicated by this circumstance—that his aggressions upon their religion are described as a purpose to "change times and laws"—a phrase by which a Jewish writer would mean and Jewish readers would understand, the times and laws of the Mosaic ritual service. [This point will be amply confirmed when we reach the parallel account of the little horn's aggressions upon God's people as given in chap. 8: 10-14, 23-25, and 11: 31-35.]——(5.). Hence it is entirely legitimate to infer that this fourth beast is dreadful and terrible to Daniel chiefly *as seen from his Jewish stand-point*, in the light of his intense love for his own people, his sympathy with their fortunes, and his responsibilities for their protection and welfare. I infer this from considerations drawn in part from the known relations sustained by Daniel to the Jewish people; in part from numerous testimonies throughout this entire book to the great strength of these feelings of love, sympathy, and solicitude in his heart for them; and in part from palpable indications in this very vision as above shown. The point is one of great importance in determining the ultimate significance of this fourth beast and his horns, since it shows that this beast is not seen as great and terrible *relatively to the whole world*, and certainly not relatively to the great European world, onward to the end of time, and quite apart from any bearing upon the Jews while 'they were the visible church and kingdom of God; but *is* seen as terrible to the Jews mainly, and to them *before* the kingdom of God was taken from them and given to the Gentiles.——This kingdom, said repeatedly to be "diverse from all the beasts that were before it" (v. 7); "diverse from all others" (v. 19); "a kingdom diverse from all kingdoms" (v. 23)—may have been diverse in this particular respect, viz., of hostile bearing against the Jewish people and their religion. This would make that power specially formidable to the Jews.——In the absence of any specific showing of the point wherein this diversity lies, this is obviously the most probable supposition.——The characteristics of the little horn; "eyes as of a man and a mouth speaking great things," will be unfolded more fully in the sequel. Suffice it to say here that these symbols indicate keen intelligence, sharpened by a malign spirit and purpose, and by blasphemous hostility against the true God and his people.——The plucking up of three of the first horns is alluded to and in part explained in v. 20. This will be a matter for future consideration.

9. I beheld till the thrones were cast down, and the Ancient of days did sit, whose garment *was* white as snow, and the hair of his head like the pure wool: his throne *was like* the fiery flame, *and* his wheels *as* burning fire.

10. A fiery stream issued and came forth from before him: thousand thousands ministered unto him, and ten thousand times ten thousand stood before him: the judgment was set, and the books were opened.

11. I beheld then because of the voice of the great words which the horn spake: I beheld *even* till the beast was slain, and his body destroyed, and given to the burning flame.

The vital question on this passage is; Does it refer to the final and general judgment; or to providential judgments *in time*, for the destruction of the fourth beast and his horns?——I adopt the latter view and defend it on the following grounds.——(1.) The general final judgment *is not in place here;* would have no connection with the subject in hand; is not indicated by any thing said in the context, or by the nature of the subject.——On the contrary, an allusion to God's providential judgments upon guilty nations *is in place here*, precisely so, being the very thing that such blasphemous hostility to his kingdom and people calls for and should lead us to expect.——(2.) In the government of God over men, individuals will be judged at the end of this world, and punished or rewarded in the next; but nations can be punished only *in time*—only in this world, for the sufficient reason that they exist as nations only here. They are not known as nations after this life. The awards made at the final judgment are upon *individuals* only; the retributions of eternity are on individuals alone. Hence if this judgment falls on the fourth beast and his horns, it must be in this world; it can not be at and after the end of it.——(3.) The declared result and outcome of this judgment is that this fourth beast "is destroyed, and his body given to the burning flame" (v. 11). Conclusive to the same point is v. 26. "The judgment shall sit" (i. e., on the little horn-king, then representing the fourth beast), "and they shall take away his dominion to consume and destroy it" utterly. ——What could be more decisive? A nationality swept away; indeed the last one in a long series of Asiatic world-kingdoms; kings cut down in their pride and rage against God,—these are the declared results of this judgment.——But if this were the judgment scene of the last day, its result and outcome ought to be like that of Mat. 25: 31-46—the assigning of the righteous and of the wicked each to their eternal destinies—"these into everlasting punishment;" "those into life eternal."——(4.) But further, the distinctive characteristics of the final judgment are *not* here.——These are, (*a*) That it takes place at the end of the world.——(*b*) Is preceded by the general resurrection.——(*c*) Embraces all the human race from the beginning to the end of time; and even the fallen angels.——(*d*) That men are judged in it as individuals and not as nations. They are not known as nations there. There "Every one of us shall give account of himself unto God."——(*e*) In the final judgment, Jesus Christ is to be the Judge. In this, the Judge is "the Ancient of days," the Eternal Father. (See v. 13.)——(*f*) Its results are not transient, as these appear to be, but eternal, even the eternal award of destiny to the righteous and to the wicked.——(*g*) The final judgment *follows* Christ's second advent; this *precedes* his first advent.——The latter statement, it will soon be seen, must be true. The next verses (viz., 13, 14) describe Christ's ascension and inauguration as King—events that follow close after his resurrection—which itself belongs to his first, not his second advent.——All these points are characteristic features of the final judgment. They are all wanting here. Their absence forbids our interpreting this passage of the final judgment. Hence we are shut up to the other alternative—a special providential judgment, of such sort as God sends on guilty nations in time.——(5.) It can scarcely be necessary to adduce any other argument to prove that this passage refers to God's providential judgments on the fourth beast and his horns; yet it will interest the thoughtful Bible reader, and is entirely legitimate to the sphere of an expositor, to add that the descriptive points in this passage are fully in analogy with those theophanies which occur somewhat frequently in the Old Testament scriptures, in which God is seen enthroned, or coming down in fire, often with attending angels, and perhaps with the forms of a judicial tribunal, to visit retribution on guilty nations.——That is to say, the analogies of this passage are *with those* which describe the judgments of God upon guilty nations in time. Its main points and features are identical with this class of passages, and therefore it belongs with them and denotes the same class of judgments.

Taking the main points of this passage in the order in which they stand, we have—(*a*) The Almighty God *enthroned*. Here, "I beheld till the thrones were cast down, and the Ancient of days did sit." "Cast down," is not (as the English reader might suppose) overthrown, demolished, but means *firmly set*, preparatory to being used as a royal judgment-seat.——Correspondingly in other Hebrew theophanies; Isaiah (6: 1) "saw the Lord sitting on a throne, high and lifted up." Micaiah (1 Kings 22: 19) "saw the Lord sitting on his throne, and all the host of heaven standing by him on his right hand and on his left." The Psalmist (11: 4, 6) writes, "The Lord's throne is in heaven; his eyes behold, his eyelids try the children of men:" . . . "Upon the wicked he will rain fire and brimstone and an horrible tempest," etc.——"His garments white as snow, and the hair of his head like the pure wool," has its analogy in the Apocalypse (1: 14). "His head and his hairs were white like wool, as white as snow." Age is venerable; its incidents are clustered upon this personage to bespeak for him reverence and homage. He is "the Ancient of Days." But this feature does not point to the final judgment.——(*b*) This throne is on wheels, and has the aspect of fire and flame.——So in Ezek. 1. The visible glory of Jehovah appears upon a throne, which itself reposes upon a "firmament" or elevated platform, supported by four living creatures who are singularly connected with living wheels. Here also is the aspect of fire. "As for the likeness of the living creatures, their appearance was like burning coals of fire, and like the appearance of lamps; it went up and down among the living creatures, and the fire was bright, and out of the fire went forth lightning" (Ezek. 1: 13).——It should be borne in mind that Ezekiel and Daniel were both residents in Chaldea, and were therefore familiar with those very peculiar modes of representing the divine attributes which appear in the ruins of Nineveh as exhumed within the last thirty years. Also, that they were contemporary; that Ezekiel wrote his first chapter B. C. 595 (see chap. 1: 2), and Daniel this chapter about B. C. 540; *i. e.*, fifty-five years later; so that Daniel might have had the writings of his elder brother before him many years. Hence perhaps their close resemblance.
——(*c*) Fire issues forth from God to devour his enemies. Here in Daniel, "A fiery stream issued and came forth from before him." So Ps. 50: 5, "Our God shall come . . . . a fire shall devour before him; it shall be very tempestuous round about him." And Ps. 97: 3, "A fire goeth before him and burneth up his enemies round about." In David's glowing description of the Lord's coming to his aid against his foes (Ps. 18: 8) we read; "There went up a smoke out of his nostrils; fire out of his mouth devoured." So also Moses (Deut. 5: 24), "For the Lord thy God is a consuming fire, even a jealous God." So in Heb. 12: 29, "For our God is a consuming fire." The fire sent on Sodom seems to have been a standing type or model of God's judgments on corrupt nations and

to have supplied the figures of speech to express this idea. In Isa. 34: 9, 10, the allusion to that model is specially palpable. Of Idumea, the prophet said, "The streams thereof shall be turned into pitch and the dust thereof into brimstone, and the land thereof shall become burning pitch. It shall not be quenched night nor day; the smoke thereof shall go up forever."——Hence fire became the usual symbol to denote the judgments which the Lord in his providence brings upon guilty nations in time, of which fact it may suffice to quote but one more passage (Isa. 66: 15, 16); "For behold the Lord will come with fire and with his chariots like a whirlwind, to render his anger with fury and his rebuke with flames of fire; for by fire and by his sword will the Lord plead with all flesh; and the slain of the Lord shall be many." The reader may add Mal. 4: 1, 3.——(*d*) Thousands of attendant ministering angels. Here it stands; "Thousand thousands ministered unto him; ten thousand times ten thousand stood before him." The fact that they *ministered* to him shows them to be, not culprits at his bar, but servants awaiting his command. To "stand before him" is also the customary attitude of his attendant angels. Not in the final judgment alone, but wherever the Lord appears in his glory and majesty and lets men see the realities of the spiritual world, angels are seen about him as his executive agents. Micaiah saw all the host of heaven standing by him on his right hand and on his left (1 Kings 22: 19). When on Sinai there "went forth from the Lord's right hand a fiery law for them" (Deut. 33: 2), "he came with ten thousand of saints," holy ones; said by the Psalmist (68: 17) to have been "thousands of Angels." Zech. 14: 5, has the same feature; "There comes the Lord my God! All the holy ones are with Thee."——(*e*) The forms of a judicial tribunal. The close analogy between the judicial proceedings of human courts and of the divine, accounts most amply for these allusions. Thus Daniel; "The judgment was set and the books were opened;" and v. 26, "The judgment shall sit." So elsewhere in those cases where the Lord comes down for the judgment of wicked nations. Ps. 50 is a case where the Lord "calls to the heavens from above and to the earth, that he may judge his people" .... "for God is judge himself." Joel 3 is wholly in this strain. "Let the heathen be wakened and come up to the valley of Jehoshaphat; for there will I sit to judge all the heathen round about."——I am not aware that any other Hebrew theophany save this of Daniel introduces the symbol of "the books" as witnessing records against the ungodly, but there is surely no reason for assuming that this symbol can be used of no other judgment than that at the end of the world. All the rest of these symbols are used, elsewhere than in Daniel, to denote the visitations of divine judgment on guilty nations in time.——(*f*) It may seem to be superfluous to argue this point further; yet in a word let me add that this destruction of the fourth beast and his horns must correspond with the stone smiting the great image upon his feet of iron and clay (chap. 2: 34, 35). As this smiting was not the final judgment, but a judgment in time; so is the judgment in the verses before us. As that of chap. 2 occurs *before* the New Testament kingdom of heaven is set up; precisely so should this, and precisely so it does, as will be seen when we pass on from this judgment (vs. 9–11), to the next act of the drama (vs. 13, 14). This latter point is of itself an independent and most conclusive argument for the position I have taken in regard to the character of this judgment scene. Succession in the several points of this vision indicates succession in time as to the events predicted. Hence there can be no doubt that the Son of Man coming to the Ancient of Days and receiving his kingdom *follows* the destruction of the fourth beast and of the little horn. But this inauguration of the Son of Man in earth and especially in heaven, occurred at his ascension, as will be shown when the passage comes under consideration.——It should be noted that the interpretation of this part of the vision gives the same order of events; first, the judgment of God sits to destroy the little horn, and then the kingdom is given to the saints of God (vs. 26, 27).

12. As concerning the rest of the beasts they had their dominion taken away: yet their lives were prolonged for a season and time.

The "rest of the beasts" are the first three. The thing said of them here is that, although they lost their supreme dominion, the scepter over the kingdoms of the East passing into other hands, yet they had still for a season a sort of existence without sovereignty. At least so much as this seems to be implied, viz., that the judgments of God did not fall on them so terribly and with so sudden devastation as on the fourth beast. It is plain that the first three are contrasted with the fourth. V. 11 shows that the fourth beast came to his fearful doom because of the blasphemies of the little horn-king. It is fair to presume, therefore, that at the time this judgment fell, this kingdom was represented by the little horn, and hence that the terribleness of this judgment pertains especially to him. This is the obvious sense of the entire passage, vs. 9–12, and is fully confirmed by the inspired interpretation (v. 24–27); where it is the little horn-king who is judged and slain, and then next in order the kingdom is given to Messiah and his people.

13. I saw in the night visions, and, behold, *one* like the Son of man came with the clouds of heaven, and came to the Ancient of days, and they brought him near before him.

14. And there was given him dominion, and glory, and a kingdom, that all people, nations, and languages, should serve him: his dominion *is* an everlasting dominion, which shall not pass away, and his kingdom *that* which shall not be destroyed.

This passage has decisive bearings on the interpretation of this vision. It should therefore be expounded with the utmost care.——Its vital question is, *Does this event take place at the close of Christ's first advent, or shortly after his second?* Does this passage describe his coming to set up his New Testament "Kingdom of heaven;" or, on the contrary, some inauguration of Christ as King *after* the universal resurrection and the general judgment? One or the other it must be.——I hold the former view most decidedly, for the reasons that follow.——(1.) This kingdom and this setting up of it must be the same as that of chap. 2: 44. *There* was a kingdom which should "never be destroyed;" "should stand forever;" should not pass over to other hands; should demolish and then supersede all that had been named before it. *Here* is a kingdom universal, everlasting, and never to pass over to other hands. This is the fifth kingdom of this vision: that is the fifth in that. The identity is complete.——(2.) That kingdom and this too are, beyond all question, the very "kingdom of God" (otherwise called "kingdom of heaven"), of which so much is said in the New Testament. The reader is referred to the argument on this point in the notes on chap. 2: 44.——(3.) The New Testament determines the precise point of Christ's inauguration over this kingdom to be at his ascension. For when John Baptist and our Lord began to preach, they both said in the same identical words, "The kingdom of heaven is at hand." During Christ's public ministry, even down to his death, he continually speaks of it as very near, on one occasion saying; "The time is fulfilled" (Mark 1: 15). Immediately before his death, and also after it and before his ascension, he speaks of this regal power as already given him, although the public inauguration in heaven was yet really future, saying in his prayer (Jn. 17: 2), "As thou hast given him power over all flesh;" and to his disciples shortly before his ascension (Mat. 28: 18), "All power is given unto me in heaven and in earth." It need not surprise us that he should thus anticipate a great event which was so near.——After his ascension, the apostles with one voice testify that Christ has now become really King and Lord of all. They preached this with astonishing effect on the day of Pentecost (Ac. 2: 33–36): "This Jesus hath God raised up." "Being by the right hand of God exalted," etc. "God hath made that same Jesus whom ye have crucified both Lord and Christ." And subsequently (Ac. 5: 31); "Him hath God exalted with his right hand to be a Prince and a Savior to give repentance to Israel," etc. So in Peter's first Gentile sermon (Ac. 10: 36); "He is Lord of all." Further, the Epistles definitely locate this inauguration immediately after his resurrection and ascension; *e. g.,* Eph. 1: 20–22, "When he raised him from the dead and set him at his own right hand in the heavenly places, far above all principality and power and might and dominion, and every name that is named; not only in this world, but also in that which is to come, and hath put all things under his feet, and gave him to be head over all things to the church," etc. And 1 Pet. 3: 22; "Who is gone into heaven and is on the right hand of God, angels and authorities and powers being made subject unto him." Compare also Jn. 3: 35, and Mat. 11: 27, and Rom. 14: 9, and Phil. 2: 9, 10, and Heb. 2: 9, and 1: 3, and 12: 2, and Rev. 3: 21, and 17: 14. Even this list is not exhaustive, but it is amply sufficient.——Remarkably, the scriptural record of our Lord's history is closely continuous from his death on Calvary to his completed inauguration on the throne at the right hand of the Father. New Testament history follows him step by step through his successive manifestations to his disciples during forty days, until at length he led them out to Bethany; the last words were spoken; he lifted up his hands and blessed them; and while they were beholding, he was taken up and a *cloud received him out of their sight.* Here the New Testament history loses sight of him for the moment, for their strained eyes can follow him no farther; but the cloud and the glorious Personage whom it embosomed were caught by the eye of Daniel in this night-vision; "He saw and behold one like a Son of man came with the clouds of heaven and came to the Ancient of Days; and they brought him near before him, and there was given him dominion and glory and a kingdom"—universal, never to be transferred to other hands, and never to be destroyed. The connection is complete; Jesus was inaugurated as king and seated on his throne immediately upon his ascension to heaven. Then and thenceforward the empire of this world is his. He rules it in the interests of his church and people. He rules it to convert the nations to himself. He is head over all things for the sake of his church—till this church shall embrace the wide earth, and "the kingdoms of this world shall become the kingdom of our Lord and of his Christ, and he shall reign forever and ever."

Does the question arise, Why should Christ have been inaugurated then? Was he not "Lord of all" before? Were not the worlds made by him and ruled by him also as well? And was not all this known in heaven?——The answer is involved in the very language of Daniel; "I saw one *like a Son of Man* coming in the clouds of heaven," etc. Jesus, *as incarnate,* had not been in heaven before. The man Jesus had not been visibly recognized there up to that hour. The divine Lord of all appears there now in new relations, and it was fitting that *in these new relations* he should be publicly recognized and duly-inducted into his exalted station and dignity. Hence the pertinence of Paul's logic; "*wherefore,*" (*i. e.,* because Christ Jesus had so benevolently and sublimely "humbled himself"—therefore) "God hath highly exalted him and given him a name above every name" (Phil. 2: 9).——(4). But yet further: no such inauguration occurs at his second coming. It would be superfluous to repeat its forms then; nay, more, worse than superfluous, since it would practically ignore *this* inauguration and impeach its validity—not to say deny its reality. But we are not left to such reasonings however strong; the silence of the Bible as to any such inauguration *at that time* is sufficient to explode the assumption. There is not a word in the sacred Scriptures to show any inauguration of Christ or setting up of his kingdom *at his second advent.* Beyond all question, therefore, this inauguration in our passage must be (as above explained) that which immediately followed his ascension and first advent.——Consequently these verses give us a definite limit over which the fourth beast and his horns (kings) can not pass;—prior to which they must have their life and meet their destruction. This limit is what interpreters call technically the "terminus ad quem"—the point where the events of the vision must close, and below which in time they can not extend.——It is every thing gained for the just and sure interpretation of prophecy when we are able to fix with unerring certainty this "terminus ad quem." It is fixed here by the complete identity between this inauguration of the Son of Man seen by Daniel, and the same event located by the New Testament at his ascension, connected with his first advent. For it can not be reasonable to evade this argument by dislocating the order of events in this vision. This order is closely consecutive. The inauguration (vs. 13, 14), follows the destruction of the fourth beast (vs. 9-11) by the same law by which the fourth beast himself follows the third; the third the second; and the second the first. Nothing but capricious violence can sever this consecutive order.——Moreover, the Angel-interpreter (vs. 25-27) gives precisely the same order of succession as the vision. The fourth beast develops itself into the little horn, or rather the little horn was at the time of this judgment the reigning king in this fourth kingdom. Vs. 24 and 25 give his sins; v. 26, his punishment; v. 27, the subsequent and consequent setting up of Messiah's kingdom. The order of succession here is unquestionable and gives its whole strength to confirm the same closely consecutive order in the vision (vs. 9-11 and 13, 14).——It is pleasant to notice the law of mental association by which the mind of the Spirit passes from the judgment and destruction of the fourth beast and little horn to the setting up of Christ's kingdom and to its glorious though somewhat remote triumphs. This law is quite common in the prophetical writings. Under it Isaiah makes use of the signal destruction of the invading hosts of Assyria, passing over from that startling event to the far more grand and glorious victories of King Messiah in the latter days. See Isa. 10: 28-34, with chaps. 11 and 12. He passes in the same way (chaps. 34 and 35) from the fall of Idumea to the victories of Messiah. So also does Joel; and so indeed do all the prophets. The course of thought is this: The Lord who works the lesser and nearer deliverance can also work the greater and more remote. The power that can achieve the one can achieve the other. The love and care for his people that secure the one secure also the other. The will and purpose to do the one are therefore the pledge of a like will and purpose to do the other. This is the real law of mental connection—the course of logical thought that links the latter event to the former; yet the minds of most men leap from the former class of events to the latter by spontaneous inference. Following this law of mind, the Divine Spirit adapts his teachings to the natural course of human thought.

"His love in time past
Forbids me to think
He'll leave me at last
In trouble to sink."

So Zion cleaves to the record of God's marvelous works of power and grace in her behalf in days of old, and builds thereon her faith for more and greater works in exigencies yet to come. So the Lord himself teaches his people.

15. I Daniel was grieved in my spirit in the midst of *my* body, and the visions of my head troubled me.
16. I came near unto one of them that stood by, and asked him the truth of all this. So he told me, and made me know the interpretation of the things.

Daniel has a painful sense of something sorely afflictive to the people of God in this vision, and therefore seeks its interpretation from an attendant angel. "Asked him the truth," etc., does not imply that he doubted God's veracity, but only that he was in doubt what this truth might be. It was the substance and meaning, and not the reliability, that he sought to learn. The angel kindly explains.

17. These great beasts, which are four, *are* four kings, *which* shall arise out of the earth.
18. But the saints of the Most High shall take the kingdom, and possess the kingdom forever, even forever and ever.

This first explanation is exceedingly brief—so brief that it does not meet Daniel's felt wants, and he therefore proceeds at once to make his inquiries more specific.——The word used here in explaining the meaning of the beasts is king, not kingdom. Yet the more full and specific interpretation (vs. 23, 24) makes them definitely kingdoms and the horns kings. Beyond all question, the whole course of Daniel's visions in chaps. 7 and 8 requires this construction—the beasts, kingdoms, and the horns, kings. The more full and precise statements must prevail over the one that is more brief and general.——The nature of the symbol also requires this. The king finds his type in the horn, for the horn is the executive power *of* the beast, but has no power *apart from* the beast. So of the king. The beasts in these visions are nationalities, embracing many kings in succession.——Two reasons may be assigned for this peculiar use of "king" in this passage instead of kingdom.——(1.) The very brevity of the statement.——(2.) The fact that (in the case of the first three especially) each kingdom was mainly embodied in one several king; Chaldea in Nebuchadnezzar; the Medo-Persian empire, in Cyrus; the Grecian, in Alexander. So far forth as these successive dynasties affected the ancient people of God, these kings severally were every thing. To all practical purposes, they were *the kingdoms.* And with nearly as much propriety may the same be said of the fourth. So far as it affected the Jews, it was chiefly embodied in Antiochus Epiphanes.

19. Then I would know the truth of the fourth beast, which was diverse from all the others, exceeding dreadful, whose teeth *were of* iron, and his nails *of* brass; *which* devoured, brake in pieces, and stamped the residue with his feet;

20. And of the ten horns that *were* in his head, and *of* the other which came up, and before whom three fell; even *of* that horn that had eyes, and a mouth that spake very great things, whose look *was* more stout than his fellows.

21. I beheld, and the same horn made war with the saints, and prevailed against them;

22. Until the Ancient of days came, and judgment was given to the saints of the Most High; and the time came that the saints possessed the kingdom.

Daniel here recites that part of the vision which he specially wishes the angel to explain. It is that which relates to the fourth beast, his ten horns, and more than all, that little horn.——The word rendered "stout," means impudent, arrogant.——Daniel seems already to understand somewhat more than is distinctly stated in the vision as he gives it, (vs. 7, 8,) this for instance; that "the same horn made war with the saints and prevailed against them." The manner of introducing this: "I beheld," etc., seems to imply another scene in the vision, in addition to those narrated vs. 2–14.—— It will be noted also that he supposes this war to continue, with success on the side of this horn, "until the Ancient of Days shall come" (as stated vs. 9–10), and interpose his judgment on this little horn-power to deliver his saints and give them the kingdom. This shows Daniel's idea of the consecutive order of these events. It seems to imply also that he expected this giving of the kingdom to the saints would ensue very soon after the destruction of the little horn. Yet it may be that this vision did not aim to give minutely the intervals between great and somewhat remote events. They may be seen in vision in close connection because of their mutual relation as cause and result, and not because of their close relation in time.—— Or we might say, the interval between the destruction of the little horn and the giving of the kingdom to Christ's people is passed in silence and practically ignored *as a time-interval* because there was nothing in it to be noticed; none of that class of events which the vision takes note of. The series of great world-monarchies, swaying the populations of Western Asia had utterly perished. The Chaldean, the Medo-Persian, the Alexandrian-Greek, and every one of the four kingdoms that became his successors, are now dead. They have gone down forever; and on that territory, of that class of powers, there is nothing to succeed them. Most fitly and beautifully therefore does the spirit of prophecy represent the kingdom of the Messiah as coming next upon the stage and supplanting all these world-monarchies, to stand forever. It comes next, for nothing of the sort intervened before its development in the personal advent of Christ and his triumphal inauguration as king at his ascension.

23. Thus he said, The fourth beast shall be the fourth kingdom upon earth, which shall be diverse from all kingdoms, and shall devour the whole earth, and shall tread it down, and break it in pieces.

24. And the ten horns out of this kingdom *are* ten kings *that* shall arise: and another shall rise after them; and he shall be diverse from the first, and he shall subdue three kings.

25. And he shall speake *great* words against the Most High, and shall wear out the saints of the Most High, and think to change times and laws: and they shall be given into his hand until a time and times and the dividing of time.

This explanation is of prime importance in the interpretation of this vision. The main points made in it are; that the beasts are kingdoms: that the fourth is the fourth consecutive kingdom, diverse from all the preceding probably in the respect of being more hostile to the Jews while they are the recognized people of God; that it should devour the whole earth, making widespread devastations; that its ten horns are ten kings; that the little horn is yet another king arising after them, diverse from the preceding ten; and here, also, probably diverse in the point of more bitter hostility to God's people: that he shall speak haughty and blasphemous words against God; shall wage sore and wasting wars against the Jews and purpose to subvert their religion—(for a Jewish prophet should use this language in such a connection only of the Mosaic system, and Jewish readers could understand by it nothing else;) and finally, that they should be given into his hand so that he would effectually arrest the established worship of the sanctuary during three and a half years. This construction as to the duration of this period, "a time, times and the dividing of time," follows Daniel's use of the same word in his account of Nebuchadnezzar's insanity (chap. 4: 16, 23, 25, 32), where, beyond a doubt, a "time" means a year. But this point will be resumed at a later stage of the discussion.

26. But the judgment shall sit, and they shall take away his dominion to consume and to destroy *it* unto the end.

27. And the kingdom and dominion, and the greatness of the kingdom under the whole heaven, shall be given to the people of the saints of the Most High, whose kingdom *is* an everlasting kingdom, and all dominions shall serve and obey him.

This "judgment" interprets the scene described vs. 9-11, and, as already suggested, shows that it fell specially on the little horn who was largely the embodiment and impersonation of the fourth kingdom. The fall of this fourth kingdom is soon followed by the setting up of the Messiah's kingdom which is represented as "given to the people of the saints of the Most High" because they are its instrumental agents, and because its triumphs are identical with their real success and prosperity.

28. Hitherto *is* the end of the matter. As for me Daniel, my cogitations much troubled me, and my countenance changed in me: but I kept the matter in my heart.

Here this vision and its interpretation close. Daniel is personally very much affected. His great heart, ever intensely anxious for "his people," feels keenly under the prophetic view of their future trials, persecutions, and sufferings. He thinks intently and with troubled thought; but having no pious bosom friend near, he "kept the matter in his heart."

Having now considered the sense of the several clauses in this chapter, both in themselves and in their relations to each other, we are prepared to take up the great question of interpretation upon which critics so widely differ, viz., *What is the fourth kingdom, and who is this little horn?*——Is this kingdom Rome Pagan, and this horn Rome Papal?——Or, is the fourth kingdom that of Alexander's successors; and the little horn, Antiochus Epiphanes?—— These are the only theories that specially claim attention. Hence the question is narrowed down to a choice between these.——I adopt the last-named theory, understanding by the fourth beast those portions of the cleft empire of Alexander which lay geographically nearest the Jews, with whom politically they stood in close and potential relations, and which chronologically follow immediately after the death of Alexander and continue very nearly down to the coming of Christ. These were primarily and chiefly the Syrian kingdom founded by Seleucus Nicator, B. C. 312, and much less prominently the Egyptian, founded by Ptolemy Lagus, B. C. 323.——This theory assumes that in many respects the fourth beast and all his horns are a unit. They are so in being alike portions of the great Grecian empire of Alexander, also in the respect of being Grecian in name, in language, in customs and in national spirit; and more than all, in the point of sustaining the closest foreign relations with the Jews.——This theory, with this view of its import, I adopt,

1. Because this political power comes in the natural order of succession. It holds this place of natural order, (1.) *Chronologically;* (2.) Geographically; (3.) Politically; (4.) In respect to its relations to the Jewish people.

(1.) Chronologically, Alexander's successors come next in time. He died B. C. 325. The Greco-Egyptian kingdom was founded in the same year. The Greco-Syrian—the result of long and bloody wars, became settled only after eleven years of conflict. Then it became the most potent foreign power in its relations to the Jews. ——On the contrary, the Roman empire came into no important relations to the Jews until the Christian era; never disturbed their repose effectually until A. D. 70—nearly four hundred years after Alexander's death, and bore no part among the foreign powers controlling the fortunes of the Jews until they aided Herod to the Jewish throne, B. C. 37; *i. e.*, nearly three hundred years after the death of Alexander. Such a chronological hiatus should not be assumed without the most cogent reasons. It is "violently improbable." (2.) Geographically, the Syrian kingdom appears on the same territory which had been the theater and home of the Chaldean, Medo-Persian, and essentially of the Grecian empires. But Rome belonged to an entirely different and then nearly unknown part of the world. Rome never was Asiatic, never was Oriental; never therefore was a legitimate successor of the first three of these great empires.——(3.) Politically, these kingdoms, Syria and Egypt, should be the fourth beast, especially Syria, because made up of the same nationalities—the same tribes, nations, and peoples—that composed successively the Chaldean, the Medo-Persian, and the Grecian empires. As these successively were composed in large measure of the same populations, only recast and clustering round a new political center, covering essentially the same territory; so this fourth kingdom should be sought on the same territory, among the same populations.——Rome had the seat of her power and the masses of her population in another and remote part of the world. ——(4.) But especially should this complex power be the fourth beast and kingdom of Daniel, because it stood in close proximity to the Jews, in fact embosoming it on the south and on the north, and constituting *the* foreign nations with which Jews stood in the closest relations of war or peace. The genius and scope of this vision demand that this fourth beast should represent such nations, and utterly forbid us to think of a power far away in the recesses of Europe, and which in the period in question, *i. e.*, during the three centuries onward from B. C. 323, had absolutely nothing to do with the fortunes of the Jewish people.

II. This theory follows the analogy of the first three kingdoms. ——I have already presented this as one of the laws by which these visions should be interpreted;—the parts less fully explained should follow the analogy of the parts more fully explained. The fourth beast should follow the analogy of the first three. Since there remains no doubt as to the meaning of the first three, let us carefully gather up all we can learn there and apply it to the interpretation of the fourth. Why not?——Now, the first three kingdoms stand in the closest political relations to the Jews. In fact, they are here for this reason and no other. The great moral lessons which these four parallel visions address to Daniel's people begin with and grow out of these historic facts;—*The great kingdoms which successively overshadow your nationality, under which you sigh in captivity, or live in dependent subjection, or against which you war for your very existence, or for the faith and worship of your fathers,—shall soon be subverted and swept away, and Messiah's kingdom take their place and fill all the earth.*——Consequently the first three kingdoms are precisely those under which the Jews lived. Analogy requires that the fourth should bear the same relations.——Again, of the first three, each follows closely upon his predecessor. the Medo-Persian subverting and succeeding the Chaldean, B. C. 538; the Grecian in like manner subverting and succeeding the Medo-Persian, B. C. 335–323. The powers that closely succeeded the death of Alexander, and were the persecutors, or, as the case may be, the protectors, of the Jews, were the Egyptian, founded in the same year, and the Syrian, which became established eleven years later. These, then, must answer by analogy to the fourth beast.——As those first three covered substantially the same territory, so by analogy should the fourth. On this theory it does.——But every point of this analogy forbids us to think of Rome Pagan as the fourth beast, and much more, of Rome Papal as the little horn.

III. The fourth beast, or rather the little horn, one of its kings, assails the Jewish religion and aims to subvert it. This must be the sense of the passage, "He shall wear out the saints of the Most High and think to change times and laws." The only "times and law" (the Chaldee is singular) known to Daniel and to his first readers, were those of the Jewish ritual service. This language must therefore refer to Judaism. "The saints of the Most High," so sorely pressed and exhausted by this king, must have been Jews—in the age before Christ. All just principles of interpretation compel us to apply this language to an attack on Jews and Judaism while the latter was in force; and forbid us to apply it to Papal Rome. The books of Maccabees constantly use the phrase, "change the law," or "the laws," for the very change which Antiochus sought to bring about.

IV. The more terrible beast is manifestly such mainly because of his hostility against the people of Daniel and their divinely authorized system of worship. This point has been already adduced. In respect to malignity against the Jewish religion, he is diverse from all the other beasts. Especially is this true of the little horn-king. Indeed, this horn is seen first *in* the fourth beast, and subsequently developed out of it, and seen in his own individuality. For *his* sins, the fourth beast is "destroyed and given to the burning flame." On him specially the terrible judgments of God fell.——All this, and specially its obvious relations to Judaism, utterly fail of application to Papal Rome. Applied to Antiochus Epiphanes, it is precisely his history—as will erelong be more fully shown.

V. The application of the "terminus ad quem" is decisive. The limit below which none of these beasts or their horns can be found, is the ascension of Christ and his inauguration as king. All the special, definite points embraced in this vision, not only all that relate to the first three beasts, but also all that relate to the fourth and to his horns, must precede this giving of the kingdom to Christ and to his people. No part of this vision comes after that "giving," except the general facts of the eternal duration and universal sway of this kingdom. Of the details given in the vision, no other occurs subsequent to the ascension of Christ.——It is, therefore, simply impossible that the Roman theory can be true. It is under the sternest demands of the laws of interpretation that the fourth beast represents the dominion of Alexander's successors, and the little horn, Antiochus Epiphanes.

VI. There are yet other arguments of no small weight. The two remaining visions—that of chap. 8 and that of chaps. 10–12—are yet to be considered. In its place I intend to examine carefully the indications that they are parallel to this, and therefore confirm the interpretation given of this. Each of those visions gives a much more full account than this of the vital point—the little horn-power. We shall find on examination that every feature given of the little horn here is found there, only in general more fully expanded and with additional but never with conflicting points. Nothing beyond this can be reasonably asked to prove identity. But this argument need not be anticipated further in this place.

VII. It is altogether in favor of this Antiochean theory that it requires no violation of the laws of prophetic language in respect to notations of time. The "time, times, and dividing of time," 1 simply make three and a half years, following Daniel's own use of these words in chap. 4: 16, 23, 25, 32. How fitly this applies to Antiochus Epiphanes, desecrating the sanctuary and holding it desolate three and a half years, will be shown in its place. In its place also I shall call special attention to the baseless theory that in prophecy all notations of time must be multiplied by three hundred and sixty to get actual time. See Appendix A.

VIII. This theory adequately meets the demands of history. Its complete fulfillment, proven without violence to the laws of interpretation on the one hand, or to the facts of history on the other, closes the argument in its support.——Legitimately the argument from historic fulfillment should always come last in order. The full sense of the prophecy should be obtained from other sources than conjectural hypothetic fulfillment. This done, a facile, natural fulfillment comes in to close the argument and place it beyond controversy or doubt. The capital vice in many interpretations of these prophecies has lain in the violation of this rule. Some foregone theory of fulfillment has superseded all other laws of interpretation, and has been allowed to shape and fix the sense of words and phrases, often in palpable violation of the laws of Hebrew speech—not to say, of all speech. Hence an untold amount of caprice, speculation, and palpable violation of very obvious laws of language.——But to our point.——1. Fulfillment verifies the interpretation given above of the first three beasts. The Chaldean kingdom under Nebuchadnezzar was, among the nations of the East, a lion with eagle's wings. Under Belshazzar, his wings were plucked, his courage gone; he had no longer the power to stand before a fierce northern bear. This is history.——The Medo-Persian power followed immediately, pushing its conquests westward and southward, "devouring much flesh," supplanting and succeeding the Chaldean empire, and especially, coming into the same close political relations to the Jews, and sustaining them during the period B. C. 538–337. This too is history.——The Grecian empire of Alexander comes next, swiftly subverting the Medo-Persian, and becoming during its short continuance the protector of the Jews. So far history simply translates the obvious sense of these prophetic symbols.——2. With equal facility, on the same principles, in the same line of thought and course of analogy, history verifies the interpretation above given of the fourth beast. He represents the powers that immediately followed Alexander and lay contiguous to the Jews, standing toward them in close political relations.——Out of the cleft empire of Alexander the Great arose two kingdoms, Egypt on the south, and Syria on the north of Palestine, between whom the Jews alternated in their allegiance, greatly dependent for their political welfare upon their relations of peace or war with these adjacent powers. Of these two, the Syrian, founded by Seleucus Nicator B. C. 312, was the stronger and by far the more terrible to the Jews. It is this kingdom that mainly constitutes the fourth beast and fills out the prophetic description. The kingdom of Egypt is quite subordinate; yet because of its close political relations to the Jews, but yet more, because it certainly appears in the more full predictions in chap. 11, it can not be altogether excluded. Both were fragments of the great empire of Alexander; both were among his successors; both were Grecian in language, customs and general character. Each in turn were in close relations of alliance and of protection or oppression as to the Jews. The Syrians had long wars with them.——These points substantially constitute the conditions of the prophecy to which the facts of history should and do correspond.——The Syrian kingdom was great, and terrible, relatively to the Jews; and not only so, it was great absolutely, and its founder was a great conqueror and a terrible scourge upon the nations of the East. From the testimony of Justin, Arrian, and Appian, it appears that he was called "Nicator" (the conqueror) on account of his gaining so many great victories; that he obtained the most extensive dominion and became the greatest king after Alexander; and that he ruled over all Western Asia from the Hellespont to India—those very countries which for nearly three hundred years had been the seat of empire for the three great prophetic dynasties before him.——Further, Daniel himself recognizes his greatness, using the very same language of his dominion as of Alexander's. The latter "shall rule with great dominion" (chap. 11: 3). Of the former, Seleucus Nicator, he says (chap. 11: 5), "His dominion shall be a great dominion."——The era of the Seleucidæ dates from the beginning of his reign B. C. 312, or as some nations held it, B. C. 311.——These two kingdoms, and especially the Syrian, fill the right place for the fourth beast, territorially, politically, chronologically, and in the line of special relations to the Jews. They come in immediately after Alexander and pass away before the Son of man receives his everlasting kingdom.——So much for the fourth beast.——But what of the ten horns?——It is remarkable that very many interpreters seem to have had no guide in searching for the horns of this fourth beast save mere conjecture. The process has been *tentative*—to go forth into the broad field of history, and find somewhere ten kings or ten kingdoms that seem to cluster easily together, and conscript them into service to do duty on this beast of Daniel. Probably a score of different expositions could be found among those who adopt the Roman theory, who (by the way) universally make the horns kingdoms, not kings, and European kingdoms at that (utterly at variance with God's own interpretation), some of them counting off their ten kingdoms in the fifth century; some finding other ten in the sixth; and some yet another ten at some point along the middle ages, etc. Scarcely any two commentators fix upon the same set.—— Another score could probably be found of those who adopt the Grecian theory, who usually look for kings, not kingdoms—in so far, following, and not disregarding the divine interpreter. Some assume that they were contemporary, and look for them among the rival claimants for the throne and dominion of Alexander the Great; others think them consecutive, and look for them in the Syrian line only, down to Antiochus Epiphanes; others select out of the two kingdoms, Egypt and Syria, the number of ten who bore the most intimate relations to the Jews. It would be tedious to recite these lists and could not be very profitable.——In view of them all, I have it to say, that if there were no better clew, I should adopt the one last named as being most in harmony with the scope of the vision; viz., select ten consecutive kings, falling between the death of Alexander and the rise of Antiochus Epiphanes who came most into contact with the Jews, and who most fully represented the relationship of the Jewish nation to foreign powers.——But there is no occasion to throw ourselves upon conjecture at all. There is no occasion even to do the next best thing—take the clew just referred to and trace out those kings of Egypt or Syria whose agency was most vital for good or evil to the fortunes of the Jews. For the selection is substantially made ready to our hand in Daniel's last vision. There, dropping all figure and symbol, he gives us the very kings themselves. So clear is this description that the great body of commentators have followed the same track of interpretation and name these kings as they occur (chap. 11: 5–27) in precisely the same way. The wonder is that with so much agreement in respect to these kings, no commentator within my knowledge seems to have counted them or to have noticed that the kings of any prominence in this narrative prophecy are ten. But such is the fact.——In this prophecy (chap. 11,) which bears from beginning to end the appearance of being explanatory of the visions in chap. 7 and 8, these ten kings lie in their order, filling precisely the interval between the death of Alexander and the rise of the little horn, Antiochus Epiphanes. How then can we doubt that these are the ten kings (horns) of this fourth beast? They come to us named and defined on the highest possible authority—that of the revealing Spirit himself. Let us accept them and so end the long controversy, and invite to harmony and peace the immensely diversified opinions of those who have sought to find these ten horns.—— When I come to treat of chap. 11, it will be more in place to give the history of these kings with some detail. Suffice it here to say that five of them are kings of the south, in the Greco-Egyptian dynasty, viz., Ptolemy Lagus in v. 5; Ptolemy Philadelphus in v. 6; Ptolemy Euergetes in vs. 7-9: Ptolemy Philopater in vs. 11, 12, and Ptolemy Philometer in vs. 25-27.——Five of them are kings of the north, in the Greek-Syrian dynasty; viz., Seleucus Nicator in v. 5; Antiochus Theos in v. 6; Seleucus Callinicus in vs. 7, 8; Antiochus the Great, vs. 10-19; and Seleucus Philopator in v. 20. This brings us in the line of chap. 11, to Antiochus Epiphanes, the little horn-king, making a perfect correspondence in respect to all the vital points of the case between this vision of chap. 7 and that of chap. 11. But this parallelism will be more fully brought out when chap. 11 shall come under consideration in its order. Suffice it to say here that these parallel prophecies of Daniel mutually sustain each other, a fact which will become more abundantly manifest hereafter.——Moreover, as we proceed in developing this theory of interpretation, every point is amply confirmed by the historic facts. These ten kings sustained specially important relations to the Jews. It was because of these relations that they find a place in the eleventh chapter.——As to the number of these kings comprised in both the Egyptian and Syrian kingdoms, from their foundation down to Antiochus Epiphanes, the question will arise, Does the prophecy (Dan. 11: 5-27) touch them all, and were there actually but ten?——To this I answer: From the full list of those two dynasties during the period specified, I omit one Egyptian king, Ptolemy Epiphanes, put upon the throne at the age of five years, and never any thing but a tool for others to use; and two Syrian kings; one, the second in the series, Antiochus Soter, he being intentionally passed over in the prophecy which leaps a chasm of at least thirty-two years by saying (chap. 11: 6) "In the end of years," etc. Here and thus the sketch passes unnoticed the entire reign of Anti. Soter. I therefore omit him. The other Syrian king omitted reigned but two years (Seleucus Ceraunus), and did nothing to entitle him to notice in this prophecy. With these exceptions, the list of ten, as above named, includes not only all that are spoken of in this prophetic sketch, but all that appear in the full tables of those kings. Such omissions as these justify themselves. The prophetic sketch touches only those whose exploits were worthy of notice. These are ten in number. Yet it may well be said that ten is often a round number; so that if there had been in fact either nine or eleven, it should create no difficulty if the number had been spoken of as ten.——The little horn is Antiochus Epiphanes. We shall see much more of him in chap. 8 and chap. 11, and his history will be given more fully there. It may properly be said here, in anticipation of its proof, that with one exception every several feature of his character, exploits, and destiny, given here in chap. 7, is brought out and consequently confirmed in the description given of him in chap. 8, and again yet more in chap. 11. The points made here are expanded there, and some new points added, but nothing is diverse; not a line, not a shade of coloring appears there that does not fit perfectly to the outline first drawn here in chap. 7. So that the fact of parallelism will appear with such a sort, variety, and amount of evidence as constitute complete demonstration.——Let it also be said here (to be shown more fully hereafter) that history confirms all these points of his character, exploits, and destiny. He was a most bitter persecutor and deadly foe of the Jewish nation; he did assail their religion with the fell purpose of uprooting it from the earth; he did speak both blasphemously and proudly against Almighty God. He knew he was fighting against the God of Israel, and when at last he fell, the stings of remorse in his awakened conscience bore their testimony that God had conquered and that his own malign purposes were utterly blasted. The special unfolding of these facts of his history should naturally be reserved till we come to the more full prophetic detail in chaps. 8 and 11.——A few points however may be as well presented here.——(1.) *Three of the first horns removed before the little horn.*——In his first account of the vision Daniel said (v. 8), "I considered the horns and behold there came up among them a little horn before whom there were three of the first horns plucked up by the roots." Daniel inquired particularly respecting this feature, "of the other that come up and before whom three fell" (v. 20). The interpretation states (v. 24), "and he shall subdue three kings." He does not say in the most precise language, three of *those ten* kings; yet this is the more obvious meaning, and is required by the language of the vision, "Three of the first horns were plucked up." The original word rendered "subdue," means to humble, to bring down.——This is the point which I excepted from the general statement that all the points made of the little horn in chap. 7, appear also in chaps. 8 and 11. This point is not in chap. 8. It does appear, however, in a very peculiar way in chap. 11.——This vision (chap. 7) obviously means that three of the first horns were in some special manner put out of the way of this little horn. Only the last statement, "he shall subdue," etc., necessarily involves any active agency of the *little* horn in their removal.——Who are these three kings? Do they appear in history and in such a way as to verify this minute statement?——On this question commentators have differed widely—a natural result of their differing so widely over the ten horns.——As above explained, I find these ten horns precisely in chap. 11: 5–27. The little horn also is there, his history filling twenty-five verses, viz., vs. 21–45. But of the three kings that he "subdued;" that "were plucked up," or that "fell before him," the history of only one is given here so fully and specifically as to show that this "vile king," alias the little horn, had an active agency in subduing him. This one is Ptolemy Philometor of Egypt (vs. 25–27) of whom this passage, after giving the history of their conflicts and wars, says, "he shall not stand" (*i. e.*, he shall fall) before Antiochus. This very brief historic prophecy does speak, however, of the death of two others as being somewhat peculiar and remarkable. Of Antiochus the Great, it records, "he shall stumble and fall and shall not be found." This king was the father of Antiochus Epiphanes. Of the next, his brother Seleucus Philopator, "a raiser of taxes," and his immediate predecessor on the throne, the record says; "But within a few days he shall be destroyed, neither in anger nor in battle." But in neither of these cases is it said that Antiochus Epiphanes was in any way the cause of his death. Still the fact that the manner of their death is hinted at in this somewhat enigmatic way, taken in connection with the prophecy that before this *little* horn three of the first horns should be plucked up by the roots," and "should fall," is surely very noticeable.——Does profane history give any hint that Antiochus Epiphanes was concerned in the death of either Antiochus the Great, his father, or of Seleucus Philopator, his brother?——It is stated in Poole's Synopsis that Antiochus the Great came to his death in a drunken frolic, under these circumstances: In a state of intoxication, he had abused certain persons and thereby incurred their ill-will. His son, this Antiochus Epiphanes, took advantage of their exasperated feelings and instigated them to mob and murder his own father! One ancient author, Aurelius Victor, states that he died in this way. On the other hand Strabo and Justin concur in stating that he fell in an attempt to pillage a rich temple of Belus in Elymais. The weight of historic evidence is for this view.—— Of his brother, Seleucus Philopator, Grotius states that he was slain by Antiochus Epiphanes or by his order. It is said this vile king caused him to be poisoned. Livy and Appian, however, attribute his murder by poison to Heliodorus, who seems to have aspired to the throne for himself.——The weight of historical evidence seems to exonerate Antiochus Epiphanes from direct participation in the death of either his father or his elder brother. Yet this evidence is somewhat conflicting, and perhaps can not be regarded as decisive. Antiochus was artful enough to keep his active hand out of sight. He was wicked enough for the most unnatural crimes, provided only that they promised to favor his ambitious schemes. The fact that he is called (chap. 11: 21) "a vile person," in such close proximity with the extraordinary deaths of the two kings next before him on the Syrian throne, may be significant.——Finally, the form of the statement—three distinct horns "*plucked up* before him"— makes room for some diversity in the manner of the thing and particularly in the personal agency of the little horn in it. Indeed the diverse statements in the prophecy (chap. 7.) favor some diversity in the historic facts as to an active agency of the little horn. "Plucked up;" "fall;" are intransitive or passive: "to subdue," in the sense, to *humble*, is active. All these varieties find their adequate fulfillment in the diversity of these three cases brought before us in chap. 11. The two kings next preceding in the Syrian line were certainly "plucked up," did certainly "fall," before him. The one king in the Egyptian line he did certainly humble and "subdue."——These three, therefore, I must account as the three horns referred to in chap. 7: 8, 20, 24.——(2.) "He thought to change times and laws." The legitimate sense of these words, as written by a Jew and for Jewish readers, can be nothing else than changing the religious institutions given by God through Moses. Every writer should be presumed to use language in the sense in which his readers must understand it. Prophecy is no exception to this rule. The prophets wrote in order to be understood. If, to refute this, it be said that Daniel as a prophet might look far down into the Christian age and see another system of religious "times and laws," the legitimate answer is that his readers were not prophets even though he was; and he certainly wrote for their reading and to their understanding.——Let us now notice the historic fulfillment of this clause. On this point the books of the Maccabees are the best of testimony. The first book witnesseth thus; "Moreover king Antiochus wrote to his whole kingdom that all should be one people, and every one should leave his laws; so all the heathen agreed according to the commandment of the king. Yea, many also of the Israelites consented to his religion, and sacrificed unto idols, and profaned the sabbath. For the king had sent letters by messengers unto Jerusalem and the cities of Judah, that they should follow the strange laws of the land, and forbid burnt-offerings and sacrifices and drink-offerings in the temple, and that they should profane the sabbaths and festival days; and pollute the sanctuary and holy people; set up altars and groves, and chapels of idols, and sacrifice swine's flesh and unclean beasts; that they should also leave their children uncircumcised, and make their souls abominable with all manner of uncleanness and profanation; *to the end they might forget the law and change all the ordinances.* And whosoever would not do according to the commandment of the king, he said, he should die. (chap. 1: 41-50.) "Now the fifteenth day of the month Casleu, in the hundred and forty-fifth year, they set up the abomination of desolation upon the altar, and builded idol-altars throughout the cities of Judah on every side" (v. 34).——The author of the second book of Maccabees makes his statements thus: "Not long after this the king sent an old man of Athens to compel the Jews to depart from the laws of their fathers, and not to live after the laws of God, and also to pollute the temple in Jerusalem and to call it the temple of Jupiter Olympius..... The coming in of this mischief was sore and grievous to the people; for the temple was filled with riot and reveling by the Gentiles, who dallied with harlots and had to do with women within the circuit of the holy places, and besides that, brought in things that were not lawful. The altar also was filled with profane things which the law forbiddeth. Neither was it lawful for a man to keep sabbath days or ancient feasts, or to profess himself at all to be a Jew. And in the day of the king's birth, every month they were brought by bitter constraint to eat of the sacrifices; and when the feast of Bacchus was kept, the Jews were compelled to go in procession to Bacchus, carrying ivy" (2 Mac. 6: 1–7).——These extracts from Jewish historians, writing not long after the events, testify amply both to the fact and to the intent. They also show that the language of Daniel, "change times and laws," is perfectly *Jewish*, and indeed could not be understood by them to mean any thing else than subverting the Mosaic ritual service.——(3.) "They shall be given into his hand until a time, times, and dividing of time."——Do the facts of history verify this on the interpretation above given? They do most fully.—— First, of the precise·sense of this clause. The proper antecedent of "they," representing who or what shall be given into his hand, is "times and laws." Hence the meaning must be that he will have power to subvert the Mosaic rites of worship, or at least suspend their observance, during the period specified. Or, if it be still insisted that "they" refers to the saints, yet the sense must be that they are given into his hand to this special extent and result, viz., that he may suspend their "times and laws"—the same ultimate significance as before. Consequently the period hereby limited in time with its contained events, is just that during which the little horn-king was allowed of God·to suspend the ritual services of the Jewish worship. The passage does not say how long the little horn shall live, nor how long he should make war upon the saints, nor does it put any thing else into this limitation of time except this one thing—how long he shall be able to prevent the normal action of those Jewish "times and laws."——The facts of history on this point are derived originally from Josephus and from the two books of Maccabees. Of the latter, the first book has the reputation of being very exact and reliable history. The second moralizes more and confines itself less closely to history; yet is regarded as in the main reliable. Josephus may be presumed to give us the traditions of his countrymen as current in his day (A. D. 75–100). His Jewish war was published about A. D. 75; his Antiquities, A. D. 93.—— On the historic period now before us, Josephus states (Proem to his Jewish War, sec. 7) that "Antiochus called Epiphanes seized Jerusalem and held it three years and six months." In the same work (1: 1: 1.) of the same Epiphanes; "He caused the customary daily sacrifice to cease three years and six months." But in his Antiquities (XII: 7: 6) he computes only three years, saying, "The temple, desolated by.Antiochus, continued in this state three years." These statements constitute precisely his testimony.

The testimony of the first book of Maccabees is entirely explicit as to the point when the sanctuary was cleansed. It was on the twenty-fifth day of the ninth month, *i. e.*, Casleu, which was the one hundred and forty-eighth year of the era of the Seleucidæ. (See 1 Mac. 4: 52.) As this era usually counts from B. C. 312, the one hundred and forty-eighth year would be B. C. 164.—— The point of commencing in these several statements is various. This first book states (chap. 1: 54) that, on the fifteenth day of the month Casleu, in the one hundred and forty-fifth year (B. C. 167), they set up the abomination of desolation upon the altar and builded idol altars throughout the cities of Judah on every side." This gives an interval, down to the cleansing of the sanctuary, of three years and ten days. In the same connection (v. 59), he says; "On the twenty-fifth day of the month they sacrificed upon the idol-altar which was upon the altar of God."——The author of the second book of Maccabees is unfortunately sparing of dates. On the point now in hand, he only says (chap. 10: 5); "Now upon the same day that the strangers profaned the temple, on the very same day it was cleansed again, even the twenty-fifth day of the same month which is Casleu."——These statements, though unlike, are yet not seriously conflicting. Observe that while in all cases the period they limit terminates at the same point, viz., the cleansing of the sanctuary, yet it does not profess to begin at the same. Thus the first book of Maccabees gives us first the day when they set up the abomination upon the sacred altar, viz., the fifteenth day of Casleu; and next the day when they offered their first idol sacrifices upon it which was ten days after, on the twenty-fifth of Casleu.——Josephus gives us in one passage the period during which Antiochus held Jerusalem by military force at three and a half years. Next, he makes the time during which he caused the daily sacrifice to cease three and a half years. In still another passage he says that the temple lay desolated three years. The somewhat full history in the first chapter of first Maccabees shows that the whole work of subduing the Jewish force, getting possession of the temple, desecrating the holy altar, setting up another for idol-offerings, and getting in readiness to commence idol-worship, occupied no little time—not improbably six months. The entire period, therefore, will be estimated variously according as the writer may commence at an earlier or a later point, to take in more or less of the preliminary steps.—— The reader will notice that the form of statement before us (in chap. 7: 25, and with this also chap. 12: 7) should naturally be the longer rather than the shorter period—the entire duration of this horn's ascendant power over the city and the holy people, to prevent their customary temple-worship, rather than the shorter term in which idol sacrifices were offered in the temple.——This seems to me to be a fair and rational solution of this slight apparent discrepancy. The marvel is not that the history should seem to fail in the point of accurate dates; but that in periods so short and at a time so remote, it should be possible to obtain so much accuracy.——(4.) Another prominent point in respect to this little horn-king is his *destruction*.——As already suggested, vs. 11, 12, plainly intimate that, being for the time the representative and embodiment of the fourth beast, he falls by some striking form of judgment. V. 26 certainly refers primarily to this king, and implies also a special judgment from God upon him—beyond question the same which is described vs. 9–11.——Correspondingly, chap. 8: 25, says; though "he shall stand up against the Prince of princes" (in his pride and rage) "yet he shall be broken without hand." (For this last expression, "broken without hand," compare Job 34: 20, "The mighty shall be taken away without hand.") By no human arm, but by one invisible and divine, he shall be utterly broken. ——So chap. 11: 45; "Though he shall plant his palace-like tents between the great Sea" (the Mediterranean) "and the glorious holy mountain, yet he shall come to his end, and none shall help him;" *i. e.*, though he gained possession of Mt. Zion and held it as his fortress for several years, exceedingly afflicting the people of God and long time desecrating his sanctuary, yet he shall come down wonderfully, and "there shall be none to help him."—— Such are the statements of Daniel's prophecy respecting the death of this king.——What are the facts of history?——The original witnesses are mainly the first and second books of Maccabees. The first book gives a clear, calm, orderly and trustworthy statement, thus; "About that time King Antiochus, traveling through the high countries, heard say that Elymais in the country of Persia was a city greatly renowned for riches, silver and gold; and that there was in it a very rich temple, wherein were coverings of gold and breast-plates and shields, which Alexander, son of Philip the Macedonian king, who reigned first among the Grecians, had left there. Wherefore he came and sought to take the city and to spoil it; but he was not able, because they of the city, having had warning thereof, rose up against him in battle; so he fled, and departed thence in great heaviness and returned to Babylon. Moreover there came one who brought him tidings into Persia, that the armies, which went against the land of Judea, were put to flight; and that Lysias who went forth first with a great force was driven away of the Jews, and that they were made strong by the armor and power and store of spoils which they had gotten of the armies whom they had destroyed; also that they had pulled down the abomination which he had set up upon the altar in Jerusalem, and that they had compassed about the sanctuary with high walls as before. Now when the king heard these words, he was astonished and sore moved; whereupon he laid himself down upon his bed and fell sick for grief because it had not befallen him as he looked for. And there he continued many days; for his grief was ever more and more, and he made account that he should die. Wherefore he called for all his friends and said unto them, 'The sleep is gone from mine eyes and my heart faileth for very care. And I thought with myself into what tribulation am I come, and how great a flood of misery is it wherein I now am! for I was bountiful and beloved in my power. But now I remember the evils that I did at Jerusalem, and that I took all the vessels of gold and silver that were therein, and sent to destroy the inhabitants of Judea without a cause. I perceive therefore that for this cause these troubles are come upon me, and behold, I perish through great grief in a strange land.' .... So King Antiochus died there in the hundred and forty-ninth year." (1 Mac. 6: 1-13, 16.)—— In the second book this narrative fills the ninth chapter, expanding and commenting somewhat freely, and making the invisible hand of God very prominent among the causes of his awful death. The outline of historic circumstances is much the same as in the first book. Antiochus goes to a remote city of Persia to pillage a very rich temple; is driven off by the people; on his way back, he hears that his armies in Judea are defeated and the Jews enriched by their spoil. Enraged to fury "he commands his charioteer to drive without ceasing and to despatch the journey, the judgments of God now following him. For he had spoken proudly in this sort that he would come to Jerusalem and make it the common burying-place of the Jews. But the Lord Almighty, the God of Israel, smote him with an invisible and incurable plague, for as soon as he had spoken these words, a pain of the bowels that was remediless came upon him, and sore torments of the inner parts; and that most justly; for he had tormented other men's bowels with many and strange torments. Howbeit he nothing at all ceased from his bragging, but still was filled with pride, breathing out fire in his rage against the Jews, and commanding to haste the journey; but it came to pass that he fell down from his chariot, carried violently, so that having a sore fall, all the members of his body were much pained. And thus he that a little afore thought he might command the waves of the sea (so proud was he beyond the condition of man) and weigh the high mountains in a balance, was now cast on the ground, and carried in a horse-litter, showing forth unto all the manifest power of God. So that the worms rose up out of the body of this wicked man, and while he lived in sorrow and pain, his flesh fell away, and the filthiness of his smell was noisome to all his army." In short, convicted of his great guilt, stung with remorse, appalled with fear of the Almighty hand, he makes vows and promises to God, even to beautify the temple he had despoiled, defray the cost of its sacrifices, and become himself a Jew and go through all the world declaring the power of God; "but for all this his pains would not cease, for the just judgment of God was come upon him." . . . "Thus this murderer and blasphemer, having suffered most grievously, as he had treated other men, so died he a miserable death in a strange country in the mountains."——It is perhaps impossible to say whether this account may not be somewhat exaggerated; yet there can be no reasonable doubt that in its main features it is correct. Assuming this, the death of this impious blasphemer classes itself with that of the Herod who murdered the elder James, and witnesses to the fearfulness of those special judgments from the Almighty which are designed to stand as his testimony and warning to those who set at naught his power and defy his vengeance.——Thus this point of the prophetic description of the little horn as Antiochus Epiphanes is amply verified by the historic facts.

At the cost of a little repetition, I proceed now to give a brief summary of the grounds on which I am compelled to reject the Roman theory in this seventh chapter.——In general my plan of commentary mostly excludes the presentation of opinions from which I dissent. But the very extensive prevalence of this Roman theory induces me to deviate in this case from my general plan. ——Briefly then, I must reject the theory which makes the fourth beast Rome Pagan; the ten horns, some ten European kingdoms; and the little horn Rome Papal,——1. Because it is out of analogy with the preceding beasts, this fourth considered as Rome, not being in any proper sense, the successor to the other three; not located in the same part of the world; not composed mainly of the same populations; not following in the same closely consecutive order of time, but involving a huge chasm—for Pagan Rome, of four hundred years, and for Papal Rome as a great persecuting power near six hundred more: and finally not standing in the same political relations to the Jews, while yet they are the recognized people of God.——2. It disregards the relation of these visions to Daniel's own people and to his special circumstances as their patron, protector and father.——3. It overlooks the manifest indications that the great conflict, the "war with the saints of the Most High," is between this little horn and the Jews while they are yet the people of God and while the Mosaic system is yet standing.——4. Both the vision and its explanation assume that the fourth beast and its little horn are in some vital respects a unit, or at least stand in the closest connection with each other; but the Roman theory makes them utterly unlike—alike in nothing indeed but the name Roman. The one is a Pagan, political empire; the other is a nominal church, and moreover far removed from each other in time. ——5. Inasmuch as v. 11 shows that the fourth beast is destroyed because of the sins of the little horn, this theory carries with it the absurdity of destroying Pagan Rome for the sins of Papal Rome—sins committed by an entirely different set of sinners, and several hundred years *after* the punishment had been inflicted and the sufferers destroyed! That is, because Papal Rome *will* drink the blood of saints and martyrs in the fourteenth and fifteenth centuries, therefore let Pagan Rome be destroyed in the fourth and fifth!——Of course neither of these parties are known in this vision save as persecuting powers. This fact must guide us as to dates and durations.——6. The Roman theory is absolutely set aside and rendered impossible by the "terminus ad quem" of the fourth beast and all his horns; i. e., by the fact that this kingdom and all its kings are destroyed before the Messiah's first advent.——7. It is also set aside by the scope and significance of the undeniably parallel visions of chap. 8 and of chap. 11. This will be shown more fully in its place.——8. It must be rejected because it conflicts with the inspired explanation of the symbol of the horn. This inspired explanation (v. 24) makes the ten horns ten *kings*, and the little horn also a king. Any system of interpretation *must be false* which disregards and overrides God's own interpretation, especially in a point so fundamental as this.——The proper significance of a horn as a symbol might be elaborated in the light of its natural relations. It might be urged that a horn is nothing apart from the beast that wears it; that it is the beast's own instrument of power, just as the king is the executive force of his kingdom; that in every point of view the natural significance of the horn on a beast is a king in his kingdom. But, waving this form of argument, I now put the case simply on the positive interpretation of God himself, and insist that this ought to be respected.——9. In reference to the little horn, the Roman theory must be rejected because it departs yet more widely from the inspired interpretation inasmuch as it makes the little horn not even a *kingdom* in the sense of this vision, but a great religious organization—a nominal church.——In view of the manifest drift and scope of this vision, this interpretation of the little horn must be pronounced pure caprice, having no support whatever in the vision itself.——10. It involves the inconsistency of making ten of these horns political kingdoms, and the eleventh a great nominal church.——11. Finally, it must be rejected because it requires for its support the utterly baseless theory of prophetic times which multiplies them by three hundred and sixty to get actual time. See this theory examined in the Appendix, Dissertation A. It is hoped these reasons for rejecting the Roman theory will be deemed satisfactory and sufficient.

It is still due to the advocates of the Roman theory to take respectful notice of the grounds on which mainly their theory is supported and the opposite one assailed. These are:

1. That on the theory I have presented, there is a want of unity in the fourth beast and hence a want of natural analogy with the three preceding beasts.——On the contrary, I have urged and labored to show that in reference to the main drift and purpose of these visions, there is a high degree of unity in the fourth beast and all his horns; that the vision and interpretation both conspire to demand far more unity between the fourth beast and the little horn than the Roman theory can possibly admit, and just such as the Grecian theory affords; and that in view of the real purport of these visions, there is (as above presented) a close and abundant analogy between the first three beasts and the fourth.——Moreover those who make great account of the precise fitting of symbol to historic fact may well take note that in the vision of the great image, as the two arms happen to fit the double kingdom of the Medes and Persians, so the two legs equally fit the two-fold Grecian kingdom—Egyptian and Syrian, and that the ten toes are found as ten kings, five in one of these two kingdoms and five in the other.

2. It is urged that Rome is really the fourth universal kingdom, and therefore must be the fourth beast.——But here every thing turns on the question whether Daniel is giving to the world universal history in general, and this from a stand-point that has no special reference to the Jews; or whether he gives profane history only because it connects itself with the fortunes of his own people, the Jews, and only so far as it so connects itself.——I take the latter view most decidedly. I find it sustained by all the circumstances of Daniel's public life; by numerous indications throughout his entire book as well as throughout these four parallel visions; and by the analogy of all the other prophets—not to say of all the

rest of the Bible.——The former view I regard as utterly untenable, and as the fundamental mistake underlying the failures so often made in the interpretation of Daniel. If Daniel wrote universal history down to the millennium, why does he not give us America also as well as Europe?——In my view Daniel, like every other prophet, had a present moral object in reference to his first readers—the people among whom and for whom he wrote. Of course he wrote to be understood; he wrote what they could understand; and therefore he did not write about European kingdoms, and the American republic in particular. Certainly he said nothing which his readers would naturally apply to these countries and powers. He must needs have used far other language to give his readers any just views of the ten European kingdoms of the Roman theory, or of the American republic. The doctrine that prophecy was not intended to be understood until very near or after its fulfillment is radically fallacious.——Further, Daniel prophesied nothing about the kingdoms of Europe or the governments of America, because his people, prior to their rejection as the people of God, sustained no relation to these powers, and had no interest in these matters. Worldly kingdoms therefore are seen to be great and formidable in Daniel's eye chiefly by virtue of their relations to his people, and not because of their relations to each other or to universal history.

3. It is felt that the description given of the little horn fits Papal Rome too well to be set aside, and so well that it must be true.—— I answer;——(1.) Fitness, however much, does not settle the question. Prophecy must not be interpreted to mean every thing or any thing it may chance to fit and only because it fits. Suppose God himself has explained it to mean something else; or has given limits of time within which the fulfillment must fall, and which absolutely preclude its reference to those things which it fits so well! As already said, one of the worst mistakes made in the interpretation of prophecy is the exclusive use of the criterion of supposed fulfillment.——(2.) Papal Rome is bad enough doubtless; I shall not seek to lessen the testimony of history to her crimes or to her depravity. But this delineation in Daniel was not made for her. *This* persecuting power lived and perished before the first advent of Christ; vented its rage upon the Jews and upon their ritual service, not on Christians in the middle ages; and was limited in the duration of its special power over the saints and their worship to three and a half years. These and kindred points put the finger of this prophecy upon Antiochus Epiphanes, and forbid its reference, in its primary and proper sense, to Papal Rome. If any choose to say that whatever God teaches of the doom of one great Antichrist applies to every other Antichrist, very well. It applies by parity of reason, not as written and primarily meant for any other but the one who sat for the picture. Such a portraiture has its solemn lessons for every self-hardened sinner.——(3.) The warmth of our interest in finding some prophecy that denounces and dooms Papal Rome should never be allowed to prejudice our

interpretation of God's word. Truth loses every thing and gains nothing by prejudiced interpretations.

4. It is urged that the setting up of the Messiah's kingdom and giving it to the saints, must refer to the millennial times yet future. Hence fitly it follows the fall of the great Roman Antichrist.——I reply;——(1.) No special distinction can be made in this prophecy between setting up Christ's kingdom and giving it to his saints. They are thought of as simultaneous and essentially the same.——(2.) The time of this setting up is fixed, as shown above, to the ascension of Christ.——(3.) Millennial times are here in the course of Christ's indefinitely long reign—in the remote, but not in the nearer future. No specific date for Christ's Millennial triumphs can be found here. Of course no special light is thrown by this prophecy on the doings or the doom of Papal Rome.

5. It is claimed that the first vision (chap. 2: 44) dates the setting up of Christ's kingdom in the latter times of the great European kingdoms denoted by the ten horns. "In the days of these kings shall the God of heaven set up a kingdom," etc.——To this I answer;——(1.) The ten horns can not be any ten European kingdoms, for God has said they are ten *kings*, and implies that he destroyed them all before Christ's first coming.——(2.) The passage "In the days of these kings shall the God of heaven set up a kingdom," etc., (chap. 2: 44,) is general, and can not fix any dates in opposition to the much more full and specific statements of chap. 7.——(3.) The scope of the vision (chap. 2: 31–45) requires that the stone (Jesus Christ) should smite and destroy all those heathen powers, including those meant by the feet and toes, *before* he himself or his kingdom becomes the great mountain and fills all the earth. It is therefore only in the general sense of the preparatory work wrought by the agencies of divine providence that the Messiah's kingdom is set up while yet those kings are living. But see the notes on chap. 2: 44.

6. Finally, it is felt that these prophecies lose most of their practical interest and value if they do not predict the fall of the great Roman Antichrist and do not give the precise date of the millennium.——I reply; If this were true, it is a calamity that can not be helped. For, we must not, for the sake of greater interest, put an interpretation on prophecy which is not true, and is not sustained by sound, legitimate principles of interpretation. It is our business to find, not make, the sense of prophecy. And it is no part of our responsibility to interpret so as to get the greatest amount of *interest* or sensation out of it.——As to profit, God knows best what will be profitable. Perhaps he thinks it best *not* to give us precisely the date of the millennium, nor the date of Christ's second coming, nor the date of the fall of Papal Rome. It may be best in his view to leave the Church to do her work under the inspiration and impulse of only general and not specific promises as to the world's conversion, assuring her of his purpose to do it, but not giving her the time when. Would it be strange if this should be found at last to be the course of divine wisdom and of the facts

of prophecy? May it not be really wise to make due account of human free agency, and to shape prophecy so as to bear both kindly and vigorously upon the free minds of men? Has the world had no illustrations of the mischiefs of making dates for Christ's second advent which God never made, and when he never meant to reveal any date for it at all?

CHAPTER VIII.

This chapter comprises one entire vision with its explanation—the third in the series of Daniel's four essentially parallel prophecies. It is naturally divided into three parts, of which the first is purely symbolic—the ram with two horns; the he-goat with his great horn; the four that came up subsequently, and the little one (vs. 1-9.) The second part shades off from the symbol of the horn to the conception of a king, and gives his doings (vs. 9-14). The third comprises the manner of giving the explanation, and the explanation itself (vs. 15-27).——As in chap. 7, so here, I propose first, to comment upon the words and clauses, to educe their exact sense; and then to inquire more fully into the prophetic significance of the little horn—this being the only thing in this vision upon which commentators have disagreed.

1. In the third year of the reign of king Belshazzar a vision appeared unto me, *even unto* me Daniel, after that which appeared unto me at the first.

It is probably safe to assume that the third year of Belshazzar's reign was also his last, or at least very near his last. If so, the date of this vision is B. C. 539 or 538.——The previous vision referred to is that of chap. 7, two years before.

2. And I saw in a vision; (and it came to pass, when I saw, that I *was* at Shushan *in* the palace, which *is* in the province of Elam;) and I saw in a vision, and I was by the river of Ulai.

The clause in parenthesis, beginning "And it came to pass," and ending, "province of Elam," seems to have been designed to show that he was actually at Shushan in the palace of the Persian king when he had this vision. Elam was one of the chief provinces of Persia, embracing Susa, the capital. The Greeks gave this province the name, Elymais. Elam is sometimes used as another name for Persia. The name appears first among the children of Shem (Gen. 10: 22).——It was strictly in vision and only so that Daniel was by the river Ulai; as one in a dream conceives himself to be where he is not. It is only by this distinction between his actual presence and his ideal presence that I account for these two statements; as if Daniel would say, I was really when I had this vision at Shushan in the palace; but when I came to see things in vision, I seemed to be by the river Ulai.——It is noticeable that his personal stand-point is Persia—the point where his historic vision begins. Chaldea is so near extinction that it may well be dropped.——This vision is none the less truly parallel with that of chap. 2 and that of chap. 7, because, being shown him so near the extinction of the Chaldean dynasty, it drops off that as no longer of any account.

3. Then I lifted up mine eyes, and saw, and behold, there stood before the river a ram which had *two* horns: and the *two* horns *were* high; but one *was* higher than the other, and the higher came up last.

4. I saw the ram pushing westward, and northward, and southward; so that no beasts might stand before him, neither *was there any* that could deliver out of his hand; but he did according to his will, and became great.

This ram, according to the interpretation (v. 20) is the Medo-Persian kingdom. His two horns are two kings, one of Media, viz., Darius or Astyages; and one of Persia, viz., Cyrus. These kings, one from Media and the other from Persia, imply the union of these two kingdoms, since the united realm draws its kings from either. The higher of these two horns is Cyrus. He came up last in point of time. These two kings, in a sort, represent the kingdoms from which they severally came.——This ram pushes his conquests west, north, and south, omitting only the east. This is perfectly in accordance with history. This Medo-Persian power made no attempts to push eastward; but did make great conquests in the directions here specified. There was no power able to stand before him; none could pluck his prey from his grasp. Of course he became great.

5. And as I was considering, behold, a he-goat came from the west on the face of the whole earth, and touched not the ground: and the goat *had* a notable horn between his eyes.

No compend of history could draw the outline of Alexander's conquest of Asia better than this prophetic vision has done it. A "rough" personage to deal with as a foe; coming from the west; sweeping the breadth of the whole land; seeming for the rapidity of his movements not to touch the earth, (like the leopard with four wings, chap. 7: 6,) and with one notable horn between his eyes—a horn specially *noticeable* and the prominent feature in this new power;—such is the description, and such was Alexander and his Grecian kingdom. Yet still the decisive evidence of identity is the explicit affirmation of the revealing angel (v. 21), "The rough goat is the king of Grecia, and the great horn is the first king." This is absolute authority.——Note here that Daniel and his readers had nothing to do with Philip of Macedon, a vigorous king next before Alexander; for what were European kings or kingdoms to them? It was only as an oriental empire, coming into special relations to the Jews that Jewish prophecy knew Greece; only as such a monarch that it knew Alexander. Hence he is the *first* Grecian king.

6. And he came to the ram that had *two* horns, which I had seen standing before the river, and ran unto him in the fury of his power.

7. And I saw him come close unto the ram, and he was moved with choler against him, and smote the ram, and brake his two horns: and there was no power in the ram to stand before him, but he cast him down to the ground, and stamped upon him: and there was none that could deliver the ram out of his hand.

Thus with fewest words, but words full of force, Daniel gives in prophetic anticipation the history of the fall of Persia before the arms of Alexander. Profane history verifies every point most perfectly. Greece had long been nursing her revenge for the invasion of her soil by Xerxes. Alexander had the energy and the ambition to lead her vigorous armies to this retaliation. He came against the ram "in the fury of his power." The last vision (11: 2, 3) touches Xerxes and then glances from him to Alexander, as if the spirit of inspiration grasped perfectly the springs of human action which threw Greece upon Asia and made her one of the great conquering powers of the East.——It is well known history that the Medo-Persian armies, now become effeminate through luxury, had no power to stand before Alexander and his Grecian forces. He used up the armed hosts of Persia with amazing rapidity. Twelve years sufficed him to master not Persia alone, but Tyre, Egypt, and all the East, even deeper into India itself than the ancient powers of Western Asia or of Europe ever went before or after.

8. Therefore, the he-goat waxed very great: and when he was strong, the great horn was broken: and for it, came up four notable ones toward the four winds of heaven.

The he-goat became very great in the sweep of his absolute sway over the eastern world; but he had scarcely reached the summit of his power when the great horn was broken. Alexander died suddenly at Babylon. Strong drink (as some say provoking fever to its aid) smote him down. He whom none of the mighty warriors of the East could overcome fell suddenly and basely before the intoxicating cup. In such near proximity came the glory of his greatness and the shame of his fall! "When he was strong, the great horn was broken."——That this great empire was cleft into four parts is a well known fact of history. Thrace and Macedon were the nucleus of the European and Western section; Asia Minor, stretching to the Euxine and the Caspian, lay on the extreme north; Syria, north as to Palestine, pushed its empire to India, and became really the eastern and great Asiatic portion; while Egypt became the center for the southern section. "Toward the four winds of heaven" describes their location.——Of these four the Jews stood in close relations only to Egypt on the south and Syria on the north. Hence the other sections are at once dropped from these visions.——The special exigencies of the symbol require these four kingdoms to appear first as horns, inasmuch as they spring up on account of the breaking of the great horn. Indeed, they *are* at first only kings, but ultimately they secured for themselves kingdoms. Hence they stand in the vision as horns, but in the interpretation as kingdoms. Consequently this case does not disprove the position heretofore taken that the natural sense of the symbol of the horn is a king, and that this must certainly be its sense *when inspiration affirms it to be.*

9. And out of one of them came forth a little horn, which waxed exceeding great, toward the south, and toward the east, and toward the pleasant *land.*

"Out of one of these" means, in the line of one of these kingdoms, viz., Syria. That he rose up as a king in one of these four kingdoms is explicitly affirmed in the inspired interpretation (vs. 22, 23).——He is a "little horn," compared with Alexander who is a "great horn." Hence he should be, like Alexander, a king, and not (as some suppose) a church, or a system of false religion. Moreover, it is also implied that he is called "little" because he was so at the first, and grew to more greatness by dint of personal energy and effort.——Our verse gives the geographical points toward which he pushed his conquests, viz., "toward the south," Egypt; "toward the east," Babylonia and Persia; and "toward the pleasant land," where the original word is one which in Daniel's writings always means Palestine. See chap. 11: 16, 41. Also Ezek. 20: 6, 15. Primarily it means the beauty or the glory, and hence would naturally be used by the Hebrews of their own country, which they accounted the glory of all lands. Such is the historical programme of Antiochus Epiphanes.——The reader will notice how the symbol of a horn shades off at once into the reality of a king; for this description paints, not the growth of a horn as such, but the enlargement of a kingdom by the efforts of its king, pushing his conquests.

10. And it waxed great, *even* to the host of heaven; and it cast down *some* of the host and of the stars to the ground, and stamped upon them.

11. Yea, he magnified *himself* even to the prince of the host, and by him the daily *sacrifice* was taken away, and the place of his sanctuary was cast down.

The word which mainly gives the clew to the sense of this passage is "*host*." It is often used for the soldiers of an army; sometimes for the stars, and all those apparently lesser bodies that seem crowded closely together. I take it to be used here for the people of God, considered as composing his militant church and kingdom on earth, as in Josh. 5: 14; "Nay, but as captain of the Lord's *host* am I now come." The qualifying words, "of heaven," in the phrase "host of heaven," may come from Daniel's conception of this kingdom as set up by "the God of heaven" (2: 44), and hence properly called "the kingdom of heaven." This is precisely the militant church on earth, warring for her Redeemer-King.——"It cast down some of the host, even of the stars, to the ground;" where we must not think of the stars in the firmament of the sky, but of the distinguished leaders in the sacramental host. "Star" is used by the Orientals in this sense, as in the "parable" of Balaam; "There shall come a *star* out of Jacob, and a scepter shall rise out of Israel"—referring to David, a king wielding a human scepter. (Num. 24: 17.) The sense of v. 10 is that this little horn-king made war upon the people of God and destroyed some of their distinguished leaders. V. 11 states that he dared to wage war against the God of the Jews, the Immanuel who appeared to Joshua as "the Prince of the host," (translated there "Captain," but it is the same word as here, Prince;) and consequently he sacrilegiously broke up the established, divinely ordained, temple sacrifices, and "cast down" the place of his manifested presence and abode.——The original Hebrew, rendered, "*By him* the daily sacrifice was taken away," is peculiar. It means either that one sent forth from and by him took away the daily sacrifice; or more abstractly, that by reason of him—at his instance, one took away, etc. It is remarkable that precisely the same expression is used in stating the same fact (chap. 11: 31); "From him or at his command, a military force ('arms') shall be organized and sent forth." So I paraphrase the first clause of this verse—such being obviously the sense of this clause, which is obscurely rendered, "arms shall stand on his part." The prophet means to say that this military force was sent from and by him, but was not led by him in person. This is precisely the sense of his language, and this too is the historic fact. Antiochus Epiphanes sent his chief collector of tribute (1 Mac. 1: 29) and he seized Jerusalem and took away the daily sacrifice.——The Hebrew for "the daily sacrifice" is but one word. This word means, "the perpetual"—that which occurs continually. It was in established use among the Jews for their most constant and most frequently recurring sacrifice, that which was offered each morning and each evening. There can be no question of the correctness of this rendering, "the daily sacrifice," nor can there be a doubt that it should be understood in the Jewish sense. It is simply impossible that a Jewish writer should use the phrase in any other sense, or that his Jewish readers could think of any thing else than this.——Naturally it carries with it all the other customary temple sacrifices. Not this alone was taken away, but all. The implication is, If this, then all.

12. **And a host was given** *him* **against the daily** *sacrifice* **by reason of transgression, and it cast down the truth to the ground; and it practiced and prospered.**

The prophecy goes on still to say that "some of the host" (*i. e.*, of God's people), "are given into his hand, *in addition* to the daily sacrifice, by reason of sin;" for so, I translate the preposition which stands before the word for daily sacrifice. Other cases of similar usage occur, Ex. 35: 22; "And they came, the men *in addition* to the women," etc. Our English version has it, "both men and women." Also Amos 3: 15; "I will smite the winter house *in addition* to the summer house;" not strictly one *upon* the other in the same pile of ruins. So Hos. 10: 14. This sense is confirmed by the last clause of v. 13, which shows that the thing done was the giving of both the sanctuary and the host to be trodden under foot.
——This was a judgment on the Jews for their sins, "by reason of transgression." Both the authors of the books of Maccabees assign the same cause, which seems to indicate a somewhat general, perhaps national, sense of the relation between their sufferings under God's judgments, and the sins for which he sent them. See 1 Maccabees 1: 11-15, 64, and 2 Mac. 5: 17, and 6: 12.——This horn-power cast down the truth—its interests and cause—and for a time seemed to have every thing his own way.

13. **Then I heard one saint speaking, and another saint said unto that certain** *saint* **which spake, How long** *shall be* **the vision** *concerning* **the daily** *sacrifice,* **and the transgression of desolation, to give both the sanctuary and the host to be trodden under foot?**

14. **And he said unto me, Unto two thousand and three hundred days; then shall the sanctuary be cleansed.**

Daniel hears one of the holy ones (attendant angels) speaking as if about to explain some point of the vision, when lo, another of the angels led his mind to the question of *time,* asking how long that part of the vision should be which refers to the daily sacrifice and the sin that works ruin, (referring to *the* sin brought forward in v. 12, as the cause of this judgment,) and which involves giving both the sanctuary and the host to be trodden under foot. Such I take to be the meaning of this question. The three Hebrew words that next follow "vision," rendered, "the daily;" "the transgression;" "of desolation;" must have been added to limit it to a certain part of the whole. For the inquirer does not ask or care to know how long the dominion of the ram and of the he-goat should continue. There being no special intimation that they will greatly afflict *his* people, he can pass over that point readily; but he does wish to know how long the daily sacrifice will be suspended and how long this sin of the covenant people will continue to call down judgments from the Lord upon them. These are matters that lie heavily on his heart. Moreover the last clause involves precisely this limitation, viz., to that part of the vision which refers to giving the sanctuary and the host to be trodden under foot.——In the clause rendered, "the transgression of desolation," I understand the word for transgression to refer to the same word in the first clause of v. 12; "by reason of *transgression,*" both because this word is the same, and because it has here the article equivalent to, "*that* transgression." It is called *desolating* (the sense of the participle) because it is the occasion of these judgments from God upon his apostate people. Daniel would know how long these judgments for this sin will continue. It is vital to get precisely the sense of the question as the first step toward the true answer.——In v. 14 the Hebrew rendered "days" is "evening morning." Yet the meaning is no doubt merely *day* in the sense of twenty-four hours, the time of one revolution of the earth on its axis. This peculiar expression may be chosen to denote *full* days, made up of the night and the day.——Did the Spirit of Inspiration intend by this expression to throw up a barrier against the absurdity of supposing that one of these days means three hundred and sixty common days, hinting to us that his day is one evening and one morning? If so, it is only the more sad to think of so much labor lost in guarding prophecy against absurd and vicious interpretations.——The Hebrew for "cleansed" means usually "justified," but here, "set right," put into its proper condition for its appropriate use. Since the evil to be remedied was its pollution and desecration by idol-worship, "cleansed" well expresses the sense.

It remains to inquire into the historic fulfillment of these twenty-three hundred days.——As already suggested, the inquiry should begin with a clear and just apprehension of the question. Let it be carefully borne in mind that the important points made in the passage, vs. 10–12, are precisely two, viz., (1.) That this little horn-king wickedly carried desolation into the "pleasant land," casting to the ground and stamping down some of the distinguished leaders of the Jews—"the host and the stars."——(2.) That he took away the daily sacrifice, and by implication all the other sacrifices as well. The question, "How long?" refers to these two points—none other. As to these two, he would know their duration.——The answer may be expected to give this, at least proximately. It does.——The chief historical authorities still extant are the two books of Maccabees. Unfortunately these books, and especially the second, rarely give exact dates. But the following points are well established.——The sanctuary was cleansed Dec. 25, 164 B. C. See 1 Mac. 4: 52, with 1 Mac. 1: 54, 59. At this point the twenty-three hundred days (= 6 years, 3 m. and 20 days) must close. From this point we go back three and a half years, spanning the period during which the daily sacrifice was suspended, to June 25, 167 B. C. So long the altar-fires ceased to burn; the daily sacrifice was not made. But six and a quarter years carry us back yet further. So also, the "treading down" of some of the host and of the stars lies yet farther back. Just two years before this, viz., in June, 169 B. C. Antiochus Epiphanes returned from his second military expedition into Egypt, greatly enraged against the Jews because he had heard that they had been making great demonstrations of joy over a report of his death. He fell upon the city with the sword, making a terrific slaughter of "the host" of the Lord's people. The first book of Maccabees says of this event; "After Antiochus had smitten Egypt, he returned in the one hundred and forty-third year" (of the Seleucidæ, B. C. 169) "and went up against Israel and Jerusalem with a great multitude," etc.; pillaged the temple and city; then "went into his own land, having made a great massacre and spoken very proudly" (1 Mac. 1: 20-24). "And *after two years fully expired,* the king sent his chief collector of tribute," etc. This was the expedition which bears date June, 167 B. C., and which desecrated the temple and suspended the sacrifices (1 Mac. 1: 29).——The second book of Maccabees is more in detail on this point, but without very exact dates, connecting it, however, with the second expedition of Antiochus into Egypt, and showing further that immediately upon the receipt of the false rumor of the king's death, Jason, one of his minions in Judea, "took at least a thousand men and suddenly made an assault upon the city, and slew his own citizens without mercy." Here some of "the host" fell, at a period considerably earlier than June, 169 B. C. His account of the massacre made by the king is full, showing it to have been terrific. From what the king heard in Egypt, "he thought Judea had revolted, whereupon removing out of Egypt in a furious mind, he took the city by force of arms and commanded his men of war not to spare such as they met, and to slay such as went up upon the houses. Thus there was killing of young and old, making away of men, women, and children; slaying of virgins and infants. And there were destroyed within three whole days four score thousand, whereof forty thousand were slain in the conflict, and no fewer sold than slain" (2 Mac. 5: 11-14). But the full period of twenty-three hundred days runs back yet a fraction of a year further. The onslaught of Jason was probably in May, 169 B. C. The period named in our passage (six years, three months and twenty days) should begin about Sept. 5, 170 B. C. The author of the second book of Maccabees, in his fourth chapter, immediately preceding that quoted above, records the murder of the good Onias, long time high priest, a "Star" of the first magnitude, whose influence had long withstood the wickedness of the times; the murder also of the three Jewish deputies who went to meet the king at Tyre, and obtain his interposition against Menelaus. This Menelaus was a vile apostate; a minion of Antiochus, subserving his interests by drawing the people into Grecian customs and idolatry. Indirectly, what he did in the way of persecuting the Jews was done by Antiochus himself. Hence these murders of four distinguished Jewish leaders should be set to the account of this little horn. They all seem to have occurred in the year 170 B. C. More-

over it was in the year B. C. 170 that Antiochus made his first expedition into Egypt, in which he naturally passed through Judea. It is not strange that a period intended to cover the whole time of casting down "some of the host and of the stars," unto the "cleansing of the sanctuary" should embrace the murder of Onias and of the three deputies to Tyre, and also the period of his first military expedition through their country.——This is the amount of historical verification which I am able to obtain from any authentic source at my command.——It may fitly be added here that the materials for a full history of Antiochus Epiphanes, in the line of profane historians, are scanty. Jahn remarks that "the writings which treat of this period by Callinicus Sutoricus, Diodorus Siculus, Hieronymus the historian, Polybius Posidonius, Claudius Theon and Andronicus Alypius, are all lost except a few fragments preserved by other authors, and we have these only from the second or third hand." Porphyry, a learned infidel of the third century, wrote against the Christians in fifteen books, of which the twelfth was devoted to Daniel, to prove from the great accuracy of his prophecy when applied to Antiochus Epiphanes and his times, that it must have been written *as history after the events.* He drew largely from the classic authors above named; but unfortunately his work is lost, except as quotations from it have come down to us in Jerome's commentary on Daniel in reply to Porphyry. Three other Christian writers replied to his work, but all these are lost except a few fragments copied into other authors. Of these three, that by Apollinarius is much lamented, having the reputation of being very accurate.
——This paucity of historic material is an ample apology for any apparent deficiency in making out the precise historic verification of this time-period which refers to events so remote, and which gives us periods so very minute as the number of days. And even this number (2300) may be round and general, and not precise and particular. Yet the approximation which is obtained, despite of such difficulties, will satisfy fair-minded readers.

15. And it came to pass, when I, *even* I Daniel, had seen the vision, and sought for the meaning, then behold, there stood before me as the appearance of a man.

16. And I heard a man's voice between *the banks of* Ulai, which called, and said, Gabriel, make this *man* to understand the vision.

17. So he came near where I stood: and when he came, I was afraid, and fell upon my face: but he said unto me, Understand, O son of man: for at the time of the end *shall be* the vision.

18. Now as he was speaking with me, I was in a deep sleep on my face toward the ground: but he touched me, and set me upright.

19. And he said, Behold, I will make thee know what

shall be in the last end of the indignation: for at the time appointed the end *shall be.*

This passage describes the way in which Daniel obtained from the Angel Gabriel an explanation of this vision. As bearing upon the date of its fulfillment and the occasion of these calamites sent on the Jews, the words (vs. 17 and 19) "at the time of the end shall be the vision;" "what shall be in the last end of the indignation;" "for at the time appointed the end shall be;" should be carefully considered. The same or similar expressions occur chap. 11: 27, 35, 36, 40, and 12: 4, 9. Other passages illustrative of these, are Dan. 10: 14, and 8: 26. Whoever shall carefully examine these passages will see that they refer to the time when these great persecutions and calamities upon the Jews will occur; that they speak of it as a time of God's indignation against them for their sins; and as determined in his divine counsels. Furthermore, they approximate toward the definite time for these events by calling it, "the time of the end," or as chap. 10: 14, has it, "In the latter days." The passage chap. 8: 17, rendered "at the time of the end shall be the vision," I take to mean that this vision looks toward the time of the end for its fulfillment: it relates to events which shall take place near "the time of the end." The *end* here is manifestly, not the final end of all earthly things, but the end of the *age before Christ.* The Jews were accustomed to speak of the times of the Messiah as "the last times;" the "last" or the "latter days." Very naturally, therefore, the period before his coming was definitely marked off by that coming, and it would be the end of the previous age of the world. Now, we have already seen in chap. 7 that these calamities must precede Christ's inauguration in his great kingdom; but since they lie very near it, they are near "the time of the end." Hence these expressions refer to the cruel and bloody persecutions of the Jews by Antiochus Epiphanes and the long wars which, commenced by him, continued about twenty-four years, inflicting great calamities upon the Jewish nation. The period was specially one of God's indignation against the apostate Jews for their fall into heathenism under the influences then pervading the East. The revealing angel declares (v. 19); "I will make thee know what shall be in the last end of the indignation," for this "end shall be at the time appointed." This implies that the Lord had indignation toward the people for their general relapse into idolatry, and had fully purposed to scourge them sorely by the little horn-power for this great sin.——As going to show that there was at this time an amount of national degeneracy truly alarming, and such as demanded from their divine Shepherd the sternest methods of national discipline and judgment, let us pause here a moment to look at the facts of their case in this respect. ——Taking our stand-point at the commencement of the reign of Antiochus Epiphanes (B. C. 175), it is now two hundred and twenty-five years since the age of Malachi and Nehemiah, when we may remember that the last reformation recorded in Old Testament history found its main work to be to withstand the tendencies to a dangerously intimate association, social and commercial, with the idolaters around them. These tendencies did not cease with that reformation. It is more than three hundred and sixty years since the age of Daniel, Cyrus and Zerubbabel, when this prophecy was given, and when the great moral lessons of a seventy years' captivity had for once impressed on the national mind a solemn warning against idolatry. In the lapse of ten generations, it is not strange that those lessons should have lost much of their vividness and power. Yet further, note that it is now one hundred and fifty years since the conquests of Alexander the Great, sweeping over all Western Asia and Northern Africa, brought with them all the great elements of Grecian life and civilization— their literature, their manners, their public amusements, their dress, and not least, their attractive idolatry. These new elements fell upon the less vigorous and more susceptible Oriental mind with the greater power because borne by the hand of the conquering people, and backed by the influence and authority of the ruling class.——To all these circumstances add yet further that ever since the captivity, *i. e.*, during now five hundred and thirty years, the Jews have been, not mainly concentrated as of old, in Palestine, but more or less widely dispersed abroad among the various tribes and peoples throughout Asia even to India, and in Egypt. It is supposed that in the great restoration, full as many remained behind as returned to Judea. And subsequently, even down to our present stand-point, B. C. 175, colonization had drained many of their families from their mother-land. The Jews were regarded as desirable colonists. In point of industry, vigor, and especially of fidelity to their friends, they stood far above any other Oriental population. Hence it was no uncommon thing that kings, desiring to build up strong cities and a substantial state, bid high for Jewish colonists. By this means they became yet more widely dispersed, and more mingled with idolaters.——And finally, let us make due account of this fact that since the death of Alexander, the frequent wars between Egypt on the south and Syria on the north, caused Judea to be repeatedly traversed to and fro by foreign armies, which of course brought the people into various contact with their heathen neighbors, and quite broke up that seclusion which the genius of the Jewish theocracy fostered and needed for its best working. Here then is a broad array of social and political influences, all tending to weaken their piety and relax the tone of their national feeling. Under these influences they were in imminent peril of being utterly swept away into Grecian heathenism.

——Let us notice some of the indications of this fact in the books of the Maccabees.——Starting at precisely our stand-point, where Antiochus Epiphanes began his reign, the author of the first book says (1: 11–15); "In those days went there out of Israel wicked men, who persuaded many, saying, Let us go and make a covenant with the heathen that are round about us; for since we departed from them we have had much sorrow. So this device pleased them

DANIEL.—CHAP. VIII.

well. Then certain of the people were so forward herein that they went to the king, who gave them license to do after the ordinances of the heathen. Whereupon they built a place of exercise for the Grecian athletic games at Jerusalem according to the customs of the heathen, and made themselves uncircumcised, and forsook the holy covenant and joined themselves to the heathen, and were sold to do mischief." "Many of the Israelites consented to the king's religion, sacrificed to idols and profaned the Sabbath." (V. 43.) When the king sent overseers to enforce his own religious system, "many of the Jewish people were gathered unto them, to-wit, every one that forsook the law; and so they committed evils in the land, and drove the Israelites into secret places" (vs. 52, 53).——The author of the second book gives some telling details (as usual) to the same point; how Jason, the apostate, "brought up new customs against the law, for he built gladly a place of exercise under the tower itself, and brought the chief young men under his subjection, and made them wear a hat. Now such was the height of Greek fashions and increase of heathenish manners through the exceeding profaneness of Jason, that ungodly wretch and not high priest, that the priests had no courage to serve any more at the altar, but despising the temple and neglecting the sacrifices, hastened to be partakers of the unlawful allowance in the place of exercise after the game of Discus called them forth" (2 Mac. 4: 11-14).
——He gives his views of these great afflictions permitted of God to come upon his people, thus; "Now I beseech those that read this book that they be not discouraged for these calamities, but that they judge those punishments not to be for destruction, but for a chastening of our nation. For it is a token of his great goodness when wicked doers are not suffered any long time, but forthwith punished. For not as with other nations whom the Lord patiently forbeareth to punish till they be come to the fullness of their sins; so dealeth he with us" (2 Mac. 6: 12-14).——Smith's Bible Dictionary (art. "Antiochus") presents similar views forcibly. "The reign of Antiochus was the last great crisis in the history of the Jews before the coming of our Lord." "The conquest of Alexander had introduced the forces of Greek thought and life into the Jewish nation, which was already prepared for their operation. For more than a century and a half, these forces had acted powerfully both upon the faith and upon the habits of the people; and the time was come when an outward struggle alone could decide whether Judaism was to be merged in a rationalized Paganism, or to rise not only victorious from the conflict, but more vigorous and more pure. There were many symptoms that betokened the approaching struggle. The position which Judea occupied on the borders of the conflicting empires of Syria and Egypt, exposed equally to the open miseries of war and the treacherous favors of rival sovereigns, rendered its national condition precarious from the first, though these very circumstances were favorable to the growth of freedom. The terrible crimes by which "the wars of the north and the south" were stained must have

alienated the mind of every faithful Jew from his Grecian lords, even if persecution had not been superadded from Egypt first, and then from Syria. Politically nothing was left for the people in the reign of Antiochus but independence, or the abandonment of every prophetic hope. Nor was their social position less perilous. The influence of Greek literature, of foreign travel, of extended commerce, had made itself felt in daily life. At Jerusalem the mass of the inhabitants seem to have desired to imitate the exercises of the Greeks; and a Jewish embassy attended the games of Hercules at Tyre (2 Mac. 4: 9-20). Even their religious feelings were yielding; and before the rising of the Maccabees no opposition was offered to the execution of the king's decrees. Upon the first attempt of Jason, the priests had no courage to serve at the altar, and this not so much from willful apostasy as from a disregard to the vital principles involved in the conflict. Thus it was necessary that the final issues of a false Hellenism should be openly seen that it might be discarded forever by those who cherished the ancient faith of Israel."——These views suffice to show the significance of the allusion in our passage to "the last end of the indignation," "at the time appointed," and why (as v. 23 indicates) this scourge of God, Antiochus Epiphanes, was suffered to come down on them precisely when "the transgressors were come to the full."

20. The ram which thou sawest having *two* horns *are* the kings of Media and Persia.

21. And the rough goat *is* the king of Grecia: and the great horn that *is* between his eyes *is* the first king.

22. Now that, being broken, whereas four stood up for it, four kingdoms shall stand up out of the nation, but not in his power.

This interpretation, given through Gabriel, the revealing angel, definitely affirms and therefore proves that the ram with two horns is the Medo-Persian empire, its composite character being indicated by the two horns, each of which represents one of the original kingdoms. So also it shows that the goat is the Grecian power as developed in Alexander. It is not strange that the angel should say first that the goat is (not the *kingdom*, but) the "*king* of Grecia;" and next that "the great horn is the first king." For as seen in the vision, it was not the kingdom but the king. The one great power was Alexander. As seen by Daniel there was yet virtually no kingdom—certainly no Asiatic, oriental kingdom. It was only a vigorous, conquering king, moving on to *make* a great kingdom.

——When Alexander was suddenly broken down by death, four new kingdoms arose out of the loose fragments of his great empire —not in his power indeed, but entirely independent of any will of his or of any influence growing out of any organization or arrangement made by him while he lived. No monarch so great ever left so little behind him to determine the question of succession. When near death, and asked by his friends to whom he would leave his vast empire, he said only, "To the worthiest." In fact he left it to be fought for with rivers of blood one quarter of a century.—— The four powers have been already indicated in the notes on v. 8. There they were four horns, yet really four kingdoms, located geographically toward the four cardinal points. Here they are definitely four kingdoms.

23. *And in the latter time of their kingdom, when the transgressors are come to the full, a king of fierce countetenance, and understanding dark sentences, shall stand up.*

This verse explains v. 9. "Out of one of them" (*i. e.*, one of those four kingdoms) "came forth a little horn." Here the angel interpreter has it; "In the latter time of their kingdom, a king shall stand up." The horn *there* is a king *here*. It is of course assumed here that he is a king in one of those four kingdoms. The angel therefore proceeds to locate him yet more definitely in point of time. "In the latter time of their kingdom," and "when the transgressors" (the Jews) "have filled up the measure of their sins," so that discipline and judgment from the Lord's hand must needs come to save them. This king is Antiochus Epiphanes. He fills the description in every particular: no other personage does or can.——As to his point of time in the Syrian line of kings, one hundred and thirty-seven years had passed when he came to the throne; about one hundred remained after his death. Moreover, the kingdom had waned very much as compared with its extent and vigor under its founder Seleucus Nicator; and hence in this point of light might naturally be thought of as in its latter stages. As the interpreter said, "in the latter time of *their* kingdom," it is proper to note that two out of these four kingdoms had already run their course and become extinct when Antiochus ascended his throne. As a whole those kingdoms were manifestly "in their latter time."——His "fierce countenance" here refers, probably, not to his physique so much as to his character; *i. e.*, to him as seen in vision with his character written on his very face, rather than as seen by merely human eyes in the flesh. It means therefore that he was ferocious, passionate, cruel. Precisely the same expression is used, Deut. 28: 50, of the people who should invade and spoil the Jews for their sins—"A nation of *fierce countenance* who shall not regard the person of the old, nor show favor to the young."——That he "should understand dark sentences," intricate matters, testifies to his resources for cunning, craft and policy, as is indicated also v. 25: "Through his policy he shall cause craft to prosper in his hand."

24. *And his power shall be mighty, but not by his own power: and he shall destroy wonderfully, and shall prosper, and practice, and shall destroy the mighty and the holy people.*

"He shall be strong," but shall not obtain this power by legitimate means, shall not be the rightful heir to the throne. Such is the history of Antiochus. He was the youngest son of Antiochus the Great. His elder brother, Seleucus Philopator, reigned eleven years. Just before his death, he sent his only son, Demetrius, to Rome as a hostage, thus exchanging and releasing his own brother, Antiochus Epiphanes, who had been there in that capacity twelve years. The king fell by poison at the hand of Heliodorus, who sought to seize the kingdom. Antiochus heard of his brother's death while at Athens on his way home, and immediately made interest with powerful foreign parties to gain the kingdom for himself, and succeeded—ungratefully displacing the real heir to the throne.——Some have supposed that the phrase, "not by his own power," looked to the agency of divine providence, since the Lord had occasion to use him as his scourge upon his sinning people. I incline to the former view.——He shall make fearful havoc among the nominal people of God, the Jews. So the reader of the books of the Maccabees will see. The Jewish wars commenced by him continued long after his death, in all about twenty-four years, resulting at length in the independence of the Jewish nation B. C. 143, but at the cost of many thousands of Jewish lives.

25. And through his policy also he shall cause craft to prosper in his hand; and he shall magnify *himself* in his heart, and by peace shall destroy many: he shall also stand up against the Prince of princes; but he shall be broken without hand.

The sense of the first clause is, that by means of cunning, keen-eyed sagacity, he will make deception work successfully toward his ends. The points made in the entire verse are—successful cunning and deceit, unbounded pride and self-esteem; destroying many suddenly, in the midst of apparent tranquillity; daring to array himself against the Almighty; and his utter fall before some superhuman hand.——This king's sharp-minded sagacity has been noticed before; "understanding dark sentences." This feature of his character, and his abundant and successful use of it stand out with great prominence in chap. 11: 21–32. "He comes in peaceably and obtains the kingdom by flatteries;" "works deceitfully;" "enters peaceably" (not by force of arms) "upon the fattest places of the provinces;" "forecasts devices and corrupts the wicked Jews by flatteries," etc.——History shows that he obtained the kingdom by precisely such means, and also that he plied these arts in their full strength upon the Jews, drawing many of them into apostasy from their religion and from their country's cause, into coöperation with himself. "He shall have intelligence with them that forsake the holy covenant."——His supreme pride and self-esteem appear also in chap. 11. "The king shall do according to his will;" "he shall exalt himself and magnify himself above every god;" "regarding neither the god of his fathers, nor the desire of women, nor any god, he shall magnify himself above all." History gives him the same character.——That he dared to fight against the God of the Jews, even while he had sufficient means of knowing that He was the true and Almighty God, has been noted on v. 11, and stands out prominently in his history as given in the books of Maccabees. It was perhaps specially manifest (as usual) in that hour which most tries men's souls—the hour of impending death. The author of second Maccabees, chap. 9, says; "Here, therefore, being plagued, he began to leave off his great pride and to come to the knowledge of himself by the scourge of God, his pain increasing every moment. And when he could not abide his own smell, he said; "It is meet to be subject unto God, and that a man that is mortal should not proudly think of himself as if he were God." Also in his distress and remorse, he vowed that if God would spare him, he "would become a Jew himself and go through all the world declaring the power of God." This shows that he had arrayed himself against Jehovah God with his eyes open, standing up intelligently against the Prince of princes. No wonder therefore that he was suddenly "broken without hand," or as in 11: 45, that "he came to his end with none to help him;" or yet as in 7: 26, that "the judgment did sit and they took away his dominion to consume and destroy it to the end." For the circumstances of his sudden and horrible death, see notes on 7: 26. Thus closes this brief but somewhat specific and minute description of the little horn-king.

26. And the vision of the evening and the morning which was told *is* true: wherefore shut thou up the vision; for it *shall be* for many days.

27. And I Daniel fainted, and was sick *certain* days; afterward I rose up, and did the king's business; and I was astonished at the vision, but none understood *it*.

This vision is spoken of as "the vision of the evening and the morning," with reference to the use of this phrase in the Hebrew of v. 14—"twenty-three hundred evening morning." There can be no doubt that "the vision of the evening and the morning" in this v. 26, is the vision of this eighth chapter, especially that part of it in which this phrase occurs, and which shows how long the little horn shall tread down "the sanctuary"and the sacramental "host."——The direction "to shut up this vision" indicates that its time of more special interest and value to its readers was yet somewhat remote. When this day of trial should come, those heroic men and women who fell martyrs to the faith of their fathers, or who fought with lion-hearted courage and prowess against fearful odds, would read these visions and dwell on these predictions of the fall of their great foe with surpassing interest. The passage implies that *relatively* less interest would be felt in the vision at that time and for some time to come.——The Hebrew word rendered "I fainted," is the passive form of the verb *to be*—a usage of a very peculiar sort, somewhat idiomatic, as "I was done for;" "was gone up;" "it was all over with me." The scene affected him so powerfully as to disqualify him temporarily for any service. That he afterward "rose up and did the king's business," seems to imply that he was there as an embassador for the king of Babylon. This accounts for his being at Shushan when he had the vision.——The last clause may mean, "There was none to make me understand it"—this form of the verb (hiphil) being very often causative. The statement would seem to imply that his mind was still "inquiring and searching diligently what or what manner of time the revealing Spirit did signify." He greatly desired to know these matters yet more particularly than the Lord had yet revealed them. "In the third year of Cyrus" this great desire was gratified. The vision recorded, chap. 10-12, was amply specific to these very points.

In concluding this chapter, I must sum up in few words my reasons for finding the little horn and the king of fierce countenance in Antiochus Epiphanes.——The reader will have noticed that neither Alexander, the "great horn," nor Antiochus, the "little horn," is called by name. Only Media, Persia, and Grecia are given by name. And yet these horns are described so precisely that, with the history of those times before us, we can identify each one as surely as if he had been actually called by name. Thus the "great horn," the first king of the Asiatic Grecian empire, can not possibly be any other than Alexander. The historical evidence is perfect. He, and nobody else but he, was the first king.——There is the same sort of evidence; and an amount of it no less decisive, to prove that the little horn is Antiochus Epiphanes. The description embraces many more points. Every one of these points, pertaining to his historical place in the four kingdoms, his date, the direction of his military exploits and successes—in short, the things he did, the spirit and character of the man, and his final destiny—every one of these minute points fit him perfectly, fit him in their obvious, legitimate, and well-established significance.——Even this is not all. Of itself alone, this might not be absolutely decisive, for it might still be said, Many of these points fit some other personage too; possibly some of them may fit another as well as they fit Antiochus Epiphanes. It is supposable (not at all probable) that a score of definite particulars of this sort might fit each of two or more kings. Hence we need yet another fact to make the evidence absolutely decisive. We need to find points that fit Antiochus, and *fit no other man ;*—points that never have been fulfilled in any other and never can be. Then the proof will be complete. Now, we have precisely this evidence. Here are some special points that never have been met in any other man, and never can be. Go through all Jewish history from Moses to Christ, *i. e.*, from the establishment of their religious ritual to its final abolishment, and ask what persecuting heathen king caused the daily sacrifices to be temporarily suspended. There is but one possible answer; Antiochus Epiphanes. ·Traverse the same history from beginning to end, and ask for the celebrated event of "cleansing the sanctuary" after a brief desecration—an event which never happened but once—the memory of which was celebrated quite down to the times of our Lord's personal ministry among the Jews as "the feast of dedication" when "it was winter" (*i. e.*, Dec. 25; see John 10: 23). Then ask, Who had been polluting the sanctuary? There is but one possible answer; Antiochus Epiphanes. These great facts of Jewish history put their finger on this heathen king with unmistakable precision. It is simply impossible that any other king can fill these points of this description. It is, therefore, impossible that this little horn can be any one else than Antiochus Epiphanes. Coupling, then, these two great lines of argument— (1.) That a great number of very minute and specific points, half a score or more, pertaining to this little horn-king, meet in him when legitimately interpreted—meet naturally, easily, and precisely: and (2.) That at least these two or more, last mentioned, *can not possibly apply to any other personage*, we have ample demonstration. Candid minds will be satisfied with it.

The *general parallelism of Daniel's four great visions* has been more than once alluded to. The present is a favorable point for renewed attention to the evidence of this fact.——I forbear to notice yet the last vision, that of chap. 10–12, because it has not yet come under our special consideration. I also omit the vision in chap. 2: 31–45, partly because, being undeniably parallel with chap. 7, there is no need of giving special attention to it in our present inquiry; and partly because it gives us no details respecting the great personage who becomes more and more prominent as the visions advance—the little horn-king. Hence we have now to consider only the parallelism of the vision chap. 7 with this of chap. 8.—— Note, then, that chap. 8 omits Chaldea, for its course is already run; its end is near; there is nothing more to say of it.——Chap. 2: 31–45, began with the reigning dynasty, in its glory, as it then was; chap. 7, with the same reigning dynasty, already waning to its fall; chap. 8, with the dynasty just about to appear, probably within a twelve-month.——In chap. 7 the Seer is present bodily in the kingdom which is the starting point in the series. In chap. 8 the same is true; he is bodily in Persia (at the capital), with which kingdom his visions begin.——In chap. 7 he gives us the Medo-Persian kingdom, and next the Grecian kingdom of Alexander. In chap. 8 the same, only making yet more prominent the manner in which the latter smote and overpowered the former, and then succeeded to his dominion.——In chap. 7 the power next in order is the fourth beast and his horns; yet remarkably nothing is said of the doings of the ten horns, and nothing distinctively of the terrible fourth beast *except as he appears in the little horn*. The fearfulness of this fourth beast; his sins that call for the judgments of God; and the visitation of those judgments—all seem to belong to him *as represented in the little horn*. So much is obviously apparent in chap. 7.——Correspondingly, in chap. 8, the fourth beast scarcely appears at all in his distinctive character. The four kingdoms that spring up on the breaking down of Alexander's are apparently introduced only to fill up the historic links, and give us more definitely the historical place and relations of the little horn. This done, we come at once to the great central personage—the little horn; to his deeds, his spirit, and his doom. Hence, we have now simply to compare the little horn of chap. 7 with the little horn of chap. 8. If these are identical, the two visions are essentially parallel.——Each bears the same distinctive name, "the little horn." Whatever this name may mean, it is safe to assume that it means the same in each vision. Such similarity of character and sameness of name go far to prove identity.——Each is declared by the angel-interpreter to be a "king"—another point toward identity. ——Chap. 7 makes him sagacious, far-seeing, for this must be the sense of eyes in a horn. Chap. 8 defines him to be a king "understanding dark sentences," and "by his policy making craft to prosper in his hand."——Chap. 7 gives this horn "a mouth speaking great things" (v. 8); "very great things" (v. 20); and "great words against the Most High" (v. 25). Correspondingly, chap. 8 represents him as elated with pride and self-esteem, and as confronting himself with horrible impiety against the true God and his people. "He magnifies himself in his heart;" "he casts down the truth to the ground;" "he stands up against the Prince of princes." ——Chap. 7 makes a definite and prominent point of his persecution of the saints; "wearing them out." Chap. 8 makes the same point not less definitely and prominently. "He casts down some of the host and of the stars to the ground and stamps upon them;" the "host is given up" to his power; he "destroys the mighty and the holy people;" and in the midst of apparent "peace, destroys many."——In chap. 7 the holy people whom he "wears out" are Jews, for it is their "times and laws" that he "thinks to change." In chap. 8 the same is true; it is their own sanctuary that he casts down;" their "daily sacrifice that he takes away."——In chap. 7 it is declared that the Jewish institutions of worship shall be given into his hand for a season, so that he will do his own will as to them; i. e., change them for heathen institutions and worship. Chap. 8 says the same. Not the "host" only, but the daily sacrifice is given up to his power (v. 12); "the sanctuary and the host are given him to be trodden under his feet" (v. 13).——In chap. 7 the duration of this dominant control over Jewish institutions and worship is set at three and a half years. In chap. 8 the period defined includes more than simply the time of his suspending the daily sacrifice. It embraces also the giving of the host, the Lord's people, to be trodden under foot, and therefore is extended to six and one-third years. But the two periods are in no sense conflicting. They are indeed essentially parallel, and apply to the same series of historic facts respecting Antiochus Epiphanes. I do not claim that one of these visions is an exact copy of the other. General parallelism does not require this. The two visions are truly independent; but the same great historic personage is the central figure in each. We proceed.——In chap. 7 it is manifestly implied throughout that he impiously sets himself against Almighty God. Not less so in chap. 8, "He magnifies himself against the

Prince of the host;" "he stands up against the Prince of princes."
——Finally, in chap. 7, special judgments from the Almighty cut him down and put an end to his power against the saints. In chap. 8 he "is broken without" (human) "hand."——So much for the points of close and unquestionable analogy. They embrace almost every special point made in chap. 7—every one indeed of any prominence except this, that the little horn-king there "subdues three of the" former "kings" (v. 24), and they "fall before him" (v. 20).——On the other hand, chap. 8 makes some new points, as might be expected from its more full descriptions. It gives (v. 9) the direction of his conquests, viz., toward Egypt, Persia, and Palestine. It intimates that he is made God's instrument for discipline and judgment on apostate Jews; "When the transgressors are come to the full" (v. 23); "In the last end of the indignation" (v. 19). It gives very definitely the historical point of "the cleansing of the sanctuary"—one of the great facts of Jewish history, celebrated during several centuries by an annual "feast of dedication," "in the winter." See John 10: 22. But these additional points by no means impair the evidence of real parallelism, or of the actual identity of this little horn with that. This evidence seems to me to be conclusive. How can it be doubted that the little horn of chap. 7 is also the little horn of chap. 8—the same personage, standing in the same political relations to heathen powers; in the same relations also to the Jews; breathing the same spirit; doing the same things; coming to the same end?

A few words are due here respecting the theory of interpreting this chapter, which makes the little horn Papal Rome.——This little horn of chap. 8 can not be Papal Rome, 1. Because he *is* Antiochus Epiphanes, as has been shown.——2. Because this horn is a king, and therefore is *not a church;* is *not* a great religious organization; is not even a kingdom.——Let it be remembered that this is put epsecially on the ground of God's own interpretation. The current strain of the vision proper (vs. 9–14) most fully implies that this horn is a king; but the interpretation (vs. 23–25) affirms it, and so describes him throughout. This authority ought to be respected. Of course it will be by those who admit that he who presents thought to others, whether by symbols or in ordinary speech, is the best interpreter of his own thought; and that this universal law is *preëminently applicable to the Omniscient God.* He surely ought to know what he himself means, and ought to be trusted to give his own meaning fairly.——Consequently this argument settles the question. More is really gratuitous—useful mainly to show how many things seem to have been overlooked, or, at least, unaccountably disposed of, that should have compelled every student of these prophecies to reject the theory that makes the little horn Papal Rome.——3. This king rises in one of the four kingdoms into which Alexander's empire was cleft. Papal Rome did not. In fact, Papal Rome could not, for the reason that every one of these four kingdoms had ceased some time before the Christian era; *i. e.,* some seven hundred years before any historian dates the rise of Papal Rome.——4. He pushes his conquests "toward the south," Egypt; "toward the east," Persia; and "toward the pleasant land," Palestine. But Papal Rome had on the south the Mediterranean Sea; made no footing in Egypt or Africa; had to give up the great East to the Greek Church; never made any show in "the pleasant land"—all her crusades through two fearful centuries of blood and toil becoming a magnificent failure. Yet she did push her conquests in precisely every other direction—thus reversing this description of the little horn.——5. This horn persecuted the Jews while yet Judaism was in force and the Jews were the only known people of God. This Papal Rome did not do and *could* not, for the reason that they had ceased to be the recognized "saints" of God, and Judaism had "waxed old and vanished away" long before Papal Rome was born.——6. This horn takes away the daily sacrifice—which Papal Rome never did, for God had taken it away forever, at least six hundred years before Papal Rome came into being.——7. After a definite period of these persecutions and desecrations by the little horn, his power is broken and "the sanctuary is cleansed"—in all which Papal Rome was not, for the same very sufficient reason as above; she was not yet in existence.——8. Finally, there is not one solitary point in this description which applies to Papal Rome so specifically as to define her and distinguish her from any other persecuting power. Nothing in this chapter applies to Papal Rome except those very general features which must pertain to any persecutor of the church. The Papal-Rome theory, therefore, violates all just principles of interpreting prophecy. Especially it goes in the very face of God's own interpretation of this little horn as a king. Hence it *can not possibly be true.* It has absolutely nothing in its support and every thing against it.——From this position I infer that the little horn of chap. 7 can not be Papal Rome, for that horn and this are identical. As this can not be Papal Rome, neither can that.—— This entire course of reasoning applies in every particular with equal force against the theory that this little horn of chap. 8 is the Mohammedan power. There is not the first shade of an argument in its support. It would not pay to go over the ground to refute it.

CHAPTER IX.

This chapter has a subject of its own, complete in itself, and not connected with the two that precede, or the three that follow. Its place here in the order of the chapters of this book is determined by its *date.* It is here because it was written after the eighth (probably not more than one year after), and four years before chapters 10–12.——Its occasion is given definitely. Daniel had learned by reading the prophecies of Jeremiah that the captivity was limited to seventy years (Jer. 25: 11, 12). This period

was now near its close. It was this circumstance that moved him to seek the face of the Lord with such earnest prayer that he would most fully and freely forgive the sins of his people; rightly judging that as the captivity was sent upon the people in judgment for their sins, it could cease only upon condition of the most humble confession and repentance on the part of the people and their free forgiveness on the part of God. In this point of light, the whole chapter yields the richest moral instruction, and legitimately awakens the deepest interest. It is indeed an admirable model of intercessory prayer, and may be applied equally to prayer for guilty nations or for guilty individuals.——The manner in which God was pleased to answer this prayer will call for our special attention. He does not answer it by reaffirming what he had said by Jeremiah, fixing the duration of the captivity at seventy years; does not give any additional particulars respecting the manner of this restoration under the decree of Cyrus. Indeed, Daniel does not ask to be informed or assured on these or kindred points. He seems to have had no doubt but that the Lord would fulfill his word, nor any fear lest he should not do it in the very best time and way. In the spirit of one whose heart is full of sympathy with God and his glory, his great burden is, the people's sins. Hence his prayer scarcely touches any other point than this one—that the Lord in his great mercy would forgive the people and wholly put away their transgressions for his name's sake.——With this point distinctly in mind, the reader will readily see the entire fitness of the answer which comes by the hand of Gabriel from the loving heart of God. It stands in the last four verses, and constitutes one of the richest promises ever made to our lost world. I shall endeavor to develop its specific import fully in its place. Suffice it to say here that it is essentially the promise of an atoning Messiah, whose violent death should provide amply for the free and full pardon of sin, and for the mission of the Spirit to seal these blessings to "many." It fixes the date of his coming; the duration of his public labors on earth; the time of his death; and of those striking effusions of the Spirit which were designed to open and illustrate the genius of the gospel age.——The chapter is therefore properly in two parts;—
(1.) Daniel's prayer that God would forgive the sins of his people (vs. 1-19);—(2.) The sending of Gabriel with the answer and the answer itself (vs. 20-27).

1. In the first year of Darius the son of Ahasuerus, of the seed of the Medes, which was made king over the realm of the Chaldeans;

2. In the first year of his reign I Daniel understood by books the number of the years, whereof the word of the Lord came to Jeremiah the prophet, that he would accomplish seventy years in the desolations of Jerusalem.

In reference to this Darius, see notes on Dan. 5: 31.——The Ahasuerus named here is not the same who bears this name in the book of Esther. This was a common name with the kings of Media and Persia, as Pharaoh was with the kings of Egypt. It is supposed to signify, "*the lion-king.*"——Daniel understood "*by books,*" in tacit antithesis to other modes, e. g., dreams and visions, by which he had come to understand many things otherwise unknown to mortals. In this case he learned from the sacred books, the written prophecies of Jeremiah which had been already incorporated into the canon of the Jewish scriptures. The plural, *books*, does not imply that Jeremiah had written more than one prophetic book, but does imply that this one was already embraced with others in one volume which was fitly spoken of therefore in the plural, even as we use the appellation, "the scriptures."——"Accomplish," is to fill out. The captivity was to continue until seventy years were past, and the amount was in this sense "*filled out*" in the desolations of Jerusalem. This specific prophecy is found Jer. 25: 11, 12; "And this whole land shall be a desolation and an astonishment; and these nations shall serve the king of Babylon seventy years. And it shall come to pass, when seventy years are accomplished that I will punish the king of Babylon," etc.——The punishment thus threatened on Babylon's king and nation had already been meted out; so that if Daniel had needed such evidence to assure him that God would fulfill his words of promise, it was here, at hand. The work had already begun. But there is no hint that Daniel's faith needed this support.——This is a suitable place for the suggestion, bearing upon the whole drift of this chapter, that Daniel prayed none the less but rather the more because he was so confident that the purpose of God was fixed to restore his people from their captivity and to redeem the nation. He did not sympathize with those who abuse the idea of God's agency in fixing future events. He did not say, "Since this thing is certain to be, why should I trouble myself to pray about it?" Not thus did he seek to evade his moral responsibilities under the wise government of a God who foreknows and determines all, and sometimes reveals the future to his people. How much he reasoned upon this matter of fate and freedom, or better, of man's duty under the reign of a God who knows and determines all his own future acts, and virtually, all the actions of other beings throughout his universe—we are not told. If he did reason upon it, he might fitly have said; God's purposes reach the means and the antecedents as truly as the ends and results, and by no means fix the latter, whether the former occur or not. If he assigns some agency in these means and antecedents to me or to any free agent, he gives us herein *duties to do*, and we neglect them at our peril. I must see to my duty! God's promise to *do* is a summons to me to prepare the way for that doing.——Perhaps he did not give much thought to the metaphysical aspects of this subject. He may have simply said, Blessed be the God of my fathers that the time draws nigh for redeeming my people from this long and fearful captivity. He sent this scourge upon our nation for their sins: it came in all justice and loving kindness. It can not pass away save upon our repentance as a nation before God, our hearty confession of our sins, and our earnest prayer for his mercy. My heart must lead the people in this confession, penitence and prayer. Thus in the exercise of a true sympathy with the God he loved and adored, he might have approached this subject on its practical side only; and with this common sense view, in the spirit of a sincere piety, he might have set himself to penitence, confession and prayer, without one thought of any complication in the subject growing out of the joint action of human freedom and divine purpose. Is not his course in this thing, an admirable—nay more, a perfect model?——The objection made to prayer, as above referred to, "Why should I trouble myself to pray when God has made the thing certain by special promise?" should not be passed over without yet another remark; viz., that the spirit which can make it is utterly foreign from the spirit of true prayer. The heart in living sympathy with God loves to pray, and goes forth in longings for the privilege and the opportunity; but never into metaphysical subtleties for an excuse from praying. Has God promised to do this great thing for his kingdom? Then let me commune with him about it; let me thank him for the promise; let me humbly ask if there be yet any thing for me to do to hasten the result or to prepare the way for it: let me at least have fellowship with him in trust and love and gratitude for this great promise.——When men labor to excuse themselves from praying, their own hearts are the witness that they have none of the spirit of true prayer.

3. And I set my face unto the Lord God, to seek by prayer and supplications, with fasting, and sackcloth, and ashes:

4. And I prayed unto the Lord my God, and made my confession, and said, O Lord the great and dreadful God, keeping the covenant and mercy to them that love him, and to them that keep his commandments;

5. We have sinned, and have committed iniquity, and have done wickedly, and have rebelled, even by departing from thy precepts and from thy judgments:

6. Neither have we hearkened unto thy servants the prophets, which spake in thy name to our kings, our princes, and our fathers, and to all the people of the land.

This language is beautifully expressive of true prayer; "I set my face unto the Lord God to seek," etc. So true prayer turns one's thought and desire to the Lord; looks to him for blessings. Prayer makes direct application to God, bearing its petition at once to him and laying its case before his throne.——In harmony with his state of mind, and as fitly expressive of his genuine humility of soul, he fasted, put on sackcloth, and cast ashes on his head and garments. The people of the East made more account of these external manifestations of humility and grief than Europeans and

Americans are wont to do. The vital thing is that the heart be humble and contrite. These manifestations were not with Daniel mere forms, but rather were the natural and truthful expression of his feelings.——He says, "I prayed and made my confession." Personally, Daniel had not worshiped idols, had not cast off the fear of God, had not involved himself in those great sins for which these judgments were sent on the Jewish city and nation, and yet he does not stand upon his exemption from these gross sins, and say, "I thank God that I am not as other men are." But we can not suppose Daniel incapable of discriminating between such a life (e. g.) as that of Manasseh and his own. He could not confess himself guilty of the same sins that Manasseh had committed, and in the same degree, for the good reason that to do so would not be according to truth. Yet how far Daniel was conscious of heart-sins before God, lying in this direction, none of us can say, nor how much this confession was due to his intensely strong sympathy with his people, of such sort as *seems* to create a positive identity of conduct and culpability as well as of suffering and punishment. However this may be, this case of Daniel suggests that there is little danger that the holiest of men will confess too much in reference to their own personal sins.——While on the one hand Daniel thought of God as great and greatly to be feared, he did not forget on the other hand that he evermore "Kept covenant and mercy to them that love him and keep his commandments." This sustained his hope. God had shown great mercy in condescending ever to enter into covenant with his people. His past mercy is good for present faith.——The reader will observe that Daniel said, "Keeping *the* covenant." The Hebrew has it also, "*the* mercy," with manifest reference to the special covenant and the special mercy which God had made and shown to his Hebrew people. Upon this great fact, Daniel's faith took strong hold in this hour of his need.
——In v. 5 the repetition is peculiarly expressive. As one whose soul is full of the thought, Daniel groups together nearly or quite all the different words known to the Hebrew language conveying the idea of sinning. This sin was greatly aggravated by the fact that God had sent his prophets to rebuke the people and forewarn them of impending judgments, but they had not hearkened to his voice in these warnings.

7. O Lord, righteousness *belongeth* unto thee, but unto us confusion of faces, as at this day; to the men of Judah, and to the inhabitants of Jerusalem, and unto all Israel, *that are* near, and *that are* far off, through all the countries whither thou hast driven them, because of their trespass that they have trespassed against thee.

8. O Lord, to us *belongeth* confusion of face, to our kings, to our princes, and to our fathers, because we have sinned against thee.

9 To the Lord our God *belong* mercies and forgivenesses, though we have rebelled against him;

10. Neither have we obeyed the voice of the Lord our God, to walk in his laws, which he set before us by his servants the prophets.

There is great force as well as fitness and beauty in the antithesis between the righteousness and the mercies that belong to God, and the shame and the sin that belong to his people. God had been all right; they, all wrong. On God's side had been ever abounding mercies and forgivenesses; on their side, only perpetual rebellion and most ungrateful, abusive sinning. Alas, that human life should almost perpetually bear precisely this record as toward God!—that the millions live on and sin on just so; their course toward God, perpetual sinning; his bearing toward them, the most amazing patience, forbearance, long-suffering, forgiveness and mercy, that seem to flow from a vast outgushing fountain, as if they could not cease! And if his hand has sometimes turned to judgment, we must still say, "Righteousness belongeth unto thee, O God, forever!"

11. Yea, all Israel have transgressed thy law, even by departing, that they might not obey thy voice; therefore the curse is poured upon us, and the oath that *is* written in the law of Moses the servant of God, because we have sinned against him.

12. And he hath confirmed his words, which he spake against us, and against our judges that judged us, by bringing upon us a great evil: for under the whole heaven hath not been done as hath been done upon Jerusalem.

13. As *it is* written in the law of Moses, all this evil is come upon us: yet made we not our prayer before the Lord our God, that we might turn from our iniquities, and understand thy truth.

14. Therefore hath the Lord watched upon the evil, and brought it upon us: for the Lord our God *is* righteous in all his works which he doeth: for we obeyed not his voice.

The central thought in these verses is that God has been righteously visiting upon the nation the very judgments he had threatened against them in the law of Moses for precisely these sins of which they had been so greatly guilty. The reader will find these passages in their impressive fullness, in Lev. 26: 14–46, and in Deut. chapters 28–30. It is there declared most distinctly that for such sins, God would send them into captivity in a foreign land, and would lay their city and homes desolate. Now Daniel recognizes the entire fulfillment of those fearful threatenings. The Lord "had watched upon the evil and brought it upon them" as one who has made positive threatenings, and for the honor of his truth as well as for the support of his throne, can not forget them, but must see to their timely execution.——Daniel felt it to be a sore aggravation of the people's sin that under this fearful scourge they had not promptly turned to God with confession, penitence and prayer, as they might and should have done, nor had they desisted from their ways of sin.

15. And now, O Lord our God, that hast brought thy people forth out of the land of Egypt with a mighty hand, and hast gotten thee renown, as at this day; we have sinned, we have done wickedly.

16. O Lord, according to all thy righteousness, I beseech thee, let thine anger and thy fury be turned away from thy city Jerusalem, thy holy mountain: because for our sins and for the iniquities of our fathers, Jerusalem and thy people *are become* a reproach to all *that are* about us.

17. Now therefore, O our God, hear the prayer of thy servant, and his supplications, and cause thy face to shine upon thy sanctuary that is desolate, for the Lord's sake.

The tone in these verses is that of imploring entreaty; importunate prayer for pardon, resting mainly on the pleas that God delights in great mercies; that he has shown the nation such mercies in delivering them from Egypt; and that the honor of his name is implicated before the nations of the earth since they are his covenant people, now for a long time in the bonds of captivity, nationally eclipsed, and according to the ideas of idolatrous nations, a standing reproach to the God they worship as being unable to redeem and save them.

18. O my God, incline thine ear, and hear; open thine eyes, and behold our desolations, and the city which is called by thy name: for we do not present our supplications before thee for our righteousnesses, but for thy great mercies.

19. O Lord, hear; O Lord, forgive; O Lord, hearken and do; defer not, for thine own sake, O my God: for thy city and thy people are called by thy name.

Beautifully he puts the contrast—we do not ask this for our righteousness, but for thy great mercies. How true!—true in their case; true in the case of every sinner who comes before God for pardon and life!——The great points of his prayer, whether of confession or of plea, being now fully brought out, Daniel pours forth the full tides of his soul's emotion and desire in most earnest pleading with God. He implores him to listen, to open his eyes and look on the desolations of his people and of the city upon both which he had called his own name. He begs that God will not defer but will grant him an answer of peace and mercy now.——Such importunity may sometimes startle us as unbecoming, obtrusive and almost irreverent—out of place and character for a frail, sinful mortal before his Holy Sovereign! The thing to be said of it is that on the one hand it should never be assumed for form's sake; nor forced by working up one's own feelings for the mere sake of reaching such a fervor and form of prayer; nor should it ever be prompted by objects that are purely our own and not identified with the honor and glory of God;—but on the other hand, when it is the spontaneous utterance of a heart in deep sympathy with the honor and cause of God; when it comes of taking firm hold of his great love and of his unfailing promises; when one falls into it, being sweetly and mightily drawn by the Spirit of God himself, then nothing can be more pleasing to him. He lets us come very near to him to "order our cause before him and to fill our mouth with arguments." "The Spirit itself maketh intercession with our spirits." God never fails to answer such prayer.

20. And while I was speaking, and praying, and confessing my sin, and the sin of my people Israel, and presenting my supplication before the Lord my God for the holy mountain of my God;

21. Yea, while I *was* speaking in prayer, even the man Gabriel, whom I had seen in the vision at the beginning, being caused to fly swiftly, touched me about the time of the evening oblation.

22. And he informed *me*, and talked with me, and said, O Daniel, I am now come forth to give thee skill and understanding.

23. At the beginning of thy supplications the commandment came forth, and I am come to shew *thee;* for thou *art* greatly beloved: therefore understand the matter, and consider the vision.

"The sin of *my* people Israel," indicates how exceedingly intimate were the heart-relations sustained by Daniel toward the Jewish people.——He felt toward them as a father toward his children. He bore them tenderly in his heart, as Paul did his Christian converts; "Now we *live*, if ye stand fast in the Lord" (1 Thess. 3: 8). This intense devotion to his own people goes far to prove that his four parallel visions have respect to the future fortunes—the struggles, oppressions, persecutions and deliverances of this same people. They put this point beyond rational doubt.——In this passage we have the preliminary steps for revealing to Daniel God's prophetic answer to his prayer. He had only begun to pray when the divine mandate came forth commissioning the angel Gabriel—the same whom he had seen in the last preceding vision (chap. 8: 16), to go and meet him at the hour of evening worship. This was doubtless the season of this prayer, above recorded—this being with pious Jews one of the usual seasons of daily prayer. See Acts 3: 1, and 10: 3, 30. On the phrase rendered, "Being caused to fly swiftly," modern lexicographers raise grave doubts whether the sense be not rather, "being wearied with a great weariness,"* as one from a long journey. The point is of no special importance. It might seem at first sight to lessen our sense of the powers of an angel to conceive of him as *weary* with the effort of transit from heaven to earth; but really why should this be more improbable than that he should *fly* at all? In both cases we have figures of speech, used to give us the conception of an angel's change of place. Of the reality, what can we know beyond the mere fact of such change? No doubt the clause is introduced for the sake of showing that Gabriel came from a far distant world to bring to Daniel an important answer to his accepted prayer. It is very idle for us to speculate on the manner and velocity of an angel's locomotion, or on its draft upon his strength.——"For thou art greatly beloved;" in the Hebrew, "a man of delights," *i. e.*, as to God. It is a most affecting thought that mortals may by grace come into a state of holiness in heart and life, in which God can feel complacency toward them and testify to his great love for them. Who would not aspire toward such holiness and such favor with God, as infinitely before all things else?——"Therefore now, understand the matter and consider the vision;" give attention to the revelations which I am about to make. The vision referred to is, beyond a doubt, the same which the angel has come to reveal, standing in vs. 24-27.

24. Seventy weeks are determined upon thy people and upon thy holy city, to finish the transgression, and to make an end of sins, and to make reconciliation for iniquity, and to bring in everlasting righteousness, and to seal up the vision and prophecy, and to anoint the Most Holy.

25. Know therefore and understand, *that* from the going forth of the commandment to restore and to build Jerusalem unto the Messiah the Prince, *shall be* seven weeks, and threescore and two weeks: the street shall be built again, and the wall, even in troublous times.

26. And after threescore and two weeks shall Messiah be cut off, but not for himself: and the people of the prince that shall come shall destroy the city and the sanctuary:

---

* The question is one of etymology, viz., whether the two words קָצַץ בְּ קָצַץ come from קָצַץ to fly, or from יָקַץ to be weary. The forms favor, not to say demand, the latter.

and the end thereof *shall be* with a flood, and unto the end of the war desolations are determined.

27. And he shall confirm the covenant with many for one week: and in the midst of the week he shall cause the sacrifice and the oblation to cease, and for the overspreading of abominations he shall make *it* desolate, even until the consummation, and that determined shall be poured upon the desolate.

This passage requires and will reward a careful and thorough study. I propose to give first a translation; then a paraphrase; and finally such special comments as may seem necessary.——
"Seventy sevens [of years] are determined in reference to thy people and thy holy city, to shut up sin, to seal transgression, to cover iniquity, to bring in everlasting righteousness, to seal up vision and prophet, and to anoint the holy of holies.——Know and understand: From the going forth of a decree for restoring and rebuilding Jerusalem unto Messiah the Prince are seven sevens [of years] and sixty-two sevens [of years]; the streets shall be restored and built again; it is decided and shall be, though in distress of times.——
And after sixty-two sevens [of years] Messiah shall be cut off and there shall be nothing more to him. Then the people of a prince that shall come shall destroy the city and the sanctuary; its end shall be with that sweeping flood; even unto the end of the war, desolations are determined.——One seven [years] shall make the covenant effective to many. The middle of the seven shall make sacrifice and offerings cease: then down upon the summit of the abomination comes the desolator, even till a complete destruction, determined, shall be poured upon the desolate."

Next, to give a partial explanation, blended with the translation, I paraphrase thus:——"Seventy sevens of years, equal to four hundred and ninety years, are cut off from the course of future time, for thy people and thy holy city, at the end of which provision shall be made for the full pardon of sin and for putting it utterly out of my sight, as a thing shut up, sealed and covered; and to bring in a system of everlasting righteousness whereby pardoned sinners may both be accounted and may become righteous before me. This, by amply fulfilling, will close up those visions of the prophets which respect the Messiah to come. Then will I anoint my church, the spiritual temple of the new dispensation, with the gracious unction of the Holy Ghost.——This in general. I will now repeat and give more particulars. Know, then, and consider, that from the issuing of the decree of Artaxerxes for restoring and rebuilding Jerusalem unto the public ministry of Messiah, the Prince, shall be forty-nine years and four hundred and thirty-four years; *i. e.*, forty-nine up to the point of completing the rebuilding of the city, and four hundred and thirty-four from that point till the Messiah shall appear before the public, to commence his gospel ministry. This city shall be restored and rebuilt; the thing is settled in the counsels of the Almighty, and shall be done, although in times of much distress.——After the four hundred and thirty-four years shall have expired, the Messiah shall be cut off by a violent death; his relationship to his ancient covenant people will cease; they will reject him, and he will abandon them to their righteous doom. Then the people of the Roman prince, coming from afar, shall destroy the city and the sanctuary; its end shall be with that sweeping flood of ruin; even till the end of this war, there is a divine decree for desolations. During one heptad of years the covenant of God's mercy shall become effective to many: at the middle point of this heptad, he will make sacrifice and offering cease by becoming himself the one great atoning sacrifice, complete thenceforth and forever, and superseding all the sacrifices of the Mosaic ritual. Then down upon the summit of the temple, now an abomination before God for the apostasy of those that worship therein, comes the desolator, the Roman legions—even until a complete, terrible, and predetermined destruction shall have been poured forth upon the desolate city."

Several points now demand a more particular explanation.——"*Seventy weeks.*" This English phrase suggests only the ordinary week of seven days, making the whole duration four hundred and ninety days. Inasmuch as the fulfillment seems to require instead four hundred and ninety *years*, it has been often assumed that this passage at least must be admitted to be a case of a prophetic day used for a year. A closer examination removes this case from the list of those proofs, explaining the phrase in another and much more reliable way.——A Hebrew reader coming to this phrase,* would say at once, This first word is not the usual form for weeks of days. The word means a seven; a heptad; and is formed from the numeral seven. The feminine plural is the form which is constantly used to denote weeks of days. This is the masculine plural, indicating at least something different from a mere week of seven days. There is no instance in the Hebrew Bible where this masculine plural form is used *alone* for weeks of days. In a few cases, where it means sevens of days, the word for days follows it to make the sense clear, showing that of itself it would not be taken in this sense of seven days. See these cases, Dan. 10: 2, 3. In Ezek. 45: 21, the feminine plural has the word *days* after it, meaning the feast of sevens of days, *i. e.*, the Passover, which was held seven days—a case which shows that the primary sense of even the feminine plural is a *heptad*, and not properly a *week*. The use of the feminine plural in the sense of our common week may be seen in Ex. 34: 22; Num. 28: 26; Deut. 16: 9, 10, 16; 2 Chron. 8: 13; Jer. 5: 24.——Further; when any thoughtful reader should meet the word *sevens*, he would naturally ask, Sevens of what? Is this sevens of *days*, or sevens of *years*, or sevens of *centuries?* He would expect to find the clew to his answer in the context. What has the writer been saying? There must be something in what he has said to give a definite clew to his meaning, for to say only

* שָׁבֻעִים

"sevens" is to leave his meaning entirely indefinite. Pursuing this train of inquiry, he would see in the present case a manifest allusion to the seventy years of captivity which is so vividly before Daniel's mind. It can not be overlooked that Daniel is praying with the great thought of the seventy years' captivity before his mind. When the Lord sends his answer by Gabriel, he too understands that the seventy years of captivity are present to Daniel's thought, and therefore he only needs to say, not that seventy *years* are assigned before the next great event, but seventy *sevens*. Daniel will supply "*years.*" The talk and the thought are about *years*. Years, therefore, is the word to be supplied after "*sevens.*"——On the strength, then, of these two considerations, either of them sufficient alone, and both together entirely decisive, I account this period precisely seventy sevens *of years*, or four hundred and ninety years.——The same usage prevails throughout this passage in the "seven weeks," the "sixty-two weeks," and the "one week."——The word heptad, transferred from the Greek language, precisely translates the original Hebrew. Or we might say *a seven*, meaning a period of seven units, leaving the particular sense of the unit to be learned from the context.——Hence this is not by any means a case of a day for a year. It is only a case of using a Hebrew word meaning a seven, a heptad, a period of seven units, selecting a form that does not suggest units of days but units of years.——The historic fulfillment of all these periods of time will be considered in its place.——"Are determined," etc., means in the original precisely, *are cut off*, *i. e.*, from all future time. A limit is set at the end of it, inside of which these events shall occur.——This cutting off or determining has reference to "thy people" and "thy holy city"—here again recognizing the very intimate relations which Daniel sustained to the Jews as their patron and father.——*What* shall be done at or near the end of this seventy heptads is next stated.——The first two verbs in this series, rendered in the received version, "to finish transgression," and "to make an end of sins," present in the marginal Hebrew a slightly different reading, which our English text follows, and the English margin does not. I adopt the reading of the Hebrew text and the English margin; to "shut up" or "restrain;" and to "seal." Sins are thought of as shut up, sealed, covered—a climax of figures. Dr. Hengstenberg well remarks; "Sin, which hitherto lay naked and open before the eyes of a righteous God, is now by his mercy shut up, sealed and covered, so that it can no more be regarded as existing—a frequent designation of the forgiveness of sin, analogous to those where it is said 'to conceal the face from sin and to cause it to pass away,'" etc. (Christology 2: 305).—— The last of these three verbs is the Levitical word for *atonement*— a cover for sins to hide them from view.——This gives us the central thought of the passage—one which stands in the closest connection with Daniel's prayer. No point stands out so prominently and strongly in this prayer as the distress and solicitude he feels in respect to the great sins of his people. The agonizing solicitude of his heart centers upon this one question; How can this sin be removed? How can the Lord pass over and forgive it so that the people can again come under his mercy and favor? It was therefore to meet precisely this main point of his distress and anxiety that the Lord replies; After seventy heptads of years I will bring forth a perfect provision to atone for sin. Then it will be seen how I can honorably and safely forgive the penitent sinner and restore him to favor.——"To bring in everlasting righteousness," is only another form of stating the same thing. The sinner forgiven and his sins all covered *stands right* before God. Christ is made of God unto him righteousness as well as redemption. On the ground of what Christ is, and has suffered for him, he is accounted righteous before God.——This way of accounting sinners righteous is "*everlasting*" as contrasted with the transient duration of the Mosaic system, and the temporary effects of those frequent sacrifices required under that system, which indeed were only typical at best, and "could never with those sacrifices which they offered, year by year, make the comers thereunto perfect" (Heb. 10: 1). This new system is to stand through all time, and its blessed effects will be enduring.——"To seal up vision and prophet," is the literal rendering of the original, and obviously refers to the fulfillment, and hence, in this sense, to the closing up of those prophecies which for many ages had predicted the Messiah, but which, having now done their work of ministry to the faith of God's waiting people, may be considered as sealed up and laid aside—superseded by the Messiah's actual coming.——"To anoint the most holy." The Hebrew has it, "the holy of holies."——In determining the sense of this phrase, we have to choose between three possible or at least supposable meanings:—(*a*.) The most holy place in the temple.—(*b*.) The Messiah himself.—(*c*.) The Christian Church.——The first is set aside by the fact that this very passage (v. 26) predicts the destruction of the sanctuary.——The second is set aside by the fact that the Old Testament never uses this phrase for the Messiah; indeed, never for persons, but always for things. Also by the further fact that if applied to the Messiah, it should relate to his baptism and not to his death, and the exact fulfillment could not be made out.——(*c*). The third meaning suggested above has in its favor both Old Testament usage and New. The Old Testament presents the work of the Messiah in building up his kingdom under the figure, "He shall build the temple of the Lord" (Zech. 6: 12, 13). The same figure runs through Isa. 60, and many kindred prophecies. They make the great facts of the Mosaic dispensation the ground-work of their portrayals of analogous things in the gospel age. Hence the temple of the Old Testament economy becomes the gospel church of the New. This becomes the current usage of the New Testament writers. "Ye are the temple of the living God; as God hath said, 'I will dwell in them and walk in them,'" etc., (2 Cor. 6: 16).——Hence there is ample authority in the line of usage for taking the phrase, "the holy of holies," to mean in our passage, the gospel church.——Anointing is a common symbol of

DANIEL.—CHAP. IX.   405

the effusions of the Spirit. Messianic prophecy has it; "The Spirit of the Lord is upon me because he hath *anointed* me to preach good tidings," etc. (Isa. 61: 1). The Messiah himself indorsed this usage and accepted its application to himself (Luke 4: 18-21). The Apostles use this figure freely. See Ac. 4: 27, and 10: 38— 1 Jn. 2: 20, 27. Hence the phrase, "to anoint the most holy," looks toward those signal manifestations of the Holy Spirit's power which were the preëminent glory of the great Pentecost, and which shed their luster over the first few years of the gospel age.——Let it now be noted that v. 24 is a comprehensive and general statement of most of the great points embraced in this prophetic answer to Daniel's prayer. It omits the desolation brought on the holy city and temple by the Roman arms under Titus, and this only. The other points are mainly comprehended in general form in this first verse of the passage. Then in the remaining verses the same topics are restated with more specific details, especially as to dates. Let us see.——"Know, therefore, and understand," urges special attention to this more minute statement. Practically, these verbs must be taken as imperatives, though in form the Hebrew has them both in the future. The use of the future for the imperative is not uncommon.—— *What commandment* or decree is this for restoring and rebuilding Jerusalem?——The reader might very naturally think first of the nearer one by Cyrus, which appears in Ezra 1: 1-4 and 2 Chron. 36: 22, 23, rather than the more remote one by Artaxerxes referred to, Neh. I. Yet the latter is undoubtedly the one intended, inasmuch as the description, which is rather minute, describes this and does not describe the decree by Cyrus. The description given here in this prophecy is that of a decree for restoring and rebuilding Jerusalem—"the city and its streets," in the sense probably of the buildings upon them. Precisely such is the decree from Artaxerxes obtained by Nehemiah. The words of the decree are not recorded by Nehemiah, but its subject-matter can be determined no less clearly from what is said of it than if the document itself were preserved. Look at the circumstances. Nehemiah hears that the wall of Jerusalem is broken down and the gates thereof burnt with fire (Neh. 1: 3). He gives himself to fasting, weeping, and mourning. The king inquires the cause of his grief. He replies: Why should not my countenance be sad when the city, the place of my father's sepulchers, lieth waste, and the gates thereof are "consumed with fire?" (Neh. 2: 3). The king says, "What is thy request?" He answers promptly: An order from the king that I be "sent to the city of my father's sepulchers *that I may build it.*" To this the king consented; so that there can be no doubt as to the substance of this decree. It said nothing about building the temple; it began and ended with rebuilding the city. The temple-building was already complete.—— On the other hand, the decree by Cyrus said not a word of rebuilding the city, but did speak expressly and only of "building an house for God in Jerusalem," *i. e.*, the temple. Hence all doubt is removed as to the particular decree referred to. It must be that

sent forth by Artaxerxes, with Nehemiah, for rebuilding the city.
——It might be added that the facts in the line of historic fulfillment go entirely against the decree of Cyrus. For, taking this decree of Cyrus for our starting point, our four hundred and ninety years would expire before the Messiah came—this decree being issued about B. C. 536. There is no occasion, however, to make use of the argument from fulfillment for help in the interpretation of this prophecy. And prophecy ought to have its meaning settled before we come to the question of fulfillment.——
Dr. Hengstenberg gives this turn to the clause now before us: "From the going forth of the commandment unto the restoring and rebuilding of Jerusalem, and from that, unto the Messiah, shall be seven sevens and sixty-two sevens"—*i. e.*, dividing the whole period into two parts, the first period of seven sevens extends to the point where the city is restored and rebuilt; the second reaches from that point to the Messiah.——I fully concur in this division of the whole period into these two portions, limited as above stated; but I think it better to read, "From the commandment *for* restoring," etc., rather than, "From the commandment *until* the restoring," etc. The latter is by no means a facile rendering. It leaves too much to be grammatically supplied.——The word rendered in our received version, "the wall," I take to be a participle in the sense of a verb; "it is determined," fully settled and decided on. For the comfort of Daniel and of his pious Jewish readers, it is here declared that this rebuilding of the city is firmly fixed in the counsels of God and will be done, although the obstacles be great—in great "straitness of times." The book of Nehemiah is a comment on this clause.——"After the sixty-two sevens shall Messiah be *cut off*," *i. e.*, by a violent death. This is the current Jewish word to denote a death by violence.——"But not for himself," shows that our translators supposed the original to mean that he died for the sins of others and not for his own. This is undoubtedly a truth, but it may not be *the* truth taught here. The original, rendered closely, would give us this; "And nothing to him." The verb of existence must be implied between "nothing" and "him," thus; Nothing shall be to him, or he shall have nothing. The ellipsis can not well be supplied with the next preceding verb, "cut off," in the sense, He shall not be cut off for him. "For him" can not well mean for himself. The Hebrews use other forms and not this to express the reciprocal sense. Hence we must look for another meaning here. I find it in the negation of all further relations between him and his ancient covenant people, the Jews, his murderers. "There is nothing more to him" *with them.* They ignore and repudiate him; He rejects them and gives them up to their just doom. Zech. 11: 8, treating of precisely the same subject, says; "My soul loathed them; and their soul abhorred me." They said, "Away with him;" "crucify him;" "his blood be on us and on our children." His sad answer, fulfilled through the judgments of his righteous providence, was; "Your house is left unto you desolate." "O that thou hadst known, even thou, at least

in this thy day, the things that belong unto thy peace; but now they are hid from thine eyes." That blood ye have so ruthlessly invoked shall come on you in an avalanche of woes till your city is in ruins, and your children are given to the slaughter.——Further, it is very much in favor of the interpretation above given to this clause, that it makes a natural transition from the violent death of Christ to the coming of that other Prince and his Roman legions to destroy the city and sanctuary. The intermediate link between these two great historic facts was the rejection by the Messiah of his ancient covenant people. Without this link, the transition is violent; with it, natural and easy.——"The Prince that shall come" is without doubt the Roman general Titus, and "the people" are his armed legions. They came and did precisely this; they "destroyed the city and the sanctuary."——"Its end was with that flood," i. e., of ruin: This word, "flood," is a favorite one with Daniel for the sweeping desolations of war. See 11: 22, 26, 40. ——"And unto the end is war; a decree of ruins." This I take to be the most exact and literal rendering of the last clause. The sense is obvious. The Jewish and Roman war shall continue until their city and nationality shall be completely broken down and the site of their noble city shall become a pile of ruins.——"He shall confirm," etc. The grammatical construction here is obviously this. "One seven shall make the covenant effective to many"—a case in which, for brevity's sake, the period of time is itself said to do that which is done within it, as e. g., Mal. 4: 1; "The day that cometh shall burn them up; or Job 3: 3, 7, 10, "The night which said, A man-child is conceived." "Let that night be solitary because it shut not up the doors of my mother's womb."—— The next clause has the same construction; The middle of the seven shall cause sacrifice and oblation to cease."——The sense of this entire passage is that during the last seven years, the closing heptad, which embraces the three and a half years of our Lord's public ministry, and the same length of time after his death, there would be extraordinary efficiency in the sealing gifts of the Spirit. God's gracious covenant with repenting sinners would become strong and effective to many. Great numbers would be savingly converted during our Lord's public ministry: so, also, during an equal length of time after his resurrection, including that blessed pentecostal season, protracted through several years, in which great multitudes were added to the Lord. At the middle point of this seven-year period, the Lord himself would die on the cross. In that death all further demand for sacrifice and oblation would cease. Dying as himself the great atoning Sacrifice, he forever superseded all other sacrifices.——"And for the overspreading of abominations he shall make it desolate." This translation seems to be rather unusually wide of the literal one, though less wide of the sense. The following is a closely literal rendering of the original: "And upon the wing [or summit] of abominations is the desolator."——The difficulties involved in the quotation of this passage into Mat. 24: 14, and Mark 13: 13, seem to require a specially careful explanation.——The word which I render "wing," is very common in Hebrew for the wing of a bird; the wing of an army; the wing or corner of a garment; the wings (extreme corners) of the land; and, as here, the wing, highest point, pinnacle, of the temple. As it stands here, it must be *the wing of* that which is called an "abomination."——This word, "abominations," is used almost exclusively (more than a score of times) for idols or things connected with idol worship, the idols being always thought of as existing, loved and worshiped *by God's professed people*, and for this reason indefinitely more abominable and detestable to God. Passages specially significant and illustrative of the sense here are, Jer. 7: 30—"For the children of Judah have done evil in my sight, saith the Lord; they have set their abominations in the house which is called by my name to pollute it." Jer. 32: 34, repeats the same idea. Also Ezek. 5: 11 : "Wherefore as I live, saith the Lord God, because thou hast defiled my sanctuary with all thy detestable things and with all thine abominations; therefore will I also diminish thee, neither shall mine eyes spare, neither will I have any pity." These passages clearly indicate the reason why the temple is called an abomination and is doomed to destruction.——The word which I translate "the desolator," being a causative participle, one who *causes* desolation, can bear no other sense than "*the desolator*," conceived of as actually doing the deed. Hence the sentence can scarcely bear any other construction than this; "Then down upon the pinnacle of the temple" (made abominable by the corruption of priests and people) "comes the desolator"—as with the swoop of an eagle pouncing on his prey.—— This is the prophecy to which our Lord refers in Mat. 24: 15, and Mark 13: 14: "When ye shall see the abomination of desolation, spoken of by Daniel the prophet, standing in the holy place," ("where it ought not;" Mark) then let them that be in Judea flee into the mountains."——This quotation is obviously made from the Septuagint version. The sense of the words there used, "abomination of desolation," I take to be the abomination which, under a righteous God, becomes the *cause* of desolation. This abomination is fundamentally the fearful religious corruption of the Jews, because of which God sent on them the Romans as his scourge of desolation. The Hebrew words used by Daniel seem to demand this sense, and the Greek of both the Septuagint and of the New Testament admits it. But precisely *what indications* of this moral corruption, or of this approaching scourge, the disciples were to look for, and were supposed to see, as a warning to flee, it is by no means easy to determine. On this point commentators differ widely. It may perhaps suffice to put the case in the general form; *Any indication* that God had given up the city to destruction by the Romans, whether it be in the horrible corruption of the Jews or in the approach of the Roman legions, was to be accepted as a warning to fly. In this general form no serious difficulties are encountered. When we attempt to describe the sign precisely, we find the data wanting.——In construing the words of Daniel, I have felt bound to follow the usual laws of language. Quotations from the Septuagint of the Old Testament into the New sometimes involve difficulties, as here.——Luke makes no specific reference to Daniel. He says, "When ye shall see Jerusalem encompassed with armies," etc. Of course he makes no allusion to the sins of the Jews as causing this destruction. But this does not prove that Matthew and Mark make none. Our Lord may have made the statements in both forms. Neither is at all inconsistent with the other.

It remains to look more closely into the designations of time in this passage.——As we have seen, the seventy weeks are to be counted from the decree of Artaxerxes, obtained by Nehemiah, as appears Neh. 1 and 2, in the twentieth year of that king. The first point to be settled then is, the year in which Artaxerxes began to reign.——It has been common with chronologists to put this B. C. 464. But Dr. Hengstenberg (Christology II, 394), by a most elaborate and conclusive examination, shows that it must have been B. C. 474, so that Xerxes his father reigned only eleven years instead of twenty-one, and Artaxerxes the son fifty-one instead of forty-one. Adopting his view, the case stands thus.——The twentieth year of Artaxerxes is B. C. 454. Sixty-nine sevens of years is four hundred and eighty-three years. Deducting from this what precedes the birth of Christ, we have 483—454=29, which is of course A. D. 29, the time when our Lord began his public ministry. So this prophecy would locate it.——On the side of N. T. history, we have (*e. g.*, Luke 3: 1) the commencement of John's ministry in the fifteenth year of Tiberius, *i. e.*, in the year of Rome 782. The birth of Christ is usually put in the year of Rome 753. But 782—753=29, which is A. D. 29. This, then, would be about the time that John commenced his public ministry. There is good reason for supposing that Christ commenced his about six months later, when not far from thirty years of age.——Thus this great prophecy of Daniel's weeks fixes the time of the Savior's appearing before the public within at farthest one year of the best historic results.——This prophecy also assumes that Christ's public ministry continued three and one-half years, so that his violent death fell in the middle of the last seven-year period. That this was proximately the duration of his ministry is generally admitted. The proof in brief may be made from the Gospel of John thus.——(1.) Jn. 2: 13, gives us one passover, the first after his ministry began, and manifestly not long after his first miracle, say six months after he began to preach.——(2.) John 5: 1, gives another feast, which with almost a certainty was a passover.——(3.) John 6: 1, is certainly another and doubtless the next.——(4.) John 19: 16, is certainly another and the last; at which his death occurred.——This makes up three and one-half years. The only point of uncertainty turns on John 5: 1. This is not said in the record to be a passover, yet that it was is evident from the following considerations. John 4: 35, shows that eight months had already elapsed since the previous passover. Of course the feast of Pentecost, fifty days after the passover, and the feast of Tabernacles,

18

six months after, had both gone by. No "feast of the Jews" remained for that year save the feast of Purim, one month before the next passover. But this can not have been the feast of Purim, for the temple is here filled with Jews (5: 14); but they kept the feast of Purim mostly by assembling, not in their temple, but in their several homes. Moreover, this feast included a Sabbath (v. 9), which the feast of Purim never did, because a divine institution must never give way to one merely human.

This very brief view of the argument must suffice.——Thus with remarkable accuracy this wonderful prophecy brings out its dates in harmony with the best authenticated facts of history.

CHAPTER X.

This entire chapter is introductory to the fourth and last of the parallel visions, the vision proper occupying the two remaining chapters. This introduction is very full on the points of the prophet's overwhelming agitation, grief, and physical prostration; the renewed ministries of his revealing angel to comfort and strengthen him; certain remarkable yet little known conflicts between the angel-guardians of the Jews and other angels standing in perhaps analogous relations toward other kingdoms—coupled with several intimations that the matters to be revealed relate to long and grievous wars, some of which would befall Daniel's people in future years.

1. In the third year of Cyrus king of Persia a thing was revealed unto Daniel, whose name was called Belteshazzar; and the thing *was* true, but the time appointed *was* long: and he understood the thing, and had understanding of the vision.

The third year of Cyrus is the latest known date in the life of Daniel. Chap. 1: 21, states that "he continued to the first year of the reign of Cyrus;' but does not say he died then; does not deny that he lived longer. That passage may mean only that he continued so long in active public service. He is now far advanced in age, it being not far from seventy-four years since he was brought, a captive youth, from Jerusalem to Babylon.——"A thing was revealed;" in the Hebrew a "word," *i. e.*, a matter, not presented largely (as in the previous visions) by symbols, but without symbols, in mere words. "The thing was true;" the "*word*" again; the original being the same.——In the phrase, "the time appointed was long,"•our translators fail to give the precise sense of the original, which means, "and of great wars" or warfare; *i. e.*, the subject-matter of this prophecy pertains to great wars—as the study of chap. 11 will show. The original word, commonly rendered *host* is used for martial host, *i. e.*, an army, and for warfare; often of going out to *war*, as in Num. 31: 27, 28, 36, and Deut. 24: 5.——"True is the word revealed, and great the warfare" of which it treats.——"He understood the thing," the sense of which seems rather to be that he gave diligent heed to it, bending the entire powers of his mind to it; for chap 12: 8, implies that there were at least some things in it that he did not understand.

2. In those days I Daniel was mourning three full weeks.

3. I ate no pleasant bread, neither came flesh nor wine in my mouth, neither did I anoint myself at all, till three whole weeks were fulfilled.

So deeply affected was he with the anticipation of these things, even before they were definitely revealed. But it should be remembered that he has had the same general subject before his mind in at least two previous visions, those of chaps. 7 and 8. In both those visions, the wars to be waged by the little horn against the saints of the Most High had been the leading theme, and had manifestly impressed his mind powerfully. Now, even before the details of this vision commence, his mind again comes under the strong impression of those scenes, and the deep fountains of his grief are broken up.——The statements as to time here; "three full weeks" (v. 2), and "three whole weeks" (v. 3), are the same in the original, and are literally, "three sevens" (or heptads) "as to days"— the word "days" being added to exclude what otherwise a Hebrew reader would think of—a week of years. The word for "seven" is precisely the same in form that occurred repeatedly in the passage 9: 24–27.——This abstaining from pleasant food and from anointing his person, were the usual indications of great grief.

4. And in the four and twentieth day of the first month, as I was by the side of the great river, which *is* Hiddekel;

5. Then I lifted up mine eyes, and looked, and behold a certain man clothed in linen, whose loins *were* girded with fine gold of Uphaz:

6. His body also *was* like the beryl, and his face as the appearance of lightning, and his eyes as lamps of fire, and his arms and his feet like in color to polished brass, and the voice of his words like the voice of a multitude.

The river Hiddekel is better known as the Tigris.——The personage described here was his angel-interpreter in human form, and in his whole appearance, splendid, majestic, awe-inspiring. Of the two usual Hebrew words for man, the one used here is that which involves most dignity. The other suggests frailty and mortality from the dust of the earth.——"His body like the beryl," where modern lexicographers say rather the *topaz*. The Hebrew is Tharshish, with reference to Spain whence it was brought. The topaz is still found there.

7. And I Daniel alone saw the vision: for the men that were with me saw not the vision; but a great quaking fell upon them, so that they fled to hide themselves.

8. Therefore I was left alone, and saw this great vision, and there remained no strength in me: for my comeliness was turned in me into corruption, and I retained no strength.

9. Yet heard I the voice of his words: and when I heard the voice of his words, then was I in a deep sleep on my face, and my face toward the ground.

10. And behold, a hand touched me, which set me upon my knees and *upon* the palms of my hands.

11. And he said unto me, O Daniel, a man greatly beloved, understand the words that I speak unto thee, and stand upright: for unto thee I am now sent. And when he had spoken this word unto me, I stood trembling.

Daniel does not mean that he was alone when he saw the vision, but that *he only* saw it. His attendants did not see it, but were impressed with a sense of something supernatural, and hence were affrighted and fled to hide themselves. The seeing in this case seems to have been, not with the eye of sense, but with the eye of the spirit. Similar phenomena occurred in the conversion of Saul. He heard audible words; his attendants heard a noise but no words. The Spirit manifests himself to whom he will.——Daniel was powerfully affected. "My comeliness" is rather my *strength*, my physical vigor, which now became mere weakness.——In v. 10 the original gives a stronger sense than our received version. "And lo, a hand touched me, and set me shaking upon my knees and the palms of my hands." "Caused me to be shaking" is the precise sense of the Hebrew.

12. Then said he unto me, Fear not, Daniel: for from the first day that thou didst set thy heart to understand, and to chasten thyself before thy God, thy words were heard, and I am come for thy words.

13. But the prince of the kingdom of Persia withstood me one and twenty days: but lo, Michael, one of the chief princes, came to help me; and I remained there with the kings of Persia.

From the first day of those three eventful weeks of fasting and prayer (says the angel) thy words were heard and I am come because of thy words. But I was hindered during the whole twenty-one days. The Prince of the realm of Persia withstood me. I was detained till Michael, the archangel whose strength is with me and with thy people (v. 21) came to help me. The last clause, "I remained there with the kings of Persia," repeats the main idea of the verse—his detention for twenty-one days because of the opposition experienced from that Prince of the realm of Persia.——The subject here introduced is very extraordinary. Who is this Prince of the kingdom of Persia? What are his functions? Whence his power? What is his moral character, and what are his relations to God? What had he to do to detain this angel who is specially commissioned to comfort Daniel and to reveal to him future events?——The same subject appears again in the last two verses of this chapter, and will receive more attention there.

14. Now I am come to make thee understand what shall befall thy people in the latter days; for yet the vision *is* for *many* days.

This statement is of prime importance as giving a clew to the interpretation of this prophecy, and equally so, of those that are parallel with it. It positively affirms that this prophecy (chap. 11 and 12) relates to the fortunes of the Jews, Daniel's own people, in future times. How far down in the future can not be definitely determined from this general expression, "in the latter days." There are instances in which this phrase refers to the times of the Messiah—the gospel age of the world; *e. g.*, Isa. 2: 2, and Mich. 4: 1. But there are also other instances in which it refers to events far less remote, *e. g.* Gen. 49: 1, which looks to the various fortunes of the tribes, mostly long prior to the gospel age. Also Num. 24: 14—the outlook of Balaam, which primarily goes not beyond the overthrow of Moab by David. So that the usage of this phrase does not of necessity carry us into the latter times of the Messiah's kingdom. In the present case it manifestly had its fulfillment prior to the first advent of Christ.——" For yet the vision is for days "— not necessarily "*many* days," for our translators supplied the word "many" to meet their own views, and not because they found any thing for it in the Hebrew text. Some years must elapse before these main events would transpire. It was in fact about three hundred and sixty years to the reign of Antiochus Epiphanes—the "vile king" whose case occupies the greater part of this vision.

15. And when he had spoken such words unto me, I set my face toward the ground, and I became dumb.

16. And behold, *one* like the similitude of the sons of men touched my lips: then I opened my mouth, and spake, and said unto him that stood before me, O my lord, by the vision my sorrows are turned upon me, and I have retained no strength.

17. For how can the servant of this my lord talk with this my lord? for as for me, straightway there remained no strength in me, neither is there breath left in me.

Again Daniel becomes completely prostrate in point of physical strength. Sorrows, wave after wave, come up and dash over him; he loses his strength and almost his breath. How can he talk with his angel-interpreter, or receive communications from him? This great prostration may be due in part to his extreme age; more, we must suppose, to the great depth of his sympathy and love for his people.

18. Then there came again and touched me *one* like the appearance of a man, and he strengthened me,

19. And said, O man greatly beloved, fear not: peace *be* unto thee, be strong, yea, be strong. And when he had spoken unto me, I was strengthened, and said, Let my lord speak; for thou hast strengthened me.

The manner of introducing the angels (vs. 16, 18) may seem to favor the opinion that these were severally distinct from each other and from the one introduced in vs. 5, 6. But the notice of the revealing angel in vs. 20, 21, supports the view that he is one only, and that these are his several manifestations. He now gives Daniel strength, and the way is prepared to proceed with his revelations.

20. Then said he, Knowest thou wherefore I come unto thee? and now will I return to fight with the prince of Persia: and when I am gone forth, lo, the prince of Grecia shall come.

21. But I will shew thee that which is noted in the scripture of truth: and *there is* none that holdeth with me in these things, but Michael your prince.

Now he returns to renew the struggle with the prince of Persia. The prince of Grecia will come in also—we must suppose in the same relation of antagonism to God's revealing angel and to Michael who "*makes himself strong*" for the aid of this good angel-interpreter and of Daniel's people.——What does all this import? Is this prince of Persia a good angel, or an evil one? in allegiance to God, or to Satan? If to God, why is he fighting with this good angel sent of God to the prophet Daniel?——Some of these questions are readily answered. The prince of Persia shows himself an adversary to God and to God's people. In his efforts and hence in his character, he is opposed to Michael who stands up for God and for the interests of his kingdom. He must belong to that order of beings commonly represented in Scripture by Satan, the great adversary of God and of his people. Satan often appears in Scripture, not as one alone in his rebellion among the higher orders of created beings, but as having legions associated with him. They are of various grades or orders. As good angels are put by their Maker in charge over the nations of his people, nothing forbids that these bad angels should in some sense be put in charge over wicked nations by their chief who directs and inspires their antagonism to the living God. This view is fully in harmony with the teachings of the New Testament.——Traces of the opinion that the heathen nations had each its own presiding angel are supposed to appear in the Septuagint translation of Deut. 32: 8. The Hebrew of this passage should be translated, "When the Most High in apportioning the sons of men gave their inheritance to the nations, he fixed the bounds of the peoples with reference to the number of the sons of Israel." But the Septuagint has the last clause, "according to the number of the angels of God," *i. e.*, so as to give one angel to each several nation.——This Septuagint translation was made (as is supposed) about B. C. 285. The allusions in the Scriptures to Michael suffice to show his relations to God and to his people very clearly. See Dan. 12: 1; Jude 9, and Rev. 12: 7.——"I will show thee that which is noted (written) in the scripture of truth," where by the scripture of truth we are not to understand our Bible, as if the angel proposed only to make a quotation from what we call the sacred Scriptures. He thinks rather of the book of God's eternal purposes, from which he is commissioned to make an extract, prophetically, for Daniel and his people, of what shall befall them in future days.——The introduction being now finished, the next chapter proceeds to the prophecy.

CHAPTER XI.

As already intimated, this is precisely "a word," see 10: 1, there called a "thing," but in Hebrew a "word." It is a word in the sense of being revealed in *words*, and not at all in symbols, as the previous visions on this general theme had been. Consequently this may well be accounted as an *interpretation* of those.——Like the other visions, this starts with the time then present, or rather it sets back some four or five years, *i. e.*, from the third year of Cyrus (10: 1) to the first year of Darius, his immediate predecessor, who reigned two years. The revealing angel simply remarks that in the first year of Darius he "stood to confirm and strengthen him." The prophecy proper begins with v. 2, at the point then present; "there shall stand up yet," etc., *i. e.*, after Cyrus, then on the throne.——Then the course of prophetic thought in the chapter is a rapid sketch of the Persian kings to Xerxes; then by a natural transition to Alexander and his great kingdom; then its four-fold division; then the two of these four kingdoms, with which alone the Jews were concerned; Egypt on the south, and Syria on the north, running through the history of ten kings, five of the former kingdom, and five of the latter, till he reaches Antiochus Epiphanes in v. 21. He then gives *his* history through the chapter to his death (v. 45).——In this, as in the other parallel visions, I propose first to give special comments on the words and phrases as may seem requisite, postponing till afterward any general discussion in defense of my interpretation and against opposing views.

1. Also I, in the first year of Darius the Mede, even I, stood to confirm and to strengthen him.

This passage seems to show that even heathen kings, when doing service for the true God, were confirmed and strengthened by good angels.

2. And now will I shew thee the truth. Behold, there shall stand up yet three kings in Persia; and the fourth shall be far richer than *they* all: and by his strength through his riches he shall stir up all against the realm of Grecia.

"Yet" (after Cyrus) there were in order these three kings of Persia; viz., Cambyses, reigning seven and a half years; Smerdis, the Magian, seven months; Darius Hystaspis, thirty-six years. Of these there is no occasion here to give any details.——The fourth must be described more particularly. He is Xerxes the Great; distinguished for his riches. The exploits of his life are summed up in precisely one thing—his great military expedition against Greece. "He shall stir up all"—and truly it was all Western Asia, organizing itself for war to come down upon the small territory, and relatively very insignificant numbers, of Greece. Universal history gives no record of a military expedition so vast and so imposing, nor of any one which achieved a more signal failure. Armed men and retainers—his host is estimated at five millions. Uncounted wealth was lavished upon their outfit. All the provinces of the east contributed to the splendor of this array and to the mass of living mortality that pressed toward the shores of the Hellespont to pour itself over the narrow fields of Greece.——Remarkably the revealing angel has not a word to say of the achievements of this martial host. "He stood up against the realm of Greece"—that is all he says. And, historically, that *was* all. The expedition came utterly to naught.

3. And a mighty king shall stand up, that shall rule with great dominion, and do according to his will.

4. And when he shall stand up, his kingdom shall be broken, and shall be divided toward the four winds of heaven; and not to his posterity, nor according to his dominion which he ruled: for his kingdom shall be plucked up, even for others besides those.

Alexander comes next, reached not closely in the order of time, but in the order of cause and effect. As already suggested in my notes on 8: 5-7, the Greeks never could forgive or forget the insult and the wrong done them by this imposing though futile invasion by Xerxes. Alexander became at length (after about one hundred and fifty years) God's instrument to avenge it. Prophecy, therefore, leaps over the intervening events as not to its purpose, and strikes next on this great conqueror of the decayed and effete Persian empire. "A mighty king stands up, ruling with great dominion and doing according to his will." Who could. tell the history of Alexander in fewer or more forcible words? When he had gained this standing, and his great empire seemed established for all time, it is suddenly broken by his death. It is then "divided toward the four winds of heaven," as we have seen (chap. 8: 8), "but not to his posterity" (not a son of his ever gained any standing); "not according to the dominion which he ruled," but on entirely other principles, and in a manner altogether foreign from any plan or wish of his. His kingdom was plucked up and torn into fragments for others to enjoy besides his own family. All this is a condensed but accurate epitome of the history of those times, of which the part relating to Xerxes has been given with great minuteness by Herodotus and others; the part borne by Alexander, by Arrian, Plutarch and Diodorus.

5. And the king of the south shall be strong, and *one* of his princes; and he shall be strong above him, and have dominion; his dominion *shall be* a great dominion.

Here begins a rapid sketch of the rise of the two kingdoms, Egypt and Syria, glancing at the wars, intrigues, treaties, and perfidies that fill the interval down to Antiochus Epiphanes in v. 21. It is remarkable that all the commentators of any celebrity concur precisely in their interpretation of these verses. They find the same kings, give them the same names, give the same sense to the prophecy, and find the same historic facts for its fulfillment. Hence there is little occasion for me to go minutely into arguments for the defense of the interpretation given so harmoniously· to this portion of the chapter.——This fifth verse introduces the two kings who respectively founded the new kingdoms of Egypt on the south and Syria on the north. The king of the south is Ptolemy Lagus, said by Jerome to be a man of very great wisdom, bravery, wealth, and power. He was one of Alexander's generals. He founded his kingdom of Egypt B. C. 323.——The last clause of the verse unquestionably means, "but this one (*i. e.*, another) shall be stronger than he and shall have dominion, and his shall be a great dominion." This more powerful monarch is Seleucus Nicator, who founded the Syrian kingdom B. C. 312. His kingdom was indeed very powerful, embracing almost all that Alexander ever held in Asia. The angel uses the same language to describe his greatness as that of Alexander. Each has great dominion. See notes on Dan. 7: p. 358.

6. And in the end of years they shall join themselves together; for the king's daughter of the south shall come

to the king of the north to make an agreement: but she
shall not retain the power of the arm: neither shall he
stand, nor his arm: but she shall be given up, and they
that brought her, and he that begat her, and he that
strengthened her in *these* times.

"In the end of years" indicates a considerable interval between these transactions and the founding of the two kingdoms as stated in the fifth verse. Ptolemy reigned thirty-nine years; Seleucus thirty-two. We pass over these reigns; also the entire reign of the next Syrian king, Antiochus Soter (twenty years) into the latter part of the reign of his successor, Antiochus Theos, who reigned fifteen years. This Theos, after long and fruitless wars with his Egyptian rival, Ptolemy Philadelphus, at last patched up a compromise ("they joined themselves together"), which being utterly iniquitous, could not stand.——The historical facts are these: He divorced his own wife, Laodice, and married Berenice, daughter of Philadelphus. Two years after, Philadelphus, now aged, died. Theos soon divorced his Egyptian wife and restored his Syrian. But the latter had lost confidence in her husband, and, stung by his abuse, took him off by poison. She then secured the kingdom for her own son, Seleucus Callinicus, who managed to murder his mother's rival, Berenice, with her son and servants. Thus the compromise availed only to the ruin of both the guilty parties to this infamous marriage. Neither of them "retained the power of the arm," the military power, not even to the extent of self-protection.

7. But out of a branch of her roots shall *one* stand up in his estate, which shall come with an army, and shall enter into the fortress of the king of the north, and shall deal against them, and shall prevail:

8. And shall also carry captives into Egypt their gods, with their princes, *and* with their precious vessels of silver and of gold: and he shall continue *more* years than the king of the north.

9. So the king of the south shall come into *his* kingdom, and shall return into his own land.

Here are the exploits of the third Ptolemy, brother of Berenice; "one out of the branch of her roots," in the sense of being from the same parentage. He gained great victories over Seleucus Callinicus, the fourth Syrian king; swept over the great eastern portion of the Syrian kingdom; took immense spoil, not less than forty thousand talents of silver, and, among the rest, recovered and took back into Egypt twenty-five hundred idols, most of which Cambyses had carried from Egypt into Persia nearly three hundred years before. For this service especially the Egyptians honored him with the title, "Energetes," the Benefactor. He reigned twenty-live years; his rival but twenty. He thus "continued more years than the king of the north."——In v. 9, it seems better to modify the translation, placing the phrase, "king of the south," immediately after "kingdom of," as in the original; thus; "Then he" (the king of the north just before spoken of) "marched into the kingdom of the king of the south, but was compelled to return" defeated "into his own land." The sense is better so, since there was no occasion to say that the king of the south, after his successful expedition, recorded vs. 7, 8, returned home again. What else should he do? Moreover, by the reading I suggest, the relation of the pronouns to their antecedents is more easy, in the commencement of both v. 9 and v. 10. The king of the north named in the end of v. 8 is *he* that comes into the kingdom of the king of the south with a vain effort to retrieve his losses; and "*his* sons" (v. 10) are the sons of this Syrian king, Seleucus Callinicus, who was compelled to return with shame to his own land.——My brief comments on vs. 10–19 may best take the form, for the most part, of a paraphrase.

10. But his sons shall be stirred up, and shall assemble a multitude of great forces: and *one* shall certainly come, and overflow, and pass through: then shall he return, and be stirred up, *even* to his fortress.

These are the two sons of Seleucus Callinicus, viz., Seleucus Ceraunus, who reigned two years, and Antiochus the Great, who reigned thirty-seven. They arouse themselves to prodigious efforts and raise a vast army. Ceraunus soon dies, and leaves Antiochus to prosecute these plans. He shall certainly come and sweep like a flood and pass through the countries of Western Asia toward Egypt. He shall make a second expedition ("return again")—the first being that of v. 9, and shall push the war even to the fortress which was the key to that kingdom.

11. And the king of the south shall be moved with choler, and shall come forth and fight with him, *even* with the king of the north: and he shall set forth a great multitude; but the multitude shall be given into his hand.

Then the king of the south, Ptolemy Philopator, greatly exasperated, rouses himself from his voluptuous lethargy, and comes forth to fight with Antiochus the Great, the king of the north; and though this king of the north had brought into the field an immense army, yet in a great battle at Raphia, near Gaza (B. C. 217), he was utterly defeated, and the power passed into the hands of Philopator, king of Egypt.

12. *And* when he hath taken away the multitude, his heart shall be lifted up; and he shall cast down *many* ten thousands: but he shall not be strengthened *by it*.

By this great victory his heart is elated; he casts down many; but is not permanently strengthened by it.

13. For the king of the north shall return, and shall set forth a multitude greater than the former, and shall certainly come after certain years with a great army and with much riches.

For the king of the north, Antiochus the Great, raises a greater army than his former one, and comes again with great resources for war.

14. And in those times there shall many stand up against the king of the south: also the robbers of thy people shall exalt themselves to establish the vision; but they shall fall.

Philopator, the miserably effeminate and dissolute king, dies (B. C. 204), leaving as the heir to his throne, his son Ptolemy Epiphanes, but five years old; whereupon Philip of Macedon, a powerful monarch, makes alliance with Antiochus against Egypt. —— "Many shall stand up against the king of the south." Violent men from among the people (the Jews) arouse themselves to cast off the Egyptian yoke. In fact, they only established the vision, for their object entirely failed; they only brought on themselves disaster.

15. So the king of the north shall come, and cast up a mount, and take the most fenced cities: and the arms of the south shall not withstand, neither his chosen people, neither *shall there be any* strength to withstand.

Antiochus of the north successfully besieged Zidon, Gaza, and other strong cities. The arms of Egypt could not stand before him.

16. But he that cometh against him shall do according to his own will, and none shall stand before him: and he shall stand in the glorious land, which by his hand shall be consumed.

The assailing party, still Antiochus the Great, coming against his feeble opponent of Egypt, shall do according to his own will and none shall stand before him. He obtains footing even in Palestine, "the glory of all lands," which under his power is fearfully wasted. He was obliged to spend a long time in besieging Jerusalem, to wrest it from the Egyptian power, subsisting his army meanwhile on Palestine, and thus wasting its supplies.

17. He shall also set his face to enter with the strength of his whole kingdom, and upright ones with him; thus

shall he do: and he shall give him the daughter of women, corrupting her: but she shall not stand on *his side*, neither be for him.

He sets himself with resolute purpose and with all his strength to invade Egypt; the Jews, even the better class, the "upright ones," with him; but the Romans intervene to frustrate his plans. He makes a treaty with Ptolemy and gives him his own daughter, Cleopatra, in marriage, with the provinces of Phenicia as her dower and hoping that she would subserve his interests. His efforts to "corrupt her" to play into his hands and prove false to her husband were unsuccessful. She abandoned her father's cause, was true to her husband, and hence "did not stand on his (her father's) side, nor be for him."

18. After this shall he turn his face unto the isles, and shall take many: but a prince for his own behalf shall cause the reproach offered by him to cease; without his own reproach he shall cause *it* to turn upon him.

Then to meet the Romans to better advantage, Antiochus the Great carried the war into Greece; took several of the Grecian islands; but the Roman Prince gained a great victory over him at Thermopylæ (B. C. 191), and another final one at Magnesia in Lydia (B. C. 190), which completely broke down the power of Antiochus the Great. The glory of his former achievements was turned into reproach. The Roman armies had no reverses; with no reproaches on themselves, they turned all reproach upon the vanquished Syrian king.

19. Then he shall turn his face toward the fort of his own land: but he shall stumble and fall, and not be found.

Compelled to relinquish all his possessions West of Mt. Taurus, and to pay the entire expenses of the war, Antiochus found himself amerced in fifteen thousand talents, of which a large portion was by installments of one thousand per annum—completely exhausting his finances, subjecting his kingdom to immense taxes and putting him upon that raid into Elymais for pillage which cost him his life. In an attempt to plunder a rich temple he was resisted by the exasperated people and slain. Some of the ancient historians, however, assert that he was slain by his own men in a drunken carousal. If so, the "vile" king—the little horn of chapters 7 and 8, may have had some agency in "plucking him up by the roots" and causing him to "fall." See notes on the three kings, removed before the little horn-king, page 366.——This rapid sketch of Antiochus the Great (vs. 10–19), is drawn so accurately that commentators have almost universally agreed in the main as to its exposition and application to all the points of his eventful history. The revealing angel was in fact *writing history* more than three hundred years before its time.

20. Then shall stand up in his estate a raiser of taxes in the glory of the kingdom: but within few days he shall be destroyed, neither in anger, nor in battle.

"In his estate," means, in his place as king; upon his throne, or in his stead. "A raiser of taxes in the glory of his kingdom," would be more closely and better rendered; "One who will send tax-gatherers over all the glory, *i. e.*, wealth, of his kingdom;" one whose great work as a king will be to raise taxes to pay the enormous sum of a thousand talents per year, pledged to the Romans. This was Seleucus Philopator, eldest son of Antiochus the Great, and heir to his throne. His reign of eleven years ended with his sudden death by poison at the hand of Heliodorus; his chief tax-gatherer, "neither in anger nor in battle," but under the promptings of ambition to mount the throne.——We have now reached Antiochus Epiphanes in the regular line of kings as sketched in this historic prophecy. Let us pause here a moment to note the very extraordinary character of this sketch of history given as prophecy throughout this chapter thus far (vs. 2–20). While it must be admitted that without the help of the actual history to guide us, some few passages would be rather obscure, yet this obscurity is due to its brevity; and even this quite disappears the moment you suppose a tolerably fair acquaintance with the outlines of the history in question. But such a case of history written out so definitely; history and nothing else; history with no hint at the moral purpose in view—is without a parallel elsewhere in the Scriptures. It is not strange that it should appear very extraordinary;—perhaps I might safely say, it is not strange that it should suggest the inquiry whether its date is really antecedent to the events narrated; in other words, whether it is real prophecy. But this investigation brings back no reason for a doubt. It only certifies us the more that Daniel had this vision when the book claims, viz., in the third year of Cyrus, and that it is all real prophecy.——Hence we fall back upon the question, What can be the object of such a prophecy, put in this straight-forward, purely historic form?——My answer is ready. This entire vision is parallel (as will be shown in its place) to chap. 7, and this portion of it corresponds to the fourth beast of that vision, "dreadful, terrible, and strong exceedingly, with great iron teeth, devouring, breaking in pieces, and stamping the residue with his feet." What is the outcome of this historic prophecy, beginning with Xerxes and ending with Seleucus Philopator who made tax-gatherers pass over and consume the glory of his kingdom? What are the achievements of Xerxes, Alexander, Seleucus Nicator, Antiochus the Great, and all the rest, but the robbery and murder of millions of human beings; wars, unceasing wars, continued through scores of years and even centuries, with untold slaughter and no offset of resulting good;—and not wars alone, but treacheries, bad faith, treaties made only to be broken; compromises all iniquitous; divorces; deceptions; taxations; the waste and destruction of human sustenance; poverty, unpaid toil, wretchedness, and starvation, and all with not the least resulting good? This is human depravity working out its legitimate fruits of crime and woe. It is a huge nondescript but horrible wild beast, "dreadful, terrible, and strong," let loose among masses of living men, women and children, to make his utmost havoc in their flesh and blood. If we could gather the statistics of the human lives cut off in those centuries of war, and could add to that sum all the incidental waste of life and treasure, the sum would appal us!—— And will it still be asked, To what end is all this portrayed in this historic prophecy? The answer is that, in chap. 7, as that fourth beast and kingdom stand next before the fifth, so they stand in tacit yet strong and palpable antithesis with it. Things are seen better in the light of contrast. Here is the rule and sway of human ambition over against the rule and sway of the gospel kingdom of peace and love. It is war and ruin set off in contrast against universal peace and blessedness.——And this historico-prophetic sketch given by the revealing angel to Daniel and to us in chap. 11: 2–20, was intended to set before us with considerable detail the real significance of that fourth beast and his ten horns, so dreadful and terrible to the weal of mankind. As already said, it expresses in words what Dan. 7: 7–27, sets forth in symbols. The nondescript but dreadful wild beast there becomes the historic record of war, crime, and death here. That is a symbolic scene given in prophetic vision; this is really its inspired explanation.——Yet further as to the purpose and the bearing of this delineation of the fourth beast. Its horrid ravages on human well-being are not only designed to stand in contrast with the next succeeding kingdom, one of universal peace and love, but also to indicate the reasons why God brought down on that fourth beast a doom so dire and so completely exterminating. When God sweeps a cluster and a series of great nations into utter destruction, it is well that he should indicate clearly why he does it. This is a case of the sort. From the age of Nimrod to the fall of the Greek, Syrian, and Egyptian kingdoms, the great empires of the world lay in Western Asia and North-eastern Africa, for the most part making their centers of power in the valleys of the Euphrates, the Orontes, and the Nile. In the age of Daniel, the Great Assyrian empire had recently passed away. His merely human eye saw both the rise and the fall of Chaldea; and the rise of Medo-Persia. With the eye of an inspired seer, he looked through to the end of this marvelous series of world-monarchies—the Medo-Persian; the Greek empire of Alexander, and its cleft fragments under his Greek successors. Those nationalities, long time so magnificent, so proud, so mighty, so cruel, so truly the terror and the scourge of mankind, are now to be utterly wiped out from the face of the earth and their succession to cease forever. Why should not the justice of God in this fearful scene of retribution be amply vindicated? Why should not the visions of prophecy which foretold this doom set forth also the catalogue of appalling crimes which preceded and demanded this fall of the great Asiatic sovereignties, never to rise again?——Hence this ample unfolding of the long, black record of their crimes. They culminated in those scenes of artful treachery, mad persecution, and terrible slaughter of God's own people which have consigned to infamy and abhorrence the name of Antiochus Epiphanes.

21. And in his estate shall stand up a vile person, to whom they shall not give the honor of the kingdom: but he shall come in peaceably, and obtain the kingdom by flatteries.

Here we arrive at Antiochus Epiphanes, in his place in the line of Syrian monarchs, and, as here described, meeting all the great facts recorded of him in history.——He comes "into the estate" of his elder brother, who had preceded him. He is "a vile person," fit only to be despised, *despicable*, for so the original imports. ——"To whom they shall not give the honor of the kingdom." It was not his by established right of succession, but belonged to the eldest son of his deceased brother, just previously sent to Rome to take his place and release him after thirteen years of hostage life in the Roman capital. Hence those whose business it was to see that the succession was determined according to usage could not give to him the honor of the kingdom. He "came in peaceably and obtained it by flatteries." He was at Athens, on his way home from Rome, when he heard of the death of his brother, and instantly laid his plans to obtain the kingdom for himself. He forthwith secured the aid of Eumenes, king of Pergamos, and of his brother Attalus, and with this help expelled Heliodorus and gained the crown.——This king was preëminently "a vile person" —vile, both in the sense of being wicked, and in the sense of being mean and despicable. So far from deserving his surname, Epiphanes, *the Illustrious*, his merits seemed to justify the slight change of his name, which reversed its meaning, "Epimanes, *the madman*. He had a low passion for aping the foolish things he had seen at Rome. He seemed to delight in playing the buffoon, in getting half drunk, and then putting himself below the common level of even tipsy, silly drunkards. It is hard to believe that a king would rise from his dinner-table, heated with wine, strip himself utterly naked, and dance round the hall as one frantic, with the lowest comedians. History can scarcely produce another like case of a man wearing a crown who debased himself so low, and made himself so vile as this same Antiochus Epiphanes.

22. And with the arms of a flood shall they be overflown from before him, and shall be broken; yea, also the prince of the covenant.

The human arm is a favorite figure with Daniel for an army and its military power. The sweep of such a host is also with him often an inundation. It "overflows," bearing down and breaking away all before it. So here. Though Antiochus began with flatteries and a pacific bearing, yet as soon as the scepter was fairly in his grasp, he was not slow to create an armed force and to wield it with energy.——"The prince of the covenant" can be no other here than the High Priest Onias—a most excellent and venerable man, who, after withstanding the current of popular sentiment toward Grecian life and idolatry, fell before the machinations of his apostate countrymen.

23. And after the league *made* with him he shall work deceitfully: for he shall come up, and shall become strong with a small people.

Continuing the same subject, this historic prophet touches the league made between Antiochus and the apostate Jew whom he constituted High-priest in place of the good Onias, and who took the Grecian name of Jason. This Jason promised to pay Antiochus large sums for his aid in obtaining the high-priesthood and for license to set up a Grecian gymnasium in Jerusalem and to institute the Grecian idolatrous rites associated with it. For three years (B. C. 175–172) he labored assiduously to seduce the Jews into the Grecian life and religion. At length he sent his younger brother, Menelaus, to carry to Antiochus the money he had promised for his high-priesthood, when both Menelaus and Antiochus "worked deceitfully;" the former, bidding higher for the priesthood than his brother had done, the latter repudiated his previous contract with Jason and gave the priesthood to him. Thus Antiochus gained a foothold in Judea and became strong, though commencing "with a small people."——This kingdom of Syria had been greatly reduced in territory and also exhausted in its finances during the two previous reigns. Hence the frequent allusions to the small beginnings of this little horn-king.

24. He shall enter peaceably even upon the fattest places of the province; and he shall do *that* which his fathers have not done, nor his fathers' fathers; he shall scatter among them the prey, and spoil, and riches: *yea*, and he shall forecast his devices against the strongholds, even for a time.

This verse is thought to refer to an expedition into Armenia, a kingdom adjacent on the north, whose king, Artaxias, Antiochus took captive. There he found rich booty and scattered it profusely to whom he would, for few kings have surpassed him in the prodigality with which he scattered his largesses of money upon cities or individuals, as the caprice might take him, apparently with no other motive than the silly ambition of being more liberal than any king ever was before him. This was a brief expedition, only "for a time."

25. And he shall stir up his power and his courage against the king of the south with a great army; and the king of the south shall be stirred up to battle with a very

great and mighty army; but he shall not stand: for they shall forecast devices against him.

26. Yea, they that feed of the portion of his meat shall destroy him, and his army shall overflow: and many shall fall down slain.

27. And both these kings' hearts *shall be* to do mischief, and they shall speak lies at one table; but it shall not prosper: for yet the end *shall be* at the time appointed.

Here begins the prophetic record of the military expeditions of Antiochus into Egypt, of which history gives account of at least four in as many successive years, B. C. 170–167. The first was short, involving but one great battle, the victory with Antiochus, after which he wintered at Tyre, and marched on Egypt again early in the ensuing spring. In this campaign he practically subjugated the whole country; became the nominal protector of the young king, Ptolemy Philometor; had precisely those intrigues with him which v. 27 describes—both kings' hearts being set on mischief, and both speaking lies to one another at one table; yet in neither case availing to frustrate the great results which God in his providence had in view, "for yet the end would surely be at the time appointed." The Egyptian king was young and was imbecile even for his youth. He was formally inaugurated at the age of fourteen; had been kept in ignorance and inefficiency by the artful management of his tutors, who loved and sought to retain the regal power which his minority and incompetence gave them. "They that fed of the portion of his meat destroyed him." So closely does the prophetic description fit the historic facts.——In v. 26 it is the army of Antiochus that "overflows" victoriously, and many of his Egyptian foes fall down, slain.

28. Then shall he return into his land with great riches; and his heart *shall be* against the holy covenant; and he shall do *exploits*, and return to his own land.

It was in June, B. C. 169, that Antiochus, having been entirely successful in Egypt, returned toward his own land with great riches. His return was hastened by a report that all Judea had risen in revolt from his authority. A rumor had reached Jerusalem that Antiochus was dead. Some public manifestations of joy ensued, which being reported to Antiochus with no little exaggeration, greatly exasperated him against the Jews. He hastened back with his victorious army and at once assailed and took Jerusalem. Of this terrific onslaught, the author of 2 Mac. says (5: 11–16); "Removing out of Egypt in a furious mind, he took the city by force of arms, and commanded his men of war not to spare such as they met and to slay such as went up upon the houses. Thus there was killing of young and old, making away of men, women and children, slaying of virgins and infants. And there were destroyed within three whole days four-score thousand, whereof forty thousand were slain in the conflict; and no fewer sold than slain. Yet was he not content with this, but presumed to go into the most holy temple of all the world, Menelaus, that traitor to the laws and to his own country, being his guide; and taking the holy vessels with polluted hands, and with profane hands pulling down the things that were dedicated by other kings to the augmentation and glory and honor of the place, he gave them away." In this scene of pillage and sacrilege, Antiochus found and took away from the temple eighteen hundred talents of gold, and then offered swine's flesh on the altar and sprinkled the whole temple with the broth of this flesh. These things exasperated the Jews against him exceedingly. They could regard him only as a monster of cruelty and wickedness. After these exploits, he returned to his own land.

29. At the time appointed he shall return, and come toward the south; but it shall not be as the former, or as the latter.

30. For the ships of Chittim shall come against him: therefore he shall be grieved, and return, and have indignation against the holy covenant: so shall he do; he shall even return, and have intelligence with them that forsake the holy covenant.

The third expedition of Antiochus into Egypt (B. C. 168) is not distinctly referred to, having in it nothing that specially affected the fortunes of the Jews. He went there to depose Physcon, the younger brother of Philometor, his protegé—the Egyptians having raised him to power because Philometor was practically under the absolute control of Antiochus. He defeated the army of Physcon in battle. Physcon and his party sought help from the Romans. ——The next year (B. C. 167) Antiochus made his fourth expedition into Egypt, of which these verses give the substance. The last clause of v. 29 means that this last expedition was not, like all his former, successful. "Not as the former, so is the latter." The reason of his failure was the intervention of the powerful Romans. ——Chittim, in its more restricted sense, is a town on the island of Cyprus, or the island itself; but in its larger sense, was used for the northern and eastern islands and coasts of the Mediterranean, including Greece and Rome. There is no doubt that Rome is meant here. So Josephus and numerous other authorities affirm. ——An embassy of three men from the Roman Senate met him just as he was about to lay siege to Alexandria; told him they had taken young Physcon under their protection, and that he must desist or have war with Rome. Antiochus indicating a wish to procrastinate, Topilius drew a circle in the sand about his feet and said, "Give me an answer before you cross that circle." He yielded, and pledged himself to do all the Senate should require. He dared not offend the Roman power. . But he chafed like a tiger under his chain, and came back to vent his rage on a fallen people, the Jews. He was "*grieved*" in this very selfish sense, and let loose "his indignation against the holy covenant" and its people. At this time, as for several years previous, he "had intelligence" with Jewish apostates; kept up a mutual understanding and cooperation with them; and made great use of their aid to further his designs.

31. And arms shall stand on his part, and they shall pollute the sanctuary of strength, and shall take away the daily *sacrifice*, and they shall place the abomination that maketh desolate.

He now sent out an army of 22,000, under Appollonius (June, B. C. 167), who seized Jerusalem, took possession of the castle and made it a stronghold; forcibly prevented the Jews from worshiping in their temple; desecrated the altar by erecting an idol-altar directly upon it, and there offering sacrifices to idols; and of course entirely superseding and suspending the daily sacrifices of the Jews. This was "the taking away of the daily sacrifice." The original word, meaning the constant, the continuous, or, rather, the regular, every-day routine, embraced really more than the morning and the evening sacrifices. It included all the services of the Mosaic ritual. (See notes on Dan. 8: 11.)——The last clause, rendered, "the abomination that maketh desolate," may be translated either "the abomination that maketh desolate," or "the abomination of the desolator"—the sense in either case being essentially the same, viz., that, instead of the sanctuary which was a tower of strength and symbolized the strength God gives to his obedient people, this abominable idol-altar was the symbol of ruin and desolation. It was set up by a force bent on desolating the city and people of God; it was permitted of God in judgment on his apostate people; it therefore carried with it only desolation.

32. And such as do wickedly against the covenant shall he corrupt by flatteries: but the people that do know their God shall be strong, and do *exploits*.

The books of Maccabees make the fact very prominent that in these times many Jews were utterly apostate from the service and worship of God. Of these, the first clause speaks. It might be rendered, "the wicked apostates of the covenant." These persons, this vile king "corrupts by his flatteries"—by his intrigues, bribes, encouragements.——On the other hand, "the people who know their God," in the sense of loving and approving both him and his service, "shall be strong." These were at first the venerable Mattathias of Modin and his sons—a most noble family, of extraordinary faith and Christian heroism. Later, the company embraced many others who joined them. No one can read their history as recorded in the first book of Maccabees without concurring in this brief but just testimony to their transcendent heroism, valor, and energy. "They were strong and they performed exploits." The zeal and courage of the aged Mattathias are inspiring. "And when he saw the blasphemies that were committed in Judea and Jerusalem, he said, Woe is me! Wherefore was I born to see this misery of my people and of the holy city and to dwell there when it was delivered into the hand of the enemy and the sanctuary into the hand of strangers? Her temple is become as a man without glory. Her glorious vessels are carried away into captivity, her infants are slain in the streets, her young men with the sword of the enemy. Behold, our sanctuary, even our beauty and our glory, is laid waste and the Gentiles have profaned it. To what end, therefore, shall we live any longer? Then Mattathias and his sons rent their clothes and put on sackcloth and mourned very sore."——When the king's officers came to Modin, and plied Mattathias with flattery and with bribes, pressing him to be the first to fulfill the king's command as all the heathen had done, he cried with a loud voice, "Though all the nations that are under the king's dominion obey him, and fall away every one from the religion of their fathers, and give consent to his commandments, yet will I and my sons and my brethren walk in the covenant of our fathers. God forbid that we should forsake the law and the ordinances! We will not hearken to the king's words to go from our religion, either on the right hand, or on the left." "Now when he had left speaking these words, there came up a Jew in the sight of all, to sacrifice on the altar at Modin, according to the king's commandment. Which thing when Mattathias saw, he was inflamed with zeal, and his reins trembled, neither could he forbear to show his anger according to judgment; wherefore he ran and slew him upon the altar. Also the king's commissioner, who compelled men to sacrifice, he killed at that time, and the altar he pulled down. Then he cried throughout the city, Whosoever is zealous of the law, and maintaineth the covenant, let him follow me." 1 Mac. 2: 6-27.——This small but heroic band retired to the mountain fastnesses of Southern Palestine; were pursued by their persecutors, were attacked upon the Sabbath, and full one thousand of them were cut down unresisting. They would not take up arms to resist on the Sabbath, but fell saying, "Let us die in all our innocency; heaven and earth shall testify for us that ye put us to death wrongfully." V. 37. The survivors, upon second thought, determined to defend their lives whenever attacked. Others, fleeing from persecution, came in and were a stay unto them. "So they joined their forces and smote sinful men in their anger and wicked men in their wrath; but the rest fled to the heathen for succor. Then Mattathias and his friends went round about and pulled down the altars; and what children soever they found within the coast of Israel uncircumcised, they circumcised valiantly. They pursued also after the proud men, and the work prospered in their hand. So they recovered the law out of the hand of the Gentiles and out of the hand of kings, neither suffered they the sinner to triumph" (1 Mac. 2: 43-48).

Now when the time drew near that Mattathias should die, he said unto his sons, Now hath pride and rebuke gotten strength, and the time of destruction and the wrath of indignation [have come.] Now therefore, my sons, be ye zealous for the law, and give your lives for the covenant of your fathers. Call to remembrance what acts our fathers did in their time; so shall ye receive great honor and an everlasting name. Was not Abraham found faithful in temptation, and it was imputed unto him for righteousness? Joseph, in the time of his distress, kept the commandment, and was made lord of Egypt. Phineas, our father, in being zealous and fervent, obtained the covenant of an everlasting priesthood. Joshua, for fulfilling the word, was made a judge in Israel. Caleb, for bearing witness before the congregation, received the heritage of the land. David, for being merciful, possessed the throne of an everlasting kingdom. Elias, for being zealous and fervent for the law was taken up into heaven. Ananias, Azarias, and Misael, by believing, were saved out of the flame. Daniel, for his innocency, was delivered from the mouth of the lions. And thus consider ye throughout all ages that *none who put their trust in Him shall be overcome.* Fear not, then, the words of a sinful man, for his glory shall be dung and worms. To-day he shall be lifted up, and to-morrow he shall not be found, because he has returned into his dust, and his thought is turned to nothing. Wherefore, my sons, be valiant and show yourselves men in behalf of the law; for by it ye shall obtain glory" (1 Mac. 2: 49–64). So Mattathias closes his testimony.—— His son Judas becomes military chieftain. His record is grand and thrilling. "Then his son Judas, called Maccabeus, rose up in his stead. And all his brethren helped him, and so did all they that held with his father; and they fought with cheerfulness the battle of Israel. So he gat his people great honor, and put on a breast-plate as a giant, and girt his warlike harness about him, and he made battles, protecting the host with the sword. In his acts he was like a lion, and like a lion's whelp roaring for his prey. For he pursued the wicked and sought them out and burnt up those that vexed his people. Wherefore the wicked shrunk for fear of him and all the workers of iniquity were troubled, because salvation prospered in his hand. He also grieved many kings, and made Jacob glad with his acts, and his memorial is blessed forever. Moreover he went through the cities of Juda, destroying the ungodly out of them and turning away wrath from Israel, so that he was renowned unto the utmost part of the earth, and he received unto him such as were ready to perish" (1 Mac. 3: 1–9).—— When the first great host of Syrians came down upon Judas, his puny band said to him, "How shall we be able, so few, to fight against so great a multitude and so strong, seeing we are ready to faint with fasting all this day? To whom Judas answered; "It is no hard matter for many to be shut up in the hands of a few, and with the God of heaven it is all one to deliver with a great multitude or a small company, for the victory of battle standeth not in the multitude of a host, but strength cometh from heaven. They come against us in much pride and iniquity to destroy us, and our wives and children, and to spoil us; but we fight for our lives and our laws. Wherefore the Lord himself will overthrow them before our face; and as for you, be not afraid of them." "Now as soon as he left off speaking, he leaped suddenly upon them, and so Seron and his host were overthrown before him" (1 Mac. 3: 17-23). ——In those times the whole army sought the mighty God in prayer. "How shall we be able to stand against them, unless Thou, O God, be our help?" "Arm yourselves then, said Judas, and be ready to fight with these nations who come against us to destroy us and our sanctuary; for it is better for us to die in battle than to behold the calamities of our people and our sanctuary. Nevertheless as the will of God is in heaven, so let him do" (1 Mac. 3: 53, 58-60).——Truly these are the words and the deeds of Christian heroes!

33. And they that understand among the people shall instruct many: yet they shall fall by the sword, and by flame, by captivity, and by spoil, *many* days.

This first clause might be rendered either "the wise ones among the people," or "the teachers of the people," with no great difference in the ultimate meaning. They devote themselves to teaching the people the law and the claims of God. Yet, one after another, they fall in war for many days. The venerable father Mattathias first; after him, Jonathan, Eleazar, Judas, Simon—a noble band, yet within the course of this twenty-four years' war with the Syrians they fell.

34. Now when they shall fall, they shall be holpen with a little help: but many shall cleave to them with flatteries.

Nevertheless God aided them with a little help. The results of the war gradually worked toward their political independence, which at length (B. C. 143) they achieved. This help was small compared with that which the Lord gave his people in the days of Joshua and of David.——That "many clave to them with flatteries" is a matter of history. Their cause suffered more than once from treacherous friends.

35. And *some* of them of understanding shall fall, to try them, and to purge, and to make *them* white, *even* to the time of the end: because *it is* yet for a time appointed.

Some of their wisest and best men fell—Jonathan, Judas and others; God's purpose in this affliction being to chastise his people the more thoroughly; to make them cease from man and put their trust in the Lord alone. This is in harmony with his usual course of moral discipline in this world of trial.——Such would be the state of things "to the time of the end," until the period assigned of God for this scene of trial should close. All was "noted in his scripture of truth" (chap. 10: 21); it should transpire accordingly. The Lord had certain ends to answer in respect to the moral discipline of his people. These scenes of conflict and trial would continue until those ends were answered.

36. And the king shall do according to his will; and he shall exalt himself, and magnify himself above every god, and shall speak marvelous things against the God of gods, and shall prosper till the indignation be accomplished: for that that is determined shall be done.

37. Neither shall he regard the God of his fathers, nor the desire of women, nor regard any god: for he shall magnify himself above all.

38. But in his estate shall he honor the God of forces: and a god whom his fathers knew not shall he honor with gold, and silver, and with precious stones, and pleasant things.

39. Thus shall he do in the most strongholds with a strange god, whom he shall acknowledge *and* increase with glory: and he shall cause them to rule over many, and shall divide the land for gain.

By all the established laws of language, this passage must treat of the same king whose wars and whose persecutions of the saints have been the subject of remark from v. 22 onward to this point. He is *the* king—the same before spoken of, the Hebrew article being explicit testimony to this point. Further, the connection of *thought* as well as of grammatical construction is close and decisive; for this king is able to "do according to his will" only because the Lord has indignation against his apostate people, and therefore sees fit to make use of this "vile king" as the rod of his scourging and discipline. Hence he shall prosper till the indignation shall be accomplished, and the thing determined of God for chastisement and reformation shall be done. This sort of logical reference to the preceding context and to the reasons assigned in the parallel vision (chap. 8: 19) for the great power of this same vile king constitutes the strongest possible connection between "*the king*" of v. 36 and the king of the north, whose case fills the passage chap. 11: 21-35.——His character, and his deeds as illustrative of character, are the subject in these verses. He is proud and self-conceited; thinks himself above every god; speaks marvelous things against the God of gods—things that excite the wonder of mankind for their horrid blasphemy and pride. This is the prophecy; to which accords the history of Antiochus in the books of the Maccabees. "Having spoken very proudly" (1 Mac. 1: 24). See also 2 Mac. 9 throughout. In this chapter, the author, commenting on his fall from his chariot, says; "Thus he who a little afore thought he might command the waves of the sea (so proud was he above the condition of man) and weigh the high mountains in a balance, was now cast on the ground and carried in a horse-litter, showing unto all the manifest power of God." Also this; "The man who thought a little afore that he could reach to the stars of heaven," etc. Throughout, the historical testimony to his pride and self-conceit is remarkably in harmony with this prophetic portrayal.——V. 37 shows that he had no reverence for the gods of his fathers, but took license to change not his own religious system alone, but the systems of every people throughout his great empire. With this agrees chap. 7: 25: "Shall think to change times and laws." His own will was supreme.——By "the desire of women," in this connection, must be meant some god or goddess who was a favorite of the Syrian women; perhaps Astarte or Anaitis.——V. 38 speaks of the god he did worship and put in the place of the gods of his fathers. He is the "god of forces," or military fortresses—this being the sense of the original word here used. Commentators differ as to the god specially intended, some supposing him to be Jupiter; others, Hercules, who is known to be of Syrian origin; and others, Mars, the Roman god of war. ——In v. 39 the received translation does not make it plain who is meant by "*them*" whom "he" (the king) "will cause to rule over many." The sense of the latter part of the verse would be better expressed by this translation; "Whosoever will recognize [his war-god, before spoken of,] he will greatly honor and give him rule over many, and apportion to him the lands for reward." The last words may mean either as a reward for his homage to the war-god or for pay, *i. e.*, for a money consideration to himself. The former view is more in harmony with the previous context; the latter, with the known avarice of this king. Probably the general doctrine of the verse is that whoever will fall in with the king's views as to his god he will pay him well for it.——The first clause of the verse is not altogether lucid. I take it to mean; This is his policy in the matter of strong fortresses, with the aid of his war-god; *i. e.*, he carries on war and defends his strongholds by making great account of his god of war; and he takes care to draw his people into the same homage by amply rewarding them.

40. And at the time of the end shall the king of the south push at him: and the king of the north shall come against him like a whirlwind, with chariots, and with horsemen, and with many ships; and he shall enter into the countries, and shall overflow and pass over.

41. He shall enter also into the glorious land, and many *countries* shall be overthrown: but these shall escape out of his hand, *even* Edom, and Moab, and the chief of the children of Ammon.

42. He shall stretch forth his hand also upon the countries: and the land of Egypt shall not escape.

43. But he shall have power over the treasures of gold

and of silver, and over all the precious things of Egypt: and the Libyans and the Ethiopians *shall be* at his steps.

44. But tidings out of the east and out of the north shall trouble him: therefore he shall go forth with great fury to destroy, and utterly to make away many.

45. And he shall plant the tabernacles of his palace between the seas in the glorious holy mountain: yet he shall come to his end, and none shall help him.

The legitimate sense of the several words and phrases in this passage is not difficult, but the general meaning of the whole, as related to the subject of the chapter, does involve one very grave and difficult question.——We look first to the sense of the several words and phrases.——"The time of the end," must doubtless be construed as in the cases where it has already occurred, *e. g.*, v. 27, "For yet the end shall be at the time appointed;" and v. 35, "even to the time of the end; because it is yet for a time appointed:" and essentially v. 36, "till the indignation be accomplished." Also in the parallel prophecy, chap. 8: 19, "I will make thee know what shall be in the last end of the indignation, for at the time appointed the end shall be." It is not, therefore, the end of the world in our modern sense, but is toward the end of the first age, that is, before the Messiah, in the Jewish sense; but yet more particularly, the time of the end of God's visitations of judgment on his apostate Jewish people by the hand especially of Antiochus Epiphanes. So I have been compelled to explain it in the passages where it has occurred already; so I must explain it here.
——"The king of the south" and "the king of the north" can be no other than Ptolemy Philometor of Egypt, and Antiochus Epiphanes of Syria. They have been before us under these descriptive names repeatedly, vs. 21–39: they are here again.——The king of the south "*pushes*" at his antagonist—the figure being taken from the fighting of horned animals, *e. g.*, rams and bulls. The fighting of the king of the north is compared to a storm, a whirlwind coming down in its fury, and with its fierce blasts sweeping away all before it.——"The glorious land," here, as in chap. 8: 9, and 11: 16, 45, can mean nothing else than Palestine, the Hebrew word being the same in each passage. See notes on chap. 8: 9.
——"The chief of the children of Ammon," some take to mean their princes, chief men; while others think it implies a degree of superiority in the Ammonites as a whole compared with the people of Edom and Moab; "and the superior children of Ammon." The difference is not here of much importance.——"He shall stretch forth his hand upon the countries," implies an effort to get them into his possession. "To put forth the hand," is used (Exod. 22: 8, 11) for one who steals or robs his neighbor's goods.——"The Ethiopians and Lybians at his steps," or at his feet, implies that they go before him as his soldiers or servants, to march at his orders and do his bidding. The analogous Hebrew phrase, "at

his feet," occurs in this sense Exod. 11: 8; Judg. 4: 10; and 2 Sam. 15: 16, 17.——"Tidings out of the east and out of the north shall trouble him." While attempting to crush the heroic bands of Judas Maccabeus, he heard of rebellion among the provinces then tributary to him, viz., Persia and Armenia, on the north and east, and was compelled to divide his army, leaving part under Lysias to prosecute the war against Judas, and taking the other part himself to subdue those insurgents. This new rebellion exasperated him greatly. It was occasioned by the same tyrannous interference with their religion which had caused the Jewish war. The Magians of the East were outraged by the mandates of Antiochus, requiring every people in all his realm to renounce their ancestral religion and adopt his Grecian idolatry.——V. 45 may be paraphrased thus: "And though he shall set up his palace-like tents between the Mediterranean Sea" (used in the plural for the sense of the superlative—the *great* sea) "and the glorious holy mountain, yet he shall come to his end ingloriously, and there shall be none to help him." The sense is, Though he impiously pushed his assaults and conquests up to the very temple of Jehovah, he shall fall like a mortal man, and there be none to save. ——Such I take to be the sense of the several words and phrases in this passage, vs. 40-45.

It remains to inquire into its general sense as related to the previous context (vs. 21-39) and to the history of Antiochus Epiphanes.——I defer for the present any notice of those interpretations which find here some other Antichrist than Antiochus Epiphanes; Papal, Mussulman, or Turk.——Of those who refer this passage to Antiochus, one class see in it a fifth and last expedition into Egypt, and in general a continuous narrative of new events down to his death. Another class suppose it to be a recapitulation and summing up of his exploits.——In the former class Porphyry leads off, first in time. I quote from Rosenmueller on v. 40, thus; "The things stated in this verse, Porphyry, as quoted in Jerome, rightly refers to Antiochus Epiphanes—'his military expedition in the eleventh year of his reign against Ptolemy Philometer, his sister's son. The latter, hearing that Antiochus was coming, assembled many thousand soldiers. But Antiochus, like a fierce storm, swept over many countries with chariots, horsemen, and a great fleet, and laid all waste as he passed.' [The single quotation marks indicate Porphyry's statements.]——Rosenmueller subjoins—'Of this new expedition of Antiochus into Egypt we find nothing in the still extant works of the Greek and Roman historians. But we are wholly destitute of any entire and continuous history of Antiochus, written by a trustworthy author of his own age."——That the history of those times WAS written, and that somewhat fully, may be inferred from the following passage in Jerome's Commentary on Daniel.—— "To understand the last portion of Daniel, the copious and various histories of the Greeks are needed, *e. g.*, Sutorius Callinicus, Diodorus, Hieronymus, Polybius, Posidonius, Claudius Theon and Andronicus, surnamed Alypius, whom Porphyry affirms that he has followed; Josephus also, and those whom he quotes, and especially our Livy and Trogus Pompeius and Justin, who wrote the entire history of the last vision, and from Alexander to Augustus Cesar, describes the wars of Syria and Egypt, i. e., of Seleucus and Antiochus on the one part, and of the Ptolemies on the other. If at any time we are compelled to appeal to secular history, it is not of our choice, but as I may say, of our stern necessity, in order to prove that the things predicted many ages since by the holy prophets have their fulfillment contained in the history as well of Greek authors as Latin, and indeed of other nations also."——But almost the entire mass of those histories here referred to have perished, past recovery, and we are left to make up the history of those times as best we can with the scanty materials still preserved.——The testimony of Porphyry to a fifth expedition of Antiochus into Egypt in his eleventh and last year would certainly be entitled to great consideration, provided it did not conflict rather seriously with other facts that seem well authenticated. One of these is that he was headed and turned back from his fourth expedition (vs. 29, 30) by the Romans. They positively forbade his interference with Egyptian affairs, and themselves assumed the protectorate of the young king. Hence it is scarcely supposable that Antiochus attempted another invasion of Egypt. Besides, the books of Maccabees are silent as to any such expedition in his eleventh and last year. If it had occurred, it could scarcely have escaped some notice from them. True, they devote themselves chiefly to Jewish interests; but such an expedition must touch Jewish interests seriously. And still further, they fill up his time quite thoroughly, scarcely leaving him even a few weeks for such an expedition as this. Hence after a somewhat careful examination, I give the preference to the latter of the two theories above named, and account the last six verses of the chapter a recapitulation of the history of Antiochus with some new incidents. The most serious difficulty to be overcome in this view is the manner of introducing the passage, "at the time of the end," etc. But some latitude of meaning may be given to this phrase. The reader is prone to think of it as meaning, just at the end of the life of Antiochus. Whether it does mean this in the present case is the vital question. For if it may be so general as to take in the eleven years' reign of Antiochus, it bears not at all against the construction of these last six verses as a recapitulation of his public life.——Now on this precise question, the testimony of usage is perhaps not altogether uniform and decisive. In chap. 12: 4, "Seal the book even to the time of the end," the phrase obviously looks to the whole period of the life of Antiochus; and indeed probably to the entire duration of this Syrian war; about twenty-four years. In chap. 11: 35, it looks toward the closing period of this great war, obviously beyond the death of Antiochus. "The time of the end," seems to be nearly or quite synonymous with "the last end of the indignation" and the "time appointed" as these phrases occur chap. 8; 19, and in so far may be understood to refer to the reign of Antiochus as a whole.

———At best some difficulty still hangs over this verse, whichever of the two constructions may be chosen. Yet we are clearly shut up to one of these two; for every other theory, especially every one which applies the passage to any other personage than Antiochus Epiphanes, is involved in tenfold greater difficulty.———As already shown, his reign of eleven years was at the last end of God's indignation toward the Jews. It was his "time appointed" for fearful judgments upon them for their sins. In this broad view his reign as a whole was "at the time of the end." Hence no violence is done to the established sense of this expression when we paraphrase the general scope and sense of the passage thus:———Having now spoken of the wars of Antiochus with Egypt; of his sacrilegious assaults upon Jerusalem and its temple; of his persecutions of the pious Jews; of the gods he did not worship and the gods he did, it remains to sum up briefly his exploits and then record his death.———His first great exploit was his terrific onslaught upon Egypt, given first in detail (vs. 25–30) and then in general, as here (v. 40). Next, his invasion of "the glorious land," given in the particulars, vs. 22, 23, 28, 30–35; and in the general, vs. 41, 45. Next in this recapitulation, the countries that did escape; Edom, Moab, Ammon, (which in fact sympathized with him and aided him in his wars against the Jews and hence did not incur his displeasure;) and the countries that did not escape;—Egypt, and with her, the Lybians and Ethiopians; and also Palestine. Next, he was a great robber of the wealth of cities and nations. This is referred to in detail (vs. 24, 28), in general statement (in v. 43). Then appears a new fact in the prophecy. In the height of these desolating conquests, he was somewhat seriously diverted by uprisings against his authority in his Northern and Eastern provinces—a fact fitly introduced here because so closely connected with his death. [For the circumstances of this horrid death, see notes on chap. 7.]———Then naturally the chapter and the record of this vile king close with his death, which is fitly put in a sort of antithesis with his horrid impiety against the house and people of the living God. Though he had the power and the hardihood to pitch his magnificent tents upon God's holy mountain, yet he came down wonderfully; he came to his end and there was none to help. Such I take to be the general drift and scope of these last six verses.

In addition to the points already made, the following considerations strongly favor this theory of recapitulation.———(1.) The statements in this passage are for the most part general in their character, and not specific and minute as in the previous portion of this prophetic history. Thus, "he shall enter into the *countries*" (v. 40); "shall overthrow *many countries*" (v. 41); "he shall put forth his hand" to pillage and plunder "the countries" (v. 42); "shall go forth with great fury to destroy many" (v. 44). V. 45, in the form of its statements, groups in antithesis with his death those great deeds of impiety and blasphemy that have made his name notorious with infamy.———(2.) The history of Antiochus, so far as known to us through any extant writings, had been already given in detail (vs. 21-39); while nearly all the statements in this closing passage either allude to or state the same great facts in a more comprehensive and general form.——(3.) The order and method of the prophetic narrative throughout vs. 21-39 is precisely such as to bring the writer to a recapitulation here at the close. Thus there is in the outset a hint at his general character; "a vile person" and an artful flatterer (v. 21); then the way he gained the crown; then his principal exploits in their chronological order through vs. 22-35, viz., his interference with the Jewish priesthood (vs. 22, 23); his expedition into Armenia (v. 24); several expeditions into Egypt (vs. 25-30); his malign persecutions of the Jews; his wars against them; his desecration of their temple and the breaking up of its worship; with their heroic endurance and earnest labors for the truth (vs. 28, 30-35); then, general views of his character as self-conceited, proud, impious, contemning all the established religions of his realm whether true or false, and assuming to set up a new religion; the gods he would not let men worship and the gods he would compel them to worship. This is a rounded and complete view of his deeds and character, and fully prepares the way for recapitulating the main points and general features—to be closed with his death.——(4.) The next chapter bears very much the same character of recapitulation, coupled with practical application both to the faithful Jews and to the unfaithful. Very few additional facts are introduced. The scenes of the history of Antiochus are the groundwork of the whole chapter. ——All these facts, conspiring to one and the same point, coupled with the arguments adduced above, render it at least strongly probable that this closing passage of the chapter is chiefly a recapitulation of the main events in the reign, and the salient points in the character, of Antiochus Epiphanes.

The meaning and scope of this chapter having now been presented, two topics remain; first, its relations to the other visions of Daniel; second, the diverse and opposing views of some interpreters.

1. Its parallelism with the other three visions.——*This "vile king" in chap. 11 is the "little horn" of chap. 7, and hence this entire vision in chap. 11 is in general parallel with that of chap. 7.* ——In proof, I adduce the following points.——(1.) The little horn-power was the central point of interest there in chap. 7. It is so here in chap. 11.——(2.) He was a *king* there; and is also here. ——(2.) He came forth there in the kingdom that next succeeded Alexander; precisely so here.——(4.) In addition to the little horn, chap. 7 has ten other horns which are kings; all on the beast that follows Alexander, and obviously all preceding the little horn, or cotemporary with him.——They are here in chap. 11 precisely in their place and of the right number—so clearly defined that no commentator hesitates to call their names respectively, and no one dissents from the universal testimony which names and locates them—ten horns which are ten kings between Alexander and the little horn.——(5.) From before this little horn-king of chap. 7

three of those ten were plucked up, or in some way removed or overthrown.——They are here in chap. 11 two of them falling in a very remarkable manner directly before he came to the throne, and the third subdued and subjugated by his arms.——(6.) In chap. 7 this little horn-power was specially terrible because it fell grievously upon the Jews while they were God's professed people.——Precisely so here, the passage chap. 10: 14, affirming, "I am come to make thee understand what shall befall *thy people;*" and chap. 11: 22, 23, 28, 30–35, 45, all concurring to show how terribly he harrassed the pious Jews; desecrated their temple, broke up their worship, and murdered their sons and daughters.——(7.) The persecutions which the little horn of chap. 7 brought on the Jews afflicted Daniel most deeply. The same is manifest throughout chaps. 10 and 12, in the near prospect of what is revealed in chap. 11.——(8.) The great points of personal character made prominent in the little horn of chap. 7 are keen sagacity, and daring, blasphemous hostility against God and his people.——Identically the same qualities of character and spirit appear in the vile king of chap.11.——(9.) In chap. 7 his specified deeds are, "wearing out the saints of the Most High;" a purpose and effort to subvert their religion and break up their worship, in the latter of which he was successful for a limited specified time—three and one-half years. ——The vile king of chap. 11 does the same things precisely; "his heart is against the holy covenant;" "he has indignation against the holy covenant;" "he pollutes the sanctuary;" "takes away the daily sacrifice;" causes the righteous to "fall by the sword, by flame, by captivity and by spoil many days;" and as to the length of time during which they are given into his hand, chap. 12: 7, 11, corresponds fully with chap. 7: 25.——(10.) In chapter 7, this king dies by the special judgments of God. Expressly so in chap. 11.—— Here let it be noted that these are not merely incidental but are *main* points. They are not culled, a few out of many, but embrace every thing of any importance that appears in chap. 7, except that there his judgment precedes the first advent, resurrection and ascension of Christ—a point which the *history* of the vile king of chap. 11 fully verifies, although the prophecy had nothing more to add on that point. Chap. 11 makes several new points, that do not appear in chap. 7, but not a line, not a feature, inconsistent with what is said in chapter 7.——Hence the evidence of identity between the little horn-king of chap. 7 and the vile king of chaps. 11 and 12, amounts to demonstration. Any additional proof would be quite superfluous.——If needful it might also be shown that both visions have the same Persian power and the same Grecian Alexander. The visions therefore as a whole are in the main parallel.

I now advance to a second main point in this question of parallelism. ——*This "vile king" of chapter* 11 *is the same personage as the little horn-king of chapter* 8; *and hence there is a close analogy between this entire vision of chapter* 11 *and that of chap.* 8.——The following points, made very briefly, might be more expanded, but will suffice.—— (1.) The little horn is the main theme in chap. 8, as the vile king is in chap. 11.——(2.) He is a king in chap. 8, and so also in chap. 11.——(3.) He is reached in each chapter by the same historic thread, beginning in each case at the prophet's stand-point in time and space; passing from the Persian line to Alexander; then in the line of his successors to Antiochus Epiphanes. The track pursued in each chapter is identically the same.——(4.) Yet more definitely; in chap. 8, the little horn comes up in one of the four kingdoms of Alexander's cleft empire. Precisely so in chap. 11.——(5.) In chap. 8 he pushes his conquests toward the south, the east, and the pleasant land. The very same thing is brought out with much more detail in chap. 11.——(6.) The things he does against the Jews and their Mosaic ritual service and temple are given with considerable detail in chap. 8: 10-14, 24, 25. Suffice it to say that we have the same details in chap. 11.——Compare "casting down some of the host and of the stars" (chap. 8: 10) with chap. 11: 22, 33, 35; desecrating the sanctuary (chap. 8: 11-13) with chap. 11: 31; daring to confront the Almighty (chap. 8: 11, 25) with chap. 11: 28, 30, 36.——(7.) He is successful against God's people and suspends their established worship for a time. This is said in chap. 8: 12-14, and is fully implied in chap. 11: 31-35. The designations of time are not identical because chap. 8: 13, 14, covers more events than chap. 12: 7, or 12: 11. But even in this there is not the least discrepancy. The diversity as to the amount of time embraced, really strengthens rather than weakens the argument for parallelism, since it shows that the two visions are really independent statements of the same grand series of events. Such statements will be undesignedly coincident, as these are.——(8.) The *animus* of this king and of his persecutions is in each vision the same. In both he is utterly vain, self-conceited, proud, arrogant and blasphemous toward Almighty God.——(9.) The main points of his character, as put in chap. 8, make him cunning, wily, crafty and fearfully malignant against God's people. So also in chap. 11 we have the same man in every shade of his character.——(10.) The references to God's indignation toward his people for their apostasy and to "the time of the end," are the same in both visions. See chap. 8: 17, 19, 26, and also chap. 11: 27, 35, 36, 40, and chap. 12: 4.——(11.) In each chapter the manner of his death is essentially the same, even to the minute point of an antithesis between his bold assault against the Almighty, and his helpless fall. In chap. 8: 25, Though he shall be impious enough to "stand up against the Prince of princes," yet "he shall be broken without hand." In chap. 11: 45, Though he shall have the hardihood and daring to "pitch his magnificent tents in the glorious holy mountain, yet he shall come to his end and none shall help him."——These points might be amplified and perhaps some others added. I have not attempted to make the comparison exhaustive. But it is surely sufficient. For here, as in the former case, the points of comparison are not relatively small but are main points. They are not a few out of many, but embrace all that are of any importance; all that are needed to give a fair view of the history and character of this personage. There can therefore be no manner of doubt of the absolute identity of the little horn of chap. 8 with the vile king of chap. 11; and consequently no doubt as to the general parallelism of that chapter with this.—— I see no occasion here to speak further in respect to the first vision, recorded chap. 2: 31–45. It is very brief; very general in its statements; and by universal admission so manifestly parallel with chap. 7 as to require no additional remark here. Hence my argument for the general parallelism of these four visions is now complete.

It is now in place to say that this point of parallelism, so abundantly manifest, is of the utmost importance in the interpretation of all these four parallel visions. *For chapters 11 and 12 now become God's own interpretation in plain words of the symbols that are used in each of the other visions, and especially in chaps. 7 and 8.* This is God's own angel coming down to interpret for us no less than for Daniel the full significance of those symbols, and especially, of that terrible little horn of chap. 7 and of chap. 8. This prophecy in chap. 11 stands in the same relation to what is said and to what is shown by symbols of the little horn in chap. 7: 8–11, 21, 22, and also in chap. 8: 9–14, as the limited interpretations, given in those two chapters bear to the portions which they professedly explain. That is, we have here just so much additional explanation of those symbols in plain English words. This is a fact of the gravest importance and one which has often been strangely overlooked.——In view of this fact, I was for several years in the habit, in my efforts to instruct classes in the prophecies of Daniel, of beginning with the last vision instead of the first, and indeed, of reversing the order throughout. The fact that each successive vision goes more and more into detail; and also shades off more and more from symbols into literal language, amply justifies this arrangement. There is wisdom in beginning with what is most plain and easy, and so advancing to what is more difficult.

II. It remains to notice other and diverse interpretations of chap. 11.——As already said, all commentators agree with remarkable unanimity throughout the first thirty verses. They all begin with Cyrus and the Persian line to Xerxes; they all pass over thence to Alexander and his successors of the Egyptian and Syrian kingdoms, and keep company through the ten kings to Antiochus Epiphanes, and without exception (among those of any note), they find Antiochus in vs. 21–30. But here they begin to diverge, and from this point they scatter indefinitely. Some break off at v. 31, and find pagan Rome in vs. 31–35; then Papal Rome vs. 36–40, and some unknown yet still future Antichrist in vs. 40–45. Others apply the chapter to Antiochus up to v. 36, and then find the Mohammedan system onward; and perhaps the Turks in the last six verses. Yet others make v. 40 the point of divergence from Antiochus Epiphanes.——Against all these, I maintain that Antiochus is the great theme of this vision from v. 21 to the end of the chapter; and that, to diverge from him at any one of the points named or at any other point, is to violate the laws of language and can not be justified; can not give the true interpretation.

1. *Antiochus can not be left at v.* 31.——(1.) Because there is not the least occasion for it. The verses that follow apply to him as naturally and are fulfilled in him as completely as the verses that precede. Hence there is not the least occasion to diverge from him, and hence it can not be done except through mere caprice and through violence done to the laws of language.——(2.) Because the grammatical construction forbids it. Vs. 28-30 all speak of Antiochus throughout. The pronouns, "he," "his," "him," all represent this king. It is he who "returns into his land;" whose "heart is against the holy covenant;" against whom "the ships of Chittim shall come," and who "has intelligence" (a secret understanding) with those Jews that "forsake their holy covenant."—— Now v. 31 refers to precisely this same man. The first clause ought to be rendered, "And an armed force goes forth from him"— the "him" referred to being Antiochus and no one else. Grammatically, it can be no other man.——(3.) Antiochus can not be dropped at the beginning of v. 31, and another person be introduced here, because of the close connection of historic thought. We see him in v. 28 enraged against God's covenant and people; in v. 30 yet more enraged and mad against them, his naturally bad temper being now exasperated by his being baffled in Egypt by the Romans;—so he is nursing his wrath, preparing for an outbreak of vengeance upon the feeble Jews. In v. 31 the storm-cloud bursts— just as we might expect.——But no! these dissenting critics break the thread of this continuous history at this very point. They tell us that this vengeance is executed, not by Antiochus, but by Pagan Rome, from two hundred to five hundred years after Antiochus is dead! Such interpretation is simply monstrous! To say that it violates all just laws of language, is only a moderate statement of the facts. One might as well break the continuous thread of any narrative, or history, or biography that can be written.——At the commencement of v. 31, Antiochus has just begun to afflict the Jews. The writer has reached this point in his prophetic narrative. Why should he not be allowed to finish what he would say? And more yet; why shall he not be allowed to go deeper than the mere fact of his outrages, persecutions, and profanations, to those elements of character that lay at the foundation, as he does in vs. 36-39? And why not let him recapitulate this vile king's exploits, and bring down the narrative in regular order to his striking, awful death? When an author makes his connections of thought so close, he does all he can do to guard his writings against being ruthlessly rent into fragments, and those fragments assigned to parties and subjects he never dreamed of!——(4.) Of this chapter, the portion before v. 31 and the portion after are closely related, inasmuch as on both sides of this line persecution rages against precisely *the Jews*. It is so in vs. 22, 28, 30; it is so also in vs. 31-35, 45. Hence a very strong probability that the persecution is throughout identically the same. At all events, the persecution vs. 31-35 *can not possibly be* that by pagan Rome upon the primitive church, for they were not God's ancient covenant people with

their sanctuary and ritual worship.——Again to the same point; the geographical location of the events in these two sections of the chapter is the same. This king, returning from Egypt to Syria, naturally passes through Palestine, and vs. 28, 30 imply that he is there. On the other side of this line the events are also in Palestine, where the sanctuary stands (v. 31) and where the daily sacrifice belongs. Vs. 41 and 45 each contains the usual distinctive term in Daniel for Palestine, "the glorious land;" fixing the same location for the events of the last portion of the chapter. But the persecutions by pagan Rome or Papal Rome were not exclusively or even chiefly done in Palestine. Therefore no portion of this chapter can apply to those persecutions.——(5.) The portion before this line and the portion after are connected *in time.* This is shown by the use on both sides of this line of the phrases, "the end," "the time appointed," as in v. 27, before it; and in vs. 35, 36, 40, after it. This test also is decisive. For it utterly precludes the application of any part of the chapter to Rome, whether pagan or Papal, or to Mohammed, or to any other personage or power than Antiochus. It can not for a moment be supposed that these allusions to "the time of God's indignation" against the apostate Jews; to "the time appointed" for these judgments; or to "the time of the end"—mean nothing; or that, despite of their meaning, we may go on to locate the events of this chapter, with no reference to them, anywhere along during the next two thousand years after Antiochus lived and died! To do so would utterly ignore God's own landmarks of time!——(6.) The wresting of vs. 31-35 away from Antiochus is utterly forbidden, by the fact that the parallel prophecies of chaps. 7 and 8 ascribe to Antiochus precisely the things here recorded. The proof of this has been given already. Just what is said here of his deeds—*c. g.*, that he polluted the sanctuary; took away the daily sacrifice; made war upon the saints and wore them out by persecution; in short, had them very much in his power for a limited time—constitute the substance of his deeds as given in those parallel chapters, 7 and 8. Therefore these verses, 31-35, must refer to Antiochus.

2. The thread can not be broken at v. 36, and only what precedes be applied to Antiochus, and all that follows to Papal Rome or to the Mohammedan power. Why not?-——(1.) Because this personage is not only *a* king but "*the* king"—the same before spoken of and spoken of as *a* king in every verse since we saw him take his throne in v. 21. His being *a king* forbids the application of these verses to Papal Rome or to Mohammedanism. His being "*the* king" forbids their application to any other king than Antiochus Epiphanes.——(2.) Because this is the place to give a general view of his character. His deeds have been rehearsed; now let the revealing angel go deeper than deeds, even to the elements of his character out of which such deeds came. Why forbid him? Why torture his words by wresting them from so fitting a theme and insisting that they look toward Papal Rome?——(3.) The character as here drawn precisely accords with the deeds as narrated above. Hence

this view of his character can not be severed from those deeds without violence to the course of thought and the laws of language.——
(4.) The statement in v. 36, that this king shall "prosper until the indignation shall be accomplished and the things determined shall be done," shows that the same personage is spoken of and the same series of events also as in v. 35, which limits those persecutions to "the time appointed," and as in v. 27; and also as in the case of the little horn-power of chap. 8. See chap. 8: 17, 19.——This portion, vs. 36–45, must certainly belong to the same history and the same personage as the portion that precedes—Antiochus Epiphanes being the grand persecutor throughout. Why he prospers at all, and how long he prospers, are important data. They are the same in the portion before this line and in the portion after it; therefore this line is only a fiction. There can be no legitimate cutting asunder of the narrative here.——(5.) As already shown, this prophecy throughout the portion vs. 21–45 applies aptly to Antiochus Epiphanes. History confirms this application of the prophecy. The same can not be shown of any other person.

3. The thread of this prophetico-historic sketch can not be cut at v. 40, and the portion, vs. 40–45, be applied to some other person or power. Why not?——(1.) Because the king of the north must be the same here as before, this phrase being absolutely appropriated throughout this chapter to the kings of Syria. So of the king of the south, who has precisely this designation twice in v. 25.
——(2.) "The time of the end" must be the same period repeatedly referred to both in this chapter and in chap. 8. This phrase limits the events to the same period of time.——(3.) This passage is in fact a resumé—a recapitulation of the deeds of Antiochus; and therefore can not be severed from the previous portions of this prophecy respecting him without the utmost caprice and violence.
——(4.) It is reasonable to expect some notice of the death of Antiochus;—the more so because the death of each of the two kings next before him is noticed; and yet the more so because the previous and parallel visions (chap. 7: 9-11, 26, and chap. 8: 25) show that his death was extraordinary—by some superhuman agency, involving special judgments from God. If we sever off this last portion, we refer this striking account of his death (v. 45) to somebody else—violently.——(5.) We must have the same Antiochus in chap. 12, as will be seen when we reach it; therefore we can not legitimately part company with him here at v. 40, and give the rest of this chapter to some other person or power.——These points may serve as a series of hints at the difficulties and the violations of sound criticism which are involved in any and every attempt to sever this portion (vs. 21–45) and to give any part of it to another personage.

There is yet another modification of the same thing which requires a brief notice. Some are understood to hold that this prophecy does indeed begin with Antiochus at v. 21, and go on with him a little way more or less; and then shade off into some other great Antichrist, losing sight at length of Antiochus altogether.——

I can see no reason for such an interpretation. No such departure from the obvious historic sense of such language should be allowed save under the sternest demands of necessity; i. e., because the historic sense is obviously inadmissible throughout.——But on what ground is this construction given to the passage vs. 21-45, or to any portion of it? Is it claimed that here are things that can not be applied to Antiochus Epiphanes? If so, the claim is made without reason. It is an entire mistake.——Is it claimed that there are clear intimations of this shading off into some unknown Antichrist? How can that be known if indeed this supposed Antichrist be yet *unknown* and wholly in the future? And what are those indications? Where do we leave the veritable Antiochus, of flesh and blood, and where does the unknown Antichrist begin to appear? What signs herald his approach? What word or phrase indicates the transition from the one to the other?——Such questions as these should be answered somewhat definitely before we sacrifice the laws of grammatical construction and the connecting bonds of historic and logical thought, and ignore the strong proofs of precise historic fulfillment in this great persecutor of the saints.——If the reference of this passage to some other Antichrist means only that moral lessons may be drawn from the prophetic and the actual history of Antiochus Epiphanes and applied to some other great Antichrist, very well. This is a very harmless thing. Indeed it is better than merely harmless: it may be made very useful. No doubt the same God who put a hook in the nose of this great Antichrist will do the same by every other. The same God who used him for the discipline and purifying of his ancient church will use every other as he may choose for the same ends, making the wrath of man work out his own praise. And the same God who protected his chosen people, then, through that fearful storm of persecution, and made those fires the salvation of his trustful children, will be no less wise and no less good when the next great persecution shall be sent on the same mission. He who loveth Zion will never let the fires of persecution burn too hotly or miss their intended result of purification to his people and triumph to his kingdom.——Before I pass from the subject of diverse and opposing views upon this chapter, I must say briefly that I recollect only three reasons assigned for applying any portion of our passage (vs. 21-45) to any other than Antiochus; viz.: (1.) That some of it does not apply historically to Antiochus; which I hold to be a mistake.——(2.) That the course of thought in the chapter must bring us down to the millennium, or to the end of the world, because the resurrection comes in early in the next chapter.——The mistake of this assumption it will be in place to show under chap. 12.——(3.) And finally, that prophecy in this same eleventh chapter makes a long stride from Xerxes to Alexander, and therefore we are justified in making other historic strides, wherever it may seem good to us to make them.——To which I answer; *That* leap from Xerxes to Alexander has its own good and sufficient reasons. Every other should have reasons equally good. That was not indeed a *chronological* connection; but it was precisely *logical*—the relation of cause and effect, and therefore by no means justifies chronological chasms except on like valid grounds.

CHAPTER XII.

This chapter speaks of a time of extraordinary trouble, from which, however, the people "written in the book of life" shall be delivered (v. 1); alludes to the resurrection and to the eternal retribution of the righteous and the wicked (vs. 2, 3); directs Daniel to seal up the vision against the time of the end (vs. 4, 9); gives designations of time (vs. 5–12), and finally assures Daniel that he shall have his lot with the righteous (v. 13).

Widely various opinions have been held as to the scope of this chapter. Its true interpretation must turn very much upon the question whether it is so connected with the previous chapter and with the entire body of Daniel's four great parallel visions as to determine its reference to the same series of events, and of course to the same age of the world.——A class of modern English expositors assume that the close of chap. 11 brought us down to the latter part of this nineteenth century; that in this twelfth chapter, we enter upon the very last age of time; reach the resurrection in its chronological order, v. 2, and the glorified state of the righteous (most of them would say *upon this* earth) at "the time of the end" of these earthly scenes.——Whether this is, or is not, the true interpretation, will turn (as above suggested) very much upon the sort of connection which obtains between this chapter and the eleventh, and also the other parallel visions. Let us then begin with examining this point.

1. And at that time shall Michael stand up, the great prince which standeth for the children of thy people: and there shall be a time of trouble, such as never was since there was a nation *even* to that same time: and at that time thy people shall be delivered, every one that shall be found written in the book.

2. And many of them that sleep in the dust of the earth shall awake, some to everlasting life, and some to shame *and* everlasting contempt.

3. And they that be wise shall shine as the brightness of the firmament; and they that turn many to righteousness as the stars forever and ever.

4. But thou, O Daniel, shut up the words, and seal the book, *even* to the time of the end: many shall run to and fro, and knowledge shall be increased.

5. Then I Daniel looked, and behold, there stood other

two, the one on this side of the bank of the river, and the other on that side of the bank of the river.

6. And *one* said to the man clothed in linen, which *was* upon the waters of the river, How long *shall it be to* the end of these wonders?

7. And I heard the man clothed in linen, which *was* upon the waters of the river, when he held up his right hand and his left hand unto heaven, and sware by him that liveth forever, that *it shall be* for a time, times, and a half; and when he shall have accomplished to scatter the power of the holy people, all these *things* shall be finished.

8. And I heard, but I understood not: then said I, O my lord, what *shall be* the end of these *things?*

9. And he said, Go thy way, Daniel: for the words are closed up and sealed till the time of the end.

10. Many shall be purified, and made white, and tried; but the wicked shall do wickedly: and none of the wicked shall understand; but the wise shall understand.

11. And from the time *that* the daily *sacrifice* shall be taken away, and the abomination that maketh desolate set up, *there shall be* a thousand two hundred and ninety days.

12. Blessed *is* he that waiteth, and cometh to the thousand three hundred and five and thirty days.

13. But go thou thy way till the end *be:* for thou shalt rest, and stand in thy lot at the end of the days.

The very first verse begins with saying that these events occur "*at that time,*" *i. e.,* at the same time of which the previous chapter speaks, especially the time when those scenes of violent persecution of the Jews took place, noticed specially vs. 31-35. This alone should go far to decide our main question. A time of great trouble had been already indicated; it is resumed and reäffirmed here for the sake of further remark upon it.——"Shall Michael stand up," etc. But this Michael has been already introduced to us, and in precisely the same relations, "standing up for thy people"—the Jewish nation, considered as the Lord's chosen ones, and also as being somewhat under Daniel's care also. See chap. 10: 13, 21. "Stand up," is a favorite phrase with Daniel in the sense of arousing one's self to earnest help, often with military power, force of arms. Hence the view of some that this Michael is the Messiah, must be wrong.——At that time "thy people shall be delivered:"— but "*thy people*" has become the established phrase for the Jews considered as under the patronage of Daniel, and hence accounted *his* people, yet none the less the chosen people of God. See chap. 10: 14 and 9: 24.——In v. 3, "they that be wise" ["the maschilim"] are plainly the same whom we saw in chap. 11: 33, 35, there rendered, "they that understand;" "them of understanding;"

but in the Hebrew precisely the same word, "the maschilim."—— In v. 4 the direction to "shut up the words and to seal the book," reminds us that the same direction was given for the third vision (chap. 8: 26), and that "the time of the end" has been repeatedly before us (in chap. 8: 17, 19, and 11: 27, 35, 40), and practically in chap. 11: 26 also, plainly showing that these events and those, being brought within the same limitations of time, are substantially identical.——In v. 6 "these wonders" can be none other than those which have been presented in the preceding parallel visions. There are no other to which the phrase can refer. Chap. 8: 24, says "he shall destroy wonderfully"—the same Hebrew word as here.——In v. 7 "the holy people," must be the same as before in chap. 11: 32–35; the same as "the host and the stars" of chap. 8: 10–13, and "the mighty and the holy people" whom he "shall destroy" (chap. 8: 24), and "the saints of the Most High" (chap. 7: 25). And the duration, three and a half years, is precisely the same as in chap. 7: 25.——In vs. 8, 9, Daniel says he does not yet understand all he would of these things, just as he had said before, chap. 8: 27.——The revealing angel speaks here also of "the time of the end"—a phrase with which we are already entirely familiar, and which connects these disclosures most perfectly with those of the previous part of this vision and with those of the other visions parallel to this.——The allusions in v. 10 to "the *wise*" carry us to chap. 11: 35, while the case of the wicked corresponds with the view given of the apostates in chap. 11: 30, 32.——In v. 11 "the taking away of the daily sacrifice and the setting up of the abomination that maketh desolate," can not possibly be separated from the same thing put in the same words, chap. 11: 31, chap. 8: 11, and also in substance in chap. 7: 25. There is therefore the most abundant evidence of the closest connection between this chapter, on the one hand, and the eleventh, and also the parallel visions of chaps. 7 and 8, on the other. The events referred to are the very same; the time of their occurrence is the same. The bonds of philological connection are of the very strongest kind. It would seem to be simply impossible for one accustomed to study, observe and obey the laws of philology, and to interpret language in view of *what it is*, to have even the least doubt on this point.

The way is now open for the special exposition of the chapter. ——To the first verse we have only to give the obvious sense, already made plain by its manifest allusion to things previously introduced.——"At that time," must be near the time of the death of Antiochus, with which the previous chapter closed.——"Michael," we know already as the great archangel-protector of the Jewish people. "The children of thy people," have been sufficiently identified as the Jews—thought of in their peculiar relations to Daniel. This "time of trouble" is the same terrible persecution which Antiochus waged against the pious Jews—as we saw in the vision of the seventh chapter; also in that of the eighth, and in that of the eleventh. But "at that time thy people shall be delivered, every one found written in the book," *i. e.*, of life—the book which records those destined to life. This "book" appears in Ps. 69: 28, "Let them be blotted out of the book of the living, and not be written with the righteous." The earliest Scriptural reference to this "book" is from Moses (Ex. 32: 32), "If not, blot me, I pray thee, out of thy book which thou hast written." The thought seems to be of a book of God's own purposes, in which he records the names of those who *live*—this life being supposed to be a good from the hand of God.——This second verse I understand to allude to the literal resurrection. But the manner and purpose of this allusion should be closely studied.——Negatively, the revealing angel does *not* allude to it, because his prophetic narrative has reached the literal resurrection in its chronological order; *i. e.*, has brought down the world's history to that point. This is simply impossible in view of the manifest connection of this entire chapter with the previous parallel visions, and especially with chap. 11. Nor does he allude to it for the sake of teaching the doctrine of the general resurrection as a new truth. For he does not here affirm or even imply a general universal resurrection. He does not say "*all that are in their graves* shall hear his voice and shall come forth." It remained for the great Author of the resurrection to make the first full announcement of the universal resurrection. All that is said here is that "*many*," not *all*, but "many out of those that sleep in the dust shall wake to a new life." Yet again, the angel does not affirm that *then*, *at that time*, many shall arise. He might have said this; probably would if he had meant so. But he did not say this.—— Positively; in my view the resurrection is suggested here because of its relations to eternal retribution. So the last clause of this verse and also v. 3 would indicate. This eternal retribution is suggested by his thought of the noble Maccabean heroes, on the one hand, and of the vile apostates from their Jewish faith and of the cruel Syrian persecutors, on the other. To see holiness and sin in such intensive forms; to see some men so nobly good and others so meanly and malignantly wicked, naturally leads the mind to eternal retribution. Remember (the revealing angel would say), remember for your consolation and for the relief of your burdened heart, that God is surely just, and that his justice will not sleep forever. There will be a glorious reward for the righteous; and prominent among these will be the righteous dead who "fell by the sword, by flame, by captivity, and by spoil for many days" (chap. 11: 33). There will also be a fearful doom of shame and everlasting contempt for those guilty apostates and their cruel Syrian associates who inflict these sufferings on the faithful servants of God. That this is the very thought of the revealing angel is made yet more sure by v. 3, where he refers explicitly to those noble Jewish martyrs; "They that be wise;" (in Heb. "the maschilim") the very name given them in chap. 11: 33, 35. Those who suffered so heroically and labored so earnestly to turn their Jewish brethren from idolatry to righteousness "shall shine as the brightness of the firmament and as the stars forever and ever." They stood and fell as "stars"—distinguished servants of God. See chap. 8: 10.

Now their joyous reward shall be to shine as the stars in the glorious firmament of heaven forever and ever.——This explanation of a passage, usually accounted very difficult, seems to me to be entirely satisfactory. The thought of final eternal retribution is certainly altogether in place here in view of the circumstances. It was legitimately reached through the resurrection. This great fact of our being was neither new nor strange to the people of God in that age. The allusion, in Isaiah 26 and Ezekiel 37 to the resurrection, and especially the use made of it as a figure of speech, show that the idea was by no means unknown—was even familiar. Hence his casual allusion to it, with no effort to state the doctrine of a universal resurrection in its full rounded form.——Some may perhaps ask, by way of objection to this construction, Why did not the angel give a more just, clear, and full view of the general resurrection?——The answer is simply, It was not his purpose to teach this doctrine in its dogmatic form. He could not turn aside from the subject before him to give theological lectures (may not I say?) on the doctrine of the resurrection. . He wanted the thought of it only for its relation to the subject he had in hand, and he therefore used it for this purpose and for this only. This is precisely as every writer or speaker does whose mind is full of his subject.——Moreover, these views as presented and left by the angel-interpreter must have been full of the richest consolation and quickening as read by those Maccabean heroes while they were nobly doing, daring, suffering, dying for the faith of their fathers' God. They are good to be read even now by all who live, labor, and endure unto the same high example of suffering affliction and of patience.——
In v. 4 the "shutting up and sealing of the book" until near the time when the events should occur seems to imply that men will have less interest in it during the intervening period, and a far deeper interest when that time shall have come, so that it will be read then; would be read but little before.——Some have said (with less probability), Men will misinterpret prophecy until the near approaching or actually transpiring events shall shed their light upon it; *therefore* shut it up "till the time of the end."——
"Many shall run to and fro;" coursing through the book, traversing it from point to point, comparing one vision with another (as my aim has been in this commentary) to get a clear and just view of it as a whole; so, *the* knowledge of it shall be greatly increased. The word for "knowledge" has the article in Hebrew, and seems to refer to the knowledge of the contents of this prophecy.——In vs. 5–7 it will be noted that the manner of bringing out the point to be revealed is by causing Daniel to hear a conversation between two angels, standing remote from each other, one on either bank of the river. The question, "How long to the end of these wonderful things?" asks for the duration of the chief transactions; here manifestly, as in chap. 7: 25, the length of time during which the worship of God's people at the temple would be broken up by the violence of this impious persecutor. In the answer, the phrase, "time, times, and a half," must be construed (as in chap. 7: 25) to

be three and a half years. Then, when the power of the holy people shall have been scattered and broken; themselves humbled and thrown upon God for help; shall these things be finished. See notes on chap. 7: 25.——Daniel does not yet understand so definitely as he would, and therefore asks again what shall be the end of these things. The form of his question and his choice of words (*What* rather than *When*); and his word rendered "end," the *after part*, the result or conclusion, seem to indicate a somewhat wider range than simply the idea of duration. That is, he asks not merely *how long*, but *what shall be the issues;* including, however, the length of time. Consequently the answer teaches both points; first indicating that the words are closed and sealed up till the time of the end, and therefore will not be much known till near that time; next, that active agencies of moral discipline will surely do their work, some being made better and some made worse by these events of God's providence: also that "the wise," the studious, humble and docile, shall readily understand, but none of the wicked, for their sin darkens their intellect while it sears their conscience and hardens their heart.——Next as to the time. It has been twice put at three and one-half years, in obviously very general terms—"a time, times, and the dividing of times," or "a half." Hence in answer to a question for the more precise time, we may expect greater precision. I therefore take this answer, twelve hundred and ninety days, to be a more accurate statement of the time. The terminus *from* which this period dates is plain, viz: "from the taking away of the daily sacrifice and the setting up of the abomination that maketh desolate"—from either of these, and if they differed in time, from the earliest. The terminus down to which the period comes and at which it closes should doubtless be the point where the sanctuary was cleansed and the Mosaic sacrifices were resumed. The books of Maccabees give this latter date with precision. Both 1 Mac. 4: 52-54, and 2 Mac. 1: 9, 18, and 10: 5, affirm that the cleansing of the sanctuary took place on the twenty-fifth day of the month Casleu (corresponding to December) in the one hundred and forty-eighth year of the Seleucidæ, which corresponds to B. C. 164. The other terminus *from which* to count is less distinctly marked. There is no doubt as to the time when the idol-altar was set up on the sacred one, nor as to the time when the heathen began to offer idol sacrifices upon it. The former was Dec. 10, 167 B. C.; the latter Dec. 25, following. But the daily sacrifice must have been taken away a considerable time—not less than six months—earlier. For it was very early in June, 167 B. C. that Antiochus returned from Egypt, and sent Apollonius with a strong force into Judea. He seized Jerusalem and put a stop to the temple worship. Josephus distinctly states in two passages that the daily sacrifices were suspended three and a half years. See notes on Dan. 7. Now three and a half years include accurately 1279 days, lacking only eleven of the number here given. Possibly this number 1290 may be somewhat a round number; or more probably the three and a half years is the less exact date and this of 1290 days the more exact. The number may have been precisely 1290 days; i. e., eleven days over three and a half years. It should be remembered that Daniel has nowhere used the designation, 1260 days, and though it is common loosely to estimate the year at 360 days, yet this is a round and not an exact number. The years were then as long as they are now, and we very well understand that we now find in the long run about 365¼ days in each year. Hence the above calculation.——This reaches as high a degree of accuracy as can be expected, under the general methods of time-computation which prevailed in that age.——In v. 12 still another period is given, viz.: 1335 days; 45 days longer than the preceding. There can be but little doubt that this dates *from* the same point of time, and therefore runs over one month and a half beyond the cleansing of the sanctuary, which would bring us nearly to the middle of February, B. C. 163. Nor can there be any doubt that it looks to the death of Antiochus as the joyful event which then occurred.——Both the first and the second books of Maccabees give some details of his death; but neither has given the day. It is not strange that they omit it. 1 Mac. 6: 1-16, gives the year, the one hundred and forty-ninth year of the Seleucidæ; equal to B. C. 163. It also gives us the means of estimating yet more definitely the exact time, for it states that Antiochus, being in the remote countries of Persia, heard of the victories of Judas over his armies in Palestine, and of the cleansing of the sanctuary, which occurred, as we may remember, Dec. 25, 164 B. C., and that the Jews had compassed the sanctuary about with high walls as before. These tidings affected him greatly, and indeed induced him to set off at once for home, and brought on the fall from his chariot and the violent sickness of which he died. Now if we allow a reasonable time for this news to reach him, and for the journey, the fall and the sickness, which preceded his death, we shall find that forty-five days is a fair estimate. The testimony of the second book of Maccabees (chap. 9) corresponds with that of the first book in these particulars, as far as it goes.——Well might the revealing angel say, "Blessed is he that waiteth" in patient hope so long, for there would be great joy over the death of that arch enemy of the people of God.——V. 13, closing the vision, directs Daniel to go on his accustomed path of life, and assures him that he shall rest from his labors and share at last in the blessed lot of the risen saints, as had been said vs. 2, 3 of the martyrs of the Maccabean age. This will be the precise sense if we take "stand in thy lot" to mean *arise* from *the dead to thy reward*. Most of the commentators and lexicons give this sense to the words in this passage. I account it the most probable sense. But yet I find no other case in which this verb "stand" means to rise from the dead. It may therefore mean only, Thou shalt be in thy place (the intermediate place of departed saints) at the end of these days of trouble upon thy people. In so far as a tacit allusion to vs. 2, 3 is probable, the sense of resurrection becomes so.

Neither construction seems bad. Either corresponds with the facts, and is pertinent to the closing scene of this vision.

It has been already intimated that this twelfth chapter is built upon the eleventh, assuming the facts therein stated, and aiming to make a practical application of those facts for the moral benefit of the people specially interested. We shall best appreciate the pertinence and force of this practical application, if we transfer ourselves back to those times, and suppose ourselves to be among and of the parties affected, or at least to be observers of its influence upon them. Let us then suppose ourselves to be there, "at the time of the end." The book is unsealed; the words long shut up are now opened. Our Jewish brethren who have been looking with alarm on the apostacy of such numbers of their people into Grecian manners and idolatry, are now well assured that this is the hand of Almighty God and this the time of his indignation, and they tremble for the results. Alas! the sanctuary is desecrated; that wicked persecutor is successful in his most wicked schemes; thousands of their brethren have fallen in battle already; women have seen their children tortured and have themselves suffered tortures worse than death; immense armies have swept through their land and have made their own Zion-hill their stronghold. Now conceive how they read this twelfth chapter. "At that time shall Michael stand up, the great prince that standeth for thy people." Precious words! God's help shall come!——"There shall be a time of trouble such as never was before since there was a nation"—a truth they well understand, for they have felt it in the anguish of their souls. Judah and Jerusalem have never before passed through such an ordeal of fire and flame, of blood and torture and desolation. But pause; What is this that comes next? "*At that time thy people shall be delivered*," "every one that shall be found written in the book." Blessed words are these! Then this desolation shall cease erelong, and this fearful Persecutor will not utterly blot out the name and memorial of God's people from under heaven. The kingdom and people of the great God will survive and will yet see better days! And then these next words, how much in point are they! Our martyrs dead are "not lost but only gone before." Not one of them will lose his reward. How will our good Mattathias and Eleazar shine as stars in the firmament forever and ever! And those apostates, too, are to have their eternal reward—of shame and contempt! They sought the glory that comes from men. God gave them the disgrace that goes forth with his unutterable reprobation! And so they read on through this subsequent record of dates, pondering deeply how long it shall be to the end of these wonders. They are glad the time can be counted *by days*. They rejoice to find that the time of thickest darkness is only three and a half years. So long, they say, our suffering people can hold out. Let us bless God that he gave us, centuries ago, a prophet by whom he might tell us how long. "Blessed is he that waiteth and cometh to the one thousand three hundred and thirty-five days!" Ah, indeed! and will our great persecutor fall—that great king who vowed in his wrath to make Jerusalem one vast burying-place for our nation—is he so soon to be cut down in his horrid wickedness, and leave the land we love to breathe again in freedom?——So we may suppose this chapter to be read and read again. So men will course through and through its precious words, and here they will get more and more knowledge of God and of their own eventful future. Verily, God has been mindful of them in making his servant Daniel, long time before, his messenger and scribe to convey and record such words of comfort and strength against their time of so great need! The prophecies of Daniel in respect to this "wearing out of the saints of the Most High," could not be complete without this closing chapter. The people would need these timely, precious words, assuring them that Michael, their great Prince, would stand up in their behalf; that deliverance could not be long delayed; that eternal glories would wreathe the brows of their martyred dead, and equally immortal shame would sink to infamy their guilty persecutors; and that the time of their sorest afflictions would be short. So they will come to feel a tenfold assurance that the living God is the strength and the hope of his people, and from their sorest chastenings will bring them forth as gold seven times purified by the fires that eat its dross away.——And who can tell how much this very chapter may have done to create such faith, courage, and heroism as that of the lion-hearted Judas Maccabeus! Who knows how much it sustained the martyr-spirit of that mother who saw her seven sons murdered before her eyes, and knew that her own torture was to follow if she would not abjure her faith and her God! Such doing, daring, and suffering need the ministry of words of cheer and hope like these. Did not God prepare this ministry for those hours of need?

Some special objections to the system of interpretation here adopted should be briefly noticed. I. That this system involves *too much repetition*. What can be the use, it is said, of so much repetition?——(1.) I might answer; Why did the Lord double the symbols to Pharaoh in his dreams of the seven years of plenty and seven of famine, giving him both kine and corn? The facts taught in each were identically the same, with no shade of difference. Or why did he reiterate so many facts respecting the Messiah and his coming kingdom? Why does he ever "give line upon line and precept upon precept?"——(2.) Again I answer; Our great inquiry should be after the *fact* rather than after the *reasons* of the fact. The *fact* of repetition is the thing for us to decide. If it be a fact, let us know it, and then, as humble learners, use it. The *reason* of the fact is quite another matter, as to which we have very little responsibility indeed. It would be very unwise for us to reject the proofs of the fact because we can not determine satisfactorily to ourselves the reasons of it.——(3.) The fact that there is a considerable degree of repetition, no sensible commentator, or even ordinary reader, can doubt. In each of the four visions which I have claimed to be in their great points parallel, who can doubt that we have the Medo-Persian kingdom, and in the last vision, some of its particular kings? Who has ever doubted that in each vision of the four, we have the Grecian empire of Alexander, and as the visions become much more specific toward the close, Alexander himself? Who has ever doubted that in the first and second visions we have the Chaldean power? There is some repetition, then, manifestly, by the inevitable admission of all intelligent readers. How much soever any one objects to the principle of repetition in several successive prophecies, he can not deny that it is here, at least to the extent just indicated. Through the first three out of the four great kingdoms, there must be parallelism. Hence it is no violation of the established analogy of these visions to find essential parallelism in the remaining fourth kingdom. Those who claim this have the manifest analogy of the first three of the four in their favor.——(4.) Furthermore, it should very much abate the force of the objection on the score of repetition to note that these visions were not originally given all in one night, nor all written at one sitting, and published to the world at one and the same time. The reader may perhaps unconsciously assume this. He can now read them all at once, and grasp them all as if they were all shown the prophet and his people at once. But this is a simple mistake of ignorance, or, more mildly, inadvertence. It comes of not observing the dates. These will show that full seventy years lay between the first and the last—the first being in the second year of Nebuchadnezzar; and the last in the third year of Cyrus. Here was ample time to note whether the great points were adequately understood. The successive visions, involving a great amount of repetition, coupled with more and more detail and the addition each time of some new matter, show that the Lord wished to have the whole subject understood more perfectly.—— (5.) The reason which the Lord usually assigns for giving line upon line is the dullness of men's hearts to apprehend the things taught them. See Isa. 28. This may be in part his reason for repeating the main points in those parallel visions. This supposition becomes the more probable from the fact that as we advance in their order they become more minute and definite on the great points that would have most interest to Daniel and his people, viz.: the terrible conflict which the Jewish faith and worship are to have with their great assailant, Antiochus Epiphanes. In fact this law of progressive clearness and definiteness is carried so far that in the last of these visions, all symbol is dropped; the whole vision becomes virtually an explanation; the usual forms of prophecy give way to the literal statements of history, and we have a plain narrative (though prophetic) of what the vile king would do, of his character and his doom. We must conclude that the Lord meant to make these points entirely plain to all that ancient Jewish people.

II. The second objection which I note lies really *in the feelings* of the reader, rather than in his convictions. He says, "How can I afford to give up my long-cherished views of these prophecies? How can I lose all I have been wont to find here in respect to the doom of the Pope and indeed of all the great Antichrists of our world, and in respect to the time of Christ's final triumph in the great millennium?"——I am quite well aware that some will feel as men do when robbed of a cherished treasure, or outraged by some theft which knows no rights of property. They can not feel very kindly disposed toward the rough hand that would tear away a cherished good. Those who have found here an epitome of the conflicts of the church down to the millennium, and who have been able (as they suppose) by some ingenuity to decipher the enigmas of this book and bring out dates that locate the millennium and almost or quite determine in what year or even day the Lord will come, will find it hard to reconcile themselves to the idea that those things are not here—not the first one of them!——What can I say to help this class of readers?

1. *Let the truth stand* before all things else. Let us go where legitimate evidence bears us, and leave the issues with God. It can not be too deeply realized that it does not devolve on us to *make* prophecy for Daniel to say, but only to *interpret* properly and truly what he has said. What he never meant is no prophecy at all. Nothing beyond the true meaning of his words—nothing other than that—has a particle of additional value because it is supposed or assumed to be in this book. The pages of Daniel are not white paper, put before the speculating interpreter for him to write therein what he will and call it the prophecy of Daniel. Nor are these pages obscure dark words, upon which ingenious men can put any foregone construction they will and call it Daniel's meaning. In short, nothing but the very sense of his words which he himself intended is his prophecy; and this must be ascertained according to the usual laws by which all language is to be interpreted.——2. False theories of Daniel's prophecies are liable to do indefinite mischief—of which the Millerism of our own age is both an instance and an illustration. Such facts as lie in the history of this sad delusion should be a caution to all interpreters of prophecy to beware lest they unwittingly become the occasion of like evils in future times. The genius of this system of Mr. Miller and its main points of argument, so far as they rest on Daniel, will be the subject of a special dissertation found in the Appendix [B.]——3. To those who cling to that interpretation of Daniel which finds precise dates for great events supposed to be now near at hand, I have to say, It may be that God saw fit not to give the church such definite dates of the fall of Antichristian powers, of the millennium, and of the second coming of Christ, as modern prophetic theories have assumed. He may have seen that to reveal these great *facts* without revealing their *dates* would insure the best pressure of motive for zeal and for faith, and would harmonize most kindly and efficiently with human free agency.——I state this here in a hypothetical way; He *may* have seen that this course would be wisest and best. A stronger form of statement might be safely made; but this will suffice for my present purpose. It is not well for men to assume that God *must have foretold* the year of those great events of our world; the fall of the last Antichrist; the ushering in of

millennial peace; and the last coming of the Son of God.——I do not assume that God *never* gives precise prophetic dates of any future events, for here are such in Daniel, much more close and near, when taken, as they say, "days," than when taken, as many do, for years. But contemplating the entire field of Scripture prophecy, precise dates are the exception and not the rule. Out of scores of prophecies respecting the Messiah's first advent and his earthly kingdom, it would be hard to find any single one that gives us definite dates except that at the close of Dan. 9.——4. The four great parallel visions of Daniel (as I understand and explain them) show how God in ancient times made use of prophecy to sustain and encourage such servants of his as Daniel and such a people as the Maccabean heroes. No doubt Daniel himself needed and felt such quickening as these visions were adapted to impart. The same was true of his people, especially in those times of fearful trial. In this view they testify to the unceasing care of Jehovah for his cause and people.——5. While this view of Daniel's prophecies fails to gratify the curiosity of those who would pry into the unrevealed times of God's purposed blessings, it does show us how all human forces hostile to the church fall before his providential judgments. These visions show how, from the fiery flame of the Ancient of Days, these judgments came down on the fourth beast and his little horn, before the first coming of the Messiah;—then how this same glorious power was solemnly invested in the new King Messiah, and he was inaugurated to do essentially what the Ancient of Days had done before him to the great Grecian kingdom and its blasphemous persecuting king; aye, and to do also a spiritual work on the hearts of men far greater and more glorious!——It also assures us that in this new form the Messiah's kingdom will stand forever; will not be transferred to other hands; that under it the influence of Christianity will be unbounded over the vast populations of the earth, and God and his truth will triumph long and gloriously. And here, amid the blaze of glory which invests this final consummation, the vision resteth!

Yet ere we close, let us again revert to Daniel, at once the great historian and the great prophet of his time; who more than any other man wrote contemporary history along with his prophecies and future history *in* his prophecies; who wonderfully blended his own present life with that future in which the Lord suffered him to live so intensely; who did so much for his people while he lived, so much for the age in which he lived, and who yet, through his wonderful prophecies, projected himself down into that most terrible age of Jewish persecution, more terrible by far than any other through which the Jewish church as such was ever called to pass;—raised up of God for these special ends—to help the nation first through the Babylonish captivity, and next, through the yet more fierce and fiery ordeal of torture and blood to which they were subjected in the age of the Maccabees;—a wonderful man! endowed with wisdom almost superhuman, of marvelous capacities for public business, for bearing great responsibilities, and for winning the confidence of men who never loved his religion and never worshiped his God, but who yet felt the presence of his piety and the power of his intrinsic greatness and worth;—such a man was justly held in the highest esteem by his countrymen; nay, more; such a man impresses us with a new sense of the wealth of resources at God's command for making great men for his own use on great occasions. The beauty of his character shines in his pure simplicity; in his modesty and humility; in the fact that he filled a sphere of thought and purpose high above the seductions of human ambition; that he dwelt in communion with God and drew his mighty impulses to goodness and even to greatness from the very sanctuary of Jehovah's presence;—that hence his heart was full to overflowing with the tenderest sympathies for his people, so that he truly lived in their life, and felt borne down and crushed in utter prostration by the views God gave him prophetically of their future afflictions and perils. What did not the grace of God do for this great and good man! Verily, God raised him up and made him what he was for use among his own people! This same God is never short of fit instruments for great emergencies. Let him be joyfully trusted to raise up other men no less great and good, what time new and great emergencies shall occur to call them forth!

DISSERTATION I.

ON THE THEORY THAT "DAY," IN PROPHECY, MEANS "YEAR."

Does the word "day" in prophecy mean a year?——And on the same principle, must other periods of time, e. g., months and years, be multiplied by three hundred and sixty to get the real time intended?——This is our question.——Technically and in short, this is often called the "day-for-a-year-theory;" but it is supposed to apply not only to the usage of the word for day, but equally to the word for month and at least to the word "time," which Daniel uses for a year. So that the broad principle is that prophetic notations of time must be multiplied by three hundred and sixty to get the real historic duration.——I am compelled to discard this theory as utterly baseless, false, and of course mischievous and delusive; for the following reasons:——1. All reasonable presumption is utterly against it. For prophecy comes from God to men in the common language of men. If it did not, it would reveal nothing, without a special revelation to explain it—a new revelation to teach the meaning of the new prophetic language. Symbols in prophecy are no exception. For in the statements made respecting these symbols, words are used in their well-known sense. The word "lion" means a lion, and the word "bear" means a bear. When a lion is seen in vision as a symbol, we fall back upon the known qualities of the lion and his known relations to other animals to find the significance of the symbol. But this is in no way peculiar to prophecy. We should do just the same in poetry, or in common conversation. So that symbols in prophecy are no exception to the common law that prophecy comes to us in merely human language, using its words in their established and well-known sense. Hence the presumption is entirely against this theory of day for year. If God speaks to men, the presumption is wholly in favor of his using the common language of men in its usual sense. The Hebrews had suitable words for both day and year, and they used them as correctly as we do ours. If God had occasion to speak to them of time in the future, why should he not use their language as they did?——2. No reason lying in the nature or objects of prophecy affords the least presumption in favor of this theory.——The only reason which I have ever heard of, or seen, assigned for this usage of day for year, is that God meant to make

his statements as to time unintelligible until their fulfillment. That is, he meant to lock up this part of the truth and hide the key.——
I reply, 1. There is no evidence that God has intended or tried to hide what he seemed to reveal. There is no evidence of his resorting to enigma lest prophecy should be understood too soon. It does not appear that he has been specially careful to hide the point of duration *while professing to reveal it.* When he chooses not to reveal the *time* of events, he manifestly forbears to give it; this is all-sufficient for that purpose. What would be gained by putting his revelations in the form of a puzzle or riddle? Not to say here that this would seem to be beneath the dignity of the great God, I still press this question; Why should the Lord thus tantalize his people and mock their desire to understand what he has said in prophecy as to the time of predicted events? Where the Lord sees fit to say nothing about the time, we bow to his wisdom. Where he has spoken of the time, why may we not try to understand what he says; and further, why should we not assume that he has revealed these notations of time *to be studied and understood* and *not* to puzzle and confound the honest inquirer? Yet further: the notion that God meant to put things in such a shape that the real time should come to light only after the event, and only by means of the event, is utterly without support; for there is no *prophecy* in that; it *foretells* nothing about the time; of itself it means nothing; and no good reason can be given why God should in this way profess to communicate prophecy and yet communicate nothing!

2. If this precise plan of day for year had been adopted, a few well-authenticated facts would have brought the key to light, and would have effectually frustrated the object of concealment. For, after the key is found, it is a very simple matter to use it. Nothing can be more simple or more certain in its results than a process of multiplication in pure mathematics. Multiplying a given period of time by three hundred and sixty is soon done and done surely.——The appearance of artifice in this scheme seems to me beneath the dignity of the great and holy God. It is altogether out of harmony with the rest of the Bible. All else is lucid, honest, and manifestly said in order to be understood by the docile, humble, diligent reader.——Nor let it be thought that the case of our Lord's speaking to the Jews in parables, and explaining them only to his disciples, refutes my position. For that was judicial—a judgment sent on self-hardened and self-blinded sinners because of their chosen blindness. But this prophetic theory, if true, would be a judgment on *good men* who love the truth, and who honestly wish to learn all that God has been pleased to reveal.

3. This theory is entirely without foundation. It has no legitimate evidence for its support. It is a castle built in the air.——There is not a single case of prophetic time, in which the fulfillment has verified this principle of multiplying the prophetic time by three hundred and sixty to get the actual time. It is thought there are some events yet future—almost ready to come—which

DISSERTATION I.

will be in point and will prove it to every body's satisfaction; but they have not come yet!——On the contrary there are numerous cases of prophetic time already fulfilled which prove that designations of time in prophecy mean what they say, and are to be taken in their usual sense.——These statements should be carefully considered and well supported. Let us have patience to examine in sufficient detail the alleged evidence that a prophetic day means year.——
(1.) Appeal is made to Num. 14: 33, 34; "Your children shall wander in the wilderness forty years. After the number of the days in which ye searched the land, even forty days, each day for a year, shall ye bear your iniquities, even forty years."——Is this a case of the word day used for year? or of the word day used for only one three hundred and sixtieth part of the time really meant? By no means. Nothing of the sort. Throughout this passage, the word day means a common day,—nothing more. The word year needs no multiplying by three hundred and sixty to find the time intended.——The only *prophecy* in this passage—here in the form of a denunciation, or threatened punishment—is, "Ye shall wander forty years." But does this mean, Ye shall wander in the wilderness three hundred and sixty times forty years; *i. e.*, fourteen thousand and four hundred years? Who can believe that? If God had said, "Ye shall wander forty *days*," and the event had proved that he truly meant forty years, using the word day to mean year, the case would have been in point. But he did not say that, and no good reason can be assigned why he should have said it.——Will the reader still ask, Does not the Lord say, "Each day for a year?" and is not that precisely what we claim?——I answer; Those are the words he uses, but their meaning is nothing like what you claim. He means only that the years of their wandering shall correspond to the days of their searching the land through their committee, the twelve spies. The one purpose of the Lord in this form of threatening was to make their punishment a perpetual reminder of their sin—a thing which he often does for the best of moral reasons. All through their weary wanderings, they could say; "Forty days our brethren searched out the land, and brought back that unbelieving report; we heard it, and, indorsing all its unbelief, we practically said, Save us from going there! The Lord gave us our prayer in judgment, and we have forty years before us in this dreary wilderness!" This is all.

(2.) Another proof text very analagous to the preceding is Ezek. 4: 4-6. Ezekiel is commanded to lie on his right side forty days and on his left three hundred and ninety days, before all Israel, to indicate that he bears (in symbol) the iniquity of Judah forty years, and of Israel three hundred and ninety. The language is; "For I have laid upon thee the years of their iniquity according to the number of the days, three hundred and ninety days:—So shalt thou bear the iniquity of the house of Israel. Then lie again on thy right side, and thou shalt bear the iniquity of Judah forty days:—I have appointed thee each day for a year."——But observe throughout this passage that in every instance the word day is used for a common day—never in the sense of year; and the word year means only one year; never three hundred and sixty years. True, the *symbolic act* of lying on one side forty days denoted that in this symbolic, representative manner he bears their forty years of sinning; but this extension of time from one day of symbol to one year of sin lies not in any peculiar use of the word "day," for there *is* no peculiar use of it here; but it is in the symbol, and is there only by special divine arrangement and statement.——If the Lord had said "forty *days*" when he meant forty *years*, it would be somewhat to the point. But he did not use his words so. There is no proof that he ever did. Certainly this case does not afford the least particle of such proof.

(3.) Another somewhat analagous passage is 2 Pet. 3: 8: "One day is with the Lord as a thousand years and a thousand years as one day." Unfortunately if this means any thing to the purpose, it means far too much. For if it applies to the case in hand, the word day means, not one year only, but one thousand years! And then, further, one thousand years mean one day, and our long millennium is cut down wofully! And then it would be impossible to tell which way to work out this problem—whether we must *multiply* by one thousand or *divide* by it! Who could tell us whether in any given prophecy a day means one thousand years, or a thousand years means one day?——Happily that little word "*as*" relieves us of all our perplexities, showing that the passage has nothing to do with this theory that God says day when he means year.

(4.) Much the most important passage ever thought of as proof of the theory in question is Dan. 9: 24–27—the celebrated prophecy of the "seventy weeks." But this has been already examined in my commentary on the passage in its place, to which the reader can refer. He will there find these main points made, viz.: that the original word means in its singular number, a seven—a heptad; and this may be a seven of days or a seven of years: that the feminine plural is currently used for heptads of days; the masculine plural (which we have here) never by itself for the common week of days, but when a week of days is meant, the word *days* is appended, as in Dan. 10: 2, 3; and finally that after a word and a special form of a word which simply suggests the idea of a seven—a seven of something, we must ask—a seven of what? and must look for our answer in the context—in the thought already before the mind. In the present case, there can be no doubt that this thought is, the seventy *years* of captivity. Then seventy sevens of *years* must be the sense of this phrase, and it involves no usage of the word day to mean year—no usage of any current notations of time in a way to need multiplying by three hundred and sixty to get the actual time.

(5.) All individual proof texts failing, some will still fall back upon the general idea that prophecy has a special fondness for highly figurative language;—so that they seem to themselves to make a pretty strong argument for their theory when they call it an instance of strong *figurative language*—such as abounds in

DISSERTATION I. 463

prophecy.——But this is a simple fallacy. Those who say this fail altogether to notice what figures in rhetoric are. Perhaps they confound figures in rhetoric with figures in mathematics—two things most unlike in sense, however like in the word. If men would only notice that there is no rhetoric and no scope for the imagination in a mathematical process; *e. g.*, in multiplying by three hundred and sixty, they might be disabused of this fallacy. Figures in language turn on some resemblances which only the imagination can recognize and appreciate. But figures in mathematics make no appeal to the imagination. This "day-for-a-year theory" needs no function of the imagination to solve and apply it. It requires only a short process in multiplication—in simple mathematics. Has this the least analogy with the use of the word "light" for what is joyous and "darkness" for what is sad? Not the least imaginable. The failure to note such distinctions may serve to mislead and delude; it can serve no other purpose.

(6.) Of the proofs from usage for the theory in question, all the rest, known to me, are in the class yet to be fulfilled and verified; or rather, like Mr. Miller's Second Advent in 1843—yet to be exploded. Those which assign the final fall of Romanism to A. D. 1866 are soon to follow Mr. Miller's. It will be soon enough to believe this theory on the strength of *fulfilled prophecy* when the cases of suitable sort and in sufficient number do actually occur. ——It is simply amazing that this theory has obtained so much credence on absolutely not the least foundation. Against all reasonable presumption—in the face of the strongest prima facie evidence against it, there should be a very imposing array of substantial argument for it before it gains any credence. How strange, then, that it has gained so much without the first particle of reliable proof?

4. It still remains to assume the offensive against this theory and show that fulfilled prophecy is all against it. So far as Bible history gives us the fulfillment of Bible prophecy in which notations of time are involved, the "usus loquendi" proves that words in prophecy denoting *time* are used in their common, normal sense, and never in the enigmatical, peculiar way affirmed by this theory. ——Thus the Lord through Noah predicted the flood after one hundred and twenty years (Gen. 6: 3). Did it turn out to be 43,200 years, or only 120?——Again in reference to this flood, the Lord said to Noah (Gen. 7: 4), "Yet seven days and I will cause it to rain forty days and forty nights." That would have been awful at forty years, and Noah and his company all that time shut up in the ark!——To Abraham (Gen. 15 · 13) the Lord said, "Thy seed shall be a stranger in a land not theirs" (Egypt), "and they shall afflict them four hundred years." Does this need to be multiplied by three hundred and sixty? Was the actual time four hundred years, or one hundred and forty-four thousand?——In Num. 14: 34, the prophecy stands, "Your children shall wander in the wilderness forty years." Did it prove to be forty, or three hundred and sixty times forty—*i. e.*, fourteen thousand and four hundred?

―――In Isa. 7: 8 is this prophecy: "Within sixty-five years shall Ephraim be broken that it be not a people." Was this really sixty-five, or was it prophetic time" (so called); *i. e.*, twenty-three thousand and four hundred years? Even sixty-five carries the end several years beyond the end of the kingdom as destroyed by Shalmaneser, B. C. 722, for the reign of Ahaz, son of Remaliah, lay B. C. 759-740. The prophet included a final crowning act by Esarhaddon, filling the country with colonists from other countries, and embraced this within the sixty-five years.―――Isaiah (16: 14) predicted of Moab, "Within three years as the years of a hireling, shall the glory of Moab be contemned." Should this be accounted as really three years, or as one thousand and eighty years? But if this is three, why is not three and a half in Dan. 7: 25, and 12: 7, just three and a half?―――In Jer. 25: 4 it is predicted, "These nations (Judah included) shall serve the king of Babylon seventy years." And Jer. 29: 10 reads, "After seventy years be accomplished at Babylon, I will visit you, and perform my good words toward you, in causing you to return to this place." Now it was because these time-designations meant just what they said that Daniel could "understand by books the number of the years" of this captivity and adjust himself to it. It is plain that he had not a particle of confidence in this theory of a day for a year, and of one year named when three hundred and sixty years are really meant. If he had believed this theory, he would have set the restoration twenty-five thousand and two hundred years after the captivity; *i. e.*, 25,200—606=A. D. 24,594—and he must have despaired of living in this world to see it!―――And now shall it be assumed that after having had such welcome proof that God means just what he says when he gives dates and numbers in prophecy, he will himself darken his own dates by enigmas that none can understand? Or if it be replied, This was not Daniel but the revealing angel, then I ask, Would not Daniel have protested against it, saying, I have myself been exceedingly comforted, aided, and blessed by being able to understand by books when the divine numbers in prophecy would end; but how of this? No mortal can ever understand it! O, if Daniel might only speak out of heaven to those who so darken his plain words and so magnify his simple numbers, would he not rebuke them?―――It can scarcely be necessary to refer to Ezek. 29: 11, 13, which predicts a temporary captivity of Egypt; forty years; not fourteen thousand and four hundred years; nor to Jonah's prophecy against Nineveh; "Yet forty days and Nineveh shall be overthrown." It would have changed the case very essentially if he had meant forty years. But why in such a case should not the Lord say what he means, even as he expects and requires men to do? Is there any conceivable reason why he should say day when he means year? Is this according to *truth*? And what can be the use of it?―――One case yet, more important than any other, is that of Daniel's own usage (Dan. 4: 16, 23, 25, 32). In each of these four verses it is predicted that king Nebuchadnezzar's insanity would continue "until *seven times* should have passed over him." So long he would be with the beasts of the field, would eat grass as oxen, and be wet with the dew of heaven. How long a period is this?——The advocates of the theory in question maintain strenuously that Daniel's "time, times, and the dividing of time," or "an half," (chap. 7: 25, and 12: 7,) equals three and a half years, and that these being prophetic years are really twelve hundred and sixty years. On no one point are they more united and strenuous than on this. Now the same writer, in the same book, will use the same word in the same sense. Unless there be some very great difference in the circumstances, this rule must hold good. No rule of interpretation can be more vital or more reliable than this. But in the present case no difference of circumstance can be shown. Both are prophecy. Both use the same word; therefore it must be used in both cases in the same sense. If three years and a half in prophecy is really of actual time twelve hundred and sixty years, then "seven times," equal to seven years of prophetic time, becomes, when converted into actual time, twenty-five hundred and twenty years!—a long time, truly, for one man to eat grass!——Some people will think there must be something very special and even mysterious in this word, "a time," when used for a year, and hence they readily admit this theory of (so called) "prophetic time," when applied to Daniel's word, a "*time.*" But the seven "times" [years] of the king's insanity is just as truly prophetic time as the three and a half "times" [years] of ascendency of Antiochus over the Mosaic institutions and sacrifices—"times and laws."——The cases above adduced are not culled out—a few of this sort from amid many of the opposite. There *are none* of the opposite sort. There is not one case in all the Bible in which fulfilled prophecy shows that prophetic time is estimated on the rule of a day for a year. The usage of the Bible goes solid against this theory. When, from its nature, this theory ought to have the very strongest support from Bible usage before it can be reasonably accepted, it has not the first particle of proof in its behalf, either from Bible usage or from any other source.——As we might rationally expect, all scriptural usage shows that when God has given prophetic time, he *meant to have it understood*, and therefore used the language of men as men use it. One of his special objects in giving prophetic time has been to afford to his people the benefit of knowing the duration, or the era, as the case may be, beforehand. Therefore, he could no more employ a myth or a riddle to puzzle his people over his dates, than he could give precepts and inculcate duty in so blind a way that none could understand him without a new revelation to reveal his meaning. Is it not a marvel that interpreters of prophecy could so far ignore the veracity and the sober honesty of the Holy One as to impute to him such a use of language as this theory involves?

5. There is yet one more objection to this theory, lying in the fact that its advocates apply it only to the periods of Zion's calamity and persecution: never, or almost never, to the period of her prosperity. They apply it to the prophecies of the sway of Anti-

christ; never to the prophecies of the true Messiah's reign. Scarcely a man within my knowledge has applied this enormous multiplier to the thousand years of Messiah's promised reign!—— Now, it is bad enough to attempt to make capricious discriminations at all as to the usage of words, and say in one set of prophecies day means only day and year only year; while in another set, day means year, and one year means three hundred and sixty. This, I say, is bad enough at the best. But it is ineffably bad to apply this awful multiplier to the eras of antichristian rule and not to the duration of the Messiah's reign! Look at the reason why this discrimination is so revolting.——(1.) It assumes that God aims and plans to hide from his people the actual duration of their calamities until the time arrives; or, rather—worse yet—he purports to reveal it; gives us the usual words for well-known periods of time; but uses them so that his people will see only one three hundred and sixtieth part of the truth! He calls the time a day when really it is a year; he calls it three years and a half when really it is twelve hundred and sixty years!——Believe this of our God—who can? ——If he had seen fit not to disclose the duration of the church's great calamity, very well. All his trustful children would bow submissively to his wisdom, and would still trust his love. But that he should profess to reveal it, and then state it at only one three hundred and sixtieth part of the actual time—that is simply horrible! And then to cap the climax, that he should state the duration of her prosperity in a way to make it seem all that it is,—this sets off the other usage in a still more strange and revolting light.——(2.) A second reason why this discrimination is so objectionable is, that it makes the reign of Antichrist relatively long and the reign of the real Christ relatively short. Antichrist triumphs twelve hundred and sixty years; Jesus Christ only one thousand! The eras of persecution, straitness and calamity, surpass the era of peace, truth, righteousness and salvation! I take it this is incredible. I have a full conviction that the greatness of God's mercy toward our world forbids it. The sure word of prophecy is absolutely and mightily against it—as witness what the Lord said by Isaiah (54: 7, 8); "For a small moment have I forsaken thee" (Zion) "but with great mercies will I gather thee. In a little wrath I hid my face from thee *for a moment;* but *with everlasting kindness* will I have mercy upon thee, saith the Lord thy Redeemer." Does a moment compare with everlasting duration, as twelve hundred and sixty years to one thousand?——These points may, I trust, suffice to show why this theory never ought to be true and never can be.

DISSERTATION II.

ON THE DATA WHICH MR. MILLER CLAIMED TO FIND IN DANIEL FOR THE DESTRUCTION OF THIS WORLD IN 1843.

About the year 1840, Mr. Wm. Miller produced considerable sensation among some portions of the American churches by his views of the second advent of Christ. He taught that this great event would occur precisely in 1843, at which time the world would be burned up and cleansed by fire for the abode of the risen righteous. He claimed, with the utmost assurance, that he had found these dates in the prophecies of Daniel, viz., in chaps. 8 and 9. He professed, and indeed seemed, to hold these opinions with most entire confidence, virtually declaring that if any reliance could be placed upon the word of the Lord, these calculations of his must be true, and his conclusions as to the time of the end of the world must be valid. A considerable number of apparently good Christian people embraced his views with a degree of confidence like his own. It served to strengthen the confidence of some of them that they devoted themselves much to prayer, and indeed assumed that the Lord, in answer to their prayers, taught them by the immediate inspiration of his Spirit how to interpret prophecy infallibly. With their views of this divine teaching, they supposed they could dispense with the natural means of ascertaining the sense of a written prophecy, being lifted at once above the labor of thought and study upon the laws of language and the principles of interpretation. The confidence of presumption is often fearfully strong.——Mr. Miller and his followers, having fixed upon the very day of Christ's coming, (in October, 1843,) it is easy to see that influences of great power were at work to rouse their minds to the most intense pitch of excitement up to that decisive day, and then subject them to a scarcely less terrible reaction when on that day the sun rose and set as usual and other days followed it as of old, and the established policy of God's plan of the world refused to verify their prophetic calculations. Some went crazy under the strain of this prodigious twofold excitement. Some set themselves to recast the scheme and fix other dates, a little further off. A much greater number sunk into a dark and often morose skepticism, their confidence in prayer lost, and their faith in God's word shaken to its very foundation. Several of their leading men soon fell victims to a degree and sort of mental excitement too severe for even the stoutest physical frame to bear. Mr. Miller, Rev. Charles Fitch, and others, survived the failure of their hopes and predictions but a short time. In general the results followed the common law of nature, that action and reaction are equal. By how much the greater influence the system had gained in any community, by so much the more fearful and calamitous was the reactionary influence when the shock of disappointment came. Truth lost ground fearfully; Error left on the minds of men its usual results of moral mischief and desolation.——Hence it may be for a warning to future speculators in prophecy to put on record in this place the links of Miller's chain of argument—the series of false and groundless assumptions by which he arrived with such confidence at a conclusion which was just as false in view of its principles before 1843 came as it was proved by the facts of history to be then. He made these points:——1. The little horn of Dan. 8 is the Roman Papal power.——2. The "daily sacrifice" which the little horn "took away" (chap. 8: 11–13) was the pagan worship of idols in old Rome.——3. The Papal power abolished this pagan idolatry in A. D. 508 or A. D. 538.——4. The "sanctuary" which was "cleansed" (chap. 8: 14) is this entire world, and its cleansing is to be by fire in 1843.——Now, to find the exact time of this great conflagration and cleansing, he called in the aid of chap. 9: 23–25.

Here he took the following positions: 1. The exhortation at the close of chap. 9: 23; "Therefore, understand the matter and consider the vision," refers to the vision in chap. 8; and hence what follows is an explanation of the eighth chapter.——2. The two points in the vision of chap. 8 which Daniel did not understand; which he was very anxious to understand, and which the angel now reveals to him were, (1.) The key to prophetic time, viz.: that he must multiply it by three hundred and sixty, i. e., account each day for a year.——(2.) The starting point from which to count the twenty-three hundred days, alias years.——These two points, he claimed, are clearly explained in these two verses (chap. 9: 24, 25). They showed Daniel that he must count a day to be a year, and that he must begin to count his twenty-three hundred years from the going forth of that certain decree for restoring and building Jerusalem. This Mr. Miller fixed at B. C. 457.——Now his data are all in readiness, for 2300—457=1843; that is, taking out from 2300 years, those 457 years which fell before Christ, you have remaining those that must come after Christ, viz., 1843; which brings you to "the cleansing of the sanctuary;" i. e., the purifying of this entire world by fire for the abode of the risen saints at least one thousand years.——3. Then further, to make assurance doubly sure, new confirmations are found in chaps. 7 and 12. For both chap. 7: 25, and chap. 12: 7, fix the duration of the Papal power at 1260 years. Historically this power began in A. D. 538 and ended in 1798. Then, since chap. 12: 12, pronounces him blessed who waiteth and cometh to the 1335th day, there were forty-five years more to be added—"the time of the end"—and this brings us down to 1843 for the perfect blessedness of the righteous.——4. Yet again; since chap. 12: 11, makes the duration of the Papal power 1290 days, alias years, you have only to begin to count from A. D. 508 and you bring up, as before, at 1798; and if you add to this "the time of the end," (45 years) wonderful to tell, you have again the end of the world in 1843! Thus, with astonishing facility, all the mystic numbers of Daniel are found to converge upon 1843, and combine their testimony to prove that the world shall be burned up and cleansed by fire in this identical year!——The reader will notice that in general these successive points are precisely *links* in a chain, all necessary to the conclusion, so that

"Whatever link you strike,
Tenth, or ten thousandth, breaks the chain alike."

Thus, if you strike the day-for-a-year link, the whole system vanishes into thin air. If you touch the little-horn-Papal-power link, all goes down. If you show that the Jewish sanctuary is not this entire world, Miller's system has nothing left, and so of the rest.

Let us now pass these successive points—the links of Miller's chain—under a brief review, and see if there is even one sound link in the entire chain. 1. The first is that the *little horn of Daniel, and particularly of chap. 8, is Papal Rome.*——This can not be true. As shown in the notes on that chapter, it is absolutely impossible. If we will believe God's own explanation, we can not believe this. 2. His second position is that "the daily sacrifice" which the little horn "took away" was the pagan worship of idols in Ancient Rome.——Nothing can be more absurd than this; nothing could be a grosser violation of the laws of language. The "daily sacrifice" was a well-known Jewish phrase for their own stated worship at their temple. It knows no other meaning in the Hebrew Bible. Hence Mr. Miller might as well have said that it refers to the carnivals in Milton's Pandemonium, as to say it means the pagan idol-worship of the Roman empire. Such outrages upon all just principles of interpretation can never be denounced too severely. As we value the book of God; as we prize its treasures of blessed truth; we must frown down and reprobate the reckless, ignorant, presumptuous trifling that throws off such interpretations under the solemn sanction of God's revealed truth!——3. Mr. Miller's third position is that the Papal power abolished this pagan idolatry in A. D. 508 or 538.——It will scarcely pay to follow out historical statements so made at random as these are. Plainly, if this was done at one of these dates, it was not done at the other. In fact neither date is historically good for any thing. For, long before any properly Papal power came into existence, primitive Christianity had abolished paganism by permeating society with its holy doctrines and spirit; by the legislation of Constantine about A. D. 325; and finally by the acts of Theodosius, A. D. 390–395. The usual date for the rise of the Papal power is about A. D. 606. Be this as it may, however, it was never any thing distinctively Papal that abolished paganism. If he had said that the Papal power baptized paganism, and then smuggled it into the Christian church and gave it thus a new lease of life for at least twelve hundred years longer, he would have announced one of the startling facts of veritable history. Note here that if the Papal power is in Daniel at all, it is merely and only as an antichristian, persecuting power. Hence to maintain that, *as such a power*, it "took away" and abolished the idol-worship of Pagan Rome, is simply absurd in idea and false in fact. So that this link of Mr. Miller's chain is not half so strong as a gossamer thread. 4. Mr. Miller's fourth position is that "the sanctuary" which was "cleansed" (chap. 8: 14) is this entire world.——If Mr. Miller had read his Bible with common intelligence, he would have seen that "the sanctuary," as spoken of by the Jews, always meant their own temple. What plain, unprejudiced Bible reader ever failed to see this?——Further, the sanctuary cleansed (v. 14) should be the same which the little horn-power had just previously desecrated by "taking away the daily sacrifice" and "casting down the place of his sanctuary." According to Mr. Miller's holding, therefore, the sanctuary to be cleansed should be the pagan shrines of old Rome, and not the whole world.

But let the reader note especially, that with Mr. Miller this world is called God's sanctuary precisely *when*, and apparently *because*, it has become so hopelessly rotten in its moral corruption as to be fit only for conflagration! That is, it is God's sanctuary, not as made in innocence, wisdom, and beauty—"all very good;" not as having some nobly good men in it, walking softly by faith and holding communion with Jehovah; not in either of these points of light, but as utterly corrupt and ripe for the fires of remediless judgment! Such a world, so considered, the Lord calls his *sanctuary*. The same in principle as if he were to call hell itself his sanctuary! ——Was such nonsense ever put into a system of prophetic interpretation before? And yet, with crimson cheek, I must admit that there were men and women in enlightened America who believed in Mr. Miller's interpretations of Daniel and in his argument and his dates for the burning of the world in 1843!——Shall we follow him now into chap. 9, and take note first of the logic by which he connects this chapter with chap. 8?——He says that Daniel did not understand the vision of chap. 8, but continued in great perplexity until the Lord sent this new vision, recorded at the close of chap. 9, to explain it and to relieve his mind. Specially he affirms that the last clause of v. 23, "Therefore understand the matter and consider the vision," refers explicitly to the vision of chap. 8.——These statements of his are entirely without foundation, and against all the evidence in the case. I admit that Daniel did not fully understand all the points in the vision of chap. 8. Hence chaps. 10-12 came at length in further explanation—real *explanation*—as its parallelism and its additional light on the same points abundantly show. But there is not the least hint in chap. 9 which implies an allusion to the topics of chap. 8.——Again, the Hebrew of chap. 9: 23, is absolutely decisive against Mr. Miller's position. "At the beginning of thy supplications, a word came forth and I have come to set it before thee; therefore understand *the word*—this same word which came forth at the beginning of thy supplications, and not some other word, revealed years before, viz., in the third year of Belshazzar. This same word, now sent you, understand; and consider *the* vision, *i. e., this* vision.——Yet further, the word for "vision" here is "march," but in chap. 8: 1, it is another word, "hhazon," which essentially forbids the assumption that this vision of chap. 9 refers to that of chap. 8. These two words for "vision" are not precisely synonymous; that in chap. 8: 1, being applied more properly to a vision in the sense of something *seen;* this in chap. 9: 23, to one in which something is merely *heard.* Yet further, a little attention to the scope of chap. 9 will show that the burden on Daniel's heart was not the dark points of the vision of chap. 8, but was the great sins of his people which he feared might stand in the way of their deliverance from their captivity in Babylon—the time for which, according to the word of the Lord by Jeremiah, was now close at hand. It was precisely to lift this burden from his heart that the Lord showed him here how at the end of sixty-nine sevens of years, he would provide through the death of the Messiah for the taking away of all sin and the fulfilling of all his good words of prophecy and promise. So that Mr. Miller has utterly failed to see the drift of this entire ninth chapter, and has most erroneously assumed and affirmed a connection with chap. 8 which never existed.

2. Yet further Daniel could not learn (as Mr. Miller claims) from the seventy weeks that the days in prophecy mean years; for, as shown already, the passage teaches no such thing. Nor could he learn that the twenty-three hundred days, at the end of which the sanctuary should be cleansed, begin with the decree for restoring and rebuilding Jerusalem. There is no shadow of connection between the one thing and the other. What had the decree of Artaxerxes to do with the beginning of that "vision concerning the daily sacrifice and the transgression of desolation, and the giving of both the sanctuary and the host to be trodden under foot?" Absolutely nothing. It is only a fancy, a mere dream of Mr. Miller's. He might as well have fixed his starting-point at the creation, or at the flood.——It is remarkable that he utterly ignores the question in chap. 8: 13, to which the twenty-three hundred days of v. 14 is the answer. By what right does any man so distort and pervert the words of this holy book?

3. Yet another remarkable confirmation is found by Mr. Miller in the twelve hundred and sixty years of the Papal power which (as he asserts) begins with A. D. 538 and ends with A. D. 1798. ——Historically, Mr. Miller has first to show that the Papal power began in A. D. 538. Was there any great event in that year which brought into being the identical persecuting, antichristian Papal power which figures so boldly in the world's history? Nothing special; no more in that year than in many other years. But passing that, did Mr. Miller prove that the Papal power perished and came to an utter end in A. D. 1798? Who does not know that the Papal power as truly lives to-day as it lived in 1797, or at any point of the eighteenth century? It is simply a great historical falsehood to assert that the Papal power perished and ceased from the earth in A. D. 1798! A man might just as well

say it ceased three hundred years ago.——Let this examination of Mr. Miller's chain of assumed proofs that the world must burn up in 1843 suffice. Let that system stand as a fearful illustration of the mischiefs of reckless tampering with prophetic interpretation—a solemn warning to men who lack every quality of a safe interpreter, who have neither the learning, nor the judgment, nor the plain common sense that are indispensable—that they refrain from mangling and torturing the prophetic words of the Lord! It was not without good reason that through the last great revelator, the Lord closed the last Bible prophecy with the terrible denouncement: "I testify to every man that heareth the words of the prophecy of this book; If any man shall add unto these things, God shall add unto him the plagues that are written in this book; and if any man shall take away from the words of the book of this prophecy, God shall take away his part out of the book of life." Rev. 22: 18, 19.——Mr. Miller's system found some of the pillars of its strength in the mistakes of previous interpreters, especially in these two, viz., that days in prophecy mean years, and that the little horn in Daniel's visions is the Roman papal power. The former of these is entirely fundamental in all those schemes which attempt to fix the time for the second advent of Christ, or the precise time for the millennium to begin.——The latter is beyond all question a mistake, a fallacy in the interpretation of Daniel, and one that can not fail to be fraught with mischief. Let the use made of these errors by Mr. Miller be an admonition to the churches!——Of the day and the year of Christ's second coming, no man will know till it comes. At what time the great Roman Antichrist shall fall, no prophecy of Daniel teaches, for the good reason that he says nothing on this subject. It is safer to conclude that it will fall when Evangelical Protestant Christendom shall do her duty, and through God's help shall make the sword of the Spirit, which is the Word of God, mighty to cast down all the formalities, idolatries, and corruptions of that great system of religious delusion. For even if God shall some day send the fires of his judgment upon her to her destruction, he will first exhaust the force of his truth for her salvation—till it shall prove itself in vain! This, as we have seen in the case of American slavery, is the law of God's mercy toward great systems of iniquity. Try them with moral appliances first; these failing, his red thunderbolts fall when and where they must! May God hasten and bless the pressure of the gospel's power upon the heart of the Papal Church! And may his people be content to be workers together with God for her salvation rather than prophets of her fall!

www.ingramcontent.com/pod-product-compliance
Lightning Source LLC
Chambersburg PA
CBHW022100300426
44117CB00007B/526